The Literature of California, Volume 1

California: Selected Sites

THE LITERATURE OF CALIFORNIA

VOLUME 1

NATIVE AMERICAN
BEGINNINGS TO 1945

EDITED BY   Jack Hicks

James D. Houston

Maxine Hong Kingston

Al Young

UNIVERSITY OF CALIFORNIA PRESS
Berkeley   Los Angeles   London

University of California Press
Berkeley and Los Angeles, California

University of California Press, Ltd.
London, England

Library of Congress Cataloging-in-Publication Data

The literature of California / edited by Jack Hicks . . . [et al.].
    p.   cm.
   Includes bibliographical references and index.
   Contents: v. 1. Native American beginnings to 1945
   ISBN 0-520-21524-9 (alk. paper : v. 1) —
   ISBN 0-520-22212-1 (pbk. : alk. paper : v. 1)
   1. American literature—California.   2. California—Literary
collections.   I. Hicks, Jack, 1942–
PS571.C2 L5   2000
810.8'09794—dc21

                                00-037410
                                    CIP

Printed and bound in Canada

9 8 7 6 5 4 3 2 1 0
10 9 8 7 6 5 4 3 2 1

The paper used in this publication meets the minimum
requirements of ANSI/NISO Z39.48-1992 (R 1997)
(Permanence of Paper).

THE PUBLISHER GRATEFULLY ACKNOWLEDGES THE GENEROUS
CONTRIBUTION TOWARD THE PUBLICATION OF THIS BOOK
PROVIDED BY THE GENERAL ENDOWMENT FUND AND THE
DIRECTOR'S CIRCLE OF THE ASSOCIATES OF THE UNIVERSITY OF
CALIFORNIA PRESS:

Jola and John M. Anderson

Elaine Mitchell Attias

Jody Upham Billings

Janice and Thomas Boyce

June and Earl Cheit

Margit and Lloyd Cotsen

Sonia Evers

Phyllis K. Friedman

Susan and August Frugé

Sheila and David Gardner

Harriett and Richard Gold

Ellina and Orville Golub

Ann and Bill Harmsen

Florence and Leo Helzel

Mrs. Charles Henri Hine

Jeannie and Edmund Kaufman

Nancy and Mead Kibbey

Lisa Sawyer and John Lescroart

Susan and James McClatchy

Hannah and Thormund Miller

Margery and Herbert Morris

Elvira Nishkian

Ann and Richard Otter

Joan Palevsky

Lisa See and Richard Kendall

Shirley and Ralph Shapiro

Sharon and Barclay Simpson

Mary and Benjamin Parker Tipton

CONTENTS

ILLUSTRATIONS

(following p. 390)

John Rollin Ridge
California Geological Survey field party
Mark Twain
Ina Coolbrith
Thocmetony (Sarah Winnemucca)
Theodore Roosevelt and John Muir
Gertrude Atherton
Yone Noguchi
Charles Fletcher Lummis
Jack London and his wife Charmian
Robinson Jeffers, Judith Anderson, and Una Jeffers
Jaime de Angulo
William Saroyan
John Steinbeck
Josephine Miles
John Fante
Raymond Chandler
Idwal Jones
Toshio Mori
Jade Snow Wong
Chester Himes

ACKNOWLEDGMENTS

A project of this magnitude is a collaborative effort, and the editors thank the many people and organizations who have contributed to *The Literature of California*, volume I. First, our hearty gratitude to Charles J. Soderquist. A former University of California regent and a continuing and tireless friend of the institution, a writer, and a patron of the arts and sciences, Dr. Soderquist offered early support that made this collection possible. The University of California at Davis was our research and logistical base of operations, and we thank the following UC Davis administrators and offices for timely assistance: Robert Kerr, executive director, and the Cal Aggie Alumni Association; Kevin Smith, vice chancellor, and the UC Davis Office of Research; JoAnn Cannon, dean, and the UC Davis College of Letters and Sciences; Karl Zender and Linda Morris, chairs, and the Department of English; the UC Davis Committee for Faculty Research and the Teaching Resources Center; Marilyn J. Sharrow, head librarian, and the UC Davis library.

UC Davis staff Terry Antonelli, Shirley Martin, Vita Simonsen, and Ron Ottman provided key assistance at every stage, and volume I would not have been possible without the involvement of numerous undergraduate and graduate students: the hundreds in Literature of California classes, and project interns Ryan Saunders and Tony Swofford. We especially commend research assistants Christopher Sindt and D. Foy O'Brien. Your efforts made this volume a reality.

Many colleagues assisted our editorial choices and writing, and we thank particularly Malcolm Margolin, David Madden, Jose Saldivar, Louis Owens, William Penn, Karl Zender, Michael Hoffman, Linda Morris, Elizabeth Davis, Oakley Hall, and Robert Hass.

We used ten libraries in researching this volume; we appreciate the assistance of these professionals and the special collections they opened to us: Susan Snyder (the Bancroft Library, UC Berkeley), Gary Kurutz (California State Library), John Skarstad (UC Davis), Rita Bottoms (UC Santa Cruz), Diane Curry (the Oakland Museum of California), John A. Harrison (the University of Arkansas Library), and Kim Walters (the Southwest Museum, Los Angeles).

We are proud to be partners with the University of California Press in this venture, and we especially acknowledge the efforts and support of director Jim Clark, executive editor Naomi Schneider (who walked every step with us), managing editor Marilyn Schwartz, editor Will Murphy (now at Random House), and the many others who assisted.

We also thank many others who offered direct and indirect counsel, assistance, and advice, and especially our families, who were helpful and supportive throughout the demanding process of creating this volume.

Jack Hicks, James D. Houston, Maxine Hong Kingston, and Al Young

General Introduction

A hundred and fifty years ago, when California first captured the attention of the wider world, it took months to get here. For gold seekers setting out from Long Island, Hamburg, Canton, and Santiago, this was a little-known province of Mexico, far removed from the centers of trade and government. From those days until now, California has been perceived as a place apart: linked by air and rail and asphalt to the rest of North America, yet somehow a separate region, with its own mystique and climate and economic history, its own legend—ever tied to that first tumultuous era of settlement—and a crossroads culture that grows increasingly complex. While geography still plays its role—with the Pacific shoreline as the western edge, and the massive Sierra Nevada range rising to the east—the physical boundaries that shape the place on the map have come to contain a singular and always seductive place in the mind.

Over time this region has produced a distinct body of writings that are a part of America's literature, yet can also be considered separately. The 150th anniversary of California's statehood, coinciding as it does with the end of one century and our entry into the next, is a fitting time to compile a literary anthology more comprehensive than any heretofore attempted, one that looks again at the sources of this region's creative output and addresses the full range of what has been accomplished.

Writers long familiar to the California canon are represented, from Richard Henry Dana and Mary Austin to Robinson Jeffers, Raymond Chandler, and John Steinbeck. These are joined by a number of earlier writers whose contributions have been reassessed during the past twenty-five years or so, thanks to a healthy climate of cultural reexamination. A growing body of scholarship and commentary by Ishmael Reed, Shawn Wong, Ida Egli, Jo Ann Levy, Luis Valdez, Gerald Vizenor, and others has reconsidered voices once thought marginal. At the same time, our overview of the literature and its history has been illuminated by Gerald Haslam, David Fine, Michael Kowalewski, and Kevin Starr, whose vast multivolume study of California culture has redefined our understanding of the state. To these have been added a shelf of significant works brought back into to print for contemporary audiences by writers such as Pablo Tac, the Luiseño neophyte trained in Rome in the 1830s; Louise Amelia Smith Clappe, who chronicled the Gold Rush; John Rollin Ridge (Yellow Bird), the first American Indian novelist; María Amparo Ruiz de Burton, the first Mexican American novelist; Yone Noguchi, the late-nineteenth-century Japanese traveler and poet; Sui Sin Far, the Eurasian short story pioneer; Jaime de Angulo, the Spanish expatriate storyteller; and the L.A. novelists John Fante and Chester Himes. During this same period a new generation of voices has emerged, broadening our sense of this region's cultural richness, past and present, offering new ways of perceiving history, community and oneself.

In short, the last quarter of the twentieth century has witnessed a sea change, and the time is ripe for the state's literary map to be redrawn.

The literature did not begin with statehood, of course. It began long before the word "California" had been heard along these shores. Until 1769, this was a world of disparate tribes, each with its own language and mythology. They did not have one name for it all, as we do now. They had thousands of names for the thousands of places between Oregon and what has become the Mexican border, and each of these places had a story. Every mountain and river and valley and bay and point of land had a song or a prayer or a memory that over time became a legend. For countless centuries, these were passed from one generation to the next within the hundred and more tribes inhabiting a huge and varied terrain. In this anthology, their rich oral tradition holds an essential place, having preceded all that has followed. The tribal songs and legends draw on features of the natural world still familiar to us— the hawks, the peaks, the ocean shore, the floods, the fearful shakes and shudders of earthquake country. Yet it is only in hindsight that we presume to call these songs and prayers and legends "Californian." In the tribal mind and in the tribal world, such a place did not exist. California began somewhere else.

It began as a novelist's invention. Long before the name appeared on maps, California had a place in the European mind. The vision of a legendary land glittering at the farthest edge of the known world was planted some two and a half centuries before this coast was explored overland by the first Spanish expedition. *The Adventures of Esplandian* by Garcí Ordóñez de Montalvo is a tale of chivalry and preposterous exploits by a bold Spanish knight. It has survived into postmodern times only because one of the knight's adventures takes him to an exotic island ruled by a queen named Calafia. Montalvo's description seems eerily prophetic:

> Know then, that on the right hand of the Indies, there is an island called California, very close to the side of the Terrestrial Paradise, and it was peopled by black women, without

any man among them, for they lived in the fashion of Amazons. They were of strong and hardy bodies, of ardent courage and great force. Their island was the strongest in all the world, with its steep cliffs and rocky shores. Their armaments were all of gold, and so was the harness of the wild beasts which they tamed and rode. For in the whole island there was no metal but gold.

This novel was published in Madrid in 1510, twenty-five years before Hernando Cortés, or one of his officers, sighted and named what is now the tip of Baja California. The name has no Indian source, nor is it Spanish. It is a Spanish-sounding word that has beguiled etymologists for years. One nineteenth-century researcher asked, Could *cali*, like *calor*, refer to heat? Could *fornia* have come from *fornax*, the Latin root for furnace? Recent scholarship suggests that Montalvo, whose hero does battle against the Moors, may have been playing with the Arabic term *khalifa*, or caliph—a successor to Mohammed. Whatever the origins, in the end it was an invented and fantastical name, the kind science fiction writers conjure up today for worlds a million light-years out in space.

In all likelihood Cortés had read Montalvo's novel, since it is the only known source for this name. Even so, why would conquistadors on a mission to claim land for God and Spain depart from the Christian habit of christening newfound sites for saints and holy days? John Steinbeck may provide an explanation. In 1940 he sailed the Baja coast. In *The Log from the Sea of Cortez*, he describes the look of the lower peninsula: "As we moved up the Gulf the mirage we had heard about began to distort the land. . . . As you pass a headland it suddenly splits off and becomes an island and then the water seems to stretch inward and pinch it to a mushroom-shaped cliff, and finally to liberate it from the earth entirely so that it hangs in the air." Perhaps Cortés, sailing north from Acapulco, thought he had reached a place as strange and improbable as the island Montalvo had invented. When Juan Cabrillo moved the Spanish exploration farther north in 1542, the name came with him.

What then does it tell us, this vision of Montalvo's? It tells us California is an island. It tells us it is filled with gold. It also tells us the dream came first. The place came later. His novel was a concoction that actually fed the hopes of the region's earliest explorers. And this sequence, the dream preceding the reality, has influenced the life and the ways it has been written about ever since.

California was not the first place to get such advance billing. Explorations of every kind have been fueled by heady visions and inflated hopes. An essential feature of this region's history is the extent to which its many endowments—splendid climate, spectacular landscape, abundant resources—lived up to some of the visions and fleshed out the hopes for a promised land. When gold was discovered in 1848—when this distant frontier actually delivered pockets and seams of the fabled ore so many had dreamed about—the imagination of the entire world had a new touchstone. There was an Eldorado after all. And the Gold Rush was to become California's formative event, economically, politically, symbolically, mythologically.

For every success story there were several tales of disillusionment, loss or disaster, none more notorious than that of the Donner Party, a parallel event from the 1840s, a kind of prologue to the Gold Rush from the same mountain range. Starting late from Missouri, they fell prey to squabbling along the trail, entered the Sierra past the season when it was considered wise to cross, and found themselves trapped in the early winter of 1846. It is a saga not only of seekers pushed past their limits, who devoured human flesh in order to survive. It is a cautionary tale from a place where the weather can turn on you in an hour, where landscape is no longer a bountiful provider, in which nature is an adversary, or a mentor you can never afford to take for granted.

These twin legends from the early years of settlement tell us the Land of Promise is really a Land of Two Promises, where fertile possibilities and the potential for disaster coexist in the elements themselves. But that is not how the myth of California has come down to us. Even now, 150 years later, the Donner Party saga gets bleached out by the blinding light of the boom times so many prefer to remember, the great example of the dream coming true. It continues to be news when things go wrong in the Golden State, for a great many who live here, as well as for many who regard it from afar.

The California Dream, it should be pointed out, has seldom been promoted by serious fiction and poetry. Chambers of commerce have done this, along with popular songs, quick-draw journalism, and ad campaigns for railroads, sports cars, and real estate. Among the first influential books about the West Coast was *The Emigrant's Guide to Oregon and California* by the Ohio lawyer Lansford Hastings. In the years just before the Gold Rush it was the Bible for transcontinental travelers. Hastings had led his first wagon party west in 1842 and returned with visions of a California republic, like Texas, free from Mexican control and led by himself as president. An early promoter and land developer, he also had plans to subdivide and sell land along the banks of the Sacramento River. A guidebook celebrating the region, he hoped, would lure west the Americans he needed to help his personal dream come true. Here is the California he was selling to the folks back east: "The purity of the atmosphere is most extraordinary and almost incredible. So pure it is, in fact, that flesh of any kind may be hung in the air for weeks together, in the open air, and that too in the summer season, without undergoing putrefaction . . . disease of any kind is very seldom known in any portion of the country. Cases of fever of any kind have seldom been known."

What literary writers have provided time and again is *counterpoint*, playing under or against such promotional copy—exploring the ironies, looking around the edges of the promise where so many Donner Passes have lurked right beside the seams of gold. Among the first to do so was Louise Smith Clappe (Dame Shirley), who traveled to San Francisco with her physician husband by way of Cape Horn in 1850. Hers is the first original voice to emerge from the writings of that era. Her husband set up shop along the North Fork of the Feather River, above Marysville, and from there she composed a series of letters addressed to her sister in Massachusetts. They were first published in the 1850s in San Francisco's earliest literary journal, *The Pioneer*. As one of four women in an isolated mining community of several hundred men, she brought a rare perspective to this sudden-growth world. In "Letter 15th" she writes:

> Our countrymen are the most discontented of mortals. They are always longing for "big strikes." If a "claim" is paying them a steady income, by which, if they pleased, they could lay up more in a month than they could accumulate in a year at home, still they are dissatisfied and, in most cases, will wander off in search of better "diggings." There are hundreds now pursuing this foolish course, who, if they had stopped where they first "camped," would now have been rich men.

In two years, Dame Shirley witnessed hangings, stabbings, amputations, births and burials, runaway drunkeness, and Anglos and Hispanics pitted against one another. The daily drama was acted out in an amphitheater of stunning Sierra scenery, where trout wriggled in the gurgling stream and quilts of wildflowers bloomed in springtime. Attentive to nature's gifts and to the pathos of human ambition, she conveys more effectively than any other writer of her era the bizarre reality of the gold country adventure.

Dame Shirley's *Letters* foreshadow many later stories. For one thing, she inhabits a world of immigrants who have only been in California a year or two. And in her epistles she takes great pains to make this new land meaningful to the sister three thousand miles away. It is a frequent situation, in writing from the far West, that a character's present will be played against a past from another region, or another country: the East Coast, or the South, or Mexico, or China. In writing from the American South, a frequent theme is the play between the present and some resonant moment in history, often the Civil War. It has been a feature of the West Coast that people arrive continually from somewhere else, with high hopes or no hopes, to start over or to play the final card. The edge of the continent looms as a kind of psychospiritual border, so that the dialogue between California and realms left behind is among several recurring themes.

A related theme has been the struggle for control of the land and for shares of its vast resources. California's much-heralded economic success has gone hand in hand with a century and a half of land abuse, exploitation, enormous theft, and epic encounter. Implicit in the greed of the miners among whom Dame Shirley lived, this struggle is at the heart of California's first large narrative, *The Life and Adventures of Joaquín Murieta* (1854) by John Rollin Ridge. From that time onward the conflict propels story after story, from Helen Hunt Jackson's *Ramona* (1884) and Frank Norris's *The Octopus* (1901) to Upton Sinclair's *Oil!* (1927) and Luis Valdez's ingenious *actos*, satirical one-act dramas first performed from flatbed trucks during the Central Valley farmworkers' strikes of the 1960s.

Coastal harbors, fertile croplands, water, timber, huge reserves of oil and gas—endowments such as these have fueled fortunes and also helped to fuel the deathless legends of what the far West holds in store. First there was the legend of mineral riches, later the legend of golden opportunities and the Golden Gate, the legend of open space and oranges, a land of promise where you can change your luck or change your life, a land of new beginnings. Some say California is the final haven for the ancestor of all such legends, the great American Dream. The atmosphere of possibility has appealed to religious cults and to generations of spiritual seekers as well as to the entrepreneurs who created the new boomtown called Silicon Valley. High expectations can move people to try things they might not otherwise try, and sometimes achieve things they might not otherwise achieve. At the same time, large hopes can also lead to particularly sharp, often crippling disappointment.

In Nathanael West's *The Day of the Locust* (1939), Tod Hackett, a Hollywood set designer from the East Coast, is working on an enormous painting he calls "The Burning of Los Angeles." It is an apocalyptic crowd scene that shows the city on fire, the result of communal arson, a final rebellion of frustrated and dissatisfied multitudes who feel deceived by the mythologies of filmland. West was in the first wave of literary writers drawn to the West Coast by the huge prices being paid for scripts. Like others before and after him, he was driven by the artificial and contradictory world he had entered to explore it in fiction. He found in Hollywood a potent metaphor for the underside of the American Dream. Written in the midst of the Great Depression, this novel offers an eerie foreshadowing of the explosive night of fire half a century later, when South Central Los Angeles went up in flames after the jury's first decision in the 1992 Rodney King case. West's prophetic vision suggests that a volatile tension was already in the air above the city, keyed to a sense of betrayal that runs so much deeper when the place itself seems to promise opportunities that have somehow passed us by.

If any one feature of the Western world has provided a distinct theme or thrust for California writing, it has been the Pacific shoreline. Much more than a thousand-mile scenic wonder, it has acquired the high symbolic role of Outer Limit and Farthest Edge, where land ends and dreams are put to some final test. Just as early Indian songs imagined dancing on the brink of the world, this fateful presence has loomed in the mind of writer after writer. In *Slouching toward Bethlehem* (1968), Joan Didion notes, "The mind is troubled by some buried but ineradicable suspicion that things had better work here, because here, beneath that immense bleached sky, is where we run out of continent." Beat poet Lew Welch wrote, in "The Song Mount Tamalpais Sings":

> This is the last place. There is nowhere else to go.
> This is why
> once again we celebrate the
> Headland's huge, cairn-studded fall
> into the sea.

No writer voiced this perception more passionately and deliberately than Robinson Jeffers. Like so many from the 1840s to the present day—from John Muir and Mary Austin to Jane Hirshfield and Robert Hass—he paid tribute to the far West's natural blessings and expansive terrain. For him, the meeting of shore and sea was a scene of wild and holy magnificence. It was also the cultural edge, where cross-continental destinies were somehow completed. Jeffers moved west from Pennsylvania in 1903, eventually settled in Carmel, and for half a century, in poem after poem, laid claim to the wind-torn Big Sur coastline. His view of it was announced in his famous "Continent's End" (1924). The title itself tells much of the story, helping readers of his generation begin to grasp not only the work of Jeffers but an essential feature of this region and its literature. The image was also used twice elsewhere as a title— twenty years apart—by San Francisco literary editors to characterize collections of breakthrough writing in California, most notably in 1944 by the critic and bookman Joseph Henry Jackson to name the first important West Coast anthology. In addition to Jeffers, Jackson's landmark collection included works by William Saroyan, M. F. K. Fisher, Josephine Miles, and Kenneth Rexroth.

This picture of the western shore has its place in the broader picture of a continent that has been settled from east to west. As "the farthest edge," its meaning derives in part from a long history of travel, migration, and settlement that began in Europe five centuries ago. It is a Eurocentric view, reinforced explicitly and implicitly by the literature of the last 150 years, because until recently most of the prominent writers associated with the West Coast originated in Europe—or their ancestors did. What this picture tends to leave out are the waves of people who continue to arrive from other directions. For Asian American writers such as Toshio Mori, Carlos Bulosan, David Wong Louie, Marilyn Chin, Lawson Inada, Cynthia Kadohata, and Amy Tan, history has been pushing toward this coastline eastward, from across the Pacific. For them—or their forebears—this is not the end of the line. It is the point of arrival in the new world.

Maxine Hong Kingston was the first American writer of Asian ancestry to appear on the front page of the *New York Times Book Review*. The occasion was the publication of *Woman Warrior* in 1976. Subtitled *A Memoir of a Girlhood among Ghosts*, it tells of a young woman coming of age in a valley town inland from San Francisco, much influenced by the tales and transplanted beliefs of her Chinese mother: "After I grew up, I heard the chant of Fa Mu Lan, the girl who took her father's place in battle. Instantly, I remembered that as a child I had followed my mother about the house, the two of us singing about how Fa Mu Lan fought gloriously and returned alive from war to settle in the village. I had forgotten this chant that once was mine, given me by my mother, who may not have known its power to remind." In Kingston's transpacific tale, an old chant has crossed the ocean from a village near Canton, in southern China, where the mother first heard it, to empower the daughter-writer growing up in Stockton, in the delta lands of the San Joaquin.

While Asians have moved from west to east, other generations of travelers and settlers trace their lineages to such places as Chile, Guatemala, Guadalajara, and Michoacán. In the works of Chicano writers like Luis Valdez, Gary Soto, Ana Castillo, Lucha Corpi, Alurista, and Francisco Alarcón, the famous coastline is neither an end nor a beginning. It parallels the long line of an archetypal journey, laid out by the earliest overland explorers and reenacted in family after family, as well as in fiction and nonfiction, from José Antonio Villareal's short novel *Pocho* (1959) and Ernesto Galarza's classic autobiography *Barrio Boy* (1971) to the multigenerational epic *Rain of Gold* (1991) by Victor Villaseñor.

In his essay "Nothing Lasts a Hundred Years," Richard Rodriguez describes growing up in Sacramento in a household where the north-south continuities are a feature of daily life:

> After mass on Sunday, my mother comes home, steps out of her high-heel shoes, opens the hatch of the mahogany stereo, threads three Mexican records onto the spindle. By the time the needle sinks into the artery of memory, my mother has already unwrapped the roast and is clattering her pans and clinking her bowls in the kitchen.
>
> It was always a man's voice. Mexico pleaded with my mother. He wanted her back. Mexico swore he could not live without her. Mexico cried like a woman. Mexico raged like a bull. He would cut her throat. He would die if she didn't come back.
>
> My mother hummed a little as she stirred the yellow cake.

Meanwhile, in stories and poems by American Indian writers such as Greg Sarris, William Penn, Wendy Rose, and Louis Owens, ancestry pushes straight up from the soil beneath their feet. In his historical memoir, "Diamond Island: Alcatraz," Darryl Babe Wilson (of the Atsugewi/Atchumawi tribes) describes a grandfather's shack in the flat country east of Redding, at the upper end of the Great Central Valley: "It was like a museum. Everything was very old and worn. It seemed that every part of the clutter had a history—sometimes a history that remembered the origin of the earth, like the bent pail of obsidian that he had collected from Glass Mountain many summers before, just in case."

If El Dorado is California's first large metaphor, continent's end is the second. In recent years a third has risen into view as a way of describing this region's place on the map and in the mind. *Pacific Rim* suggests a circle. The term itself locates the western shoreline not at the outer edge of European expansion—or rather, not only there—but also on a great wheel of peoples who surround a basin, an ocean whose shores touch the South Pacific, Asia, and Latin America. The term is geographical, and it also speaks to California's extraordinary cultural mix. This has been a culturally diverse region since 1769, when the Portolá expedition started up the coast from San Diego—a band of explorers that happened to include European Spaniards, *mestizos* (men of mixed blood), and soldiers of African descent. But only in the past quarter century or so have we begun to see a literature that truly reveals this region's multiple histories and diversity.

California is a kind of borderland where the continent meets the sea, where

Asia meets America, where cultures and subcultures touch, collide, ignite, and sometimes intermingle. And like the life, the writing nowadays moves in many directions at the same time. This is due in part to the continuing influx of people from so many backgrounds, in part to the so-called open society for which the far West is noted, in part to the sheer multitude of writers. More live here—roughly along the corridor between Mendocino and the Mexican border—than in any other part of the country, save a similar corridor that includes Boston, New York and Washington, D.C. In and of itself, this does not make California a worse or a better place, a poorer or a richer place. It does mean an abundance of prose and poetry and drama has been produced here, of every imaginable kind. For a century and a half writers have been drawn here by the action, or by the climate, or by the movies or a campus job. As often as not they have lived here and written about other climes, other countries, sometimes other planets and galaxies.

To compile a comprehensive collection of the literature, where then does one begin? How do you chart a path through this mass of material? In our view, it is not so much a matter of an author's birthplace or time in residence as it is the nature of the writing itself. We have looked for works that in content or in method or in sensibility have some relevant tie to or engagement with the region's past or present life. Thus our selections are chosen from the range of significant works that in one way or another bear on the experience of California, the lives lived, the dreams dreamed, the various histories that have crossed and gathered here.

Some of the writers included here are internationally known and read. Some, such as Pablo Tac, are anthologized for the first time. There are writers born in California—Robert Frost, to take a famous example—whose work would have little relevance in this collection. Others native to the state have found here their inspiration and best material. Gertrude Atherton was not only born in San Francisco in 1857, but she spent most of her writing life on this coast. In a dozen novels and two volumes of stories, she drew on the lore, legends, and terrain of her home region. An early voice in the debate on gender and society, Atherton was during her lifetime one of the most widely read novelists in the United States.

Among the numerous writers who arrived from somewhere else, Chester Himes was one who did not remain for long. Born in Missouri and raised in Ohio, he came to Southern California at the age of thirty-one. Four years later he departed for New York, and he spent most of his later writing life in Europe. But in his short time in California he started a semiautobiographical novel that it is now a classic. In *If He Hollers Let Him Go* (1945), Himes told a story no one else was telling, about black Americans caught between the legend of new opportunity and the social and political ironies of World War II Los Angeles.

With guidelines such as these in mind, we have divided the collection into two volumes. This first volume follows four broad stages of development.

Part 1 deals with the stories, legends, and songs of the indigenous tribes, a collective cultural bedrock for later work by writers of Indian ancestry, who are represented throughout volumes 1 and 2.

Part 2 presents letters, diaries, reports, and travel narratives that trace a century of discovery, exploration and conquest—from the diaries of Fray Juan Crespí, traveling with Portolá, to the passionate essays of Clarence King and the reports of the California Geological Survey. While they offer an early expression of some recurring themes, these accounts also serve as a kind of prologue to the literary flowering that begins in the 1860s.

Part 3 opens with Mother Lode tales by Mark Twain and Bret Harte, stories that made their early reputations and also signaled an emergence of themes, forms, and relationships specific to California terrain and its cultural milieu. During the next half-century, we see the first signs of a California poetry, the rise of narrative by California women (Atherton, Ruiz de Burton, Mary Hallock Foote), the inspirational nature writing of John Muir and Mary Austin, the earliest prose from the West Coast by writers of Asian background, and the maturing fiction of Jack London and Frank Norris, now regarded as significant in the American literature of the era.

Part 4 covers the period between the world wars, when California literature came into its own. From the continent's edge, Robinson Jeffers began to speak of this region in an original poetic voice. He was soon joined by a new generation of distinctive poets, among them Yvor Winters, Hildegarde Flanner, and Josephine Miles. In fiction, Dashiell Hammett and Raymond Chandler were inventing the hard-boiled private eye and the new detective novel, while Horace McCoy, Nathanael West, F. Scott Fitzgerald, and others were shaping the novel of filmland. In the 1930s, John Steinbeck emerged from the Salinas Valley, writing the stories that would eventually earn him the Nobel Prize. By the mid-1940s a cluster of works appeared by Carlos Bulosan, Toshio Mori, Chester Himes, and Jade Snow Wong that now seems prophetic, anticipating the diversity of voices and backgrounds that would characterize the literature from the 1970s onward.

Presented in chronological sequence, the selections in these four parts can be read for their individual values and at the same time allow us to track interweaving features of the aesthetic and cultural history. While we follow the development of predominant themes—as noted in this introduction—and the emergence of ethnic voices from the waves of settlement that have shaped the state, we also trace the rise of various geographical subregions. The first was San Francisco, launchpad for the Gold Rush, home of the first journals and presses west of the Mississippi, and a literary center ever since. Helen Hunt Jackson's *Ramona* (1884) might be called the first Southern California novel. As Los Angeles grew from a pueblo into the largest city in the West, it spawned literary traditions of its own, advanced in the early 1900s by the editor and historian Charles Fletcher Lummis, by the enormous popularity of L. Frank Baum, and later the fiction of Upton Sinclair, Wallace Thurman, John Fante, and James M. Cain. In the years before World War I, Bay Area writers discovered Carmel and Big Sur, "the Seacoast of Bohemia" that ignited Jeffers and figured in later works by Henry Miller, Jack Kerouac, and others. In the 1930s the Central Valley, the state's agricultural heartland, began to take its place on the literary map in the San Joaquin poems of William Everson (Brother Antoninus), the Fresno stories that made William Saroyan a celebrity, and Steinbeck's epic *The Grapes of Wrath*.

The reach of volume 1, then, is from precontact tribal times to 1945. Looking forward briefly to Volume 2: it will cover the second half of the twentieth century, during which California became one of the most active literary regions on earth. From the days of the San Francisco Renaissance onward, California was increasingly seen as an oasis for aesthetic innovation, populist politics, and alternative styles of living. During the 1950s the Bay Area was a headquarters for the poets and novelists of the Beat Generation, a movement officially ushered in with Allen Ginsberg's performance of "Howl" at the legendary Six Gallery reading in San Francisco in November 1955. Shapers of the counterculture which soon followed, their influence is still being felt, nationally and internationally. Volume 2 will include the broadening range of ethnic voices since the 1970s, the evolution of the Los Angeles novel, and the impact of film on fiction, as well as the complex role of nature in the nation's most populous and fastest-growing state. The works themselves testify to the flavor, vitality, and variety of contemporary writing—from lyrical meditation to standup performance poetry, from bioregional essay to bilingual drama and cross-cultural memoir, from retold Coyote fables to high-tech visions of the apocalypse. The volume will conclude with three original essays by editors James D. Houston, Maxine Hong Kingston, and Al Young, bringing their individual perspectives to the literary situation as we contemplate the new millennium.

California is an intricate mosaic of subcultures, subregions, and microclimates, easy to locate yet hard to find, it seems, in part because there are so many layers and so many ways of seeing it. There is the California of the evening news, with the emphasis on catastrophe and urban mayhem. There is the California of the guidebooks, where a thousand opportunities are listed for recreation, nightlife, and travel. There is the California of polls and statistics (it leads the nation in Nobel Prize winners, cars per capita, uninsured motorists, border guards). There is the mythical California still referred to in magazines and in Sunday feature headlines as a "Paradise" that has somehow been "lost." Meanwhile, it has been the role of literature to give us something else, to go behind the headlines and underneath the numbers, to provide a window into the hearts and visions and obsessions and quirks and passions of a people—in this case, of the many peoples who have inhabited a state that continues to be both a region of the earth and a region of the mind. This collection brings together a unique body of work, gathered here in the belief that there can be a meaningful relationship between a place and the forms of expressions it produces. A place can bear upon the stories and the essays, the plays and the poems, and these in turn help us to grasp the place, to see it with clearer eyes.

Indian Beginnings

Introduction

The archived literature of California's indigenous tribes offers traces of what was once a rich, deep culture. With a population estimated at three hundred thousand, this was the most densely peopled region of the Americas north of Mexico. Archeologists tell us the earliest inhabitants arrived at least ten thousand years ago. By the late eighteenth century, and the first Spanish overland explorations, there were a hundred separate tribes, with diverse modes of living suited to the wide regional variations of climate and terrain, from salmon-gathering communities on the north coast (Yurok) to the desert dwellers in the far south (Mojave and Cahuilla). The songs and stories that come down to us from this varied tribal world reveal vision, wit, inventiveness, and all the highs and lows of human feeling.

These tribes lived somewhat simpler lives than had been observed elsewhere. With no stone temples (as had been built in central Mexico) and no signs of the horse culture or high warrior tradition characterizing the Great Plains clans, they were often perceived as indolent and culturally inferior. Almost from the beginning of European penetration, Indians were held in low regard, commonly referred to as "diggers" in the north. Such perceptions provided a rationale for systematic exploitation and unparalleled decimation, which occurred more rapidly in pre-California than in any other region of the continent. By the end of the nineteenth century, scarcely sixteen thousand indigenous people remained.

Survivors went underground, frequently changing their names. Some merged with other ethnic groups. A scattered few worked quietly to keep the cultural flame alive, passing traditional practices through the generations for the next hundred years. Since the 1970s, thanks to the reawakened tenacity of an ancient spirit, Californians of Indian ancestry have resurfaced, reviving their heritage and bringing many of the old traditions to life, often in startling new forms. One aim of this anthology is to chart their vital literary contributions, starting with the early songs, prayers, and legends, through the later memoirs and tales by Pablo Tac, T'tcetsa (Lucy Young), John Rollin Ridge (Yellow Bird), and Sarah Winnemucca (Thocmetony), to twentieth-century works by new generations of poets and storytellers.

. . .

For peoples from the Tolowa along the Smith River to the Kumeyaay in the mountains and deserts of the far south, daily life in pre-California verged on the magical. The profusion of birds, fish, beasts of every sort, great swards of wildflowers and berries, stands of redwoods and acorn-laden oaks made the land bounteous in every sense. Yet as sweet as the world seemed, life could be short and its end sudden, and Indians knew disaster and death from cradleboard to funeral pyre. Floods, earthquakes, drought, rattlesnakes, and grizzly bears—such powers warned of the dangers of unmindful solitary action and taught the importance of the clan and of interconnectedness with the natural world. From such a blend of ecstasy and terror grew a deep sense of the need to live in balance, within a great cycle of natural rhythms. This is reflected in a powerful sense of ritual in California Indian culture and art. Since one "dances on the brink of the world," according to the Costanoans, such ritual chants as the Miwok "Ordered World" speak to the need for careful orchestration of individual life within the tribe and the great wheel of nature. Thus we organize this section in a cycle, from themes of creation, birth, and the emergence of the child to loss, death, and the journey to the spirit afterworld.

It begins with myths of creation. In their many languages, the peoples of pre-California told multiple versions of how this world came to be. For the Maidu, who made their home in the northern Sierra Nevada, creation starts in medias res:

> And Earthmaker, they say,
> When this world was covered with water,
> Floated and looked about him.

The first word here is a conjunction, "and," connecting this world to what untold previous ones? Was there another world before ours began? Creation seems to occur in an infinite continuum of mysterious time. According to the Chumash, who inhabited the lower end of the Coast Range (near what is now Santa Barbara), there were three worlds: one above, one below, and the one we now live on:

> Here where we live is the center of the world:
> it is the biggest island. And there are two giant serpents, the *malaqsiqitasup*,
> that hold our world up from below . . .

Indians throughout the West tell of terrain resting on the backs of great amphibians. One such story gave North America its recently rediscovered name, "Turtle Island."

Another view of creation comes from the Central Valley Yokuts. In "Origin of the Mountains," they describe the natural geography surrounding them: a broad plain bordered on both sides by distant ridges. From this and other texts, readers today can take pleasure in recognizing creatures and places still familiar to us: kingfisher, eagle, pelican, Mount Shasta, the Coast Range, Tehachapi Pass.

The selections in this volume are drawn from an abundant treasury of California Indian literature and offer only a taste of the larger individual works. The Maidu creation story, for example, is but the first part of a four-part epic called "In the Beginning of the World." After the final line ("That is all, they say"), three more parts follow, during which Earthmaker and Coyote "negotiate" (gamble) for the fate of living creatures. Coyote argues for death, and a great flood comes to cover the earth and drown him. When his son dies instead, the trickster regrets his words. In part 4, a great fire ensues, and then another flood, and once again the terse conclusion: "That is all, they say."

We selected "About-the-House Girl" and the chants because they define common events of human life: puberty, becoming a man, love and courtship, inaugurating a young chief, reuniting a community, prayer, gaining skills and power, old age and death. Though the individual texts all address universal matters, they are rooted in the specific ways of the California groups, family clans enjoying a plentiful land. While all the tribes had weapons and fought one another—making raids, avenging wrongs, and dancing before and after battles—there are no Homeric epics of martial adventures or warrior heroes. When About-the-House Girl, her flute-playing husband, and her father leave, they sail to a heavenly country almost as familiar as home.

We included several Coyote stories because of the character's broad appeal; the sexy, naughty trickster has made his way into the general American culture. Indians and non-Indians have long enjoyed Coyote as he luxuriates in his appetites and gleefully destroys taboos. "Coyote Cooks His Daughter" is a good example of the shock and surprise that jar us in tales of his exploits. He is both a god and a fool, and his world is so utterly strange, so different from the imagination that shapes most of English and American literature, that he pushes us toward new levels of awareness. What to make of "Coyote Turns into Driftwood," for example, or "Coyote Gives Birth," "Coyote Sucks Himself," or "Coyote Baptizes the Chickens"? Body parts exploding, strung together in vulgar combination, the smothering of the bear children—what do these things mean? Are there rules? Perhaps the insistence on linear meaning and a moral to the story are merely evidence of a limited Euro-American mindset.

Coyote gets pulverized; in the next instant, he is on his feet, reanimated, and up to his old goofiness. His adventures are not told in sequences familiar to us: news of his sudden death can appear anywhere in the Coyote cycles. We sense arrangements of time, cause and effect, and consequence that run contrary to Western modes of thought. Coyote muddies all our convenient boundaries: good and evil, right and wrong. Both godlike and gross, he finally disturbs and challenges customary and comforting assumptions.

To consider the myths, stories, and poems of the original peoples as an integral part of the canon of California literature raises questions about the nature of literature itself, a category which customarily refers to *letters*, the art of writing. Are these oral stories and poems merely folklore, or, at best, pre-literature? Perhaps they require us to rethink our own terms. We embrace the position that literature continues to mean much more than works written by a single author and read from a page by a solitary reader. It is not merely *text*. In the oral tradition, the medium is still language; there is imagery, story, voice, poetry—all the features the study of literature has taught us to look for and honor. We might well also reconsider conventional Western habits of thought that parse literature into separate genres: fiction, nonfiction, poetry, drama. In *Shaking the Pumpkin: Traditional Poetry of the Indian North Americas* (1972), Jerome Rothenberg never refers to Indian materials as chants, stories, tales, legends, or myths, but only as *poetry*, in its original mythic, communal, declamatory senses. The concept of poetry as discourse in its original preprint state also guided the anthropologist William Shipley to translate and organize the Maidu Creation as a poem with stanzas, refrains, and meter.

Considering remnants of the American Indian oral tradition as literature also tests fundamental assumptions about individual authorship. If a story changes each time it is told, which of the myriad versions is the definitive, "authentic" one? And if there is a problem with a literary form that evolves with each expression, there is also the paradox of authorship. Who "owns"—who is the author of—a work that is in a state of constant re-creation by a communal tribal group? And how do we date narratives created over thousands of years that we have just now rediscovered? Seen most broadly, such concerns about the literary "authenticity" of Native American materials should be leavened by the fact that oral literatures have been—and frequently continue as—the dominant expressive forms in human history.

Ishi, the last survivor of the Yahi tribe, came out of the wild in 1911, and for the remainder of his life he recounted stories and poems to anthropologists. Among them was the field's major scholar, Alfred Kroeber. After he died, his wife and distinguished colleague, Dorothea Kroeber, deposited the records of Ishi's accounts in the Bancroft Library at UC Berkeley. In 1986, Leanne Hinton supervised the development of computer programs to analyze the grammar of Ishi's Yahi texts. Her book *Ishi's Tale of Lizard* (with Susan L. Roth) appeared in 1992. Ishi's accounts drew from a thousand-year-old stream of oral narratives that was finally brought to the printed page by a chain linking tribal vision, the teller's own unique flavor, and the work of field recorders, anthropologists, ethnologists, translators, computer scientists, and literary editors.

The Maidu creation myth entered into mainstream literature in 1902–1903 when Hanc'ibyjim, also known as Tom Young (whom the editor Malcolm Margolin calls "the last great Maidu storyteller"), transmitted a cache of stories to Roland B. Dixon on the Huntington Expedition, an Indian collection project sponsored by the American Museum of Natural History. In 1912, Dixon published Hanc'ibyjim's wonderful Creation account in Maidu and English. In 1956, William Shipley rediscovered Dixon's book and took it to his teacher and mentor Maym Hannah Gallagher, a bilingual Maidu and English speaker and the daughter of Lena Thomas Benner, a Maidu in her nineties. After the whole family tutored Shipley in Maidu culture and language, he crafted the poetic Creation myth that was published in 1991 as *The Maidu Indian Myths and Stories of Hanc'ibyjim* (1991). We excerpt it here.

The stories and poems of Native Californians were performed orally and dramatically, not written down to be read individually. Thus each teller shaped the tradition according to his or her own power and desires and the temper of the evening audience. Shipley referred to the form he used as "poetry and theater," which would be most dramatic if read aloud. This journey from oral narration to printed text, from the tribe to the individual voice, is typical of the complex (and often elusive) process by which traditional Indian stories were conveyed to their audiences, and, later, to readers.

Indian culture frequently resisted such transmission: ceremonies were kept inside the circle, shielded from outsiders. Such secrecy was and is the last defense against pillagers taking land, slaves, animals, artifacts, and even intangible valuables like stories, poetry, and songs. It contains a belief that mystery and power must be concealed, in contrast to present-day ideas that authenticity comes from documentation and mass recognition. One way to learn and preserve the old cultures was to meet and befriend storytellers, who transmitted the narratives mouth-to-ear. Today, a more feasible alternative is to examine the many texts available to us both in library collections and in recent publications.

From the first post–Civil War surveys of Indian culture—motivated by a recognition that the coming of whites threatened Indians and native culture with extinction—ethnologists and anthropologists sought to collect and preserve Indian languages. The Smithsonian Institution created a department of field specialists who gathered oral accounts and invented orthographies for accurate transcription, finally printing them with word-by-word interlinear translations. Bulletins and reports by the Bureau of American Ethnology and the University of California Publications in American Archeology and Ethnology gathered troves of raw material, much of it yet to be recast in some semblance of its original powerful form. Recent work by contemporary scholars and publishers (such as Malcolm Margolin at Heyday Books) has further added to the rich body of recovered Indian literature emerging in California.

As native speakers of ancient languages die off, we are losing something valuable, and it is urgent that we help save their stories. One way to keep their visions alive is to publish the sorts of transmitted early textual versions included in this volume. And just as contemporary Indian "fancydancers" at a powwow draw vividly on an ancient tradition of communal expression, the creations of later writers—Louis Owens, Wendy Rose, Greg Sarris, and Darryl Babe Wilson, to name a few—originate in these early visions, refer to them, refashion or work against them to make something simultaneously ancient and thoroughly contemporary. That such narratives reach us speaks for the power and endurance of California tribes and their literature.

Origins and the Way of the World

The Creation (Maidu)

And Earthmaker, they say,
when this world was covered with water,
floated and looked about him.

As he floated and looked about,
he did not see anywhere, indeed,
even a tiny bit of land.

No various creatures of any kind—
none at all were flying about.

And thus he traveled over this world,
over the engulfed land.

It seemed transparent,
like the land in the Meadows of Heaven.

And he felt sad, they say.
"How, I wonder—how, I wonder—
in what place, I wonder—
where, I wonder—
in what sort of place might we two see a bit of land?"

This is what he asked.

"Well, you are very powerful
to have thought this world into being!
Imagine where in this world
some land might be, then,
and when you have done so,
let us two float to that place.
If, in this world, you keep floating and looking around you,
floating and looking around you,
hungering, but indeed eating nothing,

you will die of hunger, I fear,"
said the other.

Then Earthmaker pondered.
"I shall not starve," he said.
"There's nothing I don't know.
The world is very big, it is true.
If, somewhere or other, I should see a bit of earth,
then I shall make something good of it."

Thereupon, he sang.

"Where are you, little bit of earth?"
He said it, singing.
He kept singing and singing.

"Enough," he said.
He stopped singing.

Coyote said:
"Indeed, there are not many songs that I don't know."
And then, after that, he sang,
kept on singing and singing.

"Where is there land?" he asked.
He sang and sang.

"Enough! I'm tired," he said.
"You try again!"

And then, they say Earthmaker sang.
"Where are you, my great mountain ranges?
O, mountains of my world, where are you?"

Then, "Enough!" he said.
"See what you can do."

Coyote tried. He kept on singing.
"If, indeed, we two shall see nothing at all,
traveling about the world,
then, perhaps,
there may be no misty mountain ranges there!"

Earthmaker said:
"If I could but see a little bit of land
I might do something very good with it."

Floating along, then,
they saw something like a bird's nest.
Earthmaker said:
"It really is small.
It would be good if it were a little bigger,
but it is really small.
I wonder how I might stretch it apart a little.
What would be good to do?
In what way can I make it a little bigger?"

As he talked, he transformed it.

He stretched it out to where the day breaks;
he stretched it out to the south;
he stretched it out to the place where the sun goes down;
he stretched it out to the North Country;
he stretched it out to the rim of the world;
he stretched it out!

When Earthmaker had stretched it out,
he said: "Good!
You who saw of old this earth, this mud,
and made this nest, sing!
Telling old tales, humans will say of you:
'In ancient times, the being who was Meadowlark,
making the land and sticking it together in just that way
built the nest from which the world was made.' "

Then Meadowlark sang—
sang a beautiful song about Earthmaker's creation.

And when they had stretched all the world out with ropes,
Coyote sang and sang, and by and by he stopped.
And Coyote said: "Now, you sing again."

And Meadowlark sang again:
"Lo, my world

where one may travel along the edge of the meadow—
Lo, my world
where one may travel here and there, this way and that.
Lo, my mountains piled upon mountains.
Lo, my world where one may travel about!
I am one who will travel about in a world like that!"

Then the being who was Earthmaker sang—
he sang of the world which he had made.
He sang and sang; then, by and by, he stopped singing.
"Now," he said, "if this world were a very little bit bigger,
then that would be good.
Therefore, let us all stretch it."

Just then, Coyote said:
"Wait! I speak wisely!
It would be good to paint this world with something
so that it will be beautiful to see.
What do you two think of that?"

Then the being who was Meadowlark spoke.

He said: "I am a creature who knows nothing.
You two wise beings will, yourselves, be making this world,
thinking and talking together about it.
Then, indeed, seeing whatever is bad,
you two will make it good."

That was what Meadowlark said.

And then, Coyote said:
"Very well! I shall paint it with blood,
and, in this world, there will be blood,
and all kinds of creatures will be born with blood—
deer—all kinds of birds—all kinds of creatures—
all of them, without fail—
every kind will be born with blood in this world.
In various places, rocks, being red, will stay that way.
It will be, in this world, as if all is mingled with blood.

Then the world will be beautiful to look at.
Ay! What do you think of that?"

Meadowlark said: "What you say is good."

And then, Meadowlark went away.
And, as he left, he said:
"I am a creature who will travel like this."
And up and away he flew.

Earthmaker spoke.
"Please lie down here on your belly," he said.

"All right," said Coyote, and he lay on his belly.

He stretched out the land with his feet.
Pushing it out, little by little,
he stretched it out to where the sun rises—
first, he stretched it out to there.
Then, to the south, and to where the sun sets,
he stretched it out, little by little—
then, to the land beyond, to the North Country,
he stretched it out, little by little—
then, he stretched it out in all directions,
little by little.

Having stretched it all apart a little ways, not very far,
he said: "Enough!"

Then, Earthmaker looked up.
"Well," he said,
"It would be good
if this world were big enough to travel around in."

And then, by and by he said:
"Please lie down again, and,
when you have stretched out on your belly,
don't look up. Don't do it!"

"All right," said Coyote. "I won't look up."
He lay down on his belly.

Stretching the land out, little by little,
toward where the sun rises,
he pushed it with his foot as far as he could.
Stretching it around, little by little,
toward the North Country,
he pushed it with his foot as far as he could.
Stretching it around, little by little,
toward where the sun goes down,
he pushed it with his foot as far as he could.

Stretching it around on all sides, little by little,
he pushed it with his foot as far as he could.
And then, he said: "Enough!"
and jumped up.
When he had jumped up, he stepped along hither,
to somewhere around here.

And then, Earthmaker was standing there alone.

Standing there, they say he went somewhere to the south.
He went traveling along.

Afterwards, going across the rim of the world
to somewhere near where the sun floats away,
he came elsewhere, into a different part of the country,
traveling always from one place to another.
And, when he had gone toward where the sun rises,
he came to a place where he had once turned aside before,
and he stopped and got things ready.

Then, he made creatures, two by two.

He made a pure white creature,
and then he made another one which, though also white,
was a little different.

He kept on, and made a black one;
then he made one, a little different, which was also black.

He made them only in pairs.

And then, he told off all the lands,
and, when he had counted them,
he gave to the lands the creatures he had made.

He said:
"This place will have this creature.
Each one of you will have a place to be.
These creatures will keep growing and growing
while many winters come and many mornings dawn.
They will grow and grow until the winters pass
and the mornings pass.
When they are done growing, they will be born.
When very many winters have gone by they will be born.
Then they will have young, both female and male,
and when these are grown, they will also have young,
and when many winters have gone by
there will be many creatures."

In this way he gave to various creatures each its own place.

Then he spoke again.

"I have put all of you in this world.
Henceforth, this world will belong to you.
You will be creatures with names.
All of you will have names
and the places where you live will also have names.
Your places will all be places with names
and you will also have names.

You will be in this world,
and your descendants will fill it up.
Each and every one of them will have a name.

"Growing there,
as many winters pass and many days pass,
you will be grown,
and then this land will be yours."

He gave a different kind of creature to the land,
then he spoke once more again.

"You are creatures who speak differently—
creatures who look different.
You also will have a place of your own.
Your young,
growing weary,
wanting to live in another land,
going from this place,
will live there.
Being born there,
they will live on every bit of the land."

Then he divided out the lands among them.
"You take the land over that way,
And you others go to that country.
All of you various creatures will be called different things."

And then, later,
setting out another time,
he came back this way,
and, after he had traveled far,
and, when he had arrived at the middle of the world,
he made ready.

When he had made two beings, he put them there.

He said:
"You will grow and grow.
So, when a number of winters have gone by—
very many winters, many days have gone by—
you will be grown.
Then you will be born as human beings.

"And this country will have a name.
On the other side of this mountain is another country,
and that, also, shall have a name.

"But you will not be born soon."

Having set out from the center of the world,
he went away.
He kept going—going to certain places,

and, at those places where human beings were to live,
he stopped.

Then, he made things ready again.

He made two people,
then two more and then two more.
He kept count of them,
and, when he had counted them all,
he spoke.

"You will live here.
You and your country will have a name.
Living in a country that is little, not big,
you will be content.

"When I have gone hence,
you will grow and grow,
and, when a number of winters are past,
a great many winters, a great many days are gone by,
you will be grown.
And then, when you are grown,
you will be born.

"When you have been born,
different kinds of food,
all kinds of food will grow.
Then, after you are born,
you will be clever enough to survive."

Then he shoved them under the ground.

He made more people.
Then he spoke again.
"You will also have a small country."

And he spoke to all the people.

"You will not drive one another from each other's meadows,
saying: 'All right now! Clear out of our country!'

"You will call your countries by different names,
and you will also be differently named peoples.
Then, growing and growing—
when many days have passed—
many winters have passed—
when the day you will be born has passed—
then you will go on living, having children.
As other winters go by, and they get a little bigger,
going on like that,
going on growing,
after enough winters have passed,
you will have many children,
and there will be enough people.
Each and every one of your children will have a name.
In the same way
this country will also have a name.
Every country will have a name.
If you go somewhere to have a look around,
and you say as you set out,
'I'm going to such and such a country,'
calling it by name,
then everyone will know where you are going."

And, after that,
he picked out a creature from around here.
And he said:
"You, too, are going to be a human being
when several winters have passed.
When many winters have gone by,
you will be born.
Growing and growing,

you will get a little bigger each winter.
Though you are very small,
you will grow,
and, when winters have passed,
after many winters,
you will be grown.

And, when you are grown,
you will be born.

"You, too, will have a country there.
Your country will have a name.
You, too, will have a name,
and you will beget children.

"When they have gotten a little bigger,
your children will know the country,
having seen it all,
and having talked about it—
having given it a name.

"So, you will teach your children to name things:
'This place is called this;
that place is called that.'
Then, when you have taught them,
they will know what you know."

And, with the flick of a finger,
he sent the little being across the mountains.

As he was about to finish counting them all,
one still remained. He said:
"You, also, will be one who speaks another language.
You will beget a greater number of descendants.
You will be like the others,
and have a country of a certain size—
a big country.
It will be there where I used to wander about,
and you will, indeed, want for nothing."

With a sweep of his hand, he pointed out the land.

"The country I am speaking of
will be here forever,
and the last thing I shall tell you is to dwell here.
You are the last of my creatures.
Now that I have told you to dwell here,

I shall return to my own country and stay there.
If things are not just right in this country,
I shall make them so.
And, when I have done that, then, later,
you will be born."

Long before, Coyote divined all this.

He said:
"This earth is going to shift.
Since it is flat and thin, it will be an unstable world.
After the world has all been created,
then, by and by,
I shall tug on this rope from time to time,
making the earth shift."

"Now then, enough!" said Earthmaker.
"There will be songs—
there will always be songs,
and all of you will have them."

And after that, he sang—and sang—and sang;
then he stopped singing.

"These are the songs that you human beings will have,"
he said.
And then, he sang some other songs;
singing some other songs, he started off.

He went a long way
until he finally came to the middle of the world.
When he got that far,
he sat down and stayed there.

But, telling about the world,
Meadowlark sang very beautifully.
He was the first being created,
the first being to go across the meadows.
He was the being who saw the dry land,
very beautiful;

singing from the beginning—
a being who sang songs.

Then, traveling,
Earthmaker went past the middle of the world,
built a house,
and lived there.

He was there, at the ends of the earth.

That is all, they say.

The Creation: Turtle Island (Maidu)

In the beginning there was no sun, no moon, no stars. All was dark, and everywhere there was only water. A raft came floating on the water. It came from the north, and in it were two persons—Turtle and Pehe-ipe. The stream flowed very rapidly. Then from the sky a rope of feathers, called *Pokelma*, was let down, and down it came Earth-Initiate. When he reached the end of the rope, he tied it to the bow of the raft, and stepped in. His face was covered and was never seen, but his body shone like the sun. He sat down, and for a long time said nothing.

At last Turtle said, "Where do you come from?" and Earth Initiate answered, "I come from above." Then Turtle said, "Brother, can you not make for me some good dry land, so that I may sometimes come up out of the water?" Then he asked another time, "Are there going to be any people in the world?" Earth-Initiate thought awhile, and then said, "Yes." Turtle asked, "How long before you are going to make people?" Earth-Initiate replied, "I don't know. You want to have some dry land: well, how am I going to get any earth to make it of?" Turtle answered, "If you will tie a rock about my left arm, I'll dive for some." Earth-Initiate did as Turtle asked, and then, reaching around, took the end of a rope from somewhere, and tied it to Turtle. When Earth-Initiate came to the raft, there was no rope there: he just reached out and found one. Turtle said, "If the rope is not long enough, I'll jerk it once, and you must haul me up; if it is long enough, I'll give two jerks, and then you must pull me up quickly, as I shall have all the earth that I can carry." Just as Turtle went over the side of the boat, Pehe-ipe began to shout loudly.

Turtle was gone a long time. He was gone six years; and when he came up, he was covered with green slime, he had been down so long. When he reached the top of the water, the only earth he had was a very little under his nails: the rest had all washed away. Earth-Initiate took with his right hand a stone knife from under his left armpit, and carefully scraped the earth out from under Turtle's nails. He put the earth in the palm of his hand, and rolled it about till it was round; it was as large as a small pebble. He laid it on the stern of the raft. By and by he went to look at it: it had not grown at all. The third time that he went to look at it, it had grown so that it could not be spanned by the arms. The fourth time he looked, it was as big as the world, the raft was aground, and all around were mountains as far as he could see. The raft came ashore at Tadoiko, and the place can be seen today.

The Origin of the Mountains (Yokuts)

Once there was a time when there was nothing in the world but water. About the place where Tulare Lake is now, there was a pole standing far up out of the water, and on this pole perched a hawk and a crow. First one of them would sit on the pole a while, then the other would knock him off and sit on it himself. Thus they sat on top of the pole above the waters for many ages. At length they wearied of the lonesomeness, and they created the birds which prey on fish such as the kingfisher, eagle, pelican, and others. Among them was a very small duck, which dived down to the bottom of the water, picked its beak full of mud, came up, died, and lay floating on the water. The hawk and the crow then fell to work and gathered from the duck's beak the earth which it had brought up, and commenced making the mountains. They began at the place now known as Ta-hi-cha-pa Pass, and the hawk made the east range, while the crow made the west one. Little by little, as they dropped in the earth, these great mountains grew athwart the face of the waters, pushing north. It was a work of many years, but finally they met together at Mount Shasta, and their labors were ended. But, behold, when they compared their mountains, it was found that the crow's was a great deal the larger. Then the hawk said to the crow, "How did this happen, you rascal? I warrant you have been stealing some of the earth from my bill, and that is why your mountains are the biggest." It was a fact, and the crow laughed in his claws. Then the hawk went and got some Indian tobacco and chewed it, and it made him exceedingly wise. So he took hold of the mountains and turned them around in a circle, putting his range in place of the crow's; and that is why the Sierra Nevada is larger than the Coast Range.

The Three Worlds (Chumash)

There is this world in which we live, but there is also one above us and one below us. The world below is *coyinasup*, the underworld, the other world. That is where the *nunasis*, the angry ones, live. This world here is that of *itiasup*, humans, and the world above is *alapay*, although one can also say *misupasup* and *alapayasup*. Here where we live is the center of our world—it is the biggest island. And there are two giant serpents, the *malaqsiqitasup*, that hold our world up from below. When they are tired they move, and that causes earthquakes. The world above is sustained by the great *Slo:w*, who by stretching his wings causes the phases of the moon. And the water in the springs and streams of this earth is the urine of the many frogs who live in it.

The Making of Man (Chumash)

After the flood *Snilemun* (the Coyote of the Sky), Sun, Moon, Morning Star, and *Slo:w* (the great eagle that knows what is to be) were discussing how they were going to make man, and *Slo:w* and *Snilemun* kept arguing about whether or not the new people should have hands like *Snilemun*. Coyote announced that there would be people in this world and they should all be in his image, since he had the finest hands. Lizard was there also, but he just listened night after night and said nothing. At last *Snilemun* won the argument, and it was agreed that people were to have hands just like his. The next day they all gathered around a beautiful table-like rock that was there in the sky, a very fine white rock that was perfectly symmetrical and flat on top, and of such fine texture that whatever touched it left an exact impression. *Snilemun* was just about to stamp his hand down on the rock when Lizard, who had been standing silently just behind, quickly reached out and pressed a perfect handprint into the rock himself. *Snilemun* was enraged and wanted to kill Lizard, but Lizard ran down into a deep crevice and so escaped. And *Slo:w* and Sun approved of Lizard's actions, so what could *Snilemun* do? They say that the mark is still impressed on that rock in the sky. If Lizard had not done what he did, we might have hands like a coyote today.

Initiation Song (Yuki)

This rock did not come here by itself.
This tree does not stand here of itself.

There is one who made all this,
Who shows us everything.

Cottontail and the Sun (Owens Valley Paiute)

Cottontail lived at Black Rock. He decided that the sun was too hot. With his bow and arrow he lay in wait for it one morning in his little cave in the rocks. He lay there, and just as the sun came up, he shot it and brought it down. Then he took a piece of liver, which he cut thin, and put it over the sun. Since then the sun has not been so bright.

Storyteller Tom Stone

Love, Marriage, Family

Puberty Dance Song (Wintu)

Thou art a girl no more,
Thou art a girl no more;
The chief, the chief,
The chief, the chief,
  Honors thee
In the dance, in the dance,
In the long and double line
Of the dance,
  Dance, dance,
  Dance, dance.

Three Love Songs (Wintu)

 1

Before you go over the snow-mountain to the north,
Downhill toward the north,
Oh me, do look back at me.

You who dwell below the snow-mountain,
Do look back at me.
 Storyteller Harry Marsh

 2

When he walks about,
When he walks about,
Pushing the deer decoy back away from his face,
Right there in front of him
May I come gliding down and fall!
 Storyteller Harry Marsh

 3

The sleeping place
Which you and I hollowed out

Will remain always,
Will remain always,
Will remain always,
Will remain always.

Storyteller Fanny Brown

About-the-House Girl (Karok)

Patapir lived with his father and mother in a comfortable house near the mouth of the river. He liked to sit on a flat rock by the river and play his flute. The music he made carried across to the village of Rekwoi on the other side, and it drifted upstream, sometimes shrill and sharp with the trills and runs of songbirds, sometimes bright with the ripples of running water, sometimes low and sad with the sighing of the wind through the trees. He was a man grown, strong and tall, his hair reaching to his hips; but Patapir had never known any woman. He hunted and fished, he cut down trees and adzed and split the wood for the sweat house or other building, he carved and burned out his own canoe and made the long storage boxes to hold his accumulating treasure, he cut and carried ceremonial wood for sweat house fires, and he sweated himself and prayed. Between working and hunting and praying, he played his flute, and songs of love and lonesomeness and longing came from his flute.

Ifapi lived far upriver with her father in the village of Merip. Her mother died when she was a little girl. Theirs was a good family and the father could have married well again had he wished to. Instead he took care of Ifapi, and the two of them lived on in their home together until she was grown—quiet, loving, and gentle. Ifapi was a shy girl who hid herself when young men came to the house. Instead of fixing on one of them as a husband for her, the father sent Ifapi to stay for some moons with an old aunt, his elder sister, who lived alone in Rekwoi. As far as the aunt's neighbors knew, Ifapi stayed indoors all day. She was never seen about the village, and when people asked for her the old woman said only that she was not well.

One day while Patapir played his flute, he kept looking across to the village of Rekwoi and up to its topmost house, far up the hill where the sun shone on it all day and where its terrace overlooked the mouth of the river, the sand bar, and the ocean beyond. This was the house of Ifapi's aunt. His mother spoke often of the aunt and sometimes of the niece who was staying with her now. Patapir had questioned his mother about the young girl but she had said that she knew nothing of her, that the old woman appeared to keep her away from men altogether, even from Patapir, although his was an aristocratic family and one long acquainted with Ifapi's people. His mother also told him that the gossip in the village was that the girl was not strong.

Patapir continued to think about her, wondering what she was like, wishing he might have a glimpse of her. But today there was no sign of a girl or even of an old woman, and Patapir saw instead, on the terrace of a house farther downhill, two strange young women. He put his flute on the rock beside him and looked more closely. They were certainly pretty, he decided, and they looked friendly sitting there sunning themselves on the terrace, their feet tucked under, their bark skirts spread wide. He did what he had never done before—untied his boat and crossed the river deliberately to get acquainted with them.

The two young women had seen Patapir, even as he had seen them. They watched while he got into his boat and rowed across to Rekwoi. When he came up to their terrace they were sitting as he had seen them, their feet tucked under and their skirts spread out, and he thought they were prettier close up than from a distance. He spoke shyly to them, and they motioned him to sit down on a redwood stool between them, pleased to have attracted the handsome flute player. He was silent except for answering their questions briefly, for he did not know how to talk to them. This made them giggle, and they chattered and flirted with him and teased him. The three of them stayed for some time in this way, when a smell of seaweed filled the air; not of the broken plants washed ashore and rotting on the beach but of the deep-ocean seaweed, whole and fresh. Patapir looked around to find where it came from. Uphill, he saw the house of Ifapi's aunt, and the old woman herself out on her roof spreading fresh seaweed over the boards to dry. Patapir could almost taste the acrid ocean flavor, and he wanted more than anything else to have some of it to eat. He got up absent-mindedly from the stool on which he had been sitting, murmured something about seaweed and about being back soon, and left them, walking quickly to the house at the top of the hill.

As for his new friends, they shrugged their shoulders when he left them and laughed at him. "He is a strange one, the Flute Player," said one of them. "Yes, but he'll be back, you'll see," said the other.

Patapir meanwhile was greeting the old aunt, whom he had known since childhood, and telling her how the smell of seaweed had drawn him up the hill to her house. She broke off a leaf, newly dried, and gave it to him, inviting him to come indoors with her. There she dipped up a small basket of acorn mush from the large one by the fire and gave it to him to eat with the seaweed. And there, for the first time, he saw Ifapi.

Ifapi lay close to the fire, a deerskin blanket covering her. She did not get up while Patapir was there. Pale and quiet, looking smaller under the heavy blanket than in fact she was, she took little part in the conversation. None-theless Patapir thought of her all the while he was inside the house.

He did not stay long. When he had finished the mush, he returned the basket and spoon to the old woman, thanking her and saying goodbye to her and to Ifapi. Then he went back down the hill to the two young women. As soon as they saw him one of them asked him, "Where did you go?" And the other one asked him, "What is so interesting up the hill there?"

"I was talking with the old woman in the upper house," said Patapir. "She gave me some mush and seaweed." The girls shrugged their shoulders and looked at each other and laughed. Patapir stopped for only a few minutes with them before crossing back to his side of the river. During the rest of the day he cut and carried loads of wood for a sweat house fire, and at the end of the day he played long, long on his flute.

While he played he made plans for the next day, and in the morning he crossed the river as soon as he saw his new friends out on their terrace. He said to them, "I want to sleep with you. May I come to your house tonight?"

The young women laughed when he asked this, and one of them said, "Don't try to fool us—you are only pretending you want us." And the other one said, "You really want that girl up the hill. You just come here to be near her!" But after more teasing, they agreed that he might come. "Come tonight. . . . But wait till it is dark!" they told him.

Patapir fished during most of the day. Then he sweated himself again. As the sun neared the rim of the sky he was restless, already seated in his canoe waiting to paddle across as soon as the sun was set. Thus it happened he was outside the young women's house before they were expecting him. They were dressing, calling back and forth to each other while they dressed. Patapir stayed at a little distance from the house, but even so their voices reached him plainly: "How shall we dress tonight?"

"We could wear our good skirts."

"Or our new aprons."

"No one can see what we wear in the dark. Why not the same as last night?"

"But we must be sure to take capes. It is cold on the water." This was the way they talked.

Patapir waited, and the young women came out onto the terrace dressed for the out-of-doors and carrying canoe paddles. They stopped when they saw that Patapir was there, but before he could say anything they began to laugh, and then they ran as fast as they could away from him, downhill. He ran after them but it was already dark. He heard men's voices calling softly to them from the river, and as he came out onto the bank the girls were already seated with several men in a canoe which was headed downstream, one of a long line of canoes filled with men and an occasional woman or two, and being paddled toward the mouth of the river. Last of all there came a small canoe with only two men in it. They called to Patapir as he stood, uncertain what it all meant, and what he should do. "Come. Come with us," they said. "We have plenty of room."

"But where do you go?"

"To the dancing across the ocean! Come!"

Patapir got into the canoe. He saw that there were blankets for keeping warm, pipes for smoking when they should wish to rest from paddling, and baskets for gathering fresh seaweed.

The canoes, ten in all, cleared the bar and the offshore breakers and set out to sea. They stopped once at a large sea stack to rest and fill their baskets with seaweed and to have a smoke. Patapir noticed that where they knocked out their pipes the grass and flowers growing in the crannies of the rock were charred, showing that pipes had been knocked out there many times before.

Beyond the sea stack, they paddled steadily on, ten boats one after another to the edge of the world where sky and ocean meet. Patapir watched, breathless, as the boats lined up side by side. Truly it was as his grandfather had told him: the sky moves up and down, up and down; when it drops it strikes the ocean with a force so strong it starts the waves which beat unendingly against the shores of the distant earth. Patapir counted, and as his grandfather had told him, every twelfth lifting of the sky was slower than the in-between ones, leaving a gap for a long enough time that a canoe, set and ready, could pass under the sky, out beyond the edge of the world and into the outer ocean. This the ten boats lined up at the edge succeeded in doing, counting the waves, and going under as one with the slower wave. Patapir looked back. He saw that the sky was again down against the water, and that he and his companions were outside the world, paddling through the waters of the outer ocean. They went as far as the Land-Beyond-the-World, where they beached their canoes on the flat and sandy shore.

There was a fire up the beach a short distance and a circle of people around it watching a Life Renewing Dance. Patapir and the others from the ten boats went to the fire and stood quietly where they could see the dancing.

As he watched, Patapir wondered why this that was so new and strange seemed somehow familiar. Then he recalled that it was the dancing the old ones in the sweat house at home told him of when they were in a mood to talk to him of their own youth. He had thought their tales of dancing across the ocean to be no more than old men's imaginings about bygone days. They told him that such night voyages down the river and over the sea were only for the young and the strong, and they hinted that sometimes a man persuaded his sweetheart to go along. They spoke of this adventuring as something in the past—their past, when they were young and carefree, hunting and fishing by day, and paddling across the ocean and outside the world, dancing and making love by night—a time when sleep was something for the old.

Patapir was wide awake and aware and alive as never before—what had been the old one's dream was become his own reality. Never had he imagined such dancing and such singing. The singing rose from a low wail to the strident shrillness of the highest notes of songbirds. The rhythm of the dancing feet was strong and pure and steady on the earth. There was beauty and authority in the voice and gestures of the Leader as he offered incense and tobacco to fire and to Spirits, and recited the prayers for each.

Patapir and his two companions in the canoe were seeing this for the first time. So interested were they, they pressed forward, nearer to the fire, nearer to the dancers. By now, the men from the other canoes had joined the line of dancers. Patapir saw that the old ones spoke truly—the dancers were all in their young manhood, strong and tall. Some of them could leap in the dancing, high, and with the long-legged grace of the crane; and some could sing, sending their voices higher than the flickers' call. Little by little, Patapir forgot the dancers and singers as his attention gathered more and more about the person of the Leader's assistant. This was scarcely surprising; the young men beside him had eyes for nothing else, nor did Patapir, once he really looked at her.

Women never dance in the Life Renewing Dance, but the Leader is served by one woman who makes and tends the fire for him, hands him angelica root and tobacco and his pipe, removing them when he has taken what he wants of the incense or finished the pipe ritual. It is a position of honor for a woman, and since she must not have borne a child and must submit to training, to prescribed diet, and to purification, it follows that the Leader will select her with care. She is sure to be young and good-looking, with proud bearing, gracious and graceful.

The assistant Patapir was gazing at was young, the delicate oval of her face shadowed by shyly lowered lids, the young breasts shadowed by long hair braided and tied with mink and by the cloak she wore over her shoulders— a cloak made of hundreds of closely sewn crests of the red-headed woodpecker, seeming itself a sheet of flame from the fire as she moved. Her skirt and front apron were heavy fringes of shells strung close together, each string tufted with a red woodpecker crest. She was barefoot, and as she bent to the fire or lifted a basket of incense to the Leader, the play and motion of thigh and leg showed through the fringe of shells which answered her every movement with a low rustle as of a receding surf playing shell against shell on the beach.

She brought a piece of driftwood and put it on the fire, facing Patapir as she did so. The fire blazed high, lighting her shadowed face, and Patapir saw that she was Ifapi—Ifapi, the little pale girl whom he had seen lying in the old woman's house at home. She did not raise her eyes or look at him, but for the rest of that night's dancing he watched her, and during the early morning hours of paddling home, back under the sky rim and all the way across the ocean, he thought of her.

He went far into the hills that same day, cutting the topmost branches of tall fir trees according to old ceremonial rule, bringing them home in bundles. With these he made a sweat house fire, and sweated and prayed until almost sundown. Then he swam and washed himself in the river, and when the sun was quite gone, he crossed to the other side in his canoe. The aroma of drying seaweed wafted down to him, pungent and sea-filled, and he went uphill toward the old aunt's house.

Patapir had quite forgotten the two young women who had seemed so pretty to him the day before, but they were waiting for him on their terrace. He spoke to them and they knew from his manner that he was not meaning to come in with them this time. One of them said, "I don't believe you have come to see us at all. You don't even want to stop and talk!" And the other one said, "You only want to see the girl who is sick all the time up there with the old woman!"

Patapir, whose thoughts were far away, answered them, "Yes. She is the one I want to see," and he went on without more talk. They laughed, shrugging their shoulders and turning their backs to him.

When Patapir got to her house the old woman was on the roof gathering in the dried seaweed. She gave him a leaf and invited him inside to have some of her acorn mush. He followed her through the round door and there, just as before, he saw Ifapi covered with the heavy blanket, looking pale and ill. Her aunt climbed down the ladder into the pit to see if the mush was done, and Patapir jumped lightly after her, going to Ifapi, and patting her shoulder to draw her attention. Ifapi turned toward him; but before she could speak, her aunt saw what he was doing and spoke up sharply. "Do not touch her," she said. "She is very sick. You mustn't ever do that again!" She could not think what was in Patapir's mind, and she was frightened, unable for the moment to move, a wooden stirrer still in her hand, watching him and repeating over and over, "You mustn't . . . she's sick . . . she's always sick . . . you can't . . ."

Patapir paid no attention to her. He slid his arms carefully under the blanket on which Ifapi lay, lifted her, deerskin blanket and all, and carried her up the ladder. Only then did he speak to the aunt, saying, "I know that she is not sick! I saw her at the dancing across the ocean last night."

This brought the old woman back to herself. She threw aside the stirrer and followed Patapir up the ladder. Taking his arm, she said imploringly to him, "Then go—go outside. . . . Leave her!" Patapir shook his head, but she held him still. "Leave her I say! I must speak with her—only for a breath—I will call you back. . . . Please to do what I say—this is the right thing, I tell you!"

Patapir had had every intention of carrying Ifapi off without talk or delay, but something in the old woman's tone made him listen to her; and when he turned to Ifapi, she nodded her head and, in a voice so low he scarcely caught her words, said to him, "Do what she says."

"Call me then," he said, leaving Ifapi and stepping outside. And before his impatience drove him back, the aunt called him in.

Stooping to go through the low door, he looked first for Ifapi. She was there, but the shadowed face was no longer pale and indifferent, but awake as at the dancing. She was dressed in the shell fringe skirt and apron, and the red-crested feather cloak was around her shoulders. Patapir went to her and took her arm, but the old aunt's voice interrupted, "Flute Player of Rekwoi, what are you doing?"

"I am taking this little one with me, aunty."

"Wait! Let the shadows grow longer while I tell you . . ."

"Tell quickly, aunty, for I would be away from here . . ."

"Flute Player, this child is not an old woman's nobody. She has a father, my brother, upriver. I must answer to him for her, and you must answer to him for her."

"This I know, aunty. My father knows the brother of whom you speak."

"There is another thing that I must tell you so you do not misjudge me. It was she and not I who wished to make this look of sickness. I helped her to it only because she begged me to."

"I believe you, old woman, and I believe that, just now, she laid aside her sickness of her own wish. Isn't that true?"

"It is true, Flute Player. But what do you do with her?"

"Do you not worry, aunty. I am taking her with me and I am marrying her—tonight. But tomorrow, as soon as it is light, we shall go upriver, she and I, and her bride price goes with us to her father. You've known me all my life, aunty, and you know my father and my mother. You and her father and the Leader across the ocean will say she was proudly bought."

The old woman had to content herself with this promise. She was wise as well as old, and she knew that she could do very little, for what Patapir wished, Ifapi wished also. She looked on without interfering when Patapir went to Ifapi and again took her arm, saying, "Come!"

Ifapi said, "Goodbye, aunty. Thank you for helping me. I shall tell my father that you were very good to me."

Ifapi followed Patapir through the low round door. On the terrace, he lifted her gently into his arms, the feather cloak flowing about them like a flame as he carried her into the darkness, down the hill to the river, to his canoe. They crossed to his side of the river, and there in a hollow under a redwood tree he made a soft sweet bed of ferns laid over with deerskin rugs, and there he and Ifapi spent their wedding night.

In the early dawn, Rekwoi was a village asleep. No one stirred or wakened as Patapir stowed his long boxes of treasure in the canoe or as he and Ifapi took their places at either end and headed upstream. He pulled against the current, and the strong smell of seaweed again filled his senses as in a re-membered dream, while far up the hill an old woman spread fresh seaweed over her roof and watched the sun rise above the canyon wall and a canoe move out of her sight upriver, disappearing behind the same canyon wall.

Paddling steadily, stopping for short rests, Patapir and Ifapi came to her old home. Ifapi ran ahead to greet her father. He was surprised to see her, and he questioned her, saying, "All is well?"

"All is well, my father."

"What brings you home?"

"That you may know my husband."

Her father sighed, speaking half to himself, half to Ifapi, "Ahhh—that old woman, my sister, she was not careless with you?"

"No, no, my father. She was good to me and cared for me and helped me."

"But then whom could you have married? I have heard nothing of any man looking at you—only that you were serving the Leader across the ocean . . ."

"So I have served him—I alone." Ifapi said this with quiet pride.

"Tell me then—who is this man, your husband—you must know, my child, that when I let you go away from me, it was with the foolish thought that you might continue to keep yourself from men, and that the Flute Player of Rekwoi might one day come to know of your being chosen by the Leader and wish to marry you. I know his family, and perhaps you have not forgotten how we used to listen together to his songs as they floated up the river—before you were grown and went away from me."

"It was as you say, my father. I hid from men, going only to the dancing, and I, too, thought always of the Flute Player. At last, he saw the dancing—and wished to marry me."

Patapir then came up to Ifapi's father to greet him and to offer the boxes of treasure, his bride payment for Ifapi. As he had promised the old aunt, he brought a proud man's payment for a beloved daughter.

The father was satisfied. He said, "It is good, my son-in-law, my daughter."

The young people stayed with Ifapi's father until it was time to dance the Life Renewing Dances again. The father was much beyond the age of those who usually make the long voyage, but his heart was set on hearing his son-in-law sing there. He had heard Patapir singing alone in the hills, practicing against the calls and whistles of the birds, and he knew that it was a good voice for the sacred songs. So they were three in Patapir's canoe. Other canoes joined them farther downstream until there were ten of them in all. As on Patapir's first trip, they cleared the bar and went the way of the setting sun, stopping for a rest and a smoke at the lonely rock, and then going on—one boat after the other—across the ocean, under the sky rim and across the outer ocean to the Land-Beyond-the-World.

There was such dancing and singing that night as those who stood in the circle never forgot. For Ifapi, it was the last time she might make and tend the fire, the last time she might offer incense and tobacco and pipe to the Leader and receive these back from his hands, the last time she might move in and out of the line of dancers, the one woman in the sacred ceremony. Before another season of the Life Renewing Dances she would no longer be eligible to serve at them. But Ifapi was without regrets or sadness. The eyes of all the men followed her this night as never before, for the oval face was unshadowed. Whenever she raised her arms to the Leader to give him a basket or to take his pipe, she raised her eyes, too, to look down the line of dancers to the new one there, the one with the voice so strangely low and high like a flute—to Patapir, her husband.

The two young women of Rekwoi were at the dancing that night, and this is how it went with them. They watched and saw how beautiful Ifapi was, and they listened and heard the new voice among the singers. They crowded nearer and nearer, and looking in the direction Ifapi looked, they saw Patapir.

They stared a long time at him. At last, one of them said, "That new singer there—he looks like the young man across the river from us." And the other one said, "Yes. Of course. He is the one we tease all the time." Then the first one said, "I didn't know he could sing. All he ever does around home is to play his old flute and go see that sick girl up the hill." Her companion answered, "He'll go and see her again—the sick one—you just see if he doesn't!"

One of the men standing in the circle interrupted their talk. "Yes, that is the Flute Player of Rekwoi. Everyone knows him because of his playing."

A second man said, "But don't you Rekwoi people know? She," motioning toward Ifapi, "she is the 'little sick girl.' The Flute Player married her, and took the bride price to her father in Merip—my village. No one in our time has given treasure to equal it. The father is well satisfied."

"*She* is the sick girl. . . . *He* is married . . ." The young women could only repeat this over and over. They looked at one another, but they did not shrug their shoulders this time.

When the men said, "We must start home, we have far to go before daybreak," the young women did not answer them. They felt such fools they had slipped away and were never seen in Rekwoi or at the dancing again. Only their little round basket hats were left lying on the ground, marking the place where the girls were last seen.

The long night of singing and dancing came to an end at last. Patapir and Ifapi and her father went off somewhere, and for half a moon's time no one saw them or knew anything of them. Then one morning Patapir's parents sighted their canoe far out at sea, seeming to skim the water like a bird, and soon it was over the bar and they were home once more. Patapir put into the canoe the long boxes which held his dance outfits and treasure, his ten precious sacks of sacred tobacco and his flute. When they were ready to leave again, Patapir's parents asked him where they meant to go, and he answered, "Far across the ocean in the wake of the fresh seaweed! Do not worry. You will have word of us and know that all is well."

His father and mother cried when the canoe with its three passengers and its load of treasure went out over the bar, on and on like a sea bird, out of their sight and knowledge.

Patapir spoke truly when he said they would have word of him, for he was the great singer in the sacred ceremonies in the Land-Beyond-the-World for many, many moons. News of him and his family came over the bar to Rekwoi and on upriver as far as the music of his flute used to carry—all the way to Merip—as often as the ten canoes returned from the dancing.

We know that Patapir and Ifapi lived out their lives in that far land beyond the sky rim, and that Ifapi and her children and her father, as long as he lived, came with Patapir to the dancing. And we know the pet name Patapir gave to Ifapi. Because he never forgot the first time he saw her, he named her "About-the-House Girl."

The Girl Who Married Rattlesnake (Pomo)

At a place called Cobowin there is a large rock with a hole in it and there were many rattlesnakes in this hole. At Kalesima nearby there was a village with four large houses. In one of these large houses which had a center pole there lived a girl. This was in the spring of the year when the clover was just right to eat. This girl went out to gather clover and one of the rattlesnakes watched her. When she had a sufficient amount of this food she took it home and gave it to her mother.

Rattlesnake went to the village and when he had approached very near to the house he transformed himself into a young man with a head-net on his head and fine beads around his neck. He made himself look as handsome as possible. Then he climbed up onto the top of the house and came down the center pole. He went to this girl and told her that he wanted to marry her and he remained there with the family. The following morning he went home again. This he did for four days. On the fifth evening he came back but this time he did not change his form. He simply went into the house and talked just as he had before. The girl's mother said that there was someone over there talking all the time. She made a light and looked over in the place where she heard the sound, and there was Rattlesnake. He shook his head and frightened her terribly. She dropped the light and ran.

On the following morning Rattlesnake took the girl home with him and she remained there. Finally this girl had four children and as they grew up, whenever they saw any of the people from the village, they would say to their mother, "We are going to bite those people." But she would say, "No, you must not do that. Those are your relatives." And the children would do as she told them.

Now these four rattlesnake boys were out playing around one day as they grew a little older. Finally they became curious. They came in and asked their mother, "Why do you not talk the way we do? Why are you so different?"

"I am not a rattlesnake," she replied. "I am a human being. I am different from you and your father."

"Are you not afraid of our father?" asked the boys. "No," she answered.

Then the oldest of the rattlesnake boys said that he had heard the other rattlesnakes talking and that they too thought it strange that she was so different from them and that they were going to investigate and see just why it was that she was so different. They were going to crawl over her body and find out why she was so different from themselves. She was not at all afraid; when the rattlesnakes all came they crawled over her and she was not alarmed in any way.

Then she said to her oldest boy, "It is impossible for you to become a human being and I am not really a human being any longer, so I am going back to my parents and tell them what has happened." She did go home and she said to her parents, "This is the last time that I shall be able to talk to you and the last time that you will be able to talk with me." Her father and mother felt very sad about this, but they said nothing. Then the daughter started to leave, but her mother ran after her and caught her right by the door, brought her back into the house and wept over her because she was so changed. Then the girl shook her body and suddenly she was gone. No one knew how or where she went, but she really went back to Rattlesnake's house where she has lived ever since.

Storyteller Charley Brown

The Man and the Owls (Yokuts)

A man and his wife were traveling. They camped overnight in a cave. They had a fire burning. Then they heard a horned owl *(hutulu)* hoot. The woman said to her husband: "Call in the same way. He will come and you can shoot him. Then we will eat him for supper." The man got his bow and arrows ready and called. The owl answered, coming nearer. At last it sat in a tree near the fire. The man shot. He killed it. Then his wife told him: "Do it again. Another one will come." Again he called and brought an owl and shot it. He said: "It is enough now." But his wife said: "No. Call again. If you call them in the morning they will not come. We have had no meat for a long time. We shall want something to eat tomorrow as well as now." Then the man called. More owls came. There were more and more of them. He shot, but more came. The air was full of owls. All his arrows were gone. The owls came closer and attacked them. The man took sticks from the fire and fought them off. He covered the woman with a basket and kept on fighting. More and more owls came. At last they killed both the man and the woman.

Coyote Cooks His Daughter (Cupeño)

So Coyote was there,
   and his daughter,
   just one was there.
And their brush house stood at the foot of the mountain.
And there they were.
And then Coyote said,
   they had no food put away.
And Coyote went hunting,
   he fetched his bow.
And he went,
   he took his daughter.

So he kept circling around in a wash,
   his tail went switch-switch-switch,
   gallop-gallop-gallop he went,
   he kept coming along running.
And his daughter kept coming slowly behind him.
So Coyote look-look-looked behind him,
   his ears he twitch-twitch-twitched
And he kept coming, coming, coming,
   he was jump-jump-jumping,
   he trot-trot-trotted.

So there at the mountain they arrived.
And there he kept walking around,
he would go looking for something to eat.
So he kept jumping,
   he would catch an ant.
And he kept coming, coming, coming,
   they arrived there.

So there was a lake there,
   there he drank water.
So his daughter kept coming behind him.
So she kept coming slowly,
Coyote kept jump-jump-jumping,
   his tail went switch-switch-switch,
   he look-look-looked behind him,

he turn-turn-turned his head,
he shook-shook-shook-shook his head.
So he kept coming.
And his wife was there at home.

So she was gathering all the grass,
to cook something for him there.

And then it was evening.
And Coyote saw nothing there.
So he didn't see anything to kill.
So grabbing his daughter,
he hit her with a stick.
So it was a pine stick,
the stick.
And he killed that daughter of his.
And from there he carried her home on his back,
he came.

So he kept slowly coming along,
dragging his tail.
So he arrived there,
his wife was there by the door of the brush house.
And he arrived there.
So then he took all that hair off his daughter.
And there was a big place for cooking
something in the way of food,
he cut up his daughter there,
Coyote did.

And he cooked her.
So he boil-boil-boiled it,
her meat.
And he licked his hand like this,
he took it out,
he kept lick-licking it.
And he boiled it,
it got real green.

And then she came from there,
his daughter.

And she spoke,
    as she came,
    "Pine tree, stick,
    pine tree, grass stick
    jingle-ingle-ingle."
And still she came.
And her mother was there by the door.
And the girl's beads went,
    "Jingle-jingle-jingle."
And she said,
    "Pine tree, stick,
    pine tree, grass stick
    Jingle-ingle-ingle."

So the mother looked around,
    she looked,
    Coyote was still there cooking,
    the dust was still rising like this.
So he kept brushing his tail like this.
And the daughter was a ghost.
And she said,
    "Pine tree, stick,
    pine tree, grass stick
    jingle-ingle-ingle."
And her mother said,
    "Ah! it must be her voice I hear,
    it must be her,"
    she said.

"She's turned into a ghost,"
    she said.
    "Pine tree, stick,
    pine tree, grass stick
    jingle-ingle-ingle."
"Well," said the woman,
    "this guy must have killed her already,
    and here he is walking around."

And she went around her house.
    "Pine tree, stick,

        pine tree, grass stick
        jingle-ingle-ingle."
"Already she speaks to me,"
        said the woman,
"This guy must have killed her."

"And now for sure you come here to me,"
        said the woman,
        "and I'll burn you now."
So right then she got up,
        the old woman Coyote.
And she gathered all the grass,
        while Coyote was cooking his food.
And right away she fetched it.

And she burn-burn-burned everything.
So then their house went up in smoke.
And he said, "Oh,
        old woman, old woman,
        don't burn me, don't burn me!"
So all that house of theirs burned
And Coyote burned,
        he burned up.
And he died.

Order, Community

An Ordered World (Miwok)

The young chief is going to do the same as his father used to do.
Now all of you men get ready.
Put those poles up for him.
All of you men get ready.
Have the ceremonial house ready just the same as for his father.
The young chief is going to do just the same as his father.
He is going the same way as his father did.
It is just the same, just the same.

Storyteller Tom Williams

Prayer for Good Fortune (Yokuts)

My words are tied in one
With the great mountains,
With the great rocks,
With the great trees,
In one with my body
And my heart.
Do you all help me
With supernatural power,
And you, day,
And you, night!
All of you see me
One with this world!

Feast Oration (Wintu)

Yes!
Come on! Come on! Come on!
Come on!
Girls come on! Girls come on!
Youths come on!

Children come on!
At eating assembled. At eating assembled.
At this eating.
At this eating assembled.
At this *pinole* assembled.
At this acorn-soup assembled.
At this acorn-bread assembled.
You say "yes" to one another!
Say "yes" to one another!
Say "yes" to one another!
That is how you will do it!
You will call one another "nephew" or "niece."
At eating that.
At healthy eating assemble.
At eating that assemble. At eating this assemble.
At this pleasant eating assemble.
At this healthy eating assemble.
At that say "yes" to one another's eating!
Say "yes" to one another's eating!
Say "yes" to one another's eating!
Rejoice at one another.
Rejoice, "maternal uncle."
Rejoice, "father."
Rejoice, "younger brother."
Rejoice!
At him who causes you to eat.
At him who gives to you.
At him who gives food.
Who gives this *pinole*.
Who gives this acorn-bread.
At that be glad.
At that be glad.
So rejoice!
Rejoice for you.
My nephews and nieces, eat!
In this way eat! In this way eat! In this way eat!
You children.
You girls, you youths.
You children.

So eat!
So satisfied.
Satisfied, rejoice!
Satisfied, say "yes!"
Heed his word.
His word, his teaching.
He who teaches you.
So eat! So eat! So eat! So eat!

CHANTS, DREAMS, AND DANCES

To the Edge of the Earth (Poisoning Shaman's Song, Wintu)

To the edge of the earth
To the edge of the earth
To the edge of the earth
Snap all the people!
Snap all the people!
To the edge of the earth
To the edge of the earth.

Storyteller Fanny Brown

Rattlesnake Ceremony Song (Yokuts)

The King Snake said to the Rattlesnake:
Do not touch me!
You can do nothing with me
Lying with your belly full,
Rattlesnake of the rock pile,
Do not touch me!
There is nothing you can do,
You Rattlesnake with your belly full,
Lying where the ground-squirrel holes are thick
Do not touch me!
What can you do to me?
Rattlesnake in the tree clump,
Stretched in the shade,
You can do nothing;
Do not touch me!
Rattlesnake of the plains,
You whose white eye
The sun shines on,
Do not touch me!

Dream Time (Ohlone)

I dream of you,
I dream of you jumping.
Rabbit,
Jackrabbit,
Quail.

Four Dream Cult Songs (Wintu)

DOWN WEST

Down west, down west we dance.
     We spirits dance.
Down west, down west we dance,
     We spirits dance.
Down west, down west we dance,
     We spirits weeping dance,
     We spirits dance.
     Storyteller Sadie Marsh

THERE ABOVE

There above, there above,
     At the mystical earthlodge of the south,
     Spirits are wafted along the roof and fall.
There above, there above,
     At the mystical earthlodge of the south,
     Spirits are wafted along the roof and fall.
There above, there above,
     Spirits are wafted along the roof and fall,
     Flowers bend heavily on their stems.

IT IS ABOVE

It is above that you and I shall go;
     Along the Milky Way you and I shall go;
It is above that you and I shall go;
     Along the Milky Way you and I shall go;
It is above that you and I shall go;

Along the flower trail you and I shall go;
    Picking flowers on our way you and I shall go.
    Storyteller Harry Marsh

Above where the minnow maiden sleeps at rest
    The flowers droop,
    The flowers rise again.
Above where the minnow maiden sleeps at rest
    The flowers droop,
    The flowers rise again.
Above where the minnow maiden sleeps at rest
    The flowers droop,
    The flowers rise again.

Dancing on the Brink of the World (Costanoan)

Dancing
on the brink
of the world
dancing
on the brink
of the world

OLD AGE, DEATH, AND THE AFTERLIFE

Old Gambler's Song (Konkow)

I am the only one, the only one left.
An old man, I carry the gambling-board;
An old man, I sing the gambling song.
The roots I eat of the valley.
The pepper-ball is round.
The water trickles, trickles.
The water-leaves grow along the river bank.
I rub the hand, I wiggle the tail
I am a doctor, I am a doctor.

Grandfather's Prayer (Wintu)

Oh Olelbes, look down on me.
I wash my face in water, for you,
Seeking to remain in health.
I am advancing in old age; I am not capable of anything any more.
You whose nature it is to be eaten [i.e., deer],
You dwell high in the west, on the mountains, high in the east, high in the
north, high in the south;
You, salmon, you go about in the water.
Yet I cannot kill you and bring you home.
Neither can I go east down the slope to fetch you, salmon.
When a man is so advanced in age, he is not in full vigor.
If you are rock, look at me; I am advancing in old age.
If you are tree, look at me; I am advancing in old age.
If you are water, look at me; I am advancing in old age.
Acorns, I can never climb up to you again.
You, water, I can never dip you up and fetch you home again.
My legs are advancing in weakness.
Sugar-pine, you sit there; I can never climb you.
In my northward arm, in my southward arm, I am advancing in weakness.
You who are wood, you wood, I cannot carry you home on my shoulder.

For I am falling back into my cradle.
This is what my ancestors told me yesterday, they who have gone, long ago.
May my children fare likewise!

Death Song (Cupeño)

My heart is lost, lost.
My heart sets, sets.
My heart goes to the other world.
My heart goes to the other world.
My heart goes to the ocean foam.
My heart goes to the ocean foam.

Burial Oration (Wintu)

You are dead.
You will go above there to the trail.
That is the spirit trail.
Go there to the beautiful trail.
May it please you not to walk about where I am.
You are dead.
Go there to the beautiful trail above.
That is your way.
Look at the place where you used to wander.
The north trail, the mountains where you used to wander,
        you are leaving.
Listen to me: go there!

The Soul's Journey to *Similaqsa* (Chumash)

Three days after a person has been buried the soul comes up out of the grave in the evening. Between the third and fifth day it wanders about the world visiting the places it used to frequent in life. On the fifth day after death the soul returns to the grave to oversee the destruction of its property before leaving for *Similaqsa*, the Land of the Dead. The soul goes first to Point Conception, which is a wild and stormy place. It was called *humqaq*, and there was no village there. In ancient times no one ever went near *humqaq*. They only went near there to make sacrifices at a great *sawil* (shrine). There is a place at *humqaq* below the cliff that can only be reached by rope, and there is a pool of water there like a basin, into which fresh water continually drips. And there in the stone can be seen the footprints of women and children. There the spirit of the dead bathes and paints itself. Then it sees light to the westward and goes toward it through the air, and thus reaches the land of *Similaqsa.*

Sometimes in the evening people at La Quemada village would see a soul passing by on its way to Point Conception. Sometimes these were the souls of people who had died, but sometimes they were souls that had temporarily left the body. The people of La Quemada would motion with their hands at the soul and tell it to return, to go back east, and they would clap their hands. Sometimes the soul would respond and turn back, but other times it would simply swerve a little from its course and continue on to *Similaqsa.* When the people of La Quemada saw the soul it shone like a light, and it left a blue trail behind it. The disease from which the person had died was seen as a fiery ball at its side. When the soul turned back, as it sometimes did, anyone at La Quemada who might have recognized it would hurry to the village where the man whose soul it was lived, and if the sick man then drank a lot of toloache he might recover and not die. Maria heard that a short time after the soul passed La Quemada the people there would hear a report like a distant cannon shot, and know that that was the sound of the closing of the gate of *Similaqsa* as the soul entered.

The old people said that there were three lands in the world to the west: *Wit, Ayaya,* and *Similaqsa.* These were somewhat like purgatory, hell, and heaven. When the soul leaves Point Conception and crosses the sea, it first reaches the Land of Widows. When the women there get old, their friends dip them in a spring and when they awake they are young again. And they never eat, though they have all kinds of food there. They merely take a handful of food and smell it and throw it away and as soon as they do so it turns to feces. And when they are thirsty they just smell the water and their thirst is quenched. Once past the Land of Widows the soul comes to a deep ravine through which it must pass. The road is all cut up and consists of deep, fine earth as a result of so many souls passing over it. In the ravine are two huge stones that continually part and clash together, part and clash together, so that any person who got caught between them would be crushed. Any living person who attempted to pass would be killed, but souls pass through un-harmed.

Once past the clashing rocks the soul comes to a place where there are two gigantic *qaq* (ravens) perched on each side of the trail, who each peck out an eye as the soul goes by. But there are many poppies growing there in the ravine and the soul quickly picks two of these and inserts them in each eyesocket and so is able to see again immediately. When the soul finally gets to *Similaqsa* it is given eyes made of blue abalone. After leaving the ravine the soul comes to La Tonadora, the woman who stings with her tail. She kills any living person who comes by, but merely annoys the soul who passes safely.

Just beyond this woman lies a body of water that separates this world from the next, with a bridge that the soul must cross to reach *Similaqsa*. The souls of murderers and poisoners and other evil people never reach the bridge, but are turned to stone from the neck down. They remain there on the near shore forever, moving their eyes and watching other souls pass. When the pole begins to fall the soul starts quickly across, but when it reaches the middle two huge monsters rise from the water on either side and give a loud cry, attempting to frighten it so that it falls into the water. If the soul belongs to someone who had no *atsiswin* (spirit helper), or who did not know about the old religion and did not drink toloache—someone who merely lived in ignorance—it falls into the water and the lower part of the body changes to that of a frog, turtle, snake, or fish. The water is full of these beings, who are thus undergoing punishment. When they are hungry they crawl out of the water and wander through the hills nearby looking for cacomites to eat. The old people used to say that someone who drank toloache always passed the pole safely for they were strong of spirit.

Once the soul has crossed the bridge it is safe in *Similaqsa*. There are two roads leading from the bridge—one goes straight ahead and the other goes to the left. Maria [the teller] knows nothing about souls being born again in this world. Souls live in *Similaqsa* forever and never get old. It is packed full of souls. They harvest islay, sweet islay, and there is no end of it. Every kind of food is there in abundance. When children die they take the same route as adults. The *qaq* peck out their eyes, but they have no other troubles on the journey. They pass the bridge easily, for the monsters that try to frighten other souls do not appear.

The Land of the Dead (Serrano)

A great hunter brought home a wife. They loved each other, and were very happy. But the man's mother hated the young wife, and one day when the husband was out hunting, she put a sharp pointed object in the wife's seat, and the woman sat down upon it and was killed.

The people immediately brought brush and piled it up. They put her body upon it, and burned it, so that when her husband returned that night the body was all consumed.

The man went to the burning-place, and stayed there motionless. Curls of dust rose and whirled about the charred spot. He watched them all day. At night they grew larger, and at last one larger than all the rest whirled round and round the burned spot, and set off down the road. The man followed it. At last when it was quite dark, he saw that it was the figure of his wife that he was following, but she would not speak to him.

She was leading him in the direction of the rock past which all dead people must go. If they have been bad in their lives, the rock falls on them and crushes them. When they came to this rock, she spoke to him. "We are going to the place of dead people," she told him. "I will take you on my back so that you will not be seen and recognized as one of the living."

Thus they went on until they came to the river the dead have to ford. This was very dangerous, because the man was not dead, but the woman kept him on her back, and they came through safely. The woman went directly to her people. She went home to her parents and brothers and sisters who had died before. They were glad to see her, but they did not like the man, for he was not dead. The woman pleaded for him, however, and they let him stay. Special food had to be always cooked for him, for he could not eat what dead people live on. Also in the daytime he could see nothing; it was as if he were alone all day long; only in the night could he see.

When the people were going hunting, they said to each other that they ought to take the man along. So they took him, and stationed him on the trail the deer would take. Presently he heard them shouting, "The deer, the deer," and he knew they were shouting to him that the deer were coming in his direction. But he could see nothing. Then he looked again, and he could see two little black beetles; he knocked them over, and these were the deer the dead people hunted. And when all the people had come up, they praised him for his hunting, and after that they did not complain of his being there.

The people were sorry for him. They said, "It is not time for him to die yet. He has a hard time here. The woman ought to go back with him." So they planned that it should be so. They instructed the man and the woman to have nothing to do with each other for three nights after their return to earth; but three nights for the dead meant three years for the living.

So the man and the woman returned to earth, and they were continent for three nights. But they did not know that the dead people meant three years, and when the husband woke on the morning of the fourth day he was alone.

Storyteller Rosa Marongo

Summons to a Mourning Ceremony (Miwok)

Get up! Get up! Get up! Get up! Get up!
Wake up! Wake up! Wake up!
People get up on the south side,
East side, east side, east side, east side,
North side, north side, north side,
Lower side, lower side, lower side!
You folks come here!
Visitors are coming, visitors are coming.
Strike out together!
Hunt deer, squirrels!
And you women, strike out, gather wild onions, wild potatoes!
Gather all you can! Gather all you can!
Pound acorns, pound acorns, pound acorns!
Cook, cook!
Make some bread, make some bread!
So we can eat, so we can eat, so we can eat.
Put it up, and put it up, and put it up!
Make acorn soup so that the people will eat it!
There are many coming.
Come here, come here, come here, come here!
You have to be dry and hungry.
Be for a while.
Got nothing here.
People get up, people around get up!
Wake up!
Wake up so you can cook!
Visitors are here now and all hungry.
Get ready so we can feed them!
Gather up, gather up, and bring it all in, so we can give it to them!
Go ahead and eat!
That's all we have.
Don't talk about starvation, because we never have much!

Eat acorns!
There is nothing to it.
Eat and eat!
Eat! Eat! Eat! Eat!
So that we can get ready to cry.
Everybody get up! Everybody get up!
All here, very sad occasion.
All cry! All cry!
Last time for you to be sad.

Storyteller Chief Yanapayak

PART TWO

ONE HUNDRED YEARS OF
EXPLORATION AND CONQUEST
1769–1870

INTRODUCTION

The first writings from the region now called California are dated 1769. In July of that year, a small band led by the Spanish army captain Gaspar de Portolá began an overland expedition, following the coastline north from San Diego to San Francisco Bay. It was late in the days of conquest, settlement, and the advances of the written word. Elsewhere on this continent, Benjamin Franklin had already published numerous editions of *Poor Richard's Almanac*. William Byrd, the Virginia surveyor and prominent man of letters, had accumulated a personal library of 3,600 volumes. Settlers in New Mexico had been performing Spanish miracle plays annually for over two hundred years. But on the Pacific coast, as of 1769, there were only the diaries of a few men like Portolá and his chaplain, Fray Juan Crespí. From these come the earliest writings about the life and look of the region. Making daily entries as their caravan of mules and horses crept up the coast, Crespí was the first to report at length on the fauna and the flora, the climate, the habits of local tribes, and the habits of the land.

For the next hundred years the stories and reports come from other travelers—ship's captains, missionaries, soldiers and trappers, fortune hunters, homesteaders, geologists, and newspapermen. With one or two exceptions the significant writing is nonfiction: journals, letters, royal reports, guidebooks, and travel narratives. Taken together they chart a century of cultural and political ferment as California was dramatically transformed from the age-old habitat of disparate native tribes into a far-flung outpost of the Spanish empire, the most northerly province of Mexico, and then the thirty-first state admitted to the Union.

After Juan Cabrillo's early sightings in 1542, the region had been included in the Spanish sphere of influence. But for over two hundred years, apart from a few scattered landings by explorers and merchant ships, the Pacific coast went unaltered by the European expansion reshaping so many other shorelines around the globe. In the late eighteenth century Spain finally decided to push north from Mexico, prompted in part by reports of Russian and British ambitions in the Pacific and in part by the expansionist visions of José de Galvez, then visitador general of New Spain. He launched the Sacred Expedition to explore possibilities for settlement and for coastal defense in the little-known province of Alta California.

Over the next fifty years military governors like Pedro Fages and Franciscan padres like Crespí and Junípero Serra founded a string of missions, *presidios*, and civil towns along the five-hundred-mile coastal strip between San Diego and Sonoma. Their efforts to Christianize and "civilize" the indigenous tribes began a process of cultural suppression and population decline that continued under successive governments, through the nineteenth century and into the twentieth. While colonists gradually built up sizable cattle herds on vast land-grant *ranchos*, establishing an economic base, the *presidios* were chronically underprovided with money, weapons, and troops. Early visitors, such as England's Vancouver, France's La Pérouse and Russia's Rezanov, could see that the region's only real defense was its remote location.

Spain never had a firm hold on California. The old empire was tottering. In 1821, after Mexico's bitterly fought war for independence, the provincial government changed hands without a struggle. The war had never reached this far north. Life went on. The missions were secularized, freeing up large tracts of land for more ranchos. The original landed families grew, as did the interests of foreign powers, now that the ports, under Mexican rule, were legally open to international trade.

Following Rezanov's visit in 1806, the Russian American Company founded Fort Ross as a base for gathering seal and sea otter pelts. From the Oregon territory the British were also eyeing California. Hudson Bay Company trappers had penetrated the Central Valley in search of beaver and had been seen as far south as Needles. There was a British vice consul stationed at Monterey. By the mid-1830s, when Richard Henry Dana first saw this coastline from the deck of the brig *Pilgrim*, most of the trade into and out of California's ports was with the young nation called the United States, on the farther side of North America. Trade around the Pacific region was on the rise. Boston sea captains were not only bringing home hide and tallow; they brought back glowing accounts of the Bay of San Francisco, one of the finest harbors anyone had seen, ideally placed to link this shoreline with the rest of the Pacific and open wide the doors of trade with Asia.

Though the dream of Eldorado had propelled conquistadors of an earlier age, and though it still lurked in the atmosphere of the Americas, a hope that precious metals might be waiting somewhere at this farthest edge of the New World had little to do with the first years of our western migration or with the political ambitions that forced the war with Mexico in 1846. The dreams and schemes all had to do with trading opportunities and the appeal of large quantities of land. In 1835, when President Andrew Jackson first expressed a serious interest in acquiring California, San Francisco Bay was the main attraction. In the national imagination this already famous port had its role in the larger drama of manifest destiny, the idea that the entire continent, by a kind of divine right, now belonged to the United States. Through the early decades of the century, this idea had acquired an almost religious fervor.

While politicians and diplomats maneuvered in Washington and in Mexico City, while sea traffic around Cape Horn increased, travelers began to trickle west across the continent, first on foot or on horseback, then by wagon. The first overland expedition into California was led by the trapper Jedediah Smith in 1826, from Salt Lake down to San Diego. During the 1840s the numbers began to increase, from 34 in 1841 to 1,500 in 1846. The various accounts of these pioneering trips form an illuminating chapter in the Western story and in the national story: among them are Smith's *Southwest Expedition; A Journey to California* (1841) by John Bidwell, who, at age twenty-two, led the first wagon party into the region; *Journal of a Mountain Man* (c. 1845) by James Clyman; *From St. Louis to Sutter's Fort* (1846) by the young Swiss adventurer Heinrich Leinhard; *The Emigrants' Guide* (1845) by Lansford Hastings, the first popular handbook for overland travelers; John C. Frémont's *Reports* of his epic far West surveys in 1843–1844; and *What I Saw in California* (1848) by the Kentucky journalist Edwin Bryant.

When gold was discovered on the American River in January 1848, the timing was as lucky as the gold itself, coming just at the moment when a restless nation was eager to head in this direction. Argonauts and opportunists were soon arriving from all parts of the world, from Chile, Hawai'i, Australia, Malaya, China, Italy, Germany, Ireland, France. Most of them, of course, came from "the States," trekking overland on trails blazed in the previous decade, or by ship around the Cape, or by way of Panama.

This multitude included a cluster of writers who documented life in the "diggings" and in the sudden-growth communities. Over four or five years they all passed through or lingered in San Francisco: a transient group that included the mining-country chronicler Dame Shirley (Louise Clappe); the feminist reformer Eliza Farnham; the novelist and travel writer Bayard Taylor; the poet and journalist John Rollin Ridge; Edward Gould Buffum, who had arrived with General Stevenson's New York Regiment during the Mexican War and stayed long enough to write *Six Months in the Gold Mines* (1850); and Ferdinand Ewer, who founded the far West's first literary magazine, *The Pioneer,* in 1854. The new city would be a gathering place for writers and editors from this time onward.

It was a raucous and boisterous era, characterized by greed, near-anarchy, and a lust for adventure, along with a self-conscious sense that history was being made and that some kind of new society was taking shape, with new possibilities. Statehood seemed inevitable. In fact, it happened so quickly that California was the only region to become a state without first doing apprenticeship as a territory. In such a climate, cultural clashes were also inevitable. The resident *Californios* (as the original Mexican settlers were known), outnumbered, divided among themselves, and with little support from the Mexican government, had been unable to resist the tide. Though many *Californio* families had been in the region for two or three generations, they now found themselves regarded as foreigners, with fewer and fewer rights, just as the Indians, who had been here for centuries, found themselves on the run in their own homeland.

The plight of north county tribes was voiced by T'tcetsa (Lucy Young), whose people were uprooted when settlers and state legislators began to covet their ancestral lands. The power struggle between Anglos and Hispanics was described in several reminiscences and memoirs by former *Californio* leaders, most notably Mariano Vallejo in his *Recuerdos* (1875). The mixed-blood writer John Rollin Ridge (whose Cherokee name meant Yellow Bird) gave fictional life to a notorious bandit whose experience at the hands of white miners turned him into a brutal but charismatic outlaw. Ridge's *Life and Times of Joaquín Murieta* (1854) launched the legend of California's first folk hero.

As the new society grew, however, as Americans and Europeans continued to arrive and settle, such voices were few. The prevailing mood was expansive, as the nation now reached from coast to coast. The formation of the California Geological Survey, authorized by the state legislature in 1860, was emblematic of the times. Excitement over the discovery of gold and silver had stirred a wider interest in the region's mineral resources. The survey also offered a way to map and chart the huge terrain, thus another step in laying claim to a new and still only dimly understood possession.

From members of the survey team came two significant books still read today. As the survey's field leader, William Brewer spent four years roaming the state from Los Angeles to Mount Shasta, through the Central Valley and the full length of the Sierra. His *Up and Down in California, 1860–64* is remarkable for its vivid and accurate observation as well as for the range of places visited. With four years to travel and record his impressions, Brewer covered more territory within the state's boundaries than any previous observer. His protégé and field companion Clarence King wrote *Mountaineering in the Sierra Nevada* (1872), a high-spirited tribute to the scale, challenge, and mystery of the Western landscape. King's mix of passion and poetic prose anticipated the work of John Muir, Robinson Jeffers, Gary Snyder, and other celebrators of the region's natural endowments.

In these books, and throughout the writings from this first century of exploration and conquest, we see early signs of themes that shaped the literature in the decades to come: the inspirational power of landscape; extraordinary cultural diversity and the mingling and collision of cultures; the shaping of the long legend we call the California Dream; and its ironic underside, as the dream collides with wilderness realities and daily life in the semi-formed social terrain.

GARCÍ RODRIGUEZ ORDÓÑEZ DE MONTALVO

c. 1500

Little is known about Montalvo except that he wrote Las Sergas de Esplandián *(The Adventures of Esplandian), published in Madrid in 1510. A sequel to the popular* Amadis of Gaul, *it is a fictional romance, a tale of improbable deeds by Esplandían, a heroic knight and the son of Amadis. The story has survived only because one of Esplandían's adventures takes him to an island the author dubbed "California." No one has discovered any earlier source for this name. In an* Atlantic Monthly *article in March 1864, Edward Everett Hale (author of* The Man without a Country *and translator of the following excerpt) was the first to propose that an early Spanish explorer familiar with this novel—Hernando Cortés, or one of his officers—gave the name to the tip of what is now the Baja California peninsula.*

"The Queen of California"
from *Las Sergas de Esplandián*

Now you are to hear the most extraordinary thing that ever was heard of in any chronicles or in the memory of man, by which the city would have been lost on the next day, but that where the danger came, there the safety came also. Know, then, that, on the right hand of the Indies, there is an island called California, very close to the side of the Terrestrial Paradise, and it was peopled by black women, without any man among them, for they lived in the fashion of Amazons. They were of strong and hardy bodies, of ardent courage and great force. Their island was the strongest in all the world, with its steep cliffs and rocky shores. Their arms were all of gold, and so was the harness of the wild beasts which they tamed and rode. For, in the whole island, there was no metal but gold. They lived in caves wrought out of the rock with much labor. They had many ships with which they sailed out to other countries to obtain booty.

In this island, called California, there were many griffins, on account of the great ruggedness of the country, and its infinite host of wild beasts, such as never were seen in any other part of the world. And when these griffins were yet small, the women went out with traps to take them. They covered themselves over with very thick hides, and when they had caught the little griffins they took them to their caves, and brought them up there. And being themselves quite a match for the griffins, they fed them with the men whom they took prisoners, and with the boys to whom they gave birth, and brought them up with such arts that they got much good from them, and no harm. Every man who landed on the island was immediately devoured by these griffins; and although they had had enough, none the less would they seize them, and carry them high up in the air in their flight; and when they were tired of carrying them, would let them fall anywhere as soon as they died.

Now, at the time when those great men of the Pagans sailed with their great fleets, as the history has told you, there reigned in this island of California a Queen [Calafia], very large in person, the most beautiful of all of them, of blooming years, and in her thoughts desirous of achieving great things, strong of limb, and of great courage, more than any of those who had filled her throne before her. She heard tell that all the greater part of the world was moving in this onslaught against the Christians. She did not know what Christians were; for she had no knowledge of any parts of the world excepting those which were close to her. But she desired to see the world and its various people; and thinking that with the great strength of herself and of her women, she should have the greater part of their plunder, either from her rank or from her prowess, she began to talk with all of those who were most skilled in war, and told them that it would be well if, sailing in their great fleets, they also entered on this expedition, in which all these great princes and lords were embarking. She animated and excited them, showing them the great profits and honors which they would gain in the enterprise,—above all, the great fame which would be theirs in all the world; while, if they stayed in their island, doing nothing but what their grandmothers did, they were really buried alive,—they were dead while they lived, passing their days without fame and without glory, as did the very brutes.

Garcí Rodriguez Ordóñez de Montalvo

FRAY JUAN CRESPÍ

1721–1782

Crespí was the first writer to provide a detailed account of what this region looked like before European settlement began. Born on the Spanish island of Majorca, he studied there with Junípero Serra and was ordained into the Franciscan order. With Serra he went to the Franciscan College of San Fernando in Mexico to further his missionary training. In 1769 Crespí joined the Sacred Expedition. Traveling with the party led by Gaspar de Portolá, he became the official diarist for the first overland exploration of the shoreline. Three years later he traveled with Pedro Fages in search of a land route from Monterey to Point Reyes. His record of that journey provides the first written view of the Central Valley. From the slopes of Mount Diablo Crespí described "a great plain as level as the palm of a hand" and a river so wide it appeared to be "the largest that has been discovered in New Spain." After a voyage to Alaska with the 1774 Perez expedition, Crespí lived out his final years at Mission Carmel, where he is buried.

"The Naming of Santa Ana and Los Angeles"
from *Fray Juan Crespí: Missionary Explorer of the Pacific Coast*

Friday, July 28.—About seven in the morning we set out, continuing our way to the northwest along the skirts of the mountains which we have on the right, to the north, and after traveling a league and a half we came to the banks of a river which has a bed of running water about ten *varas* wide and half a *vara* deep. It is not at all boxed in by banks. Its course is from northeast to southwest, and it empties through this place, according to the judgment of those who sailed to the bay of San Pedro. It apparently has its source in the range that we have in sight on the right, about three leagues from the road that we are following. The bed of the river is well grown with sycamores, alders, willows, and other trees which we have not recognized. It is evident from the sand on its banks that in the rainy season it must have great floods which would prevent crossing it. It has a great deal of good land which can easily be irrigated.

We pitched camp on the left bank of this river. On its right bank there is a populous village of Indians, who received us with great friendliness. Fifty-two of them came to the camp, and their chief told us by signs which we understood very well that we must come to live with them; that they would make houses for us, and provide us with food, such as antelope, hares, and seeds. They urged us to do this, telling us that all the land we saw, and there was certainly a great deal of it, was theirs, and that they would divide it with us. We told him that we would return and would gladly remain to live with them, and when the chief understood it he was so affected that he broke into tears. The governor made them a present of some beads and a small silk handkerchief, and in gratitude the chief gave us two baskets of seeds, already made into *pinole,* together with a string of beads made of shells such as they wear. I called this place the sweet name of Jesús de los Temblores, because we experienced here a horrifying earthquake, which was repeated four times during the day. The first, which was the most violent, happened at one in the afternoon, and the last one about four. One of the heathen who were in the camp, who doubtless exercised among them the office of priest, alarmed at the occurrence no less than we, began with frightful cries and great demonstrations of fear to entreat heaven, turning to all the winds. This river is known to the soldiers as the Santa Ana.

Tuesday, August 1.—This day was one of rest, for the purpose of exploring, and especially to celebrate the jubilee of Our Lady of Los Angeles de Porciúncula. We both said Mass and the men took communion, performing the obligations to gain the great indulgence. At ten in the morning the earth trembled. The shock was repeated with violence at one in the afternoon, and one hour afterwards we experienced another. The soldiers went out this afternoon to hunt, and brought an antelope, with which animals this country abounds; they are like wild goats, but have horns rather larger than goats. I tasted the roasted meat, and it was not bad. Today I observed the latitude and it came out for us thirty-four degrees and ten minutes north latitude.

Wednesday, August 2.—We set out from the valley in the morning and followed the same plain in a westerly direction. After traveling about a league and a half through a pass between low hills, we entered a very spacious valley, well grown with cottonwoods and alders, among which ran a beautiful river from the north-northwest, and then, doubling the point of a steep hill, it went on afterwards to the south. Toward the north-northeast there is another river bed which forms a spacious water-course, but we found it dry. This bed unites with that of the river, giving a clear indication of great floods in the rainy season, for we saw that it had many trunks of trees on the banks. We halted not very far from the river, which we named Porciúncula. Here we felt three consecutive earthquakes in the afternoon and night. We must have traveled about three leagues today. This plain where the river runs is very extensive.

It has good land for planting all kinds of grain and seeds, and is the most suitable site of all that we have seen for a mission, for it has all the requisites for a large settlement. As soon as we arrived about eight heathen from a good village came to visit us; they live in this delightful place among the trees on the river. They presented us with some baskets of *pinole* made from seeds of sage and other grasses. Their chief brought some strings of beads made of shells, and they threw us three handfuls of them. Some of the old men were smoking pipes well made of baked clay and they puffed at us three mouthfuls of smoke. We gave them a little tobacco and glass beads, and they went away well pleased.

Thursday, August 3.—At half-past six we left the camp and forded the Porciúncula River, which runs down from the valley, flowing through it from the mountains into the plain. After crossing the river we entered a large vineyard of wild grapes and an infinity of rosebushes in full bloom. All the soil is black and loamy, and is capable of producing every kind of grain and fruit which may be planted. We went west, continually over good land well covered with grass. After traveling about half a league we came to the village of this region, the people of which, on seeing us, came out into the road. As they drew near us they began to howl like wolves; they greeted us and wished to give us seeds, but as we had nothing at hand in which to carry them we did not accept them. Seeing this, they threw some handfuls of them on the ground and the rest in the air. We traveled over another plain for three hours, during which we must have gone as many leagues. In the same plain we came across a grove of very large alders, high and thick, from which flows a stream of water about a *buey* in depth. The banks were grassy and covered with fragrant herbs and watercress. The water flowed afterwards in a deep channel towards the southwest. All the land that we saw this morning seemed admirable to us. We pitched camp near the water. This afternoon we felt new earthquakes, the continuation of which astonishes us. We judge that in the mountains that run to the west in front of us there are some volcanoes, for there are many signs on the road which stretches between the Porciúncula River and the Spring of the Alders, for the explorers saw some large marshes of a certain substance like pitch; they were boiling and bubbling, and the pitch came out mixed with an abundance of water. They noticed that the water runs to one side and the pitch to the other, and that there is such an abundance of it that it would serve to caulk many ships. This place where we stopped is called the Spring of the Alders of San Estévan.

PEDRO FAGES

1730–1794

Fages was twice named governor of Alta California. Born in Catalonia, he arrived in Mexico as a Spanish infantry lieutenant in 1767. He was second in command of the first overland expedition to explore and settle the region. When Portolá returned to Mexico City in 1770, Fages became the second com-mandante and governor of the "New Establishments." His travels took him up and down his command, from San Diego to the Sacramento delta, east through Cajon Pass to the Imperial Valley, the Mojave Desert, and then north into the San Joaquin Valley. While Crespí's Diary stands as the earliest written report, Fages's Historical, Political, and Natural Description—addressed to the Spanish viceroy in Mexico—is one of the first attempts to craft and organize a systematic account of the region. Like the Diary, his writings describe California just before it began to feel the influence of the outside world. He also helps us see the conquistador's view of a virgin terrain and its native peoples. In 1771 Fages was promoted to captain and in 1777 to colonel. From 1782 to 1791 he served again as governor, after which he returned to Mexico.

"Report to the Viceroy"
from *A Historical, Political, and Natural Description of California*

STATE OF THE NEW MISSIONS

The mission of San Luís Obispo de Toloso is the only one established in the third and fourth stages of the journey. It was founded September 1, 1772, and is situated on a hill three leagues distant from the beach and the bay called La Ensenada del Buchón. It has near it many fields excellent for cultivation, and abundant water for everything. At the foot of the hill runs a ditch from which water is taken for the fields, which have now been tested, and have proved to yield prolifically of whatever is sown. I was there about the first of November in '73, to interview the Reverend Father-President Francisco Palóu, who was coming from Lower California. There was then a field of two *almudes* sowing from which the corn, heavily eared, was just ready to be harvested. They were plowing and preparing the soil for sowing eight *fanegas* of wheat to be irrigated. Certainly, with the measures which the reverend father-president has taken to settle there half of the families of married and single Indians whom he brought with him from the peninsula, everything may turn out well. And as he has done the same thing at the mission of San Gabriel, which is no less well supplied with land, water, and pasture, as has been said, it is to be expected that these two missions alone may soon succor and provide for the rest, that of San Gabriel for those below, and that of San Luís Obispo for those in the upper part, rendering unnecessary the exportation of grains from the port of San Blas.

Not only is there the water supply spoken of, running at the foot of the hill, which will supply this mission and provide irrigation for its crops, but there is still another ample stream at a short distance and in its vicinity are good localities possessing fertile soil. In addition, abundant water is found in every direction, and pasture for the cattle, so that no matter how large the mission grows to be and however great the number of Indians reduced, the land promises sustenance, without prejudice either to the mission or the Indians, and for many settlers as well, who may desire to establish themselves here—an efficacious means for the advancement of the spiritual conquest and for the secure conservation of that which has been conquered temporally. The father-president assured me that some settlers from Lower California and some cuirassiers had offered voluntarily to bring their wives and families to this country, and that they had gone to Loreto to make the proposal to their governor, Don Felipe Barry. To him this zealous minister of God and good vassal of the king had written with reference to the enterprise, informing him how desirable and advantageous this emigration would be for the service of both majesties. It is certain that if this colonization should some day happen, the Indians would soon cease to consider (as they now do) that we are exiles from our own lands who have come here in quest of their women; for they would then see coming here to settle men who had their own wives, instead of noting, as at present, that we have come neither to oppose them in arms nor to settle the country, since only men have come. They would then cease to feel the disquietude and misgiving in which they have lived from the first as a result of apprehension or whim.

Nearly all the natives of this middle district possessing, as they do, abundance of seeds to store and use, and those along the beach having all the fish they want, to such a degree that this nation may be considered the richest among them all, it may with reason be feared that collecting and reducing the Indians to mission life will be difficult; there remains only the hope of interesting and attracting them by gifts of clothing,—which they lack without confusion or shame,—but chiefly by the suavity and kindliness which through love of God and desire for the welfare of these poor souls is edifyingly manifested by the reverend fathers the missionaries.

As a result, a few adults are submitting; for their instruction continuous effort is made, and they are being catechised that they may prepare to receive holy baptism. This benefit only twelve boys and girls have availed themselves of at this mission in more than a year, and no adults whatever during that time.

The church, the dwelling of the missionary fathers, and the offices, are all within the stockade, and all made in the ordinary manner described in preceding chapters. Of the same construction is the barrack of the guard, a body which is here composed of eight cuirassiers with a corporal and a servant. In the neighborhood of this mission there is no well-established village, but the parents of the new Christians have settled close to the stockade, and in the same place small houses were being built for receiving the Indians who, with their families, were expected from Lower California.

OBSERVATIONS ON POLITICAL AND NATURAL HISTORY

At the mission of San Luís Obispo and for a radius of about twelve leagues around it, I have observed the following: The natives are well appearing, of good disposition, affable, liberal, and friendly toward the Spaniard. As to their government, it is by captaincies over villages, as in the others; the captains here also have many wives, with the right of putting them away and taking maidens only; here also the other Indian men have not this privilege, for they have only one wife, and do not marry a second time, until they are widowed. They have cemeteries set apart for the burial of their dead. The god whom they adore, and to whom they offer their seeds, fruits, and all that they possess, is the sun. . . .

Their dress and clothing are like those of the Indians of San Gabriel, except that here one sees the hair oftener worn flowing, and of fine texture. The women wear toupés made by burning, and their coiffure is of shells, as I said in a previous chapter. On their cloaks or skirts, stained a handsome red, they put as a trimming or decoration various fabrications made from tips of shells and small snail shells, leaving numerous pendants hanging from the margins, after the style of the trinkets of our children. For an ornament and as a protection from the sun, they cover their heads with little woven trays or baskets, decorated with handsome patterns and shaped like the crown of a hat. Both men and women like to go painted with various colors, the former especially when they go on a campaign, and the latter when they are having a festal occasion, to give a dance.

When an Indian woman is in childbirth, she makes a small hole wherever she may be when her labor begins, even though it be in the open field; she digs out the soil, puts in a little hay or grass neatly arranged, warms the hole with fire, of which she always carries a supply ready, and composes herself tranquilly to give birth. She removes from her child the envelope and adhesions bestowed by nature, strokes it, and deforms the cartilaginous part of the nose by flattening; then she goes without delay to bathe herself with cold water, whereupon the entire operation is completed without further ceremony. The child is then swaddled from the feet to the shoulders with a band to shape its body; thus enveloped, it is fastened against a coffin-shaped board, which the Indian woman carries suspended from her shoulders by cords; she takes the child in her arms without removing it from the frame every time she needs to give it milk, or to soothe it if it cries. Thus the Indian women are left unencumbered for all their duties and occupations without on account of them having to leave off caring for and nursing their children, a very natural course of procedure.

In their manufactures, these Indians, men and women alike, are more finished and artistic than those of the mission of San Gabriel. They know how to make very beautiful inlaid work of mother-of-pearl on the rims and sides of stone mortars, and various other utensils. The women weave nearly all their baskets, pitchers, trays, and jars for various uses, interweaving with the reeds or willows, or embroidering upon them, long, flexible, fibrous roots, which keep their natural color, white, black, or red. They also do the same with shells, and small stones of the same three colors for decorating their cloaks and embroidering the bands of their headgear. The tools of these skillful artisans are only two, the most simple ones in the world, the knife and the punch. This latter, used by the women, is a piece of bone as sharp as an awl, from the foreleg, next to the shinbone, of the deer. The other is more particularly a tool for the men. They usually carry it across the head, fastened to the hair. It is a flint cut tongue-shaped, with very sharp edges; they affix it to a very small handle of straight polished wood inlaid with mother-of-pearl. These knives are made, as is perhaps natural, by rubbing and rubbing away the stone (or natural glass) in contact with harder ones, with water and fine sand. With these knives they supply their lack of iron and steel by dint of much labor and industry.

For starting a fire, which can be communicated to, and made to inflame, other materials, they use the only means they have,—since they lack steel, as has been said, or instruments for focusing the rays of the sun,—namely, that of rubbing one stick forcibly against another.

These natives always carry their means of making fire in the shape of two small sticks attached to the net with which they are accustomed to gird themselves; one stick is like a spindle, and the other is oblong, or it might properly be called a parallelepiped; in it there is a hole in the middle, in which the end of the other stick may be rotated. When they want to make fire, they secure the square stick firmly on the ground between the feet, and the round one, stuck into the hole, they rotate rapidly between the hands. It begins to smoke instantly, and both sticks are burned a little.

JEAN FRANÇOIS DE GALOUP DE LA PÉROUSE
1741–1788

Born in the south of France, Comte la Pérouse began his naval training at fifteen. As a young lieutenant he fought against the British during the American Revolution. In 1785 he was put in command of two frigates for a voyage around the world. It would become the basis for his classic explorer's narrative, Voyage autour du Monde. *The stated purpose of this expedition was to increase geographic knowledge and look for the elusive Northwest Passage. The less public motive was to explore the Pacific area with an eye to advancing French trade and possible colonization. In September 1786 the expedition dropped anchor off Monterey, then the provincial capital, where they were welcomed by Governor Pedro Fages and stayed for ten days. While his geologists and botanists gathered data, La Pérouse gave the world its first close look at daily life in the newly established mission system. His expedition was never completed. A year and a half later he was killed when his ship hit a reef and sank near the Santa Cruz Islands, northeast of Australia.*

"A Visit to Carmel"
from *Voyage autour du Monde*

The fathers of the mission of San Carlos, at the distance of two leagues from Monterey, soon arrived at the presidio. No less obliging than the officers of the two vessels and the fort, they invited us to dine with them and promised to inform us minutely concerning the government of their missions, the manner of living of the Indians, their arts, their newly acquired habits, and in general everything that could rouse the curiosity of travelers. We eagerly accepted this invitation, which we should not have failed to solicit if we had not thus been anticipated. It was agreed that we should set out in two days. Mr. Fages wanted to accompany us and undertook to procure horses.

After crossing a small plain covered with herds of cattle and in which there were only a few trees, which were necessary to shelter these animals against the rain and the sun, we ascended the hills. From there we heard the sound of bells announcing our arrival, of which the missionaries had been previously informed by a horseman from the governor.

We were received like the lords of manors when they first take possession of their estates. The president of the missions, in his ceremonial vestments and with his holy water sprinkle in his hand, awaited us at the gate of the church, which was illuminated in the same manner as on the greatest feast days. He conducted us to the foot of the high altar, where he chanted the *Te Deum* in thanksgiving for the happy outcome of our voyage.

Before we entered the church, we had passed through a square in which the Indians of both sexes were ranged in a line. They exhibited no marks of surprise in their countenance, and left us in doubt whether we should be the subject of their conversation for the rest of the day.

The church is neat though thatched with straw. It is dedicated to Saint Charles, and adorned with some tolerable pictures, copied from originals in Italy. Among them is a picture of hell, in which the painter appears to have borrowed from the imagination of Callot; but as it is absolutely necessary to strike the imagination of these new converts with the most lively impressions, I am persuaded that such a representation was never more useful in any country. It would be impossible for the Protestant worship, which proscribes images and almost all the ceremonies of our church, to make any progress with this people. I doubt whether the picture of paradise, which sits opposite that of hell, produces so good an effect upon them. The state of tranquillity which it represents, and that mild satisfaction of the elect who surround the throne of the Supreme Being, are ideas too sublime for the minds of uncultivated savages. But it was necessary to place rewards by the side of punishment, and it was a point of duty that no change should be permitted in the kind of enjoyments which the Catholic religion promises to man.

On coming out of the church we passed through the same row of Indians, whom the *Te Deum* had not induced to abandon their post. Only the children had removed to a small distance and formed groups near the house of missionaries, which, along with the different storehouses, is opposite the church. The Indian village stands on the right, consisting of about fifty huts which serve for seven hundred and forty persons of both sexes, including their children. . . .

The Indians as well as the missionaries rise with the sun, and immediately go to prayers and mass, which last for an hour. During this time three large boilers are set on the fire for cooking a kind of soup, made of barley meal, the grain of which has been roasted previous to its being ground. This sort of food, of which the Indians are extremely fond, is called *atole*. They eat it without either butter or salt, and it would certainly to us be a most insipid mess.

Each hut sends for the allowance of all its inhabitants in a vessel made of the bark of a tree. There is neither confusion nor disorder in the distribution,

Jean François de Galoup de la Pérouse

87

and when the boilers are nearly emptied, the thicker portion at the bottom is distributed to those children who have said their catechism the best.

The time of repast is three quarters of an hour, after which they all go to work, some to till the ground with oxen, some to dig in the garden, while others are employed in domestic occupations, all under the eye of one or two missionaries.

The women have no other employment than their household affairs, the care of their children, and the roasting and grinding of corn. This last operation is both tedious and laborious, because they have no other method of breaking the grain than with a roller upon a stone. Mr. de Langle, who saw this operation, made a present of his mill to the missionaries. It was difficult to have rendered them a greater service, since four women will now do the work of a hundred, thus leaving them time to spin the wool of their sheep and manufacture some coarse cloths.

But the missionaries have hitherto been more attentive to their heavenly than their earthly concerns, and have greatly neglected the introduction of the most common arts. They are so austere as to their own comforts that they have no fireplace in their chambers, though the winter is sometimes severe. The greatest anchorites have never lived a more edifying life. Father Fermín de Lasuén, president of the missions of New California, is one of the most worthy and respectable men I have ever met. His mildness, charity, and affection for the Indians are beyond expression.

At noon the bells give notice of the time of dinner. The Indians then quit their work, and send for their allowance in the same vessel as at breakfast. But this second soup is thicker than the former, and contains a mixture of wheat, maize, peas, and beans; the Indians call it *pozole*.

They return to work from two to four or five o'clock, when they repair to evening prayer, which lasts nearly an hour and is followed by a distribution of *atole*, the same as at breakfast. These three distributions are sufficient for the subsistence of the greater number of these Indians, and we might perhaps adopt this economical food in years of scarcity, with the addition of some seasoning.

The whole art of this cookery consists in roasting the grain before it is reduced to meal. As the Indian women have no clay or metallic vessels for this operation, they perform it in baskets of bark by using small burning wood coals. They turn these vessels with such dexterity and rapidity that they succeed in causing the grain to swell and burst without burning the basket, though made of combustible material. (We can affirm that our best coffee is far from being roasted with equal skill.) It is distributed to them every morning, and the slightest embezzlement is punished by the whip, though it seldom happens that they expose themselves to the danger.

These punishments are adjudged by Indian magistrates, called *caciques*. There are three in each mission, chosen by the people from among those whom the missionaries have not excluded. However, to give a proper notion of this magistracy, we must observe that these *caciques* are like the overseers of a plantation: passive beings, blind performers of the will of their superiors. Their principal functions consist in serving as beadles in the church, to maintain order and the appearance of attention.

Women are never whipped in public, but in an enclosed and somewhat distant place that their cries may not excite a too lively compassion, which might cause the men to revolt. The latter, on the contrary, are exposed to the view of all their fellow citizens, that their punishment may serve as an example. They usually ask pardon for their fault, in which case the executioner diminishes the force of his lashes but the number is always irrevocable.

The rewards are small distributions of grain, of which they make little thin cakes, and bake them on hot wood ashes. On high festivals an allowance of beef is distributed which many eat raw, particularly the fat, considered by them as delicious as the finest butter or the most excellent cheese. They skin all animals with the greatest dexterity, and when an animal is fat they make, like the ravens, a croaking of pleasure, devouring with their eyes those parts for which they have the greatest desire.

The Indian men are often permitted to hunt and fish for their own benefit, and upon their return they generally make a present to the missionaries of a part of their fish or game. But they proportion the quantity to what is strictly necessary for their consumption, taking care to increase it when they know that their superiors have any visitors or guests.

The women raise some poultry about their huts, the eggs of which they give to their children. These fowls are the property of the Indians, as are their clothes, small articles of furniture, and implements of hunting.

There is no example of theft among them, though the door of their hut consists merely of a bundle of straw which they place across the entrance when the inhabitants are absent. These manners may appear patriarchal to some of our readers, who may not reflect that in these huts there is no article which can excite the avarice of a neighboring hut. The food of the Indians is secured to them, and they have therefore no other want than that of giving life to beings who are sure to be as simple as themselves.

The men in these missions have made greater sacrifices to Christianity than the women, because, before its introduction, they were accustomed to polygamy, and were even in the habit of espousing all the sisters of the same family. The women, on the contrary, have acquired the right of receiving exclusively the caresses of a single man.

I must confess, however, notwithstanding the unanimous report of the missionaries concerning this pretended polygamy, that I am at a loss to conceive how it could have been established in a nation of savages; with the number of men being nearly equal to that of the women, the consequence must have been a forced continence in many individuals, unless conjugal fidelity were less rigorously observed than in the missions, where the holy fathers have constituted themselves guardians of the virtue of the women. An hour after supper, they take care to secure all the women whose husbands are absent, as well as the young girls above the age of nine years, by locking them up, and during the day they entrust them to the care of elderly women. All these precautions are still inadequate, and we have seen men in the stocks and women in irons for having eluded the vigilance of these female Arguses, whose eyes are not sufficient for the complete performance of their office.

The converted Indians have preserved all the ancient customs which their new religion does not prohibit. They have the same huts, the same games, and the same clothes. The clothing of the richest consists of a garment of otter skin, which descends from the waist somewhat lower than the groin. The most indolent have simply a piece of cloth, which the mission supplies, to conceal nudity, and a small cloak of rabbit skin, tied under the chin, which covers their shoulders, and descends to their waist. The rest of their body is absolutely naked, as is their head. Some of them, however, have straw hats which are neatly made.

NIKOLAI PETROVICH REZANOV

1764–1807

Count Rezanov was a founder of the Russian-American Company, which established a post at Fort Ross in 1812. Born in Irkutsk, the capital of eastern Siberia, he married a daughter of the wealthy Siberian merchant who had established the first permanent Russian post in North America (on Kodiak Island in 1784). Thus he became involved in his father-in-law's trading empire as well as in Russia's imperial expansion into Alaska and points farther south. In 1803, soon after his wife passed away, Rezanov took charge of a round-the-world expedition with the double aim of opening Russia's trade to Japan and investigating transpacific supply routes. At New Archangel (now Sitka) they nearly starved to death, eventually setting sail for San Francisco Bay in search of food to resupply the impoverished outpost. His forty-two-page report of this visit, in the form of a letter to the minister of commerce, was written after returning to New Archangel. He had intended to travel from there to Saint Petersburg and then—after receiving the czar's approval and a papal blessing from Rome—to return to California to marry young Concepción Arguello, daughter of the presidio commandante. *But he died en route while crossing his native Siberia. After waiting many years for his return, Concepción entered a nunnery. Their story became one of California's first romantic legends, giving rise to poems such as Bret Harte's "Concepción Arguello" and Gertrude Atherton's popular novel* Rezanov *(1906).*

A Letter to the Minister of Commerce

June 17, 1806

Gracious Sire Count Nikolai Petrovich:

From my recent reports to Your Excellency and to the Board of Directors of the Company you are sufficiently informed of the calamitous situation which I found in the Russian-American possessions. You know of the starvation which we had to endure the entire winter, the men barely subsisting on provisions purchased with the ship *Juno*. You are aware of the disastrous condition of the country caused by sickness, and of my determination to undertake a voyage to New California, setting forth with inexperienced men, sick with scurvy, resolved to save the region or perish in the attempt. Having with God's help completed this journey, so difficult considering the circumstances we were in, I am now pleased to report to Your Excellency on the first step of the Russians in this land.

We left Sitka on February 25th, on the ship *Juno,* which I had purchased from the Bostonians. The crew, disabled by scurvy, soon became exhausted and hardly half were able to man the sails. . . . Thanks to God, a change in the moon brought us a continuing and favorable wind, and with pallid, death-like faces we at last reached the entrance to San Francisco Bay on the night of March 24th and on account of dense fog we anchored outside to wait for the morning.

On the following morning a favorable wind and current enabled us to enter the port. Knowing the suspicious nature of the Spanish Government, and in view of our desperate situation, I thought it best to go straight through the [Golden] Gate and past the fort. I deemed it useless to ask for permission to enter, since in the event of refusal we should perish at sea, and decided that two or three cannon-balls would make less difference to us than refusal. With all sails full, we ran for the harbor. As we neared the fort we could see a great commotion among the soldiers. When we were abreast of it one of them asked through a speaking-trumpet: "What ship is that?"

"Russian!" we replied.

They shouted to us several times to anchor, but we merely replied: "Si Señor! Si Señor!", simulating confusion, meanwhile passing the fortress, un-til, running up in the port, we finally complied with their demand, anchoring at a cannon-shot's distance.

Soon about twenty horsemen, among whom were the commandant and a missionary, demanded the surrender of the ship, but we could afford to be bold, as their cavalry was within range of our grapeshot.

I dispatched Midshipman Davydov to inform them that I was the one of whose coming I hoped they had been notified by their Government; that I was proceeding to Monterey but my ship had been damaged by storms, which compelled me to seek shelter in the first port; and that I should leave as soon as the repairs were made. The answer was brought back that orders had already been received from the King to render us all necessary assistance, and that the commandant invited me to dine with him at the presidio, at the same time assuring me that all my requests should be promptly attended to. Grat-itude forced me to go ashore, where I was met by Don Luis de Arguello, a son of the commandant, taking his father's place during the latter's absence. We were proffered saddle-horses, but as the presidio is not more than a *verst*

[0.66 mile] away from the shore, we went on foot with the commandant and the missionary, Father José de Uria. The cordial reception by the hospitable family of the commandant overwhelmed us. We remained until evening after dinner, and then returned to the ship. In the meantime veal, vegetables, bread and milk were already sent on board the ship and our men after restoring their exhausted strength felt as gratified and pleased as we.

Don Luis informed me with marked courtesy that he was obliged to send a courier to the governor to advise him of my arrival, and that he therefore found himself compelled to ask where our ships the *Nadezhda* and *Neva* were, of which they were previously notified. I replied that I had ordered them back to Russia; that I had been entrusted by the Emperor with the command over all the American territories, had visited them during the past year, wintered in Norfolk Sound and finally decided to visit the Governor of New California to confer with him, as the chief of a neighboring territory, as to our mutual interests.

Do not think, Gracious Sire, that I made this declaration from personal ambition. No, it was solely to impress the Spaniards with the importance of our territories in the north and to further our interests with them that I proclaimed myself Commandant General. The interests of our country required it. Even here I did not transgress, as I really have the chief command by the Emperor's orders and by the power of attorney given to me by the shareholders. I made no improper use of these, but on the contrary, sacrificed myself every hour for the benefit of those whom I represented. With the same courier I sent a letter to the Governor thanking him for the gracious manifestations of hospitality and informed him that I would sail to Monterey as soon as the vessel was repaired.

On the following day the missionaries of San Francisco invited us to dinner. The mission is about an hour's ride from the presidio, and I went there with my officers. In our conversation with the missionaries there we touched upon the subject of trade, and their strong wish for it was very clear to us. Later, in a more fitting connection, I shall have the honor to describe to Your Excellency the condition of all the missions, presidios, trade, surplus and requirements of this province but now, Gracious Sire, be kind enough to permit me to occupy your attention with what are perhaps but trifling matters, that I may show you how, imperceptibly to those of whom I shall speak, I accomplished my purpose, in spite of our desperate straits, and the means I employed.

After our return from the mission I sent fitting and valuable presents both to the Commandant and to the missionaries, to repay them for their invita-

Nikolai Petrovich Rezanov

tions and to hide from them our poverty and need, of which the Boston vessels had told them to our disadvantage. I accomplished my purpose to perfection. There was not one who did not receive something especially desired, and the hearts of all inhabitants were won for us. Good reports about the Russians drew the missionaries from afar, while those nearby voluntarily offered to supply us with a cargo of grain.

Seeing the possibility of obtaining a cargo of grain from this port, I decided to go overland to Monterey, which was eighty miles distant. I sent a courier to the Governor with a letter in which I explained that as the repairs to my ship would perhaps detain me a considerable time, I would beg him to allow me to visit him. His reply was full of courtesies. He would not permit me to go to so much trouble, but he himself would undertake this journey the following day, and he had sent orders that I should be assisted in everything. At the same time he sent me the Commandant to congratulate me officially upon my arrival. I recognized in that the suspicious nature of the Spanish Government, which prevents foreigners everywhere from gaining a knowledge of the interior of their territories and from observing the weakness of their military forces.

In the meantime the excellent climate of California, the abundance of breadstuffs there as compared to our lack of them, and the prospect of facing starvation again in the future were the hourly subject of conversation among our men. We noticed their inclination and desire to remain permanently and took measures against their desertion.

The third day after we arrived, three Bostonians and a Prussian who had entered the Company's service as sailors when we purchased the *Juno* expressed to me their wish to stay. I told them that I would consult the Commandant, and after he refused to grant them his permission I ordered them removed to a barren island, where they were held until our departure. In the meantime we placed pickets on shore and established rounds. The Spaniards gave us mounted patrols, but in spite of all measures taken, two very good men who were well cared for, Mikhailo Kallianin and Peter Polkanov, ran away when they went to the creek to wash clothes and disappeared without a trace. Subsequently the Spanish authorities gave me their word of honor to deport the deserters, if found, to Russia by way of Vera Cruz. I will ask to have them punished and returned to America to remain forever. Without severe punishment as an example, it will be hard to control others.

While awaiting the arrival of the Governor we spent our time in the residence of the hospitable Arguellos and soon became on intimate terms with them. Of the lovely sisters of the acting commandant, Doña Concepcion is the recognized beauty of New California, and Your Excellency will agree with me when I say that our past sufferings were requited, for our time passed joyfully. Pardon me, Gracious Sire, if I mingle something of the romantic in such a serious letter, but perhaps it is best to be sincere. Meanwhile the favorable reports concerning us which were constantly reaching Monterey had disposed in my favor the Governor himself who luckily for us had been a friend of this family from his youth.

At last, on April 7th, Don José de Arillaga, governor of the two Californias, arrived. The fortress saluted him with nine cannons, and a battery concealed behind our ship around a point opened fire with the same number.

Weak as the Spanish defenses are, they have nevertheless increased their artillery since Vancouver's visit. We later secretly inspected this battery. It has five brass cannons of twelve pound caliber. I heard that there are seven guns in the fortress. As I was never there and in order to disarm suspicion did not allow others to go either, I do not know if there are more or less guns there.

When the Governor came I at once sent an officer to congratulate him upon his arrival. Replying graciously, he informed me that he had a bad foot, was tired from his journey, but hoped to see me soon. And really this venerable old man, whose hair was white, was extremely fatigued from horseback riding, as there is no other mode of traveling in California. . . .

In the meantime rumors of war with the French grew day by day. They were also expecting a frigate from San Blas to arrive to patrol the coast. I found out that a part of the Monterey garrison had been transferred to the mission of Santa Clara, a distance of one day's journey on horseback from the port. The inclination of our men to prove treasonable and to leave us, and the actual desertion of two men, rendered our position still more critical. But the respect always manifested by the Spaniards showed no signs of diminishing. I always had dragoon soldiers as a guard of honor. The Spanish pickets always saluted. The Governor met and took leave of me graciously every day; and the general courtesy everywhere displayed disarmed me of all suspicion.

From day to day, though in a way imperceptible to the Governor, the graciousness of the house of Arguello was drawing us closer and the confidence of Arguello in me was increasing. He apologized for not having visited me on my ship.

"Let us set aside all useless formality of etiquette," I said. "I know the ways of your government. I know that if you had followed the impulses of your heart you would have visited me long ago. Anyway, I am with you every day."

"We have become accustomed to your presence," said Don José de Arillaga, "and I assure you that the good family of my friend Arguello appreciate the pleasure of seeing you in their house just as highly as they are grateful to you for the manifestation of your benevolence."

Here I must make a confession to Your Excellency of my purely personal adventures. Seeing that our situation was not improving, expecting every day that some big trouble would arise, and having but little confidence in my own men, I decided that I should assume a serious bearing where I had before been but formally polite and gracious. Associating daily with and paying my compliments to the beautiful Spanish señorita, I perceived her active, venturesome disposition and character, her unlimited ambition, which at her age of fifteen, made her, alone among her family, dissatisfied with the land of her birth. She always referred to it, when we were joking, as "A beautiful country, a warm climate, an abundance of grain and cattle—and nothing else." I described Russia to her as more severe in climate, but still abounding in everything, and she was willing to live there. At length I created imperceptibly in her an impatient desire to hear something more explicit from me, and when I proposed marriage she accepted. My proposal was a shock to her parents, whose religious upbringing was fanatical. The difference in religion, and the separation from their daughter was like a stroke of lightning to them. They sought the council of the missionaries, who did not know what to do, took poor Concepcion to church, made her confess, and tried to make her refuse me, but her determination finally quieted everybody down. The holy fathers left everything to the decision of the throne of Rome. Even if I could not bring about the marriage, I had a written conditional agreement made, and forced a betrothal. Consent was given on condition the betrothal be kept secret pending the decision of the Pope. Thereafter my position in the house of the Commandant was that of a near relative and I managed the port of his Catholic Majesty as my interests required.

The Governor was now very much perplexed and perceived that he had made a mistake when he assured me of the high esteem with which I was regarded by the family of the Commandant, as he now found himself to be in fact my guest. A rare friendship of thirty years standing obliged him to consult the Commandant in everything. Every official paper received by the Governor passed through the hands of Arguello and consequently through mine. The Governor was soon won over, placed a like confidence in me, and at length they did not keep the slightest secret from me. I spoke Spanish better every hour, and was in Arguello's house from morning till evening. When their officers saw that I had almost become hispanicized, they began to compete with one another to be first to inform me of any new occurrence, so that now I did not dread hearing of the possible arrival of any courier. . . .

Excuse me, Gracious Sire, that I have mixed purely personal matters, writing about them and of my personal adventures as they were happening. Perhaps I should not have done so, but I have no time to put everything in system and write separate letters to Your Excellency on each subject, so I have described here the chain of events in order of their occurrence. My romance began not in hot passion, which has no place at my age, but from entirely different motives and perhaps also under the influence of remnants of feelings that in the past were the source of happiness in my life. Considering the circumstances, remoteness, and my duties I acted carefully and made the beginning subject to conditions. Should fate decree its completion, I shall be in a position to render new services to my country by personally examining the harbor of Vera Cruz, Mexico and by a trip through the interior part of America. Hardly anybody but me could do it, the suspicious Spanish government forbidding such investigations. I should be able to inform you fully as to their trade, their surplus and their needs. Upon becoming acquainted with the Viceroy I could be of benefit to my countrymen by an attempt to secure entry for Russian vessels to the eastern ports, as I hope that during the reign of such a gracious Emperor the Russians will begin to trade from Petersburg with such natural and industrial products as can be used by the foreigners. At the same time upon visiting the American States I can investigate the prospects of trading with them, and seek to establish business connections for our Company. Here, Gracious Sire, is a new sacrifice of a man who has dedicated himself to serve others, and I only hope that my strength will equal my intentions.

Nikolai Petrovich Rezanov

JEDEDIAH STRONG SMITH

1799–1831

One of the great mountain men and early explorers of the far West, Smith led the first American trek overland into California. He was born in Jericho, New York. In 1822, determined to make his way in the fur trade, he traveled to Saint Louis and went to work for William Ashley, eventually becoming co-owner of the Rocky Mountain Fur Company. In 1826 Smith led a historic trapping expedition from Salt Lake south across the deserts. At the end of November, after crossing through the San Bernardino Mountains, they reached the Franciscan mission at San Gabriel. Father José Sanchez welcomed these unexpected visitors, but Governor Echeandía later asked Smith to leave the Mexican province, fearing he was an American spy. From San Diego the party headed north and east through the San Joaquin Valley, trapping beaver, then became the first white men to cross the Sierra Nevada range. Four years later Smith met an early end, killed by Comanches in New Mexico. His Journal *of the Southwest Expedition, for many years thought lost, was discovered in a Saint Louis attic in 1967.*

"The Trapper and the Padre"
from *The Southwest Expeditions of Jedediah S. Smith: His Personal Account of the Journey to California*

The next day following the valley of a creek alternately sinking and rising and passing through a range of Mt for 8 miles where I was obliged to travel in the bed of the creek as the hills on both sides which were thick covered with cedar came in close and rugged to the creek. About ten miles from camp I came out into a large valley having no timber except what was on the creeks coming from the Mountains. Here we found a plenty of grass and what was still more pleasing we began to see track of Horses and Cattle and shortly after saw some fine herds of Cattle in many directions. As those sure evidences of Civilization passed in sight they awakened many emotions in my mind and some of them not the most pleasant. It would perhaps be supposed that after numerous hardships endured in a savage and inhospitable desert I should hail the herds that were passing before me in the valley as harbingers of better times. But they reminded me that I was approaching a country inhabited by Spaniards. A people whose distinguishing characteristic has ever been jealousy a people of different religion from mine and possessing a full share of that bigotry and disregard of the rights of a Protestant that has at times stained the Catholic Religion.

They might perhaps consider me a spy imprison me persecute me for the sake of religion or detain me in prison to the ruin of my business. I knew such things had been and might be again. Yet confiding in the rectitude of my intentions I endeavored to convince myself that I should be able to make it appear to them that I had come to their country as the only means by which I could extricate myself from my own embarrassing situation and that so far from being a spy my only [wish] was to procure such supplies as would enable me to proceed to my own country.

When we left the Mts our course was W S W. Close on the right was a range of Mts out of which poured several beautiful streams watering a fertile valley extending many miles on the left. Having traveled about 18 miles I encamped. We had nothing to eat and knowing that it would take two days to reach the settlements I determined to help myself to one of the hundreds of fine cattle in view. In endeavoring to kill one I had to use all the precaution necessary in approaching Buffalo. Having succeeded I found the animal branded on the hip. I therefore saved the skin to carry in to the owner. At this place I remained during the following day. Again moving onward in two days travel I arrived at a farm house. The country through which we passed was strikingly contrasted with the Rocky and Sandy deserts through which we had so long been traveling. There we had passed many high mountains rocky and Barren. Many plains whose sands drank up the waters of the river and spring, where our need was the greatest. There sometimes a solitary Antelope Bounded by to vex our hunger and the stunted useless sedge grew as in mockery of the surrounding sterility. There for many days we had traveled weary hungry and thirsty drinking from springs that increased our thirst and looking in vain for a boundary of the interminable waste of sands. But now the scene was changed and whether it was its own real Beauty or the contrast with what we had seen it certainly seemed to us enchantment. Our path was through a fertile and well watered valley and the herds of Cattle and the bands of wild horses as they sniffed the wind and rushed wildly across our way reminded me of the Plains of the Buffalo East of the mountains that seemed to me as a home or of the cattle of the more distant prairies of Missouri and Illinois.

Even in the Idea that we were approaching the abode of comparative civilization there was a pleasure not however entirely unmixed with dred for we knew not how we might be received. As we advanced the white Brant and

Mallard were seen in great numbers it being now their season, and we passed a farm on a creek where a number of indians were at work. They gazed and gazed again considering us no doubt as strange objects in which they were not much in error. When it is considered that they were not accustomed to see white men walking with horses packed as mine were with Furs Traps Saddlebags Guns and Blankets and every thing so different from any thing they had ever seen and add to this our ragged and miserable appearance I should not have been surprised if they had run off at first sight for I have often been treated in that manner by savages. Arrived at the farm houses I was kindly received by an elderly man an indian who spoke spanish and immediately asked me if I would have a Bullock killed. I answered that I would and away rode two young Indians in a moment It being the custom in this country as I have since learned to keep a horse or horses constantly tied at the door Saddled and Bridled and of course ready to mount at a moments warning. In a short time the indians returned bringing a cow as fast as she could gallop. She was held between the two horsemen by ropes thrown over her horns and having the other end fast to the Pomel of the spanish Saddle one riding before and the other behind she was forced along without the power of resistance. They were anxious that I should shoot the cow which I did. Novel as the scenery of this country was to me It seemed that we ourselves were a still greater wonder to our semi-civilized friends. As I afterwards learned they wondered how indians could be so white having no Idea that civilized people lived in the direction from which we came. It was also a great wonder to them that we had guns and other articles and more than all that there should be with us one of the people of Reason this being the name by which they were learned to distinguish Spaniards from indians and which they readily applied to one of my men who spoke spanish.

The farm house consisted of Two Buildings each about 100 feet long 20 feet wide and 12 feet high placed so as to form two sides of a square. The walls are of unburnt brick about 2 feet thick and at intervals of 15 feet Loop holes are left for the admission of light. The roofs were Thatched. It should be premised that I had at this time but a vague idea of the peculiarities of the country in which my fortune had placed me. I therefore was in the dark as to the manner in which I should conduct myself and determined to be guided by circumstances as they should transpire. In pursuance of this plan when the old overseer asked me if I was not going to write to Father I told him I was and immediately set down and wrote a few lines briefly stating where I was from and the reason of my being there an Indian mounting one of the horses that are always in readiness took my note and was off in an instant.

In about an hour the answer was returned by a man who the overseer told me was the commandant but in fact a Corporal. He asked me how I did and congratulated me that I had escaped the Gentiles and got into a christian country and offering me some Segars made with paper according to the common custom of the country when I would take one he insisted that I should take the bunch. He then presented the note from the Father written in Latin and as I could not read his Latin nor he my english it seemed that we were not likely to become general correspondents. I however ascertained that he wished me to ride to the Mission so giving Mr. Rogers instructions how to proceed in my absence I took my interpreter and in Company with the corporal and a soldier moved on at the gate that appears quite common in this country a gallop passing large fields laid out on both sides of the road and fenced with Posts set in the ground with rails tied to them by means of strong pieces of raw hide there being also thousands of Cattle skulls in rows on each side of the road conveying the Idea that we were approaching an immense slaughter yard. Arrived in view of a Building of ancient and Castle-like appearance and not knowing why I was brought there or who I was to see the current of my thoughts ran so rapidly through my mind as to deprive me of the power of coming to any conclusion so that when we passed in front of the Building and the Corporal after pointing to an old man sitting in the portico and observing that there was the father immediately rode off I was left quite embarrassed hardly knowing how to introduce myself. Observing this I presume the father took me by hand and quite familiarly asked me to walk in making at the same time many enquiries. Soon some bread and cheese were brought in and some rum of which I drank to please the Father but much against my own taste. I then related to him as well as in my power the course of my being in that country but it was being to him a thing so entirely new and my interpreter perhaps not giving a correct translation of my words he was not able to comprehend the subject and told me there was an American residing in the vicinity for whom he would send as he spoke good Spanish and on his arrival we might have a good understanding. In the mean time he told me to make myself as contented as possible and consider myself at home. He ordered the steward to show me to a room about 20 feet square in which there was a bed taking possession of it I was left alone to reflect on my singular situation for about two hours when the bell ringing for Supper a boy came and invited me in. The Old Father invited me to pass up next to him. We were seated on a long bench with a back to it one of these occupying each side of the table. On The opposite side of the table sat a Spanish Gentlemen and a father from the neighboring village of the Angels and the steward of the mission. at my side sat my interpreter. As soon as we were seated the Father said Benediction and each one in the most hurried manner asked the blessing of heaven—and even while the last words were pronouncing the fathers were reaching for the different dishes. About a dozen Indian boys were in attendance who passing the different dishes to the fathers they helping themselves and passing them to the next. Our knives and forks according to the common custom of the country were rolled up in a napkin and laid by the side of the plates. The supper consisted principally of meats, and an abundance of wine. Before the cloth was removed Cigars were passed around. I may be excused for being this particular in this table scene when it is recollected that It was along time since I had had the pleasure of sitting at a table and never before in such company.

PABLO TAC
1822–1841

*Pablo Tac was born at the Mission of San Luis Rey de Francia, north of San Diego. His people called themselves Quechnajuichom. His Con-*version of the San Luiseños of Alta California, *composed in Rome in the 1830s, is the first known written document by a California Indian. As a student in the mission school, he was recognized for his high promise and skill with languages. At age eleven he was one of two youths chosen to travel with Fray Antonio Peyri, first to the Franciscan College of San Fernando in Mexico City, in 1832, then to Spain, and on to Rome, where Tac was registered at the Urban College in September 1834. During the next seven years, preparing for mission work, he studied Latin grammar, rhetoric, humanities, and philosophy. Under the direction of Guiseppe Caspar Mezzofanti, chief custodian of the Vatican library, he began a grammar and dictionary of his native tongue; before his early death, he had made 1,200 entries. During this time Tac also began a cultural history of his people, which is excerpted here. It is the only account of California mission life written by an Indian. It also reveals a remarkable young mind, with early signs of a rare cross-cultural perspective. Speaking three languages, Tac can compare the origins of place-names, noting that the Spanish named his region for a French king, and his people named it for the local stones. Having traveled on two continents, he has a fresh view of his own tribal dances and how they serve the communal life. Like the dictionary, his essay was unfinished at the time of his death in Rome at age nineteen.*

"Our Songs and Dances"
from *Conversion of the San Luiseños of Alta California*

The Fernandino Father made five big gardens, that is to say, three in the Mission itself, one in the district we call Pala, the fifth in another district whose name I do not now remember, all very fruitful with what is sown. Four districts, the Mission, Pala, Temeco, and Usva, three ranchos. The Mission of San Luis Rey de Francia, thus the Fernandino Father named it after having completed all the house, because our patron is St. Louis the King.

But we call it *Quechla* in our language. Thus our grandparents called it, because in this country there was a kind of stones that were called *quechlam* in the plural, and in the singular *quechla*, and we inhabitants of Quechla call

ourselves Quechnajuichom in the plural, Quechnajuis in the singular, meaning inhabitants of Quechla. In Quechla not long ago there were 5,000 souls,
with all their neighboring lands. Through a sickness that came to California
2,000 souls died, and 3,000 were left.

The Fernandino Father, as he was alone and very accustomed to the usages
of the Spanish soldiers, seeing that it would be very difficult for him alone to
give orders to that people, and, moreover, people that had left the woods just
a few years before, therefore appointed *alcaldes* from the people themselves
that knew how to speak Spanish more than the others and were better than
the others in their customs. There were seven of these *alcaldes,* with rods as
a symbol that they could judge the others. The captain dressed like the Spanish, always remaining captain, but not ordering his people about as of old,
when they were still gentiles. The chief of the *alcaldes* was called the general.
He knew the name of each one, and when he took something he then named
each person by his name. In the afternoon, the *alcaldes* gather at the house
of the missionary. They bring the news of that day, and if the missionary tells
them something that all the people of the country ought to know, they return
to the villages shouting, "Tomorrow morning . . ."

Returning to the villages, each one of the *alcaldes* wherever he goes cries
out what the missionary has told them, in his language, and all the country
hears it. "Tomorrow the sowing begins and so the laborers go to the chicken
yard and assemble there." And again he goes saying these same words until
he reaches his own village to eat something and then to sleep. In the morning
you will see the laborers appear in the chicken yard and assemble there according to what they heard last night. . . .

OF THE DANCE OF THE INDIANS

Each Indian people has its dances, different from other dances. In Europe
they dance for joy, for a feast, for any fortunate news. But the Indians of
California dance not only for a feast, but also before starting a war, for grief,
because they have lost the victory, and in memory of grandparents, aunts and
uncles, parents already dead. Now that we are Christians we dance for ceremony.

The dance of the Yumas is almost always sad, and thus the song; the same
of the Diegueños. But we Luiseños have three principal kinds for men alone,
because the women have others, and they can never dance with the men.
Three principal ones, two for many, and the other for one, which is more
difficult. Many can dance in these two, and in this kind it is possible to dance
day and night, and in the other only at night.

No one can dance without permission of the elders, and he must be of the same people, a youth of ten and more years. The elders, before doing the dances publicly, teach them the song and make them learn perfectly, because the dance consists in knowing the song, because they act according to the song. According to the song he makes as many kicks, as many leaps as the singers make, who are the old people, the old and others of the same people. When they have learned, then they can perform the dance, but before this they give him something to drink, and then that one is a dancer; he can dance and not stop when the others dance.

On this occasion the clothing is of feathers of various colors, and the body painted, and the chest is bare, and from the waist to the knees they are covered, the arms without clothing. In the right hand they carry a stick made to take off the sweat. The face is painted. The head is bound with a band of hair woven so as to be able to thrust in the *cheyatom,* our word. This *cheyat* is made of feathers of any bird, and almost always of crow and of sparrow hawk, and in the middle a sharp stick in order to be able to insert it. Thus they are in the house when immediately two men go out, each one carrying two wooden swords and crying out, without saying any word, and after stopping before the place where they dance, they look at the sky for some time. The people are silent, and they turn and then the dancers go out. These two men are called by us *Pajaom,* meaning crimson snakes. In California there are large red snakes. These do not bite but lash out at those who come near them.

The dancers in this dance can be as many as thirty, more or less. Going out of the house, they turn their faces to the singers and begin to give kicks, but not hard ones, because it is not the time, and when the song is finished the captain of the dancers touching his feet cries, "Hu," and all fall silent. He again comes to the singers and sings, and all dance, and at last cries, "Hu," and the singers fall silent and they make the sound of the horse who is looking for his son. The sound *hu* means nothing in our language, but the dancers understand that it means "be silent." When the captain does not say, "Hu," the singers cannot be silent, and they repeat and repeat the song until the captain wants them to stop. Then they go before the singers and all the people who are watching them, and the captain of the dancers sings and dances, and the others follow him. They dance in a circle, kicking, and whoever gets tired stays in the middle of the circle and then follows the others. No one can laugh in this dance, and all follow the first ones with head bent and eyes toward the earth. When this stops, all take off the *cheyat* to end the dance and holding it in the right hand they raise it to heaven, blowing at each kick that they give to the earth, and the captain ends the dance with a "Hu," and all return to the houses of the costumes, and at this the old men begin to suck or smoke, and all the smoke goes up to heaven three times before ending the dance. This done, it ends. The old man returns to his house tired, because the dance lasts three hours, and it is necessary to sing for three hours. It is danced in the middle of the day when the sun burns more, and then the shoulders of the dancers appear fountains of water with so much sweat that falls. This dance is difficult, and among 2,000 men there was one who knew how to dance well. . . .

BALL GAME

The place where they play is all level, in length a quarter and half a league, in width the same, the players all men of thirty to sixty years. In all they can be seventy or eighty, thirty or forty men on one side, thirty or forty on the other. They choose two leaders from this and from that side. Each one of the men holds his stick, four hands high, five joined fingers thick, arched below. The ball of the game is of wood, bigger than the egg of a turkey. There are two marks where they must throw the ball, and when the enemy crosses this mark, he has won.

The rule is that they cannot carry it in the hand very long, but on the ground with the stick. In the middle of the game they bury the ball, and the two leaders must get it out with their sticks, each one staying toward his mark, and his companions behind with sticks raised waiting for the ball, and when it goes out, each one wants to carry it to his mark. And here tumult, shoves, the strength of Hercules is necessary if one by chance gets the ball, hurling it with all force to his mark, throws it in the middle of the mark. The enemies follow it. Others hinder others. One falls running, having slipped. One with equal running comes up to the ball, and from there carries it to the other part running for fear that they will take it from him, and seeing his companions at a distance, throws them the ball through the air. They carry it to their mark, running at all haste. The enemies attack them, and here riot, running like a deer to flee so that they do not catch up or reach them, and this game lasts three or four hours.

The women play also, and this each Sunday with permission. The Luiseños know how to play well, strong men. Once thirty Luiseños went off to San Juan, another mission near the Mission of San Luis Rey de Francia, our mission. They arrived there and were invited to play ball. They said, "We want to, but let us make a rule that you cannot carry the ball in your hand." Those indeed said, "Thus we will do. We will play with all justice." Sunday during the afternoon the Luiseños take their sticks and go off to the place for the game.

They go out to meet them and brought them to the place for the game. They began to play with the same rule as the Luiseños, as we have already said before. All the people of this district were watching the game, and the captain of that district too was watching on horseback. All thirty Luiseños played well and were speedily defeating the Sanjuaneños, when one Sanjuaneño takes the ball and carries it in his hand. Then a Luiseño comes up, and seizing him by the waist throws him up and makes him fall. Another Sanjuaneño came to defend his countryman. Other Luiseños go to help the first. After these came the captain, and he beat a Luiseño. Then one of the Luiseños, stronger and with a huge body, gave a leap, knocked him down. The horse stepped on him and dragged him beneath his feet. He was not able to get up. Attracted by the uproar the people came up with sticks in hand. The women followed a Luiseño who had no stick but could defend himself well with leaps, although they might be warded off, and the women threw stones anywhere, but they did not hurt him.

The Sanjuaneños fled with their split heads. The Luiseños remain alone. One wanted to give a blow to another, believing that he was a Sanjuaneño. Such was their rage they did not recognize each other, and they were afraid of nothing. The Spanish soldiers arrive, although the uproar was ended, because they too were trembling, and they wished to end the tumult with words. The chief of the thirty Luiseños was an Indian and spoke like the Spanish. The Indian said to him, "Raise your saber, and then I will eat you," but in his language, and afterwards there was no trouble.

RICHARD HENRY DANA

1815–1882

Born in Cambridge, Massachusetts, Dana was a sophomore at Harvard when a bad case of measles endangered his eyesight. To restore his health he put aside his studies and went to sea. At age nineteen he shipped out on the brig Pilgrim, *bound for Cape Horn and California in the hide and tallow trade. He spent sixteen months on the Pacific Coast, from January 1835 to May 1836, with stops at the main ports: San Diego, San Pedro, Santa Barbara, Monterey, and San Francisco Bay. All the while he kept a journal and extensive notes, which became the basis for his first and best-known book. Dana went back to Harvard to complete his legal training. In 1840, at age twenty-five, he was admitted to the bar, the same year that Harper Brothers published* Two Years before the Mast: A Personal Narrative of Life at Sea. *In the long history of voyaging, his was one of the first accounts from the perspective of a deckhand, rather than of a passenger or a ship's officer. "My design," said Dana in his preface, "is to present the life of a common sailor as it really is." While contributing a classic to the literature of voyaging, he also gave us an extended look at life in Mexican California in the 1830s: the towns, the ports, the mix of peoples, and the cross-cultural world of trade, sailors, and seamanship.*

"Haole and Kanaka"
from *Two Years before the Mast*

Friday, May 8, 1835. Arrived at San Diego. Here we found the little harbor deserted. The Lagoda, Ayacucho, Loriotte, and all, had left the coast, and we were nearly alone. All the hide-houses on the beach, but ours, were shut up, and the Sandwich Islanders, a dozen or twenty in number, who had worked for the other vessels and been paid off when they sailed, were living on the beach, keeping up a grand carnival. A Russian discovery-ship, which had been in this port a few years before, had built a large oven for baking bread, and went away, leaving it standing. This, the Sandwich Islanders took possession of, and had kept, ever since, undisturbed. It was big enough to hold six or eight men—that is, it was as large as a ship's forecastle; had a door at the side, and a vent-hole at top. They covered it with Oahu mats, for a carpet; stopped up the vent-hole in bad weather, and made it their head-quarters. It was now inhabited by as many as a dozen or twenty men, who lived there in complete idleness—drinking, playing cards, and carousing in every way. They bought a bullock once a week, which kept them in meat, and one of them went up to the town every day to get fruit, liquor, and provisions. Besides this, they had bought a cask of ship-bread, and a barrel of flour from the Lagoda, before she sailed. There they lived, having a grand time, and caring for nobody. Captain Thompson was anxious to get three or four of them to come on board the Pilgrim, as we were so much diminished in numbers; and went up to the oven, and spent an hour or two trying to negotiate with them. One of them,—a finely built, active, strong and intelligent fellow,—who was a sort of king among them, acted as spokesman. He was called Mannini,—or rather, out of compliment to his known importance and influence, *Mr.* Mannini,—and was known all over California. Through him, the captain offered them fifteen dollars a month, and one month's pay in advance; but it was like throwing pearls before swine, or, rather, carrying coals to Newcastle. So long as they had money, they would not work for fifty dollars a month, and when their money was gone, they would work for ten.

"What do you do here, Mr. Mannini?" said the captain.

"Oh, we play cards, get drunk, smoke—do anything we're a mind to."

"Don't you want to come aboard and work?"

"*Aole! aole make make makou i ka hana.* Now, got plenty money; no good, work. *Mamule,* money *pau*—all gone. Ah! very good, work!—*maikai, hana hana nui!*"

"But you'll spend all your money in this way," said the captain.

"Aye! me know that. By-'em-by money *pau*—all gone; then Kanaka work plenty:"

This was a hopeless case, and the captain left them, to wait patiently until their money was gone.

We discharged our hides and tallow, and in about a week were ready to set sail again for the windward. We unmoored, and got everything ready, when the captain made another attempt upon the oven. This time he had more regard to the "mollia tempora fandi," and succeeded very well. He got Mr. Mannini in his interest, and as the shot was getting low in the locker, prevailed upon him and three others to come on board with their chests and baggage, and sent a hasty summons to me and to Sam Hooper the boy to come ashore with our things, and join the gang at the hide-house. This was unexpected to me; but anything in the way of variety I liked; so we got ready, and were pulled ashore. I stood on the beach while the brig got under weigh, and watched her until she rounded the point, and then went up to the hide-house to take up my quarters for a few months.

Here was a change in my life as complete as it had been sudden. In the twinkling of an eye, I was transformed from a sailor into a "beach-comber" and a hide-curer; yet the novelty and the comparative independence of the life were not unpleasant. Our hide-house was a large building, made of plain clap boards, and intended to hold forty thousand hides. In one corner of it, a small room was parted off, in which four berths were made, where we were to live, with mother earth for our floor. It contained a table, a small locker for pots, spoons, plates, &c., and a small hole cut to let in the light. Here we put our chests, threw our bedding into the berths, and took up our quarters. Over our head was another small room, in which *Mr.* Russell lived, who had charge of the hide-house; the same man who was for a time an officer of the Pilgrim. There he lived in solitary grandeur; eating and sleeping alone, (and these were his principal occupations), and communing with his own dignity. The boy Sam was to act as cook; while myself, a giant of a Frenchman named Nicholas, and four Sandwich Islanders, were to cure the hides. Sam, the Frenchman, and myself, lived together in the room, and the four Sandwich Islanders worked and ate with us, but generally slept at the oven. My new messmate, Nicholas, was the most immense man that I had ever seen in my life. He came on the coast in a vessel which was afterwards wrecked, and now let himself out to the different houses to cure hides. He was considerably over six feet, and of a frame so large that he might have been shown for a curiosity. But the most remarkable thing about him was his feet. They were so large that he could not find a pair of shoes in California to fit him, and was obliged to send to Oahu for a pair; and when he got them, he was compelled to wear them down at the heel. He told me once, himself, that he was wrecked in an American brig on the Goodwin Sands, and was sent up to London, to the charge of the American consul, without clothing to his back or shoes to his feet, and was obliged to go about London streets in his stocking-feet three or four days, in the month of January, until the consul could have a pair of shoes *made for him.* His strength was in proportion to his size, and his ignorance to his strength—"strong as an ox, and ignorant as strong." He neither knew how to read nor to write. He had been to sea from a boy, and had seen all kinds of service, and been in every kind of vessel: merchantmen, men-of-war, privateers, and slavers; and from what I could gather from his accounts of himself, and from what he once told me, in confidence, after we had become better acquainted, he had even been in worse business than slave-trading. He was once tried for his life in Charleston, South Carolina, and though acquitted, yet he was so frightened that he never would show himself in the United States again; and I could not persuade him that he could never be tried a second time for the same offence. He said he had got safe off from the breakers, and was too good a sailor to risk his timbers again.

Though I knew what his life had been, yet I never had the slightest fear of him. We always got along very well together, and, though so much stronger and larger than I, he showed a respect for my education, and for what he had heard of my situation before coming to sea. "I'll be good friends with you"; he used to say, "for by-and-by you'll come out here captain, and then you'll *haze* me well!" By holding well together, we kept the officer in good order, for he was evidently afraid of Nicholas, and never ordered us, except when employed upon the hides. My other companions, the Sandwich Islanders, deserve particular notice.

A considerable trade has been carried on for several years between California and the Sandwich Islands, and most of the vessels are manned with Islanders; who, as they, for the most part, sign no articles, leave whenever they choose, and let themselves out to cure hides at San Diego, and to supply the places of the men of the American vessels while on the coast. In this way, quite a colony of them had become settled at San Diego, as their head-quarters. Some of these had recently gone off in the Ayacucho and Loriotte, and the Pilgrim had taken Mr. Mannini and three others, so that there were not more than twenty left. Of these, four were on pay at the Ayacucho's house, four more working with us, and the rest were living at the oven in a quiet way, for their money was nearly gone, and they must make it last until some other vessel came down to employ them.

During the four months that I lived here, I got well acquainted with all of them, and took the greatest pains to become familiar with their language, habits, and characters. Their language, I could only learn orally, for they had not any books among them, though many of them had been taught to read and write by the missionaries at home. They spoke a little English, and by a sort of compromise, a mixed language was used on the beach, which could be understood by all. The long name of Sandwich Islanders is dropped, and they are called by the whites, all over the Pacific ocean, "Kanakas," from a word in their own language which they apply to themselves, and to all South Sea Islanders, in distinction from whites, whom they call "Haole." This name, "Kanaka," they answer to, both collectively and individually. Their proper names, in their own language, being difficult to pronounce and remember, they are called by any names which the captains or crews may choose to give them. Some are called after the vessel they are in; others by common names, as Jack, Tom, Bill; and some have fancy names, as Ban-yan, Fore-top, Rope-yarn, Pelican, &c. &c. Of the four who worked at our house, one was named "Mr. Bingham," after the missionary at Oahu; another, Hope, after a vessel that he had been in; a third, Tom Davis, the name of his first captain; and the fourth Pelican, from his fancied resemblance to that bird. Then there was Lagoda-Jack, California-Bill, &c. &c. But by whatever names they might be called, they were the most interesting, intelligent, and kindhearted set of people that I ever fell in with. I felt a positive attachment for almost all of them; and many of them I have, to this time, a feeling for, which would lead me to go a great way for the mere pleasure of seeing them, and which will always make me feel a strong interest in the mere name of a Sandwich Islander.

Tom Davis knew how to read, write, and cipher in common arithmetic; had been to the United States, and spoke English quite well. His education was as good as that of three quarters of the Yankees in California, and his manners and principles a good deal better, and he was so quick of apprehension that he might have been taught navigation, and the elements of many of the sciences, with the most perfect ease. Old "Mr. Bingham" spoke very little English—almost none, and neither knew how to read nor write; but he was the best-hearted old fellow that I ever met with. He must have been over forty years of age, and had two of his front teeth knocked out, which was done by his parents as a sign of grief at the death of Tamahamaha, the great king of the Sandwich Islands. We used to tell him that he ate Captain Cook, and lost his teeth in that way. That was the only thing that ever made him angry. He would always be quite excited at that; and say—"Aole!" (no). "Me no eat Captain Cook! Me pikinini—small—so high—no more! My father see Captain Cook! Me—no!" None of them liked to have anything said about Captain Cook, for the sailors all believe that he was eaten, and that, they cannot endure to be taunted with.—"New Zealand Kanaka eat white man;—Sandwich Islands Kanaka,—no. Sandwich Island Kanaka ua like pu na haole—all 'e same a' you!"

Mr. Bingham was a sort of patriarch among them, and was always treated with great respect, though he had not the education and energy which gave Mr. Mannini his power over them. I have spent hours in talking with this old fellow about Tamahamaha, the Charlemagne of the Sandwich Islands; his son and successor Riho Riho, who died in England, and was brought to Oahu in the frigate Blonde, Captain Lord Byron, and whose funeral he remembered perfectly; and also about the customs of his country in his boyhood, and the changes which had been made by the missionaries. He never would allow that human beings had ever been eaten there; and, indeed, it always seemed like an insult to tell so affectionate, intelligent, and civilized a class of men, that such barbarities had been practised in their own country within the recollection of many of them. Certainly, the history of no people on the globe can show anything like so rapid an advance. I would have trusted my life and my fortune in the hands of any one of these people; and certainly, had I wished for a favor or act of sacrifice, I would have gone to them all, in turn, before I should have applied to one of my own countrymen on the coast, and should have expected to have seen it done, before my own countrymen had got half through counting the cost. Their customs, and manner of treating one another, show a simple, primitive generosity, which is truly delightful; and which is often a reproach to our own people. Whatever one has, they all have. Money, food, clothes, they share with one another; even to the last piece of tobacco to put in their pipes. I once heard old Mr. Bingham say, with the highest indignation, to a Yankee trader who was trying to persuade him to keep his money to himself—"No! We no all 'e same a' you!—Suppose one got money, all got money. You;—suppose one got money—lock him up in chest.—No good!"—"Kanaka all 'e same a' one!" This principle they carry so far, that none of them will eat anything in sight of others, without offering it all round. I have seen one of them break a biscuit, which had been given him, into five parts, at a time when I knew he was on a very short allowance, as there was but little to eat on the beach.

My favorite among all of them, and one who was liked by every one, both officers and men, and by whoever had anything to do with him, was Hope. He was an intelligent, kind-hearted little fellow, and I never saw him angry, though I knew him for more than a year, and have seen him imposed upon by white people, and abused by insolent officers of vessels. He was always civil, and always ready, and never forgot a benefit. I once took care of him when he was ill, getting medicines from the ship's chests, when no captain or officer would do anything for him, and he never forgot it. Every Kanaka has one particular friend, whom he considers himself bound to do everything for, and with whom he has a sort of contract,—an alliance offensive and defensive,—and for whom he will often make the greatest sacrifices. This friend they call *aikane;* and for such, did Hope adopt me. I do not believe I could have wanted anything which he had, that he would not have given me. In return for this, I was always his friend among the Americans, and used to teach him letters and numbers; for he left home before he had learned how to read. He was very curious about Boston (as they call the United States); asking many questions about the houses, the people, &c., and always wished to have the pictures in books explained to him. They were all astonishingly quick in catching at explanations, and many things which I had thought utterly impossible to make them understand, they often seized in an instant, and asked questions which showed that they knew enough to make them wish to go farther. The pictures of steamboats and railroad cars, in the columns of some newspapers which I had, gave me great difficulty to explain. The grading of the road, the rails, the construction of the carriages, they could easily understand, but the motion produced by steam was a little too refined for them. I attempted to show it to them once by an experiment upon the cook's coppers, but failed; probably as much from my own ignorance as from their want of apprehension; and, I have no doubt, left them with about as clear an idea of the principle as I had myself. This difficulty, of course, existed in the same force with the steamboats; and all I could do was to give them some account of the results, in the shape of speed; for, failing in the reason, I had to fall back upon the fact. In my account of the speed I was supported by Tom, who had been to Nantucket, and seen a little steamboat which ran over to New Bedford.

A map of the world, which I once showed them, kept their attention for hours; those who knew how to read pointing out the places and referring to me for the distances. I remember being much amused with a question which Hope asked me. Pointing to the large irregular place which is always left blank round the poles, to denote that it is undiscovered, he looked up and asked— "Pau?" (Done? ended?)

The system of naming the streets and numbering the houses, they easily understood, and the utility of it. They had a great desire to see America, but were afraid of doubling Cape Horn, for they suffer much in cold weather, and had heard dreadful accounts of the Cape, from those of their number who had been round it.

They smoke a great deal, though not much at a time; using pipes with large bowls, and very short stems, or no stems at all. These, they light, and putting them to their mouths, take a long draught, getting their mouths as full as they can hold, and their cheeks distended, and then let it slowly out through their mouths and nostrils. The pipe is then passed to others, who draw, in the same manner, one pipe-full serving for a half a dozen. They never take short, continuous draughts, like Europeans, but one of these "Oahu puffs," as the sailors call them, serves for an hour or two, until some one else lights his pipe, and it is passed round in the same manner. Each Kanaka on the beach had a pipe, flint, steel, tinder, a hand of tobacco, and a jack-knife, which he always carried about with him.

That which strikes a stranger most peculiarly is their style of singing. They run on, in a low, guttural, monotonous sort of chant, their lips and tongues seeming hardly to move, and the sounds apparently modulated solely in the throat. There is very little tune to it, and the words, so far as I could learn, are extempore. They sing about persons and things which are around them, and adopt this method when they do not wish to be understood by any but themselves; and it is very effectual, for with the most careful attention I never could detect a word that I knew. I have often heard Mr. Mannini, who was the most noted *improvisatore* among them, sing for an hour together, when at work in the midst of Americans and Englishmen; and, by the occasional shouts and laughter of the Kanakas, who were at a distance, it was evident that he was singing about the different men that he was at work with. They have great powers of ridicule, and are excellent mimics; many of them discovering and imitating the peculiarities of our own people, before we had seen them ourselves.

These were the people with whom I was to spend a few months; and who, with the exception of the officer, Nicholas the Frenchman, and the boy, made the whole population of the beach. I ought, perhaps to except the dogs, for they were an important part of our settlement. Some of the first vessels brought dogs out with them, who, for convenience, were left ashore, and there multiplied, until they came to a great nation. While I was on the beach, the average number was about forty, and probably an equal, or greater number are drowned, or killed in some way, every year. They are very useful in guarding the beach, the Indians being afraid to come down at night; for it was impossible for any one to get within half a mile of the hide-houses without a general alarm. The father of the colony, old Sachem, so called from the ship in which he was brought out, died while I was there, full of years, and was honorably buried. Hogs, and a few chickens, were the rest of the animal tribe, and formed, like the dogs, a common company, though they were all known and marked, and usually fed at the houses to which they belonged.

I had been but a few hours on the beach, and the Pilgrim was hardly out of sight, when the cry of "Sail ho!" was raised, and a small hermaphrodite brig rounded the point, bore up into the harbor, and came to anchor. It was the Mexican brig Fazio, which we had left at San Pedro, and which had come down to land her tallow, try it all over, and make new bags, and then take it in, and leave the coast. They moored ship, erected their try-works on shore, put up a small tent, in which they all lived, and commenced operations. They made an addition to our society, and we spent many evenings in their tent, where, amid, the Babel of English, Spanish, French, Indian, and Kanaka, we found some words that we could understand in common.

Richard Henry Dana

John Charles Frémont

1813–1890

*As an officer with the U.S. Army's Topographical Corps, Frémont led
expeditions to the Rocky Mountains in 1842 and to Oregon and California
in 1843. His Reports of these trips, published by an order of Congress, had an
enormous influence on western migration during the 1840s. Their impact and popularity
were due in part to the extent of Frémont's travels, the precision of his maps, and the
unprecedented geological and botanical data he presented and in part to the literary
contribution of his young wife, Jesse Benton Frémont (1824–1902), the daughter of
Frémont's chief backer, Senator Thomas Hart Benton. She edited his dictated material
and field notes and added pictorial flourishes, enlivening what could have been a much
less readable and overly scientific document. Together they crafted a best-selling narrative
that changed the way overland parties viewed North America. Returning west in 1845–
1846, Frémont played a controversial role in the U.S. takeover of Mexican California.
He instigated the Bear Flag Revolt, then led his notorious battalion south, reaching
Cahuenga Pass in time to accept the final military surrender. For five weeks he served
as California's third American governor, in defiance of contradicting orders brought
from Washington by General Stephen Kearney. Tried and convicted of mutiny, Frémont
resigned from the Army, then went on to serve as a U.S. senator representing California
in the first year of statehood.*

"Some Points in Geography"
from *Report of the Exploring Mission to Oregon and North California*

April 13. In the evening a Christian Indian rode into the camp, well dressed,
with long spurs, and a *sombrero,* and speaking Spanish fluently. It was an
unexpected apparition, and a strange and pleasant sight in this desolate gorge
of a mountain—an Indian face, Spanish costume, jingling spurs, and horse
equipped after the Spanish manner. He informed me that he belonged to one
of the Spanish missions to the south, distant two or three days' ride, and that
he had obtained from the priests leave to spend a few days with his relations
in the Sierra. Having seen us enter the pass, he had come down to visit us.
He appeared familiarly acquainted with the country, and gave me definite and
clear information in regard to the desert region east of the mountains. I had

entered the pass with a strong disposition to vary my route, and to travel directly across towards the Great Salt Lake, in the view of obtaining some acquaintance with the interior of the Great Basin, while pursuing a direct course for the frontier; but his representation, which described it as an arid and barren desert, that had repulsed by its sterility all the attempts of the Indians to penetrate it, determined me for the present to relinquish the plan; and, agreeably to his advice, after crossing the Sierra, continue our intended route along its eastern base to the Spanish trail. By this route, a party of six Indians, who had come from a great river in the eastern part of the desert to trade with his people, had just started on their return. He would himself return the next day to *San Fernando;* and as our roads would be the same for two days, he offered his services to conduct us so far on our way. His offer was gladly accepted. The fog, which had somewhat interfered with views in the valley, had entirely passed off and left a clear sky. That which had enveloped us in the neighborhood of the pass, proceeded evidently from fires kindled among the tulares by Indians living near the lakes, and which were intended to warn those in the mountains that there were strangers in the valley. Our position was in latitude 35° 17' 12", and longitude 118° 35' 03".

April 14. Our guide joined us this morning on the trail; and, arriving in a short distance at an open bottom where the creek forked, we continued up the right-hand branch, which was enriched by a profusion of flowers and handsomely wooded with sycamore, oaks, cottonwood, and willow, with other trees, and some shrubby plants. In its long strings of balls, this sycamore differs from that of the United States, and is the *Platanus occidentalis* of Hooker—a new species recently described among the plants collected in the voyage of the *Sulphur.* The cottonwood varied its foliage with white tufts, and the feathery seeds were flying plentifully through the air. Gooseberries, nearly ripe, were very abundant on the mountain; and as we passed the dividing grounds, which were not very easy to ascertain, the air was filled with perfume, as if we were entering a highly cultivated garden; and, instead of green, our pathway and the mountain-sides were covered with fields of yellow flowers, which here was the prevailing color. Our journey to-day was in the midst of an advanced spring, whose green and floral beauty offered a delightful contrast to the sandy valley we had just left. All the day snow was in sight on the butt of the mountain, which frowned down upon us on the right; but we beheld it now with feelings of pleasant security, as we rode along between green trees and on flowers, with hummingbirds and other feathered friends of the traveller enlivening the serene spring air. As we reached the summit of this beautiful pass, and obtained a view into the eastern country, we saw at once that here was the place to take leave of all such pleasant scenes as those around us. The distant mountains were now bald rocks again; and below, the land had any color but green. Taking into consideration the nature of the Sierra Nevada, we found this pass an excellent one for horses; and with a little labor, or perhaps with a more perfect examination of the localities, it might be made sufficiently practicable for wagons. Its latitude and longitude may be considered that of our last encampment, only a few miles distant. The elevation was not taken—our half-wild cavalcade making it too troublesome to halt before night, when once started.

We here left the waters of the bay of San Francisco, and, though forced upon them contrary to my intentions, I cannot regret the necessity which occasioned the deviation. It made me well acquainted with the great range of the Sierra Nevada of the Alta California, and showed that this broad and elevated snowy ridge was a continuation of the Cascade Range of Oregon, between which and the ocean there is still another and a lower range, parallel to the former and to the coast, and which may be called the Coast Range. It also made me well acquainted with the basin of the San Francisco bay, and with the two pretty rivers and their valleys (the Sacramento and San Joaquin), which are tributary to that bay; and cleared up some points in geography on which error had long prevailed. It had been constantly represented, as I have already stated, that the bay of San Francisco opened far into the interior, by some river coming down from the base of the Rocky mountains, and upon which supposed stream the name of Rio Buenaventura had been bestowed. Our observations of the Sierra Nevada, in the long distance from the head of the Sacramento to the head of the San Joaquin, and of the valley below it, which collects all the waters of the San Francisco bay, show that this neither is nor can be the case. No river from the interior does, or can, cross the Sierra Nevada—itself more lofty than the Rocky mountains; and as to the Buenaventura, the mouth of which seen on the coast gave the idea and the name of the reputed great river, it is, in fact, a small stream of no consequence, not only below the Sierra Nevada, but actually below the Coast Range—taking its rise within half a degree of the ocean, running parallel to it for about two degrees, and then falling into the Pacific near Monterey. There is no opening from the bay of San Francisco into the interior of the continent. The two rivers which flow into it are comparatively short, and not perpendicular to the coast, but lateral to it, and having their heads towards Oregon and southern California. They open lines of communication north and south, and not eastwardly; and thus this want of interior communication from the San Francisco bay, now fully ascertained, gives great additional value to the Columbia, which stands alone as the only great river on the Pacific slope of our continent which leads from the ocean to the Rocky mountains, and opens a line of communication from the sea to the valley of the Mississippi.

Four *compañeros* joined our guide at the pass; and two going back at noon, the others continued on in company. Descending from the hills, we reached a country of fine grass, where the *Erodium cicutarium* finally disappeared, giving place to an excellent quality of bunch grass. Passing by some springs where there was a rich sward of grass among groves of large black oak, we rode over a plain on which the guide pointed out a spot where a refugee Christian Indian had been killed by a party of soldiers which had unexpectedly penetrated into the mountains. Crossing a low sierra, and descending a hollow where a spring gushed out, we were struck by the sudden appearance of *yucca* trees, which gave a strange and southern character to the country, and suited well with the dry and desert region we were approaching. Associated with the idea of barren sands, their stiff and ungraceful form makes them to the traveller the most repulsive tree in the vegetable kingdom. Following the hollow, we shortly came upon a creek timbered with large black oak, which yet had not put forth a leaf. There was a small rivulet of running water, with good grass.

April 15.—The Indians who had accompanied the guide returned this morning, and I purchased from them a Spanish saddle, and long spurs, as reminiscences of the time; and for a few yards of scarlet cloth they gave me a horse, which afterwards became food for other Indians.

We continued a short distance down the creek, in which our guide informed us that the water very soon disappeared, and turned directly to the southward along the foot of the mountain; the trail on which we rode appearing to describe the eastern limit of travel, where water and grass terminated. Crossing a low spur, which bordered the creek, we descended to a kind of plain among the lower spurs; the desert being in full view on our left, apparently illimitable. A hot mist lay over it to day, through which it had a white and glistening appearance; here and there a few dry-looking *buttes* and isolated black ridges rose suddenly upon it. "There," said our guide, stretching out his hand towards it, "there are the great *llanos*, (plains); *no hay agua; no hay zacate—nada:* there is neither water nor grass—nothing; every animal that goes out upon them, dies." It was indeed dismal to look upon, and hard to conceive so great a change in so short a distance. One might travel the world over, without finding a valley more fresh and verdant—more floral and sylvan—more alive with birds and animals—more bounteously watered— than we had left in the San Joaquin: here, within a few miles' ride, a vast desert plain spread before us, from which the boldest traveller turned away in despair.

Directly in front of us, at some distance to the southward, and running out in an easterly direction from the mountains, stretched a sierra, having at the eastern end (perhaps 50 miles distant) some snowy peaks, on which, by the information of our guide, snow rested all the year.

Our cavalcade made a strange and grotesque appearance, and it was impossible to avoid reflecting upon our position and composition in this remote solitude. Within two degrees of the Pacific ocean; already far south of the latitude of Monterey; and still forced on south by a desert on one hand and a mountain range on the other; guided by a civilized Indian, attended by two wild ones from the Sierra; a Chinook from the Columbia; and our own mixture of American, French, German—all armed; four or five languages heard at once; above a hundred horses and mules, half wild; American, Spanish, and Indian dresses and equipments intermingled;—such was our composition. Our march was a sort of procession. Scouts ahead, and on the flanks; a front and rear division; the pack animals, baggage, and horned cattle in the centre; and the whole stretching a quarter of a mile along our dreary path. In this form we journeyed; looking more like we belonged to Asia than to the United States of America.

LANSFORD HASTINGS
1819–1870

A lawyer from Ohio, Hastings was an early promoter of what would become an essential feature of the California Dream: a place you can go to change your life. He led his first wagon party west in 1842, at the age of twenty-three. His book The Emigrants' Guide *was published in Cincinnati in the spring of 1845, and its appearance was followed by an East Coast lecture tour. It has been said that in 1846, the year of the "Great Migration," every wagon on the trail bore a copy of his* Guide. *Promising such things as perpetual spring and freedom from disease, it became almost a sacred text. Among his readers were members of the Donner Party, whose ill-fated decision to follow the Hastings Cut-off cost precious weeks and contributed to their epic misfortune in the Sierra Nevada snows. Like countless promoters in years to come, Hastings also had real estate to sell. After leading a second party west in 1845, he and a partner laid out an early version of a subdivision called Sutterville, just below the site of the future city of Sacramento. As a delegate to the constitutional convention in 1849, he first proposed what would become the state's eastern boundary. He later served as a San Francisco judge.*

From *The Emigrants' Guide to Oregon and California*

Considering the very short space of time, which has elapsed, since the different governments have turned their attentions to this country, and little which is, as yet, known in reference to it, its present commerce scarcely paralleled; some conception, of which, may be drawn at has been said upon a former page, in reference to its extensive imports and duties. Fifteen or twenty vessels are, not infrequently, seen in many of the various ports at the same time, displaying the national flags of all the principal powers of the world. Merchant vessels of the United States, England, France, Russia, and Mexico, as well as the ships of war, and the whale ships of the four former governments, are to be seen, at almost any time, in the different ports of this country, and of all of which there are frequent arrivals and departures. The ships of war, which cruise in the Pacific, touch very frequently at the various ports of entry, for the purpose of obtaining fresh supplies of water, and provisions, and maintaining the rights of their respective governments, as well as for the purpose of capturing, now and then, a small town, or seizing, here and there, upon an island of the Pacific. The merchant vessels are much the most numerous, and are, chiefly, those of the United States, which arrive in that country each spring, and depart for the States every autumn or winter. Arriving in the spring, they are engaged in the coasting trade, until the latter part of the fall, or the early part of the winter, when they depart for the States, with cargoes of hides, tallow, or furs, which have been collected during the previous year. About one half of the merchant vessels, engaged in this trade, always remain in the country, engaged in the coasting trade, while the residue return to the States, England, or France, for the purpose of renewing their stock of goods. Several of these vessels usually belong to the same houses, either of Boston or New York, which always keep a number in the country, while they employ others, constantly, in exporting the products of California, and importing goods for that trade, which they dispose of at most extraordinary prices. The whale ships touch at the various ports, for the purpose of obtaining supplies of provisions and water, and also for the purpose of trade with the inhabitants. Besides the ships and vessels above enumerated, there are numerous others, as well as various barques and brigs, which annually touch at the various ports of this country, not only from the States, England, France, and Russia, but also from the Sandwich Islands, the Russian settlements, and China.

The foregoing will enable us to form very correct conclusions, in reference to the present and future commerce of this infant country, the former of which, considering the newness of the country, and the sparseness of the population, is scarcely equaled, and, if the present may be considered as a prelude to the future, the latter is destined, in a very few years, to exceed, by far, that of any other country of the same extent and population, in any portion of the known world. We are necessarily driven to this conclusion, when we consider the vast extent of its plains and valleys, of unequaled fertility and exuberance; the extraordinary variety and abundance, of its productions, its unheard of uniformity, and salubrity of climate; in fine, its unexhausted and inexhaustible resources, as well, as its increasing emigration, which is annually swelling its population, from hundreds to thousands, and which is destined, at no distant day, to revolutionize the whole commercial, political, and moral aspect of all that highly important and delightful country. In a word, I will remark that in my opinion, there is no country, in the known world, possessing a soil so fertile and productive, with such varied and inexhaustible resources, and a climate of such mildness, uniformity and salubrity; nor is there a country, in my opinion, now known, which is so eminently calculated, by nature herself, in all respects, to promote the unbounded happiness and prosperity, of civilized and enlightened man.

MARIANO GUADALUPE VALLEJO
1808–1890

Vallejo was born in Monterey, the son of Ignacio Vallejo of Jalisco, Mexico, who came to Alta California as a soldier in 1774. He began his own military career at the Monterey garrison at the age of fifteen. During the 1830s, Vallejo was a leader in the movement to break from Mexico and make California a separate republic. By the mid-1840s he was arguably the most powerful man in the province, and among the wealthiest landholders. He had founded the pueblo of Sonoma. As commander of the northern frontier, he presided like a feudal baron. He welcomed the American takeover, since he had come to see union with the United States as the best option for his home region. Ironically, he was the first man arrested during the semi-staged Bear Flag Revolt. Vallejo's account of that escapade comes from a massive history he began to compose in the 1860s, after his retirement from public life. When his Sonoma mansion, Casa Grande, burned down in 1867, the first version, then nine hundred pages long, was lost in the fire. He began again, completing his five-volume Historical and Personal Memories Relating to Alta California in 1875. It is among the earliest narratives written by a native Californian.

"The Bear Flag Party"
from *Recuerdos Históricos y Personales Tocante a la Alta California*

All during the first week of the month of June various interviews took place between Captain Frémont and his compatriots. What passed between them is not public knowledge, but if the antecedents may be drawn from what followed, it is easy to presume that they were perfecting the plans they thought most appropriate for seizing Alta California and devising the means to come off victorious in their undertaking. . . .

The gentlemen under Captain Frémont's command took the road leading through the Napa Hills to Sonoma and at dawn on the fourteenth of June they surrounded my house located on the plaza at Sonoma. At daybreak they raised the shout of alarm and when I heard it, I looked out of my bedroom window. To my great surprise, I made out groups of armed men scattered to the right and left of my residence. The recent arrivals were not in uniform, but were all armed and presented a fierce aspect. Some of them wore on their heads a visorless cap of coyote skin, some a low-crowned plush hat, [and] some a red cotton handkerchief. As for the balance of the clothing of the assaulters of my residence, I shall not attempt to describe it, for I acknowledge that I am incapable of doing the task justice—I suspected that the intruders had intentions harmful not to my [property] interests alone, but to my life and that of the members of my family. I realized that my situation was desperate. My wife advised me to try and flee by the rear door but I told her that such a step was unworthy and that under no circumstances could I decide to desert my young family at such a critical time. I had my uniform brought, dressed quickly and then ordered the large vestibule door thrown open. The house was immediately filled with armed men. I went with them into the parlor of my residence. I asked them what the trouble was and who was heading the party but had to repeat that question a second time, because almost all of those who were in the parlor replied at once, "Here we are all heads." When I again asked with whom I should take the matter up, they pointed out William B. Ide who was the eldest of all. I then addressed that gentleman and informed him that I wanted to know to what happy circumstance I owed the visit of so many individuals.

In reply he stated that both Captain Merritt and the other gentlemen who were in his company had decided not to continue living any longer under the Mexican government, whose representatives, Castro and Pío Pico, did not respect the rights of American citizens living in the Departamento; that Castro was every once in a while issuing proclamations treating them all as bandits and, in a desire to put a stop to all these insults, they had decided to declare California independent; that while he held none but sentiments of regard for me, he would be forced to take me prisoner along with all my family.

We were at this point when there appeared in the room Don Salvador Vallejo, don Pepe de la Rosa, Jacob P. Leese, and don Victor Prudon, all friends of mine for whom an order of arrest was suggested until it was decided what should be my fate. I thought for a moment that through some sacrifice on my part I might get rid of so many and such little desired guests, but my hopes were frustrated by the unworthy action of the Canadian, Olivier Beaulieu, who, knowing from his own experiences that liquor is an incentive for all kinds of villainous acts, had gone to his house and procured there a barrel full of brandy, which he distributed among the companions of Merritt and Ide. Once under the influence of the liquor, they forgot the chief object of their mission and broke into shouts of "Get the loot, get the loot!"

Fortunately, these seditious cries emitted by Scott, Beaulieu, Sears and others attracted the attention of Doctor Semple who stepped very angrily to the door of the entrance vestibule and by means of a speech of much feeling, in which there were not a few threats, gave them to understand that he would kill the first man who by committing robbery would cast a blot upon the expedition he had helped organize to advance a political end and that, so long as he was alive, he would not allow it to be turned into a looting expedition. . . .

I am of the opinion that it has been intentional, for it seems that a hidden but powerful hand has taken great pains to garble all the facts relative to the capture of the Sonoma plaza by the group of adventurers to whom history has given the name of "The Bear Flag Party." I, who was made the chief victim those patriotic gentlemen sacrificed upon the altar of their well-laid plans, have no interest whatsoever in bespattering them with mud, nor do I aspire to ennoble myself at the expense of their reputation. All I desire is that the impartial public may know what took place at Sonoma on fateful June 14th, 1846, and that it may, after learning all there is to know in regard to this scandalous violation of law that deprived of liberty those who for years had been making countless sacrifices to redeem from the hands of the barbarous heathen the territory known as the Sonoma Frontier, decide in favor of one or the other of the participants in the events I have just related. All I demand is that the decision arrived at may be upon a basis of fact.

On the fourth day that Mr. Ide was in command at the Sonoma plaza . . . he issued a document in which he set forth the reasons that had impelled him to refuse to recognize the authority of the Mexican government. The original proclamation, which was very brief, merely stated that, since the lives of foreigners were in imminent danger, he had felt it his duty to declare Alta California independent and that, counting as he did upon the definite support and cooperation of the "fighting men" who had rallied around him, he aimed to do all he could to prevent the Californians or the Mexicans from recovering the military post and arms which the valor of his men had seized from them. This is approximately what "Captain" Ide read aloud before the flagpole in the Sonoma plaza. . . .

After the reading of the Commander-in-chief's proclamation, they proceeded with great ceremony to hoist the flag by virtue of which those who had assaulted my home and who had by that time appropriated to themselves two hundred fifty muskets and nine cannon proposed to carry on their campaign.

This flag was nothing more nor less than a strip of white cotton stuff with a red edge and upon the white part, almost in the center, were written the words "California Republic." Also on the white part, almost in the center, there was painted a bear with lowered head. The bear was so badly painted, however, that it looked more like a pig than a bear. . . . Of course, both the

Mariano Guadalupe Vallejo

bear and the star were very badly drawn, but that should not be wondered at, if one takes into consideration the fact that they lacked brushes and suitable colors.

The running up of this queer flag caused much fear to the families of the Californians established in the neighborhood of Sonoma, Petaluma and San Rafael, for they realized that the instigators of the uprising that had disturbed the tranquillity of the frontier had made up their minds to rule, come what might, and, as the rumor had been spread far and wide that Ide and his associates had raised the bear flag in order to enjoy complete liberty and not be obliged to render any account of their activities to any civilized governments, the ranchers, who would have remained unperturbed should the American flag have been run up in Sonoma and who would have considered it as the harbinger of a period of progress and enlightenment, seized their machetes and guns and fled to the woods, determined to await a propitious moment for getting rid of the disturbers of the peace. Strange to relate, the first victim that the ranchers sacrificed was the painter of the "Bear Flag," young Thomas Cowie who, along with P. Fowler, was on his way to Fitch's ranch to get one-eyed Moses Carson (brother of the famous explorer Colonel Kit Carson), who was employed as an overseer by Captain Henry Fitch, to give them a half barrel of powder he had locked up in one of the storage closets of his farmhouse.

Fowler and Cowie were taken by surprise at the Yulupa Rancho by the party operating under the command of Captains Padilla and Ramon Carrillo. . . . Neither of the two extemporaneous commanders thought it right to take the lives of their young captives, upon whom there had been found letters that proved beyond any doubt that Moses Carson and certain others of the Americans employed at the Fitch Ranch were in accord with Ide, Merritt and others of those who had made up their minds to put an end to Mexican domination in California; so they decided to tie them up to a couple of trees while they deliberated as to what should be done with the captives, whose fate was to be decided at the meeting that night to which had been summoned all the ranchers who by their votes had shared in entrusting command of the Californian forces to those wealthy citizens, Padilla and Carrillo. I am of the opinion that the lives of Cowie and Fowler would have been spared, had it not been that a certain Bernardo Garcia, better known under the name of "Three-fingered Jack," taking advantage of the darkness of the night, approached the trees to which the captives were tied and put an end to their existence with his well-sharpened dagger.

After committing the two murders I have just told about, Bernardo Garcia entered the lonely hut in which Padilla, Carrillo and others had met and were discussing as to what disposition should be made of the prisoners. Without waiting for them to ask him any questions, he said to his compatriots, "I thought you here were going to decide to free the prisoners and, as that is not for the good of my country, I got ahead of you and took the lives of the Americans who were tied to the trees."

Those few words, spoken with the greatest of sang-froid by the wickedest man that California had produced up to that time, caused all who heard him to shudder. No one dared to object to what had been done, however, for they knew that such a step would have exposed them to falling under the knife of the dreaded Bernardo Garcia, who for years past had been the terror of the Sonoma frontier.

Equally with the relatives of the unfortunate youths, Cowie and Fowler, I regretted their premature death, for, in spite of the fact that they belonged to a group of audacious men who had torn me from the bosom of my family and done as they pleased with my horses, saddles and arms, I did not consider that the simple fact that they were the bearers of a few letters made them deserving of the supreme penalty. Until that fatal June 21st, neither they nor their companions had shed any Mexican blood and it was not right for the Mexicans to begin a war of outrage, that could not help but bring very grievous consequences upon them and their families. . . .

When we reached New Helvetia, the Canadian, Alexis, who was heading our escort, gave three knocks upon the main gate with his lance and it was immediately thrown open by Captain Sutter, who, feigning surprise at seeing us as prisoners, led us into his living quarters. He then promised to comply with the orders that Captain Frémont had delivered to him by the mouth of his lieutenant, Alexis, who had said in our presence, "Captain Frémont is turning these gentlemen over to you for you to keep as prisoners behind these walls and upon your own responsibility."

"All right," said Sutter, and without any further ceremony he turned to us and suggested that we accompany him to a large room situated on the second floor where the only furniture was a kind of rude benches. When we were all inside this room Sutter locked the door and thought no more about us that night.

I leave my readers to imagine how we cursed at finding ourselves locked up in a narrow room and forced to sleep upon the floor, without a mattress and without a blanket, even without water with which to quench our burning thirst. . . .

After a sleepless night, I greeted the dawn of the new day with enthusiasm,

Mariano Guadalupe Vallejo

for we were by then beginning to experience the urge of a voracious appetite. Our jailer, however, who had doubtless made up his mind to make us drain the last drop of gall which a perverse fate had meted out to us, sent us no food until eleven o'clock in the morning, at which time he came and opened the door to permit the entrance of an Indian carrying a jar filled with broth and pieces of meat. He did not send us a spoon or knives and forks, for Captain Sutter no doubt thought that since we had lost our liberty we had also ceased to retain our dignity. Such behavior on the part of a companion in arms (at that time Captain Sutter was still an official of the Mexican Government) could not help but inspire our disgust, for we all recognized the insult that he was inflicting upon us by taking advantage of the circumstances. There are times in life, however, when man should resign himself to suffering every kind of adversity. Doubtless, God had decreed that the month of June, 1846, should be the blackest month of my life. . . .

Let my readers not think that it is my desire to open up wounds that have healed over by now. I am very far from harboring any such thought, for ever since Alta California became a part of the great federation of the United States of North America, I have spared no effort to establish upon a solid and enduring basis those sentiments of union and concord which are so indispensable for the progress and advancement of all those who dwell in my native land, and, so long as I live, I propose to use all the means at my command to see to it that both races cast a stigma upon the disagreeable events that took place on the Sonoma frontier in 1846. If before I pass on to render an account of my acts to the Supreme Creator, I succeed in being a witness to a reconciliation between victor and vanquished, conquerors and conquered, I shall die with the conviction of not having striven in vain.

EDWIN BRYANT

1805–1869

During the Gold Rush, Bryant's book What I Saw in California *played a significant role for the new multitude of transcontinental travelers. Unlike Hastings, he set out not to promote the region but rather to record what he saw with the accurate eye of a skillful journalist. Born in Massachusetts, he was a first cousin of the poet William Cullen Bryant. He grew up in Kentucky, where he became a leading newspaperman. In April 1846 he quit his job as coeditor of the* Louisville Courier *to head west with the Great Migration. His purpose from the outset was to write a book about what he and others saw as history in the making. He followed the Emigrant Trail from St. Louis to Fort Laramie, past Salt Lake and across Nevada, and into Sutter's Fort. Entering California at the height of the conflict with Mexico, he observed the American takeover, rode as a lieutenant with Frémont's battalion, and served a short term as mayor of San Francisco (where Bryant Street is named for him). En route he kept an extensive journal, which he assembled in San Francisco before carrying the manuscript back to Philadelphia for publication. His timing was perfect. The book appeared in 1848, soon after James Marshall's discovery of gold. When this news reached the larger world, Bryant's book was widely reviewed, and he was instantly perceived as the new expert on travel to the far West. By 1850 his book had been published in England, France, and Sweden and gone through six American editions.*

"The California Battalion"
from *What I Saw in California*

November 30.—The battalion of mounted riflemen under the command of Lieutenant-colonel Fremont, numbers, rank and file, including Indians and servants, 428. With the exception of the exploring party, which left the United States with Colonel F., they are composed of volunteers from the American settlers, and the emigrants which have arrived in the country within a few weeks. The latter have generally furnished their own ammunition and other equipments for the expedition. Most of these are practiced riflemen, men of undoubted courage, and capable of bearing any fatigue and privations endurable by veteran troops. The Indians are composed of a party of Walla-Wallas from Oregon, and a party of native Californians. Attached to the battalion are two pieces of artillery, under the command of Lieutenant McLane, of the navy. In the appearance of our small army there is presented but little of "the pomp and circumstance of glorious war." There are no plumes nodding over brazen helmets, nor coats of broadcloth spangled with lace and buttons. A broad-brimmed, low-crowned hat, a shirt of blue flannel, or buckskin, with pantaloons and moccasins of the same, all generally much the worse for wear, and smeared with mud and dust, make up the costume of the party, officers as well as men. A leathern girdle surrounds the waist, from which are suspended a bowie and a hunter's knife, and sometimes a brace of pistols. These, with the rifle and holster-pistols, are the arms carried by officers and privates. A single bugle (and a sorry one it is) composes the band. Many an embryo Napoleon, in his own conceit, whose martial spirit has been excited to flaming intensity of heat by the peacock-plumage and gaudy trappings of our militia companies, when marching through the streets to the sound of drum, fife, and brass band, if he could have looked upon us, and then consulted the state of the military thermometer within him, would probably have discovered that the mercury of his heroism had fallen several degrees below zero. He might even have desired that we should not come

"Between the wind and his nobility."

War, stripped of its pageantry, possesses but few of the attractions with which poetry and painting have embellished it. . . .

December 4.—I was ordered with a small party in advance this morning. Proceeding up the valley a few miles, we left it, crossing several steep hills sparsely timbered with oak, from which we descended into another small valley, down which we continued to the point of its termination, near some narrow and difficult mountain gorges. In exploring the gorges, we discovered the trail of a party of Californians, which had passed south several days before us, and found a horse which they had left in their march. This, doubtless, was a portion of the party which captured Mr. Larkin, and had the engagement between Monterey and St. Juan, on the 17th ult. The main body coming up, we encamped at 3 o'clock. The old grass around our camp is abundant; but having been so much washed by the rains, and consequently exhausted of its nutritious qualities, the animals refuse to eat it. The country over which we have traveled to-day, and as far as I can see, is mountainous and broken, little of it being adapted to other agricultural purposes than grazing.

Thirteen beeves are slaughtered every afternoon for the consumption of the battalion. These beeves are generally of good size, and in fair condition. Other provisions being entirely exhausted, beef constitutes the only subsistence for the men, and most of the officers. Under these circumstances, the consumption of beef is astonishing. I do not know that I shall be believed when I state a fact, derived from observation and calculation, that the average consumption per man of fresh beef is at least ten pounds per day. Many of them, I believe, consume much more, and some of them less. Nor does this quantity appear to be injurious to health, or fully to satisfy the appetite. I have seen some of the men roast their meat and devour it by the fire from the hour of encamping until late bedtime. They would then sleep until one or two o'clock in the morning, when the cravings of hunger being greater than the desire for repose, the same occupation would be resumed and continued until the order was given to march. The Californian beef is generally fat, juicy, and tender, and surpasses in flavor any which I ever tasted elsewhere. Distance 10 miles. . . .

December 22.—Clear and pleasant. Being of the party which performed rear-guard duty to-day, with orders to bring in all stragglers, we did not leave camp until several hours after the main body had left. The horses of the *caballada* and the pack-animals were continually giving out and refusing to proceed. Parties of men, exhausted, lay down upon the ground, and it was with much urging, and sometimes with peremptory commands only, that they could be prevailed upon to proceed. The country bears the same marks of drought heretofore described, but fresh vegetation is now springing up and appears vigorous. A large horse-trail leading into one of the *cañadas* of the mountains on our left, was discovered by the scouts, and a party was dispatched to trace it. We passed one deserted rancho, and reached camp between nine and ten o'clock at night, having forced in all the men and most of the horses and pack-mules. Distance 15 miles.

December 23.—Rain fell steadily and heavily the entire day. A small party of men was in advance. Discovering in a brushy valley two Indians armed with bows and arrows, they were taken prisoners. Learning from them that there was a *caballada* of horses secreted in one of the *cañadas,* they continued on about ten miles, and found about twenty-five fresh, fat horses, belonging to a Californian now among the insurgents below. They were taken and delivered at the camp near the eastern base of the St. Ynes mountain. Passed this morning a rancho inhabited by a foreigner, an Englishman.

December 24.—Cloudy and cool, with an occasional sprinkling rain. Our route to-day lay directly over the St. Ynes mountain, by an elevated and most difficult pass. The height of this mountain is several thousand feet. We reached the summit about twelve o'clock, and our company composing the advance-guard, we encamped about a mile and a half in advance of the main body of the battalion, at a point which overlooks the beautiful plain of Santa Barbara, of which, and the ocean beyond, we had a most extended and interesting view. With the spyglass, we could see in the plain far below us, herds of cattle quietly grazing upon the green herbage that carpets its gentle undulations. The plain is dotted with groves, surrounding the springs and belting the small water-courses, of which there are many flowing from this range of mountains. Ranchos are scattered far up and down the plain, but not one human being could be seen stirring. About ten or twelve miles to the south, the white towers of the mission of Santa Barbara raise themselves. Beyond, is the illimitable waste of waters. A more lovely and picturesque landscape I never beheld. On the summit of the mountain, and surrounding us, there is a growth of hawthorn, manzanita, (in bloom), and other small shrubbery. The rock is soft sandstone and conglomerate, immense masses of which, piled one upon another, form a wall along the western brow of the mountain, through which there is a single pass or gateway about eight or ten feet in width. The descent on the western side is precipitous, and appears almost impassable. Distance 4 miles.

December 25.—Christmas-day, and a memorable one to me. Owing to the difficulty in hauling the cannon up the steep acclivities of the mountain, the main body of the battalion did not come up with us until twelve o'clock, and before we commenced the descent of the mountain a furious storm commenced, raging with a violence rarely surpassed. The rain fell in torrents and the wind blew almost with the force of a tornado. This fierce strife of the elements continued without abatement the entire afternoon, and until two o'clock at night. Driving our horses before us we were compelled to slide down the steep and slippery rocks, or wade through deep gullies and ravines filled with mud and foaming torrents of water, that rushed downwards with such force as to carry along the loose rocks and tear up the trees and shrubbery by the roots. Many of the horses falling into the ravines refused to make an effort to extricate themselves, and were swept downwards and drowned. Others, bewildered by the fierceness and terrors of the storm, rushed or fell headlong over the steep precipices and were killed. Others obstinately refused to proceed, but stood quaking with fear or shivering with cold, and many of these perished in the night from the severity of the storm. The advance party did not reach the foot of the mountain and find a place to encamp until night—and a night of more impenetrable and terrific darkness I never witnessed. The ground upon which our camp was made, although sloping from the hills to a small stream, was so saturated with water that men as well as horses sunk deep at every step. The rain fell in such quantities that fires with great difficulty could be lighted, and most of them were immediately extinguished.

The officers and men belonging to the company having the cannon in charge, labored until nine or ten o'clock to bring them down the mountain, but they were finally compelled to leave them. Much of the baggage also remained on the side of the mountain, with the pack-mules and horses conveying them; all efforts to force the animals down being fruitless. The men continued to straggle into the camp until a late hour of the night;—some crept under the shelving rocks and did not come in until the next morning. We were so fortunate as to find our tent, and after much difficulty pitched it under an oak-tree. All efforts to light a fire and keep it blazing proving abortive, we spread our blankets upon the ground and endeavored to sleep, although we could feel the cold streams of water running through the tent and between and around our bodies.

In this condition we remained until about two o'clock in the morning, when the storm having abated I rose, and shaking from my garments the dripping water, after many unsuccessful efforts succeeded in kindling a fire. Near our tent I found three soldiers who had reached camp at a late hour. They were fast asleep on the ground, the water around them being two or three inches deep; but they had taken care to keep their heads above water by using a log of wood for a pillow. The fire beginning to blaze freely, I dug a ditch with my hands and a sharp stick of wood, which drained off the pool surrounding the tent. One of the men, when he felt the sensation consequent upon being "high and dry," roused himself, and sitting upright, looked around for some time with an expression of bewildered amazement. At length he seemed to realize the true state of the case, and exclaimed in a tone of energetic soliloquy:

"Well, who *wouldn't* be a soldier and fight for California?"

"You are mistaken," I replied.

Rubbing his eyes he gazed at me with astonishment, as if having been entirely unconscious of my presence; but reassuring himself he said:

"How mistaken?"

"Why," I answered, "you are not fighting for California."

"What the d——l then am I fighting for?" he inquired.

"For *Texas.*"

"Texas be d——d; but hurrah for General Jackson!" and with this exclamation he threw himself back again upon his wooden pillow, and was soon snoring in a profound slumber.

Making a platform composed of sticks of wood upon the soft mud, I stripped myself to the skin, wringing the water from each garment as I proceeded. I then commenced drying them by the fire in the order that they were replaced upon my body, an employment that occupied me until daylight, which sign, above the high mountain to the east, down which we had rolled rather than marched yesterday, I was truly rejoiced to see. Distance 3 miles.

Dec. 26.—Parties were detailed early this morning, and dispatched up the mountain to bring down the cannon, and collect the living horses and baggage. The destruction of horse-flesh, by those who witnessed the scene, by daylight, is described as frightful. In some places large numbers of dead horses were piled together. In others, horses half buried in the mud of the ravines, or among the rocks, were gasping in the agonies of death. The number of dead animals is variously estimated at from seventy-five to one hundred and fifty, by different persons. The cannon, most of the missing baggage, and the living horses, were all brought in by noon. The day was busily employed in cleansing our rifles and pistols, and drying our drenched baggage.

Dec. 27.—Preparations were commenced early for the resumption of our march; but such was the condition of every thing around us, that it was two o'clock, p.m., before the battalion was in readiness; and then so great had been the loss of horses in various ways, that the number remaining was insufficient to mount the men. One or two companies, and portions of others, were compelled to march on foot. We were visited during the forenoon by Mr. Sparks, an American, Dr. Den, an Irishman, and Mr. Burton, another American, residents of Santa Barbara. They had been suffered by the Californians to remain in the place. Their information communicated to us was, that the town was deserted of nearly all its population. A few houses only were occupied. Passing down a beautiful and fertile undulating plain, we encamped just before sunset in a live-oak grove, about half a mile from the town of Santa Barbara. Strict orders were issued by Col. Fremont, that the property and the persons of Californians, not found in arms, should be sacredly respected. To prevent all collisions, no soldier was allowed to pass the lines of the camp without special permission, or orders from his officers.

I visited the town before dark; but found the houses, with few exceptions, closed, and the streets deserted. After hunting about some time we discovered a miserable dwelling, occupied by a shoemaker and his family, open. Entering it we were very kindly received by its occupants, who, with a princely supply of civility, possessed but a beggarly array of comforts. At our request they provided for us a supper of *tortillas, frijoles,* and stewed *carne* seasoned with *chile colorado,* for which, paying them *dos pesos* for four, we bade them good-evening, all parties being well satisfied. The family consisted, exclusive of the shoemaker, of a dozen women and children, of all ages. The women, from the accounts they had received of the intentions of the Americans, were evidently unprepared for civil treatment from them. They expected to he dealt with in a very barbarous manner, *in all respects;* but they were disappointed, and invited us to visit them again. Distance eight miles.

SARAH ELEANOR ROYCE

1819–1891

In the midst of the Gold Rush, Sarah Royce and her husband crossed the continent by ox-drawn wagon. Like Margaret Frink, young Sallie Hester, and other women caught up in that tumultuous era, she kept a record of the trip, calling hers a "Pilgrimage Diary." She was born in England, at Stratford-upon-Avon, and grew up in New York State. She was twenty, with a two-year-old daughter, when they departed Council Bluffs, Iowa, in April 1849. Crossing the Sierra just ahead of some early snow, they had reached the "diggings" by the end of October, stopping first at a rough and ready mining camp in the foothills east of Sacramento. They eventually settled in Grass Valley and spent the rest of their lives in California. Thirty years later, at the urging of her son, the eminent historian and philosopher Josiah Royce, she shaped her diary entries into the narrative now called A Frontier Lady. A devoutly religious woman, she had found her faith tested and strengthened by the rigors of the trek. Speaking as a wife, a mother, and a young woman in a world of uprooted men, hers is a seldom-heard voice from a legendary time.

From A Frontier Lady

The next day we climbed the first of the two ridges at the summit. And now I realized, in earnest, the value of a thoroughly trained mountain mule. In several places the way was so steep that the head of my animal was even with my eyes as I leaned forward with Mary's chief weight on my left arm while I clung with my right hand to the pommel of the saddle, obliged, for the time, to let the mule guide and drive himself. And nobly he did it, never slipping once; while the dark mule did as well with his great load. The other animals had to be driven, urged and kept in the track, while there seemed great danger of their packs being lost or torn; but, near evening, all arrived safely in camp.

That night we slept within a few yards of snow, which lay in a ravine; and water froze in our pans not very far from the fire, which, however, was rather low the last part of the night. But the morning was bright and sunny. "Hope sprang exultant"; for, that day, that blessed 19th of October, we were to cross the highest ridge, view the "promised land," and begin our descent into warmth and safety. So, without flinching I faced steeps still steeper than yesterday: I even laughed in my little one's upturned face, as she lay back against my arm, while I leaned forward almost to the neck of the mule, tugging up the hardest places. I had purposely hastened, that morning, to start ahead of the rest; and not far from noon, I was rewarded by coming out, in advance of all the others, on a rocky height whence I looked, *down,* far over constantly descending hills, to where a soft haze sent up a warm, rosy glow that seemed to me a smile of welcome; while beyond, occasional faint outlines of other mountains appeared; and I knew I was looking across the Sacramento Valley.

California, land of sunny skies—that was my first look into your smiling face. I loved you from that moment, for you seemed to welcome me with loving look into rest and safety. However brave a face I might have put on most of the time, I knew my coward heart was yearning all the while for a home-nest and a welcome into it, and you seemed to promise me both. A short time I had on those rocks, sacred to thanksgiving and prayer; then the others came, and boisterous shouts, and snatches of song made rocks and welkin ring.

We soon began to descend. Not far from the summit, on a small plateau, affording room to camp, and a little timber, we saw traces of fires, and near by, the carcasses of two fine horses evidently not very long dead; while a number of things scattered about looked like hasty flight. We concluded this must have been the scene of disaster of one of those unfortunate parties the relief man had told us of, who were caught in the two nights of snow-storm only about ten days before. And now very cheerily we found our way leading down, and down, and down; so suddenly in some places, that my mule braced his legs and slid. But the next day the descent was not so remarkable; the road became exceedingly dusty; and the spirits of the party flagged somewhat.

We still, each night, made an effort to camp near Col. J—— and his men, for we had been warned that the Indians had in several instances attempted to attack and rob lone emigrants, while still high up in the mountains; though there would be no danger when we reached the mines. On the night of October 21st we unloaded our packs and made our fires within a few rods of our courteous protectors. We had, as usual, made for our own little family a sort of barricade of packs somewhat retired from the others; the men were lying near their fire asleep; and all was still; when a sudden, loud outcry, as of mingled pain and fright followed by other hasty exclamations, and rushing footsteps, and, soon, two or three shots roused us all. We were quickly informed that two Indian arrows had been fired into our neighbors' camp, evidently aimed at the men who were sleeping in the light of their fire. One of the arrows had wounded a man, striking him directly on one of the large ribs, which had prevented its reaching the vitals. The other arrow missed its aim and fell on the ground. Several of the men rushed, armed, into the thicket whence the arrows came, fired, and pursued a short distance. But the enemy knew every turn better than strangers could, and no Indians were to be found. The wounded man proved not to be mortally wounded; and we had the satisfaction of knowing he was improving before we finally parted company—which occurred a day or two after.

On the 24th of October at evening we reached what in our Guide Book was called "Pleasant Valley Gold Mines"; where we found two or three tents, and a few men with their gold-washing pans. They had been at work there for awhile; but said the little "diggings" just there were pretty much "worked out"; and they were going, in a day or two, over to Weaver Creek where, they told us, very fine "prospects had lately been struck," and there was quite a town growing up. That night, we slept, for the first time in several months, without the fear of Indians, or the dread of perils in advance. We rested ourselves and animals for two or three days, and then moved into the village of "Weaverville," of which the miners had told us. This village was made up of tents, many of them very irregularly placed; though in one part, following the trend of the principal ravine, there was, already, something like a row of these primitive dwellings, though at considerable distances apart. We added one to that row, and soon began to gather about us little comforts and conveniences, which made us feel as though we once more had a home. In a few days after we arrived in Weaverville, rain fell heavily, and soon the mountains just above us were blocked by snow. Only one company came through after us; and they barely escaped, by means of good mules. But, with us, lovely, sunny days followed the rainy nights; and, though the season, as a whole, was unusually stormy for California, and doubtless would have been death to any caught at the mountain tops; yet there were intervals that seemed very delightful to those who had spent the preceding winter where the temperature ranged, for many weeks, below zero.

· · ·

Soon after arriving in Weaverville, my husband had met with an acquaintance who had been a traveling companion in the early part of our long journey. He had washed out a little gold, and was desirous to go into business. He had made two or three acquaintances who also thought this new mining settlement presented an opening for a store; but none of them were accustomed to trading. They understood that my husband was; so they proposed to him to enter into partnership with them, proceed immediately to Sacramento City to purchase goods, and they, by the time he returned, would have a place prepared to open a store.

An effort was made to get a house built. The plan was, to hew out timber for the frame, and to split shakes for the roof and sides. But when they tried to get men to help them, so that the building could be done in anything like reasonable time, they found it impossible. All were so absorbed in washing out gold, or hunting for some to wash, that they could not think of doing anything else. On all sides the gold-pans were rattling, the cradles rocking, and the water splashing. So the best that could be done was, to hew out some strong tent poles and ridges, and erect two good sized tents, one behind the other; the back one for dwelling, the front for a store. An opportunity occurred to buy a large cook stove, which was placed near the junction of the two tents. The back part of the back tent was curtained off for me, leaving a space round the cook stove for kitchen and dining room. One of the men slept in the store, and the other two had a small tent on one side. They managed to buy some packing boxes, and other odds and ends of lumber, and so made shelves and a counter, which did very well for those primitive times.

We were soon fixed in our new quarters, the goods arrived from Sacramento, and business was opened. As one of the partners had formerly been in the meat business, some fat cattle were purchased, and beef was added to the other articles sold. This drew quite a crowd every morning; for fresh meat had not yet become very plentiful in the mines. It had not been thought necessary for all the men of the firm to devote their time to the store. Two of them continued mining; so, when a large number of customers came together, I helped to serve them. This gave me an opportunity to see most of the dwellers in Weaverville; and observe in a small way their behavior to each other. The majority of them were, as I have said, men of ordinary intelligence, evidently accustomed to life in an orderly community, where morality and religion bore sway. They very generally showed a consciousness of being somewhat the worse, for a long, rough journey, in which they had lived semi-barbarous lives, and for their continued separation from the amenities and refinements of home. Even in their intercourse with each other, they often alluded to this feeling, and in the presence of a woman, then so unusual, most of them showed it in a very marked manner. But, mingled with these better sort of men who formed the majority, were others of a different class. Roughly-reared frontier-men almost as ignorant of civilized life as savages. Reckless bravados, carrying their characters in their faces and demeanor, even when under the restraints imposed by policy. All these and more were represented in the crowd who used to come for their meat, and other provisions in the early morning hours. There were even some Indians, who were washing out gold in the neighboring ravines, and who used to come with the others to buy provisions. It was a motley assembly and they kept two or three of us very busy; for payments were made almost exclusively in gold-dust and it took longer to weigh that, than it would have done to receive coin and give change. But coin was very rare in the mines at that time, so we had our little gold scales and weights, and I soon became quite expert in handling them. While thus busy, in near communication with all these characters, no rude word or impertinent behavior was ever offered me.

But, among this moving crowd, thus working and eating, buying and selling, sounds of discontent and sadness were often heard. Discontent; for most of them had come to California with the hope of becoming easily and rapidly rich; and so, when they had to toil for days before finding gold, and, when they found it, had to work hard in order to wash out their "ounce a day"; and then discovered that the necessaries of life were so scarce it took much of their proceeds to pay their way, they murmured; and some of them cursed the country, calling it a "God forsaken land," while a larger number bitterly condemned their own folly in having left comfortable homes and moderate business chances, for so many hardships and uncertainties. And still, many of them kept repeating this same folly, by being easily induced, when they had struck tolerably fair prospects, and were clearing twice as much per day as they had ever done before, to give up their present diggings, and rush off after some new discovery, which was sure to be heralded every few days, by the chronic "prospectors" who then, (as too commonly ever since) kept the whole community in a ferment.

BAYARD TAYLOR
1825–1878

Born in Pennsylvania, Taylor was a man of letters, a poet, a novelist, a travel writer, and the author of over forty books. In 1849, aged twenty-five, he was a journalist for the New York Tribune, *then edited by Horace Greeley, and was sent to cover the Gold Rush. He had already published a sheaf of poems and a book on Europe (*Views Afoot, *1846). What began as a series of letters for the* Tribune *became his best-known work,* Eldorado, or Adventures in the Path of Empire. *In June he sailed from New York, crossing the isthmus of Panama, and by mid-August had reached San Francisco. He visited the mining country and all the towns from Sacramento to Monterey, where he arrived in time to report on the state constitutional convention. Taylor had not come west to prospect for gold or to make his fortune in land or trading. He was here as a writer, to find the story. With remarkable clarity and telling detail he captures the spirit of the region at a crucial moment of transition. After four and a half months in California he returned to New York by way of Mexico, and his book was in the stores by the fall of 1850. In later years he wrote four novels, books on Africa, India, China, Russia, and Egypt, and several volumes of verse, which were widely read during his lifetime. In 1878 a well-regarded translation of Goethe's* Faust *led to his appointment as U.S. minister to Germany.*

"San Francisco by Day and Night"
from *El Dorado, or Adventures in the Path of Empire*

A better idea of San Francisco, in the beginning of September, 1849, cannot be given than by the description of a single day. Supposing the visitor to have been long enough in the place to sleep on a hard plank and in spite of the attacks of innumerable fleas, he will be awakened at daylight by the noises of building, with which the hills are all alive. The air is temperate, and the invariable morning fog is just beginning to gather. By sunrise, which gleams hazily over the Coast Mountains across the Bay, the whole populace is up and at work. The wooden buildings unlock their doors, the canvas houses and tents throw back their front curtains; the lighters on the water are warped out from ship to ship; carts and porters are busy along the beach; and only the gaming-tables, thronged all night by the votaries of chance, are idle and deserted. The temperature is so fresh as to inspire an active habit of body, and

even without the stimulus of trade and speculation there would be few slug-
gards at this season.

As early as half-past six the bells begin to sound to breakfast, and for an
hour thenceforth, their incessant clang and the braying of immense gongs
drown all the hammers that are busy on a hundred roofs. The hotels, restaurants and refectories of all kinds are already as numerous as gaming-tables,
and equally various in kind. The tables d'hôte of the first class, (which charge
$2 and upwards the meal,) are abundantly supplied. There are others, with
more simple and solid fare, frequented by the large class who have their
fortunes yet to make. At the United States and California restaurants, on the
plaza, you may get an excellent beefsteak, scantily garnished with potatoes,
and a cup of good coffee or chocolate, for $1. Fresh beef, bread, potatoes. and
all provisions which will bear importation, are plenty; but milk, fruit and
vegetables are classed as luxuries, and fresh butter is rarely heard of. On
Montgomery street, and the vacant space fronting the water, vendors of coffee,
cakes and sweetmeats have erected their stands, in order to tempt the appetite
of sailors just arrived in port, or miners coming down from the mountains.

By nine o'clock the town is in the full flow of business. The streets running
down to the water, and Montgomery street which fronts the Bay, are crowded
with people, all in hurried motion. The variety of characters and costumes is
remarkable. Our own countrymen seem to lose their local peculiarities in such
a crowd, and it is by chance epithets rather than by manner, that the New
Yorker is distinguished from the Kentuckian, the Carolinian from the Down-
Easter, the Virginian from the Texan. The German and Frenchman are more
easily recognized. Peruvians and Chileans go by in their brown ponchos, and
the sober Chinese, cool and impassive in the midst of excitement, look out
of the oblique corners of their long eyes at the bustle, but are never tempted
to venture from their own line of business. The eastern side of the plaza, in
front of the Parker house and a canvas hell called the Eldorado, are the general
rendezvous of business and amusement—combining 'change, park, club-
room and promenade all in one. There, everybody not constantly employed
in one spot, may be seen at some time of the day. The character of the groups
scattered along the plaza is oftentimes very interesting. In one place are three
or four speculators bargaining for lots, buying and selling "fifty *varas* square"
in towns, some of which are canvas and some only paper; in another, a company of miners, brown as leather, and rugged in features as in dress; in a
third, perhaps, three or four naval officers speculating on the next cruise, or
a knot of genteel gamblers, talking over the last night's operations.

The day advances. The mist which after sunrise hung low and heavy for an hour or two, has risen above the hills, and there will be two hours of pleasant sunshine before the wind sets in from the sea. The crowd in the streets is now wholly alive. Men dart hither and thither, as if possessed with a never-resting spirit. You speak to an acquaintance—a merchant, perhaps. He utters a few hurried words of greeting, while his eyes send keen glances on all sides of you; suddenly he catches sight of somebody in the crowd; he is off, and in the next five minutes has bought up half a cargo, sold a town lot at treble the sum he gave, and taken a share in some new and imposing speculation. It is impossible to witness this excess and dissipation of business, without feeling something of its influence. The very air is pregnant with the magnetism of bold, spirited, unwearied action, and he who but ventures into the outer circle of the whirlpool, is spinning, ere he has time for thought, in its dizzy vortex.

But see! the groups in the plaza suddenly scatter; the city surveyor jerks his pole out of the ground and leaps on a pile of boards; the vendors of cakes and sweetmeats follow his example, and the place is cleared, just as a wild bull which has been racing down Kearney street makes his appearance. Two vaqueros, shouting and swinging their lariats, follow at a hot gallop; the dust flies as they dash across the plaza. One of them, in mid-career, hurls his lariat in the air. Mark how deftly the coil unwinds in its flying curve, and with what precision the noose falls over the bull's horns. The horse wheels as if on a pivot, and shoots off in an opposite line. He knows the length of the lariat to a hair, and the instant it is drawn taught, plants his feet firmly for the shock and throws his body forward. The bull is "brought up" with such force as to throw him off his legs. He lies stunned a moment, and then, rising heavily, makes another charge. But by this time the second vaquero has thrown a lariat around one of his hind legs, and thus checked on both sides, he is dragged off to slaughter.

The plaza is refilled as quickly as it was emptied, and the course of business is resumed. About twelve o'clock, a wind begins to blow from the north-west, sweeping with most violence through a gap between the hills, opening towards the Golden Gate. The bells and gongs begin to sound for dinner, and these two causes tend to lessen the crowd in the streets for an hour or two. Two o'clock is the usual dinner-time for business men, but some of the old and successful merchants have adopted the fashionable hour of five. Where shall we dine today? The restaurants display their signs invitingly on all sides; we have choice of the United States, Tortoni's, the Alhambra and many other equally classic resorts, but Delmonico's, like its distinguished original in New York, has the highest prices and the greatest variety of dishes. We go down

Kearney street to a two-story wooden house on the corner of Jackson. The lower story is a market; the walls are garnished with quarters of beef and mutton; a huge pile of Sandwich Island squashes fills one corner, and several cabbage-heads, valued at $2 each, show themselves in the window. We enter a little door at the end of the building, ascend a dark, narrow flight of steps and find ourselves in a long, low room, with ceiling and walls of white muslin and a floor covered with oil-cloth.

There are about twenty tables disposed in two rows, all of them so well filled that we have some difficulty in finding places. Taking up the written bill of fare, we find such items as the following:

SOUPS

Mock Turtle	$0.75
St. Julien	1.00

FISH

Boiled Salmon Trout, Anchovy Sauce	1.75

BOILED

Leg Mutton, caper sauce	1.00
Corned Beef, Cabbage	1.00
Ham and Tongues	0.75

ENTREES

Fillet of Beef, mushroom sauce	1.75
Veal Cutlets, breaded	1.00
Mutton Chop	1.00
Lobster Salad	2.00
Sirloin or Venison	1.50
Baked Maccaroni	0.75
Beef Tongue, sauce piquante	1.00

So that, with but a moderate appetite, the dinner will cost us $5, if we are at all epicurean in our tastes. There are cries of "steward!" from all parts of the room—the word " waiter" is not considered sufficiently respectful, seeing that the waiter may have been a lawyer or merchant's clerk a few months before. The dishes look very small as they are placed on the table, but they are skillfully cooked and very palatable to men that have ridden in from the diggings. The appetite one acquires in California is something remarkable. For two months after my arrival, my sensations were like those of a famished wolf.

In the matter of dining, the tastes of all nations can be gratified here. There are French restaurants on the plaza and on Dupont street; an extensive German establishment on Pacific street; the *Fonda Peruana;* the Italian Confectionary; and three Chinese houses, denoted by their long three-cornered flags of yellow silk. The latter are much frequented by Americans, on account of their excellent cookery, and the fact that meals are $1 each, without regard to quantity. Kong-Sung's house is near the water; Whang-Tong's in Sacramento Street, and Tong-Ling's in Jackson street. There the grave Celestials serve up their chow-chow and curry, besides many genuine English dishes; their tea and coffee cannot be surpassed.

The afternoon is less noisy and active than the forenoon. Merchants keep within-doors, and the gambling-rooms are crowded with persons who step in to escape the wind and dust. The sky takes a cold gray east, and the hills over the bay are barely visible in the dense, dusty air. Now and then a watcher, who has been stationed on the hill above Fort Montgomery, comes down and reports an inward-bound vessel, which occasions a little excitement among the boatmen and the merchants who are awaiting consignments. Towards sunset, the plaza is nearly deserted; the wind is merciless in its force, and a heavy overcoat is not found unpleasantly warm. As it grows dark, there is a lull, though occasional gusts blow down the hill and carry the dust of the city out among the shipping.

The appearance of San Francisco at night, from the water, is unlike anything I ever beheld. The houses are mostly of canvas, which is made transparent by the lamps within, and transforms them, in the darkness, to dwellings of solid light. Seated on the slopes of its three hills, the tents pitched among the chapparal to the very summits, it gleams like an amphitheatre of fire. Here and there shine out brilliant points, from the decoy-lamps of the gaming-houses; and through the indistinct murmur of the streets comes by fits the sound of music from their hot and crowded precincts. The picture has in it something unreal and fantastic; it impresses one like the cities of the magic lantern, which a motion of the hand can build or annihilate.

The only objects left for us to visit are the gaming-tables, whose day has just fairly dawned. We need not wander far in search of one. Denison's Exchange, the Parker House and Eldorado stand side by side; across the way are the Verandah and Aguila de Oro; higher up the plaza the St. Charles and Bella Union; while dozens of second-rate establishments are scattered through time less frequented streets. The greatest crowd is about the Eldorado; we find it difficult to effect an entrance. There are about eight tables in the room, all of which are thronged; copper-hued Kanakas, Mexicans rolled in their serapes and Peruvians thrust through their ponchos, stand shoulder to shoulder with the brown and bearded American miners. The stakes are generally small, though when the bettor gets into "a streak of luck," as it is called, they are allowed to double until all is lost or the bank breaks. Along the end of the room is a spacious bar, supplied with all kinds of bad liquors, and in a sort of gallery, suspended under the ceiling, a female violinist tasks her talent amid strength of muscle to minister to the excitement of play.

The Verandah, opposite, is smaller, but boasts an equal attraction in a musician who has a set of Pandean pipes fastened at his chin, a drum on his back, which he beats with sticks at his elbows, and cymbals in his hands. The piles of coin on the monte tables clink merrily to his playing, and the throng of spectators, jammed together in a sweltering mass, walk up to the bar between the tunes and drink out of sympathy with his dry and breathless throat. At the Aguila de Oro there is a full band of Ethiopian serenaders, and at the other hells, violins, guitars or wheezy accordeons, as the case may be. The atmosphere of these places is rank with tobacco-smoke, and filled with a feverish, stifling heat, which communicates an unhealthy glow to the faces of the players.

We shall not be deterred from entering by the heat and smoke, or the motley characters into whose company we shall be thrown. There are rare chances here for seeing human nature in one of its most dark and exciting phases. Note the variety of expression in the faces gathered around this table! They are playing monte, the favorite game in California, since the chances are considered more equal and the opportunity of false play very slight. The dealer throws out his cards with a cool, nonchalant air; indeed, the gradual increase of the hollow square of dollars at his left hand is not calculated to disturb his equanimity. The two Mexicans in front, muffled in their dirty serapes, put down their half-dollars and dollars and see them lost, without changing a muscle. Gambling is a born habit with them, and they would lose thousands with the same indifference. Very different is the demeanor of the Americans who are playing; their good or ill luck is betrayed at once by involuntary exclamations and changes of countenance, unless the stake should be very large and absorbing, when their anxiety, though silent, may be read with no less certainty. They have no power to resist the fascination of the game. Now counting their winnings by thousands, now dependent on the kindness of a friend for a few dollars to commence anew, they pass hour after hour in those hot, unwholesome dens. There is no appearance of arms, but let one of the players, impatient with his losses and maddened by the poisonous fluids he has drunk, threaten one of the profession, and there will be no scarcity of knives and revolvers.

There are other places, where gaining is carried on privately and to a more ruinous extent—rooms in the rear of the Parker house, in the City Hotel and other places, frequented only by the initiated. Here the stakes are almost unlimited, the players being men of wealth and apparent respectability. Frequently, in the absorbing interest of some desperate game the night goes by unheeded and morning breaks upon haggard faces and reckless hearts. Here are lost, in a few turns of a card or rolls of a ball, the product of fortunate ventures by sea or months of racking labor on hand. How many men, maddened by continual losses, might exclaim in their blind vehemence of passion, on leaving these hells:

> "Out, out, thou strumpet, Fortune! All you gods,
> In general synod, take away her power;
> Break all the spokes and fellies from her wheel,
> And bowl the round nave down the hilt of heaven,
> As low as to the fiends!"

LOUISE CLAPPE [DAME SHIRLEY]
1819–1906

Dame Shirley was the pen name of Louise Amelia Knapp Smith Clapp[e]. Born in New Jersey, she joined her new husband, Fayette Clapp, on a trip around Cape Horn in 1850. He had some medical training, and so set up practice in a mining camp called Rich Bar on the Feather River, north of Marysville. From there, between September 1851 and November 1852, she composed twenty-three extended letters addressed to her sister Molly in Massachusetts. She had been writing poetry for years, and earlier in 1851 she had published some sketches and poems in the Marysville Herald. But something in this remote and rowdy mining camp released the voice that would secure her a permanent place in the literature of the Gold Rush. She wrote with compassion, with a poet's eye and a sense of history. She saw tragedy and comedy intertwined.

From Rich Bar the couple returned to San Francisco, where her "Letters" were soon published in the short-lived journal The Pioneer. *Thus they eventually came to the attention of influential editors and historians such as Josiah Royce, Hugh H. Bancroft, and Bret Harte, whose Mother Lode stories may in turn have been fueled by Clappe's memorable accounts. In San Francisco she and Fayette separated. He left for Hawai'i, while she became a popular local schoolteacher (the poet Charles Warren Stoddard was a student of hers). She spent nearly thirty years in California, returning to New York in 1878.*

"A Trip into the Mines"
from *The Shirley Letters*

Rich Bar,
East Branch of the North Fork of Feather River,
September 20, 1851

I intend to-day, dear M., to be as disagreeably statistical and as praiseworthily matter-of-factish as the most dogged utilitarian could desire. I shall give you a full, true and particular account of the discovery, rise and progress of this place, with a religious adherence to *dates* which will rather astonish your unmathematical mind. But let me first describe the spot, as it looked to my wondering and unaccustomed eyes. Remember, I had never seen a mining district before; and had just left San Francisco, amid whose flashy-looking shops and showy houses the most of my time had been spent, since my arrival into the Golden State. Of course, to me, the *coup d'oeuil* of Rich Bar was charmingly fresh and original. Imagine a tiny valley, about eight hundred yards in length and, perhaps, thirty in width, (it was measured for my especial information,) apparently hemmed in by lofty hills, almost perpendicular, draperied to their very summits with beautiful fir trees; the blue-bosomed "Plumas," or Feather River I suppose I must call it, undulating along their base, and you have as good an idea as I can give you of the *locale* of "Barra Rica," as the Spaniards so prettily term it.

In almost any of the numerous books written upon California, no doubt you will be able to find a most scientific description of the origin of these "Bars." I must acknowledge, with shame, that my ideas on the subject are distressingly vague. I could never appreciate the poetry or the humor, of making one's wrists ache by knocking to pieces gloomy looking stones, or in dirtying one's fingers by analysing soils, in a vain attempt to fathom the osteology, or anatomy of our beloved earth; though my heart is thrillingly alive to the faintest shade of color and the infinite variety of styles in which she delights to robe her ever-changeful and ever-beautiful *surface*. In my unscientific mind the *formations* are without form and void; and you might as well talk Chinese to me, as to embroider your conversation with the terms "hornblende," "mica," "lime-stone," "slate," "granite" and "quartz," in a hopeless attempt to enlighten me as to their merits. The dutiful diligence with which I attend course after course of lectures on Geology by America's greatest illustrator of that subject, arose rather from my affectionate reverence for our beloved Dr. H., and the fascinating charm which his glorious mind throws round every subject which it condescends to illuminate, than to any interest in the dry science itself. It is, therefore, with a most humiliating consciousness of my geological deficiencies, that I offer you the only explanation which I have been able to obtain from those most learned in such matters here. I gather from their remarks, that these bars are formed by deposits of earth, rolling down from the mountains, crowding the river aside and occupying a portion of its deserted bed. If my definition is unsatisfactory, I can but refer you to some of the aforesaid works upon California.

Through the middle of Rich Bar runs the street, thickly planted with about forty tenements; among which figure round tents, square tents, plank hovels, log cabins, &c.,—the residences, varying in elegance and convenience from the palatial splendor of "The Empire," down to a "local habitation," formed of pine boughs, and covered with old calico shirts.

Louise Clappe [Dame Shirley]

To-day I visited the "Office," the only one on the river. I had heard so much about it from others, as well as from F., that I really *did* expect something extra. When I entered this imposing place, the shock to my optic nerves was so great that I sank, helplessly, upon one of the benches which ran, divan-like, the whole length (ten feet!) of the building, and laughed till I cried. There was, of course, no floor; a rude nondescript in one corner, on which was ranged the medical library, consisting of half a dozen volumes, did duty as a table. The shelves, which looked like sticks snatched hastily from the woodpile and nailed up without the least alteration, contained quite a respectable array of medicines. The white canvas window stared everybody in the face, with the interesting information painted on it, in perfect grenadiers of capitals, that this was Dr. ———'s office.

At my loud laugh (which, it must be confessed, was noisy enough to give the whole street assurance of the presence of a woman), F. looked shocked, and his partner looked prussic acid. To him, (the partner, I mean, he hadn't been out of the mines for years)—the "Office" was a thing sacred and set apart for an almost admiring worship. It was a beautiful, architectural ideal, embodied in pine shingles and cotton cloth. Here, he literally "lived, and moved, and had his being," his bed and his board. With an admiration of the fine arts, truly praiseworthy, he had fondly decorated the walls thereof with sundry pictures from Godey, Graham and Sartain's Magazines, among which, fashion plates with imaginary monsters, sporting miraculous waists, impossible wrists and fabulous feet, largely predominated.

During my call at the office, I was introduced to one of the *finders* of Rich Bar—a young Georgian, who afterwards gave me a full description of all the facts connected with its discovery. This unfortunate had not spoken to a woman for two years; and in the elation of his heart at the joyful event, he rushed out and invested capital in some excellent champagne, which I, on Willie's principle of "doing in Turkey as the Turkies do," assisted the company in drinking to the honor of my own arrival. I mention this, as an instance, that nothing can be done in California without the sanctifying influence of the *spirit;* and it generally appears in much more "questionable shape" than that of sparkling wine. Mr. H. informed me, that on the twentieth of July, 1850, it was rumored at Nelson's Creek—a mining station situated at the Middle Fork of the Feather River, about eighty miles from Marysville—that one of those vague "Somebodies"—a near relation of the "They Says"—had discovered mines of a remarkable richness in a north-easterly direction, and about forty miles from the first-mentioned place. Anxious and immediate search was made for "Somebody" but, as our western brethren say, he "wasn't thar!" but his absence could not deter the miners when once the golden rumor had been set afloat. A large company packed up their goods and chattels, generally consisting of a pair of blankets, a frying pan, some flour, salt pork, brandy, pick-axe and shovel, and started for the new Dorado. They "traveled, and traveled, and traveled," as we used to say in the fairy stories, for nearly a week in every possible direction, when one evening, weary and discouraged, about one hundred of the party found themselves at the top of that famous hill, which figures so largely in my letters, whence the river can be distinctly seen. Half of the number concluded to descend the mountain that night, the remainder stopping on the summit until the next morning. On arriving at Rich Bar, part of the adventurers camped there, but many went a few miles further down the river. The next morning two men turned over a large stone, beneath which they found quite a sizable piece of gold. They washed a small panful of the dirt, and obtained from it two hundred and fifty-six dollars. Encouraged by this success, they commenced staking off the legal amount of ground allowed to each person for mining purposes; and, the remainder of the party having descended the hill, before night the entire bar was "claimed." In a fortnight from that time, the two men who found the first bit of gold had each taken out six thousand dollars. Two others took out thirty-three pounds of gold in eight hours; which is the best day's work that has been done on this branch of the river; the largest amount ever taken from one panful of dirt was fifteen hundred dollars. In little more than a week after its discovery, five hundred men had settled upon the bar for the summer.—Such is the wonderful alacrity with which a mining town is built. Soon after was discovered on the same side of the river—about half a mile apart, and at nearly the same distance from this place—the two bars, "Smith" and "Indian," both very rich: also another, lying across the river, just opposite Indian, called "Missouri Bar." There are several more, all within a few miles of here, called "Frenchman's," "Taylor's," "Brown's," "The Junction," "Wyandott" and "Muggin's." But they are at present of little importance as mining stations.

Those who worked in these mines during the fall of 1850 were extremely fortunate; but, alas! the Monte fiend ruined hundreds! Shall I tell you the fate of two of the most successful of these gold hunters? From poor men, they found themselves at the end of a few weeks, absolutely rich. Elated with their good fortune, seized with a mania for Monte, in less than a year, these unfortunates,—so lately respectable and intelligent,—became a pair of drunken gamblers. One of them at this present writing, works for five dollars a day and boards himself out of that; the other actually suffers for the necessaries of life,—a too common result of scenes in the mines.

Louise Clappe [Dame Shirley]

There were but a few that dared to remain in the mountains during the winter for fear of being buried in the snow, of which at that time they had a most vague idea. I have been told that in these sheltered valleys it seldom falls to the depth of more than a foot, and disappears almost invariably within a day or two. Perhaps there were three hundred that concluded to stay; of which number, two-thirds stopped on Smith's Bar, as the labor of mining there is much easier than it is here. Contrary to the general expectation, the weather was delightful until about the middle of March; it then commenced storming, and continued to snow and rain incessantly for nearly three weeks. Supposing that the rainy season had passed, hundreds had arrived on the river during the previous month. The snow, which fell several feet in depth on the mountains, rendered the trail impassable and entirely stopped the pack trains; provisions soon became scarce, and the sufferings of these unhappy men were, indeed, extreme. Some adventurous spirits, with true Yankee hardihood, forced their way through the snow to the Frenchman's ranch, and packed flour *on their backs,* for more than forty miles! The first meal that arrived sold for three dollars a pound. Many subsisted for days on nothing but barley, which is kept here to feed the pack-mules on. One unhappy individual who could not obtain even a little barley, for love or money, and had eaten nothing for three days, forced his way out to the Spanish rancho fourteen miles distant, and in less than an hour after his arrival, had devoured *twenty-seven* biscuits and a corresponding quantity of other eatables, and, of course, drinkables to match. Don't let this account alarm you. There is no danger of another famine here. They tell me that there is hardly a building in the place that has not food enough in it to last its occupants for the next two years; besides, there are two or three well-filled groceries in town.

September 22, 1851

There has been quite an excitement here for the last week, on account of a successful amputation having been performed upon the person of a young man by the name of W. As I happen to know all the circumstances of the case, I will relate them to you, as illustrative of the frightful accidents to which the gold-seekers are constantly liable; and I can assure you that similar ones happen very often. W. was one of the first who settled on this river, and suffered extremely from the scarcity of provisions during the last winter. By steady industry in his laborious vocation, he had accumulated about four thousand dollars. He was thinking seriously of returning to Massachusetts with what he had already gained, when in the early part of last May, a stone unexpectedly rolling from the top of Smith's Hill, on the side of which he was mining—crushed his leg in the most shocking manner. Naturally enough, the poor fellow shrank with horror, from the idea of an amputation here in the mountains; it seemed absolutely worse than death. His physician, appreciating his feelings on the subject, made every effort to save his shattered limb; but, truly, the fates seemed against him. An attack of typhoid fever reduced him to a state of great weakness, which was still further increased by erysipelas—a common complaint in the mountains—in its most virulent form; the latter disease settling in the fractured leg, rendered a cure utterly hopeless. His sufferings have been of the most intense description. Through all the blossoming spring, and a summer as golden as its own golden self, of our beautiful California, he has languished away existence in a miserable cabin, his only nurses men—some of them, it is true, kind and good—others neglectful and careless. A few weeks since, F. was called in to see him. He decided immediately that nothing but an amputation would save him. A universal outcry against it, was raised by nearly all the other physicians on the Bar. They agreed *en masse,* that he could live but a few weeks, unless the leg—now a mere lump of disease—was taken off; at the same time, they declared that he would certainly expire under the knife, and that it was cruel to subject him to any further suffering. You can, perhaps, imagine F.'s anxiety. It was a great responsibility for a young physician to take. Should the patient die during the operation, F.'s professional reputation would, of course, die with him. But he felt it his duty to waive all selfish considerations, and give W. that one chance—feeble as it seemed—for his life. Thank God, the result was most triumphant! For several days, existence hung upon a mere thread, he was not allowed to speak or move, and was fed from a teaspoon—his only diet being milk, which we obtained from the Spanish Rancho, sending twice a week for it. I should have mentioned that F. decidedly refused to risk an operation in the small and miserable tent in which W. had languished away nearly half a year, and he was removed to the "Empire," the day previous to the amputation. It is almost needless to tell you that the little fortune, to accumulate which he suffered so much—is now nearly exhausted. Poor fellow! the philosophy and cheerful resignation, with which he has endured his terrible martyrdom, is beautiful to behold. My heart aches as I look upon his young face, and think of "his gentle, dark-eyed mother, weeping lonely at the North," for her far away and suffering son.

As I sat by the bedside of our poor invalid, yielding myself up to a world of dreamy visionings, suggested by the musical sweep of the pine branch which I waved above his head, and the rosy sunset flushing the western casement with its soft glory, he suddenly opened his languid eyes and whispered, "the Chileno procession is returning; do you not hear it?" I did not tell him

> "That the weary sound, and the heavy breath,
>   And the silent motions of passing death,
>   And the smell, cold, oppressive and dank,
>   Sent through the pores of the coffin plank,"

had already informed me that a far other band than that of the noisy South Americans, was solemnly marching by. It was the funeral train of a young man who was instantly killed, the evening before, by falling into one of those deep pits, sunk for mining purposes, which are scattered over the bar in almost every direction. I rose quietly and looked from the window. About a dozen persons were carrying an unpainted coffin, without pall or bier (the place of the latter being supplied by ropes) up the steep hill which rises behind the Empire—on the top of which, is situated the burial ground of Rich Bar. The bearers were all neatly and cleanly dressed in their miner's costume; which, consisting of a flannel shirt,—almost always of a dark blue color— pantaloons with the boots drawn up over them, and a low-crowned, broad-brimmed, black felt hat—though the fashion of the latter is not invariable— is not, simple as it seems, so unpicturesque as you might, perhaps, imagine. A strange horror of that lonely mountain grave-yard came over me, as I watched the little company wending wearily up to the solitary spot. The "sweet habitude of being,"—not that I fear *death*, but that I love *life*, as, for instance, Charles Lamb loved it—makes me particularly affect a cheerful burial-place. I know that it is dreadfully unsentimental, but I should like to make my last home in the heart of a crowded city; or better still, in one of those social homes of the dead, which the Turks, with a philosophy so beautiful and so poetical, make their most cheerful resort. Singularly enough, Christians seem to delight in rendering death particularly hideous, and grave-yards decidedly disagreeable. I, on the contrary, would "plant the latter with laurels, and sprinkle it with lilies." I would wreath "Sleep's pale brother" so thickly with roses, that even those rabid moralists, who think that it makes us better, to paint him as a dreadful fiend, instead of a loving friend—could see nothing but their blushing radiance. I would alter the whole paraphernalia of the coffin, the shroud and the bier; particularly the first, which, as Dickens says, "looks like a high-shouldered ghost, with its hands in its breeches pockets." Why should we endeavor to make our entrance into a glorious immortality, so unutterably ghastly? Let us glide into the "fair shadow land" through a "gate of flowers," if we may no longer, as in the majestic olden time, aspire heavenward on the wings of perfumed flame.

How oddly do life and death jostle each other in this strange world of ours! How nearly allied are smiles and tears! My eyes were yet moist from the egotistical *pitie de moi-même* in which I had been indulging, at the thought of sleeping forever amid these lonely hills, which in a few years must return to their primeval solitude, perchance never again to be awakened by the voice of humanity—when the Chileno procession, every member of it most intensely drunk, really *did* appear. I never saw anything more diverting than the whole affair. Of course, *selon regle*, I ought to have been shocked and horrified—to have shed salt tears, and have uttered melancholy Jeremiads over their miserable degradation. But the world is so full of platitudes, my dear, that I think you will easily forgive me for not boring you with a temperance lecture, and will good-naturedly let me have my laugh, and not think me *very* wicked after all.

You must know that to-day is the anniversary of the Independence of Chile. The procession got up in honor of it, consisted, perhaps, of twenty men, nearly a third of whom, were of that class of Yankees, who are particularly noisy and particularly conspicuous in all celebrations, where it is each man's most onerous duty, to get, what is technically called "tight." The man who headed the procession was a complete comic poem in his own individual self. He was a person of Falstaffean proportions and coloring; and if a brandy barrel ever *does* "come alive," and, donning a red shirt and buck-skin trowsers, betake itself to pedestrianism, it will look more like my hero than anything else that I can at present think of. With that affectionateness so peculiar to people when they arrive at the sentimental stage of intoxication—although it was with the greatest difficulty that he could sustain his own corporocity—he was tenderly trying to direct the zigzag footsteps of his companion, a little withered-up, weird-looking Chileno. Alas, for the wickedness of human nature! The latter, whose drunkenness had taken a Byronic and misanthropical turn, rejected with the basest ingratitude, these delicate attentions. Do not think that my incarnated brandy cask was the only one of the party "who did unto others as he would they should do unto him;" for the entire band were officiously tendering to each other the same good Samaritan-like assistance. I was not astonished at the Virginia fence-like style of their marching, when I heard a description of the feast of which they had partaken a few hours before. A friend of mine who stopped into the tent where they were dining, said that the board—really *board*—was arranged with a bottle of claret at each plate;

and after the cloth—metaphorically speaking, I mean, for table-linen is a mere myth in the mines—was removed, a twenty-gallon keg of brandy was placed in the centre, with quart-dippers gracefully encircling it, that each one might help himself as he pleased. Can you wonder, after that, that every man vied with his neighbor in illustrating Hogarth's line of beauty? It was impossible to tell which nation was the most gloriously drunk; but this I *will* say, even at the risk of being thought partial to my own beloved countrymen; that though the Chilenos reeled with a better grace, the Americans did it more *naturally!*

ELIZA W. B. FARNHAM

1815–1864

Eliza Farnham was an early feminist and suffragist who came to California by way of Cape Horn in 1849. Her husband of fourteen years, the lawyer, traveler, and businessman Thomas Farnham, passed away unexpectedly in San Francisco, leaving some properties to be attended to. Eliza had spent the previous five years as matron of the Female State Prison at Sing Sing, New York. She would spend the next six years based on a two-hundred-acre ranch in Santa Cruz County, inland from Monterey Bay, farming, writing, settling her husband's estate, raising two young sons, and advocating for women's causes. She had already written one book, about her early married years in Illinois, titled Life in Prairie Land. *From her time in Santa Cruz came* California In-Doors and Out: Or How We Farm, Mine and Live Generally in the Gold State. *Appearing in New York in 1856, it was the first published book from the far West written by a woman. It is both personal and political, by turns a rural journal, a report on the blessings and pitfalls of Western life, and a reformer's call to action.*

In 1856 Farnham returned to New York. In 1859 she published My Early Days *(1859), a fictionalized account of her childhood, which was followed by* A Woman and Her Era *(1864). During the Civil War she volunteered as a nurse and died in New York City at forty-nine, after contracting tuberculosis while working with the wounded at the battle of Gettysburg.*

From *California In-Doors and Out*

CHAPTER I

To the struggling advocates of Woman's Rights, it may seem a hopeful sign of the times that one of their sex should put forth a book claiming to be in any degree descriptive of farming, especially when they make the delightful discovery that the writer speaks in a great measure from personal experience in the business. But it must not be forgotten that life in California is altogether anomalous, and that it is no more extraordinary for a woman to plough, dig, and hoe with her own hands, if she have the will and strength to do so, than for men to do all their household labor for months, never seeing the face nor hearing the voice of a woman during that time.

I could not seriously undertake to write even so small a volume as I intend this to be, on farming, without the etc., which the reader will perceive, has completely freed me as to my subjects. I also have an abiding faith that there is something in California besides its mines; some life worth considering besides that of the people who delve at the "dry or wet diggings," and pray, if they ever pray at all, that the Sierras might turn into huge piles of gold-dust before their eyes. The mining life is constantly so much enlarged upon in all books, pamphlets, letters, and newspapers, that there will be no just cause of complaint, if not more than a dozen pages of so unpretending a volume are found devoted to it. There are many thousand souls in the country, at least the presence of so many bodies is *prima facie* evidence in support of the assertion, who have never seen the mines, who, notwithstanding their previous silence give a side to life too apt to be forgotten by those abroad, who look only for tidings from the diggings, and the amount of gold brought by the last steamer. My own experience places me in this class, and I am the more willing to speak for it, because a large portion of it is connected with an interest not less important to the State than her mines, which is far more delightful to those who cultivate it, and which must be a chief instrumentality in her salvation, if any such fate await her. At present, the indications in that direction are too feeble to promise any clear tendency.

In truth, I believe there is up to this time a very weighty opposite preponderance, the removal of which must, in a great measure, be due to a thrifty agricultural population, such as it is probable will shortly occupy most of the arable lands of this beautiful and fertile State. There is not another on the globe, perhaps, in which agriculture can be so successfully pursued—in which fertility of soil is united to a climate affording every security for the growth and the gathering of crops, and where so great variety of products can be grown without resort to artificial processes. It is the land of the vine and the olive, and beside them the most delicious fruits of the higher latitudes come to the fullest perfection. If half the stout hearts and strong hands, that every year leave home for the mining regions of California, were as resolutely directed towards her teeming vales and plains and hills, for here all are fertile, there would be an annual saving of wealth, health, life, and virtue, that would, in these respects, soon elevate her to a level with any of her elder sisters. . . .

The region of country of which I can speak most confidently, is one in which farming has been as generally and as variously tried, perhaps, as in any other of the State, and the reader must not be surprised into a loss of his patience, if, instead of a grave disquisition on Agricultural Science, or its possibilities in California, he finds the subject chiefly illustrated by my own and my neighbor's experience in the peerless little valley of Santa Cruz, if valley it can be called, which is shut in by the ocean on its southern and western limits, and by mountains in all other directions. The region now known by the name of Santa Cruz, is the country lying contiguous to the old mission of that name, which is situated on the coast, at the north side of Monterey Bay, about seventy miles south from San Francisco, and twenty miles north from Monterey. Like the site of all the missions, it is one of the most beautiful spots to be found in the country. The old mission buildings are situated on a gentle height, about a mile from the shore, where the San Lorenzo—a considerable stream, coming down from the coast range—empties into the bay, to the left. They command a complete view of the bay, with its surrounding shores, while in front the blue Pacific stretches its endless waters, which roll in and break on the beach in all varieties of tone, from the alto of thunder to the sweet tenor of that gentle chime which, heard through the deep solitudes of the night, soothes and charms the soul . . .

CHAPTER 2

On one of the most delightful farms—or, to use a term we like better in California—on one of the most delightful *ranchos* in this beautiful region, the writer sat down, eighteen months ago, with her two little sons, a female friend, and a farmer, with the intention of trying the chances of farming-life in California—a new life to me anywhere—but the very essence of newness in this strangest of all countries peopled by our countrymen, and made doubly strange by the new and startling aspects which individual, as well as general character, not unfrequently assume in it.

We had come down from San Francisco by sea—been landed like bales of goods through the surf, partly in boats and partly in the arms of the seamen, and had walked out to our ranch, which the farmer had visited the previous evening. Behold me, then, landed, with Charlie trotting eagerly at my side, and a friend who had come down with us carrying dear Eddie on his back. My friend, Miss Sampson, had staid upon the beach—partly because she was unable to take the walk, and partly that a careful eye might be kept upon the goods as they were landed. See us, after a walk of two miles, on the 22nd of February, through clover and grass four inches high, borne down by the heavy dews that had fallen on the previous night, enter the casa of El Rancho La Libertad. There have been two men occupying it before our arrival, who are to remove in the afternoon or the next day. Their household goods consist of a table—the roughest of its species—two or three old benches, three or four bowls, as many plates, and one or two articles of hollow-ware. The casa is not a cheerful specimen even of California habitations—being made of slabs, which were originally placed upright, but which have departed sadly from the perpendicular in every direction. There is not a foot of floor, nor a pane of glass, nor a brick, nor anything in the shape of a stove. The fire is made upon the ground, and the smoke departs by any avenue that seemeth to itself good, or lingers in the airy space between our heads and the roof, which is beautifully done in bas relief of webs, dressed in pyroligneous acid.

The dimensions of the entire structure are about twenty-five feet in length by fifteen feet in width at one end, and diminishing, by beautiful convergence, to about ten feet at the other. A partition of slabs, thrown across the narrow end, rather divides the house than makes a room, of which the other three walls are so imperfect that you may walk through them almost where you will.

When Eddie, and a satchel or two that had come along with the party, had been deposited, and a brief survey taken of the beautiful spot in which this forlorn habitation stood, the men returned to the beach, and the boys and I were left to the housekeeping. Such outward apparel as I would have laid aside, I found it much against my inclination to deposit in the soot and ashes that everywhere abounded; but after some search, I found means to get rid safely of bonnet, shawl, etc., and giving the boys license to explore the course of the little stream that babbled and brawled along its deep bed, within twenty feet of the door, I strolled out alone, to enjoy the exceeding quietness and loveliness of the place—the first novel emotions at finding myself the mistress of it, and to get some idea of the capacities and resources of my future home. I had been told it was a beautiful place, but I was not prepared for the sort of impression it produced.

It was one of those peerless days, such as only a California winter affords, with a cloudless sky above the head, and the earth piled with tenderest herbage under the feet. In the deep seclusion of La Libertad I enjoyed that silence and solitude which for a day one finds so welcome a change from bustle and annoyance, such as had been our previous lot in California. Only the song of birds, the bubbling of the stream over the roots of the trees whose tops embower it, mingled with the gleeful shouts of the delighted boys, who are already deep in the mysteries of its most secret places, greet my ear. The beating of the distant surf rather aids than breaks the silence, and by ascending a gentle slope to the right, I look out on a picture so filled with repose and beauty, that while I gaze, the hateful stir of the world in which I have lately been mixed up, seems to die out of the universe, and I no longer remember it. For the hour, I forget that life subjects the spirit to jar or discord, and am only conscious of the harmony that flows from the generous breast of nature into our own, when, for a happy moment, she gets undivided audience of it. Alas, alas! that lapse of time should constantly separate such seasons further and further apart in our lives!

On either hand, at a short distance from the stream, rise hills, now beautifully rounded, now more abrupt and stern, but all clothed with richest herbage, which herds of cattle are cropping in silent satisfaction. Just back of the house these hills approach each other so nearly, that what is a broad vale below becomes a deep ravine, with wooded banks, upon which a dozen tall redwoods tower above their neighbors, and seem, to my wondering eyes, to be penetrating the very clouds. In front, the hills open generously to the right and left, quite down to the large stream to which ours is a tributary, and stretch around a broad sunny vale that looks out upon the bay, over the gentle swell of land, much lower than the hills on either side, on which the old Mission buildings stand. Beyond this, I gaze upon the sparkling waters of the great bay, whose surrounding coast is diversified by hill and plain, cloud and sunshine, so exquisitely, that I deem it a fairy scene, rather than a portion of the real, peopled earth. So bright is it, in its newness and unrevealed deformities, so tender in its solitude and purity, so holy in its beauty, overhung by a sky whose pure blue seems made only to veil the heaven we imagine above from that we gaze upon beneath, I wonder, while beholding it, that religious and devout thankfulness to God does not continually ascend from the hearts of those who dwell in so fair a portion of his creation.

But a shout of "Mother, mother," calls my attention from the dream of goodness, inspired by what I behold. I descend to the house, to learn the important and novel fact that the boys are hungry. No stores have arrived; and there seems, consequently, no lawful way of satisfying their wants. I tell them this; but Charlie, who has hungered occasionally through some four years more than his brother, is quick to suggest that a slice each might be cut, without sin, from the solid looking loaf lying upon the table. Neither its complexion nor juxtaposition make it very inviting to my housekeeping sense; but as that is a faculty rarely developed in boys, they experience no qualms, but take their lunches, when I get them off with some difficulty, and are off again with a cup, to the brook, of the wonders and beauty of which they have poured forth a stream of narrative, exclamation, and delight, as incessant as the noise of its own waters. But, for me, the charm was broken; there was no return to the world from which they had recalled me. To the child-heart the beautiful was a sufficing presence. It placed above question all that enjoyed its blessed contiguity. Faith could not waver, nor hope falter before it. Blessed season! when the visible works of God suffice to give us faith in all that is, and all that we hope shall yet be.

Neither the trees, the birds, nor the sunshine, could tempt me abroad again. I sat down in the ashes—not at the fireside, but in a remote part of the room, to look at the reverse of the picture: at the in-door world—a less delightful survey than I had made without. I had failed to secure a temporary home, as I hoped to be able to, in the house of a good old couple in the neighborhood—the fame of whose kindness had reached me in San Francisco, and now had to address myself to my own resources for that purpose, the Spanish houses being entirely out of the question, and the very few American families that I have referred to being entirely unknown to me. In my meditations I inverted the black walls, turned them inside out, laid an ideal floor, erected imaginary closets, etc., set apart corners for bed-rooms, and was far advanced in my housekeeping, before I was interrupted by a call from a neighbor—one of the prisoners of 1840—who, after many civil expressions of pleasure at seeing me and the children, invited us to make his house our home until we should be able to fit up something habitable of these ruins.

JOHN ROLLIN RIDGE [YELLOW BIRD]
1827–1867

John Rollin Ridge has been called the first American Indian to publish a novel. Writing in San Francisco in the 1850s, he often signed his poems and stories "Yellow Bird," the English version of his tribal name. Born in Georgia of a Cherokee father and a white mother, he attended school for a while in New England. He came of age during the uprootings that followed the Indian Removal Act, when the Cherokee people were transported from the eastern seaboard into what later became Oklahoma. Ridge's grandfather, a wealthy landholder and tribal leader, had supported this controversial and divisive move, contending that it would be more costly to stay and fight a losing battle against land-hungry whites. In 1839, after settling in Oklahoma, Ridge's father and grandfather were assassinated by members of the tribe's anti-removal faction while the rest of his family looked on. A few years later, perhaps caught up in these same struggles, Ridge killed a man. By 1850 he had found his way to California, and during the Gold Rush he began to write for such periodicals as The Golden Era, Hesperian, *and Ferdinand Ewer's* Pioneer *(where his work and Dame Shirley's sometimes appeared in the same issue). A fascination with the exploits of a much-talked-about Mexican bandit led to* The Life and Times of Joaquín Murieta: The Celebrated California Bandit. *Though it was offered as a true story, it was largely invented by Ridge, as he elaborated on the numerous tales then in circulation—some with a kernel of fact, some apocryphal. Transmuting the violence of his own past, he launched the reputation of this "Robin Hood of Eldorado."*

From *The Life and Adventures of Joaquín Murieta, the Celebrated California Bandit*

Joaquín Murieta was a Mexican, born in the province of Sonora of respectable parents and educated in the schools of Mexico. While growing up, he was remarkable for a very mild and peaceable disposition, and gave no sign of that indomitable and daring spirit which afterwards characterized him. Those who knew him in his school-boy days speak affectionately of his generous and noble nature at that period of his life and can scarcely credit the fact that the renowned and bloody bandit of California was one and the same being. At an early age of his manhood—indeed, while he was yet scarcely more than a boy—he became tired of the uncertain state of affairs in his own country, the usurpations and revolutions which were of such common occurrence, and resolved to try his fortunes among the American people, of whom he had formed the most favorable opinion from an acquaintance with the few whom he had met in his own native land. The war with Mexico had been fought, and California belonged to the United States. Disgusted with the conduct of his degenerate countrymen and fired with enthusiastic admiration of the American character, the youthful Joaquín left his home with a buoyant heart and full of the exhilarating spirit of adventure.

The first that we hear of him in the Golden State is that, in the spring of 1850, he is engaged in the honest occupation of a miner in the Stanislaus placers, then reckoned among the richest portions of the mines. He was then eighteen years of age, a little over the medium height, slenderly but grace-fully built, and active as a young tiger. His complexion was neither very dark or very light, but clear and brilliant, and his countenance is pronounced to have been, at that time, exceedingly handsome and attractive. His large black eyes, kindling with the enthusiasm of his earnest nature, his firm and well-formed mouth, his well-shaped head from which the long, glossy, black hair hung down over his shoulders, his silvery voice full of generous utterance, and the frank and cordial bearing which distinguished him made him be-loved by all with whom he came in contact. He had the confidence and respect of the whole community around him, and was fast amassing a for-tune from his rich mining claim. He had built him a comfortable min-ing residence in which he had domiciled his heart's treasure—a beautiful Sonorian girl, who had followed the young adventurer in all his wanderings with that devotedness of passion which belongs to the dark-eyed damsels of Mexico.

It was at this moment of peace and felicity that a blight came over the young man's prospects. The country was then full of lawless and desperate men, who bore the name of Americans but failed to support the honor and dignity of that title. A feeling was prevalent among this class of contempt for any and all Mexicans, whom they looked upon as no better than conquered subjects of the United States, having no rights which could stand before a haughtier and superior race. They made no exceptions. If the proud blood of the Castilians mounted to the cheek of a partial descendant of the Mexiques, showing that he had inherited the old chivalrous spirit of his Spanish ancestry, they looked upon it as a saucy presumption in one so inferior to them. The prejudice of color, the antipathy of races, which are always stronger and bit-terer with the ignorant and unlettered, they could not overcome, or if they could, would not, because it afforded them a convenient excuse for their unmanly cruelty and oppression.

A band of these lawless men, having the brute power to do as they pleased, visited Joaquín's house and peremptorily bade him leave his claim, as they would allow no Mexicans to work in that region. Upon his remonstrating against such outrageous conduct, they struck him violently over the face, and, being physically superior, compelled him to swallow his wrath. Not content with this, they tied him hand and foot and ravished his mistress before his eyes. They left him, but the soul of the young man was from that moment darkened. It was the first injury he had ever received at the hands of the Americans, whom he had always hitherto respected, and it wrung him to the soul as a deeper and deadlier wrong from that very circumstance. He departed with his weeping and almost heart-broken mistress for a more northern portion of the mines; and the next we hear of him, he is cultivating a little farm on the banks of a beautiful stream that watered a fertile valley, far out in the seclusion of the mountains. Here he might hope for peace—here he might forget the past, and again be happy.

But his dream was not destined to last. A company of unprincipled Americans—shame that there should be such bearing the name!—saw his retreat, coveted his little home surrounded by its fertile tract of land, and drove him from it, with no other excuse than that he was "an infernal Mexican intruder!" Joaquín's blood boiled in his veins, but his spirit was still unbroken, nor had the iron so far entered his soul as to sear up the innate sensitiveness to honor and right which reigned in his bosom. Twice broken up in his honest pursuit of fortune, he resolved still to labor on with unflinching brow and with that true *moral* bravery, which throws its redeeming light forward upon his subsequently dark and criminal career. How deep must have been the anguish of that young heart and how strongly rooted the native honesty of his soul, none can know or imagine but they who have been tried in a like manner. He bundled up his little movable property, still accompanied by his faithful bosom-friend, and again started forth to strike once more, like a brave and honest man, for fortune and for happiness.

He arrived at "Murphy's Diggings" in Calaveras County, in the month of April, and went again to mining, but, meeting with nothing like his former success, he soon abandoned that business and devoted his time to dealing "monte," a game which is common in Mexico, and has been almost universally adopted by gamblers in California. It is considered by the Mexican in no manner a disreputable employment, and many well-raised young men from the Atlantic States have resorted to it as a profession in this land of luck and chances. It was then in much better odor than it is now, although it is at present a game which may be played on very fair and honest principles; provided, anything can be strictly honest or fair which allows the taking of money without a valuable consideration. It was therefore looked upon as no departure from rectitude on the part of Joaquín, when he commenced the business of dealing "monte." Having a very pleasing exterior and being, despite of all his sorrows, very gay and lively in disposition, he attracted many persons to his table, and won their money with such skill and grace, or lost his own with such perfect good humor that he was considered by all the very beau ideal of a gambler and the prince of clever fellows. His sky seemed clear and his prospects bright, but Fate was weaving her mysterious web around him, and fitting him to be by the force of circumstances what nature never intended to make him.

He had gone a short distance from Murphy's Diggings to see a half-brother, who had been located in that vicinity for several months, and returned to Murphy's upon a horse which his brother had lent him. The animal proved to have been stolen, and being recognized by a number of individuals in town, an excitement was raised on the subject. Joaquín suddenly found himself surrounded by a furious mob and charged with the crime of theft. He told them how it happened that he was riding the horse and in what manner his half-brother had come in possession of it. They listened to no explanation, but bound him to a tree, and publicly disgraced him with the lash. They then proceeded to the house of his half-brother and hung him without judge or jury. It was then that the character of Joaquín changed, suddenly and irrevocably. Wanton cruelty and the tyranny of prejudice had reached their climax. His soul swelled beyond its former boundaries, and the barriers of honor, rocked into atoms by the strong passion which shook his heart like an earthquake, crumbled around him. Then it was that he declared to a friend that he would live henceforth for revenge and that his path should be marked with blood. Fearfully did he keep his promise, as the following pages will show.

It was not long after this unfortunate affair that an American was found dead in the vicinity of Murphy's Diggings, having been cut to pieces with a knife. Though horribly mangled, he was recognized as one of the mob engaged in whipping Joaquín. A doctor, passing in the neighborhood of this murder, was met, shortly afterward, by two men on horseback, who fired their revolvers at him, but, owing to his speed on foot, and the unevenness of the ground, he succeeded in escaping with no further injury than having a bullet shot through his hat within an inch of the top of his head! A panic spread among the rash individuals who had composed that mob, and they were afraid to stir out on their ordinary business. Whenever any one of them strayed out of sight of his camp or ventured to travel on the highway, he was shot down suddenly and mysteriously. Report after report came into the villages that Americans had been found dead on the highways, having been either shot or stabbed, and it was invariably discovered, for many weeks, that the murdered men belonged to the mob who publicly whipped Joaquín. It was fearful and it was strange to see how swiftly and mysteriously those men disappeared. "Murieta's revenge was very nearly complete," said an eyewitness of these events, in reply to an inquiry which I addressed him. "I am inclined to think he *wiped out* the most of those prominently engaged in whipping him."

Thus far, who can blame him? But the iron had entered too deeply in his soul for him to stop here. He had contracted a hatred to the whole American race, and was determined to shed their blood, whenever and wherever an opportunity occurred. It was no time now for him to retrace his steps. He had committed deeds which made him amenable to the law, and his only safety lay in a persistence in the unlawful course which he had begun. It was necessary that he should have horses and that he should have money. These he could not obtain except by robbery and murder, and thus he became an outlaw and a bandit on the verge of his nineteenth year . . .

Among the many thrilling instances of the daring and recklessness of spirit which belonged to Joaquín, there is one which I do not feel at liberty to omit—especially as it comes naturally and properly in this connection. Shortly after he parted from Reis and Luis Vulvia, he went up into the extreme north of the county. There, at the head of a branch of the South Fork of the Mokelumne River, in a wild and desolate region near the boundary line of Calaveras and El Dorado Counties, were located a company of miners, consisting of twenty-five men. They were at a long distance from any neighbors, having gone there well armed on a prospecting tour which resulted in their finding diggings so rich that they were persuaded to pitch their tents and remain. One morning while they were eating their breakfast on a flat rock—a natural table which stood in front of their tents—armed as usual with their revolvers, a young fellow with very dark hair and eyes rode up and saluted them. He spoke very good English and they could scarcely make out whether he was a Mexican or an American. They requested him to get down and eat with them, but he politely declined. He sat with one leg crossed over his horse's neck very much at his ease, conversing very freely on various subjects, until Jim Boyce, one of the partners who had been to the spring after water, appeared in sight. At the first glance on him, the young horseman flung his reclining leg back over the saddle and spurred his horse. Boyce roared out:

"Boys, that fellow is *Joaquín;* d—n it, shoot him!" At the same instant, he himself fired but without effect.

Joaquín dashed down to the creek below with headlong speed and crossed with the intention, no doubt, to escape over the hills which ran parallel with the stream, but his way was blocked up by perpendicular rocks, and his only practicable path was a narrow digger-trail which led along the side of a huge mountain, directly over a ledge of rocks a hundred yards in length, which hung over the rushing stream beneath in a direct line with the hill upon which the miners had pitched their tents, and not more than forty yards distant. It was a fearful gauntlet for any man to run. Not only was there danger of falling a hundred feet from the rocks, but he must run in a parallel line with his enemies, and in pistol-range, for a hundred yards. In fair view of him stood the whole company with their revolvers drawn. He dashed along that fearful trail as if he had been mounted upon a spirit-steed, shouting as he passed:

"I am Joaquín! Kill me if you can!"

Shot after shot came clanging around his head, and bullet after bullet flattened on the wall of slate at his right. In the midst of the first firing, his hat was knocked from his head, and left his long black hair streaming behind him. He had no time to use his own pistol, but, knowing that his only chance lay in the swiftness of his sure-footed animal, he drew his keenly polished bowie knife in proud defiance of the danger and waved it in scorn as he rode on. It was perfectly sublime to see such super-human daring and recklessness. At each report, which came fast and thick, he kissed the flashing blade and waved it at his foes. He passed the ordeal, as awful and harrowing to a man's nerves as can be conceived, untouched by a ball and otherwise unharmed. In a few moments, a loud whoop rang out in the woods a quarter of a mile distant, and the bold rider was safe!

Joaquín, knowing well the determined character of Jim Boyce, and, deeming it more than probable that he had heard of the different large rewards offered for his capture or death amounting in the aggregate to $15,000 or $20,000, he made up his mind speedily that an attack would be made upon him by the whole party of miners if he remained at his encampment, which was some five miles distant from their tents. Concluding that they could not collect their horses together and prepare their arms and ammunition in a proper manner for an attack or pursuit before night, he conceived a plan, the most brilliant and ingenious that ever entered an outlaw's brain, by which to defeat their purposes and carry out his own original intention of robbing them. Knowing that a trail could very well be made in the night but that it could only be followed in the day-time, he ordered his men, numbering fifteen, to saddle up and make ready for a ride. They obeyed with alacrity and without question, and in a few moments were on their horses and ready to move forward. The chief led the way in silence, proceeding over the pine ridges in an easterly direction. He rode on vigorously until night over very rough ground, having traversed a distance of twenty miles; but, wishing to place a still greater distance between him and the encampment which he had left, he did not come to final halt until a late hour. Building a huge fire and hitching their animals near by, the wearied bandits hastily threw their blankets down and stretched their limbs upon them for repose. Sentinels alternately sat up until day-light, so that at the first touch of dawn the whole band arose and again started, having lost only four hours in sleep. They journeyed on in the same course as briskly as possible until noon, when, having reached a nice little valley, covered with grass and wild clover, and watered by a beautiful spring which bubbled up from the roots of a clump of evergreen oaks, distant about twenty miles from their last encampment, they stopped for two hours to let their horses graze and to refresh their own rather empty stomachs with the sardines and crackers which they generally carried with them. Here they left strong indications that they had spent the night but established the contrary fact by riding on for the remainder of the day, whose close found them at another distance of twenty miles. Building fires as before and eating a hasty supper, they again mounted, and, having made a circle of five miles in their course, suddenly turned to the westward and encamped about three o'clock, A. M., at a spot distant another common day's journey from the last starting point. Thus traveling and resting, after the lapse of a few days they found themselves in the original trail upon which they had started.

Jim Boyce and company had struck the path of the robbers on the next morning after their departure and had camped each night at the fires which they had left, expecting, as was natural, that they would come to a final stopping-place when they had proceeded as far as they liked. Joaquín smiled with exquisite satisfaction when he perceived that Boyce was certainly ahead of him and, from every indication, unsuspecting in the remotest degree that his arch-enemy was at that moment in his rear.

At night, after a long day's ride over rugged mountains and deep gulches, Jim Boyce and his company, numbering twenty-five men including himself, were seated around one of Joaquín's late fires, which they had rekindled, quietly enjoying their pipes and laughing over the numerous stereotyped jokes, which had descended, like Shakespeare, from one gentleman to another, and are too good ever to be worn out. The Heavens were cloudy, and a boundary of solid darkness lay around the lighted ring in which they sat. In the ragged clouds a few stars dimly struggled, and the lonesome scream of the cougar, like the wail of a lost spirit benighted in the infinity of darkness, gave a wild terror to the surrounding woods.

Suddenly and startlingly, the simultaneous reports of fifteen pistols rent the air, the dark outer-wall of the fire-circle blazed, as if a cloud had unbosomed its lightnings, and the astonished survivors of the company bounded up to see fifteen of their number stretched upon the earth and to meet with the deadly repetition of the fifteen revolvers. Panic-stricken and bewildered, the survivors of the second discharge, numbering three men among whom was Jim Boyce, fled head-long into the darkness, and, taking no time to choose their ground, hurried madly and distractedly away from the horrible scene. Joaquín stepped quietly into the circle to see if Jim Boyce was killed, but Three-Fingered Jack leaped in like a demon with his huge knife in his mutilated hand, which had lost none of its strength, but did its three-fingered work far better than many other whole hands could do it, and soon quenched the last spark of beating life in the pale forms around him. Every one must know that death from a bullet flings a sudden and extreme paleness over the countenance, and thus the light from the fire, falling upon the ghastly faces around, displayed a sight so hideous and harrowing that Joaquín exclaimed with a shudder:

"Let's leave here, we will camp tonight, somewhere else."

Searching the bundles upon which the company had been seated, he found in different buckskin purses a sum amounting to not less than thirty thousand dollars. He also added fifteen excellent horses and ten powerful mules to his live-stock.

Jim Boyce and his surviving companions wandered to the distant settlements, which, after many hardships, they reached in safety, and it is pleasant to add that in a short time they raised another company with whom they went back to their rich diggings, and, in spite of their immense loss by Joaquín's robbery, made for themselves ample fortunes, with which they returned to the States. Should Jim Boyce chance to read this humble narrative of mine, I beg him to receive my warmest congratulations.

T'TCETSA [LUCY YOUNG]
1846–1944

A member of the Lassik tribe of northern California, T'tcetsa came of age in a period of turmoil, just as her people's ancient way of life began to feel the full impact of Western settlement. She was born near what is now Alderpoint, in Humboldt County, between Eureka and Fort Bragg. Her father was an Alderpoint Wailaki, and her mother was cousin to a Lassik chief. Neither the Spanish nor the Mexicans had ventured this far north, and, since there was no gold to lure argonauts, the region had gone relatively undisturbed until the early 1860s. T'tcetsa was in her teens when she and her family became fugitives in a region their ancestors had inhabited for thousands of years. In the 1930s she shared her memories of this traumatic time with Edith Van Allen Murphey, a friend and local botanist, who recorded T'tcetsa's testimony word for word. Hers is a rare voice from an era of profound cultural disruption.

Later in her life, a white husband renamed her Lucy. In 1914 she married Sam Young, a member of the Hayfork tribe. These two made their home at the Round Valley reservation, north of Ukiah, where she was known for her clairvoyant powers and her extensive knowledge of herbs and native plants. She lived almost a hundred years.

"Lucy's Story"
from *Out of the Past: A True Indian Story*

My grandpa, before white people came, had a dream. He was so old he was all doubled up. Knees to chin, and eyes like indigo. Grown son carry him in great basket on his back, every place. My grandpa say: "White Rabbit"—he mean white people—"gonta devour our grass, our seed, our living. We won't have nothing more, this world. Big elk with straight horn come when white man bring it." I think he meant cattle. "'Nother animal, bigger than deer, but round feet, got hair on neck." This one, horse, I guess.

My aunt say: "Oh, Father, you out your head, don't say that way."

He say: "Now, Daughter, I not crazy. You young people gonta see this."

People come long way, listen to him dream. He dream, then say this way, every morning.

They leave li'l children play by him. He watch good. Have big stick, wave round, scare snake away. He had good teeth. All old people had good teeth.

One time they travel, they come to big pile of brush. My grandpa stop, and look at it. He say: "This, good wood. When I die, burn my body to ashes on top of ground. Here gonta be big canoe, run around, carry white people's things. Those White Rabbit got lotsa everything."

"How canoe gonta run round on dry ground all round here?" we askum. "Don't know," he say. "Just run that way." He mean wagon, I guess.

I never grow much. They call me "Li'l Shorty," but I know pretty near everything that time. My grandpa put his head on my head, smoove my hair, and hold his hand there.

"Long time you gonta live, my child," he say. "You live long time in this world."

. . .

First soldiers ever I see, my li'l sister 'bout three feet high. Took us to Fort Baker and down Van Duzen River. Mother run away, twice. Last time tookted us to lower country. I run off, too, many times.

It was in August. Soldiers had all Inyan together. Gonta takum to Hoopa.

Mother run away when we hit redwoods. Hide us all in hollow tree. Lay there all day. I had li'l cup and bucket soldier give me. Mother send me hunt water.

I 'fraid lost. Break bushes every li'l way. Offus dark in redwoods. Can't see nothing. Pretty soon come to big fern. I break it, lay in my track. Pretty soon hear waterfall, fill bucket. Turn back, find stick I broke. Find fern. Good thing I do that way. Might I lost. Too dark, them redwoods.

Two days we lay in hollow log. Hear soldier in camp, go li'l ways, listen. Go li'l further, listen. . . .

We see horse track. Hide again. Somebody whistle. We drop in fern. Just see soldier hat go by. We watchum long ways. When dark come, we go way down open ridge. . . .

There we stay till sundown. Mother begin get sick. If she die, she tell us go back to soldiers, not to no other white people. We go on. From top of mountain, we come to big pond. High mountain. I pack water for poor mother. . . .

We go round behind Lassik Peak on top of ridge. Rocky. I want hunt water. I starve for water. I hunt for water like in redwoods, see li'l ferns, drink water, carry to mother, rest awhile, then go on. Too hungry we feel. I want go back on road, let soldiers catch us. Then we find sunflower, plenty. We gather head, seed dry 'nough to eat. We go down creek, catch crawfish. Mother can't eat hardtack, make it sick.

We had bedticking dresses, soldiers made us. I wear that. Mother holler: "Young ducks coming down in water." I stand in water, catch li'l ducky in my skirt. Two of 'em. Pretty good size. Can't fly yet. Run on top of water. We killum, club. . . .

We get to big spring, we stay all night, all day. Evening, mother want to go down to head of Soldier Creek. We stay there, gather brush, make basket, pounding basket, call it "Chesta-a." Pounding rock, call it "Bilt-sook." . . .

Long time we stay there, get good basket roots along river. Kinda lonesome there. Talk 'bout move over li'l gulch, get hazelnut. Bear like hazelnut, too. I 'fraid bear get mother. She laugh, tell me if bear get it, take li'l sister to soldier. They gonta take care us both. . . .

One day, I see smoke over to Kettenchaw. Me 'n li'l sister playing. We see big smoke raise over Kettenchaw. Mother come out, shade eyes with hand—look, look.

"Guess someum come back from Hoopa," he say.

Mother want go back, see who there. I 'fraid. I tell it: "You go there, some-um kill us. I gonta take li'l sister, go to soldier, *now.*"

We had thick black oak bark, we pack fire on it, save matches. Evening time, wind blow, 'way down ridge, I see big fire raise up where I drop coal.

Over Kettenchaw two women, one man, burn coals in grass for grasshopper. They see our smoke, know then we still alive.

"That's our cousin and li'l children," they say. "Them that run off from soldier." Lotsa Inyan die on road, starve.

Mother went down to river, stay all night. Morning come, we go way up ridge on top of Kettenchaw. Coming down, mother tell me: "Daughter, I dry for water." I get water. I ask it gonta flat down on Kettenchaw. He say "No, we get out on point see who is, if we know."

Had big load hazelnut to pack. "Push basket up for me, Daughter," mother say. He sit down, I lift strap, push basket up on back. Just then, I hear brush crack. Look quick, see soldier hat. I run back, way back, run in gulch. Mother call me: "Come back, don't run off." I lay there long time. After while, I come back. . . .

Fall time, then, acorns getting good. All want go back Alder Point, winter there. 'Mence rain hard. We camp, build bark house. Everybody tell li'l sister 'n me: "Go on outside, play." We get oak ball, playing, playing. We play pitch 'n catch.

White people come find us. Want take us all to Fort Seward. We all scared to dead. Inyan boy tell us: "Don't 'fraid, won't kill you."

Tookted us to Fort Seward, had Inyan women there, all man killed. Plenty house there; any Inyan escape from Hoopa, bring it to Fort Seward.

After while, Chief Lassik come in. White people went away to get grub, snowing. Find Inyan track way down some place on road. Three white men, two-three Inyan boys gonta hunt up who make track—find it.

"Don't run," Inyan boy tellum. "Gonta take you Fort Seward." They bringum, four Inyan men, five women, Fort Seward. Chief Lassik among them. He uncle-cousin my mother. They all stay there, kill deer, pack it in. Pack wood all time.

One white man come there, want take me South Fork Mountain. His woman got li'l baby. He want me stay his woman. He take me South Fork. He herd hogs, gonta takum to Weaver. I never stay long there. This Inyan woman whip me all time. Didden' talk my language. 'Bout week all I stay. Commence rain pretty hard. He tell me go get water. I go down, water muddy. I get it anyway. He ask me, make sign, "Where you get this water?" I showum down to river. He think I get water in hole near house. He throw out water, commence whip me, tell me go get water.

I go down river, pretty steep go down. I throw bucket in river. I run off. Never see bucket no more. I had soldier shoes, take off, tie around neck. Water knee deep. I just had thin dress, can run good. Come up big high bank. Keep look back see if that woman follow me.

Lotsa redwood tree stand there. I see hog got killed, laying there, neck and shoulder eat up. Hog warm yet. When I put foot on it, something come up behind me. Grizzly bear growl at me. Wind blow from river. He smell me. I fall over back in tall ferns. I feel same as dead. Grizzly set there, his paw hang down. Head turn look every way. I keep eye on him. He give up listen, look, turn around, dig hole to sleep in. I keep still, just like a dead. Fainty, too, and weak.

That's time I run—when he dig deep. Water up to my waist. I run through. Get to Fort Seward before I look back.

At last I come home. Before I get there, I see big fire in lotsa down timber and tree-top. Same time awfully funny smell. I think: Somebody get lotsa wood.

I go on to house. Everybody crying. Mother tell me: "All our men killed now." She say white men there, others come from Round Valley, Humboldt County too, kill our old uncle, Chief Lassik, and all our men.

Stood up about forty Inyan in a row with rope around neck. "What this for?" Chief Lassik askum. "To hang you, dirty dogs," white men tell it. "Hanging, that's dog's death," Chief Lassik say. "We done nothing, be hung for. Must we die, shoot us."

So they shoot. All our men. Then build fire with wood and brush Inyan men been cut for days, never know their own funeral fire they fix. Build big fire, burn all them bodies. That's funny smell I smell before I get to house. Make hair raise on back of my neck. Make sick stomach, too.

That man what herd hogs, his Inyan boy speak my language. He say: "Why you come back?"

"That woman whip me every day," I say.

"What for she whip you?"

"Everything, little or big, she whip me."

Boy say: "White man say he gonta take all you folks over there, build you house."

That white man, same evening got me, took to his house. Then took me down South Fork again. I ride behind. He talk his women. He had cowhide rope. Short one. He upped that. Give woman good whipping with that. He stay all night, next morning go back Fort Seward. 'Nother Inyan boy where I was. I didden' know he spoke my language. When man come, that woman wash clothes down by the river. Want me stay take care baby. She go on, then this boy talk with me. He tell me: "Tomorrow, 'other white man come, gonta take you off. Way down. Tomorrow, white man come."

So it did happen. He take me then. This boy say: "Better you stay white people, better for you. All your people killed. Nothing to come back for."

I didden' say nothing. Yes nor no.

He bring me back Alder Point, this white man did. From there he take me down low. I ride on packsaddle. Had big blanket over me. Winter time.

Get up on top of mountain, meet 'nother white man, got li'l Inyan boy with him. This boy talk my talk good. He ride packsaddle too. They take us way up to Blue Rock Mountain. White men live there. Dogs begin barking. We get there, ride up to gate. White man take me off. I can't walk. Ride all day. Take li'l boy off, too.

I see woman come out of door. I know that woman, one of my people. Bill Dobbins' mother. This one, her father's my aunt. She know me. I know her. She set down in chair, hug me, commence cry. I cry, too, cause think 'bout mother all time.

This woman live with old white man. He cook supper. This woman don't know how to cook. He come in, think I his daughter. "Your papoose?" he say. She say: "No." Put hand on chest. "My Inyan," she say.

"Ah-hah," white say. He bring out li'l baby tumbler, give me li'l whisky, put sugar in it, cause riding in cold.

Then they took me to Long Valley. He had 'nother wife there. Next. morning that other man was there, washing face. He come in, count my finger: "One, two, three, four, days you going down, close to ocean." That man washing was cutting wood there. I stay there and play with pups. I look back. Two small Inyan boys stand there. I look and feel afraid. Went in house.

That man cook supper. He go to bed overhead. I sleep in big blanket by chimney. He cook in kitchen in morning. "Get up," he say. "Breakfast ready."

Two Inyan women come in. Talk quick to me: "Poor my li'l sister, where you come from?" "I come from north. That bald-headed man bring me."

"He got wife and children," they say.

These women talk clipped my language. "That's way all Inyan children come here," they say. "He bringum all."

I half cry, all time for my mother. After while, bald-headed man come back, talk women long time. Gonta have big gamble over there, they say. Men got up and left. First, they give women grub, hog backbone, ribs.

These women say: "In four days you go stay old couple close by us." One um say: "I got white man, I come see you."

They leave for home. Little ridge, over hill. I hear Inyan talking, li'l way'. I stand there and think. Only show for me to run off, now. Nobody there. I run in house. Match box on shelf. I put it in dress pocket. In kitchen, I find flour sacks. Take loaf bread, take boiling meat. Take big blanket from my bed.

I went out so quick, I never shut door. Then I went out to barn, open door, let all horses out.

All day I travel on edge of valley. I forgot I gonta have to swim Eel River. Then I see white man house, and lotta Inyan house, all smoke even—good sign. I go towards white man house. I go upstream, look for foot-log. Brush thick, too. I found big trail. 'Fraid then. Stop and listen, every li'l while. Pretty soon find footbridge. Just getting dark good. Star coming up. 'Nother big stream. Shallow water.

Lotsa people there. Lotsa bell. Talk. Laugh. Pack-train stop there. I cross above camp. Water knee-deep. Go up long hill. Pretty near daylight, come out on mountain. Come out in big open country where Billy Dobbins' mother lived.

Owl commence holler, coming daylight. Way this side, great big rock. Big live-oak. Hollow place. I lay blanket down. Sleep all day; dark, I wake up. . . .

Saw big mountain, went over it. I back-track li'l way. I see white man hunt for me on white horse. I lay still long time, travel all night.

Went down in canyon, find big log all dry underneath. I sleep right there all day. Had to cross two li'l creek, went barefoot there. When I cross those two li'l creek, I home to old stamping ground, nor far from Alder Point.

Again I lay down in sun to sleep. Three days I stay there, 'fraid go down to Fort Seward. Good weather. Think 'bout mother all time. Half-time cry, once awhile. Two nights I stay alone, then I go to Fort Seward.

That white man told Inyan boys watch for me come home. Lotsa women there, man all killed.

I go where they get water, two-three places there where make buckeye soup. It ain't done yet. Nobody there. I taste buckeye, all bitter yet. I drink water, outa basket setting there. After awhile I see woman coming. I step behind brush. He never see me. He pour water in buckeye. Talk to self 'bout being bitter. It was my mother! Then I step in plain sight. He stir soup with hand, shake drops off. Look round. "Who's you," he say. "That you, my daughter?" I say: "Yes." He hug me and cry. Poor mother!

"Inyan boy watching," he whisper. "You come in 'bout morning, 'bout midnight?" "No," I told it. "Got grub, got blanket, I sleep down here, some place."

"Shall I bring buckeye soup tonight?" "No," I tell it. "Don't fetch grub out, might they follow you, find me."

Two night I hide out. I go way down creek down under big tree roots. Sleep dry. Then I go to house. All time I never leave no sign. Mother and li'l sister hunt me. Make believe gather wood, never find me.

My uncle hunt me the last night. I see him. Then I show up on open ground. He say: "Poor li'l thing, hunted, starving. 'Bout midnight I put you 'cross river in boat." I say: "Tell mother meet me out there."

He say them two li'l girl been take away from that 'nother woman. Cry all time.

Midnight, I go in, meetum. Watch stars for time. I eat. Mother give me 'nother blanket, food too. Them two men don't make no track—walk in leaves and river. Had big boat. Put my aunt and me 'cross river. If mother let li'l sister go, white men would kill mother.

We travel all night, sleep all day till sundown. Had lotsa dry meat. Left most of my white-man grub with mother. Found some of our people at Poison Rock, pretty near sundown. I see old man pack wood. He been on look-out. He go in big bark house. I look in door, big fire in middle of house.

Man say: "Li'l girl look in door." They get up, bring me in. Young girl lay there, sick, my half sister. That night she die. Snowing, raining hard. They dig hole right by house, put body in. All went out. Tore all house down, set it afire. Midnight, snow whirl, wind howl. Then we went over to 'nother house; all left there next day, went over to Soldier Basin.

We stay there awhile, went to Cottonwood. Some of our people there. We went to head of Mad River, next day to South Fork of Trinity River. We stay all night. Tired. No horses. Next day to Cottonwood.

My cousin, Ellen, Wylackie Tom's woman, was there. We found her right away. Then I stay at Cottonwood all summer. After awhile, my' cousin living with white man, he want kill her, she leave him. I stay with her and li'l boy.

Ellen's cousin-brother say to me: "Take care my li'l boy, cause I gonta Hayfork. Maybe white folks kill me," he say. "Take care my boy, takum way' off."

White man name Rogers come after this. Ellen my cousin's man, went to work for him. I go with her to Hayfork, and take li'l boy too.

Rogers, my white man, took me then to take care of, that summer. Marry me bimeby when get old enough, 'bout size ten year girl I guess, when first see soldier. I stay there at Hayfork long time. My mother come there, too. She die there after awhile at Hayfork.

My cousin, Ellen, younger than me but she got man first. We didn't neither one know much. Man told us cook beans. We cook green coffee for beans. Man cook long time for us.

Li'l sister, white man took her away. Never see her no more. If see it, maybe wouldn't know it. That's last young one tooken away. Mother lost her at Fort Seward.

I hear it, I went back, got mother, brought her to Hayfork. Lotsa Inyan there, lotsa different language, all different. Mother stay with me until she die.

You ask 'bout father. He got killed and brother in soldier war, before soldiers captured us. Three days fight. Three days running. Just blood, blood, blood. Young woman cousin, run from soldier, run into our camp. Three of us girls run. I lose buckskin blanket. Cousin run back, pick it up. I roll it up, put under arm—run more better that way.

We had young man cousin, got shot side of head, crease him, all covered his blood, everything. We helpum to water. Wash off. No die. That night all our women come to camp. I ask mother: "You see my father, big brother?" "Yes," she say, "both two of um dead." I want go see. Mother say "No."

Young woman been stole by white people, come back. Shot through lights and liver. Front skin hang down like apron. She tie up with cotton dress. Never die, neither. Little boy, knee-pan shot off. Young man shot through thigh. Only two man of all our tribe left—that battle.

White people want our land, want destroy us. Break and burn all our basket, break our pounding rock. Destroy our ropes. No snares, no deerskin, flint knife, nothing.

Some old lady wear moss blanket, peel off rock good.

I hear people tell 'bout what Inyan do early days to white man. Nobody ever tell it what white man do to Inyan. That's the reason I tell it. That's history. That's truth. I seen it myself.

T'tcetsa [Lucy Young]

WILLIAM HENRY BREWER

1828–1910

Brewer spent four years with the California Geological Survey as field leader and principal assistant to its director, Josiah Whitney. Born in New York, he studied agricultural chemistry at Yale. In Germany he pursued advanced study, and he later taught at Washington College in Pennsylvania. He was among the first trained scientists to write at length about California. As the mules and wagons of the survey party moved up and down the state, Brewer kept several sets of meticulous notes on weather, plant specimens, and geological features, as well as maintaining an extensive correspondence. He wrote a series of letters to his brother, Edgar, with instructions that these be held until his return. Never published during Brewer's lifetime, they were finally compiled, edited, and published in 1930 by Yale University Press. In 1865, Brewer was appointed to the chair of agriculture in the Sheffield School at Yale, where he remained until his retirement in 1903.

"Los Angeles and Environs"
from *Up and Down California*

Sunday, December 2, 1860.

Professor Whitney returned from Sacramento Wednesday, November 21, with the "sinews of war," and with orders to get off immediately. The next two days were spent in the greatest activity, buying blankets, getting tents made, getting harness, saddles, some groceries, tea and coffee, etc., and Saturday, November 24, we were on board a steamer for San Pedro, 380 miles southwest of San Francisco. Four of us started. Professor Whitney went to Mariposa with Colonel Frémont, intending to come down by the next steamer, about three weeks later. As first assistant, the company was placed in my charge, a heavy responsibility I would like to have had placed on someone else. We were to come down here, buy mules, provision and equip fully, and go into camp and await Professor Whitney.

Well, we sailed on Saturday, a most lovely morning, and took our course down the coast to the southeast. There are two small rocky islands just at the Golden Gate and they were completely covered with sea lions, a kind of large seal, apparently nearly as large as a walrus. They barked at us as we passed and many tumbled into the sea, but hundreds were basking in the sun or moving about with awkward motions.

The next morning we arrived at San Luis Obispo. The port is but a single house, and the village is about four miles distant. As we lay there all day, I went ashore with a friend, a doctor from the United States Army, and spent several hours, saw the country and collected some plants, all strange to me. The steamer was anchored a mile from the shore, and the freight, some seventy or eighty tons, had to be landed in yawls or rowboats. There is no dock, so it is landed on a rock.

The land was very dry, the rains had hardly begun, so the vegetation looked very scanty and the land desolate. Scrub oaks, crabbed sycamores, and scrubby undershrubs composed the scanty vegetation. We wandered along the beach and picked up a few shells, some of great beauty. The sea has worn the rocks in fantastic shapes; there are several natural arches, one of great size.

On our return to the ship, we found the passengers playing cards, singing songs, drinking whiskey, etc.—a Californian sabbath. The Boundary Commission, to run the line between California and countries east, were aboard, a hard set, who were making much noise and drinking much whiskey. They are now encamped near here. One of their men died this morning, killed most probably with bad whiskey. He was out yesterday, walked to camp last evening, and died this morning.

Well, we started that evening. The next morning, after stopping a few hours at Santa Barbara, we arrived at San Pedro, the port of Los Angeles, about twenty-five miles from here. We got in about sundown, rode six miles up the river on a small steamer, then disembarked for this place by stage. It was a most lovely night, but there were more than three times as many passengers as there was stage room, so two of us came up and left two other men with the baggage. They came up the next day. We have been here since, looking at mules, harness, bacon, stores, etc. We hope to be in camp in two days more. I have been to church once today, we had a congregation of about thirty or forty, I should think.

December 7.

Well, we are in camp. It is a cold rainy night, but I can hardly realize the fact that you at home are blowing your fingers in the cold, and possibly sleighing, while I am sitting here in a tent, without fire, and sleeping on the ground in blankets, in this month. We are camped on a hill near the town, perhaps a mile distant, a pretty place.

Los Angeles is a city of some 3,500 or 4,000 inhabitants, nearly a century old, a regular old Spanish-Mexican town, built by the old *padres*, Catholic Spanish missionaries, before the American independence. The houses are but one story, mostly built of *adobe* or sun-burnt brick, with very thick walls and flat roofs. They are so low because of earthquakes, and the style is Mexican. The inhabitants are a mixture of old Spanish, Indian, American, and German Jews; the last two have come in lately. The language of the natives is Spanish, and I have commenced learning it. The only thing they appear to excel in is riding, and certainly I have never seen such riders.

Here is a great plain, or rather a gentle slope, from the Pacific to the mountains. We are on this plain about twenty miles from the sea and fifteen from the mountains, a most lovely locality; all that is wanted naturally to make it a paradise is *water,* more *water.* Apples, pears, plums, figs, olives, lemons, oranges, and "the finest grapes in the world," so the books say, pears of two and a half pounds each, and such things in proportion. The weather is soft and balmy—no winter, but a perpetual spring and summer. Such is Los Angeles, a place where "every prospect pleases and only man is vile."

As we stand on a hill over the town, which lies at our feet, one of the loveliest views I ever saw is spread out. Over the level plain to the southwest lies the Pacific, blue in the distance; to the north are the mountains of the Sierra Santa Monica; to the south, beneath us, lies the picturesque town with its flat roofs, the fertile plain and vineyards stretching away to a great distance; to the east, in the distance, are some mountains without name, their sides abrupt and broken, while still above them stand the snow covered peaks of San Bernardino. The effect of the pepper, fig, olive, and palm trees in the foreground, with the snow in the distance, is very unusual.

This is a most peculiar climate, a mingling of the temperate with the tropical. The date palm and another palm grow here, but do not fruit, while the olive, fig, orange, and lemon flourish well. The grapes are famous, and the wine of Los Angeles begins to be known even in Europe.

We got in camp on Tuesday, December 4. We had been invited to a ranch and vineyard about nine miles east, and went with a friend on Tuesday evening. It lies near San Gabriel Mission, on a most beautiful spot, I think even finer than this. Mr. Wilson, our host, uneducated, but a man of great force of character, is now worth a hundred or more thousand dollars and lives like a prince, only with less luxury. His wife is finely educated and refined, and his home to the visitor a little paradise. We were received with the greatest cordiality and were entertained with the greatest hospitality. A touch of the country and times was indicated by our rig—I was dressed in colored woolen shirt, with heavy navy revolver (loaded) and huge eight-inch bowie knife at my belt; my friend the same; and the clergyman who took us out in his carriage carried along his rifle, he said for game, yet owned that it was "best to have arms after dark."

Here let me digress. This southern California is still unsettled. We all continually wear arms—each wears both bowie knife and pistol (navy revolver), while we have always for game or otherwise, a Sharp's rifle, Sharp's carbine, and two double-barrel shotguns. Fifty to sixty murders per year have been common here in Los Angeles, and some think it odd that there has been no violent death during the two weeks that we have been here. Yet with our care there is no considerable danger, for as I write this there are at least six heavy loaded revolvers in the tent, besides bowie knives and other arms, so we anticipate no danger. I have been practicing with my revolver and am becoming expert.

CLARENCE KING

1842–1901

King crossed the continent on horseback in 1863. He was twenty-one, a recent graduate of Yale College. In California he met fellow Yale alumnus William Brewer, who hired him to work with the Geological Survey. King spent most of the next ten years roaming and charting the Sierra Nevada range, where he acquired a reputation as a fearless and skillful climber. From these years came Mountaineering in the Sierra Nevada. *While Brewer wrote letters to his brother, and while Josiah Whitney compiled the Survey's official reports, King, in this early work, had more literary ambitions. Parts of his book first appeared in* Atlantic Monthly *and in Bret Harte's* Overland Monthly *in San Francisco. It combines geology, lively anecdote, and a lyrical gift for conveying nature's grand panorama. King later led a major, congressionally funded survey from eastern Colorado to the California border and then led a move to consolidate the various surveys around the country. As a result, in 1878 he became the first director of the U.S. Geological Survey. That year also saw the publication of his* Systematic Geology, *for years a classic text in the field.*

"Mount Shasta"
from *Mountaineering in the Sierra Nevada*

A day's march brought us from McCloud to the Sacramento, here a small stream, with banks fringed by a pleasing variety of trees and margins graceful with water-plants.

Northward for two days we followed closely the line of the Sacramento River, now descending along slopes to its bed, where the stream played among picturesque rocks and boulders, and again climbing by toilsome ascents into the forest a thousand feet up on the *cañon* wall, catching glimpses of towering ridges of pine-clad Sierra above, and curves of the foaming river deep in the blue shadow beneath us.

More and more the woods became darkened with mountain pine, the air freshened by northern life gave us the inspiration of altitude.

At last, through a notch to the northward, rose the conical summit of Shasta, its pale, rosy lavas enamelled with ice. Body and base of the great peak were hidden by intervening hills, over whose smooth rolls of forest green the bright, blue sky and the brilliant Shasta summit were sharp and strong. From that moment the peak became the centre of our life. From every crest we strained our eyes forward, as now and then, either through forest vistas the incandescent snow greeted us, or from some high summit the opening cañon walls displayed grander and grander views of the great volcano. It was sometimes, after all, a pleasure to descend from these cool heights, with the impression of the mountain upon our minds, to the cañon bottom, where, among the endlessly varying bits of beautiful detail, the mental strain wore off.

When our tents were pitched at Sisson's, while a picturesque haze floated up from southward, we enjoyed the grand uncertain form of Shasta with its heaven-piercing crest of white, and wide placid sweep of base; full of lines as deeply poseful as a Greek temple. Its dark head lifted among the fading stars of dawn, and strongly set upon the arch of coming rose, appealed to our emotions; but best we liked to sit at evening near Munger's easel, watching the great lava cone glow with light almost as wild and lurid as if its crater still streamed.

Watkins thought it "photographic luck" that the mountain should so have draped itself with mist as to defy his camera. Palmer stayed at camp to make observations in the coloring of meerschaums at fixed altitudes, and to watch now and then the station barometer.

Shasta from Sisson's is a broad triple mountain, the central summit being flanked on the west by a large and quite perfect crater whose rim reaches about twelve thousand feet altitude. On the west a broad shoulder-like spur juts from the general slope. The cone rises from its base eleven thousand feet in one sweep.

A forest of tall, rich pines surrounds Strawberry Valley, and the little group of ranches near Sisson's. Under this high sky, and a pure quality of light, the whole varied foreground of green and gold stretches out toward the rocky mountain base in charming contrast. Brooks from the snow thread their way through open meadow, waving overhead a tent-work of willows, silvery and cool.

Shasta, as a whole, is the single cone of an immense extinct volcano. It occupies almost precisely the axial line of the Sierra Nevada, but the range, instead of carrying its great wave-like ridge through this region, breaks down in the neighborhood of Lassen's Butte, and for eighty miles northward is only represented by low confused masses of mountain cut through and through by the cañons of the McCloud, Pit, and Sacramento.

A broad volcanic plain, interrupted here and there by inconsiderable chains, occupies the country east of Scott's Mountain. From this general plain, whose altitude is from twenty-five hundred to thirty-five hundred feet, rises Mount Shasta. About its base cluster hillocks of a hundred little volcanoes, but they are utterly inconspicuous under the shadow of the great peak. The volcanic plain-land is partly overgrown by forest, and in part covers itself with fields of grass or sage. Riding over it in almost any part the one great point in the landscape is the cone of Shasta; its crest of solid white, its vast altitude, the pale-gray or rosy tints of its lavas, and the dark girdle of forest which swells up over cañon carved foot-hills give it a grandeur equalled by hardly any American mountain.

September eleventh found the climbers of our party,—S. F. Emmons, Frederick A. Clark, Albert B. Clark, Mr. Sisson, the pioneer guide of the region, and myself,—mounted upon our mules, heading for the crater cone over rocks and among the stunted firs and pines which mark the upper limit of forest growth. The morning was cool and with a fresh north wind sweeping around the volcano and bringing in its descent invigorating cold of the snow region. When we had gone as far as our mules could carry us, threading their difficult way among piles of lava, we dismounted and made up our packs of beds, instruments, food, and fuel for a three days' trip, turned the animals over to George and John, our two muleteers, bade them good day, and with Sisson, who was to accompany us up the first descent, struck out on foot. Already above vegetation, we looked out over all the valley south and west, observing its arabesque of forest, meadow, and chaparral, the files of pines which struggled up almost to our feet, and just below us the volcano slope strewn with red and brown wreck and patches of shrunken snow-drift.

Our climb up the steep western crater slope was slow and tiresome, quite without risk or excitement. The footing, altogether of lodged débris, at times gave way provokingly, and threw us out of balance. Once upon the spiry pinnacles which crown the crater rim, a scene of wild power broke upon us. The round crater-bowl, about a mile in diameter and nearly a thousand feet deep, lay beneath us, its steep, shelving sides of shattered lava mantled in places to the very bottom by fields of snow.

We clambered along the edge toward Shasta, and came to a place where for a thousand feet it was a mere blade of ice, sharpened by the snow into a thin, frail edge, upon which we walked in cautious balance, a misstep likely to hurl us down into the chaos of lava blocks within the crater.

Passing this, we reached the north edge of the rim, and from a rugged mound of shattered rock looked down into a gorge between us and the main Shasta. There, winding its huge body along, lay a glacier, riven with sharp, deep crevasses yawning fifty or sixty feet wide, the blue hollows of their shadowed depth contrasting with the brilliant surfaces of ice.

We studied its whole length from the far, high Shasta crest down in winding course, deepening its *cañon* more and more as it extends, crowding past our crater cone, and at last terminating in bold ice-billows and a wide belt of hilly moraine. The surface over half of its length was quite clean, but directly opposite us occurs a fine ice cascade; there its entire surface is cut with transverse crevasses, which have a general tendency to curve downward; and all this dislocation is accompanied by a freight of lava blocks which shoot down the *cañon* walls on either side, bounding out all over the glacier.

In a later trip, while Watkins was making his photographic views, I climbed about, going to the edges of some crevasses and looking over into their blue vaults, where icicles overhang and a whispered sound of water-flow comes up faintly from beneath.

From a point about midway across where I had climbed and rested upon the brink of an ice-cliff, the glacier below me breaking off into its wild pile of cascade blocks and *séracs,* I looked down over all the lower flow, broken with billowy upheavals, and bright with bristling spires of sunlit ice. Upon the right rose the great cone of Shasta, formed of chocolate-colored lavas, its sky-line a single curved sweep of snow cut sharply against a deep blue sky. To the left the precipices of the lesser cone rose to the altitude of twelve thousand feet, their surfaces half jagged ledges of lava and half irregular sheets of ice. From my feet the glacier sank rapidly between volcanic walls, and the shadow of the lesser cone fell in a dark band across the brilliantly lighted surface. Looking down its course, my eye ranged over sunny and shadowed zones of ice, over the gray, boulder region of the terminal moraine; still lower, along the former track of ancient and grander glaciers, and down upon undulating pine-clad foot-hills descending in green steps, reaching out like promontories into the sea of plain which lay outspread nine thousand feet below, basking in the half-tropical sunshine, its checkered green fields and orchards ripening their wheat and figs.

Our little party separated, each going about his labor. The Clarks, with theodolite and barometer, were engaged on a pinnacle over on the western crater-edge. Mr. Sisson, who had helped us thus far with a huge pack-load of wood, now said good by, and was soon out of sight on his homeward tramp. Emmons and I geologized about the rim and interior slope, getting at last out of sight of one another.

In mid-crater sprang up a sharp cone several hundred feet high, composed of much shattered lava, and indicating doubtless the very latest volcanic activity. At its base lay a small lakelet, frozen over with rough black ice. Far below us, cold, gray banks and floating flocks of vapor began to drift and circle about the lava slopes, rising higher at sunset, till they quite enveloped us, and at times shut out the view.

Later we met for bivouac, spread our beds upon small débris under lee of a mass of rock on the rim, and built a little camp-fire, around which we sat closely. Clouds still eddied about us, opening now wide rifts of deep-blue sky, and then glimpses of the Shasta summit glowing with evening light, and again views down upon the far earth, where sunlight had long faded, leaving forest and field and village sunken in purple gloom. Through the old broken crater lip, over foreground of pallid ice and sharp black lava rocks, the clouds whirled away, and, yawning wide, revealed an objectless expanse, out of which emerged dim mountain tops, for a moment seen, then veiled. Thus, in the midst of clouds, I found it extremely interesting to watch them and their habits. Drifting slowly across the crater-bowl I saw them float over and among the points of cindery lava, whose savage forms contrasted wonderfully with the infinite softness of their texture.

I found it strange and suggestive that fields of perpetual snow should mantle the slopes of an old lava caldron, that the very volcano's throat should be choked with a pure little lakelet, and sealed with unmelting ice. That power of extremes, which held sway over lifeless nature before there were human hearts to experience its crush, expressed itself with poetic eloquence. Had Lowell been in our bivouac, I know he must have felt again the power of his own perfect figure of

"Burned-out craters healed with snow."

It was a wild moment. Wind smiting in shocks against the rock beside us, flaring up our little fire, and whirling on with its cloud-freight into the darkening crater gulf.

We turned in; the Clarks together, Emmons and I in our fur bags. Upon cold stone our bed was anything but comfortable, angular fragments of trachyte finding their way with great directness among our ribs and under shoulder-blades, keeping us almost awake in that despairing semi-consciousness where dreams and thoughts tangle in tiresome confusion.

Just after midnight, from sheer weariness, I arose, finding the sky cloudless, its whole black dome crowded with stars. A silver dawn over the slope of Shasta brightened till the moon sailed clear. Under its light all the rugged topography came out with unnatural distinctness, every impression of height and depth greatly exaggerated. The empty crater lifted its rampart into the light. I could not tell which seemed most desolate, that dim moonlit rim with pallid snow-mantle and gaunt crags, or the solid black shadow which was cast downward from southern walls, darkening half the bowl. From the silent air every breath of wind or whisper of sound seemed frozen. Naked lava-slopes and walls, the high gray body of Shasta with ridge and gorge, glacier and snow-field, all cold and still under the icy brightness of the moon, produced a scene of Arctic terribleness such as I had never imagined. I looked down, eagerly straining my eyes, through the solemn crater's lip, hoping to catch a glimpse of the lower world; but far below, hiding the earth, stretched out a level plain of cloud, upon which the light fell cold and gray as upon a frozen ocean.

I scrambled back to bed, and happily to sleep, a real, sound, dreamless repose.

We breakfasted some time after sunrise, and were soon under way with packs on our shoulders.

The day was brilliant and cloudless, the cold, still air full of life and inspiration. Through its clear blue the Shasta peak seemed illusively near, and we hurried down to the saddle which connects our cone with the peak, and across the head of a small tributary glacier, and up over the first débris slopes. It was a slow, tedious three hours' climb over stones which lay as steeply as loose material possibly can, up to the base of a red trachyte spur; then on up a gorge, and out upon a level mountain shoulder, where are considerable flats covered with deep ice. To the north it overflows in a much crevassed tributary of the glacier we had studied below.

Here we rested, and hung the barometer from Clark's tripod.

The further ascent lies up a long scoria ridge of loose, red, pumiceous rock for seven or eight hundred feet, then across another level step curved with rugged ice, and up into a sort of corridor between two steep, much broken, and stained ridges. Here in the hollow are boiling sulphurous springs and hot earth. We sat down by them, eating our lunch in the lee of some stones.

A short, rapid climb brought us to the top; four hours and thirty minutes working time from our crater bivouac. . . .

After we had walked along a short curved ridge which forms the summit, representing, as I believe, all that remains of the original crater, it became my occupation to study the view.

A singularly transparent air revealed every plain and peak on till the earth's curve rolled them under remote horizons. The whole great disk of world outspread beneath wore an aspect of glorious cheerfulness. The cascade range, a roll of blue forest land, stretched northward, surmounted at intervals by volcanoes; the lower, like symmetrical Mount Pit, bare and warm with rosy lava colors; those farther north lifting against the pale, horizon-blue solid white cones upon which strong light rested with brilliance. It seemed incredible that we could see so far toward the Columbia River, almost across the State of Oregon, but there stood Pit, Jefferson, and the Three Sisters in unmistakable plainness. Northeast and east spread those great plains out of which rise low lava chains, and a few small, burned-out volcanoes, and there, too, were the group of Klamath and Goose lakes lying in mid plain glassing the deep upper violet. Farther and farther from our mountain base in that direction the greenness of forest and meadow fades out into rich mellow brown, with warm cloudings of sienna over bare lava hills, and shades, as you reach the eastern limit, in pale ash and lavender and buff, where stretches of level land slope down over Madelin plains into Nevada deserts. An unmistakable purity and delicacy of tint, with transparent air and paleness of tone, give all desert scenes the aspect of water-color drawings. Even at this immense distance I could see the gradual change from rich, warm hues of rocky slope, or plain overspread with ripened vegetation, out to the high pale key of the desert.

Southeast the mountain spurs are smoothed into a broad glacis, densely overgrown with chaparral, and ending in open groves around plains of yellow grass.

A little farther begin the wild, *cañon*-curved piles of green mountains which represent the Sierras, and afar, towering over them, eighty miles away, the lava dome of Lassen Peak standing up bold and fine. South, the Sacramento Cañon cuts down to unseen depths, its deep trough opening a view of the California plain, a brown, sunny expanse, over which loom in vanishing perspective the Coast Range peaks. West of us, and quite around the semicircle of view, stretches a vast sea of ridges, chains, peaks, and sharp walls of *cañons*, as wild and tumultuous as an ocean storm. Here and there above the blue billows rise snow-crests and shaggy rock-chains, but the topography is indistinguishable. With difficulty I could trace for a short distance the Klamath Cañon course, recognizing Siskiyou peaks, where Professor Brewer and I had been years before; but in that broad area no further unravelling was possible. So high is Shasta, so dominant above the field of view, we looked over it all as upon a great shield which rose gently in all directions to the sky.

Whichever way we turned the great cone fell off from our feet in dizzying abruptness. We looked down steep slopes of *névé*, on over shattered ice-wreck, where glaciers roll over cliffs, and around the whole broad massive base curved deeply through its lava crusts in straight *cañons*.

These flutings of ancient and grander glaciers are flanked by straight, long moraines, for the most part bare, but reaching down part way into the forest. It is interesting to observe that those on the north and east, by greater massiveness and length, indicate that in former days the glacier distribution was related to the points of compass about as it is now. What volumes of geographical history lay in view! Old mountain uplift; volcanoes built upon the plain of fiery lava; the chill of ice and wearing force of torrent, written in glacier-gorge and water-curved *cañon!*

I think such vastness of prospect now and then extremely valuable in itself; it forcibly widens one's conception of country, driving away such false notion of extent or narrowing idea of limitation as we get in living on lower plains.

I never tire of overlooking these great wide fields, studying their rich variety, and giving myself up to the expansion which is the instant and lasting reward. In presence of these vast spaces and all but unbounded outlooks, the hours hurry by with singular swiftness. Minutes or miles are nothing; days and degrees seem best fitted for one's thoughts. So it came sooner than I could have believed that the sun neared its setting, sinking into a warm, bright stratum of air. The light stretched from north to south, reflecting itself with an equal depth all along the east, until a perfect ring of soft, glowing rose edged the whole horizon. Over us the ever dark heaven hung near and flat. Light swept eastward across the earth, every uplift of hill-ridge or solitary cone warm and bright with its reflections, and from each object upon the plains, far and near, streamed out dense, sharp shadows, slowly lengthening their intense images. We were far enough lifted above it all to lose the ordinary landscape impression, and reach that extraordinary effect of black-and-bright topography seen upon the moon through a telescope.

Afar in the north, bars of blue shadows streamed out from the peaks, tracing themselves upon rosy air. All the eastern slope of Shasta was of course in dark shade, the gray glacier forms, broken ridges of stone, and forest all dim and fading. A long cone of cobalt-blue, the shadow of Shasta fell strongly defined over the bright plain, its apex darkening the earth a hundred miles away. As the sun sank, this gigantic spectral volcano rose on the warm sky till its darker form stood huge and terrible over the whole east. It was intensely distinct at the summit, just as far-away peaks seen against the east in evening always are, and faded at base as it entered the stratum of earth mist.

Grand and impressive we had thought Shasta when studying in similar light from the plain. Infinitely more impressive was this phantom volcano as it stood over-shadowing the land and slowly fading into night.

Clarence King

PART THREE

THE RISE OF A
CALIFORNIA LITERATURE

1865–1914

Introduction

Samuel Clemens first saw California in the summer of 1861, adrift in a leaky skiff just off the Nevada shore of Lake Tahoe. Through a veil of smoke, he peered across ten miles of cobalt water toward what looked like calmer territories on the western shore. He had set the forest ablaze with a supper campfire and fled for his life to the boat. Before it burned out the next morning, the conflagration ate up several thousand acres of virgin pine and fir in what is now the Toiyabe National Forest. Thus Samuel Clemens experienced California, a distant green haven with disaster lurking at its edge.

Clemens had scaled the eastern slopes of the Sierra Nevada—not far from the region that trapped the Donner Party in 1846—to wildcat timber tracts in the forests around Lake Tahoe. He and a tenderfoot pal staked their claims and then watched their jackpot fantasies go up in a roaring fire, but Clemens's first vision of Tahoe and the Sierra haunted him long afterward. He described it in a breathy narrative in *Roughing It* (1872) as "a sea of royal seclusion guarded by a cordon of sentinel peaks," an earthly paradise, "the fairest picture the whole world affords."

He had heeded Horace Greeley's advice of 1850 to "Go West, Young Man"—to seek fortune and to find himself. The gold strikes of 1849 had about played out, but thousands of immigrants continued to pour in anyway. Northern California was in the throes of an exponential boom. In August 1848, shortly after word of the gold strike at Sutter's Mill, east of Sacramento, the population of San Francisco numbered eight hundred. When Clemens arrived, the city was awash with more than forty thousand fellow optimists.

Mark Twain was "born" on February 2, 1863, when Sam Clemens first used the pseudonym as a reporter for the *Virginia City Territorial Enterprise*. Bored by the facts in Nevada and later in San Francisco, he embroidered on them. His unsparing sketches attracted readers but also provoked outrage, occasionally requiring quick getaways. By the time of one such midnight flight to Jackass Hill in the Mother Lode, Twain was known widely as a wit, the literary "Moralist of the Pacific Slope." He sought refuge (and gold) in Calaveras County, but the real pay came from yarns allowed by locals like Ben Coon, to whom Twain listened impatiently for three months. One of Coon's chestnuts became Twain's story "The Celebrated Jumping Frog of Calaveras

County," and when it ran in the *New York Saturday Press* in November 1865 it won the author national acclaim and highlighted California's reputation as a mythic territory.

Although Twain stayed less than three years in California, he was the first to give full voice to many of the distinctive themes and styles of its literature. *Roughing It* was the first of many literary depictions of the regions that constituted California, but Twain sensed, as well, a larger metaphor in the land. Whether in the Sierra Nevada or the Mother Lode, or on the bustling streets of San Francisco, he read a promise in his surroundings that was both exhilarating and terrifying: a place to start over again, to find a fortune, a site on which innocence might encounter darkness—perhaps even transform it— the geographical end of the line for the westward odyssey. And, as he also grew aware, each bright promise held a shadow. He knew the seductiveness of the state's mythic power not only for the American East but for Asia and Europe, and he worked with and against it throughout his narratives.

When Twain arrived in 1864, Bret Harte ruled the San Francisco literary scene. Writing for the rival newspaper *The Californian,* Twain watched as Harte presided first over the *Golden Era* (the City's premier repository of letters) and then the *Overland Monthly.* Their two very different tempers struck a complex bond that somehow survived for ten years, until they parted bitterly after a disastrous collaboration. San Francisco was the perfect site for their shared ambitions. By 1864, with a population of sixty-five thousand, it was the major port of call and commercial center for the American West, with a vigorous if adolescent literary culture, much of it displayed in a tangle of bumptious newspapers and magazines. By the time *Roughing It* was published in 1872, the population had spiked to 165,000, with almost 40,000 living in Chinatown alone. Los Angeles, by contrast, was slowly evolving from the site the indigenous Gabrieliños had termed Yang-na (from *iyaanga*, "poison oak patch"): it was still a dusty frontier town of seven thousand inhabitants.

San Francisco was *the* place to be for adventurous European and American types looking for the next cultural wave, a wide-open city in which rowdies in buckskins, businessmen in beaver hats, and European dandies in velvet breeches jostled on the muddy boardwalks. Thus accents from New York, London, and Paris mingled with the cruder twang of the roughneck West, and the demography of the city was further mixed and remixed as fires, earthquakes, floods, and other natural pressures erased whole neighborhoods and altered the lay of the land. The resulting urban brew has supported social struggles and subcultural surges from labor fights and anarchist experiments through the Beat Generation and hippies to the campaigns for the rights of women, gays and lesbians, and ethnic minorities in the late twentieth century.

Like Twain, Bret Harte was a transplanted Easterner who never quite rooted. His editing influence on Twain was profound, and his own tales of the gold country—which he began publishing in the *Overland Monthly* in 1868—remain classics of American local color. "The Outcasts of Poker Flats" and "The Luck of Roaring Camp," enormously popular when they appeared in 1869, were considered daring, even avant-garde. Harte was among the first American writers to depict prostitutes and gamblers among his characters, and his literary depictions of blizzards, gunfights, and illegitimate births were fresh and exciting. As sentimental and dated as they may seem now, the stories took the East by storm—the *Overland Monthly* sold more copies in New York City than in all the Western territories—and made Harte a very comfortable man. When he left California, it was for a contract that made him the most highly paid writer in the United States.

If Twain and Harte were the early romancers of literary and mythic visions, their work also manifested a self-critical awareness of the character of the Golden State, an ambivalence toward the dreams that beckoned others. The early California passages of *Roughing It,* for example, question and counter the airbrushed idylls of topography, climate, and primitive innocence for which the good citizens of the East and Midwest thirsted. The longer the two writers lingered, the more their doubts grew. The skeptical Twain departed in 1868 and did not return for the remaining forty years of his life. Harte both loved and hated California during his seventeen-year stay, often despairing of it as a cultural wasteland. After leaving for New York in 1871, he never communicated with anyone he left behind.

Harte's most lasting influence was as a literary adviser and editor. Acquainted with writers across the nation, he also nurtured many early California talents, including Twain, Ambrose Bierce, and Joaquin Miller. With two protégés, Charles Warren Stoddard and Ina Coolbrith (the three were termed the "Golden Gate Trinity"), Harte sought to move California literature from the infant days of bumpkin tales by the likes of John Phoenix and the rhymed doggerel that passed for poetry in the weekly papers. He included poetry in the *Golden Era* (1860–1865) and *Overland Monthly* (1868–1871), but audiences for popular verse, declaimed by such personages as Clara Dolliver and "The California Canary," clamored for the familiar. He and others with a sense of poetry as a higher art met with great hostility from poetasters and their followers. When Harte published *Outcroppings* (1866), the first anthology of California verse, it was reviled as "hogwash . . . ladled from the slop bucket."

So great was the rancor that no subsequent anthology of California poetry followed until *The Story of the Files* in 1893. Edited by Ella Sterling Mighels (author of *Little Mountain Princess*, the first novel published by a native-born Californian), it is the sole collection of nineteenth-century poetry of interest to the contemporary reader or scholar.

Ina Coolbrith, the state's first poet laureate, wrote for forty years, and her best work was collected in *Songs from the Golden Gate* (1895). She was California's first significant poet, and she mentored three generations of writers through her Sunday afternoon salons and generous efforts as writer and advocate. She created the persona of Joaquin Miller when she advised the struggling poet Cincinnatus Hiner Miller to adopt frontier buckskins—along with mustachios, a floppy hat, boots, and spurs—a pen name, and a Byronic Western image. And she advised him further to take the whole act to England, where matters Californian were all the rage. Joaquin Miller was an instant success, and his *Songs of the Sierra* (1872) was the first attempt at a Californiad, a state epic poem. Later, as a librarian in Oakland, Ina Coolbrith hand-shaped young Jack London's reading and early development.

Poetic notables after Coolbrith, Stoddard, and Miller included Edwin Markham ("Man with a Hoe" was an international socialist success); George Sterling, a prominent poet and member of the Carmel Colony, a bohemian enclave that hosted every major California writer and artist in the first decade of the twentieth century; and Yone Noguchi, a fresh Japanese voice who prefigured Beat Generation writers such as Jack Kerouac. But there was more heat than light in the early poetry, and it was half a century before Robinson Jeffers emerged with a vision, voice, and subject that were at once unique to California and international in execution and acceptance.

Two other contrasting major prose stylists came to the San Francisco Bay region in the 1870s. A world voyager, Robert Louis Stevenson remains among the premier travel writers in English. He arrived in 1879, and although his stay was brief, he left clear prints in the literature of the state. His strongest California work was based on his honeymoon of 1880. *The Silverado Squatters* (1883) is a charming tale of a marriage launched while "squatting" at an abandoned silver mine in the Napa Valley, and it wrote that region into literary being.

Writing in a darker tone, Ambrose Bierce, fresh from the Civil War, stayed for almost twenty years. Tales of psychological trauma in war, such as "An Occurrence at Owl Creek Bridge," remain classic American short stories. He pushed his interests toward the macabre and supernatural in such tales as "Moxon's Master," an early instance of science fiction, a genre that would flourish in California some years later. Bierce became an investigative reporter and a fierce opponent of the railroad monopolies. Starting in 1896, working in an unlikely alliance with William Randolph Hearst and the *San Francisco Examiner*, he wrote a series of scathing investigative articles from Washington, D.C., exposing Collis Huntington's federal tax grabs and beginning a process that led to wholesale antitrust action against the railroads.

If Bierce was outraged at the avarice and political manipulations of the railroad barons, Josiah Royce undertook a deeper analysis of the greed that seemed so quickly to have infected the state. In *California: A Study of the American Character* (1886), he examined the watershed period 1846 to 1856. His was the first sustained critical scrutiny of the roots of California culture, one that challenged the ethics behind the forming actions of the modern state: the betrayal of the Mexican founders of the great *ranchos,* the villainy of John Frémont, and the sheer voracious anarchy of the Gold Rush. The work is a landmark in California letters, introducing a mature self-critical capacity to the state's literature and public life.

While Bierce and Royce intensified the deconstruction of the California Dream, ethnic minorities still poured into the state, and the literary voices of those denied full access to visionary promises began to emerge in the 1880s. From its founding, California has been the most ethnically diverse American state, but the assimilation of the cultures that have helped define it has rarely been harmonious, thorough, or just. With the arrival of every major immigrant group, a public outcry and discriminatory legislation have followed. The culture and plight of the earliest Californians was an abiding interest for later writers, and *Life among the Piutes* (1883) by Thocmetony (Sarah Winnemucca) was the first published autobiography by an American Indian woman. The granddaughter of Paiute Chief Truckee, she had strong ties to the state, and her narrative is a personal, historical, and ethnographic account of the brutal treatment of Western Indians. California tribes had been decimated by a century of near-genocidal practices. Thocmetony, who knew this story from the inside, was the first to bring it to literary life.

Gold Rush California was a man's world, and the paucity of women—and the limits society imposed on them when they did arrive in numbers—kept early literature by women in the background. Popular magazines and newspapers grew to include abundant examples of domestic romance and lofty verse, and occasional flamboyant poetic figures like Ada Clare (dubbed "The Queen of Bohemia") and Adah Menken (a "nude" performer and poetess who scandalized San Francisco and toyed with Mark Twain and Bret Harte) enlivened an already colorful cultural scene. But it was not until the 1880s, when the female population grew sufficiently to form an artistic critical mass, that serious literature by women established itself. Mary Hallock Foote and Gértrude Atherton limned the inner and social class lives of the generations of women who were born here or immigrated well after the Forty-niners. Best known for tales set in the hardrock mines elsewhere in the West, Foote explored life in the Grass Valley foothills in the aftermath of the gold rush. Gertrude Atherton was one of California's first distinguished persons of letters, and she created a vast social history of the state in fiction. She explored class and caste in the West, from the early Russian outpost at Fort Ross on the Mendocino coast through *rancho* times in the "splendid idle" 1840s, to contemporary privileged San Francisco life in *The Californians* (1898), which focuses on the simultaneous coming of age of her heroines and the Golden State.

Much of the enduring work by women was galvanized by the status of ethnic cultures. To the great dismay of the author, Helen Hunt Jackson's *Ramona* (1884) was a wildly popular work. An activist for American Indian causes, Jackson wrote her novel to rouse national concern for the plight of the former mission Indians, much as Harriet Beecher Stowe's *Uncle Tom's Cabin* had done for African American slaves. Instead she soon found herself famous as the author of a cult romance. The doomed alliance between the mixed-blood Ramona and her Indian lover Alessandro triggered a wave of nostalgia for the halcyon days of the California missions, a theme that became a staple in the marketing of Los Angeles and the myths that helped define and develop it.

Others knew the territory more personally, as writers of color. María Amparo Ruiz de Burton, a native of Baja California, fictionalized the plights of the *Californios,* a noble founding class dismissed as "greasers," dispossessed by legal decisions, and overrun by "American" squatters. *The Squatter and the Don* (1883) was the first major work published by a Mexican American author, a primary historical thread in a proud ethnic tradition. Ruiz de Burton's novel was a vividly imagined portrait of the Mexican families who established the great *ranchos* and their decline into poverty and bitterness. As bold and finished as her work was, it imagined the last days of old Mexican culture in California as it was stifled, and it would be many decades before social conditions encouraged the rise of a new Chicana/Latina literature.

Similarly, Chinese immigrants, a crucial workforce in the mines, railroads, and fields of California as they streamed to "Gold Mountain," found themselves branded the "Yellow Peril" and made the targets of racial antagonism, riots, hangings, political demagoguery, and exclusionary laws. Edith Maud

Eaton (Sui Sin Far), half Chinese and half English, knew well the limitations she faced because of her ethnic origin and gender. Her tales and children's stories, which appeared often in national magazines, were finally collected in *Mrs. Spring Fragrance* (1912). The book dramatized the complex daily joys and sorrows of women in San Francisco's Chinatown at the dawn of the twentieth century. Her sister Winnifred Eaton, a novelist and screenwriter in Los Angeles, chose a Japanese pen name (Onoto Watanna) to deflect the virulent anti-Chinese views of the era. Together, the works of the two sisters give us the first sustained California literary vision of Eurasian and Chinese life in a Caucasian-dominated culture. The works of both Ruiz de Burton and the Eatons, lost for almost one hundred years, have been recently republished by contemporary revisionist literary scholars.

From the time Los Angeles was connected by rail to San Francisco (1876) and to the East Coast (between 1869 and 1881), the southern half of the state grew in spasms. The economy of California was founded by the railroad trusts and the big money that flowed from them, and if the southland was born on the tracks, it was weaned on wildcat land deals, the discovery of oil (more than one thousand wells in Los Angeles alone by 1900), giant water projects (the Imperial and Owens Valley projects), and—slightly later—the film and aircraft empires. Attracted by the climate and every sort of crackpot or plausible promise of freedom, wealth, and contentment, residents of the American East and Midwest streamed toward the region. Early visions of the state as a rugged and spectacular lost world took a subtropical shape in the south, and Eden was reimagined as a maze of *rancherias* and irrigated farms. The population of the once-sleepy mission and hide ranches of Pueblo de Nuestra Señora la Reina de Los Ángeles de Porciúncula grew from 50,000 in 1890 to 100,000 in 1900 and 320,000 in 1910, and Los Angeles surpassed San Francisco in population by the end of World War I.

A flourishing literary "Arroyo Movement" (named for the region's dry watercourses and encouraged by local business interests) unfolded, positing a nostalgic return to the trappings of Indian and Spanish California. The writing of Charles Fletcher Lummis, George Wharton James, and John McGroarty helped define the southwest character of the region, and the Mission Revival found broad appeal. Born with *Ramona,* and stimulated by such magazines as *Land of Sunshine,* the sentimental cult peaked with McGroarty's pageant "The Mission Play," which opened in 1912 and ran for three thousand performances to more than two million people at Mission San Gabriel. The once-foreboding desert also attracted serious literary treatment: John C. Van Dyke and Mary Austin wrote it into print in vivid, accomplished prose. What had seemed archaic, foreign, liminal, or desolate soon provided distinctive accents for Los Angeles culture and art as the region began to evolve from a Western frontier toward what would become a postmodern borderland.

For better or worse, anything and everything has been or will be tried in the southland. For every visionary and valuable creation there are a thousand frauds and scams. Such is the mixed nature of an improvisational culture, a dynamo unchecked by the restraints of history, convention, or a sense of human limits. The region has long been an inspiration for pop culture around the globe, and Southern California during this period was especially fertile ground for writers of popular fantasy. Zane Grey's cowboy melodramas, Edgar Rice Burroughs's Tarzan epics, and L. Frank Baum's beloved Oz series all reached large national audiences. All these writers at one time resided within a ten-mile radius in greater Los Angeles.

Baum first fell in love with California during flights from Chicago winters, completing much of the Wizard of Oz series at Ozcot, his Los Angeles home. His literary fortunes were tied to a succession of Oz books, and he searched everywhere, including the fractured Southern California landscape, for inspiration. In *Dorothy and the Wizard in Oz* (1908), Baum puts his heroine on a train south from San Francisco. Soon after she disembarks at a rural depot near Los Angeles, an earthquake splits the ground in front of her carriage. She plunges into the chasm, tumbling into a subterranean world both seductive and sinister. The Glass City is colored with rainbow lights from six revolving suns, and the tallest buildings are topped with menacing spires "like great spear-points." Dorothy and party of course land safely.

Inland from the cities, a California literature of nature and wilderness emerged that now energizes an international environmental movement. The majesty and terrors of the landscape have been literary motifs from Indian times to the present, but John Muir's *The Mountains of California* (1894) and Mary Austin's *The Land of Little Rain* (1903) were watershed works. These environmental classics offered founding literary treatments of two of the state's major bioregions, raised first voices in the conflicted modern discourse on the relationship between the human and the wild, and established the personal wilderness narrative as a major literary form.

Muir, a leading advocate for environment and wilderness, founded the Sierra Club and played a crucial role in the legal preservation of Yosemite and other California wilderness regions. He is the West's counterpart to Henry Thoreau, and *The Mountains of California* is the first lengthy literary depiction of the Sierra Nevada. The line of the literature of natural discovery runs from Muir through the works of Norris, Jeffers, and Steinbeck to the present. This is a body of writing that speaks to the primacy of the land as it existed before us, now shapes us, and will survive our formidable challenges.

Austin's *The Land of Little Rain* wrote the Western American desert into modern mind, but it is more than a striking regional portrait. It is a xerophytic work, the sparseness of which conceals densely interwoven relationships between wild place, gender, class, and ethnicity. She saw in the sere Mojave an informing metaphor, first for the ways in which a powerful place could channel all sentient life, including humans, and then for the ways in which an apparently desolate region could mediate between ancient spiritual truths and the urgent demands of modern "progress." And, last, it represents the power of a locale to dictate an entire literary aesthetic, from the structure of a book to the line-by-line choices of diction, image, and syntax. Mary Austin's was the first powerful American literary voice for the desert. She was a prototypical ecofeminist visionary and a cantankerous mystic—the spiritual predecessor of Edward Abbey—whose works continue to intrigue and refresh contemporary readers.

By brute will and fevered application, Jack London made himself—from the basest of origins as a reject bastard and illiterate teenage sweatshop laborer—into the country's most widely read and commercially viable writer. He was the most vital, uneven, and contradictory of California literary figures. An autodidact and a literary primitive, he saw and wrote of life as a battle, whether between a dog and the frozen Yukon, two men in a boxing ring, or a young man battling capitalism. He wrote fifty books—seven centrally concerned with California—and died at age forty, a physical ruin, near the burned-out husk of Wolf House, his beloved Sonoma estate near Glen Ellen.

London was more a teller of riveting tales than a polished artist, an internationally popular figure rather than a critical favorite. His most enduring California novels are *Martin Eden* (1908) and *The Valley of the Moon* (1913), the latter a celebration of agrarian life in the Sonoma hill country. *Martin Eden* is a bildungsroman with a tragic close, a narrative that counters the prevalent Horatio Alger fantasies of both the nation and the state. The narrator, a compressed model of the author, moves through stages of brutish Darwinian work and battle (and ensuing escape in alcohol and women), a quest for meaning in socialism, a relentless effort to pursue the writer's calling, and eventual success as a producer of literary commodities. Martin Eden leaps into the sea at the close, simultaneously acting out London's own gathering sense of the emptiness of life at the top and literary California's increasingly self-critical view of the cost and ultimate value of the Golden Dream.

The Octopus (1901) grew from Frank Norris's research in corporate offices (including those of "the octopus," the Southern Pacific Railroad Company), courts, and the towns and wheatfields of California's agricultural valleys. An admirer of Émile Zola's documentary methods, he took the Mussel Slough tragedy of May, 1880—in which six Tulare County farmers were slain by Southern Pacific agents in the company of a U.S. marshal—as the germ for a tale of the struggle between the railroad monopolies and upstart agribusiness. His muckraking technique clearly posits Shelgrim (a loose portrait of C. P. Huntington) and S. Behrman (symbolically drowned by wheat in a ship lading for India) as the villains. His heroic figures—Presley, Annixter, Vanamee, and Hilma Tree—are all redeemed in some manner. But Norris's genius transcends a romanticized account of isolated resistance in the face of greed and evil.

To be certain, *The Octopus* summarizes the major movements of nineteenth-century California literature. Norris produces a rich composite portrait of the Great Central Valley, first via a panorama of the grand sweep of valley tableland. The land—wild, harnessed, or ruined—and its relationship to people who enter it, seek to tame or coexist with it, or are swallowed up by it, have long been central in the state's literary profile. Norris vividly evokes California's heartland through vignettes of ranch society and the fields of crops that stretched for miles by 1900. But he also offers as accurate an image of the corporate greed and social turbulence of the period (and the ensuing harm to ordinary people and minority cultures) as any American writer.

Norris intended *The Octopus* as the first volume of a trilogy, "The Epic of the Wheat," a project big and complex enough to embody the soul of a big state after a half-century of existence. Volume 2, *The Pit* (1903), published shortly after he died at age thirty-two, was as far as he got. The author saw California as a great nation-within-a-nation, with both state and country in the throes of seismic shifts that seemed beyond human control. In the battle for the San Joaquin, Frank Norris saw the saga of the "huge, conglomerate West" as it hurtled into the modern age. Presley, the central character in *The Octopus*, starts as a would-be writer who burns to compose "the great poem of the West, the primeval epic of life . . . from Winnipeg to Guadalupe," insisting that it is time for a new Homer to sing the glories of a new land and people. By the end of the novel, Presley's loss of innocence represents that of the state and the nation, as what had seemed a simple narrative of good and evil is swept aside by a vision of "a vast cyclopean power," as deep and irresistible as the currents of the Pacific, sweeping California and the United States into a strange, turbulent, twentieth century.

Mary Austin, Jack London, and Frank Norris formed a trio of mature California writers who artfully engaged with the state's growth from a patchwork of frontiers to a modern entity, and their works have found enduring places in the canon of American literature. California was a wildcat colony of the American East when it emerged as a state in 1850, yet within sixty years it morphed into a dynamic Western empire. Its literature quickly grew from an exotic backwater of sourdough tales and barroom ballads through a phase of boosterism and Victorian imitation to a writing embodying the state's own distinct history, culture, and destiny. It became a literature with a growing sense of the unique themes, styles, and forms that would both depict and shape a new world as it emerged.

Samuel Clemens [Mark Twain]

1835–1910

"To think that after writing many an article a man might be excused for thinking tolerably good," Mark Twain grumbled in a letter to his mother, "that those New York people should single out a villainous back-woods sketch to compliment me on." He was writing of "The Celebrated Jumping Frog," the story that brought him fame in East and West and put California on the American literary map. Born in Hannibal, Missouri, he started in the West as a twenty-six-year-old reporter, but he invented more than he witnessed, and his California career embodied the transition from a literature of fact (as in Fages, Dame Shirley, and William Brewer) to fiction and the fully realized works of Atherton, Norris, and London. Twain's tales were central in the American local color movement, but beneath the rowdy surfaces he saw the deep conflicts that divided regions and people. Coming to the state fresh from an aborted term as a Confederate raider, he knew the horrid moral legacy of slavery that split the country; it is a central theme of Huckleberry Finn. After life on the Mississippi, Twain was always searching for another Eden, traveling from California to Hawai'i and then to the Holy Land itself. In one of his last "Letters from Hawaii" for the Sacramento Union, he saw the seeds of a Pacific Rim culture, in which California was—for once—an easternmost point: "With the China mail steamers about to throw open to her the vast trade . . . what state in the Union has so splendid a future before her as California? We have found the true Northwest Passage—the Golden Gate of San Francisco. . . . She is about to be appointed to preside over an almost exclusive trade of 450,000,000 people." It would take a hundred years and different sets of eyes to embrace the full implications of Twain's first glimpse of what was to come. Back from Hawai'i, he made one triumphant lecture tour and then left California forever in June 1868.

The Celebrated Jumping Frog of Calaveras County

In compliance with the request of a friend of mine, who wrote me from the East, I called on good-natured, garrulous old Simon Wheeler, and inquired after my friend's friend, Leonidas W. Smiley, as requested to do, and I hereunto append the result. I have a lurking suspicion that *Leonidas* W. Smiley is a myth; that my friend never knew such a personage; and that he only conjectured that if I asked old Wheeler about him, it would remind him of his infamous *Jim* Smiley, and he would go to work and bore me to death with some exasperating reminiscence of him as long and as tedious as it should be useless to me. If that was the design, it succeeded.

I found Simon Wheeler dozing comfortably by the bar-room stove of the dilapidated tavern in the decayed mining camp of Angel's, and I noticed that he was fat and bald-headed, and had an expression of winning gentleness and simplicity upon his tranquil countenance. He roused up, and gave me good day. I told him that a friend of mine had commissioned me to make some inquiries about a cherished companion of his boyhood named *Leonidas* W. Smiley—*Rev. Leonidas* W. Smiley, a young minister of the Gospel, who he had heard was at one time a resident of Angel's Camp. I added that if Mr. Wheeler could tell me anything about this Rev. Leonidas W. Smiley, I would feel under many obligations to him.

Simon Wheeler backed me into a corner and blockaded me there with his chair, and then sat down and reeled off the monotonous narrative which follows this paragraph. He never smiled, he never frowned, he never changed his voice from the gentle-flowing key to which he tuned his initial sentence, he never betrayed the slightest suspicion of enthusiasm (but all through the interminable narrative there ran a vein of impressive earnestness and sincerity, which showed me plainly that so far from his imagining that there was anything ridiculous or funny about his story, he regarded it as a really important matter, and admired its two heroes as men of transcendent genius in *finesse*). I let him go on in his own way, and never interrupted him once.

"Rev. Leonidas W. H'm, Reverend Le—well, there was a feller here once by the name of *Jim* Smiley, in the winter of '49—Or maybe it was the spring of '50—I don't recollect exactly, somehow, though what makes me think it was one or the other is because I remember the big flume warn't finished when he first come to the camp; but anyway, he was the curiousest man about always betting on anything that turned up you ever see, if he could get anybody to bet on the other side; and if he couldn't he'd change sides. Any way that suited the other man would suit *him*—any way just so's he got a bet, *he* was satisfied. But still he was lucky, uncommon lucky; he most always come out winner. He was always ready and laying for a chance; there couldn't be no solit'ry thing mentioned but that feller'd offer to bet on it, and take ary side you please, as I was just telling you. If there was a horse-race, you'd find him flush or you'd find him busted at the end of it; if there was a dogfight, he'd bet on it; if there was a cat-fight, he'd bet on it; if there was a chicken-fight, he'd bet on it; why, if there was two birds setting on a fence, he would bet you which one would fly first; or if there was a camp-meeting, he would be there reg'lar to bet on Parson Walker, which he judged to be the best exhorter about here, and so he was too, and a good man. If he even see a straddle-bug start to go anywhere, he would bet you how long it would take him to get to—to wherever he was going to, and if you took him up, he would foller that straddle-bug to Mexico but what he would find out where he was bound for and how long he was on the road. Lots of the boys here has seen that Smiley, and can tell you about him. Why, it never made no difference to *him*—he'd bet on *any* thing—the dangdest feller. Parson Walker's wife laid very sick once, for a good while, and it seemed as if they warn't going to save her; but one morning he come in, and Smiley up and asked him how she was, and he said she was considerable better—thank the Lord for his inf'nite mercy—and coming on so smart that with the blessing of Prov'dence she'd get well yet; and Smiley, before he thought, says, 'Well, I'll resk two-and-a-half she don't anyway.'

"Thish-yer Smiley had a mare—the boys called her the fifteen-minute nag, but that was only in fun, you know, because of course she was faster than that—and he used to win money on that horse, for all she was so slow and always had the asthma, or the distemper, or the consumption, or something of that kind. They used to give her two or three hundred yards' start, and then pass her under way; but always at the fag end of the race she'd get excited and desperate like, and come cavorting and straddling up, and scattering her legs around limber, sometimes in the air, and sometimes out to one side among the fences, and kicking up m-o-r-e dust and raising m-o-r-e racket with her coughing and sneezing and blowing her nose—and *always* fetch up at the stand just about a neck ahead, as near as you could cipher it down.

"And he had a little small bull-pup, that to look at him you'd think he warn't worth a cent but to set around and look ornery and lay for a chance to steal something. But as soon as money was up on him he was a different dog; his under-jaw'd begin to stick out like the fo'castle of a steamboat, and his teeth would uncover and shine like the furnaces. And a dog might tackle him and bully-rag him, and bite him, and throw him over his shoulder two or three times, and Andrew Jackson—which was the name of the pup—Andrew Jackson would never let on but what *he* was satisfied, and hadn't expected nothing else—and the bets being doubled and doubled on the other side all the time, till the money was all up; and then all of a sudden he would grab that other dog jest by the j'int of his hind leg and freeze to it—not chaw, you understand, but only just grip and hang on till they throwed up the sponge, if it was a year. Smiley always come out winner on that pup, till he harnessed a dog once that didn't have no hind legs, because they'd been sawed off in a circular saw, and when the thing had gone along far enough, and the money was all up, and he come to make a snatch for his pet holt, he see in a minute how he'd been imposed on, and how the other dog had him in the door, so to speak, and he 'peared surprised, and then he looked sorter dis-couraged-like, and didn't try no more to win the fight, and so he got shucked out bad. He give Smiley a look, as much as to say his heart was broke, and it was *his* fault, for putting up a dog that hadn't no hind legs for him to take holt of, which was his main dependence in a fight, and then he limped off a piece and laid down and died. It was a good pup, was that Andrew Jackson, and would have made a name for hisself if he'd lived, for the stuff was in him and he had genius—I know it, because he hadn't no opportunities to speak of, and it don't stand to reason that a dog could make such a fight as he could under them circumstances if he hadn't no talent. It always makes me feel sorry when I think of that last fight of his'n, and the way it turned out.

"Well, thish-yer Smiley had rat-tarriers, and chicken cocks, and tomcats and all them kind of things, till you couldn't rest, and you couldn't fetch nothing for him to bet on but he'd match you. He ketched a frog one day, and took him home, and said he cal'lated to educate him; and so he never done nothing for three months but set in his back yard and learn that frog to jump. And you bet you he *did* learn him, too. He'd give him a little punch behind, and the next minute you'd see that frog whirling in the air like a doughnut—see him turn one summerset, or maybe a couple, if he got a good start, and come down flat-footed and all right, like a cat. He got him up so in the matter of ketching flies, and kep' him in practice so constant, that he'd nail a fly every time as fur as he could see him. Smiley said all a frog wanted was education, and he could do 'most anything—and I believe him. Why, I've seen him set Dan'l Webster down here on this floor—Dan'l Webster was the name of the frog—and sing out, 'Flies, Dan'l, flies!' and quicker'n you could wink he'd spring straight up and snake a fly off'n the counter there, and flop down on the floor ag'in as solid as a gob of mud, and fall to scratching the side of his head with his hind foot as indifferent as if he hadn't no idea he'd been doin' any more'n any frog might do. You never see a frog so modest and straightfor'ard as he was, for all he was so gifted. And when it come to fair and square jumping on a dead level, he could get over more ground at one straddle than any animal of his breed you ever see. Jumping on a dead level was his strong suit, you understand; and when it come to that, Smiley would ante up money on him as long as he had a red. Smiley was monstrous proud of his frog, and well he might be, for fellers that had traveled and been everywheres all said he laid over any frog that ever *they* see.

Samuel Clemens [Mark Twain]

"Well, Smiley kep' the beast in a little lattice box, and he used to fetch him down-town sometimes and lay for a bet. One day a feller—a stranger in the camp, he was—come acrost him with his box, and says:

" 'What might it be that you've got in the box?'

"And Smiley says, sorter indifferent-like, 'It might be a parrot, or it might be a canary, maybe, but it ain't—it's only just a frog.'

"And the feller took it, and looked at it careful, and turned it round this way and that, and says, 'H'm—so 'tis. Well, what's *he* good for?'

" 'Well,' Smiley says, easy and careless, 'he's good enough for *one* thing, I should judge—he can outjump any frog in Calaveras County.'

"The feller took the box again, and took another long, particular look, and give it back to Smiley, and says, very deliberate, 'Well,' he says, 'I don't see no p'ints about that frog that's any better'n any other frog.'

" 'Maybe you don't,' Smiley says. 'Maybe you understand frogs and maybe you don't understand 'em; maybe you've had experience, and maybe you ain't only a amature, as it were. Anyways, I've got *my* opinion, and I'll resk forty dollars that he can outjump any frog in Calaveras County.'

"And the feller studied a minute, and then says, kinder sad-like, 'Well, I'm only a stranger here, and I ain't got no frog; but if I had a frog, I'd bet you.'

"And then Smiley says, 'That's all right—that's all right—if you'll hold my box a minute, I'll go and get you a frog.' And so the feller took the box, and put up his forty dollars along with Smiley's, and set down to wait.

"So he set there a good while thinking and thinking to himself, and then he got the frog out and prized his mouth open and took a teaspoon and filled him full of quail-shot—filled him pretty near up to his chin—and set him on the floor. Smiley he went to the swamp and slopped around in the mud for a long time, and finally he ketched a frog, and fetched him in, and give him to this feller, and says:

" 'Now, if you're ready, set him alongside of Dan'l, with his fore paws just even with Dan'l's, and I'll give the word.' Then he says, 'One—two—three—git!' and him and the feller touched up the frogs from behind, and the new frog hopped off lively, but Dan'l give a heave, and hysted up his shoulders—so—like a Frenchman, but it warn't no use—he couldn't budge; he was planted as solid as a church, and he couldn't no more stir than if he was anchored out. Smiley was a good deal surprised, and he was disgusted too, but he didn't have no idea what the matter was, of course.

"The feller took the money and started away; and when he was going out at the door, he sorter jerked his thumb over his shoulder—so—at Dan'l, and says again, very deliberate, 'Well,' he says, '*I* don't see no p'ints about that frog that's any better'n any other frog.'

"Smiley he stood scratching his head and looking down at Dan'l a long time, and at last he says, 'I do wonder what in the nation that frog throw'd off for—I wonder if there ain't something the matter with him—he 'pears to look mighty baggy, somehow.' And he ketched Dan'l by the nap of the neck, and hefted him, and says, 'Why blame my cats if he don't weigh five pound!' and turned him upside down and he belched out a double handful of shot. And then he see how it was, and he was the maddest man—he set the frog down and took out after that feller, but he never ketched him. And—"

[Here Simon Wheeler heard his name called from the front yard, and got up to see what was wanted.] And turning to me as he moved away, he said: "Just set where you are, stranger, and rest easy—I ain't going to be gone a second."

But, by your leave, I did not think that a continuation of the history of the enterprising vagabond *Jim* Smiley would be likely to afford me much information concerning the Rev. *Leonidas* W. Smiley, and so I started away.

At the door I met the sociable Wheeler returning, and he buttonholed me and recommenced:

"Well, thish-yer Smiley had a yaller one-eyed cow that didn't have no tail, only just a short stump like a bannanner, and—"

However, lacking both time and inclination, I did not wait to hear about the afflicted cow, but took my leave.

Chapter 56
from *Roughing It*

We rumbled over the plains and valleys, climbed the Sierras to the clouds, and looked down upon summer-clad California. And I will remark here, in passing, that all scenery in California requires *distance* to give it its highest charm. The mountains are imposing in their sublimity and their majesty of form and altitude, from any point of view—but one must have distance to soften their ruggedness and enrich their tintings; a Californian forest is best at a little distance, for there is a sad poverty of variety in species, the trees being chiefly of one monotonous family—redwood, pine, spruce, fir—and so, at a near view there is a wearisome sameness of attitude in their rigid arms, stretched downward and outward in one continued and reiterated appeal to all men to "Sh!—don't say a word!—you might disturb somebody!" Close at hand, too, there is a reliefless and relentless smell of pitch and turpentine; there is a ceaseless melancholy in their sighing and complaining foliage; one walks over a soundless carpet of beaten yellow bark and dead spines of the foliage till he feels like a wandering spirit bereft of a footfall; he tires of the endless tufts of needles and yearns for substantial, shapely leaves; he looks for moss and grass to loll upon, and finds none, for where there is no bark there is naked clay and dirt, enemies to pensive musing and clean apparel. Often a grassy plain in California, is what it should be, but often, too, it is best contemplated at a distance, because although its grass blades are tall, they stand up vindictively straight and self-sufficient, and are unsociably wide apart, with uncomely spots of barren sand between.

One of the queerest things I know of, is to hear tourists from "the States" go into ecstasies over the loveliness of "ever-blooming California." And they always do go into that sort of ecstasies. But perhaps they would modify them if they knew how old Californians, with the memory full upon them of the dust-covered and questionable summer greens of Californian "verdure," stand astonished, and filled with worshipping admiration, in the presence of the lavish richness, the brilliant green, the infinite freshness, the spend-thrift variety of form and species and foliage that make an Eastern landscape a vision of Paradise itself. The idea of a man falling into raptures over grave and sombre California, when that man has seen New England's meadow-expanses and her maples, oaks and cathedral-windowed elms decked in summer attire, or the opaline splendors of autumn descending upon her forests, comes very near being funny—would be, in fact, but that it is so pathetic. No land with an unvarying climate can be very beautiful. The tropics are not, for all the sentiment that is wasted on them. They seem beautiful at first, but sameness impairs the charm by and by. *Change* is the handmaiden Nature requires to do her miracles with. The land that has four well-defined seasons, cannot lack beauty, or pall with monotony. Each season brings a world of enjoyment and interest in the watching of its unfolding, its gradual, harmonious development, its culminating graces—and just as one begins to tire of it, it passes away and a radical change comes, with new witcheries and new glories in its train. And I think that to one in sympathy with nature, each season in its turn, seems the loveliest.

San Francisco, a truly fascinating city to live in, is stately and handsome at a fair distance, but close at hand one notes that the architecture is mostly old-fashioned, many streets are made up of decaying, smoke-grimed, wooden houses and the barren sand-hills toward the outskirts obtrude themselves too prominently. Even the kindly climate is sometimes pleasanter when read about than personally experienced, for a lovely, cloudless sky wears out its welcome by and by, and then when the longed for rain does come it *stays.* Even the playful earthquake is better contemplated at a dis—

However there are varying opinions about that.

The climate of San Francisco is mild and singularly equable. The thermometer stands at about seventy degrees the year round. It hardly changes at all. You sleep under one or two light blankets Summer and Winter, and never use a mosquito bar. Nobody ever wears Summer clothing. You wear black broadcloth—if you have it—in August and January, just the same. It is no colder, and no warmer, in the one month than the other. You do not use overcoats and you do not use fans. It is as pleasant a climate as could well be contrived, take it all around, and is doubtless the most unvarying in the whole world. The wind blows there a good deal in the Summer months, but then you can go over to Oakland, if you choose—three or four miles away—it does not blow there. It has only snowed twice in San Francisco in nineteen years, and then it only remained on the ground long enough to astonish the children, and set them to wondering what the feathery stuff was.

During eight months of the year, straight along, the skies are bright and cloudless, and never a drop of rain falls. But when the other four months come along, you will need to go and steal an umbrella. Because you will require it. Not just one day, but one hundred and twenty days in hardly varying succession. When you want to go visiting, or attend church, or the theatre, you never look up at the clouds to see whether it is likely to rain or not—you look at the almanac. If it is Winter, it will *rain*—and if it is Summer, it *won't* rain, and you cannot help it. You never need a lightning-rod, because it never thunders and it never lightens. And after you have listened for six or eight weeks, every night, to the dismal monotony of those quiet rains, you will wish in your heart the thunder *would* leap and crash and roar along those drowsy skies once, and make everything alive—you will wish the prisoned lightnings *would* cleave the dull firmament asunder and light it with a blinding glare for *one* little instant. You would give *anything* to hear the old familiar thunder again and see the lightning strike somebody. And along in the Summer, when you have suffered about four months of lustrous, pitiless sunshine, you are ready to go down on your knees and plead for rain—hail—snow—thunder and lightning—anything to break the monotony—you will take an earthquake, if you cannot do any better. And the chances are that you'll get it, too.

San Francisco is built on sand hills, but they are prolific sand hills. They yield a generous vegetation. All the rare flowers which people in "the States" rear with such patient care in parlor flower-pots and green-houses, flourish luxuriantly in the open air there all the year round. Calla lilies, all sorts of geraniums, passion flowers, moss roses—I do not know the names of a tenth part of them. I only know that while New Yorkers are burdened with banks and drifts of snow, Californians are burdened with banks and drifts of flowers, if they only keep their hands off and let them grow. And I have heard that they have also that rarest and most curious of all the flowers, the beautiful *Espiritu Santo,* as the Spaniards call it—or flower of the Holy Spirit—though I thought it grew only in Central America—down on the Isthmus. In its cup is the daintiest little facsimile of a dove, as pure as snow. The Spaniards have a superstitious reverence for it. The blossom has been conveyed to the States, submerged in ether; and the bulb has been taken thither also, but every attempt to make it bloom after it arrived, has failed.

I have elsewhere spoken of the endless Winter of Mono, California, and but this moment of the eternal Spring of San Francisco. Now if we travel a hundred miles in a straight line, we come to the eternal Summer of Sacramento. One never sees Summer-clothing or mosquitoes in San Francisco—but they can be found in Sacramento. Not always and unvaryingly, but about one hundred and forty-three months out of twelve years, perhaps. Flowers bloom there, always, the reader can easily believe—people suffer and sweat, and swear, morning, noon and night, and wear out their staunchest energies fanning themselves. It gets hot there, but if you go down to Fort Yuma you will find it hotter. Fort Yuma is probably the hottest place on earth. The thermometer stays at one hundred and twenty in the shade there all the time—except when it varies and goes higher. It is a U. S. military post, and its occupants get so used to the terrific heat that they suffer without it. There is a tradition (attributed to John Phenix*) that a very, very wicked soldier died there, once, and of course, went straight to the hottest corner of perdition,— and the next day he *telegraphed back for his blankets.* There is no doubt about the truth of this statement—there can be no doubt about it. I have seen the place where that soldier used to board. In Sacramento it is fiery Summer always, and you can gather roses, and eat strawberries and ice-cream, and wear white linen clothes, and pant and perspire, at eight or nine o'clock in the morning, and then take the cars, and at noon put on your furs and your skates, and go skimming over frozen Donner Lake, seven thousand feet above the valley, among snow banks fifteen feet deep, and in the shadow of grand mountain peaks that lift their frosty crags ten thousand feet above the level

*It has been purloined by fifty different scribblers who were too poor to invent a fancy but not ashamed to steal one.—M.T.

of the sea. There is a transition for you! Where will you find another like it in the Western hemisphere? And some of us have swept around snow-walled curves of the Pacific Railroad in that vicinity, six thousand feet above the sea, and looked down as the birds do, upon the deathless Summer of the Sacramento Valley, with its fruitful fields, its feathery foliage, its silver streams, all slumbering in the mellow haze of its enchanted atmosphere, and all infinitely softened and spiritualized by distance—a dreamy, exquisite glimpse of fairyland, made all the more charming and striking that it was caught through a forbidden gateway of ice and snow, and savage crags and precipices.

BRET HARTE

1836–1902

When Frank Harte arrived in California from New York, he came as something of a dandy. He left Oakland to prospect for gold in patent leather shoes and a city suit, and he misread backcountry justice and paid the price as managing editor of the Northern Californian in Arcata in 1859. Harte reported the truth of a murderous local ambush of an unarmed Indian camp, and he was forced to leave soon after—hurriedly—for the Bay Area. He began publishing poems, sketches, and essays, some under the name of Bret Harte, working his way into the new literary society of San Francisco. He edited Outcroppings, the first anthology of California poetry, in 1865. In 1868 Harte became editor of the Overland Monthly, the upstart journal for which he wrote stories that made him and his magazine famous. "The Luck of Roaring Camp," which came out in the second issue, made him a celebrity, and it was followed by his most colorful tale of sagebrush realism, "The Outcasts of Poker Flats." When The Luck of Roaring Camp and Other Sketches, his first (and last) major collection of tales, was published in 1870, he became a national phenomenon. After that success he was not long for California, a strange land in which he had mostly felt a stranger. Harte agreed to join the Atlantic Monthly for an unheard-of ten thousand dollars a year, and he left in early 1871, never to return. His career foundered in the East, and the vein of frontier melodrama he had worked so successfully soon seemed formulaic and old-fashioned. When his fiction and plays failed, he moved to Europe, where he spent the last twenty-five years of his life, serving briefly as U.S. consul in Prussia and Glasgow.

The Outcasts of Poker Flats

As Mr. John Oakhurst, gambler, stepped into the main street of Poker Flat on the morning of the twenty-third of November, 1850, he was conscious of a change in its moral atmosphere since the preceding night. Two or three men, conversing earnestly together, ceased as he approached, and exchanged significant glances. There was a Sabbath lull in the air, which, in a settlement unused to Sabbath influences, looked ominous.

Mr. Oakhurst's calm, handsome face betrayed small concern in these indications. Whether he was conscious of any predisposing cause, was another question. "I reckon they're after somebody," he reflected; "likely it's me." He returned to his pocket the handkerchief with which he had been whipping away the red dust of Poker Flat from his neat boots, and quietly discharged his mind of any further conjecture.

In point of fact, Poker Flat was "after somebody." It had lately suffered the loss of several thousand dollars, two valuable horses, and a prominent citizen. It was experiencing a spasm of virtuous reaction, quite as lawless and ungovernable as any of the acts that had provoked it. A secret committee had determined to rid the town of all improper persons. This was done permanently in regard of two men who were then hanging from the boughs of a sycamore in the gulch, and temporarily in the banishment of certain other objectionable characters. I regret to say that some of these were ladies. It is but due to the sex, however, to state that their impropriety was professional, and it was only in such easily established standards of evil that Poker Flat ventured to sit in judgment.

Mr. Oakhurst was right in supposing that he was included in this category. A few of the committee had urged hanging him as a possible example, and a sure method of reimbursing themselves from his pockets of the sums he had won from them. "It's agin justice," said Jim Wheeler, "to let this yer young man from Roaring Camp—an entire stranger—carry away our money." But a crude sentiment of equity residing in the breasts of those who had been fortunate enough to win from Mr. Oakhurst overruled this narrower local prejudice.

Mr. Oakhurst received his sentence with philosophic calmness, none the less coolly that he was aware of the hesitation of his judges. He was too much of a gambler not to accept Fate, with him life was at best an uncertain game, and he recognized the usual percentage in favor of the dealer.

A body of armed men accompanied the deported wickedness of Poker Flat to the outskirts of the settlement. Besides Mr. Oakhurst, who was known to be a coolly desperate man, and for whose intimidation the armed escort was intended, the expatriated party consisted of a young woman familiarly known as "The Duchess"; another, who had won the title of "Mother Shipton"; and "Uncle Billy," a suspected sluice-robber and confirmed drunkard. The cavalcade provoked no comments from the spectators, nor was any word uttered by the escort. Only, when the gulch which marked the uttermost limit of Poker Flat was reached, the leader spoke briefly and to the point. The exiles were forbidden to return at the peril of their lives.

As the escort disappeared, their pent-up feelings found vent in a few hysterical tears from the Duchess, some bad language from Mother Shipton, and a Parthian volley of expletives from Uncle Billy. The philosophic Oakhurst alone remained silent. He listened calmly to Mother Shipton's desire to cut somebody's heart out, to the repeated statements of the Duchess that she would die in the road, and to the alarming oaths that seemed to be bumped out of Uncle Billy as he rode forward. With the easy good-humor characteristic of his class, he insisted upon exchanging his own riding-horse, "Five Spot," for the sorry mule which the Duchess rode. But even this act did not draw the party into any closer sympathy. The young woman readjusted her some-what draggled plumes with a feeble, faded coquetry; Mother Shipton eyed the possessor of "Five Spot" with malevolence, and Uncle Billy included the whole party in one sweeping anathema.

The road to Sandy Bar—a camp that, not having as yet experienced the regenerating influences of Poker Flat, consequently seemed to offer some invitation to the emigrants—lay over a steep mountain range. It was distant a day's severe travel. In that advanced season, the party soon passed out of the moist, temperate regions of the foothills into the dry, cold, bracing air of the Sierras. The trail was narrow and difficult. At noon the Duchess, rolling out of her saddle upon the ground, declared her intention of going no farther, and the party halted.

The spot was singularly wild and impressive. A wooded amphitheatre, surrounded on three sides by precipitous cliffs of naked granite, sloped gently toward the crest of another precipice that overlooked the valley. It was, un-doubtedly, the most suitable spot for a camp, had camping been advisable. But Mr. Oakhurst knew that scarcely half the journey to Sandy Bar was ac-complished, and the party were not equipped or provisioned for delay. This fact he pointed out to his companions curtly, with a philosophic commentary on the folly of "throwing up their hand before the game was played out." But they were furnished with liquor, which in this emergency stood them in place of food, fuel, rest, and prescience. In spite of his remonstrances, it was not long before they were more or less under its influence. Uncle Billy passed rapidly from a bellicose state into one of stupor, the Duchess became maudlin, and Mother Shipton snored. Mr. Oakhurst alone remained erect, leaning against a rock, calmly surveying them.

Mr. Oakhurst did not drink. It interfered with a profession which required coolness, impassiveness, and presence of mind, and, in his own language, he "couldn't afford it." As he gazed at his recumbent fellow-exiles, the loneliness begotten of his pariah-trade, his habits of life, his very vices, for the first time seriously oppressed him. He bestirred himself in dusting his black clothes, washing his hands and face, and other acts characteristic of his studiously neat habits, and for a moment forgot his annoyance. The thought of deserting his weaker and more pitiable companions never perhaps occurred to him. Yet he could not help feeling the want of that excitement which, singularly enough, was most conducive to that calm equanimity for which he was notorious. He looked at the gloomy walls that rose a thousand feet sheer above the circling pines around him at the sky, ominously clouded; at the valley below, already deepening into shadow. And, doing so, suddenly he heard his own name called.

A horseman slowly ascended the trail. In the fresh, open face of the newcomer Mr. Oakhurst recognized Tom Simson, otherwise known as "The Innocent" of Sandy Bar. He had met him some months before over a "little game," and had, with perfect equanimity, won the entire fortune—amounting to some forty dollars—of that guileless youth. After the game was finished, Mr. Oakhurst drew the youthful speculator behind the door and thus addressed him: "Tommy, you're a good little man, but you can't gamble worth a cent. Don't try it over again." He then handed him his money back, pushed him gently from the room, and so made a devoted slave of Tom Simson.

There was a remembrance of this in his boyish and enthusiastic greeting of Mr. Oakhurst. He had started, he said, to go to Poker Flat to seek his fortune. "Alone?" No, not exactly alone; in fact (a giggle), he had run away with Piney Woods. Didn't Mr. Oakhurst remember Piney? She 'that used to wait on the table at the Temperance House?' They had been engaged a long time, but old Jake Woods had objected, and so they had run away, and were going to Poker Flat to be married, and here they were. And they were tired out, and how lucky it was they had found a place to camp and company. All this the Innocent delivered rapidly, while Piney, a stout, comely damsel of fifteen, emerged from behind the pine tree, where she had been blushing unseen, and rode to the side of her lover.

Mr. Oakhurst seldom troubled himself with sentiment, still less with propriety; but he had a vague idea that the situation was not fortunate. He retained, however, his presence of mind sufficiently to kick Uncle Billy, who was about to say something, and Uncle Billy was sober enough to recognize in Mr. Oakhurst's kick a superior power that would not bear trifling. He then endeavored to dissuade Tom Simson from delaying further, but in vain. He even pointed out the fact that there was no provision, nor means of making a camp. But, unluckily, the Innocent met this objection by assuring the party that he was provided with an extra mule loaded with provisions, and by the discovery of a rude attempt at a loghouse near the trail. "Piney can stay with Mrs. Oakhurst," said the Innocent, pointing to the Duchess, "and I can shift for myself."

Nothing but Mr. Oakhurst's admonishing foot saved Uncle Billy from bursting into a roar of laughter. As it was, he felt compelled to retire up the cañon until he could recover his gravity. There he confided the joke to the tall pine-trees, with many slaps of his leg, contortions of his face, and the usual profanity. But when he returned to the party, he found them seated by a fire— for the air had grown strangely chill and the sky overcast—in apparently amicable conversation. Piney was actually talking in an impulsive, girlish fashion to the Duchess, who was listening with an interest and animation she had not shown for many days. The Innocent was holding forth, apparently with equal effect, to Mr. Oakhurst and Mother Shipton, who was actually relaxing into amiability. "Is this yer a d——d picnic?" said Uncle Billy, with inward scorn, as he surveyed the sylvan group, the glancing firelight, and the tethered animals in the foreground. Suddenly an idea mingled with the alcoholic fumes that disturbed his brain. It was apparently of a jocular nature, for he felt impelled to slap his leg again and cram his fist into his mouth.

As the shadows crept slowly up the mountain, a slight breeze rocked the tops of the pine-trees, and moaned though their long and gloomy aisles. The ruined cabin, patched and covered with pine-boughs, was set apart for the ladies. As the lovers parted, they unaffectedly exchanged a kiss, so honest and sincere that it might have been heard above the swaying pines. The frail Duchess and the malevolent Mother Shipton were probably too stunned to remark upon this last evidence of simplicity, and so turned without a word to the hut. The fire was replenished, the men lay down before the door, and in a few minutes were asleep.

Mr. Oakhurst was a light sleeper. Toward morning he awoke benumbed and cold. As he stirred the dying fire, the wind, which was now blowing strongly, brought to his cheek that which caused the blood to leave it—snow!

He started to his feet with the intention of awakening the sleepers, for there was no time to lose. But turning to where Uncle Billy had been lying, he found him gone. A suspicion leaped to his brain and a curse to his lips. He ran to the spot where the mules had been tethered; they were no longer there. The tracks were already rapidly disappearing in the snow.

The momentary excitement brought Mr. Oakhurst back to the fire with his usual calm. He did not waken the sleepers. The Innocent slumbered peacefully, with a smile on his good-humored, freckled face; the virgin Piney slept beside her frailer sisters as sweetly as though attended by celestial guardians, and Mr. Oakhurst, drawing his blanket over his shoulders, stroked his mustaches and waited for the dawn. It came slowly in a whirling mist of snowflakes, that dazzled and confused the eye. What could be seen of the landscape appeared magically changed. He looked over the valley, and summed up the present and future in two words—"snowed in!"

A careful inventory of the provisions, which, fortunately for the party, had been stored within the hut, and so escaped the felonious fingers of Uncle Billy, disclosed the fact that with care and prudence they might last ten days longer. "That is," said Mr. Oakhurst, *sotto voce* to the Innocent, "if you're willing to board us. If you ain't—and perhaps you'd better not—you can wait till Uncle Billy gets back with provisions." For some occult reason, Mr. Oakhurst could not bring himself to disclose Uncle Billy's rascality, and so offered the hypothesis that he had wandered from the camp and had accidentally stampeded the animals. He dropped a warning to the Duchess and Mother Shipton, who of course knew the facts of their associate's defection. "They'll find out the truth about us *all* when they find out anything," he added, significantly, "and there's no good frightening them now."

Tom Simson not only put all his worldly store at the disposal of Mr. Oakhurst, but seemed to enjoy the prospect of their enforced seclusion. "We'll have a good camp for a week, and then the snow'll melt, and we'll all go back together." The cheerful gayety of the young man, and Mr. Oakhurst's calm infected the others. The Innocent, with the aid of pine-boughs, extemporized a thatch for the roofless cabin, and the Duchess directed Piney in the rearrangement of the interior with a taste and tact that opened the blue eyes of that provincial maiden to their fullest extent. "I reckon now you're used to fine things at Poker Flat," said Piney. The Duchess turned away sharply to conceal something that reddened her cheeks through its professional tint, and Mother Shipton requested Piney not to "chatter." But when Mr. Oakhurst returned from a weary search for the trail, he heard the sound of happy laughter echoed from the rocks. He stopped in some alarm, and his thoughts first naturally reverted to the whiskey, which he had prudently *cachéd*. "And yet it don't somehow sound like whiskey," said the gambler. It was not until he caught sight of the blazing fire through the still-blinding storm and the group around it that he settled to the conviction that it was "square fun."

Whether Mr. Oakhurst had *cachéd* his cards with the whiskey as something debarred the free access of the community, I cannot say. It was certain that, in Mother Shipton's words, he "didn't say cards once" during that evening. Haply the time was beguiled by an accordion, produced somewhat ostentatiously by Tom Simson from his pack.

Notwithstanding some difficulties attending the manipulation of this instrument, Piney Woods managed to pluck several reluctant melodies from its keys, to an accompaniment by the Innocent on a pair of bone castinets. But the crowning festivity of the evening was reached in a rude camp-meeting hymn, which the lovers, joining hands, sang with great earnestness and vociferation. I fear that a certain defiant tone and Covepanter's swing to its chorus, rather than any devotional quality, caused it speedily to infect the others, who at last joined in the refrain:—

> "I'm proud to live in the service of the Lord,
> And I'm bound to die in His army."

The pines rocked, the storm eddied and whirled above the miserable group, and the flames of their altar leaped heavenward, as if in token of the row.

At midnight the storm abated, the rolling clouds parted, and the stars glittered keenly above the sleeping camp. Mr. Oakhurst, whose professional habits had enabled him to live on the smallest possible amount of sleep, in dividing the watch with Tom Simson, somehow managed to take upon himself the greater part of that duty. He excused himself to the Innocent, by saying that he had "often been a week without sleep." "Doing what?" asked Tom. "Poker!" replied Oakhurst, sententiously; "when a man gets a streak of luck,—nigger-luck,—he don't get tired. The luck gives in first. Luck," continued the gambler, reflectively, "is a mighty queer thing. All you know about it for certain is that it's bound to change. And it's finding out when it's going to change that makes you. We've had a streak of bad luck since we left Poker Flat—you come along, and slap you get into it, too. If you can hold your cards right along you're all right. For," added the gambler, with cheerful irrelevance,

> "I'm proud to live in the service of the Lord,
> And I'm bound to die in His army."

The third day came, and the sun, looking through the white-curtained valley, saw the outcasts divide their slowly decreasing store of provisions for the morning meal. It was one of the peculiarities of that mountain climate that its rays diffused a kindly warmth over the wintry landscape, as if in regretful commiseration of the past. But it revealed drift on drift of snow piled high around the hut—a hopeless, uncharted, trackless sea of white lying below the rocky shores to which the castaways still clung. Through the marvelously clear air the smoke of the pastoral village of Poker Flat rose miles away. Mother Shipton saw it, and from a remote pinnacle of her rocky fastness, hurled in that direction a final malediction. It was her last vituperative attempt, and perhaps for that reason was invested with a certain degree of sublimity. It did her good, she privately informed the Duchess. "Just you go out there and cuss, and see." She then set herself to the task of amusing "the child," as she and the Duchess were pleased to call Piney. Piney was no chicken, but it was a soothing and original theory of the pair thus to account for the fact that she didn't swear and wasn't improper.

When night crept up again through the gorges, the reedy notes of the accordion rose and fell in fitful spasms and long-drawn gasps by the flickering camp-fire. But music failed to fill entirely the aching void left by insufficient food, and a new diversion was proposed by Piney—story-telling. Neither Mr. Oakhurst nor his female companions caring to relate their personal experiences, this plan would have failed, too, but for the Innocent. Some months before he had chanced upon a stray copy of Mr. Pope's ingenious translation of the *Iliad*. He now proposed to narrate the principal incidents of that poem—having thoroughly mastered the argument and fairly forgotten the words—in the current vernacular of Sandy Bar. And so for the rest of that night the Homeric demigods again walked the earth. Trojan bully and wily Greek wrestled in the winds; and the great pines in the cañon seemed to bow to the wrath of the son of Peleus. Mr. Oakhurst listened with quiet satisfaction. Most especially was he interested in the fate of "Ash-heels," as the Innocent persisted in denominating the "swift-footed Achilles."

So with small food and much of Homer and the accordion, a week passed over the heads of the outcasts. The sun again forsook them, and again from leaden skies the snow-flakes were sifted over the land. Day by day closer around them drew the snowy circle, until at last they looked from their prison over drifted walls of dazzling white, that towered twenty feet above their heads. It became more and more difficult to replenish their fires, even from the fallen trees beside them, now half hidden in the drifts. And yet no one complained. The lovers turned from the dreary prospect and looked into each other's eyes, and were happy. Mr. Oakhurst settled himself coolly to the losing game before him. The Duchess, more cheerful than she had been, assumed the care of Piney. Only Mother Shipton—once the strongest of the party—seemed to sicken and fade. At midnight on the tenth day she called Oakhurst to her side. "I'm going," she said, in a voice of querulous weakness, "but don't say anything about it. Don't waken the kids. Take the bundle from under my head and open it." Mr. Oakhurst did so. It contained Mother Shipton's rations for the last week, untouched. "Give 'em to the child," she said, pointing to the sleeping Piney. "You've starved yourself," said the gambler. "That's what they call it," said the woman, querulously, as she lay down again, and, turning her face to the wall, passed quietly away.

The accordion and the bones were put aside that day, and Homer was forgotten. When the body of Mother Shipton had been committed to the snow, Mr. Oakhurst took the Innocent aside, and showed him a pair of snow-shoes, which he had fashioned from the old pack-saddle. "There's one chance in a hundred to save her yet," he said, pointing to Piney; "but it's there," he added, pointing toward Poker Flat. "If you can reach there in two days she's safe." "And you?" asked Tom Simson. "I'll stay here," was the curt reply.

The lovers parted with a long embrace. "You are not going, too?" said the Duchess, as she saw Mr. Oakhurst apparently waiting to accompany him. "As far as the cañon," he replied. He turned suddenly, and kissed the Duchess, leaving her pallid face aflame, and her trembling limbs rigid with amazement.

Night came, but not Mr. Oakhurst. It brought the storm again and the whirling snow. Then the Duchess, feeding the fire, found that some one had quietly piled beside the hut enough fuel to last a few days longer. The tears rose to her eyes, but she hid them from Piney.

The women slept but little. In the morning, looking into each other's faces, they read their fate. Neither spoke; but Piney, accepting the position of the stronger, drew near and placed her arm around the Duchess's waist. They kept this attitude for the rest of the day. That night the storm reached its greatest fury, and, rending asunder the protecting pines, invaded the very hut.

Toward morning they found themselves unable to feed the fire, which gradually died away. As the embers slowly blackened, the Duchess crept closer to Piney, and broke the silence of many hours: "Piney, can you pray?" "No, dear," said Piney, simply. The Duchess, without knowing exactly why, felt relieved, and, putting her head upon Piney's shoulder, spoke no more. And so reclining, the younger and purer pillowing the head of her soiled sister upon her virgin breast, they fell asleep.

The wind lulled as if it feared to waken them. Feathery drifts of snow, shaken from the long pine-boughs, flew like white-winged birds, and settled about them as they slept. The moon through the rifted clouds looked down upon what had been the camp. But all human stain, all trace of earthly travail, was hidden beneath the spotless mantle mercifully flung from above.

They slept all that day and the next, nor did they waken when voices and footsteps broke the silence of the camp. And when pitying fingers brushed the snow from their wan faces, you could scarcely have told from the equal peace that dwelt upon them, which was she that had sinned. Even the law of Poker Flat recognized this, and turned away, leaving them still locked in each other's arms.

But at the head of the gulch, on one of the largest pine-trees, they found the deuce of clubs pinned to the bark with a bowie-knife. It bore the following, written in pencil, in a firm hand:—

Beneath This Tree
Lies the Body
of
JOHN OAKHURST
Who Struck A Streak of Bad Luck
on the 23d of November, 1850,
and
Handed in his Checks
on the 7th December, 1850.

And pulseless and cold, with a Derringer by his side and a bullet in his heart, though still calm as in life, beneath the snow lay he who was at once the strongest and yet the weakest of the outcasts of Poker Flat.

CHARLES WARREN STODDARD
1843–1909

Charles Warren Stoddard came to San Francisco in 1855 from Rochester, New York, and his first literary endeavors were verses under the pseudonym of "Pip Pepperpod." With the publication of Poems *(1867), he became San Francisco's unofficial poet laureate and an exemplar of elegant, slightly decadent bohemianism, affecting, in Kevin Starr's words, "Chopin at twilight, Oriental bric-a-brac, incense, lounging robes, and fragrant cigarettes." He joined Bret Harte and Ina Coolbrith to edit the* Overland Monthly *in 1868 and became one of the city's most famous figures in the "golden era" of California literature. Stoddard was an inveterate traveler and a genteel connoisseur of exotic old and new Edens. While mystery shrouds his sojourns in Hawai'i and the homoerotic relationships he may have had there, there is no doubt that the Sandwich Islands released him from the social conventions of the age. He introduced Robert Louis Stevenson to the pleasures of the South Seas, and he was much taken with the nostalgic romanticism of the California missions, drawing on his reveries in such works as* In the Footsteps of the Padres *(1902). A talented editor and literary mentor, and a central figure in the making of literary San Francisco, Stoddard was nevertheless derivative and highblown in his poetry. His occasional essays and travel writing, however, have received increasing attention from appreciative modern scholars.*

Old Monterey

Sleep on in thy sunny sand-dunes and slumber in thy byways;
  In the hollow of thy drowsy hills, lo! sleep and the shadow of death.
Dream on, O dear enchantress, of the babel that filled thy highways,
  When passionate throngs sang thy song of songs and a war-cry was thy breath.

Now in thy listless languor, lo! the encircling sea-mew—
  Gulls in the wild sea-gardens; and the curve of the lateen sail
As it cleaves like a silver scimitar the mist of the sea; and dream you
  Of the treasure vast and the glory past—the visions of no avail.

Dream of the splendid trappings of the troops that met and mingled—
  Mexican cavaleros and hidalgos of old Castile:

Hark to the music of the spurs of silver that jolted and jingled;
  And loudly laugh, as the wine you quaff, at the past beyond appeal.

Where are they now, O dreamer? thy treasures have vanished whither?
  Thou who wast first to the headland-front and Queen of the western sea:
Long have I watched and have waited and have wandered hither and thither
  Asking a word with a voice unheard and now I would ask it of thee.

The bitter tang of the sea is ours and the winds forever roaming;
  The fleecy crest of the breaking wave and the ribbons of streaming kelp;
The fishers mending their nets in the sun, and the crickets in the gloaming,
  And the seal's gruff bark, in the dew and the dark, and the whine of her
    hungry whelp.

The wind and the wave pour over the rocks that are barren and bony;
  Like ghosts of avalanches the fog sweeps down from the heights:
The star-fish sprawl in the briny meadows; the abalone
  Hides, where it lies, its rainbow dyes in a dome of dim delights.

There is spice of the pine in plenty and oak and the cypress tangle;
  And the bleaching bones of the strand whale, and sea-shells near and far—
No soft refrain of old, old Spain, or voices in musical wrangle;
  Nor the click of the clashing castanets nor the throb of the hushed guitar.

There is never a day in the year but tells of thy glory gone forever,
  And never a dusk that hovers near in the sea-shell pink of the sky,
But we sit in the chill adobe shade with hearts that are past endeavor—
  While the mists unfurl like the gates of pearl, as we watch the daylight die.

INA COOLBRITH

1841–1928

Born in Nauvoo, Illinois, the niece of the Mormon founder Joseph Smith, Josephine Donna Smith spent her early California days in Los Angeles. She assumed the name Ina Donna Coolbrith on moving to San Francisco in 1862. Her poetry was soon published in Eastern journals such as Harper's Weekly and Century, and in 1868 Bret Harte named her—with Charles Warren Stoddard—coeditor of the Overland Monthly. Under the leadership of the "Golden Gate Trinity," that journal soon became a rival to the reigning Atlantic. From 1865 on, Coolbrith conducted literary salons in San Francisco during which she met and encouraged most of the literary figures of the period, including Joaquin Miller. While her literary fortunes thrived, her personal life was marked by loss and turmoil, and a constant theme in her poetry was the contrast between the idyllic and lofty world of nature and the harsh realities of human life. Faced with the need to support a niece and nephew (as well as Joaquin Miller's abandoned daughter Cali-Shasta), she became a librarian in Oakland in 1873, a position she held for eighteen years. She continued to serve as a literary mentor and had a major influence on the young Jack London. She was named the state's first poet laureate in 1915, the first such honor to be bestowed in the United States. Coolbrith's poetry was conventional; her major collection was Songs of the Golden Gate (1895). In Oakley Hall's novel Separations (1997), a roman à clef set in San Francisco around 1870, Ina Coolbrith, Charles Warren Stoddard, Joaquin Miller, and Clarence King figure centrally in a vivid fictional glimpse of the era.

Copa de Oro (The California Poppy)

Thy satin vesture richer is than looms
   Of Orient weave for raiment of her kings!
   Not dyes of olden Tyre, not precious things
Regathered from the long-forgotten tombs
Of buried empires, not the iris plumes
   That wave upon the tropics' myriad wings,
   Not all proud Sheba's queenly offerings,
Could match the golden marvel of thy blooms.
For thou art nurtured from the treasure-veins
   Of this fair land: thy golden rootlets sup

Her sands of gold—of gold thy petals spun.
Her golden glory, thou! on hills and plains,
  Lifting, exultant, every kingly cup
    Brimmed with the golden vintage of the sun.

The Mariposa Lily

Insect or blossom? Fragile, fairy thing,
Poised upon slender tip, and quivering
  To flight! a flower of the fields of air;
  A jeweled moth; a butterfly, with rare
And tender tints upon his downy wing
  A moment resting in our happy sight;
  A flower held captive by a thread so slight
Its petal-wings of broidered gossamer
Are, light as the wind, with every wind astir,—
  Wafting sweet odor, faint and exquisite.
O dainty nursling of the field and sky,
  What fairer thing looks up to heaven's blue
  And drinks the noontide sun, the dawning's dew?
Thou wingëd bloom! thou blossom-butterfly!

Millennium

The night falls, heavy with the coming storm!
  Far out, the ocean frets against the bar,
And the cloud-legions, gathering force and form,
  Shut, with closed ranks, all gleam of moon or star.
Tempestuous darkness! and unto the dawn,
  Long hours. Ah! with the passing will there be
The gold and crimson by the sun-rays drawn,
  Or tempest still, and moaning of the sea?

The world is heavy with the coming storm!
  No nation wars with nation, race with race,
But where the love-pulse should beat quick and warm,
  Lo! brother against brother, face to face.
Abel unto the god of blood gives blood,
  Who heeds not the fair fruitage of the land,

And wrong and rage, of viper-nests the brood,
    Arm Cain with flaming heart and flaming brand.

Where is the peace that should with thee abide
    O Earth? Art still beneath the primal ban,
Availing naught the Holy Crucified?
    No faith in God because no faith in man!
Thy helpless idols help thee not—Awake!
    Arise, and let thy weary burden fall!
Captive, the fetters of the ages break,
    And, thrall to Mammon, be no longer thrall.

O Spirit of the Holy One, from where
    On high Thou dwellest, lend Thy loving will
To quell these battle-giants of the air,
    And to the warring waters speak, "Be still."
Or if from darkness, only, springs the light,
    And but from struggle blessëd peace is born,
Loose all the awful thunders of Thy might—
    And hail, the night! that heralds the glad morn.

Retrospect

(In Los Angeles)

A breath of balm—of orange bloom!
    By what strange fancy wafted me,
Through the lone starlight of the room?
    And suddenly I seem to see

The long, low vale, with tawny edge
    Of bills, within the sunset glow;
Cool vine-rows through the cactus hedge,
    And fluttering gleams of orchard snow.

Far off, the slender line of white
    Against the blue of ocean's crest;
The slow sun sinking into night,
    A quivering opal in the west.

Somewhere a stream sings, far away;
    Somewhere from out the hidden groves,

And dreamy as the dying day,
    Comes the soft coo of mourning doves.

One moment all the world is peace!
    The years like clouds are rolled away,
And I am on those sunny leas,
    A child, amid the flowers at play.

Ina Coolbrith

Joaquin Miller
1837?–1913

Cincinnatus Hiner Miller was born in Indiana and came west in a covered wagon. He was a vivid character well before he arrived in California. An Oregon teacher, lawyer, journalist, miner, Pony Express rider, and horse thief, he alternately lived with and fought Indians, and he brought Cali-Shasta—his daughter by an Indian woman—with him when he arrived in 1869. These experiences are embellished on in the freewheeling account Life amongst the Modocs (1873). In San Francisco he came under the influence of Bret Harte, Charles Warren Stoddard, and Ina Coolbrith, and under her tutelage renamed himself after the legendary Joaquín Murieta, had a fanciful buckskin outfit tailored to wear "onstage," and moved to London to effect his literary transformation to a Western bard. His swaggering persona and declamatory Songs of the Sierras (1872) enthralled the English Pre-Raphaelites, who dubbed him "the Byron of the West." He returned to California in 1886 to build a wonderful and eccentric estate in the Oakland hills that he named—in his inventive spelling—"The Hights." Advocating free love, abundant wine, and other bohemian pleasures, he reigned from that perch as a colorful holdover from the frontier Old West, entertaining many literary visitors (including Hamlin Garland, George Sterling, and Yone Noguchi, fresh from Japan) and curiosity-seekers. Joaquin Miller was one of numerous early California writers to live a version of the California Dream, and while he was long dismissed as a kind of crackpot literary Emperor Norton, William Everson focused on Miller in his landmark Archetype West (1976), and he has been regarded seriously since.

"Californian"
from *Songs of the Sierra*

I stand beside the mobile sea;
And sails are spread, and sails are furl'd
From farthest corners of the world,
And fold like white wings wearily.
Steamships go up, and some go down
In haste, like traders in a town,
And seem to see and beckon all.
Afar at sea some white shapes flee,

With arms stretch'd like a ghost's to me,
And cloud-like sails far blown and curl'd,
Then glide down to the under-world.
As if blown bare in winter blasts
Of leaf and limb, tall naked masts
Are rising from the restless sea,
So still and desolate and tall,
I seem to see them gleam and shine
With clinging drops of dripping brine.
Broad still brown wings flit here and there,
Thin sea-blue wings wheel everywhere,
And white wings whistle through the air:
I hear a thousand sea-gulls call.

   Behold the ocean on the beach
Kneel lowly down as if in prayer.
I hear a moan as of despair,
While far at sea do toss and reach
Some things so like white pleading hands.
The ocean's thin and hoary hair
Is trail'd along the silver'd sands,
At every sigh and sounding moan.
'Tis not a place for mirthfulness,
But meditation deep, and prayer,
And kneelings on the salted sod,
Where man must own his littleness
And know the mightiness of God.
The very birds shriek in distress
And sound the ocean's monotone.

   Dared I but say a prophecy,
As sang the holy men of old,
Of rock-built cities yet to be
Along these sliming shores of gold,
Crowding athirst into the sea,
What wondrous marvels might be told!
Enough, to know that empire here
Shall burn her loftiest, brightest star;
Here art and eloquence shall reign,

Joaquin Miller

As o'er the wolf-rear'd realm of old;
Here learn'd and famous from afar,
To pay their noble court, shall come,
And shall not seek or see in vain,
But look on all with wonder dumb.

Afar the bright Sierras lie
A swaying line of snowy white,
A fringe of heaven hung in sight
Against the blue base of the sky.

I look along each gaping gorge,
I hear a thousand sounding strokes
Like giants rending giant oaks,
Or brawny Vulcan at his forge;
I see pick-axes flash and shine
And great wheels whirling in a mine.
Here winds a thick and yellow thread,
A moss'd and silver stream instead;
And trout that leap'd its rippled tide
Have turn'd upon their sides and died.

Lo! when the last pick in the mine
Is rusting red with idleness,
And rot yon cabins in the mould,
And wheels no more croak in distress,
And tall pines reassert command,
Sweet bards along this sunset shore
Their mellow melodies will pour;
Will charm as charmers very wise,
Will strike the harp with master hand,
Will sound unto the vaulted skies
The valor of these men of old—
The mighty men of 'Forty-nine;
Will sweetly sing and proudly say,
Long, long agone there was a day
When there were giants in the land.

AMBROSE BIERCE
1842–1914?

Born in Ohio and reared in Indiana, Ambrose Bierce came to California after the Civil War and stayed almost twenty years. In his California works we hear three different voices. First there is the master of tales of psychological trauma in war, depicted in such classic short stories as "Chickamauga" and "An Occurrence at Owl Creek Bridge." Bierce later extended his psychological interests to the supernatural and the macabre in stories such as "Moxon's Master." The second Bierce was a darkly comic satirist, a vitriolic essayist, and dreaded reviewer. At his height, as in his 1877 pseudonymous Dance of Death *(an "attack" on the waltz as satanic, one of the great literary hoaxes in the nineteenth century) and* The Devil's Dictionary *(1906), he was a major American satirist. The third Bierce was the investigative reporter who traveled to Washington, D.C., to expose railroad corruption. Ambrose Bierce never returned to California. He remained in the East, and his vision grew so cynical that he dismissed the California Dream and all of humanity as folly. He drifted south to tour Civil War battlefields and disappeared in 1914, apparently crossing the border into Mexico to join the Mexican revolution. This mysterious and bitter figure has been the frequent subject of novels, most recently* The Old Gringo *by Carlos Fuentes (1985) and* Ambrose Bierce and the Queen of Spades *by Oakley Hall (1998).*

Moxon's Master

"Are you serious?—do you really believe that a machine thinks?" I got no immediate reply; Moxon was apparently intent upon the coals in the grate, touching them deftly here and there with the fire-poker till they signified a sense of his attention by a brighter glow. For several weeks I had been observing in him a growing habit of delay in answering even the most trivial of commonplace questions. His air, however, was that of preoccupation rather than deliberation: one might have said that he had "something on his mind."

Presently he said:

"What is a 'machine'? The word has been variously defined. Here is one definition from a popular dictionary: 'Any instrument or organization by which power is applied and made effective, or a desired effect produced.' Well, then, is not a man a machine? And you will admit that he thinks—or thinks he thinks."

"If you do not wish to answer my question," I said, rather testily, "why not say so?—all that you say is mere evasion. You know well enough that when I say 'machine' I do not mean a man, but something that man has made and controls."

"When it does not control him," he said, rising abruptly and looking out of a window, whence nothing was visible in the blackness of a stormy night. A moment later he turned about and with a smile said: "I beg your pardon; I had no thought of evasion. I considered the dictionary man's unconscious testimony suggestive and worth something in the discussion. I can give your question a direct answer easily enough: I do believe that a machine thinks about the work that it is doing."

That was direct enough, certainly. It was not altogether pleasing, for it tended to confirm a sad suspicion that Moxon's devotion to study and work in his machine-shop had not been good for him. I knew, for one thing, that he suffered from insomnia, and that is no light affliction. Had it affected his mind? His reply to my question seemed to me then evidence that it had; perhaps I should think differently about it now. I was younger then, and among the blessings that are not denied to youth is ignorance. Incited by that great stimulant to controversy, I said:

"And what, pray, does it think with—in the absence of a brain?"

The reply, coming with less than his customary delay, took his favorite form of counter-interrogation:

"With what does a plant think—in the absence of a brain?"

"Ah, plants also belong to the philosopher class! I should be pleased to know some of their conclusions; you may omit the premises."

"Perhaps," he replied, apparently unaffected by my foolish irony, "you may be able to infer their convictions from their acts. I will spare you the familiar examples of the sensitive mimosa, the several insectivorous flowers and those whose stamens bend down and shake their pollen upon the entering bee in order that he may fertilize their distant mates. But observe this. In an open spot in my garden I planted a climbing vine. When it was barely above the surface I set a stake into the soil a yard away. The vine at once made for it, but as it was about to reach it after several days I removed it a few feet. The vine at once altered its course, making an acute angle, and again made for the stake. This manoeuvre was repeated several times, but finally, as if discouraged, the vine abandoned the pursuit and ignoring further attempts to divert it traveled to a small tree, further away, which it climbed.

"Roots of the eucalyptus will prolong themselves incredibly in search of moisture. A well-known horticulturist relates that one entered an old drain pipe and followed it until it came to a break, where a section of the pipe had been removed to make way for a stone wall that had been built across its course. The root left the drain and followed the wall until it found an opening where a stone had fallen out. It crept through and following the other side of the wall back to the drain, entered the unexplored part and resumed its journey."

"And all this?"

"Can you miss the significance of it? It shows the consciousness of plants. It proves that they think."

"Even if it did—what then? We were speaking, not of plants, but of machines. They may be composed partly of wood—wood that has no longer vitality—or wholly of metal. Is thought an attribute also of the mineral kingdom?"

"How else do you explain the phenomena, for example, of crystallization?"

"I do not explain them."

"Because you cannot without affirming what you wish to deny, namely, intelligent cooperation among the constituent elements of the crystals. When soldiers form lines, or hollow squares, you call it reason. When wild geese in flight take the form of a letter V you say instinct. When the homogeneous atoms of a mineral, moving freely in solution, arrange themselves into shapes mathematically perfect, or particles of frozen moisture into the symmetrical and beautiful forms of snowflakes, you have nothing to say. You have not even invented a name to conceal your heroic unreason."

Moxon was speaking with unusual animation and earnestness. As he paused I heard in an adjoining room known to me as his "machineshop," which no one but himself was permitted to enter, a singular thumping sound, as of some one pounding upon a table with an open hand. Moxon heard it at the same moment and, visibly agitated, rose and hurriedly passed into the room whence it came. I thought it odd that any one else should be in there, and my interest in my friend—with doubtless a touch of unwarrantable curiosity—led me to listen intently, though, I am happy to say, not at the keyhole. There were confused sounds, as of a struggle or scuffle; the floor shook. I distinctly heard hard breathing and a hoarse whisper which said "Damn you!" Then all was silent, and presently Moxon reappeared and said, with a rather sorry smile:

"Pardon me for leaving you so abruptly. I have a machine in there that lost its temper and cut up rough."

Fixing my eyes steadily upon his left cheek, which was traversed by four parallel excoriations showing blood, I said:

"How would it do to trim its nails?"

I could have spared myself the jest; he gave it no attention, but seated himself in the chair that he had left and resumed the interrupted monologue as if nothing had occurred:

"Doubtless you do not hold with those (I need not name them to a man of your reading) who have taught that all matter is sentient, that every atom is a living, feeling, conscious being. *I* do. There is no such thing as dead, inert matter: it is all alive; all instinct with force, actual and potential; all sensitive to the same forces in its environment and susceptible to the contagion of higher and subtler ones residing in such superior organisms as it may be brought into relation with, as those of man when he is fashioning it into an instrument of his will. It absorbs something of his intelligence and purpose—more of them in proportion to the complexity of the resulting machine and that of its work.

"Do you happen to recall Herbert Spencer's definition of 'Life'? I read it thirty years ago. He may have altered it afterward, for anything I know, but in all that time I have been unable to think of a single word that could profitably be changed or added or removed. It seems to me not only the best definition, but the only possible one.

" 'Life,' he says, 'is a definite combination of heterogeneous changes, both simultaneous and successive, in correspondence with external co-existences and sequences.' "

"That defines the phenomenon," I said, "but gives no hint of its cause."

"That," he replied, "is all that any definition can do. As Mill points out, we know nothing of cause except as an antecedent—nothing of effect except as a consequent. Of certain phenomena, one never occurs without another, which is dissimilar: the first in point of time we call cause, the second, effect. One who had many times seen a rabbit pursued by a dog, and had never seen rabbits and dogs otherwise, would think the rabbit the cause of the dog.

"But I fear," he added, laughing naturally enough, "that my rabbit is leading me a long way from the track of my legitimate quarry: I'm indulging in the pleasure of the chase for its own sake. What I want you to observe is that in Herbert Spencer's definition of 'life' the activity of a machine is included—there is nothing in the definition that is not applicable to it. According to this sharpest of observers and deepest of thinkers, if a man during his period of activity is alive, so is a machine when in operation. As an inventor and constructor of machines I know that to be true."

Moxon was silent for a long time, gazing absently into the fire. It was growing late and I thought it time to be going, but somehow I did not like the notion of leaving him in that isolated house, all alone except for the presence of some person of whose nature my conjectures could go no further than that it was unfriendly, perhaps malign. Leaning toward him and looking earnestly into his eyes while making a motion with my hand through the door of his workshop, I said:

"Moxon, whom have you in there?"

Somewhat to my surprise he laughed lightly and answered without hesitation:

"Nobody; the incident that you have in mind was caused by my folly in leaving a machine in action with nothing to act upon, while I undertook the interminable task of enlightening your understanding. Do you happen to know that Consciousness is the creature of Rhythm?"

"O bother them both!" I replied, rising and laying hold of my overcoat. "I'm going to wish you good night; and I'll add the hope that the machine which you inadvertently left in action will have her gloves on the next time you think it needful to stop her."

Without waiting to observe the effect of my shot I left the house.

Rain was falling, and the darkness was intense. In the sky beyond the crest of a hill toward which I groped my way along precarious plank sidewalks and across miry, unpaved streets I could see the faint glow of the city's lights, but behind me nothing was visible but a single window of Moxon's house. It glowed with what seemed to me a mysterious and fateful meaning. I knew it was an uncurtained aperture in my friend's "machine-shop," and I had little doubt that he had resumed the studies interrupted by his duties as my instructor in mechanical consciousness and the fatherhood of Rhythm. Odd, and in some degree humorous, as his convictions seemed to me at that time, I could not wholly divest myself of the feeling that they had some tragic relation to his life and character—perhaps to his destiny—although I no longer entertained the notion that they were the vagaries of a disordered mind. Whatever might be thought of his views, his exposition of them was too logical for that. Over and over, his last words came back to me: "Consciousness is the creature of Rhythm." Bald and terse as the statement was, I now found it infinitely alluring. At each recurrence it broadened in meaning and deepened in suggestion. Why, here, (I thought) is something upon which to found a philosophy. If consciousness is the product of rhythm all things *are* conscious, for all have motion, and all motion is rhythmic. I wondered if Moxon knew the significance and breadth of his thought—the scope of this momentous generalization; or had he arrived at his philosophic faith by the tortuous and uncertain road of observation?

That faith was then new to me, and all Moxon's expounding had failed to make me a convert; but now it seemed as if a great light shone about me, like that which fell upon Saul of Tarsus; and out there in the storm and darkness and solitude I experienced what Lewes calls "the endless variety and excitement of philosophic thought." I exulted in a new sense of knowledge, a new pride of reason. My feet seemed hardly to touch the earth; it was as if I were uplifted and borne through the air by invisible wings.

Yielding to an impulse to seek further light from him whom I now recognized as my master and guide, I had unconsciously turned about, and almost before I was aware of having done so found myself again at Moxon's door. I was drenched with rain, but felt no discomfort. Unable in my excitement to find the doorbell I instinctively tried the knob. It turned and, entering, I mounted the stairs to the room that I had so recently left. All was dark and silent; Moxon, as I had supposed, was in the adjoining room—the "machine-shop." Groping along the wall until I found the communicating door I knocked loudly several times, but got no response, which I attributed to the uproar outside, for the wind was blowing a gale and dashing the rain against the thin walls in sheets. The drumming upon the shingle roof spanning the unceiled room was loud and incessant.

I had never been invited into the machine-shop—had, indeed, been denied admittance, as had all others, with one exception, a skilled metal worker, of whom no one knew anything except that his name was Haley and his habit silence. But in my spiritual exaltation, discretion and civility were alike forgotten and I opened the door. What I saw took all philosophical speculation out of me in short order.

Moxon sat facing me at the farther side of a small table upon which a single candle made all the light that was in the room. Opposite him, his back toward me, sat another person. On the table between the two was a chessboard; the men were playing. I knew little of chess, but as only a few pieces were on the board it was obvious that the game was near its close. Moxon was intensely interested—not so much, it seemed to me, in the game as in his antagonist, upon whom he had fixed so intent a look that, standing though I did directly in the line of his vision, I was altogether unobserved. His face was ghastly white, and his eyes glittered like diamonds. Of his antagonist I had only a back view, but that was sufficient; I should not have cared to see his face.

He was apparently not more than five feet in height, with proportions suggesting those of a gorilla—a tremendous breadth of shoulders, thick, short neck and broad, squat head, which had a tangled growth of black hair and was topped with a crimson fez. A tunic of the same color, belted tightly to the waist, reached the seat—apparently a box—upon which he sat; his legs and feet were not seen. His left forearm appeared to rest in his lap; he moved his pieces with his right hand, which seemed disproportionately long.

I had shrunk back and now stood a little to one side of the doorway and in shadow. If Moxon had looked farther than the face of his opponent he could have observed nothing now, except that the door was open. Something forbade me either to enter or to retire, a feeling—I know not how it came—that I was in the presence of an imminent tragedy and might serve my friend by remaining. With a scarcely conscious rebellion against the indelicacy of the act I remained.

The play was rapid. Moxon hardly glanced at the board before making his moves, and to my unskilled eye seemed to move the piece most convenient to his hand, his motions in doing so being quick, nervous and lacking in precision. The response of his antagonist, while equally prompt in the inception, was made with a slow, uniform, mechanical and, I thought, somewhat theatrical movement of the arm, that was a sore trial to my patience. There was something unearthly about it all, and I caught myself shuddering. But I was wet and cold.

Two or three times after moving a piece the stranger slightly inclined his head, and each time I observed that Moxon shifted his king. All at once the thought came to me that the man was dumb. And then that he was a machine—an automaton chess-player! Then I remembered that Moxon had once spoken to me of having invented such a piece of mechanism, though I did not understand that it had actually been constructed. Was all his talk about the consciousness and intelligence of machines merely a prelude to eventual exhibition of this device—only a trick to intensify the effect of its mechanical action upon me in my ignorance of its secret?

A fine end, this, of all my intellectual transports—my "endless variety and excitement of philosophic thought!" I was about to retire in disgust when something occurred to hold my curiosity. I observed a shrug of the thing's great shoulders, as if it were irritated: and so natural was this—so entirely human—that in my new view of the matter it startled me. Nor was that all, for a moment later it struck the table sharply with its clenched hand. At that gesture Moxon seemed even more startled than I: he pushed his chair a little backward, as in alarm.

Presently Moxon, whose play it was, raised his hand high above the board, pounced upon one of his pieces like a sparrow-hawk and with the exclamation "checkmate!" rose quickly to his feet and stepped behind his chair. The automaton sat motionless.

The wind had now gone down, but I heard, at lessening intervals and progressively louder, the rumble and roll of thunder. In the pauses between I now became conscious of a low humming or buzzing which, like the thunder, grew momentarily louder and more distinct. It seemed to come from the body of the automaton, and was unmistakably a whirring of wheels. It gave me the impression of a disordered mechanism which had escaped the repressive and regulating action of some controlling part—an effect such as might be expected if a pawl should be jostled from the teeth of a ratchet-wheel. But before I had time for much conjecture as to its nature my attention was taken by the strange motions of the automaton itself. A slight but continuous convulsion appeared to have possession of it. In body and head it shook like a man with palsy or an ague chill, and the motion augmented every moment until the entire figure was in violent agitation. Suddenly it sprang to its feet and with a movement almost too quick for the eye to follow shot forward across table and chair, with both arms thrust forth to their full length—the posture and lunge of a diver. Moxon tried to throw himself backward out of reach, but he was too late: I saw the horrible thing's hands close upon his throat, his own clutch its wrists. Then the table was overturned, the candle thrown to the floor and extinguished, and all was black dark. But the noise of the struggle was dreadfully distinct, and most terrible of all were the raucous, squawking sounds made by the strangled man's efforts to breathe. Guided by the infernal hubbub, I sprang to the rescue of my friend, but had hardly taken a stride in the darkness when the whole room blazed with a blinding white light that burned into my brain and heart and memory a vivid picture of the combatants on the floor, Moxon underneath, his throat still in the clutch of those iron hands, his head forced backward, his eyes protruding, his mouth wide open and his tongue thrust out; and—horrible contrast!—upon the painted face of his assassin an expression of tranquil and profound thought, as in the solution of a problem in chess! This I observed, then all was blackness and silence.

Three days later I recovered consciousness in a hospital. As the memory of that tragic night slowly evolved in my ailing brain I recognized in my attendant Moxon's confidential workman, Haley. Responding to a look he approached, smiling.

"Tell me about it," I managed to say, faintly—"all about it."

"Certainly," he said; "you were carried unconscious from a burning house—Moxon's. Nobody knows how you came to be there. You may have to do a little explaining. The origin of the fire is a bit mysterious, too. My own notion is that the house was struck by lightning."

"And Moxon?"

"Buried yesterday—what was left of him."

Apparently this reticent person could unfold himself on occasion. When imparting shocking intelligence to the sick he was affable enough. After some moments of the keenest mental suffering I ventured to ask another question:

"Who rescued me?"

"Well, if that interests you—I did."

"Thank you, Mr. Haley, and may God bless you for it. Did you rescue, also, that charming product of your skill, the automaton chess-player that murdered its inventor?"

The man was silent a long time, looking away from me. Presently he turned and gravely said:

"Do you know that?"

"I do," I replied; "I saw it done."

That was many years ago. If asked today I should answer less confidently.

María Amparo Ruiz de Burton

1832–1894

Born into an elite Mexican family, María del Amparo Ruiz Arango met Captain Henry Burton of the United States Army in July 1847, when an American ship landed at La Paz to seize possession of Baja California. As a condition of the Treaty of Guadalupe Hidalgo in 1848, 480 Baja Californians were expatriated by ship to Monterey in Alta California, among them the sixteen-year-old María and her mother, Doña Isabel. In 1849 she married Burton, a widower, in Monterey, and their legendary romance as "enemy lovers" is recounted in Hubert H. Bancroft's California Pastoral *(1888). Ruiz de Burton accompanied her husband to Army posts in the East. While fighting in the Civil War, Henry Burton contracted malaria, from which he died in 1869. Angered at the hypocrisy and duplicity she had seen around her, she wrote* Who Would Have Thought It? *(1872), a bitterly parodic historical romance focusing on a Northern abolitionist family. She returned to San Diego with her family, where she pondered the mistreatment and political sacrifice of the Californios, and the result was* The Squatter and the Don *(1885), signed pseudonymously as "C. Loyal." The first novel by a Mexican American woman, it was an informed and telling fictional defense of one of California's founding peoples and a sharp exposé of the common practice of land "squatting." An ardent defender of a wronged and misled culture, Ruiz de Burton corresponded with the family of Mariano Vallejo. These letters, recently published, define her clearly as a proud defender not merely of the legal rights of the Californios but also of "our race," distinct from the "Anglo-Saxon race." Ruiz de Burton's novels have been republished with extensive introductions by Arte Publico Press.*

From *The Squatter and the Don*

THE DON'S VIEW OF THE TREATY OF GUADALUPE HIDALGO

If there had been such a thing as communicating by telephone in the days of '72, and there had been those magic wires spanning the distance between William Darrell's house in Alameda County and that of Don Mariano Alamar in San Diego County, with power to transmit the human voice for five hundred miles, a listener at either end would have heard various discussions upon the same subject, differentiated only by circumstances. No magic wires crossed San Francisco bay to bring the sound of voices to San Diego, but the law of necessity made the Squatter and the Don, distant as they were—distant in every way, without reckoning the miles between them—talk quite warmly of the same matter. The point of view was of course different, for how could it be otherwise? Darrell thought himself justified, and *authorized,* to "take up lands," as he had done before. He had had more than half of California's population on his side, and though the *"Squatter's Sovereignty"* was now rather on the wane, and the *"squatter vote"* was no longer the power, still, the squatters would not abdicate, having yet much to say about election times. . . .

This time, however, Darrell honestly meant to take no land but what belonged to the United States. His promise to his wife was sincere, yet his coming to Southern California had already brought trouble to the Alamar rancho.

Don Mariano Alamar was silently walking up and down the front piazza of his house at the rancho; his hands listlessly clasped behind and his head slightly bent forward in deep thought. He had pushed away to one side the many armchairs and wicker rockers with which the piazza was furnished. He wanted a long space to walk. That his meditations were far from agreeable, could easily be seen by the compressed lips, slight frown, and sad gaze of his mild and beautiful blue eyes. Sounds of laughter, music and dancing came from the parlor; the young people were entertaining friends from town with their usual gay hospitality, and enjoying themselves heartily. Don Mariano, though already in his fiftieth year, was as fond of dancing as his sons and daughters, and not to see him come in and join the quadrille was so singular that his wife thought she must come out and inquire what could detain him. He was so absorbed in his thoughts that he did not hear her voice calling him—"What keeps you away? Lizzie has been looking for you; she wants you for a partner in the lancers," said Doña Josefa, putting her arm under that of her husband, bending her head forward and turning it up to look into his eyes.

"What is the matter?" she asked, stopping short, thus making her husband come to a sudden halt. "I am sure something has happened. Tell me."

"Nothing, dear wife. Nothing has happened. That is to say, nothing new."

"More squatters?" she asked. Senior Alamar bent his head slightly, in affirmative reply.

"More coming, you mean?"

"Yes, wife; more. Those two friends of squatters Mathews and Hagar, who were here last year to locate claims and went away, did not abandon their claims, but only went away to bring proselytes and their families, and a large invoice of them will arrive on tomorrow's steamer. The worst of it all is, that among the newcomers is that terrible and most dangerous squatter William Darrell, who some years ago gave so much trouble to the Spanish people in Napa and Sonoma Counties, by locating claims there. John Gasbang wrote to Hogsden that besides Darrell, there will be six or seven other men bringing their families, so that there will be more rifles for my cattle."

"But, didn't we hear that Darrell was no longer a squatter, that he is rich and living quietly in Alameda?"

"Yes, we heard that, and it is true. He is quite well off, but Gasbang and Miller and Mathews went and told him that my rancho had been rejected, and that it is near enough to town to become valuable, as soon as we have a railroad. Darrell believed it, and is coming to locate here."

"Strange that Darrell should believe such men; I suppose he does not know how low they are."

"He ought to know them, for they were his teamsters when he crossed the plains in '48. That is, Miller, Mathews, Hughes and Hager, were his teamsters, and Gasbang was their cook—the cook for the hired men. Mrs. Darrell had a colored woman who cooked for the Darrell family; she despised Gasbang's cooking as we despise his character, I suppose."

Doña Josefa was silent, and holding on to her husband's arm, took a turn with him up and down the piazza.

"Is it possible that there is no law to protect us; to protect our property; what does your lawyer say about obtaining redress or protection; is there no hope?" she asked, with a sigh.

"Protection for our land, or for our cattle, you mean?"

"For both, as we get it for neither," she said.

"In the matter of our land, we have to await for the attorney general, at Washington, to decide."

"Lizzie was telling Elvira, yesterday, that her uncle Lawrence is a friend of several influential people in Washington, and that George can get him to interest himself in having your title decided."

"But, as George is to marry my daughter, he would be the last man from whom I would ask a favor."

"What is that I hear about not asking a favor from me?" said George Mechlin, coming out on the piazza with Elvira on his arm, having just finished a waltz—"I am interested to know why you would not ask it."

"You know why, my dear boy. It isn't exactly the thing to bother you with my disagreeable business."

"And why not? And who has a better right? And why should it be a bother to me to help you in any way I can? My father spoke to me about a dismissal of an appeal, and I made a note of it. Let me see, I think I have it in my pocket now,"—said George, feeling in his breast pocket for his memorandum book,—"yes, here it is,—'For uncle to write to the attorney general about dismissing the appeal taken by the squatters in the Alamar grant, against Don Mariano's title, which was approved.' Is that the correct idea? I only made this note to ask you for further particulars."

"You have it exactly. When I give you the number of the case, it is all that you need say to your uncle. What I want is to have the appeal dismissed, of course, but if the attorney general does not see fit to do so, he can, at least, remand back the case for a new trial. Anything rather than this killing suspense. Killing literally, for while we are waiting to have my title settled, the *settlers* (I don't mean to make puns), are killing my cattle by the hundred head, and I cannot stop them."

"But are there no laws to protect property in California?" George asked.

"Yes, some sort of laws, which in my case seem more intended to help the law-breakers than to protect the law-abiding," Don Mariano replied.

"How so? Is there no law to punish the thieves who kill your cattle?"

"There are some enactments so obviously intended to favor one class of citizens against another class, that to call them laws is an insult to law, but such as they are, we must submit to them. By those laws any man can come to my land, for instance, plant ten acres of grain, without any fence, and then catch my cattle which, seeing the green grass without a fence, will go to eat it. Then he puts them in a *'corral'* and makes me pay damages and so much per head for keeping them, and costs of legal proceedings and many other trumped up expenses, until for such little fields of grain I may be obliged to pay thousands of dollars. Or, if the grain fields are large enough to bring more money by keeping the cattle away, then the settler shoots the cattle at any time without the least hesitation, only taking care that no one sees him in the act of firing upon the cattle. He might stand behind a bush or tree and fire, but then he is not seen. No one can swear that they saw him actually kill the cattle, and no jury can convict him, for although the dead animals may be there, lying on the ground shot, still no one saw the settler kill them. And so it is all the time. I must pay damages and expenses of litigation, or my cattle get killed almost every day."

"But this is infamous. Haven't you—the cattle owners—tried to have some law enacted that will protect your property?" George asked. "It seems to me that could be done."

"It could be done, perhaps, if our positions were reversed, and the Spanish people—'the *natives*'—*were* the planters of the grain fields, and the Americans were the owners of the cattle. But as we, the Spaniards, are the owners of the Spanish—or Mexican—land grants and also the owners of the cattle ranchos, our State legislators will not make any law to protect cattle. They make laws *'to protect agriculture'* (they say proudly), which means to drive to the wall all owners of cattle ranchos. I am told that at this session of the legislature a law more strict yet will be passed, which will be ostensibly 'to protect agriculture,' but in reality to destroy cattle and ruin the native Californians. The agriculture of this State does not require legislative protection. Such pretext is absurd."

"I thought that the rights of the Spanish people were protected by our treaty with Mexico," George said.

"Mexico did not pay much attention to the future welfare of the children she left to their fate in the hands of a nation which had no sympathies for us," said Doña Josefa, feelingly.

"I remember," calmly said Don Mariano, "that when I first read the text of the treaty of Guadalupe Hidalgo, I felt a bitter resentment against my people; against Mexico, the mother country, who abandoned us—her children—with so slight a provision of obligatory stipulations for protection. But afterwards, upon mature reflection, I saw that Mexico did as much as could have been reasonably expected at the time. In the very preamble of the treaty the spirit of peace and friendship, which animated both nations, was carefully made manifest. That spirit was to be the *foundation* of the relations between the conqueror and conquered. How could Mexico have foreseen then that when scarcely half a dozen years should have elapsed the trusted conquerors would, *'In Congress Assembled,'* pass laws which were to be retroactive upon the defenseless, helpless, conquered people, in order to despoil them? The treaty said that our rights would be the same as those enjoyed by all other American citizens. But, you see, Congress takes very good care not to enact retroactive laws for Americans; laws to take away from American citizens the property which they hold now, already, with a recognized legal title. No, indeed. But they do so quickly enough with us—with us, the Spano-Americans, who were to enjoy equal rights, mind you, according to the treaty of peace. This is what seems to me a breach of faith, which Mexico could neither presuppose nor prevent."

"It is nothing else, I am sorry and ashamed to say," George said. "I never knew much about the treaty with Mexico, but I never imagined we had acted so badly." . . .

"We have had no one to speak for us. By the treaty of Guadalupe Hidalgo the American nation pledged its honor to respect our land titles just the same as Mexico would have done. Unfortunately, however, the discovery of gold brought to California the riff-raff of the world, and with it a horde of land-sharks, all possessing the privilege of voting, and most of them coveting our lands, for which they very quickly began to clamor. There was, and still is, plenty of good government land, which any one can take. But no. The forbidden fruit is the sweetest. They do not want government land. They want the land of the Spanish people, because we 'have too much,' they say. So, to win their votes, the votes of the squatters, our representatives in Congress helped to pass laws declaring all lands in California open to preemption, as in Louisiana, for instance. Then, as a coating of whitewash to the stain on the nation's honor, a 'land commission' was established to examine land titles. Because, having pledged the national word to respect our rights, it would be an act of despoliation, besides an open violation of pledged honor, to take the lands without some pretext of a legal process. So then, we became obliged to present our titles before the said land commission to be examined and approved or rejected. While these legal proceedings are going on, the squatters locate their claims and raise crops on our lands, which they convert into money to fight our titles. But don't let me, with my disagreeable subject spoil your dance. Go back to your lancers, and tell Lizzie to excuse me," said Don Mariano. . . .

PRE-EMPTING UNDER THE LAW

"All aboard for San Diego!" shouted a voice from a wagon, as it rumbled past Darrell, who walked leisurely with a satchel in his hand, swinging it unconsciously, lost in thought. He looked up and saw that the wagon whence the voice came carried ten or twelve men, sitting on trunks and packages and carpet-bags. These men Mathews and Gasbang had presented to him, saying that they were settlers already residing at the Alamar rancho, and others who were going down to take up claims, at the same time that he would locate his. Darrell looked at his future neighbors with feelings of anything but pleasure. The broad, vulgar face of Gasbang, with its square jaws, gray beard, closely clipped, but never shaved, his compressed, thin, bloodless lips, his small, pale, restless eyes and flat nose, Darrell soon recognized, though the wagon was going rapidly. Mathews' visage was equally noticeable for its ugliness, though of a different type; for his face was long and shaved; his nose was pinched and peaked and red; his cheeks were flabby; and his long, oily, dusty, hair dragged over his neck in matted, meshy locks, while a constant frown settled on his brow. As he was broad shouldered and rather tall, his face seemed made for some other man much weaker than himself. His face looked mean and discontented, while his body seemed strong and self-reliant. . . .

The voyage down the coast was made safely. Darrell had managed to keep away from his fellow-travelers, to think of home unmolested.

It was a bright morning of January, 1872, when he stood far forward, watching the course of the steamer Orizaba, as she made her way around Point Loma, then between Ballast Point and the sandy peninsula, and passing by La Playa, came in sight of San Diego city.

"Here we are," said John Gasbang; "how do you like the looks of our little city, Mr. Darrell?"

"Very well; it is larger than I supposed, and the site of it seems very pleasant."

"Pleasant! I should say it was. A perfect slope, sir, as gentle and regular as if made to order. The best drained city in the world, sir, when we put in sewers. Too poor for that, yet, sir, but we are coming to it, sir, growing, growing, sir."

"When we get the railroad," added Mathews, with a mouth full of tobacco, spitting profusely on the deck.

"Exactly, and we'll soon have that. Our news from Washington is very encouraging. Tom Scott will visit us this summer," Gasbang said.

"I like a town with plenty of trees," said Darrell, with his gaze fixed on the approaching panorama, thinking that his wife would be pleased with the place, she being so fond of trees. "I had no idea you had so many trees about you. Many are small, yet, but all seem healthy."

"And health-giving trees, they are, too. Most of them are eucalyptus and pepper trees, the healthiest in the world. You never hear of any malarial fevers in San Diego, sir, never. Our perfect climate, the fine sloping ground of our town site, our eucalyptus trees, sea breezes and mountain air, make San Diego a most healthy little city," said Gasbang.

"That is an excellent recommendation, as life is not worth having without health," Darrell observed.

"We have it here," Hughes said. "A man has to be very imprudent not to keep well in our climate, sir. All we want now is a little stimulus of business prosperity, and the railroad is sure to bring us that. Then San Diego will be the best place on the coast for a residence."

The loud report of a cannon, close by, made Darrell jump and look around quickly, not knowing what that explosion could mean.

"That is our visiting card to the people of San Diego, to announce our coming," said the captain, laughingly. "I am sorry it startled you."

"That is nothing. I didn't know I had nerves. I believe that is what women call it. I was not expecting such a military salute," Darrell said.

"Oh yes, we always give it. The San Diego people are very military. At least, I should say the settlers on Señor Alamar's rancho are, as I hear they practice rifle shooting there all the time," the captain said, looking at Mathews and Gasbang.

"That is a shot at us," Gasbang answered, laughing.

"But it is a blank cartridge, meant not to hurt," the captain replied.

"The rifle practice is on dark nights," said a young Spaniard, who had been listening at what was said by the others.

"Or in the daytime, if the cattle deserve it," Mathews said.

"That is very creditable and brave, to shoot tame cows," the Spaniard re-joined.

"Perhaps you had better come and try it," Mathews returned.

"Thank you. It is the mischievous brutes I would like to shoot, not the good, useful cattle"; so saying, the Spaniard walked away, followed by the scowls of the settlers.

"That is impudence for you," Gasbang exclaimed.

"Those greasers ain't half crushed yet. We have to tame them like they do their mustangs, or shoot them, as we shoot their cattle," said Mathews.

"Oh, no. No such violent means are necessary. All we have to do is to take their lands, and finish their cattle," said Hughes, sneeringly, looking at Darrell for approval. But he did not get it. Darrell did not care for the Spanish population of California, but he did not approve of shooting cattle in the way which the foregoing conversation indicated. To do this, was useless cruelty and useless waste of valuable property, no matter to whom it might belong. To destroy it was a loss to the State. It was folly.

"Why must cattle be shot? Can't they be kept off, away from your crops without shooting them?" he asked.

"Not always. At first, that is, for the first three years after we located our claims," Gasbang said, "we had to shoot them all the time. Now the Don has sold a good many, or sent them to the mountains, so that few have been killed."

"I suppose fencing would be too expensive."

"Phew! It would be ruinous, impossible," Mathews said. . . .

In a few hours Darrell was driving by Don Mariano Alamar's house, a one-story mansion on a low hill, with a broad piazza in front, and in the interior a court formed by two wings, and a row of rooms variously occupied at its back. That the house was commodious, Darrell could see. There was a flower garden in front. At the back there were several *"corrales"* for cattle and horses. At the foot of the hill, on the left, there was an orchard, and some grain fields enclosed with good fences.

Darrell took notice of all these particulars. He also noticed that there were females on the front piazza. He was taken to see the best unoccupied lands to make his selection. He ran his practiced eye over the valley from the highest point on the hill. He then came to the next bench; he stopped there, also, and finally came to the broad slope of the foot-hills.

"I think I'll locate here," said he, "if no one else has already filed a claim to this land." . . .

"You'll take 320 acres?" asked Hughes.

"Yes, 320 acres,—according to law," replied Darrell.

"All right. Let us measure them now," said Gasbang. "We have time to mark the limits and put the corner stakes. I have a cord here in my wagon, which is a chain's length. That will do the business."

"That will do temporarily, I suppose; but I'll have the two claims properly surveyed afterwards according to law," Darrell said.

"Of course, you will. We all know you will do the fair thing by everybody, and follow the law strictly," said Hughes. In which opinion all concurred.

"Have you all made your selections?" Darrell asked Hughes.

"Yes; Pittikin and I will locate near Hancock. We like that valley; it is further off, but better soil," said Hughes. "My oldest boy will put a claim near me, and Miller's two boys have staked theirs also. I think we'll like that location better."

"I am glad you like it. I think this is good enough soil for me," Darrell said.

"It is good enough for anybody. The whole rancho is all good soil. Let us put the stakes now," said Gasbang; and assisted by Mathews, Romeo Hancock and Sumner Pittikin, Darrell proceeded by making a rough guess to measure 320 acres (more or less), and put the corner stakes.

"This is what I call business," said Gasbang, carrying cheerfully one end of the rope used for measurement; "and all inside of the law. That is the beauty of it—all perfectly lawful."

And so it was.

The stakes having been placed, Darrell felt satisfied. Next day he would have the claim properly filed, and in due time a surveyor would measure them. All would be done "according to law" and in this easy way more land was taken from its legitimate owner.

This certainly was a more simple way of appropriating the property of *"the conquered"* than in the days of Alaric or Hannibal.

There would have been bloodshed then. Now tears only flowed, silent tears of helpless discouragement; of a presentiment of impending desolation.

Sadly Doña Josefa and her daughters had witnessed from the half-closed shutters of their bedroom windows Mr. Darrell's performance, and fully anticipated serious trouble therefrom.

Don Mariano Alamar, Gabriel and Victoriano—his two sons—had also silently witnessed Mr. Darrell's *lawful* appropriation of their own property. Gabriel was pale and calm. Victoriano was biting his lips, and his face was flushed.

"The government has for sale hundreds of millions of acres, but yet these men must come and take my land, as if there was no other," said Don Mariano sadly.

"And as we pay the taxes on the land that they will cultivate, our taxes will double next year," Gabriel added.

"Undoubtedly. That climax to injustice has been the most fatal of all the hardships imposed upon us. George could not believe me when I told him that (the land-owners) have to pay the taxes on the land cultivated by the pre-emptors, and upon all the improvements they make and enjoy. When he at last understood that such unfair laws did exist, he was amazed, but understood then why the settlers wished to prolong litigation, since it is 'the natives' who must bear the burden of taxation, while the titles are in the courts, and thus the pre-emptors hold the land free."

"I wish we were squatters," Victoriano remarked.

"During litigation, yes; but there have been cases where honest men have, in good faith, taken lands as squatters, and after all, had to give them up. No, I don't blame the squatters; they are at times like ourselves, victims of a wrong legislation, which unintentionally cuts both ways. They were set loose upon us, but a law without equity recoils upon them more cruelly. Then we are all sufferers, all victims of a defective legislation and subverted moral principles."

THOCMETONY [SARAH WINNEMUCCA]
1844–1891

Thocmetony was the first American Indian woman to publish an autobiography. Her tribe, the Northern Paiute, are native to the desert plateau of western Nevada, southeastern Oregon, and northeastern California west of the Sierra. The granddaughter of Truckee, the legendary chief who guided an early wagon party into the Sierra, she was born in western Nevada. Her name means "Shellflower." She moved to California with her father at age six, remaining for several years in the Central Valley, where she began to learn English and Spanish. In 1860 she was enrolled at the convent school in San Jose. Her activism began in 1866, when Paiutes asked her help in stopping white raids on the tribe. Thereafter she stayed active in Native American issues—as a translator, cultural broker with whites, lecturer, and writer. Life among the Piutes: Their Wrongs and Claims *(1883) was a powerful witness that mixed personal narrative and tribal ethnology, covering the period 1844 to 1883. She experienced and wrote of her people's transformation from independent free-contact tribes to reduced, isolated groups held mainly on reservations. She also lectured widely in the West and East, exposing the corrupt and degrading treatment of Western Indians and criticizing agents, missionaries, and federal policy. She was prominent in drafting new national legislation protecting Indians, but she grew disenchanted with the meager results of her labor and returned to Nevada to found a school for Paiute children. Outspoken and controversial among whites and Indians alike, Thocmetony lived with a sister in her later years and died at Henry's Lake, Idaho.*

From *Life among the Piutes*

Our children are very carefully taught to be good. Their parents tell them stories, traditions of old times, even of the first mother of the human race; and love stories, stories of giants, and fables; and when they ask if these last stories are true, they answer, "Oh, it is only coyote," which means that they are make-believe stories. Coyote is the name of a mean, crafty little animal, half wolf, half dog, and stands for everything low. It is the greatest term of reproach one Indian has for another. Indians do not swear,—they have no words for swearing till they learn them of white men. The worst they call each is bad or coyote; but they are very sincere with one another, and if they think each other in the wrong they say so.

We are taught to love everybody. We don't need to be taught to love our fathers and mothers. We love them without being told to. Our tenth cousin is as near to us as our first cousin; and we don't marry into our relations. Our young women are not allowed to talk to any young man that is not their cousin, except at the festive dances, when both are dressed in their best clothes, adorned with beads, feathers or shells, and stand alternately in the ring and take hold of hands. These are very pleasant occasions to all the young people.

Many years ago, when my people were happier than they are now, they used to celebrate the Festival of Flowers in the spring. I have been to three of them only in the course of my life.

Oh, with what eagerness we girls used to watch every spring for the time when we could meet with our hearts' delight, the young men, whom in civilized life you call beaux. We would all go in company to see if the flowers we were named for were yet in bloom, for almost all the girls are named for flowers. We talked about them in our wigwams, as if we were the flowers, saying, "Oh, I saw myself today in full bloom!" We would talk all the evening in this way in our families with such delight, and such beautiful thoughts of the happy day when we should meet with those who admired us and would help us to sing our flower-songs which we made up as we sang. But we were always sorry for those that were not named after some flower, because we knew they could not join in the flower-songs like ourselves, who were named for flowers of all kinds.

At last one evening came a beautiful voice, which made every girl's heart throb with happiness. It was the chief, and every one hushed to hear what he said today.

"My dear daughters, we are told that you have seen yourselves in the hills and in the valleys, in full bloom. Five days from today your festival day will come. I know every young man's heart stops beating while I am talking. I know how it was with me many years ago. I used to wish the Flower Festival would come every day. Dear young men and young women, you are saying, 'Why put it off five days?' But you all know that is our rule. It gives you time to think, and to show your sweetheart your flower."

All the girls who have flower-names dance along together, and those who have not go together also. Our fathers and mothers and grandfathers and grandmothers make a place for us where we can dance. Each one gathers the flower she is named for, and then all weave them into wreaths and crowns and scarfs, and dress up in them.

Some girls are named for rocks and are called rock-girls, and they find some pretty rocks which they carry; each one such a rock as she is named for, or whatever she is named for. If she cannot, she can take a branch of sage-brush, or a bunch of rye-grass, which have no flower.

They all go marching along, each girl in turn singing of herself; but she is not a girl any more,—she is a flower singing. She sings of herself, and her sweetheart, dancing along by her side, helps her sing the song she makes.

I will repeat what we say of ourselves. "I, Sarah Winnemucca, am a shell-flower, such as I wear on my dress. My name is Thocmetony. I am so beautiful! Who will come and dance with me while I am so beautiful? Oh, come and be happy with me! I shall be beautiful while the earth lasts. Somebody will always admire me; and who will come and be happy with me in the Spirit-land? I shall be beautiful forever there. Yes, I shall be more beautiful than my shell-flower, my Thocmetony! Then, come, oh come, and dance and be happy with me!" The young men sing with us as they dance beside us.

Our parents are waiting for us somewhere to welcome us home. And then we praise the sage-brush and the rye-grass that have no flower, and the pretty rocks that some are named for; and then we present our beautiful flowers to these companions who could carry none. And so all are happy; and that closes the beautiful day.

My people have been so unhappy for a long time they wish now to *disincrease,* instead of multiply. The mothers are afraid to have more children, for fear they shall have daughters, who are not safe even in their mother's presence.

The grandmothers have the special care of the daughters just before and after they come to womanhood. The girls are not allowed to get married until they have come to womanhood; and that period is recognized as a very sacred thing, and is the subject of a festival, and has peculiar customs. The young woman is set apart under the care of two of her friends, somewhat older, and a little wigwam, called a teepee, just big enough for the three, is made for them, to which they retire. She goes through certain labors which are thought to be strengthening, and these last twenty-five days. Every day, three times a day, she must gather, and pile up as high as she can, five stacks of wood. This makes fifteen stacks a day. At the end of every five days the attendants take her to a river to bathe. She fasts from all flesh-meat during these twenty-five days, and continues to do this for five days in every month all her life. At the end of the twenty-five days she returns to the family lodge, and gives all her clothing to her attendants in payment for their care. Sometimes the wardrobe is quite extensive.

It is thus publicly known that there is another marriageable woman, and any young man interested in her, or wishing to form an alliance, comes forward. But the courting is very different from the courting of the white people. He never speaks to her, or visits the family, but endeavors to attract her attention by showing his horsemanship, etc. As he knows that she sleeps next to her grandmother in the lodge, he enters in full dress after the family has retired for the night, and seats himself at her feet. If she is not awake, her grandmother wakes her. He does not speak to either young woman or grandmother, but when the young woman wishes him to go away, she rises and goes and lies down by the side of her mother. He then leaves as silently as he came in. This goes on sometimes for a year or longer, if the young woman has not made up her mind. She is never forced by her parents to marry against her wishes. When she knows her own mind, she makes a confidant of her grandmother, and then the young man is summoned by the father of the girl, who asks him in her presence, if he really loves his daughter, and reminds him, if he says he does, of all the duties of a husband. He then asks his daughter the same question, and sets before her minutely all her duties. And these duties are not slight. She is to dress the game, prepare the food, clean the buckskins, make his moccasins, dress his hair, bring all the wood,—in short, do all the household work. She promises to "be himself," and she fulfills her promise. Then he is invited to a feast and all his relatives with him. But after the betrothal, a teepee is erected for the presents that pour in from both sides.

At the wedding feast, all the food is prepared in baskets. The young woman sits by the young man, and hands him the basket of food prepared for him with her own hands. He does not take it with his right hand; but seizes her wrist, and takes it with the left hand. This constitutes the marriage ceremony, and the father pronounces them man and wife. They go to a wigwam of their own, where they live till the first child is born. This event also is celebrated. Both father and mother fast from all flesh, and the father goes through the labor of piling the wood for twenty-five days, and assumes all his wife's household work during that time. If he does not do his part in the care of the child, he is considered an outcast. Every five days his child's basket is changed for a new one, and the five are all carefully put away at the end of the days, the last one containing the navel-string, carefully wrapped up, and all are put up into a tree, and the child put into a new and ornamented basket. All this respect shown to the mother and child makes the parents feel their responsibility, and makes the tie between parents and children very strong. The young mothers often get together and exchange their experiences about the attentions of their husbands; and inquire of each other if the fathers did their duty to their children, and were careful of their wives' health. When they are married they give away all the clothing they have ever worn, and dress themselves anew. The poor people have the same ceremonies, but do not make a feast of it, for want of means.

Our boys are introduced to manhood by their hunting of deer and mountain-sheep. Before they are fifteen or sixteen, they hunt only small game, like rabbits, hares, fowls, etc. They never eat what they kill themselves, but only what their father or elder brothers kill. When a boy becomes strong enough to use larger bows made of sinew, and arrows that are ornamented with eagle-feathers, for the first time, he kills game that is large, a deer or an antelope, or a mountain-sheep. Then he brings home the hide, and his father cuts it into a long coil which is wound into a loop, and the boy takes his quiver and throws it on his back as if he was going on a hunt, and takes his bow and arrows in his hand. Then his father throws the loop over him, and he jumps through it. This he does five times. Now for the first time he eats the flesh of the animal he has killed, and from that time he eats whatever he kills but he has always been faithful to his parents' command not to eat what he has killed before. He can now do whatever he likes, for now he is a man, and no longer considered a boy. If there is a war he can go to it; but the Piutes, and other tribes west of the Rocky Mountains, are not fond of going to war. I never saw a war-dance but once. It is always the whites that begin the wars, for their own selfish purposes. The government does not take care to send the good men; there are a plenty who would take pains to see and understand the chiefs and learn their characters, and their good will to the whites. But the whites have not waited to find out how good the Indians were, and what ideas they had of God, just like those of Jesus, who called him Father, just as my people do, and told men to do to others as they would be done by, just as my people teach their children to do. My people teach their children never to make fun of any one, no matter how they look. If you see your brother or sister doing something wrong, look away, or go away from them. If you make fun of bad persons, you make yourself beneath them. Be kind to all, both poor and rich, and feed all that come to your wigwam, and your name can be spoken of by every one far and near. In this way you will make many friends for yourself. Be kind both to bad and good, for you don't know your own heart. This is the way my people teach their children. It was handed down from father to son for many generations. I never in my life saw our children rude as I have seen white children and grown people in the streets.

The chief's tent is the largest tent, and it is the council-tent, where every one goes who wants advice. In the evenings the head men go there to discuss everything, for the chiefs do not rule like tyrants; they discuss everything with their people, as a father would in his family. Often they sit up all night. They discuss the doings of all, if they need to be advised. If a boy is not doing well they talk that over, and if the women are interested they can share in the talks. If there is not room enough inside, they all go out of doors, and make a great circle. The men are in the inner circle, for there would be too much smoke for the women inside. The men never talk without smoking first. The women sit behind them in another circle, and if the children wish to hear, they can be there too. The women know as much as the men do, and their advice is often asked. We have a republic as well as you. The council-tent is our Congress, and anybody can speak who has anything to say, women and all. They are always interested in what their husbands are doing and thinking about. And they take some part even in the wars. They are always near at hand when fighting is going on, ready to snatch their husbands up and carry them off if wounded or killed. One splendid woman that my brother Lee married after his first wife died, went out into the battle-field after her uncle was killed, and went into the front ranks and cheered the men on. Her uncle's horse was dressed in a splendid robe made of eagles' feathers and she snatched it off and swung it in the face of the enemy, who always carry off everything they find, as much as to say, "You can't have that—I have it safe"; and she stayed and took her uncle's place, as brave as any of the men. It means something when the women promise their fathers to make their husbands *themselves*. They faithfully keep with them in all the dangers they can share. They not only take care of their children together, but they do everything together; and when they grow blind, which I am sorry to say is very common, for the smoke they live in destroys their eyes at last, they take sweet care of one another. Marriage is a sweet thing when people love each other. If women could go into your Congress I think justice would soon be done to the Indians. I can't tell about all Indians; but I know my own people are kind to everybody, that does not do them harm; but they will not be imposed upon, and when people are too bad they rise up and resist them. This seems to me all right. It is different from being revengeful. There is nothing cruel about our people. They never scalped a human being. . . .

The sub-chiefs are appointed by the great chief for special duties. There is no quarrelling about that, for neither sub-chief or great chief has any salary. It is this which makes the tribe so united and attached to each other, and makes it so dreadful to be parted. They would rather all die at once than be parted. They believe that in the Spirit-land those that die still watch over those that are living. When I was a child in California, I heard the Methodist minister say that everybody that did wrong was burned in hell forever. I was so frightened it made me very sick. He said the blessed ones in heaven looked down and saw their friends burning and could not help them. I wanted to be unborn, and cried so that my mother and the others told me it was not so, that it was only here that people did wrong and were in the hell that it made, and that those that were in the Spirit-land saw us here and were sorry for us. But we should go to them when we died, where there was never any wrong-doing, and so no hell. That is our religion.

My people capture antelopes by charming them, but only some of the people are charmers. My father was one of them, and once I went with him on an antelope hunt. The antelopes move in herds in the winter, and as late in the spring as April. At this time there was said to be a large herd in a certain place, and my father told all his people to come together in ten days to go with him in his hunt. He told them to bring their wives with them, but no small children. When they came, at the end of ten days, he chose two men, who he said were to be his messengers to the antelopes. They were to have two large torches made of sage-brush bark, and after he had found a place for his camp, he marked out a circle around which the wigwams were to be placed, putting his own in the middle of the western side, and leaving an opening directly opposite in the middle of the eastern side, which was towards the antelopes.

The people who were with him in the camp then made another circle to the east of the one where their wigwams were, and made six mounds of sage-brush and stones on the sides of it, with a space of a hundred yards or more from one mound to the next one, but with no fence between the mounds. These mounds were made high, so that they could be seen from far off.

The women and boys and old men who were in the camp, and who were working on the mounds, were told to be very careful not to drop anything and not to stumble over a sage-brush root, or a stone, or anything, and not to have any accident, but to do everything perfectly and to keep thinking about the antelopes all the time, and not to let their thoughts go away to anything else. It took five days to charm the antelopes, and if anybody had an accident he must tell of it.

Every morning early, when the bright morning star could be seen, the people sat around the opening to the circle, with my father sitting in the middle of the opening, and my father lighted his pipe and passed it to his right, and the pipe went round the circle five times. And at night they did the same thing.

After they had smoked the pipe, my father took a kind of drum, which is used in this charming, and made music with it. This is the only kind of musical instrument which my people have, and it is only used for this antelope-charming. It is made of a hide of some large animal, stuffed with grass, so as to make it sound hollow, and then wound around tightly from one end to the other with a cord as large as my finger. One end of this instrument is large, and it tapers down to the other end, which is small, so that it makes a different sound on the different parts. My father took a stick and rubbed this stick from one end of the instrument to the other, making a penetrating, vibrating sound, that could be heard afar off, and he sang, and all his people sang with him.

After that the two men who were messengers went out to see the antelopes. They carried their torches in their right hands, and one of them carried a pipe in his left hand. They started from my father's wigwam and went straight across the camp to the opening; then they crossed, and one went around the second circle to the right and the other went to the left, till they met on the other side of the circle. Then they crossed again, and one went round the herd of antelopes one way and the other went round the other way, but they did not let the antelopes see them. When they met on the other side of the herd of antelopes, they stopped and smoked the pipe, and then they crossed, and each man came back on the track of the other to the camp, and told my father what they saw and what the antelopes were doing.

This was done every day for five days, and after the first day all the men and women and boys followed the messengers, and went around the circle they were to enter. On the fifth day the antelopes were charmed, and the whole herd followed the tracks of my people and entered the circle where the mounds were, coming in at the entrance, bowing and tossing their heads, and looking sleepy and under a powerful spell. They ran round and round inside the circle just as if there was a fence all around it and they could not get out, and they staid there until my people had killed every one. But if anybody had dropped anything, or had stumbled and had not told about it, then when the antelopes came to the place where he had done that, they threw off the spell and rushed wildly out of the circle at that place.

My brother can charm horses in the same way.

Thocmetony [Sarah Winnemucca]

ROBERT LOUIS STEVENSON
1850–1894

Stevenson, the beloved Scottish storyteller and poet, was born in Edinburgh. He studied law and passed the bar but never practiced, drawn instead toward literature and travel. In France in 1876, he fell in love with Fanny Vandegrift Osbourne, a married American woman ten years his senior. When she returned home to Oakland, California, Stevenson soon followed. In 1879, while they awaited her divorce, he lived in San Francisco and met Charles Warren Stoddard, who first awakened his desire to visit the South Seas. With Fanny, Stevenson spent several months in Monterey. He wrote articles for the local paper and saw a spectacular point of land that some believe provided the locale for one of his most popular novels: in Cannery Row, Steinbeck remarks, "Monterey . . . remembers with pleasure and some glory that Robert Louis Stevenson lived there. Treasure Island certainly has the topography and coastal plan of Point Lobos." In 1880, he and Fanny were married in Napa Valley and honeymooned for nine weeks on the slope of Mount Saint Helena, a sojourn that gave us The Silverado Squatters (1883). Returning to Scotland, he spent several years traveling and writing such classics as A Child's Garden of Verses (1885), Kidnapped (1886), and Dr. Jekyll and Mr. Hyde (1886). Afflicted throughout his life with a complex lung disease, he had held onto a dream that the South Seas would restore his health. In 1887 he and Fanny returned to the Americas and the next year set sail from San Francisco Bay for the Marquesas, Tahiti, and Hawai'i, eventually settling in Samoa, where Stevenson is buried.

From *The Silverado Squatters*

IN THE VALLEY CALISTOGA

It is difficult for a European to imagine Calistoga, the whole place is so new, and of such an occidental pattern; the very name, I hear, was invented at a supper-party by the man who found the springs.

The railroad and the highway come up the valley about parallel to one another. The street of Calistoga joins them, perpendicular to both—a wide street, with bright, clean, low houses, here and there a verandah over the sidewalk, here and there a horse-post, here and there lounging townsfolk. Other streets are marked out, and most likely named; for these towns in the

New World begin with a firm resolve to grow larger, Washington and Broadway, and then First and Second, and so forth, being boldly plotted out as soon as the community indulges in a plan. But, in the meanwhile, all the life and most of the houses of Calistoga are concentrated upon that street between the railway station and the road. I never heard it called by any name, but I will hazard a guess that it is either Washington or Broadway. Here are the blacksmith's, the chemist's, the general merchant's, and Kong Sam Kee, the Chinese laundryman's; here, probably, is the office of the local paper (for the place has a paper—they all have papers); and here certainly is one of the hotels, Cheeseborough's, whence the daring Foss, a man dear to legend, starts his horses for the Geysers.

It must be remembered that we are here in a land of stage-drivers and highwaymen: a land, in that sense, like England a hundred years ago. The highway robber—road-agent, he is quaintly called—is still busy in these parts. The fame of Vasquez is still young. Only a few years ago, the Lakeport stage was robbed a mile or two from Calistoga. In 1879, the dentist of Mendocino City, fifty miles away upon the coast, suddenly threw off the garments of his trade, like Grindoff, in *The Miller and his Men*, and flamed forth in his second dress as a captain of banditti. A great robbery was followed by a long chase, a chase of days if not of weeks, among the intricate hill-country; and the chase was followed by much desultory fighting, in which several—and the dentist, I believe, amongst the number—bit the dust. The grass was springing for the first time, nourished upon their blood, when I arrived in Calistoga. I am reminded of another highwayman of that same year. "He had been unwell," so ran his humorous defence, "and the doctor told him to take something, so he took the expressbox."

The cultus of the stage-coachman always flourishes highest where there are thieves on the road, and where the guard travels armed, and the stage is not only a link between country and city, and the vehicle of news, but has a faint warfaring aroma, like a man who should be brother to a soldier. California boasts her famous stage-drivers, and among the famous Foss is not forgotten. Along the unfenced, abominable mountain roads, he launches his team with small regard to human life or the doctrine of probabilities. Flinching travelers, who behold themselves coasting eternity at every corner, look with natural admiration at their driver's huge, impassive, fleshy countenance. He has the very face for the driver in Sam Weller's anecdote, who upset the election party at the required point. Wonderful tales are current of his readiness and skill. One in particular, of how one of his horses fell at a ticklish passage of the road, and how Foss let slip the reins, and, driving over the fallen animal, arrived at the next stage with only three. This I relate as I heard it, without guarantee.

I only saw Foss once, though, strange as it may sound, I have twice talked with him. He lives out of Calistoga, at a ranch called Fossville. One evening, after he was long gone home, I dropped into Cheeseborough's and was asked if I should like to speak with Mr. Foss. Supposing that the interview was impossible, and that I was merely called upon to subscribe the general sentiment, I boldly answered "Yes." Next moment, I had one instrument at my ear, another at my mouth, and found myself, with nothing in the world to say, conversing with a man several miles off among desolate hills. Foss rapidly and somewhat plaintively brought the conversation to an end; and he returned to his night's grog at Fossville, while I strolled forth again on Calistoga high street. But it was an odd thing that here, on what we are accustomed to consider the very skirts of civilization, I should have used the telephone for the first time in my civilized career. So it goes in these young countries; telephones, and telegraphs, and newspapers, and advertisements running far ahead among the Indians and the grizzly bears.

Alone, on the other side of the railway, stands the Springs Hotel, with its attendant cottages. The floor of the valley is extremely level to the very roots of the hills; only here and there a hillock, crowned with pines, rises like the barrow of some chieftain famed in war; and right against one of these hillocks is the Springs Hotel—is or was; for since I was there the place has been destroyed by fire, and has risen again from its ashes. A lawn runs about the house, and the lawn is in its turn surrounded by a system of little five-roomed cottages, each with a verandah and a weedy palm before the door. Some of the cottages are let to residents, and these are wreathed in flowers. The rest are occupied by ordinary visitors to the hotel; and a very pleasant way this is, by which you have a little country cottage of your own, without domestic burthens, and by the day or week.

The whole neighbourhood of Mount Saint Helena is full of sulphur and of boiling springs. The Geysers are famous; they were the great health resort of the Indians before the coming of the whites. Lake County is dotted with spas; Hot Springs and White Sulphur Springs are the names of two stations on the Napa Valley railroad; and Calistoga itself seems to repose on a mere film above a boiling, subterranean lake. At one end of the hotel enclosure are the springs from which it takes its name, hot enough to scald a child seriously while I was there. At the other end, the tenant of a cottage sank a well, and there also the water came up boiling. It keeps this end of the valley as warm as a toast. I have gone across to the hotel a little after five in the morning, when a sea fog from the Pacific was hanging thick and gray, and dark and dirty overhead, and found the thermometer had been up before me, and had already climbed among the nineties; and in the stress of the day it was sometimes too hot to move about.

But in spite of this heat from above and below, doing one on both sides, Calistoga was a pleasant place to dwell in; beautifully green, for it was then that favoured moment in the Californian year, when the rains are over and the dusty summer has not yet set in; often visited by fresh airs, now from the mountain, now across Sonoma from the sea; very quiet, very idle, very silent but for the breezes and the cattle bells afield. And there was something satisfactory in the sight of that great mountain that enclosed us to the north: whether it stood, robed in sunshine, quaking to its topmost pinnacle with the heat and brightness of the day; or whether it set itself to weaving vapours, wisp after wisp growing, trembling, fleeting, and fading in the blue.

The tangled, woody, and almost trackless foot-hills that enclose the valley, shutting it off from Sonoma on the west, and from Yolo on the east—rough as they were in outline, dug out by winter streams, crowned by cliffy bluffs and nodding pine trees—were dwarfed into satellites by the bulk and bearing of Mount Saint Helena. She over-towered them by two-thirds of her own stature. She excelled them by the boldness of her profile. Her great bald summit, clear of trees and pasture, a cairn of quartz and cinnabar, rejected kinship with the dark and shaggy wilderness of lesser hill-tops.

THE ACT OF SQUATTING

There were four of us squatters—myself and my wife, the King and Queen of Silverado; Sam, the Crown Prince; and Chuchu, the Grand Duke. Chuchu, a setter crossed with spaniel, was the most unsuited for a rough life. He had been nurtured tenderly in the society of ladies; his heart was large and soft; he regarded the sofa-cushion as a bed-rock necessary of existence. Though about the size of a sheep, he loved to sit in ladies' laps; he never said a bad word in all his blameless days; and if he had seen a flute, I am sure he could have played upon it by nature. It may seem hard to say it of a dog, but Chuchu was a tame cat.

The king and queen, the grand duke, and a basket of cold provender for immediate use, set forth from Calistoga in a double buggy; the crown prince, on horseback, led the way like an outrider. Bags and boxes and a second-hand stove were to follow close upon our heels by Hanson's team.

It was a beautiful still day; the sky was one field of azure. Not a leaf moved, not a speck appeared in heaven. Only from the summit of the mountain one little snowy wisp of cloud after another kept detaching itself, like smoke from a volcano, and blowing southward in some high stream of air: Mount Saint Helena still at her interminable task, making the weather, like a Lapland witch.

By noon we had come in sight of the mill: a great brown building, halfway up the hill, big as a factory, two stories high, and with tanks and ladders along the roof; which, as a pendicle of Silverado mine, we held to be an outlying province of our own. Thither, then, we went, crossing the valley by a grassy trail; and there lunched out of the basket, sitting in a kind of portico, and wondering, while we ate, at this great bulk of useless building. Through a chink we could look far down into the interior, and see sunbeams floating in the dust and striking on tier after tier of silent, rusty machinery. It cost six thousand dollars, twelve hundred English sovereigns; and now, here it stands deserted, like the temple of a forgotten religion, the busy millers toiling somewhere else. All the time we were there, mill and mill town showed no sign of life; that part of the mountainside, which is very open and green, was tenanted by no living creature but ourselves and the insects; and nothing stirred but the cloud manufactory upon the mountain summit. It was odd to compare this with the former days, when the engine was in full blast, the mill palpitating to its strokes, and the carts came rattling down from Silverado, charged with ore.

By two we had been landed at the mine, the buggy was gone again, and we were left to our own reflections and the basket of cold provender, until Hanson should arrive. Hot as it was by the sun, there was something chill in such a home-coming, in that world of wreck and rust, splinter and rolling gravel, where for so many years no fire had smoked.

Silverado platform filled the whole width of the canyon. Above, as I have said, this was a wild, red, stony gully in the mountains; but below it was a wooded dingle. And through this, I was told, there had gone a path between the mine and the Toll House—our natural north-west passage to civilization. I found and followed it, clearing my way as I went through fallen branches and dead trees. It went straight down that steep canyon, till it brought you out abruptly over the roofs of the hotel. There was nowhere any break in the descent. It almost seemed as if, were you to drop a stone down the old iron chute at our platform, it would never rest until it hopped upon the Toll House shingles. Signs were not wanting of the ancient greatness of Silverado. The footpath was well marked, and had been well trodden in the old days by thirsty miners. And far down, buried in foliage, deep out of sight of Silverado, I came on a last outpost of the mine—a mound of gravel, some wreck of wooden aqueduct, and the mouth of a tunnel, like a treasure grotto in a fairy story. A stream of water, fed by the invisible leakage from our shaft, and dyed red with cinnabar or iron, ran trippingly forth out of the bowels of the cave; and, looking far under the arch, I could see something like an iron lantern fastened on the rocky wail. It was a promising spot for the imagination. No boy could have left it unexplored. . . .

Here, also, the handiwork of men lay ruined: but the plants were all alive and thriving; the view below was fresh with the colors of nature; and we had exchanged a dim, human garret for a corner, even although it were untidy, of the blue hall of heaven. Not a bird, not a beast, not a reptile. There was no noise in that part of the world, save when we passed beside the staging, and heard the water musically falling in the shaft.

We wandered to and fro. We searched among that drift of lumber—wood and iron, nails and rails, and sleepers and the wheels of trucks. We gazed up the cleft into the bosom of the mountain. We sat by the margin of the dump and saw, far below us, the green treetops standing still in the clear air. Beautiful perfumes, breaths of bay, resin, and nutmeg, came to us more often and grew sweeter and sharper as the afternoon declined. But still there was no word of Hanson.

I set to with pick and shovel, and deepened the pool behind the shaft, till we were sure of sufficient water for the morning; and by the time I had finished, the sun had begun to go down behind the mountain shoulder, the platform was plunged in quiet shadow, and a chill descended from the sky. Night began early in our deft. Before us, over the margin of the dump, we could see the sun still striking aslant into the wooded nick below, and on the battlemented, pine-bescattered ridges on the farther side.

There was no stove, of course, and no hearth in our lodging, so we betook ourselves to the blacksmith's forge across the platform. If the platform be taken as a stage, and the out-curving margin of the dump to represent the line of the footlights, then our house would be the first wing on the actor's left, and this blacksmith's forge, although no match for it in size, the foremost on the right. It was a low, brown cottage, planted close against the hill, and overhung by the foliage and peeling boughs of a madrona thicket. Within it was full of dead leaves and mountain dust, and rubbish from the mine. But we soon had a good fire brightly blazing, and sat close about it on impromptu seats. Chuchu, the slave of sofa-cushions, whimpered for a softer bed; but the rest of us were greatly revived and comforted by that good creature—fire, which gives us warmth and light and companionable sounds, and colours up the emptiest building with better than frescoes. For a while it was even pleasant in the forge, with the blaze in the midst, and a look over our shoulders on the woods and mountains where the day was dying like a dolphin.

HELEN HUNT JACKSON
1831–1885

Born in Massachusetts as Helen Maria Fiske, Jackson was an independent child in a cultured New England family. Her early literary mentor was Colonel Thomas Wentworth Higginson, the Brahmin shaper of reputations in Boston, and through him she met another talented protégé, Emily Dickinson, with whom she corresponded for the rest of her life. From 1866 she was a prolific magazine journalist, producing almost four hundred articles in her lifetime. Jackson came to California on assignment in 1872, on the newly completed transcontinental railroad, and the magazine account of her journey was republished in Bits of Travel at Home *(1878), one of her many travel books. The trip brought her first sight of Indians in the West. She found tribal culture fascinating but was appalled by the squalor to which many had been reduced. Jackson was moved to write a nonfiction book documenting their plight, and the result was the hard-hitting* Century of Dishonor *(1881), which she sent to every member of Congress. She undertook* Ramona *(1884), her most famous work, as a parallel to Harriet Beecher Stowe's* Uncle Tom's Cabin, *hoping to inspire national concern for the plight of American Indians as Stowe had done for Southern slaves. Although the book was wildly popular, it was embraced as a tragic, doomed romance between the mixed-blood Ramona and her Indian lover Alessandro. While Jackson had a high didactic purpose, her audience responded to the novel very differently. The cult of Ramona grew: girls and towns were named after her, and the book was central in the revival of the nostalgic Mission myth in Southern California. Even so, reviewers saw artistic merit in the novel, with Albion Tourgee pronouncing it in 1886 "unquestionably the best novel yet produced by an American woman."*

Chapter 4
from *Ramona*

It was longer even than the Señora had thought it would be, before Father Salvierderra arrived. The old man had grown feeble during the year that she had not seen him, and it was a very short day's journey that he could make now without too great fatigue. It was not only his body that had failed. He had lost heart; and the miles which would have been nothing to him, had he walked in the companionship of hopeful and happy thoughts, stretched out wearily as he brooded over sad memories and still sadder anticipations,—the downfall of the Missions, the loss of their vast estates, and the growing power of the ungodly in the land. The final decision of the United States Government in regard to the Mission-lands had been a terrible blow to him. He had devoutly believed that ultimate restoration of these great estates to the Church was inevitable. In the long vigils which he always kept when at home at the Franciscan Monastery in Santa Barbara, kneeling on the stone pavement in the church, and praying ceaselessly from midnight till dawn, he had often had visions vouchsafed him of a new dispensation, in which the Mission establishments should be reinstated in all their old splendor and prosperity, and their Indian converts again numbered by tens of thousands. . . .

It was with thoughts such as these that Father Salvierderra drew near the home of the Señora Moreno late in the afternoon of one of those midsummer days of which Southern California has so many in spring. The almonds had bloomed and the blossoms fallen; the apricots also, and the peaches and pears; on all the orchards of these fruits had come a filmy tint of green, so light it was hardly more than a shadow on the gray. The willows were vivid light green, and the orange groves dark and glossy like laurel. The billowy hills on either side the valley were covered with verdure and bloom,— myriads of low blossoming plants, so close to the earth that their tints lapped and overlapped on each other, and on the green of the grass, as feathers in fine plumage overlap each other and blend into a changeful color. . . .

Father Salvierderra paused many times to gaze at the beautiful picture. . . . The fairer this beautiful land, the sadder to know it lost to the Church,—alien hands reaping its fullness, establishing new customs, new laws. All the way down the coast from Santa Barbara he had seen, at every stopping-place, new tokens of the settling up of the country—farms opening, towns growing; the Americans pouring in, at all points, to reap the advantages of their new possessions. It was this which had made his journey heavy hearted and made him feel, in approaching the Señora Moreno's, as if he were coming to one of the last sure strongholds of the Catholic faith left in the country.

When he was within two miles of the house, he struck off from the highway into a narrow path that he recollected led by a short-cut through the hills, and saved nearly a third of the distance. It was more than a year since he had trod this path, and as he found it growing fainter and fainter, and more and more overgrown with the wild mustard, he said to himself, "I think no one can have passed through here this year."

As he proceeded he found the mustard thicker and thicker. The wild mustard in Southern California is like that spoken of in the New Testament, in the branches of which the birds of the air may rest. Coming up out of the earth, so slender a stem that dozens can find starting-point in an inch, it darts up, a slender straight shoot, five, ten, twenty feet, with hundreds of fine feathery branches locking and interlocking with all the other hundreds around it, till it is an inextricable network like lace. Then it bursts into yellow bloom still finer, more feathery and lacelike. The stems are so infinitesimally small, and of so dark a green, that at a short distance they do not show, and the cloud of blossom seems floating in the air; at times it looks like golden dust. With a clear blue sky behind it, as it is often seen, it looks like a golden snow-storm. The plant is a tyrant and a nuisance,—the terror of the farmer; it takes riotous possession of a whole field in a season; once in, never out; for one plant this year, a million the next; but it is impossible to wish that the land were freed from it. Its gold is as distinct a value to the eye as the nugget gold is in the pocket.

Father Salvierderra soon found himself in a veritable thicket of these delicate branches, high above his head, and so interlaced that he could make headway only by slowly and patiently disentangling them, as one would disentangle a skein of silk. It was a fantastic sort of dilemma, and not un-pleasing. Except that the Father was in haste to reach his journey's end, he would have enjoyed threading his way through the golden meshes. Suddenly he heard faint notes of singing. He paused,—listened. It was the voice of a woman. It was slowly drawing nearer, apparently from the direction in which he was going. At intervals it ceased abruptly, then began again; as if by a sudden but brief interruption, like that made by question and answer. Then, peering ahead through the mustard blossoms, he saw them waving and bending, and heard sounds as if they were being broken. Evidently some one entering on the path from the opposite end had been caught in the fragrant thicket as he was. The notes grew clearer, though still low and sweet as the twilight notes of the thrush; the mustard branches waved more and more violently; light steps were now to be heard. Father Salvierderra stood still as one in a dream, his eyes straining forward into the golden mist of blossoms. In a moment more came, distinct and clear to his ear, the beautiful words of the second stanza of Saint Francis's inimitable lyric, "The Canticle of the Sun":

"Praise be to thee, O Lord, for all thy creatures, and especially for our brother the Sun,— who illuminates the day, and by his beauty and splendor shadows forth unto us thine."

"Ramona!" exclaimed the Father, his thin cheeks flushing with pleasure. "The blessed child!" And as he spoke, her face came into sight, set in a swaying frame of the blossoms, as she parted them lightly to right and left with her hands, and half crept, half danced through the loop-hole openings thus made. Father Salvierderra was past eighty, but his blood was not too old to move quicker at the sight of this picture. A man must be dead not to thrill at it. Ramona's beauty was of the sort to be best enhanced by the waving gold which now framed her face. She had just enough of olive tint in her complexion to underlie and enrich her skin without making it swarthy. Her hair was like her Indian mother's, heavy and black, but her eyes were like her father's, steel-blue. Only those who came very near to Ramona knew, however, that her eyes were blue, for the heavy black eyebrows and long black lashes so shaded and shadowed them that they looked black as night. At the same instant that Father Salvierderra first caught sight of her face, Ramona also saw him, and crying out joyfully, "Ah, Father, I knew you would come by this path, and something told me you were near!" she sprang forward, and sank on her knees before him, bowing her head for his blessing. In silence he laid his hands on her brow. It would not have been easy for him to speak to her at that first moment. She had looked to the devout old monk, as she sprang through the cloud of golden flowers, the sun falling on her bared head, her cheeks flushed, her eyes shining, more like an apparition of an angel or saint, than like the flesh-and-blood maiden whom he had carried in his arms when she was a babe.

"We have been waiting, waiting, oh, so long for you, Father!" she said, rising. "We began to fear that you might be ill. The shearers have been sent for, and will be here tonight, and that was the reason I felt so sure you would come. I knew the Virgin would bring you in time for mass in the chapel on the first morning."

The monk smiled half sadly. "Would there were more with such faith as yours, daughter," he said. "Are all well on the place?"

"Yes, Father, all well," she answered. "Felipe has been ill with a fever; but he is out now, these ten days, and fretting for—for your coming."

Ramona had like to have said the literal truth,—"fretting for the sheep-shearing," but recollected herself in time.

"And the Señora?" said the Father.

"She is well," answered Ramona, gently, but with a slight change of tone,—so slight as to be almost imperceptible; but an acute observer would have always detected it in the girl's tone whenever she spoke of the Señora Moreno. "And you,—are you well yourself, Father?" she asked affectionately, noting with her quick, loving eye how feebly the old man walked, and that he carried what she had never before seen in his hand,—a stout staff to steady his steps. "You must be very tired with the long journey on foot."

"Ay, Ramona, I am tired," he replied. "Old age is conquering me. It will not be many times more that I shall see this place." . . .

While they were talking, they had been slowly moving forward, Ramona slightly in advance, gracefully bending the mustard branches, and holding them down till the Father had followed in her steps. As they came out from the thicket, she exclaimed, laughing, "There is Felipe, in the willows. I told him I was coming to meet you, and he laughed at me. Now he will see I was right."

Astonished enough, Felipe, hearing voices, looked up, and saw Ramona and the Father approaching. Throwing down the knife with which he had been cutting the willows, he hastened to meet them, and dropped on his knees, as Ramona had done, for the monk's blessing. As he knelt there, the wind blowing his hair loosely off his brow, his large brown eyes lifted in gentle reverence to the Father's face, and his face full of affectionate welcome, Ramona thought to herself, as she had thought hundreds of times since she became a woman, "How beautiful Felipe is! No wonder the Señora loves him so much! If I had been beautiful like that she would have liked me better." Never was a little child more unconscious of her own beauty than Ramona still was. All the admiration which was expressed to her in word and look she took for simple kindness and good-will. Her face, as she herself saw it in her glass, did not please her. She compared her straight, massive black eyebrows with Felipe's, arched and delicately pencilled, and found her own ugly. The expression of gentle repose which her countenance wore, seemed to her an expression of stupidity. "Felipe looks so bright!" she thought, as she noted his mobile changing face, never for two successive seconds the same. "There is nobody like Felipe." And when his brown eyes were fixed on her, as they so often were, in a long lingering gaze, she looked steadily back into their velvet depths with an abstracted sort of intensity which profoundly puzzled Felipe. It was this look, more than any other one thing, which had for two years held Felipe's tongue in leash, as it were, and made it impossible for him to say to Ramona any of the loving things of which his heart had been full ever since he could remember. The boy had spoken them unhesitatingly, unconsciously; but the man found himself suddenly afraid. "What is it she thinks when she looks into my eyes so?" he wondered. If he had known that the thing she was usually thinking was simply, "How much handsomer brown eyes are than blue! I wish my eyes were the color of Felipe's!" he would have perceived, perhaps, what would have saved him sorrow, if he had known it, that a girl who looked at a man thus, would be hard to win to look at him as a lover. But being a lover, he could not see this. He saw only enough to perplex and deter him.

As they drew near the house, Ramona saw Margarita standing at the gate of the garden. She was holding something white in her hands, looking down at it, and crying piteously. As she perceived Ramona, she made an eager leap forward, and then shrank back again, making dumb signals of distress to her. Her whole attitude was one of misery and entreaty. Margarita was, of all the maids, most beloved by Ramona. Though they were nearly of the same age, it had been Margarita who first had charge of Ramona; the nurse and her charge had played together, grown up together, become women together, and were now, although Margarita never presumed on the relation, or forgot to address Ramona as Señorita, more like friends than like mistress and maid.

"Pardon me, Father," said Ramona. "I see that Margarita there is in trouble. I will leave Felipe to go with you to the house. I will be with you again in a few moments." And kissing his hand, she flew rather than ran across the field to the foot of the garden.

Before she reached the spot, Margarita had dropped on the ground and buried her face in her hands. A mass of crumpled and stained linen lay at her feet.

"What is it? What has happened, Margarita mia?" cried Ramona, in the affectionate Spanish phrase. For answer, Margarita removed one wet hand from her eyes, and pointed with a gesture of despair to the crumpled linen. Sobs choked her voice, and she buried her face again in her hands.

Ramona stooped, and lifted one corner of the linen. An involuntary cry of dismay broke from her, at which Margarita's sobs redoubled, and she gasped out, "Yes, Señorita, it is totally ruined! It can never be mended, and it will be needed for the mass tomorrow morning. When I saw the Father coming by your side, I prayed to the Virgin to let me die. The Señora will never forgive me."

It was indeed a sorry sight. The white linen altar-cloth, the cloth which the Señora Moreno had with her own hands made into one solid front of beautiful lace of the Mexican fashion, by drawing out part of the threads and sewing the remainder into intricate patterns, the cloth which had always been on the altar, when mass was said, since Margarita's and Ramona's earliest recollections,—there it lay, torn, stained, as if it had been dragged through muddy brambles. In silence, aghast, Ramona opened it out and held it up. "How did it happen, Margarita?" she whispered, glancing in terror up towards the house.

"Oh, that is the worst of it, Señorita!" sobbed the girl. "That is the worst of it! If it were not for that, I would not be so afraid. If it had happened any other way, the Señora might have forgiven me; but she never will. I would rather die than tell her;" and she shook from head to foot.

"Stop crying, Margarita!" said Ramona, firmly, "and tell me all about it. It isn't so bad as it looks. I think I can mend it."

"Oh, the saints bless you!" cried Margarita, looking up for the first time. "Do you really think you can mend it, Señorita? If you will mend that lace, I'll go on my knees for you all the rest of my life!"

Ramona laughed in spite of herself. "You'll serve me better by keeping on your feet," she said merrily; at which Margarita laughed too, through her tears. They were both young.

"Oh, but Señorita," Margarita began again in a tone of anguish, her tears flowing afresh, "there is not time! It must be washed and ironed to-night, for the mass to-morrow morning, and I have to help at the supper. Anita and Rosa are both ill in bed, you know, and Maria has gone away for a week. The Señora said if the Father came to-night I must help mother, and must wait on table. It cannot be done. I was just going to iron it now, and I found it— so—It was in the artichoke-patch, and Capitan, the beast, had been tossing it among the sharp pricks of the old last year's seeds."

"In the artichoke-patch!" ejaculated Ramona. "How under heavens did it get there?"

"Oh, that was what I meant, Señorita, when I said she never would forgive me. She has forbidden me many times to hang anything to dry on the fence there; and if I had only washed it when she first told me, two days ago, all would have been well. But I forgot it till this afternoon, and there was no sun in the court to dry it, and you know how the sun lies on the artichoke-patch, and I put a strong cloth over the fence, so that the wood should not pierce the lace, and I did not leave it more than half an hour, just while I said a few words to Luigo, and there was no wind; and I believe the saints must have fetched it down to the ground to punish me for my disobedience."

Ramona had been all this time carefully smoothing out the torn places. "It is not so bad as it looks," she said; "if it were not for the hurry, there would be no trouble in mending it. But I will do it the best I can, so that it will not show, for to-morrow, and then, after the Father is gone, I can repair it at leisure, and make it just as good as new. I think I can mend it and wash it before dark," and she glanced at the sun. "Oh, yes, there are good three hours of daylight yet. I can do it. You put the irons on the fire, to have them hot, to iron it as soon as it is partly dried. You will see it will not show that anything has happened to it."

"Will the Señora know?" asked poor Margarita, calmed and reassured, but still in mortal terror.

Ramona turned her steady glance full on Margarita's face. "You would not be any happier if she were deceived, do you think?" she said gravely.

"O Señorita, after it is mended? If it really does not show?" pleaded the girl.

"I will tell her myself, and not till after it is mended," said Ramona; but she did not smile.

"Ah, Señorita," said Margarita, deprecatingly, "you do not know what it is to have the Señora displeased with one."

"Nothing can be so bad as to be displeased with one's self," retorted Ramona, as she walked swiftly away to her room with the linen rolled up under her arm. Luckily for Margarita's cause, she met no one on the way. The Señora had welcomed Father Salvierderra at the foot of the veranda steps, and had immediately closeted herself with him. She had much to say to him,—much about which she wished his help and counsel, and much which she wished to learn from him as to affairs in the Church and in the country generally.

Felipe had gone off at once to find Juan Canito, to see if everything were ready for the sheep-shearing to begin on the next day, if the shearers arrived in time; and there was very good chance of their coming in by sundown this day, Felipe thought, for he had privately instructed his messenger to make all possible haste, and to impress on the Indians the urgent need of their losing no time on the road.

It had been a great concession on the Señora's part to allow the messenger to be sent off before she had positive intelligence as to the Father's movements. But as day after day passed and no news came, even she perceived that it would not do to put off the sheep-shearing much longer, or, as Juan Canito said, "forever." The Father might have fallen ill; and if that were so, it might very easily be weeks before they heard of it, so scanty were the means of communication between the remote places on his route of visitation. The messenger had therefore been sent to summon the Temecula shearers, and Señora had resigned herself to the inevitable; piously praying, however, morning and night, and at odd moments in the day, that the Father might arrive before the Indians did. When she saw him coming up the garden-walk, leaning on the arm of her Felipe, on the afternoon of the very day which was the earliest possible day for the Indians to arrive, it was not strange that she felt, mingled with the joy of her greeting to her long-loved friend and confessor, a triumphant exultation that the saints had heard her prayers. . . .

At last supper was ready,—a great dish of spiced beef and cabbage in the centre of the table; a tureen of thick soup, with forcemeat balls and red peppers in it; two red earthen platters heaped, one with the boiled rice and onions, the other with the delicious *frijoles* (beans) so dear to all Mexican hearts; cut-glass dishes filled with hot stewed pears, or preserved quinces, or grape jelly; plates of frosted cakes of various sorts; and a steaming silver teakettle, from which went up an aroma of tea such as had never been bought or sold in all California, the Señora's one extravagance and passion.

"Where is Ramona?" asked the Señora, surprised and displeased, as she entered the dining-room. "Margarita, go tell the Señorita that we are waiting for her."

Margarita started tremblingly, with flushed face, towards the door. What would happen now! "O Saint Francis," she inwardly prayed, "help us this once!"

"Stay," said Felipe. "Do not call Señorita Ramona." Then, turning to his mother, "Ramona cannot come. She is not in the house. She has a duty to perform for tomorrow," he said; and he looked meaningly at his mother, adding, "we will not wait for her."

Much bewildered, the Señora took her seat at the head of the table in a mechanical way, and began, "But—" Felipe, seeing that questions were to follow, interrupted her: "I have just spoken with her. It is impossible for her to come," and turning to Father Salvierderra, he at once engaged him in conversation, and left the baffled Señora to bear her unsatisfied curiosity as best she could.

Margarita looked at Felipe with an expression of profound gratitude, which he did not observe, and would not in the least have understood; for Ramona had not confided to him any details of the disaster. Seeing him under her window, she had called cautiously to him, and said: "Dear Felipe, do you think you can save me from having to come to supper? A dreadful accident has happened to the altar-cloth, and I must mend it and wash it, and there is barely time before dark. Don't let them call me; I shall be down at the brook, and they will not find me, and your mother will be displeased."

This wise precaution of Ramona's was the salvation of everything, so far as the altar-cloth was concerned. The rents had proved far less serious than she had feared; the daylight held out till the last of them was skillfully mended; and just as the red beams of the sinking sun came streaming through the willow-trees at the foot of the garden, Ramona, darting down the garden, had reached the brook, and kneeling on the grass, had dipped the linen into the water.

Her hurried working over the lace, and her anxiety, had made her cheeks scarlet. As she ran down the garden, her comb had loosened and her hair fallen to her waist. Stopping only to pick up the comb and thrust it in her pocket, she had sped on, as it would soon be too dark for her to see the stains on the linen, and it was going to be no small trouble to get them out without fraying the lace.

Her hair in disorder, her sleeves pinned loosely on her shoulders, her whole face aglow with the earnestness of her task, she bent low over the stones, rinsing the altar-cloth up and down in the water, anxiously scanning it, then plunging it in again.

The sunset beams played around her hair like a halo; the whole place was aglow with red light, and her face was kindled into transcendent beauty. A sound arrested her attention. She looked up. Forms, dusky black against the fiery western sky, were coming down the valley. It was the band of Indian shearers. They turned to the left, and went towards the sheep sheds and booths. But there was one of them that Ramona did not see. He had been standing for some minutes concealed behind a large willow-tree a few rods from the place where Ramona was kneeling. It was Alessandro, son of Pablo Assis, captain of the shearing band. Walking slowly along in advance of his men, he had felt a light, as from a mirror held in the sun, smite his eyes. It was the red sunbeam on the glittering water where Ramona knelt. In the same second he saw Ramona.

He halted, as wild creatures of the forest halt at a sound; gazed; walked abruptly away from his men, who kept on, not noticing his disappearance. Cautiously he moved a few steps nearer, into the shelter of a gnarled old willow, from behind which he could gaze unperceived on the beautiful vision,—for so it seemed to him.

As he gazed, his senses seemed leaving him, and unconsciously he spoke aloud: "Christ! What shall I do!"

JOSIAH ROYCE

1855–1916

Born in Grass Valley to Josiah Royce Sr. and Sarah Royce (author of
A Frontier Lady*), Royce received his Ph.D. from Johns Hopkins University*
at age twenty-three and taught at the University of California at Berkeley from
1879 to 1882. While at Berkeley, he did the major research for his masterwork of critical
history, California: A Study of the American Character *(1886), and a novel based*
on the Mussel Slough tragedy, The Feud at Oakfield Creek *(1887). Royce was among*
the first historians of California to examine both national and state history in the period
1846–1856 and to lay bare the patterns of deceit and moral betrayal in the conquest of
the American West and the founding of California. His work was very controversial in
the state, as he suggested that the Gold Rush and the betrayal of the Californios *revealed*
cultural weaknesses that would compromise the future development of California. Royce
went on to teach at Harvard, where—as the successor to William James—he became
recognized as an eminent philosopher and historian.

From *California: A Study of American Character*

CHAPTER 2. THE AMERICAN AS CONQUEROR:
THE SECRET MISSION AND THE BEAR FLAG

In the strict sense, we Americans have seldom been conquerors; and early
California shows us our nation in this somewhat rare character. A few men
did the work for us; but their acts were in some cases directly representative
of the national qualities, and in others of far-reaching influence on the life
and character of our people in California in the subsequent days. For both
reasons these acts concern us deeply here, and are very instructive for our
purposes.

Moreover, the story of the conquest belongs, for yet other reasons, even
more to national than to local annals. Our plans for getting the coveted land,
and the actual execution of these plans, are a part of the drama of the Mexican
War, and our national honor is deeply concerned in the interpretation that
shall be given to the facts. As for the treatment of these facts here, a bare
summary would be, in the present day, more vexatious than a detailed study;
for a bare summary would either leave all the mysteries unsolved, or else
seem to fill all the gaps with mere dogmas. The whole story of the conquest

is turbid with popular legends. We cannot follow the narrative in a simple way, and tell incident after incident. The condition of our knowledge of the subject forbids such a purely narrative procedure save in fragments. What can be given might indeed be suggestively entitled "Commentaries on the Conquest," in a very literal sense of the word *commentary*. We have to employ numerous sources of information, and to use our best historical intelligence. Yet we beseech the reader not to despair of ending in this chapter the interest that properly belongs to a dramatic series of events. These very problems of the conquest, the mysteries that have hung over parts of the *story*, are, as we have just hinted, themselves dramatic, and the investigation seems to me to present many elements of exciting interest, even apart from the original fascination of the incidents.

The subsequent history of the American people in California turns, we have suggested, in large measure upon the occurrences of the conquest. The prejudices, the enmities, and the mistakes of that unhappy time bore rich fruit in the sequel, determining to a great extent the future relations of the new-comers and the natives; and these relations in their turn determined, in no small degree, both the happiness and the moral welfare of the new-comers themselves. We must understand the conquest if we are to understand what followed. The attitude that chance, the choice of one or two representative men, and our national character made us assume towards the Californians at the moment of our appearance among them as conquerors, we have ever since kept, with disaster to them, and not without disgrace and degradation to ourselves. The story is no happy one; but this book is written, not to extol our transient national glories, but to serve the true patriot's interest in a clear self-knowledge, and in the formation of sensible ideals of national greatness.

From the point of view of the study of historical fact as such, this history of the conquest is one of the strangest examples of the vitality of the truth. Never were the real motives and methods of a somewhat complex undertaking more carefully, or, by the help of luck, more successfully, hidden from the public than the methods and motives of certain of our national agents in California at the time of the conquest have for a generation been hidden. And never has accident more unmercifully turned at last upon its own creations.

I. The Confidential Agent and the Beginning of War

As the reader knows from the foregoing, our hearts were set upon California as one prize that made the Mexican War most worth fighting. The Bay of San Francisco, the future commerce of the Pacific, the fair and sunny land beyond the Sierras, the full and even boundary westward, the possible new field for the extension of slavery,—such motives were powerful with some or all of our leaders. The hasty seizure of Monterey in 1842, although wholly disavowed by our government, was a betrayal of our national feeling, to say the least, if not of our national plans, which no apology could withdraw from plain history. Meanwhile, with more or less good foundation, we had strong fears of both England and France as dangerous rivals in the acquisition of this western land. In short, to use the phrase so often repeated by opponents of the Mexican War, California formed a great part of the "Naboth's vineyard" that we coveted, and that for years we had expected some day to get by the fairest convenient means.

Nor was our desire for California in itself an evil. However difficult the righteous satisfaction of the desire might prove, this desire was inevitable. Our national duty doubtless forbade our cheerful surrender of the Pacific coast to any European power. And by sloth, neglect, and misgovernment, Mexico had done all she could do to make her California vineyard bring forth wild grapes, and to forfeit her proprietary rights in its soil. Not "Naboth" in this case was the one whom we were most in danger of wronging, although indeed we did wrong him fearfully. He, poor fellow, was distracted in his own house, tilled not his own fields, and often was stained with blood. It was the true proprietor of California that, when we coveted the land, we were most apt to injure; it was the disorganized but not wholly unpromising young nation of a few thousand cheerful, hospitable, and proud souls on the Pacific coast that we were especially bound to respect. With their good-will if possible, and at all events with the strictest possible regard for their rights, we were bound in honor to proceed in our plans and undertakings on the Pacific coast. The Mexican War, if deliberately schemed, and forced into life through our aggressive policy, would be indeed a crime; but it would be adding another great crime if we wronged these nearly independent Californians, while assailing their unkind but helpless mother.

The slow and steady growth of the American settlements in California was not the result of any definite plot on the part of our government. Yet, as the correspondence of the State Department with Consul Larkin shows, the government was curious concerning this very matter; and the American colonization was looked upon as a fortunate occurrence for us, and as a process that, if let alone by the course of events and particularly by European aggressors, might of itself suffice, here as in Texas, to secure to us the country. Yet nobody intended to leave the decision of the matter to so slow a process as this. Natural colonization would need to be assisted. . . .

The State, then, was triumphantly created out of the very midst of the troubles of the interregnum, and in the excitements of the first golden days. But the busy scenes of early California life give us, as we follow their events, little time for quiet enjoyment of the results of even the best social undertakings. The proclamation of the sovereign state itself is only as the sound of a trumpet, signaling the beginning of the real social battle. Anarchy is a thing of degrees, and its lesser degrees often coexist even with the constitutions that are well conceived and popular. The California pioneers had now to deal with forces, both within themselves and in the world beyond, that produced an exciting and not bloodless struggle for order, some of whose events, as they took place in the mines, in the interior cities, in the course of the state politics, and in San Francisco, we must try to describe, selecting what will best illustrate the problems of the time from the great mass of occurrences, and returning, where it is necessary, to the relation of some events that were antecedent to those last described. Of the romantic and heroic we shall have something to tell, as we go on; but much of our story will concern matters that only the sternest and least romantic realism can properly represent.

I. The Philosophy of California History during the Golden Days

Two very familiar errors exist concerning the California of the years between 1848 and 1856, both misconceptions of the era of the struggle for order. One of these errors will have it that, on the whole, there was struggle; while the other affirms that, on the whole there was no order. In fact there were both, and their union is incomprehensible, save as an historical program from lower to higher social conditions. Both the mentioned errors find support, not in authoritative pioneer evidence, but in some of the more irresponsible reminiscences of forgetful pioneers, reminiscences that express little save a desire to boast, either of the marvelous probity, or of the phenomenal wickedness, of their lows in the early days. Many pioneers seem to assume that, save their own anecdotes, no sound records of the early days are extant. Yet the fact is that, valuable as the honest man's memory must be, to retain and convey the coloring of the minds and moods of individuals and parties, this individual memory cannot be trusted, in general, either for the details of any complex transaction, or for an account of the whole state of any large and mixed community. And one finds this especially true when one reads some of these personal reminiscences of the more forgetful California pioneers. In one mood, or with one sort of experience, the pioneer can remember little but the ardor, the high aims, the generosity, the honor, and the good order of the Californian community. A few gamblers, a few foreign convicts, a few "greasers" there were, who threw shadows into the glorious picture. But they could not obscure it. On the other hand, however, another equally boastful memory revels in scenes of sanguinary freedom, of lawless popular frenzy, of fraud, of drunkenness, of gaming, and of ardor. According to this memory nothing shall have remained pure: most ministers who happened to be intent gambled, society was ruled by courtesans, nobody looked twice at a freshly murdered man, everybody gayly joined in lynching any supposed thief, and alike rejoiced in raptures of vicious liberty. These are the two extreme views. You can find numbers of similarly incomplete intermediate views. The kaleidoscopic effect of a series of them can be judged by read-the conflicting statements that, with a rather unnecessary liberality, Mr. Shinn has added to his own more sober, rational, and well-founded views, in some of the less authoritative citations in chapters xi and xii of his "Mining Camps."

But these impressions are, as individual impressions, once for all doomed to be unhistorical. The experience of one man could never reveal the social process, of which his life formed but one least element. This process, however, was after all a very simple though widely extended moral process, the struggle of society to impress the true dignity and majesty of its claims on wayward and blind individuals, and the struggle of the individual man, meanwhile, to escape, like a fool, from his moral obligations to society. This struggle is an old one and old societies do not avoid it; for every man without exception is born to the illusion that the moral world is his oyster. But in older societies each man is conquered for himself, and is forced in his own time to give up his fool's longings for liberty, and to do a work as he may, while in a new society, especially in one made up largely of men who have left homes and families, who have fled from before the word of the Lord and have sought safety from their old vexatious duties in a golden paradise, this struggle being begun afresh by all comes to the surface of things. California was full of Jonahs, whose modest and possibly unprophetic duties had lain in their various quiet paths at home. They had found out how to escape all these duties, at least for the moment, by fleeing over seas and deserts. Strange to say, the ships laden with these fugitives sank not, but bore them safely to the new land. And in the deserts the wanderers by land found an almost miraculous safety. The snares of the god were, however, none the less well laid for that, and these hasty feet were soon to trip. Whoever sought a fool's liberty here (as which of us has not at some time sought it somewhere?) was soon to find all of a man's due bondage prepared for him, and doubtless much more. For nowhere and at no time are social duties in the end more painful or exacting than in the tumultuous days of new countries; just as it is harder to work for months on a Vigilance Committee than once in a lifetime to sit on a legal jury in a quiet town.

What we have here to do is to understand what force worked for and against order in this community of irresponsible strangers, and how in time, for their lonely freedom, was substituted the long and wearisome toil that has caused nearly all the men of that pioneer community to die before their due season, or to live even today, when they do live at all, the life of poverty and disappointment. Let us name at the outset these forces of order and of disorder.

The great cause of the growth of order in California is usually said to be the undoubtedly marvelous political talent of our race and nation. And yet, important as that was, we must not exaggerate it. The very ease with which the State on paper could be made lulled to sleep the political conscience of the ordinary man, and from the outset gave too much self-confidence to the community. The truly significant social order, which requires not only natural political instinct, but also voluntary and loyal devotion to society, was often rather retarded than hastened in its coming by the political facility of the people. What helped still more than instinct was the courage, the moral elasticity, the teachableness of the people. Their greatest calamities they learned to laugh at, their greatest blunders they soon recovered from; and even while they boasted of their prowess, and denied their sins, they would quietly go on to correct their past grievous errors, good-humored and self-confident as ever. A people such as this are in the long run favored of heaven, although outwardly they show little proper humility or contrition. For in time they learn the hardest lessons, by dint of obstinate cheerfulness in enduring their bitter experiences, and of wisdom in tacitly avoiding their past blunders.

Against order, however, worked especially two tendencies in early California: one this aforementioned general sense of irresponsibility, and the other a diseased local exaggeration of our common national feeling towards foreigners, an exaggeration for which the circumstances of the moment were partly responsible. The first tendency pioneers admit, though not in all its true magnitude; the second they seldom recognize at all, charging to the foreigners themselves whatever trouble was due to our brutal ill-treatment of them.

As for the first tendency, it is the great key to the problem of the worst troubles of early California. The new-comers, viewed as a mass, were homeless. They sought wealth, and not a social order. They were, for the most part, as Americans, decently trained in the duties of a citizen; and as to courage and energy they were picked men, capable, when their time should come far showing true manhood, of sacrificing their vain hopes and enduring everything. But their early quest was at all events an unmoral one; and when they neglected their duties as freemen, as citizens, and as brethren among brethren, their quest became not merely unmoral, but positively sinful. And never did the journeying pillar, of cloud by day and of fire by night, teach to the legendary wanderers in the desert more unmistakably by signs and wonders the eternal law, than did the fortunes of these early Californians display to them, through the very accidents of the majesty of the same law of order and of loyalty to society. In the air, as it were, the invisible divine net of social duties hung, and descending, enmeshed irresistibly all these gay and careless fortune-hunters even while they boasted of their freedom. Every piece of neglected social work they had to do over again, with many times the toil. Every slighted duty avenged relentlessly on the community that had despised it.

However, in the early days, there was also that other agency at work for disorder, whose influence is to blame for much, although not for all, nor even for most, of the degradation that the new State passed through. This was a brutal tendency, and yet it was very natural, and, like all natural brutality, it was often, in any individual man, a childishly innocent tendency. It was a hearty American contempt for things and institutions and people that were stubbornly foreign, and that would not conform themselves to American customs and wishes. Representatives of their nation these gold-seeking Californian Americans were; yet it remains true, and is, under the circumstances, a very natural result, that the American had nowhere else, save perhaps as conqueror in Mexico itself, shown so blindly and brutally as he often showed in early California, his innate intolerance for whatever is stubbornly foreign. No American of sense can be proud when he reflects upon these doings of his countrymen, both towards the real foreigners and towards those who were usually confounded with such, namely, the native Californians. Least of all can a native American Californian, like the author, rejoice to remember how the community from which he sprang treated both their fellow-intruders in the land, and his own fellows, the born citizens of this dear soil, themselves. All this tale is one of disgrace to our people. But it is none the less true, and none the less profitable to know. For this hatred of foreigners, this blind nativism, are we not all alike born to it? And what but reflection, and our chance measure of cultivation, checks it in any of us?

If we leave out the unprovoked violence frequently offered to foreigners, we may then say that the well known crises and tragedies of violent popular justice during the struggle for order were frequently neither directly and in themselves crimes of the community, as conservative people have often considered them, nor yet merely expressions of righteous indignation on the part of an innocent and outraged society; but they were simply the outward symptoms in each case of the *past* popular crimes of disloyalty to the social order; they were social penalties, borne by the community itself even more than by the rogues, for the treason of carelessness.

MARY HALLOCK FOOTE
1847–1938

Born in New York, Mary Hallock Foote spent her early life at the center of society and the abolitionist and feminist intellectual currents of the time. At age twenty-nine she married Arthur Foote, a mining engineer, and headed west. Foote spent much of the period from 1876 to 1932 in the rugged mining towns of the American West, but she never lost her early sense of noblesse and Victorian womanhood. The couple moved from Leadville, Colorado, to Boise, Idaho, before settling in Grass Valley, California—where Arthur became manager of the North Star Mine—in 1895. Initially a distinguished magazine illustrator, she turned the harsh mining life around her into the material of novels and stories that brought her prominence—among them The Led-Horse Claim *(1883),* The Last Assembly Ball *(1889), and* In Exile *(1894). Her best work reflected the mingled romanticism and realism of the time. Foote stayed long in Grass Valley, but wrote relatively little of the experience. The fiction that emerged, including her short story "How the Pump Stopped at the Morning Watch," was, in the words of Wallace Stegner, "the only serious writing after Bret Harte to deal with mining-camp society, and virtually the only serious fiction which has dealt with the camps from intimate knowledge." Stegner draws on her letters (a matter of recent controversy) in his Pulitzer Prize–winning novel* Angle of Repose *(1971).*

How the Pump Stopped at the Morning Watch

The main shaft of the Morning Watch is an incline, sunk on the vein to a depth below daylight of eighteen hundred feet; there are lower workings still, in the twenty-one hundred, for the mine is one of the patriarchs of the golden age in northern California and its famous vein, though small, has been richly persistent.

The shaft is a specimen of good early construction in mining; it has two compartments, answering to the two vital functions of pumping and hoisting. A man walking up the hoist may step into the pump shaft between timbers to avoid a car, but he must then be wary of the pump rod.

The pump rod at the Morning Watch is half a mile long; with a measured movement, mighty, conclusive, slow, it crawls a little way up the shaft, waits a breath, then plunges down, and you hear subterranean sobs and gulpings where the twelve pumps at their stations are sucking water from the mine.

These are the water guard which is never relieved. Nights and Sundays, frost or flood or dry, the pumps never rest. Each lifts its load to the brother above him, sweating cold sweat and smeared with grease and slime, fighting the climbing waters. The stroke of the pump rod is the pulse of the mine. If the pulse should stop and the waters rise, the pumps as they go under are "drowned". In their bitter costliness, in the depths from which they rise, though born in sunlight the waters of the "sump" might typify the encroaching power of evil in man's nature—a power that springs from good that yet may be turned to good, but over which conscience, like the pumps, must keep unsleeping watch and ward.

Between the Cornish miner and the Cornish pump there is a constitutional affinity and an ancient hereditary understanding. Both are governed and driven by the power on top; both have held their own underground from generation to generation without change or visible improvement. They do their work by virtue of main strength and dogged constancy, and neither one can be hurried.

On this last head, the pump-man will answer for his pump—speaking of it as of an old comrade, in the masculine singular, if you ask how many beats of the great connecting rod are normal:—"'E 'ave been as 'igh as seven and a quarter; 'e 'ave been, but it do strain 'im. Seven, about seven, is what 'e can bear."

John Trenberth of Penzance, spoken of familiarly as "old John," was pump-man first and last at the Morning Watch. He was there when the first pump-station was put in and the rod was but four hundred feet long. He saw that mighty member grow, section by section, pump added to pump, as the shaft went down. Each new pump was as a child born to him; there was room in his pride always for one more. If one had a failing more than another, he made a study of its individual crankiness and learned to spare the fault he could not remedy nor hide. To the mining captain, to whom he was forced to go for supplies, he might confess that "No. 5, 'e do chaw up more packin' than all the pumps in the mine"; but in general it was like touching upon delicate family matters with old John to question the conduct of his pumps.

He was a just man, Trenberth, but not perfect; he had his temporal bonds. It went hard with him on the Lord's day to choose between the public duty of worship in the miners' church above ground and his private leaning towards his pumps below. Can a man do his work in this world too well? Excessive devotion to the interests of the mine was not a common fault with its employees. The boys at the Morning Watch made friendly sport of the old enthusiast, declaring that he took his pumps to bed with him and dreamed at night of their kicking and bucking. It is true that the thought of Sammy Trebilcox, and what he might be doing or not doing as his substitute underground, took the heart out of his Sabbath observances and made his day of rest, when he gave himself one, the longest of the seven. Wherefore his little wife—"a good bit older nor 'e"—and a woman of grave disposition saddened by the want of children—sat mournful in church without her man, and thought of his clean shirts folded in the drawer at home and of him in his week day livery of mud, earning unblessed wages underground. She knew it was not the extra day's pay that ensnared him; her prayer was that he be delivered from pride in carnal labors and that he make not unto himself a graven image and an idol of "they pumps".

A pump-man has his regular shifts; but so well known was the quality of John's service that not a man about the mine, from the oldest tributer to the new superintendent, would have questioned his appearance above ground at any irregular hour of the day or night. He looked, when he came on top, like some old piece of mining machinery that has been soaked underground for half a century—plastered with pallid mud of the deepest levels, coated with grease and stained with rust from fondlings of his pumps,—the recognizably human parts of him, his unsunned face and hands, pitted and drawn with steam.

The day's pay men were lively in the stopes; the car-boys romped with the landing men, and chalked the names of one another's sweethearts on the sides of the refractory cars; every tributer in the old workings had his partner to help him hammer out a "crushin' "; the contractors tunneled and drifted and argued in gangs; but old John, in the bowels of the mine, with death within a foot of him on either side, kept his one man watch alone. In his work there was no variety, no change of surroundings or of seasons, no irrelevant object to rest his fixed attention; solitude, monotony, and ceaseless nagging vigilance, imprisoned in a tube of darkness between the crashing of the cars on the one hand and the squeeze of the rod on the other.

Iron will crystallize after years of such use; lose its elasticity and cohesive strength. Old John had ceased to find pleasure in society or sunlight. He chose the darkest paths going home through the woods, the old roads deep in pine needles undisturbed by passing feet. The sound of a boy's whoop or a man's hearty halloo drove him deeper into the shade. If spoken to, he had no answer ready but would whisper one to himself later, with his eyes on the ground.

Once the night shift, going down, saw the old man bare headed in the hoist shaft standing motionless on the track, his hand up as if listening. He appeared not to hear the noise of the car, or to have heard it from some imaginary direction. They waved, they roared to him, and he vanished in the pumpshaft. Afterward they remembered his stare of bewilderment as if he had come awake suddenly in a strange place, uncertain how he had got there. Sometimes he would pop up like a stage ghost in the hoisting works, haggard and panting, as if in urgent haste. Greeted with jocular questioning, he would gaze about him vaguely, turn, and plunge down again without, a word.

The wife began to hear from relatives and neighbors disquieting comments on her husband's looks.

"It's more than a whole month 'e 'aven't 'ad a Sunday off," said the buxom wife of one of the shift bosses. "Whatever is the sense of 'im workin' so 'ard, and you only two in family? A rest is what 'e need."

"Rest, dear! 'Aven't I telled 'im so, scores and scores of times! An' 'e just like a fish out o' water when 'e's parted from they pumps. 'E talk of 'em the same as they were humans—made of the same piece wi' 'is own flesh and blood."

"Eh! It's a bad lookout when a man can't leave his work behind 'im when the day is done. We belongs to 'ave our rest sometime. Why don't 'e coax 'im out more? 'Twould do him good to see the folks."

"'E never was one to be coaxed. What 'e think right, that 'e'll do; man nor woman can't make 'im do other," Mrs. Trenberth would boast, proud of a husband's will unbroken after forty years of marriage.

One morning there was a summons for the mistress at the kitchen door of the superintendent's house.

"Clem' want see you—kitch'," was the Chinese cook's sketchy way of transmitting the message.

Clemmo was there, the gardener and general utility man. The two do not go together unless the man is good natured, as Clemmo was. He stood, hat in hand, in his deferential way, perspiring and quite noticeably pale. There was a catch in his breath from running. He had come to borrow an umbrella.

The mistress hooked at him in surprise. It was cloudless summer weather, the hot valley steaming up in the face of the foothills, dust on the cloaking pine woods, red dust deep on all the roads and trails, dust like a steamer's smoke the in wake of ore teams miles away. The shadows of the mine buildings were short and black where a group of men had gathered, though the twelve bell had not yet struck. A sun umbrella did he mean?

"Any kind, ma'am; any old one will do," Clemmo repeated apologetically. "It's just to hold over Mr. Trenberth when they're carryin' him home. Yes, Ma'am, he was hurt in the shaft just now—an hour ago. Oh, yes, the doctor's seen him. He's pretty bad. It was an empty car struck him; dragged quite a way before the shaft men heard him scream. They can't tell just how it happened; he hasn't spoken since they brought him up. Yes, Ma'am, one of the boys has gone to tell the wife. They've got an old mattress to carry him on; they have brandy. No, Ma'am, there ain't anything, thank you—only the umbrella. Any old one will do."

When the umbrella was brought and it proved to be a silk one, Clemmo took it reluctantly, protesting that "any old one—", but the mistress cut him short. He went off with it finally, assuring her over his shoulder that he would carry it himself and see that it "came right back."

The Chinaman looked on calmly. "I think he pletty ole—he die pletty soon," he remarked.

Three little children were frolicking in the swing under the pine trees. Their mother quieted them out of respect for what was soon to pass the house; but she could not moderate the morning's display of pink faced roses, nor suggest to the sun to go under a brief cloud. All was heartless radiance and peace as the forlorn little procession came down the road—the workers carrying him home whose work was done; three men on a side, and between their stout backs and faces red with exertion, a broken shape stretched out and a stark white profile crowned with a bloody cloth.

What had the old man been doing in the hoist? "Fixin' up the bell rope," the mining captain said; "but it didn't look like any of John's work," he added meaningly. "He wasn't all there when he rigged up that thing. He'd slipped a cog, somehow.—Yes sir, you bet! A man in a shaft he's got to keep his eye out. He can watch for forty years, and the minute he forgets himself, that minute he's gone."

About the turn of the night, when the old man was nearing his end, he gave a loud cry and sprang up in bed, where he had lain speechless and helpless three days. The startled watchers flew to his side.

"Take your 'ands off me, women!" he panted. "I must up. Th' pump 'e's stopped!"

"Don't 'ee, deary!" The wife trembled at the look in his pinched gray face. "Don't 'ee be thinkin' o' they pumps no more. 'Owever could 'ee hear 'em, two miles away? Hark, now! 'Tis all as still as still."

It was so still, that windless summer night, they could hear the clock tick across the passage, and the hoarse straining of the dying man's breath as they struggled to hold him down. His weakness, not their strength, prevailed. He fell back on his pillows, and a passive, awestruck stare succeeded the energy of horror and resistance. His eyes were fixed, as one who watches spellbound the oncoming of a great disaster. They touched his still face; it was damp and cold. His chest pumped hard and slow.

"Two thousan' gone under! Drowned, drowned!" he whispered.

'Tis all nothin' but they pumps!" the old wife grieved distractedly. She knew his time was short. "Oh, dear Savior, don't mind it of 'im! 'E were a hard worker, and a good man to me."

At that same hour, the night of John's release, when he had given his loud cry, the watchman at the mine heard above the roar of forty stamp heads a sound like a cannon smothered within walls. He rushed across to the hoisting works. There lay the great crown wheel of the pump, in pieces on the floor. The pump rod, settled on its chocks, had stopped with its last stroke.

One little cog, worn out, had dropped from its place; then two cogs came together, tooth to tooth, and the ten-ton wheel burst with a groan that had arrested the passing soul of the pump-man, duty bound to the last.

An old mine, or an old man, that is nearly worked out may run for years at small expense if no essential part gives way; but the cost of heavy repairs is too great a strain upon halting faith and an exhausted treasury. Even so small a thing as the dropping out of one little cog, in a system worth thousands to rebuild, may decide the question whether to give up or keep on.

In that moment of ultimate consciousness, the mystery of which is with the dead, it may be that old John beheld the whole sequence of disaster that was to follow the breaking of the pump. If he did foresee it all, as his ghostly eyes seemed to say, he accepted it as well; and that look of awe-struck, appealing submission in the face of immeasurable calamity he carried to the grave. Perhaps he had seen beyond the work of this world to some place of larger recompense where the unpaid increment of such service as his is waiting on the books. Perhaps he heard already the Master's patient "Well done."

While they were preaching the funeral sermon, his old enemy, the water of the black deeps, was creeping up, regaining ground which he and the pumps had fought for and defended, inch by inch and year by year.

"Two thousan' gone under!" The lowest pump is lost. Leave it where it drowned, at its post. Now there is hurry and rush of tearing up tracks before the levels are flooded; the order to shut down has come late. Pull out the pumps; the fight is over! They have taken up the track in the main incline; the water has reached the nine hundred, like the chill creeping up the limbs of a dying man. The old tributers take down their muddy mine suits from the change house walls; families will live poorer this winter for all that water in the mine. They go trooping home, boots and bundles over shoulder, by the paths their own feet have made. They meet no night shift coming on. Another year and those paths of labor will be deep in hushing pine needles; shadows of morning and evening will be the change of shifts. The payrolls are closed; the last crushing has gone to the mill. The grave of ten millions is for sale cheap, with a thousand feet of water in it.

Mary Hallock Foote

EDWIN MARKHAM

1852–1940

Born in Oregon, Markham grew up in San Jose and later near Vacaville. He attended Christian College in Santa Rosa and taught school in Placerville and then Oakland, while beginning to write poetry. "The Man with the Hoe" (1899) made him famous overnight and secured his place in California literary history. Published as a four-page leaflet in William Randolph Hearst's San Francisco Examiner *on Sunday, January 15, 1899, the poem occasioned a firestorm of support and controversy, and by the end of Markham's long life it had appeared in ten thousand magazines and newspapers in more than forty languages. Tame as it is by current standards, the poem—which pits farmers against greedy corporations—was both attacked for its socialist views and exalted for its idealistic portrait of the noble worker in the field. Knowing news when he saw it, Hearst also published Markham's "Lincoln, the Man of the People" in his chain of newspapers on February 12, 1900, and by the next weekend it had been reprinted in virtually every newspaper in the country. Like many of his generation, Markham, known as "the Placerville Schoolmaster," fell under the sway of numerous utopian and socialist visionaries of the time (including Marx and Swedenborg). His ability to transform political dreams into popular poetry won him enormous audiences and financial comfort. He was a mesmerizing orator, and at the end of his four-month continental tour in 1915 an amazed fellow poet, Joyce Kilmer, noted that crowds surged in to touch the poet "as if he was Roosevelt or Jess Willard." Frank Norris modeled the idealistic Presley in* The Octopus *after Markham.*

The Man with the Hoe

Written after seeing Millet's World-Famous Painting

God made man in His own image,
in the image of God made He him.
            —*Genesis*

Bowed by the weight of centuries he leans
Upon his hoe and gazes on the ground,
The emptiness of ages in his face,
And on his back the burden of the world.
Who made him dead to rapture and despair,
A thing that grieves not and that never hopes,

Stolid and stunned, a brother to the ox?
Who loosened and let down this brutal jaw?
Whose was the hand that slanted back this brow?
Whose breath blew out the light within this brain?

Is this the Thing the Lord God made and gave
To have dominion over sea and land;
To trace the stars and search the heavens for power;
To feel the passion of Eternity?
Is this the Dream He dreamed who shaped the suns
And pillared the blue firmament with light?
Down all the stretch of Hell to its last gulf
There is no shape more terrible than this—
More tongued with censure of the world's blind greed—
More filled with signs and portents for the soul—
More fraught with menace to the universe.

What gulfs between him and the seraphim!
Slave of the wheel of labor, what to him
Are Plato and the swing of Pleiades?
What the long reaches of the peaks of song,
The rift of dawn, the reddening of the rose?

Through this dread shape the suffering ages look;
Time's tragedy is in that aching stoop;
Through this dread shape humanity betrayed,
Plundered, profaned and disinherited,
Cries protest to the Judges of the World,
A protest that is also prophecy.

O masters, lords and rulers in all lands,
Is this the handiwork you give to God,
This monstrous thing distorted and soul-quenched?
How will you ever straighten up this shape;
Touch it again with immortality;
Give back the upward looking and the light;
Rebuild in it the music and the dream;
Make right the immemorial infamies,
Perfidious wrongs, immedicable woes?

Edwin Markham

O masters, lords and rulers in all lands,
How will the Future reckon with this Man?
How answer his brute question in that hour
When whirlwinds of rebellion shake the world?
How will it be with kingdoms and with kings—
With those who shaped him to the thing he is—
When this dumb Terror shall reply to God,
After the silence of the centuries?

The Sower

Written after seeing Millet's painting with this title

Soon will the lonesome cricket by the stone
Begin to hush the night; and lightly blown
Field fragrances will fill the fading blue—
Old furrow-scents that ancient Eden knew.
Soon in the upper twilight will be heard
The winging whisper of a homing bird.

Who is it coming on the slant brown slope,
Touched by the twilight and her mournful hope—
Coming with hero step, with rhythmic swing,
Where all the bodily motions weave and sing?
The grief of the ground is in him, yet the power
Of Earth to hide the furrow with the flower.

He is the stone rejected, yet the stone
Whereon is built metropolis and throne.
Out of his toil come all their pompous shows,
Their purple luxury and plush repose!
The grime of this bruised hand keeps tender white
The hands that never labor, day nor night.
His feet that know only the field's rough floors
Send lordly steps down echoing corridors.

Yea, this vicarious toiler at the plow
Gives that fine pallor to my lady's brow.
And idle armies with their boom and blare,
Flinging their foolish glory on the air—

He hides their nakedness, he gives them bed,
And by his alms their hungry mouths are fed.

Not his the lurching of an aimless clod,
For with the august gesture of a god—
A gesture that is question and command—
He hurls the bread of nations from his hand;
And in the passion of the gesture flings

His fierce resentment in the face of kings.
This is the Earth-god of the latter day,
Treading with solemn joy the upward way;
A lusty god that in some crowning hour
Will hurl Gray Privilege from the place of power.
These are the inevitable steps that make
Unreason tremble and Tradition shake.
This is the World-Will climbing to its goal,
The climb of the unconquerable Soul—
Democracy whose sure insurgent stride
Jars kingdoms to their ultimate stone of pride.

Edwin Markham

John Muir

1838–1914

A naturalist and ardent conservationist, Muir was a pioneer voice for wilderness preservation. Born in Dunbar, Scotland, he came to the United States with his family in 1849. After studying chemistry, geology, and botany at the University of Wisconsin, he designed machine parts and began the extended tramps and explorations of the natural world that would occupy him for the rest of his days. He traveled first into Canada. In 1867 he made his famous journey from Indiana to the Florida coast, his account of which was published forty years later as A Thousand Mile Walk to the Gulf *(1916). From there he sailed around Cape Horn to San Francisco, and in 1869 he found himself herding sheep into the mountains he would later dub "the range of light." The notebooks he kept that summer not only chart his study of astonishing terrain;* My First Summer in the Sierra, *finally published in 1914, has the luminous and passionate quality of one man's testament to personal transformation through the splendor of a natural region. As Muir traveled and studied the Western landscape from Mount Shasta to Alaska, he was recognized by many as the world's foremost expert on glaciers and their power. In 1892 he cofounded the Sierra Club and became its first president. Through writings such as* The Mountains of California *(1894) and* The Yosemite *(1921) and his public advocacy, he had a significant influence on U.S. environmental policy. Largely through his efforts, the Yosemite area was named a national park, and a portion of the Grand Canyon was set aside as a national monument. Today more sites in California are named for him than for any other person, among them Muir Woods in Marin County and the Sierra Nevada's famous John Muir Trail.*

From *The Mountains of California*

Go where you may within the bounds of California, mountains are ever in sight, charming and glorifying every landscape. Yet so simple and massive is the topography of the State in general views that the main central portion displays only one valley, and two chains of mountains which seem almost perfectly regular in trend and height: the Coast Range on the west side, the Sierra Nevada on the east. These two ranges coming together in curves on the north and south enclose a magnificent basin, with a level floor more than 400 miles long, and from 35 to 60 miles wide. This is the grand Central

Valley of California, the waters of which have only one outlet to the sea through the Golden Gate. But with this general simplicity of features there is great complexity of hidden detail. The Coast Range, rising as a grand green barrier against the ocean, from 2000 to 8000 feet high, is composed of innumerable forest-crowned spurs, ridges, and rolling hill-waves which enclose a multitude of smaller valleys; some looking out through long, forest-lined vistas to the sea; others, with but few trees, to the Central Valley; while a thousand others yet smaller are embosomed and concealed in mild, round-brewed hills, each with its own climate, soil, and productions.

Making your way through the mazes of the Coast Range to the summit of any of the inner peaks or passes opposite San Francisco, in the clear spring-time, the grandest and most telling of all California landscapes is outspread before you. At your feet lies the great Central Valley glowing golden in the sunshine, extending north and south farther than the eye can reach, one smooth, flowery, lake-like bed of fertile soil. Along its eastern margin rises the mighty Sierra, miles in height, reposing like a smooth, cumulous cloud in the sunny sky, and so gloriously colored, and so luminous, it seems to be not clothed with light but wholly composed of it, like the wall of some celestial city. Along the top, and extending a good way down, you see a pale, pearl-gray belt of snow; and below it a belt of blue and dark purple, marking the extension of the forests; and along the base of the range a broad belt of rose-purple and yellow, where lie the miner's gold-fields and the foot-hill gardens. All these colored belts blending smoothly make a wall of light ineffably fine, and as beautiful as a rainbow, yet firm as adamant.

When I first enjoyed this superb view, one glowing April day, from the summit of the Pacheco Pass, the Central Valley, but little trampled or plowed as yet, was one furred, rich sheet of golden composite, and the luminous wall of the mountains shone in all its glory. Then it seemed to me the Sierra should be called not the Nevada, or Snowy Range, but the Range of Light. And after ten years spent in the heart of it, rejoicing and wondering, bathing in its glorious floods of light, seeing the sunbursts of morning among the icy peaks, the noonday radiance on the trees and rocks and mow, the flush of the alpenglow, and a thousand dashing waterfalls with their marvelous abundance of irised spray, it still seems to me above all others the Range of Light, the most divinely beautiful of all the mountain-chains I have ever seen.

The Sierra is about 500 miles long, 70 miles wide, and from 7000 to nearly 15,000 feet high. In general views no mark of man is visible on it, nor anything to suggest the richness of the life it cherishes, or the depth and grandeur of its sculpture. None of its magnificent forest-crowned ridges rises much above the general level to publish its wealth. No great valley or lake is seen, or river, or group of well-marked features of any kind, standing out in distinct pictures. Even the summit-peaks, so clear and high in the sky, seem comparatively smooth and featureless. Nevertheless, glaciers are still at work in the shadows of the peaks, and thousands of lakes and meadows shine and bloom beneath them, and the whole range is furrowed with cañons to a depth of from 2000 to 5000 feet, in which once flowed majestic glaciers, and in which now flow and sing a band of beautiful rivers.

Though of such stupendous depth, these famous cañons are not raw, gloomy, jagged-walled gorges, savage and inaccessible. With rough passages here and there they still make delightful pathways for the mountaineer, conducting from the fertile lowlands to the highest icy fountains, as a kind of mountain streets full of charming life and light, graded and sculptured by the ancient glaciers, and presenting, throughout all their courses, a rich variety of novel and attractive scenery, the most attractive that has yet been discovered in the mountain-ranges of the world.

In many places, especially in the middle region of the western flank of the range, the main cañons widen into spacious valleys or parks, diversified like artificial landscape-gardens, with charming groves and meadows, and thickets of blooming bushes, while the lofty, retiring walls, infinitely varied in form and sculpture, are fringed with ferns, flowering-plants of many species, oaks, and evergreens, which find anchorage on a thousand narrow steps and benches; while the whole is enlivened and made glorious with rejoicing streams that come dancing and foaming over the sunny brows of the cliffs to join the shining river that flows in tranquil beauty down the middle of each one of them.

The walls of these park valleys of the Yosemite kind are made up of rocks mountains in size, partly separated from each other by narrow gorges and side-cañons; and they are so sheer in front, and so compactly built together on a level floor, that, comprehensively seen, the parks they enclose look like immense halls or temples lighted from above. Every rock seems to glow with life. Some lean back in majestic repose; others, absolutely sheer, or nearly so, for thousands of feet, advance their brows in thoughtful attitudes beyond their companions, giving welcome to storms and calms alike, seemingly conscious yet heedless of everything going on about them, awful in stern majesty, types of permanence, yet associated with beauty of the frailest and most fleeting forms; their feet set in pine-groves and gay emerald meadows, their brows in the sky; bathed in light, bathed in floods of singing water, while snow-clouds, avalanches, and the winds shine and surge and wreathe about them as the years go by, as if into these mountain mansions Nature had taken pains to gather her choicest treasures to draw her lovers into close and confiding communion with her.

Here, too, in the middle region of deepest cañons are the grandest forest-trees, the Sequoia, king of conifers, the noble Sugar and Yellow Pines, Douglas Spruce, Libocedrus, and the Silver Firs, each a giant of its kind, assembled together in one and the same forest, surpassing all other coniferous forests in the world, both in the number of its species and in the size and beauty of its trees. The winds flow in melody through their colossal spires, and they are vocal everywhere with the songs of birds and running water. Miles of fragrant ceanothus and manzanita bushes bloom beneath them, and lily gardens and meadows, and damp, ferny glens in endless variety of fragrance and color, compelling the admiration of every observer. Sweeping on over ridge and valley, these noble trees extend a continuous belt from end to end of the range, only slightly interrupted by sheer-walled cañons at intervals of about fifteen and twenty miles. Here the great burly brown bears delight to roam, harmonizing with the brown boles of the trees beneath which they feed. Deer, also, dwell here, and find food and shelter in the ceanothus tangles, with a multitude of smaller people. Above this region of giants, the trees grow smaller until the utmost limit of the timber line is reached on the stormy mountain-slopes at a height of from ten to twelve thousand feet above the sea, where the Dwarf Pine is so lowly and hard beset by storms and heavy snow, it is pressed into flat tangles, over the tops of which we may easily walk. Below the main forest belt the trees likewise diminish in size, frost and burning drought repressing and blasting alike.

The rose-purple zone along the base of the range comprehends nearly all the famous gold region of California. And here it was that miners from every country under the sun assembled in a wild, torrent-like rush to seek their fortunes. On the banks of every river, ravine, and gully they have left their marks. Every gravel-and boulder-bed has been desperately riddled over and over again. But in this region the pick and shovel, once, wielded with savage enthusiasm, have been laid away, and only quartz-mining is now being carried on to any considerable extent. The zone in general is made up of low, tawny, waving foot-hills, roughened here and there with brush and trees, and outcropping masses of slate, colored gray and red with lichens. The smaller masses of slate, rising abruptly from the dry, grassy sod in leaning slabs, look like ancient tombstones in a deserted burying-ground. In early spring, say from February to April, the whole of this foot-hill belt is a paradise of bees and flowers. Refreshing rains then fall freely, birds are busy building their nests, and the sunshine is balmy and delightful. But by the end of May the soil, plants, and sky seem to have been baked in an oven. Most of the plants crumble to dust beneath the foot, and the ground is full of cracks; while the thirsty traveler gazes with eager longing through the burning glare to the snowy summits looming like hazy clouds in the distance.

The trees, mostly *Quercus Douglasii* and *Pinus Sabiniana*, thirty to forty feet high, with thin, pale-green foliage, stand far apart and cast but little shade. Lizards glide about on the rocks enjoying a constitution that no drought can dry, and ants in amazing numbers, whose tiny sparks of life seem to burn the brighter with the increasing heat, ramble industriously in long trains in search of food. Crows, ravens, magpies—friends in distress—gather on the ground beneath the best shade-frees, panting with drooping wings and hills wide open, scarce a note from any of them during the midday hours. Quails, too, seek the shade during the heat of the day about tepid pools in the channels of the larger mid-river streams. Rabbits scurry from thicket to thicket among the ceanothus bushes, and occasionally a long-eared hare is seen cantering gracefully across the wider openings. The nights are calm and dewless during the summer, and a thousand voices proclaim the abundance of life, notwithstanding the desolating effect of dry sunshine on the plants and larger animals. The hylas make a delightfully pure and tranquil music after sunset; and coyotes, the little, despised dogs of the wilderness, brave, hardy fellows, looking like withered wisps of bay, bark in chorus for hours. Mining-towns, most of them dead, and a few living ones with bright bits of cultivation about them, occur at long intervals along the belt, and cottages covered with climbing roses, in the midst of orange and peach orchards, and sweet-scented hay-fields in fertile flats where water for irrigation may be had. But they are mostly far apart, and make scarce any mark in general views.

Every winter the High Sierra and the middle forest region get snow in glorious abundance, and even the foot-hills are at times whitened. Then all the range looks like a vast beveled wall of purest marble. The rough places are then made smooth, the death and decay of the year is covered gently and kindly, and the ground seems as clean as the sky. And though silent in its flight from the clouds, and when it is taking its place on rock, or tree, or grassy meadow, how soon the gentle snow finds a voice! Slipping from the heights, gathering in avalanches, it booms and roars like thunder, and makes a glorious show as it sweeps down the mountain-side, arrayed in long, silken streamers and wreathing, swirling films of crystal dust.

The north half of the range is mostly covered with floods of lava, and dotted with volcanoes and craters, some of them recent and perfect in form, others in various stages of decay. The south half is composed of granite nearly from base to summit, while a considerable number of peaks, in the middle of the range, are capped with metamorphic slates, among which are Mounts Dana and Gibbs to the east of Yosemite Valley. Mount Whitney, the culminating point of the range near its southern extremity, lifts its helmet-shaped crest to a height of nearly 14,700 feet. Mount Shasta, a colossal volcanic cone, rises to a height of 14,440 feet at the northern extremity, and forms a noble land-mark for all the surrounding region within a radius of a hundred miles. Residual masses of volcanic rocks occur throughout most of the granitic southern portion also, and a considerable number of old volcanoes on the flanks, especially along the eastern base of the range near Mono Lake and southward. But it is only to the northward that the entire range, from base to summit, is covered with lava.

From the summit of Mount Whitney only granite is seen. Innumerable peaks and spires but little lower than its own storm-beaten crags rise in groups like forest-trees, in full view, segregated by cañons of tremendous depth end ruggedness. On Shasta nearly every feature in the vast view speaks of the old volcanic fires. Far to the northward, in Oregon, the icy volcanoes of Mount Pitt and the Three Sisters rise above the dark evergreen woods. Southward innumerable smaller craters and cones are distributed along the axis of the range and on each flank. Of these, Lassen's Butte is the highest, being nearly 11,000 feet above sea-level. Miles of its flanks are reeking and bubbling with hot springs, many of them so boisterous and sulphurous they seem ever ready to become spouting geysers like those of the Yellowstone.

The Cinder Cone near marks the most recent volcanic eruption in the Sierra. It is a symmetrical truncated cone about 700 feet high, covered with gray cinders and ashes, and has a regular unchanged crater on its summit, in which a few small Two-leaved Pines are growing. These show that the age of the cone is not less than eighty years. It stands between two lakes, which a short time ago were one. Before the cone was built, a flood of rough vesicular lava was poured into the lake, cutting it in two, and, overflowing its banks, the fiery flood advanced into the pine-woods, overwhelming the trees in its way, the charred ends of some of which may still be seen projecting from beneath the snout of the lava-stream where it came to rest. Later still there was an eruption of ashes and loose obsidian cinders, probably from the same vent, which, besides forming the Cinder Cone, scattered a heavy shower over the surrounding woods for miles to a depth of from six inches to several feet.

The history of this last Sierra eruption is also preserved in the traditions of the Pitt River Indians. They tell of a fearful time of darkness, when the sky was black with ashes and smoke that threatened every living thing with death, and that when at length the sun appeared once more it was red like blood.

Less recent craters in great numbers roughen the adjacent region; some of them with lakes in their throats, others overgrown with trees and flowers, Nature in these old hearths and firesides having literally given beauty for ashes. On the northwest side of Mount Shasta there is a subordinate cone about 3000 feet below the summit, which has been active subsequent to the breaking up of the main ice-cap that once covered the mountain, as is shown by its comparatively unwasted crater and the streams of unglaciated lava radiating from it. The main summit is about a mile and a half in diameter, bounded by small crumbling peaks and ridges, among which we seek in vain for the outlines of the ancient crater.

These ruinous masses, and the deep glacial grooves that flute the sides of the mountain, show that it has been considerably lowered and wasted by ice; how much we have no means of knowing. Just below the extreme summit hot sulphurous gases and vapor issue from irregular fissures, mixed with spray derived from melting snow, the last feeble expression of the mighty force that built the mountain. Not in one great convulsion was Shasta given birth. The crags of the summit exposed by the glaciers down the sides display enough of its internal framework to prove that comparatively long periods of quiescence intervened between many distinct eruptions, during which the cooling lavas ceased to flow, and became permanent additions to the hulk of the growing mountain. With alternate haste and deliberation eruption succeeded eruption till the old volcano surpassed even its present sublime height.

Standing on the icy top of this, the grandest of all the fire-mountains of the Sierra, we can hardly fail to look forward to its next eruption. Gardens, vineyards, homes have been planted confidingly on the flanks of volcanoes which, after remaining steadfast for ages, have suddenly blazed into violent action, and poured forth overwhelming floods of fire. It is known that more than a thousand years of cool calm have intervened between violent eruptions. Like gigantic geysers spouting molten rock instead of water, volcanoes work and rest, and we have no sure means of knowing whether they are dead when still, or only sleeping.

Along the western base of the range a telling series of sedimentary rocks containing the early history of the Sierra are now being studied. But leaving for the present these first chapters, we see that only a very short geological time ago, just before the coming on of that winter of winters called the glacial period, a vast deluge of molten rocks poured from many a chasm and crater on the flanks and summit of the range, filling lake basins and river channels, and obliterating nearly every existing feature on the northern portion. At length these all-destroying floods ceased to flow. But while the great volcanic cones built up along the axis still burned and smoked, the whole Sierra passed under the domain of ice and snow. Then over the bald, featureless, fire-blackened mountains, glaciers began to crawl, covering them from the summits to the sea with a mantle of ice; and then with infinite deliberation the work went on of sculpturing the range anew. These mighty agents of erosion, halting never through unnumbered centuries, crushed and ground the flinty lavas and granites beneath their crystal folds, wasting and building until in the fullness of time the Sierra was born again, brought to light nearly as we behold it today, with glaciers and snow-crushed pines at the top of the range, wheat-fields and orange-groves at the foot of it.

This change from icy darkness and death to life and beauty was slow, as we count time, and is still going on, north and south, over all the world wherever glaciers exist, whether in the form of distinct rivers, as in Switzerland, Norway, the mountains of Asia, and the Pacific Coast; or in continuous mantling folds, as in portions of Alaska, Greenland, Franz-Joseph-Land, Nova Zembla, Spitzbergen, and the lands about the South Pole. But in no country, as far as I know, may these majestic changes be studied to better advantage than in the plains and mountains of California.

Toward the close of the glacial period, when the snow-clouds became less fertile and the melting waste of sunshine became greater, the lower folds of the ice-sheet in California, discharging fleets of icebergs into the sea, began to shallow and recede from the lowlands, and then move slowly up the flanks of the Sierra in compliance with the changes of climate. The great white mantle on the mountains broke up into a series of glaciers more or less distinct and river-like, with many tributaries, and these again were melted and divided into still smaller glaciers, until now only a few of the smallest residual topmost branches of the grand system exist on the cool slopes of the summit peaks.

Plants and animals, biding their time, closely followed the retiring ice, bestowing quick and joyous animation on the new-born landscapes. Pine-trees marched up the sun-warmed moraines in long, hopeful files, taking the ground and establishing themselves as soon as it was ready for them; brown-spiked sedges fringed the shores of the new-born lakes; young rivers roared in the abandoned channels of the glaciers; flowers bloomed around the feet of the great burnished domes,—while with quick fertility mellow beds of soil, settling and warming, offered food to multitudes of Nature's waiting children, great and small, animals as well as plants, mice, squirrels, marmots, deer, bears, elephants, etc. The ground burst into bloom with magical rapidity, and the young forests into bird-song: life in every form warming and sweetening and growing richer as the years passed away over the mighty Sierra so lately suggestive of death and consummate desolation only.

It is hard without long and loving study to realize the magnitude of the work done on these mountains during the last glacial period by glaciers, which are only streams of closely compacted snow-crystals. Careful study of the phenomena presented goes to show that the pre-glacial condition of the range was comparatively simple: one vast wave of stone in which a thousand mountains, domes, cañons, ridges, etc., lay concealed. And in the development of these Nature chose for a tool not the earthquake or lightning to rend and split asunder, not the stormy torrent or eroding rain, but the tender snow-flowers noiselessly falling through unnumbered centuries, the offspring of the sun and sea. Laboring harmoniously in united strength they crushed and ground and wore away the rocks in their march, making vast beds of soil, and at the same time developed and fashioned the landscapes into the delightful variety of hill and dale and lordly mountain that mortals call beauty. Perhaps more than a mile in average depth has the range been thus degraded during the last glacial period,—a quantity of mechanical work almost inconceivably great. And our admiration must be excited again and again as we toil and study and learn that this vast job of rockwork, so far-reaching in its influences, was done by agents so fragile and small as are these flowers of the mountain clouds. Strong only by force of numbers, they carried away entire mountains, particle by particle, block by block, and cast them into the sea; sculptured, fashioned, modeled all the range, and developed its predestined beauty. All these new Sierra landscapes were evidently predestined, for the physical structure of the rocks on which the features of the scenery depend was acquired while they lay at least a mile deep below the pre-glacial surface. And it was while these features were taking form in the depths of the range, the particles of the rocks marching to their appointed places in the dark with reference to the coming beauty, that the particles of icy vapor in the sky marching to the same music assembled to bring them to the light. Then, after their grand task was done, these bands of snow-flowers, these mighty glaciers, were melted and removed as if of no more importance than dew destined to last but an hour. Few, however, of Nature's agents have left monuments so noble and enduring as they. The great granite domes a mile high, the cañons as deep, the noble peaks, the Yosemite valleys, these, and indeed nearly all other features of the Sierra scenery, are glacier monuments.

Contemplating the works of these flowers of the sky, one may easily fancy them endowed with life: messengers sent down to work in the mountain mines on errands of divine love. Silently flying through the darkened air, swirling, glinting, to their appointed places, they seem to have taken counsel together, saying, "Come, we are feeble; let us help one another. We are many, and together we will be strong. Marching in close, deep ranks, let us roll away the stones from these mountain sepulchers, and set the landscapes free. Let us uncover these clustering domes. Here let us carve a lake basin; there, a Yosemite Valley; here, a channel for a river with fluted steps and brows for the plunge of songful cataracts. Yonder let us spread broad sheets of soil, that man and beast may be fed; and here pile trains of boulders for pines and giant Sequoias. Here make ground for a meadow; there, for a garden and grove, making it smooth and fine for small daisies and violets and beds of heathy bryanthus, spicing it well with crystals, garnet feldspar, and zircon." Thus and so on it has oftentimes seemed to me sang and planned and labored the hearty snow-flower crusaders; and nothing that I can write can possibly exaggerate the grandeur and beauty of their work. Like morning mist they have vanished in sunshine, all save the few small companies that still linger on the coolest mountain-sides, and, as residual glaciers, are still busily at work completing the last of the lake basins, the last beds of soil, and the sculpture of some of the highest peaks.

George Sterling
1869–1926

Best remembered as the model for Brissenden, a debonair and jaded poet in Jack London's Martin Eden, *George Sterling met London, Joaquin Miller, and Ambrose Bierce after he moved to Oakland from Sag Harbor, New York, in 1890. He adopted Bierce as his unlikely mentor, publishing highly dramatic romantic poetry exemplified in "Beyond the Breakers." He was one of the first Bay Area free spirits to take up residence in Carmel (in 1905), and over the next ten years he was a significant force in the growth of the "Seacoast of Bohemia" as an artists' colony. Sterling was a handsome and magnetic figure, and he reciprocated London's admiration in a warm friendship that endured until the novelist's death in 1916, a tragedy that darkened his own life considerably. He admired Robinson Jeffers's style and work, and his book* Robinson Jeffers: The Man and the Artist *(1926) was one of the first important evaluations of that poet's writing and significance. He spent his last years in San Francisco, living at the fabled Bohemian Club, where he was a major contributor to the secret society's lavish Bohemian Grove pageants in the redwoods north of the city. Depressed by his wife Carrie's suicide in 1918 and convinced time had passed him by, George Sterling killed himself with cyanide—just as she had—in 1926.*

Beyond the Breakers
to James Hopper

The world was full of the sound of a great wind out of the West,
And the tracks of its feet were white on the trampled ocean's breast.
And I said, "With the sea and wind I will mix my body and soul,
Where the breath of the planet drives and the herded billows roll."

And down through the pines I went, to the shore-sands warm and white,
Till I saw from the ocean's verge the gulls in clamorous flight,—
Till the wind was sharp in my face, and pure and strong in its sweep
From the smokeless dome of the world and a thousand leagues of the deep.

The breakers rose before me where the hard, wet sands were grey—
Each in its colored robe, fronting the new-born day;
The singing waves of the sea, clean beyond all of clean,
Beautiful, swift, alive, undulant, apple-green.

Who shall grapple with lions or wrestle with seraphim?
Even so can the surf come forth in its power to him—
Legion crying to legion, hurled to the steadfast shore;
Rampart answering rampart, where the flame-shaped summits roar.

And I flung me forth at their strength, at their might of motion and sound,
Till the foam-bolts stung my brow and the foam-chains ringed me around,
And the hissing ridges ran like dragons driven by gods—
Mad with the battle-cries and their unseen lashes and rods.

From fighting nostrils to feet the ocean clad me in cold,
Tingling, thrilling and sweet, a raiment none could behold,
As I rose with urging of arms to the shattered foam-crests' rain,
To look far over the deep and sink from the wind again.

O hills of voices and snows, O valleys of sapphire and calm,
That smote and wrenched and released to moments of respite and balm!
Splendid, young and eternal, from bridals of wind and sea,
Tho I sleep at last in your vaults, yet first ye shall war with me!

Furious, swift, they came, the pulse and surge of the deep,
Rank on rank in their beauty, poised for the shoreward leap,
Lifting my form in crystal to gaze out over the West,—
Clutching in sudden wrath at limbs and loins and breast.

Then was it as tho companions, godlike, alert, unseen,
Swam under and at my sides, with sight unerring and keen,
Touching, splashing and laughing (and I hear their laughter still),
Where the foam shot sudden veils in the waters torn and chill.

And I shouted to them in kinship, in ocean ardor and love,
Lifting an arm to the sun and the azure far above,—
Mixing my voice with theirs and the sea-wind's lordly song,—
Feeling them stir about me, the swimmers happy and strong.

Felt I not with them, the invisible at mirth,
The wind and wonder of life, the thrill and union of earth?—
More intimate, more sure, for the sea's high loneliness,
Than the blinded sages dream, or the land-bound people guess.

George Sterling

The great embrace of ocean was closer than love's can be;
Its clasp was sharp on my limbs, yet went I supple and free.
The breast of the deep unheaved as a mother's under a child—
Terrible, tender, strong, imperial, undefiled.

So for a space I lived with life intense and aware,
Far from the human swarm and mortal folly and care—
I, the foam of earth, assailed by the ocean-foam,
I, the homeless of worlds, forgetting the dream of Home.

Yet in the end it was earth that called me in from the vast,
Till the salt, wild waters boiled and the spray was thin on the blast,
And the undertow swept out, laughing at strength like mine,
Till I rode to shore on a wave that stung with its hurtled brine.

    Carmel, California

The Black Vulture

Aloof within the day's enormous dome,
He holds unshared the silence of the sky.
Far down his bleak, relentless eyes descry
The eagle's empire and the falcon's home—
Far down, the galleons of sunset roam;
His hazards on the sea of morning lie;
Serene, he hears the broken tempest sigh
Where cold sierras gleam like scattered foam.

And least of all he holds the human swarm—
Unwitting now that envious men prepare
To make their dream and its fulfilment one,
When, poised above the caldrons of the storm,
Their hearts, contemptuous of death, shall dare
His roads between the thunder and the sun.

GERTRUDE ATHERTON
1857–1948

Born in San Francisco, Gertrude Franklin Horn married George Atherton, the son of an affluent merchant and an aristocratic Chilean mother. She was freed from their unhappy union when her husband died at sea and was grotesquely returned to land preserved in a barrel of rum—an event she recalled in Adventures of a Novelist *(1923). Atherton wrote fifty books between 1888 and 1946, and the core of her work was the eighteen volumes that made up a "story-chronicle" of Northern California life from 1840 to World War II. Prolific and accessible, she was a writer of best-sellers. She is now often remembered as the author of* The Splendid Idle Forties, *a collection of tales that evoked a romanticized vision of mission life before statehood. Her best works were the novels of manners that captured privileged and middle-class life in San Francisco between 1890 and 1910, especially* The Californians *(1898), her ninth novel.*

Atherton loved San Francisco, but she saw it wryly as "a fool's paradise," her female protagonists navigating a maze of genteel privilege and restraint as they made the journey from the Victorian age to the modern. A self-schooled expert in matters Californian, Atherton wrote perhaps too much, but she was an astute cultural critic and a sound fictional technician. She drew her California in national and international contexts, and she endures as the state's first major woman writer of fiction.

From Chapter 6 of *The Californians*

Magdaléna had failed at every point. She had expected to fail, but she felt miserable and discouraged, nevertheless. After dinner she went up to her room and prayed to the Virgin. In time she felt comforted, her tears ceased, and she sat thinking for some time at the foot of her little altar. With the sad philosophy of her nature she put the impossible from her, and considered the future. It had been arranged long ago that she and Helena, Ila and Tiny, were to come out at the same time; the great function which should introduce to San Francisco three of its most beautiful girls, and its most favoured by lineage and fortune, was to be given by Mrs. Yorba. The other girls would come out a year earlier or later. Ila and Tiny were already in Europe. She had three uninterrupted years before her. In those years she could do much. When she was not studying, she would read the best authors and learn their secret.

Her father had no library, but Colonel Belmont had, and she was a life member of the Mercantile Library; the membership had been presented to her two birthdays ago by her luncheon guests, who respected what they would not emulate. She pressed her face into her hands, striving to arrange the nebulous thoughts and ambitions which burned in her brain.

There was a wild ringing of bells. She raised her head and saw a red glare, then rose and walked over to the window. She thought a fire very beautiful; and as there were many in that city of wood and wind, she had had full opportunity to observe their manifold phases. Her bedroom adjoined the schoolroom, but was on the corner of the house at the back, and overlooked not only the business part of the city between the foot of the hill and the bay, but the region known as "South of Market Street." This large valley had its aristocratic quarter, but it was now largely given over to warehouses, dépôts, and streets of the poor. A month seldom passed without a big blaze in this closely built combustible section. Tonight there was a long narrow ribbon of flame twisting in the wind, which in a few moments would leap from block to block, licking up the flimsy dwellings as a cat licks up milk. Above the ribbon flew a million sparks, turning the stars from gold to white. Every moment the wind twisted the ribbon into wonderful fantastic shapes, which beset Magdaléna's brain for words as beautiful.

She listened intently. Someone was climbing a pillar of the balcony. It was Helena, of course: she often chose that laborious method of entering a house whose doors were always open to her. Magdaléna opened the back window and stepped out on to the balcony.

"Is that you, Helena?" she whispered.

"Is it? Just you wait till you see me!"

A moment later she had clambered over the railing and stood before the astonished Magdaléna.

"What—what—"

"Boys' clothes. Can't you see for yourself? I'm going to the fire, and you're going with me."

"Of course I shall not. What possessed you—"

But the astute Helena detected a lack of decision in her friend's voice. "You're just dying to go," she said coaxingly . "You adore fires, and you'd love to see one close to. Put a waterproof on and a black shawl over your head. Then if anybody notices you, they'll think you're a *muchacha* from Spanish town. As I am a boy, I can protect you beautifully. We'll go to the livery stable and I'll make old Duff give me a hack. I've a pocket full of boodle; papa gave me my allowance today. Here, come in." She dragged the unresisting Magdaléna into the room, arrayed her in a waterproof, and pinned a black shawl tightly about the small brown face. "There!" she said triumphantly, "you look like a poor little greaser, for all the world. Don Roberto would have a fit. Do you think you can slide down the pillar?"

"I don't know—yes, I am sure I can if you can." Her Spanish dignity was aghast, but her newborn creative instinct stung her spirit into a sudden overpowering desire for dramatic incident. "Yes, I'll go," she whispered, closer to excitement than Helena had ever, save once, seen her. "I'll go." . . .

When they reached the livery stable, Helena marched in, holding Magdaléna firmly by the hand. "I want a hack," she said peremptorily to the man in charge. "And double quick, too." The man stared, but Helena rattled the gold in her pocket, and he called to two men to hitch up.

"Upon my soul," he whispered to his associates, "it's those kids of Jack Belmont's and old Yorba's, or I'm a dead man. But it ain't none of my business, and I ain't one to preach. I like spirit."

"We're going to the fire, and I wish the hack to wait for us," said Helena, as he signified that all was ready. "I'll pay you now. How much is it?"

"Ten dollars," he replied unblushingly.

Helena paid the money like a blood, Magdaléna horrified at the extravagance. Her own allowance was five dollars a month. "Can you really afford this, Helena?" she asked remonstrantly, as the hack slid down the steep hill.

"I got fifty dollars out of Jack to-night. He's feeling awfully soft over my going away. Poor old Jack, he'll feel so lonesome without me. But we'll have a gay old time travelling together in Europe when I'm through."

Magdaléna did not speak of her conversation with her own parent. She did not want to think of it. This night was to be one of uniform joy. They were a quarter of an hour reaching the fire. As they turned into the great central artery of the city, Market Street, they leaned forward and gazed eagerly at the dense highly coloured mass of men and women, mostly young, that promenaded the north sidewalk under a blaze of gas.

"What queer-looking girls!" said Magdaléna. "Why do they wear so many frizzes, and sailor hats on one side?"

"They're chippies," said Helena, wisely.

"What's chippies?"

"Girls that live south of Market Street. They work all day and promenade with their beaux all evening. As I live, 'Léna, we're going down Fourth Street. We'll go right through Chippytown."

They had been south of Market Street before, for Ila and Tiny lived on the aristocratic Rincon Hill; but their way had always lain down Second Street, which was old, but stately and respectable. Fourth Street, like Market Street by night, would be a new country; but after a few moments' eager attention Helena sniffed with disappointment. The narrow street and those branching from it were ill-lighted and deserted; there was nothing to be seen but low-browed shops. But there was always the red glare beyond; and in a few moments the conflagration burst upon them in all its terrible magnificence.

They sprang out of the hack and walked rapidly to the edge of the crowd, which filled the street in spite of the warning cries of the firemen and the angry shouts of the policemen. The fire was devouring four large squares and sending leaping branches to isolated dwellings beyond. A great furniture factory and innumerable tenements were vanishing like icicles under a hot sun.

The girls, careless of the severe jostling they received, stared in fascinated amazement at the red tongues darting among the blackened shells, the crashing roofs, the black masses of smoke above, cut with narrow swords of flame, the solid pillar of fire above the factory, the futile streams of water, the gallant efforts of the firemen. Magdaléna, hardly knowing why, reflected with deep satisfaction that a fire was even more wonderful at close quarters than when viewed from a distance. Every detail delighted her; but when a clumsy boy stepped on her toes, she drew Helena into a sand lot opposite, where it was less crowded. It was then that she noticed for the first time the weeping women gathered about their household goods. She stared at them for a moment, then shook the rapt Helena by the arm.

"Look!" she whispered. "What is the matter with those people?"

"What?" asked Helena, absently. "Oh, don't I wish I were on that house with a hose in my hand! What a lovely exciting life a fireman's must be!" Then, yielding to Magdaléna's insistence, she turned and directed her gaze to the people in the lot behind her. "Oh, the poor things!" she said, forgetting the fire. "They've been burnt out. Let's talk to them."

The two girls approached the unfortunate creatures, who were wailing loudly, as if at a wake.

"Poor devils!" exclaimed Helena. "I am so glad I have some silver with me."

"And I have nothing to give them," thought Magdaléna, bitterly; but she was too proud to speak. She stared at them, her brain a medley of new sensations, as Helena went about, questioning, fascinating, sympathising, giving. It was the first time she had seen poverty; she had barely heard of its existence; it had never occurred to her that great romanticists condescended to borrow from life. It was not abject poverty that she witnessed, by any means. There were no hollow cheeks here, no pallid faces, no shrunken limbs. It was, save for the passing distress, to which they were not unaccustomed, a very jolly, hearty, contented poverty. Their belongings were certainly mean, but solid and sufficient. Nevertheless, to Magdaléna, who had been surrounded by luxury from her birth, and had rarely been in a street of less importance than her own, these commonly clad creatures, weeping over their cheap household goods, seemed the very dregs of the earth. Her keen enjoyment fled. . . .

A policeman had tapped her roughly on the shoulder. She gazed at him in speechless terror for a half-moment, then gasped, "W-h-a-t do you want?"

"I want you two young uns for the lock-up," he said curtly. The struggling crowd had lashed his pugnacity and ensanguined his temper. As an additional indignity, the saloon had been burned, and he had not had a drink for an hour. "I'll run you in for wearing boys' clothes; have you ever heard the penalty for that, miss? And I'll run in this little greaser as a vagrant."

Helena burst into shrieks of terror, clinging to Magdaléna, who comforted her mechanically, too terrified, herself, to speak. Even in that awful moment it was her father she feared, not the law.

"Shut up!" exclaimed the officer. "None of that." He paused abruptly and regarded Helena closely. She was searching wildly in her pockets. "Oh, if you've got a fiver," he said easily, "I'll call it square."

"I haven't so much as a five-cent piece," sobbed Helena, with a fresh burst of tears. "Oh, 'Léna, what shall we do?"

"You'll come with me! that's what you'll do." He took them firmly by the hand and dragged them through the crowd, a section of which had transferred its attentions to the victims of the officer's wrath. But the three were soon hurrying up a dark cross-street toward a car; and as they went Helena recovered herself, and began to cast about among her plentiful resources. She dared not risk telling this man their names, and bid him take them home in hope of reward, for he would certainly demand that reward of their scandalised parents. No, she decided, she would confide in the dignitary in charge at the station; and as soon as he knew who she was, he would be sure to let them go at once.

They went up town on a street-car. Helena had never been in one before, and the experience interested her; but Magdaléna sat dumb and wretched. She had been a docile child, and her father's anger had never been visited upon her; but she had seen his frightful outbursts at the servants, and once he had horsewhipped a Mexican in his employ until the lad's shrieks had made Magdaléna put her fingers in her ears. He would not whip her, of course; but what would he do? And this horrid man, who was of the class of her father's coachman, had called her a "greaser." She had all the pride of her race. The insult stifled her. She felt smirched and degraded.

Nor was this all: she had had her first precise experience of the pall that lines the golden cloud.

The officer motioned to the conductor to stop in front of a squat building in front of the Old Plaza. The man, whose gall had been slowly rising for want of drink, hurried them roughly off the car and across the sidewalk into a dark passage. Their feet lagged, and he shoved them before him, flourishing his bludgeon.

"Git on! Git on !" he said. "There's no gittin' out of this until you've served your time."

The words and the dark passage made Helena shiver. What if they would not give her a chance to speak, but should lock her up at once? She knew nothing of these dark doings of night. Perhaps the policeman would take them directly to a cell. In that case, she must confide in him.

They entered a room, and her confidence returned. A man sat at a desk, an open ledger before him. He was talking to several tramps who stood in various uneasy attitudes in front of the desk. His face was tired, but his eyes had a humourous twinkle. He did not glance at the new-comers.

"Sit down," commanded the policeman, "and wait your turn."

The girls sat down uncomfortably on the edge of a bench. In a moment they noticed a young man sitting near the desk and writing on a small pad of paper. He looked up, looked again, regarding them intently, then rose and approached the policeman.

"Hello, Tim," he said. "What have you got here? A girl in boys' clothes?"

"That's about the size of it."

Helena pulled her cap over her eyes and reddened to her hair. For the first time she fully realised her position. She was Colonel Jack Belmont's daughter, and she was waiting in the city prison as a common vagrant. Magdaléna bent her head, pulling the shawl more closely about her face.

The young man looked them over sharply. "They are the kids of some-bodies," he said audibly. "Look at their hands. There's a 'story' here."

Helena turned cold and set her teeth. She had no idea who the young man might be, but instinct told her that he threatened exposure.

A few moments later the tramps had gone, and the man at the desk asked the policeman what charge he preferred against his arrests.

"This one's a girl in boys' clothes, sir, and both, I take it, are vagrants. The House of Correction is the place for 'em, I'm thinkin'."

Magdaléna's head sank still lower, and she dug her nails into her palms to keep from gasping. But Helena, in this crucial moment, was game. She walked boldly forward and said authoritatively,—

"I wish to speak alone with you."

The sergeant recognised the great I AM of the American maiden; he also recognised her social altitude. But he said, with what severity he could muster,—

"If you have anything private to say, you can whisper it."

Helena stepped behind the desk and put her lips close to his ear. "I am Colonel Jack Belmont's daughter," she whispered. "Send me home, quick, and he'll make it all right with you to-morrow."

"A chip off the old block," muttered the sergeant, with a smile. "I see. And who is your companion?"

Helena hesitated. "Do—do I need to tell you?" she asked.

"You must," firmly.

"She's—you'll never breathe it?

"You must leave that to my discretion. I shall do what is best."

"She is the daughter of Don Roberto Yorba."

"O Lord! O Lord!" He threw back his head and gave a prolonged chuckle.

The young man edged up to the desk.

"Who is that man?" demanded Helena haughtily. She felt quite mistress of the situation.

"He's a reporter."

"What's that?"

"Why, a reporter for the newspapers."

"I know nothing of the newspapers," said Helena, with an annihilating glance at the reporter. "My father does not permit me to read them."

The sergeant sprang to his feet. "This *is* no place for you," he muttered. "That's the best thing I've heard of Jack Belmont for some time. Here, come along, both of you."

He motioned to the girls to enter the passage, and turned to the officer. "Don't let anybody leave the room till I come back," he said; and the reporter, who had started eagerly forward, fell back with a scowl. "There's no 'story' in this, young man," said the sergeant, severely; "and you'll oblige *me*," with significant emphasis, "by making no reference to it."

"I think you're just splendid!" exclaimed Helena, as they went down the passage.

"Oh, well, we all like your father. Although it would be a great joke on him,—Scott, but it would! However, it wouldn't be any joke on you a few years from now, so I'm going to send you home with a little good advice,—don't do it again."

"But it's such fun to run to fires!" replied Helena, who now feared nothing under heaven. "We *did* have a time!"

"Well, if you're set on running to fires, go in your own good clothes, with money enough in your pocket to grease the palm of people like our friend Tim. Here we are."

He called a hack and handed the girls in.

"Please tell him to stop a few doors from the house," said Helena; "and," with her most engaging smile, "I'm afraid I'll have to ask you to pay him. If you'll give me your address, I'll send you the amount first thing to-morrow."

"Oh, don't mention it. Just ask your father to vote for Tom Shannon when he runs for sheriff. It's no use asking anything of old Yorba," he added, with some viciousness. "And I'd advise you, young lady, to keep this night's lark pretty dark."

The remark was addressed to Magdaléna, but she only lifted her head haughtily and turned it away. Helena replied hastily,—

"My father shall vote for you and make all his friends vote, too. I won't tell him about this until next Wednesday, the day before I leave for New York; then he'll be feeling so badly he won't say a word, and he'll be so grateful to you that he'll do anything. Good-night."

"Good-night, miss, and I guess you'll get along in this world."

As the carriage drove on Helena threw her arms about Magdaléna, who was sitting stiffly in the corner. "Oh, darling, dearest! " she exclaimed. "*What* have I made you go through? And you're so generous, you'll never tell me what a villain I am. But you will forgive me, won't you?"

"I am just as much to blame as you are. I was not obliged to go."

"But it was dreadful, wasn't it? That horrid low policeman! The idea of his daring to put his hand on my shoulder. But we'll just forget it, and next week, to-morrow, it will be as if it never had happened."

Magdaléna made no reply.

"'Léna!" exclaimed Helena, sharply. "You're never going to own up?"

"I must," said Magdaléna, firmly. "I've done a wicked thing. I've disobeyed my father, who thinks it's horrible for girls to be on the street even in the daytime alone, and I've nearly disgraced him. I've no right not to tell him. I must!"

"That's your crazy old New England conscience! If you were all Spanish, you'd look as innocent as a madonna for a week, and if you were my kind of

Californian you'd cheek it and make your elders feel that they were impertinent for taking you to task."

"You are half New England."

"So I am, but I'm half Southerner, too, and all Californian. I'm just beautifully mixed. You're not mixed at all; you're just hooked together. Come now, say you won't tell him. He's a terror when he gets angry."

"I must tell him. I'd never respect myself again if I didn't. I've done lots of other things and didn't tell, but they didn't matter,—that is, not so much. He's got a *right* to know."

"It's a pity you're not more like him, then you wouldn't tell."

"What do you mean, Helena? I am sure my father never told a lie."

Helena was too generous to tell what she knew. She asked instead, "I wonder would your conscience hurt you so hard if everything had turned out all right, and we were coming home in our own hack?"

Magdaléna thought a moment. "It might not tonight, but it would tomorrow. I am sure of that," she said.

Helena groaned. "You are hopeless. Thank Heaven, I was born without a conscience, that kind, anyhow. I intend to be a law all to myself. I'm Californian clear through into my backbone."

The hack stopped. The girls alighted and walked slowly forward. Mr. Belmont's house was the first of the three.

"Well," said Helena, "here we are. I'm going to climb up the pillar and walk along the ledge. How are you going in?"

"Through the front door."

"Well, if you will, you will, I suppose. Kiss me good-night."

Magdaléna kissed her and walked on. A half-moment later Helena called after her in a loud whisper,—

"Take off that shawl!"

Magdaléna lifted her hand to her chin, then dropped it. When she reached her own home, she rang the bell firmly. The Chinaman who opened the door stared at her, the dawn of an expression on his face.

"Where is Don Roberto?" she asked.

"In loffice, missee."

Magdaléna crossed the hall and tapped at the door of the small room her father called his office. Don Roberto grunted, and she opened the door and went in. He was writing, and wheeled about sharply.

"What?" he exclaimed. "What the devil! Take that shawl off the head."

Magdaléna removed the shawl and sat down.

"I went to a fire," she said. "I got taken up by a policeman and went to the station. A man named Tom Shannon said he wouldn't lock me up, and sent me home. He paid for the carriage." She paused, looking at her father with white lips.

His face had turned livid, then purple. *"Dios!"* he gasped. *"Dios!"* And then she knew how furious her father was. When his life was in even tenor he never used his native tongue. *"Dios!"* he repeated. "Tell that again. You go with that little devil, Helena Belmont, I suppose. *Madre de Dios!* Again! Again!"

"I went to a fire—south of Market Street. A policeman arrested me for a vagrant. He called me a greaser—"

Her father sprang to his feet with a yell of rage. He caught his riding-whip from the mantel.

She stumbled to her feet. "Papa!" she said. "Papa! You will not do that!"

A few moments later she was in her own room. The stars shone full on her pretty altar. She turned her back on it and sat down on the floor. She had not uttered a word as her father beat her. Even now she barely felt the welts on her back. But her self-respect had been cut through at every blow, and it quivered and writhed within her. She hated her father and she hated life with an intensity which added to her misery, and she decided that she had made her last confession to any one but the priest, who always forgave her.

EDITH MAUD EATON [SUI SIN FAR]

1865–1914

Born in England to a Chinese mother and an English artist-businessman, Eaton moved with her quasi-bohemian family to New York. A lifelong traveler, she then lived in Canada, the Midwest, San Francisco, Seattle, the West Indies, and at last returned to Canada, where she died. Between 1890 and 1914 she published a large number of articles and stories in national magazines that she signed "Sui Sin Far," a courageous act of self-declaration in a time of virulent anti-Chinese sentiment and legislation. Her stories and children's tales were collected in Mrs. Spring Fragrance *(1912), the first book by a person of Chinese extraction to write in defense of the Chinese in America. Out of print for more than eighty years, the book was reissued in 1995 in an expanded edition by Amy Ling and Annette White-Parks. Set mainly in the Chinatowns of San Francisco and Los Angeles, many of the stories deal with the puzzle of mixed Caucasian-Asian identity, and more than a few explore similar blurrings of gender lines. "The Land of the Free" is her most charged social story, and here, as elsewhere, Eaton uses child characters to dramatize the human toll of exclusionary practices against immigrant Chinese.*

From *Mrs. Spring Fragrance*

I

"See, Little One—the hills in the morning sun. There is thy home for years to come. It is very beautiful and thou wilt be very happy there."

The Little One looked up into his mother's face in perfect faith. He was engaged in the pleasant occupation of sucking a sweetmeat; but that did not prevent him from gurgling responsively.

"Yes, my olive bud; there is where thy father is making a fortune for thee. Thy father! Oh, wilt thou not be glad to behold his dear face. 'Twas for thee I left him."

The Little One ducked his chin sympathetically against his mother's knee. She lifted him on to her lap. He was two years old, a round, dimple-cheeked boy with bright brown eyes and a sturdy little frame.

"Ah! Ah! Ah! Ooh! Ooh! Ooh!" puffed he, mocking a tugboat steaming by.

San Francisco's waterfront was lined with ships and steamers, while other craft, large and small, including a couple of white transports from the Philippines, lay at anchor here and there off shore. It was some time before the *Eastern Queen* could get docked, and even after that was accomplished, a lone Chinaman who had been waiting on the wharf for an hour was detained that much longer by men with the initials U.S.C. on their caps, before he could board the steamer and welcome his wife and child.

"This is thy son," announced the happy Lae Choo.

Hom Hing lifted the child, felt of his little body and limbs, gazed into his face with proud and joyous eyes; then turned inquiringly to the customs officer at his elbow.

"That's a fine boy you have there," said the man. "Where was he born?"

"In China," answered Hom Hing, swinging the Little One on his right shoulder, preparatory to leading his wife off the steamer.

"Ever been to America before?"

"No, not he," answered the father with a happy laugh.

The customs officer beckoned to another.

"This little fellow," said he, "is visiting America for the first time."

The other customs officer stroked his chin reflectively.

"Good day," said Hom Hing.

"Wait!" commanded one of the officers. "You cannot go just yet."

"What more now?" asked Hom Hing.

"I'm afraid," said the first customs officer, "that we cannot allow the boy to go ashore. There is nothing in the papers that you have shown us—your wife's papers and your own—having any bearing upon the child."

"There was no child when the papers were made out," returned Horn Hing. He spoke calmly; but there was apprehension in his eyes and in his tightening grip on his son.

"What is it? What is it?" quavered Lae Choo, who understood a little English.

The second customs officer regarded her pityingly.

"I don't like this part of the business," he muttered.

The first officer turned to Hom Hing and in an official tone of voice, said:

"Seeing that the boy has no certificate entitling him to admission to this country you will have to leave him with us."

"Leave my boy!" exclaimed Horn Hing.

"Yes, he will be well taken care of, and just as soon as we can hear from Washington he will be handed over to you."

"But," protested Hom Hing," he is my son.

"We have no proof," answered the man with a shrug of his shoulders; "and even if so we cannot let him pass without orders from the Government."

"He is my son," reiterated Horn Hing, slowly and solemnly. "I am a Chinese merchant and have been in business in San Francisco for many years. When my wife told to me one morning that she dreamed of a green tree with spreading branches and one beautiful red flower growing thereon, I answered her that I wished my son to be born in our country, and for her to prepare to go to China. My wife complied with my wish. After my son was born my mother fell sick and my wife nursed and cared for her; then my father, too, fell sick, and my wife also nursed and cared for him. For twenty moons my wife care for and nurse the old people, and when they die they bless her and my son, and send for her to return to me. I had no fear of trouble. I was a Chinese merchant and my son was my son.

"Very good, Hom Hing," replied the first officer. "Nevertheless, we take your son."

"No, you not take him; he my son too."

It was Lae Choo. Snatching the child from his father's arms she held and covered him with her own.

The officers conferred together for a few moments; then one drew Hom Hing aside and spoke in his ear.

Resignedly Hom Hing bowed his head, then approached his wife. "'Tis the law," said he, speaking in Chinese, "and 'twill be but for a little while— until tomorrow's sun arises."

"You, too," reproached Lae Choo in a voice eloquent with pain. But accustomed to obedience she yielded the boy to her husband, who in turn delivered him to the first officer.

The Little One protested lustily against the transfer; but his mother covered her face with her sleeve and the father silently led her away. Thus was the law of the land complied with.

II

Day was breaking. Lae Choo, who had been awake all night, dressed herself, then awoke her husband.

"'Tis the morn," she cried. "Go, bring our son."

The man rubbed his eyes and arose upon his elbow so that he could see out of the window. A pale star was visible in the sky. The petals of a lily in a bowl on the window-sill were unfurled.

"'Tis not yet time," said he, laying his head down again.

"Not yet time. Ah, all the time that I lived before yesterday is not so much as the time that has been since my little one was taken from me."

The mother threw herself down beside the bed and covered her face.

Hom Hing turned on the light, and touching his wife's bowed head with a sympathetic hand inquired if she had slept.

"Slept!" she echoed, weepingly. "Ah, how could I close my eyes with my arms empty of the little body that has filled them every night for more than twenty moons! You do not know—man—what it is to miss the feel of the little finger and the little toes and the soft round limbs of your little one. Even in the darkness his darling eyes used to shine up to mine, and often have I fallen into slumber with his pretty babble at my ear. And now, I see him not; I touch him not; I hear him not. My baby, my little fat one!"

"Now! Now! Now!" consoled Hom Hing, patting his wife's shoulder re-assuringly; "there is no need to grieve so; he will soon gladden you again. There cannot be any law that would keep a child from its mother!"

Lae Choo dried her tears.

"You are right, my husband," she meekly murmured. She arose and stepped about the apartment, setting things to rights. The box of presents she had brought for her California friends had been opened the evening before; and silks, embroideries, carved ivories, ornamental lacquer-ware, brasses, camphor-wood boxes, fans, and chinaware were scattered around in confused heaps. In the midst of unpacking the thought of her child in the hands of strangers had overpowered her, and she had left everything to crawl into bed and weep.

Having arranged her gifts in order, she stepped out on to the deep balcony.

The star had faded from view and there were bright streaks in the eastern sky. Lae Choo looked down the street and around. Beneath the flat occupied by her and her husband were quarters for a number of bachelor Chinamen, and she could hear them from where she stood, taking their early morning breakfast. Below their dining-room was her husband's grocery store. Across the way was a large restaurant. Last night it had been resplendent with gay colored lanterns and the sound of music. The rejoicings over "the completion of the moon," by Quong Sum's firstborn, had been long and loud, and had caused her to tie a handkerchief over her ears. She, a bereaved mother, had it not in her heart to rejoice with other parents. This morning the place was more in accord with her mood. It was still and quiet. The revellers had dispersed or were asleep.

A roly-poly woman in black sateen, with long pendant earrings in her ears, looked up from the street below and waved her a smiling greeting. It was her old neighbor, Kuie Hoe, the wife of the gold embosser, Mark Sing. With her was a little boy in yellow jacket and lavender pantaloons. Lae Choo remembered him as a baby. She used to like to play with him in those days when she had no child of her own. What a long time ago that seemed! She caught her breath in a sigh, and laughed instead.

"Why are you so merry?" called her husband from within.

"Because my Little One is coming home," answered Lae Choo. "I am a very happy mother—a happy mother."

She pattered into the room with a smile on her face.

The noon hour had arrived. The rice was steaming in the bowls and a fragrant dish of chicken and bamboo shoots was awaiting Hom Hing. Not for one moment had Lae Choo paused to rest during the morning hours; her activity had been ceaseless. Every now and again, however, she had raised her eyes to the gilded clock on the curiously carved mantelpiece. Once, she had exclaimed:

"Why so long, oh! why so long?" Then apostrophizing herself: "Lae Choo, be happy. The Little One is coming! The Little One is coming!" Several times she burst into tears and several times she laughed aloud.

Hom Hing entered the room; his arms hung down by his side.

"The Little One!" shrieked Lae Choo.

"They bid me call tomorrow."

With a moan the mother sank to the floor.

The noon hour passed. The dinner remained on the table.

III

The winter rains were over: the spring had come to California, flushing the hills with green and causing an ever-changing pageant of flowers to pass over them. But there was no spring in Lae Choo's heart, for the Little One remained away from her arms. He was being kept in a mission. White women were caring for him, and though for one full moon he had pined for his mother and refused to be comforted he was now apparently happy and contented. Five moons or five months had gone by since the day he had passed with Lae Choo through the Golden Gate; but the great Government at Washington still delayed sending the answer which would return him to his parents.

Hom Hing was disconsolately rolling up and down the balls in his abacus box when a keen-faced young man stepped into the store.

"What news?" asked the Chinese merchant.

"This!" The young man brought forth a typewritten letter. Hom Hing read the words:

"Re Chinese child, alleged to be the son of Hom Hing, Chinese merchant, doing business at 425 Clay Street, San Francisco.

"Same will have attention as soon as possible."

Hom Hing returned the letter, and without a word continued his manipulation of the counting machine.

"Have you anything to say?" asked the young man.

"Nothing. They have sent the same letter fifteen times before. Have you not yourself showed it to me?"

"True!" The young man eyed the Chinese merchant furtively. He had a proposition to make and he was pondering whether or not the time was opportune.

"How is your wife?" he inquired solicitously—and diplomatically.

Hom Hing shook his head mournfully.

"She seems less every day," he replied. "Her food she takes only when I bid her and her tears fall continually. She finds no pleasure in dress or flowers and cares not to see her friends. Her eyes stare all night. I think before another moon she will pass into the land of spirits."

"No!" exclaimed the young man, genuinely startled.

"If the boy not come home I lose my wife sure," continued Hom Hing with bitter sadness.

"It's not right," cried the young man indignantly. Then he made his proposition.

The Chinese father's eyes brightened exceedingly.

"Will I like you to go to Washington and make them give you the paper to restore my son?" cried he. "How can you ask when you know my heart's desire?"

"Then," said the young fellow, "I will start next week. I am anxious to see this thing through if only for the sake of your wife's peace of mind."

"I will call her. To hear what you think to do will make her glad," said Hom Hing.

He called a message to Lae Choo upstairs through a tube in the wall.

In a few moments she appeared, listless, wan, and hollow-eyed; but when her husband told her the young lawyer's suggestion she became as one electrified; her form straightened, her eyes glistened; the color flushed to her cheeks.

"Oh," she cried, turning to James Clancy, "You are a hundred man good!"

The young man felt somewhat embarrassed; his eyes shifted a little under the intense gaze of the Chinese mother.

"Well, we must get your boy for you," he responded. "Of course"—turning to Hom Hing—"it will cost a little money. You can't get fellows to hurry the Government for you without gold in your pocket."

Hom Hing stared blankly for a moment. Then: "How much do you want, Mr. Clancy?" he asked quietly.

"Well, I will need at least five hundred to start with."

Hom Hing cleared his throat.

"I think I told to you the time I last paid you for writing letters for me and seeing the Custom boss here that nearly all I had was gone!"

"Oh, well then we won't talk about it, old fellow. It won't harm the boy to stay where he is, and your wife may get over it all right."

"What that you say?" quavered Lae Choo.

James Clancy looked out of the window.

"He says," explained Hom Hing in English, "that to get our boy we have to have much money."

"Money! Oh, yes."

Lae Choo nodded her head.

"I have not got the money to give him."

For a moment Lae Choo gazed wonderingly from one face to the other; then, comprehension dawning upon her, with swift anger, pointing to the lawyer, she cried: "You not one hundred man good; you just common white man."

"Yes, ma'am," returned James Clancy, bowing and smiling ironically.

Hom Hing pushed his wife behind him and addressed the lawyer again: "I might try," said he, "to raise something; but five hundred—it is not possible."

"What about four?"

"I tell you I have next to nothing left and my friends are not rich."

"Very well!"

The lawyer moved leisurely toward the door, pausing on its threshold to light a cigarette.

"Stop, white man; white man, stop!"

Lae Choo, panting and terrified, had started forward and now stood beside him, clutching his sleeve excitedly.

"You say you can go to get paper to bring my Little One to me if Hom Hing give you five hundred dollars?"

Edith Maud Eaton [Sui Sin Far]

The lawyer nodded carelessly; his eyes were intent upon the cigarette which would not take fire from the match.

"Then you go get paper. If Hom Hing not can give you five hundred dollars—I give you perhaps what more that much."

She slipped a heavy gold bracelet from her wrist and held it out to the man. Mechanically, he took it.

"I go get more!"

She scurried away, disappearing behind the door through which she had come.

"Oh, look here, I can't accept this," said James Clancy, walking back to Hom Hing and laying down the bracelet before him.

"It's all right," said Hom Hing seriously, "pure China gold. My wife's parent give it to her when we married."

"But I can't take it anyway," protested the young man.

"It is all same as money. And you want money to go to Washington," replied Hom Hing in a matter of fact manner.

"See my jade earrings—my gold buttons—my hairpins—my comb of pearl and my rings—one, two, three, four, five rings; very good—very good—all same much money. I give them all to you. You take and bring me paper for my Little One."

Lae Choo piled up her jewels before the lawyer.

Hom Hing laid a restraining hand upon her shoulder. "Not all, my wife," he said in Chinese. He selected a ring—his gift to Lae Choo when she dreamed of the tree with the red flower. The rest of the jewels he pushed toward the white man.

"Take them and sell them," said he. "They will pay your fare to Washington and bring you back with the paper."

For one moment James Clancy hesitated. He was not a sentimental man; but something within him arose against accepting such payment for his services.

"They are good, good," pleadingly asserted Lae Choo, seeing his hesitation.

Whereupon he seized the jewels, thrust them into his coat pocket, and walked rapidly away from the store.

IV

Lae Choo followed after the missionary woman through the mission nursery school. Her heart was beating so high with happiness that she could scarcely breathe. The paper had come at last—the precious paper which gave Hom Hing and his wife the right to the possession of their own child. It was ten months now since he had been taken from them—ten months since the sun had ceased to shine for Lae Choo.

The room was filled with children—most of them wee tots, but none so wee as her own. The mission woman talked as she walked. She told Lae Choo that little Kim, as he had been named by the school, was the pet of the place, and that his little tricks and ways amused and delighted every one. He had been rather difficult to manage at first and had cried much for his mother; "but children so soon forget, and after a month he seemed quite at home and played around as bright and happy as a bird."

"Yes," responded Lae Choo. "Oh, yes, yes!"

But she did not hear what was said to her. She was walking in a maze of anticipatory joy.

"Wait here, please," said the mission woman, placing Lae Choo in a chair. "The very youngest ones are having their breakfast."

She withdrew for a moment—it seemed like an hour to the mother—then she reappeared leading by the hand a little boy dressed in blue cotton overalls and white-soled shoes. The little boy's face was round and dimpled and his eyes were very bright.

"Little One, ah, my Little One!" cried Lae Choo.

She fell on her knees and stretched her hungry arms toward her son.

But the Little One shrunk from her and tried to hide himself in the folds of the white woman's skirt.

"Go 'way, go 'way!" he bade his mother.

YONE NOGUCHI

1875–1947

*Born in Nagoya, Japan, Yone Noguchi studied haiku and Zen Bud-
dhism, English philosophy and poetry at a university in Tokyo, and he was
one of the first literary figures versed in two cultures to arrive in California. He
came to San Francisco by boat in 1893, and his wanderings in California are recorded
in a fascinating account,* The Story of Yone Noguchi *(1914). He spent his first years
in the bustling Asian American communities of the Bay Area, but, thirsty for American
adventures, he made his way in 1896 to Joaquin Miller and "The Hights" in the
Oakland Hills. Miller became his mentor and Miller's home the base for his hermetic
journeys—many on foot—all over California for the next three years. He soon met other
literary figures, including Charles Warren Stoddard and Edwin Markham, who were
taken with the freshness of his personality and manner on the page. Within a year of
entering the San Francisco circle, he was publishing poems, and his first book,* Seen
and Unseen; or, Monologues of a Homeless Snail, *appeared in 1896. From California, Noguchi traveled to Chicago, Boston, New York, and finally London, returning
to Japan in 1904. He was a distinguished professor of English at Keio University,
publishing poetry, criticism, art commentary, and travel writing, almost all of it written
in Japanese.*

*Noguchi was a major influence after his few years in California, and both Ezra
Pound and William Butler Yeats knew and reflected on his work. A wandering figure
with a sharp, Zen-influenced, imagistic eye, he was pivotal in California poetry, pointing
the way toward a substantial body of post–World War II work rooted strongly in Asian
philosophies and aesthetics. The prominent sculptor Isamu Noguchi is his son from an
early relationship with an American woman.*

Some Stories of My Western Life

My new life began when I left Tokyo for California; on the 3rd of November,
1893, my friends saw me off at Shimbashi Station. I felt most ambitious when
they wished me godspeed; but my heart soon broke down when my eldest
brother, who came to Yokohama to bid me a final farewell, left me alone on
the *Belgic*. That was the name of my steamer, an almost unimaginably small
affair for a Pacific liner, being only three thousand tons. I cried when the last
bell went ringing round to make the people leave the ship; I cried more when

my brother became invisible among the hurrying crowd and distance; it was my most bitter experience, as I cannot forget the pain of sadness of that moment even to-day. I stood by an iron rail on the deck, a boy only eighteen years old, alone, friendless, with less than one hundred dollars in my pocket. I immediately grew conscious of the fact that I had to face unknown America, a land of angels or devils, the darkness.

It is true that it was my first experience to see such a vastness of water, as I was born in a place out of sight of the sea; and its restless motion made me at once recall my sickness on the water which I had experienced when I joined a fishing party on the river Kiso several years before. The most unagreeable smell that filled the "Chinese steerage" made me already ill, even before the engine began to turn; I was practically thrown in as if a little bundle of merchandise for America. I could not eat, drink, for many days, and I vomited even what I did not eat, when the ship rolled. I was often obliged to tie me round the iron pole by my canvas bed; I soon became a thorough sea-hater, as I am still to-day.

The steamer duly reached San Francisco on a certain Sunday morning; we, I and a few other fellow-passengers, were taken to the Cosmopolitan Hotel, whose shabby appearance looked then palace-like and most wonderful. And within it was not less handsome. The American room was the first thing for us; even the sheets and the soft pillow, quite strange for the head acquainted only with hard wood, were a novelty. We put all the fruits we had bought (what splendid California fruits!) in a white bowl under the washing table; when we were told, to our utmost shame, that that bowl was for another purpose, we at once thought that we were, indeed, in a country alien in custom, and had a thousand things to study. We acted even more barbarously at the dinner-table; we took salt for sugar, and declared the cheese to be something rotten. We did not know which hand, left or right, had to hold a knife; we used a tablespoon for sipping the coffee, in which we did not know enough to drop a lump of sugar; we could not understand that those lumps were sugar. I stepped alone out of the hotel into a street and crowd; what attracted my immediate attention, which soon became admiration, was the American women. "What lovely complexions, what delightfully quick steps," I exclaimed. They were a perfect revelation of freedom and new beauty for my Japanese eye, having no relation whatever with any form of convention with which I was acquainted at home; it is not strange to say that I could not distinguish their ages, old or young; they appeared equally young, beautiful, even divine, because my discrimination lost its power at once. True, it took some months, though not one year, before I could venture to be critical toward their beauty; for some long time they only looked, all of them, perfectly-raised California poppies. I am happy to say that my first impression never betrayed me during my eleven years of American life; not only in California, but in any other place, they were my admiration and delight.

Now to return to the adventure of my first day in San Francisco. I again stepped out of the hotel after supper, and walked up and down, turned right, and again left, till the night was growing late. When I felt quite doubtful about my way back to the hotel, I was standing before a certain show window (I believe it was on Market Street), the beauty of which doubtless surprises me; I was suddenly struck by a hard hand from behind, and found a large, red-faced fellow, somewhat smiling in scorn, who, seeing my face, exclaimed, "Hello, Jap!" I was terribly indignant to be addressed in such a fashion; my indignation increased when he ran away, after spitting on my face. I recalled my friend, who said that I should have such a determination as if I were entering among enemies; I thrilled from fear with the uncertainty and even the darkness of my future. I could not find the way to my hotel, when I felt everything grow sad at once; in fact, nearly all the houses looked alike. Nobody seemed to understand my English, in the ability of which I trusted; many of the people coldly passed by even when I tried to speak. I almost cried, when I found one Japanese, fortunately; he, after hearing my trouble, exclaimed in laughter: "You are standing right before your hotel, my friend!"

My bed at the hotel was too soft; it even imitated, I fancied, the motion of the sea, the very thought of which made me sleepless. I sat alone on the shaky bed through the silence of midnight, thinking how I should begin my new life in this foreign country. In my heart of hearts, I even acknowledged my dead mistake in coming to America.

.　.　.

The work of "schoolboy," which I took up with much enthusiasm, served for some time as a delightful break in my American life; but its monotony soon became unbearable, and I decided to go on foot to Palo Alto, as I thought (as in a Japanese proverb, "The children who live by the temple learn how to read a sutra") I might learn something there. I slipped out of my employer's house one early morning from the window, as I was afraid the lady would not let me go if I asked my wages. When I reached the Stanford University ground, it was near evening; I called at the house of Prof. G——, where my friend was working while he attended the lecture courses. I was permitted to stay with him till I found some way to support myself. Through the kindness of the wife of Prof. G——I got a job at Mrs. C——'s to work morning and evening, and by turns I found a place at the Manzanita Hall (a sort of preparatory school for Stanford), where I was admitted to appear at the school for my service in cleaning the classrooms and waiting on table for the student-boarders. There were less than twenty students then; the work was not heavy, but if I remember rightly, I received no payment. I do not remember now how long I stayed there, what knowledge I picked up in the classroom; one thing I remember is that I read Irving's *Sketch Book* there for the first time, in which the description of Westminster Abbey incited my sudden desire for England. The general influence of Stanford, silent, not unkind, courteous, encouraging, that I felt from the buildings, the surrounding view with trees, even the group of students, was, I confess, far deeper than my first impression of Harvard, or even Oxford of England; after all, the library and lectures are not the main things. As I said, I worked without payment at the Manzanita Hall; I began to feel uncomfortable in course of time, with my heelless shoes and dirty coat. I decided to work at the Menlo Park Hotel, Menlo Park, as a dish-washer, till I could put myself in a respectable shape.

The work was not light; I had to rise every morning before four o'clock, and my work was never finished till ten o'clock at night. It was about the time when Japan declared war with China; what a delight it was to read the paper with the battle news in my spare time! When the war was quite advanced, almost reaching the zenith of interest as Li Hang Chang, the appointed Chinese Special Envoy, had already left home for Bakan to meet Ito, my mind grew restless from a sudden burst of desire to see my friends at San Francisco, and talk over the war, if it were necessary, even to fight with them. I dismissed myself from the hotel, and hurried back again to the *San Francisco News*.

Joaquin Miller was regarded most reverentially by Japanese a *sennin,* or "hermit who lived on dews." His great personality, it was said, was in his denying of the modern civilisation; his only joy of life was to raise roses and carnations. I believe it was with more than curiosity that I climbed up the hills behind Oakland to see him at the "Heights" where he sang:

"Come under my oaks, oh drowsy dusk!
The wolf and the dog; dear incense hour,
When Mother Earth hath a smell of musk
And things of the spirit assert their power—
When candles are set to burn in the West—
Set head and foot to the day at rest."

It was the ideal spot on earth with balmy air, such a wonder of view at your feet; I fell in love with the place at once, and I thought I could get plenty of the rest which was beyond my reach during two years and seven months that I had already spent in America. More than the place itself, I fell in love with Mr. Miller, whose almost archaic simplicity in the way of living and speech was indeed prophet-like; he said he would be glad to have me stay with him. I decided to do so on the spot.

He said that he had no lesson or teaching to give me, or if he had as any, it was about the full value of silence, without the understanding it of which one could never read the true heart of Mother Nature; and the heart of Nature, he said was Love.

"Silence, Love—and simplicity," he exclaimed.

When I retired in the house right next to his own to sleep that night, I secretly decided that I would become a poet. . . .

Indeed, I was left alone at Miller's "Heights" sadly or happily. It was happy to lie on the top of the hill when the poppies covered it in spring, where I often dreamed death would be, if I could be buried in such a place overlooking the bay (the Golden Gate), sweeter than life; it was happier still to rest by a brook in the canyon, with whose song I could send my mind far into the Unknown and Eternal. My life of seclusion was not without a happy break in meeting celebrities now and then.

My passion for wandering, that seemed to have ceased temporarily its flight (I was quite a traveller already in my boyhood at home), began to blaze up again; I felt it almost impossible not to heed the calling voice of trees, hills, waters, and skies in the far distance. I have read the romantic story of Gold-smith in his vagabondising in European villages, with only his beloved little flute; and the travelling note that was written by Basho, poet of moon and wind, impressed my mind, which only aspired to become a real poet. And the true poetry is not in writing, but in the union with nature. I decided to experience a 'tramp life" in poetical fashion; I thought it was the first step for my idea. I did not see at all the hard side of it; the romantic aspect of parting with the world and society, the perfect freedom, the having April when I started on my lone pilgrimage (with a book of poems all airs and flowers on equal terms, was brighter. It was the month of instead of a holy staff) toward the Yosemite Valley; my tramp life commenced at Stockton, which I reached by a river boat from San Francisco. I remember clearly, as it were yesterday, that it was already dark, a few stars sparkling in the high sky, as if a guiding spirit for a pilgrim, when I passed through Chinese Camp, the once famous place I had read of in Harte's stories of a mining camp. I felt extremely sad, the wind blowing from behind, at not finding a right place to sleep, and finally I camped under the trees, by a brook whose silver song still remains in my ears. I could not fall asleep because my blanket was so light, and I remember I put many little stones and twigs on it, that I gathered under the starlight. It was the first time that I felt such a great love in that light, which I never felt before; I thank my tramp life, which revealed many new beauties of nature, above all, how to appreciate it. . . .

I entered in the Courter Vale Road gradually, first coming into contact with California cedars, spruces, and pines. The season was still too early, as there were few travellers who had advanced into the valley; many houses by the road were still unoccupied, and consequently I could not find food and sleep at the place I wished. Once I slept in a barn, where I found no horse when I went to sleep. At midnight I felt a queer warmth and occasionally heard some biting sound, doubtless of hay; but I was too sleepy to rise. In the morning I found, to my surprise, I was sleeping right between the four legs of a horse. This and other incidents did not bring any pleasure at that time, like to-day, when I feel an almost tantalising delight in my reminiscent mood.

What a thrill of fear, which was not the thing of our world, I felt in the Yosemite Valley, as you can see in the first lines of my song of night:

"Hark! The prophecy-inciting windquake of the unfathomable concave of darkest Hell!
O, the God-scorning demon's shout against the truth-locked gate of mighty Heaven!"

What a sight of the falls reflected to the low-hanging moon! The tall trees looked no other but the ghosts or spirits who gathered and talked something wonderful and evil; and what a sound of water, besides that of the fall, which dashed down the river! I felt cold and suddenly hungry, when I became con-scious of my sad being amid such an almost frightening demonstration of Nature, particularly in the night. I was kindly treated by the clerk or manager of the Stoneman House, who needed somebody to chop wood, as the hotel had opened only a week before; I was given good food that night, and I even slept in a bed. I stayed in the valley four days, during which I chopped wood, with one Indian boy, for whose brother I was taken by one person there; I took every chance to look around the valley as much as I could. When I left the hotel, the manager wished me to stay for the whole summer; but wages and work were not my aim. I left the valley light-hearted, as I entered.

My next, far longer tramp-journey in the month of April 1898, was toward the south, down to Los Angeles; as I had decided that I would chop wood for my dinner, and sleep in a barn, I had only a few dollars for an emergency, and a mishap that I encountered on the first night robbed them away. I was sleeping in an empty wagon car, which I found near the station of Ocean

View; it was rather hot and uncomfortable; I was obliged to take off my trousers before lying down. But it was a mistake, as I found when, my car moving toward San Francisco at midnight, I hurriedly grasped my trousers upside down, and all the silver rolled away. I was glad, however, my little razor and comb were safe in the pocket of my coat; I was no more a boy, as a trifling moustache already began to bother me; and I had to have my toilet done before entering a town, by the looking-glass of a stream I might find. I wished to keep at least my appearance of a gentleman tramp.

I left San José in the early morning for Los Gatos, being given a chance to ride on a wagon by a kindly old farmer. As it was the latter part of April, both sides of the country road were perfectly covered by the cherry-blossoms in full glory. The morning freshness mingled with the fragrance of the flowers; as I was high up in the wagon, I was looking down the flat valley, and this unexpected flower-viewing (it is the Spring custom that Japanese keep at home) called my longing at once to sing my mind. The beauty of the cherry-blossom is not only Japan's; and it never happens in Japan to admire the thousand and thousand trees in one spot. I have the following in my diary of the Journey:

"*Santa Cruz, April 29th.*—Yesterday evening—a little before sunset—I crossed a long tunnel. Half a mile long, some say. The station-master did not believe me when I said that I was going to cross the tunnel. However, he assured me that there was some one hour before the next train. Enter did I. What dampness in the tunnel! It were the easiest thing to faint in it. A thievish light from the door, which was already small as a morning star, finally disappeared. Alas! Such darkness! I felt as if the darkness were an animal and about to devour my flesh. Monstrous darkness! I missed my footing and fell in the ditches. 'My God!' I exclaimed. I crawled, my hands touching the railroad track. Undoubtedly I might have been dead if I had not had Faith—Faith that would come out at the other side if I kept on. Oh, mighty Faith! Mother of hope! Yes, Faith is life! . . ."

It was fortunate, perhaps, to find a Japanese keeping a bamboo store or laundry shop, or working on a farm, wherever I went along the coast, who welcomed me, as my name was very well known to him; I was often begged to stay, if possible, indefinitely. I was glad that I could wash my stockings, or shirts even, with hot water prepared by him; he would be pleased also if I served him by writing an English letter or interpreting a business transaction. I stayed more than anywhere else at Monterey, where I learned the mystery of the sea better than ever; I inscribed my name in Japanese on the wall of the Carmel Mission, satisfied to find myself the only inscriber.

I reached San Lucas one afternoon of a certain day, feeling almost dead from hunger, as I had only breakfast on that day. The stationmaster directed me to a Japanese who kept a little vegetable garden; I found him quite ill, but his welcome was cordial. I saw plenty of charcoal fire burning to keep him warm; I think now that it was from the charcoal gas that I was suffocated and fell flat on the floor. It is true I was lying as a dead person till midnight, when the cold air brought me to my senses. I was told when I awoke that the sick man had had such a trouble in sending a message to San Francisco of my death, or at least of my being near to death. I understood the reason that I surprised my friends at Los Angeles with my presence a month later; I believe I was then supposed already dead throughout the Japanese colony of the coast. I thank the rain, the most gentle rain of Californian May, that drove me into a barn at San Miguel during two days, but made me study *Hamlet* line after line, which I carried with me; whatever I know about it to-day is from my reading in that haystack.

I cannot forget San Louis Obispo, where I entered under the bright moon, riding on the wagon of some gypsies with whom I became acquainted on the roadside; I parted from them presently with the hope of meeting again. I had not known before that it was a Spanish town full of beautiful girls; above all, with such a sweet atmosphere which only belongs to a Latin race; I observed that many of the girls were sitting with their banjos by the balconies, and singing serenades. When I appealed to them at one house with my hunger and tired feet, they stopped their songs, and rushed into a kitchen to cook something for me; I believe that it was a sort of festival in the town, as the joyous uproar could not be mistaken. How those young girls with such large black eyes and olive-skinned oval faces, sympathised with me when I told them I had walked so many miles on that day! Nothing particular happened before I reached Los Angeles in the beginning of July, except my stay of one month at Santa Barbara, picked up as a dish-washer by some Eastern visitor, who had settled there temporarily for health.

Ah, Who Says So?

Wet by the tapping sounds of rain on the roof,
My soul finding not a melodious silence—a warm
      reverie, stirs the darkness of my chamber to
      flight, while I lie on the midnight, lonely bed.
Alas! The rains nail on the roof; nay on the darkness
      of the night; nay, on the silence of the Universe!

Yone Noguchi

Being even as a lost child in the night, I hear no
        following tears of my heart-broken mother—only
        the rains, dripped down from the redwood
        boughs. What prattle! Is it the chatter of some
        unseen mortal?

Alas! Ought a man to be one who ever weeps?
Ah, who says so?

My Poetry

My Poetry begins with the tireless songs of the
        cricket, on the lean gray haired hill, in sober—
        faced evening.
And the next page is Stillness—
And what then, about the next to that?
Alas, the god puts his universe-covering hand over its sheets!
"Master, take off your hand for the humble servant!"
Asked in vain:—
How long for my meditation?

Charles Fletcher Lummis
1859–1928

Charles Fletcher Lummis walked to Los Angeles from Chillicothe, Ohio, in 1885. Accepting Harrison Gray Otis's offer to edit the new Los Angeles Times, *he took off on foot as a promotional stunt, filing stories all during the four-month journey. He gathered many of his reports in his first travel book,* A Tramp across the Continent *(1892). Lummis was smitten by the Southwest landscape on the trails to California, and was—throughout his life—as much a booster with furious energy as an enduring literary figure. He was unswerving in his defense of California Indians and the preservation of the old missions, and envisioned an emerging metropolis of Los Angeles with Mexican and Indian literary, artistic, and architectural accents. He edited* The Land of Sunshine *from 1894 to 1909, transforming the magazine from a promotional throwaway into a handsome showcase for turn-of-the-century southland art and literature. Like many another California writer, he lived out his dreams: he spoke exquisite Spanish and used it frequently, often dressed in Southwest costume. He built El Alisal, his Arroyo Seco home, from local stone with his own hands, and he surrounded himself with Mission-era appointments. With George Wharton James and Mary Austin, Lummis played a significant role in the awakening of California and Los Angeles to the splendor of the deserts. A shrewd and tireless collector, he founded the Southwest Museum in Los Angeles in 1914, and it thrives today as a center for South-western anthropology. In "As I Remember," an unpublished manuscript, Lummis recounts his memories of early Los Angeles.*

"Walking to Los Angeles"
from "As I Remember"

He [Otis] had got word to me enroute and when I reached San Gabriel, he was there to meet me. We had dinner together under the famed giant grape-vine. After the meal had settled, we walked the eleven miles to Los Angeles. I imagine it was the last long tramp the veteran ever took.

We reached Los Angeles a little after eleven that night. The memory of the earlier dinner entirely effaced by the walk, we had at Jerry Illich's on Court Street one of the famous meals that fine old Hungarian knew how to cook.

The night was largely passed in domestic pursuits in the New Hollenbeck Hotel—delousing, cleaning up, extricating my arm from its home-made splint, and getting acquainted again with my wife. At ten the next morning, I was on duty as first city editor of the *Los Angeles Times*.

When I walked into Los Angeles that winter day of 1885 it was a dull little place of some 12,000 persons. There were perhaps six buildings of three stories or better. The street railway had a few doleful miles of "bobtail" horsecars (like those which still served parts of New York City as late as 1903). I used to shoot quail and jackrabbits in the center of such a residence district as no other American city has quite the likes of.

The Los Angeles of my day was preponderantly of adobe, and the Spanish-speaking population outnumbered the Gringos two or three to one. The Pico House, the Baker Block, Nadeau Hotel, the Downey and Temple Blocks were the outstanding buildings. The streets were narrow and crooked, with an infinite capacity for mud. It was a fond joke to erect a pole at the intersection of Spring, Main and Temple Streets (where the Federal Building now stands) recording that a hack had sunk there beneath the surface.

Third Street was pretty near the southerly urban limit—beyond that were gardens and orchards and embowered residences. The *Times* Office was in the Downey Block. So was the Los Angeles Public Library—what there was of it—in a narrow room presided over by a graduate of the first L. A. High School class. (I had no premonition about this institution.)

The first City Hall was a long, one-story adobe across Spring Street from the present magnificent City Hall. The police headquarters and some other city offices were still in the aforesaid adobe. In the high-fence backyard I saw three notorious gentlemen suspended from their necks for various offences, chiefly killing wives.

The Council Chamber was over the Fire Engine House on Second Street in a two-story brick building. I had to report the council meetings, which was not so bad until dear old Dr. Sinsabaugh became president and ruled out smoking. To report a council meeting without smoking would tax the saint-hood of any reporter. Chewing of tobacco was however sanctioned. I tried to learn the mastication but could get nowhere. . . .

Col. Otis and I had hit it off from the first. The owner of the *Times* was a large paunchy man with a fine head and a gray imperial. After the Civil War he had been in the Federal Service in Alaska, then a newspaper man and printer for many years. He had a deep gruff voice and a brusque manner.

He hated anybody who was afraid of him. Because of his dominant and overbearing way a great many people were afraid of him. One of the reasons he liked me was that I wasn't. In my judgment, all the heartbreaking toil I put in on the *Times*, all the scoops I got and all the material help I gave toward making it a metropolitan daily—nothing did so much to clinch the old man's liking for me as this finding out that I wasn't afraid of him when I thought I was right.

The *Times* had been supporting the Chief of Police, a charming Irishman, in one of the periodic police fights that have characterized the city through all the years I have known it. I was greatly taken with Mac myself and fought valiantly for him. But one day I found out that he wasn't straight. "Colonel," I said, laying some revealing papers before him, "We'll have to fight the chief of police."

The Colonel shuffled over the papers. "Lummis! Don't you know this is contrary to the Policy of the *Times*?"

"To hell with the policy of the *Times!* I'm understanding that it is the policy of the *Times* to tell the truth and to be in the right. If it isn't, take it and go to hell!"

Dear old Bates, the telegraph editor, was fumbling his "flimsy" at the telegraph table, and Clarence Eddy, Foreman of the composing room, stood in the door thereof. Having seen the "Old Man" explode before, both looked to see the furniture fly.

He looked at me steadily for a moment and said very quietly, "Lummis, do you think that is the proper way to speak to your superior officer?"

It wasn't and I said so. But I also stuck to my guns.

The Old Man wasn't afraid of anything. Few people in Los Angeles realize today what they owe him. I don't exaggerate when I say as one who has known and studied this town for 44 years that it owes no other man so much as this rough old soldier.

The first fight of the *Times* was for High License [for the purpose of limiting the saloons]. Los Angeles in 1885 was wide open like any good Frontier town. The saloons bossed politics and everything else. They weren't such bad bosses at that! But feeling the urge of progress we made a fight for High License. Everybody laughed at us. We had no real expectation of winning. Both the other newspapers were against us. Yet the *Times* single-handed rolled up a majority of more than two to one in favor of High License. That was the beginning of modern law and order in the city.

An Angeleño who was probably the most popular man in Southern California, a "Prince of Good Fellows," with a wonderful mother, a beautiful wife and high social connections, ran for Secretary of State on the Republican ticket. The *Times* was Republican; but the personal character of the candidate was too much; and we fought him, tooth and nail. Every other publication in the city stood by him and bombarded us; but he was hopelessly snowed under in the election—the greatest political surprise in California up to that date.

Of course the Typographical Union controlled all the newspapers in Los Angeles. Col. Otis was a printer himself and a relentless worker. The *Times* was the only newspaper in town that never missed a payday, and it paid higher rates than any other. But the Union got greedy. They held us up time after time, presenting their demands at one or two o'clock in the morning—when to refuse would mean no issue in the morning, and that would have spelled ruin for a young and struggling paper.

We had to knuckle under many times. The Old Man would get purple in the face. I was present, I remember, when the last straw broke the camel's back—if you can call it a straw. You may recall the old patent medicine ads, two columns wide and a full column tall. These ads came to us in electrotype blocks. All the printer had to do was to pick up the block and put it in the "chase." At two one morning, Eddy and a couple of walking delegates came in and demanded that they be paid the same price for the one motion of picking up that block and laying it on the stone as they would be paid for picking up one by one the 50,000 or 60,000 letters and putting them into their printer's stick and unloading stick after stick into the column!

Col. Otis looked the committee up and down, drew himself to his full military stature and said without heat or explosion, "That is an unreasonable request and the *Times* will not accede to it. You gentlemen have black mailed the *Times* long enough. You can get your time at the window tomorrow. Good night."

They stared at him as though petrified. Going to slip an issue in the morning? Was the Old Man crazy? They lingered but he showed signs which they recognized and they hurriedly backed out.

Within half an hour a full force of Union compositors was at work in the *Times* composing room—but they were not Typographical Union. Foreseeing the inevitable, Col. Otis had imported from Ohio a band of the Typothetae. Quite undreamed of by anyone, he had them in waiting in a quiet hotel. Now at the drop of a hat they came.

So far as I know this is the only case in the United States in which the all-powerful Typographical Union has been defied and defeated. The nationwide organization rallied to the support of their brothers in Los Angeles and the war was taken up by the American Federation of Labor. The *Times* was boycotted, threatened, attacked. Advertisers were bulldozed, every house at which the *Times* was delivered was threatened and cajoled to cease subscribing. The ingenuities and the shamelessness of the boycott were almost incredible, but as Americans have a sense of fair play, that same boycott was the making of the *Times*.

Things looked particularly ugly during the countrywide railroad strike of 1904 when the dissatisfied elements marched around the streets openly threatening the *Times*. I had long been out of the paper but went up to see the Old Chief (who in the Spanish-American war had become General Otis) and asked him if he needed a man with a scatter-gun to help stand guard. He thanked me and said he thought not. "If they do dynamite the building as they threaten," he said, "I suppose it is about as good a tomb for me as any."

Several years later (Oct. 1, 1910) a little after midnight, I was writing in my den some six miles away when I heard two explosions. To my practiced ear they said *dynamite*. And though there had been no threats for a year or so, I jumped up and shouted, "By God, I believe they have got the *Times!*"

At 8 next morning there came to my door a little 4 page *Times* telling how the *Times* building had been dynamited, killing twenty men at their work. The Old Chief had not been caught napping. For a year, unknown to almost anyone, he had had an auxiliary plant half a mile away down by the railroad yards. As soon as the bleeding feet and hands of the heroic survivors could be bound up they trudged down to the new plant and got out the little paper.

It was a big thing done without a dramatic gesture and in the plain line of military duty. The dynamiting was the stupidest blunder the *Union* ever made—which is saying a great deal.

I have lived in many countries; but never in one where human life was so insecure as in this, nor any in which the criminal was so safe as he is here. In Mexico, Guatemala, Central America, Peru, Bolivia and Chile, justice is far swifter and surer than with us and murder much less endemic.

Col. Otis was brusque, rough, suspicious, vindictive, a strange combination of childlikeness, of great practicality in many things—n printing and news-papering he was a past master—very far from worldly-wise in many others. He made innumerable enemies quite needlessly, as well as a large number that were greatly to his credit. It was good that every scoundrel, every criminal, every low politician hated him. It was a pity that so many thoroughly good disliked him. He could have done a great deal more good if he had not antagonized so many good citizens. However as he did more for the community than all the other newspapermen put together, I presume we may forgive him this loss of further achievement.

The episode which gave me undying admiration and reverence for Col.

Otis involved his partner, a polished plausible gentleman known as Col. Smoothy. His ideals of citizenship and public honesty did not at all jibe with Otis's. When the latter found this out unmistakenly, the last strand of tolerance broke, and there was open war between them.

Smoothy made an offer which he felt sure would give him the paper. Col. Otis had neither money nor connections. He sweat blood to raise the necessary sum but failed.

One afternoon three gentlemen came up to the *Times* office. The Chief told me to sit still at my table. Major E. F. Spence, a heavy, stolid, honorable president of the First National Bank, had the congressional bee. There was nothing against him. Indeed there was much in his favor.

"Col. Otis," his emissaries said, "if the *Times* will give support to Maj. Spence's campaign we can adjust that financial matter for you on your own terms. Within three days you can be absolute master of the paper."

Up and down the room without saying a word walked the big, clumsy man, the sweat rolling down his cheeks. It was his Gethsemane.

He wheeled at last like a soldier. "Gentlemen, I thank you. Maj. Spence is a good man. He would make a good congressman. But I don't know what other candidates may appear, and I cannot sell the support of the *Times* to any man alive. It belongs to the community. I cannot bargain with you."

That chivalric heroism, I am glad to record, was not lost. The Colonel managed to acquire the money in another way and to buy out his partner.

Later on Col. Smoothy started a rival paper. One morning it came out with the phrase, "Otis, the Brute, Lummis, the Little Liar." I sought out Col. Smoothy and whacked him across the face with my leather cane. Next time we met he reached for his derringer. I laughed in his face. And though for several months he carried the derringer in that pocket and got his hand on it whenever we passed, he never did pull the trigger.

His paper did not live many years. Before it died he brought a violent and sensational libel suit against the *Times* for $50,000. The jury awarded him the sum of $1.00.

The Southern California Land Boom lasted from the spring of 1886 to about January 1888. The area it covered—though in varying pitch—was nearly as large as New England. I think there is no doubt that in area of land plotted and sold it exceeded any similar land gamble in history. Lands have elsewhere brought higher prices and in a few other instances been more rapidly sold; but it is probably safe to say that nowhere else (certainly never before this specific instance) did the prices rise so fast nor so unreasonably, and that never has such a stupendous sum in transfers been accomplished with so small an expenditure of cash, nor by such unwonted speculators.

The boom began by purely legitimate "additions" to towns and cities actually extant, of lands whose immediate potentialities were very little exaggerated. It is fair to remark too that counting the average of the Boom there was very little real swindling. Almost all that came after the collapse. In this desperate post-mortem gleaning thousands of the 25-foot holdings were sold in Mexican territory, 150 miles south of the California line, for enough apiece to have bought a good farm. But it is only fair to say that this was pursued wholly by professional sharks and almost without exception through the columns of Eastern newspapers.

Early in 1887 tens of thousands of acres fir only for grain or pasture, if that, were cut up into 25-ft. city lots, thousands of acres purchased from their original owners at $10 to $30 an acre were sold in lots at $1000 to $10,000 an acre.

In 1887 Los Angeles was growing at the rate of least 1500 a month, and San Diego was growing by at least half that rate. On an average business day one could not stir upon the street without encountering brass bands, transparencies and other fake sales devices. At the tract office a line would begin to form one or two days before a sale was to open. I have seen men pay $100 for a place in that line. I have seen them serpentine for a block or worse all afternoon and night and until 9 o'clock of the critical morning. There were dozens of cases in which a company or individual sold over $300,000 worth of lots in the first few days and had at least three-fourths of the land left. The barren sandspit that I used to know seaward from San Diego, on which is now one of the fine hotels of the world [Del Coronado] took in for its organized owners two and a half million dollars in cash in one year, and after paying off its debts and making its enormously costly improvements it had four-fifths of its landed property left clear of incumbrance.

Real estate transfers recorded in the county of Los Angeles for 1887 exceeded $1000 for every man, woman and child. Everyone was plunging— bankers, ministers, school teachers, policemen, tramps, judges, servant girls, bootblacks, car drivers, society ladies, counter-jumpers. At then current real estate values Southern California was worth more than perhaps New York State. Yet not one single bank, not one well-established house, not one legitimate enterprise failed in the collapse of that stupendous madness. For with all its greed, its ignorance, its idiocy, the boom was not quite a lottery. Thousands of lots were sold for far more than they were worth, but all were worth something real.

Charles Fletcher Lummis

The colossal superstructure of values that upheld a million fortunes came down as fast and as noiselessly as a castle of cards. But its victims were born game. In May 1888, fifty percent more land was plowed in Southern California than ever before. When the bank quietly raked in the chips, the greenhorn victims turned instantly and almost unanimously to developing the values with which they had diced, and from the bursting of that bubble there has not been a day's cessation of steady growth.

L. FRANK BAUM
1856–1919

Born in New York State, Baum was a traveling actor and producer, petroleum salesman, and journalist, all of which vocations provided only a marginal income. When he published his first children's book in 1897, it met with such financial success that he began to write virtually nonstop. In 1906 alone, he published six books, including his most enduring work, The Wonderful Wizard of Oz. Plagued by poor health and disastrous investments in radio plays and illuminated slide ventures, he moved to Hollywood in 1910, intent on changing his image and fortunes. He wrote two boys' adventure books, but when they did poorly his publishers insisted he return to the tried-and-true Oz formula. Inspired by the entrepreneurial fortunes being made around him in Los Angeles, Baum built Ozcot, his lavish Hollywood home, and launched an unsuccessful film company, Oz Film Manufacturing, into which he poured most of his personal fortune until it failed in 1915. He found fame and wealth as the creator of Dorothy and the rest of the fabled cast, but he could never move beyond the role of the writer of Oz fantasies. By the time of his death in Los Angeles in 1919, he had developed a profoundly ambivalent attitude toward his lot. Baum's Oz books remain both classic children's fantasy—the first truly American fairy tales—and the subject of endless adult speculations as to their "real" meaning. Oz sequels were still being written by other authors forty years after his death.

From *Dorothy and the Wizard in Oz*

THE EARTHQUAKE

The train from 'Frisco was very late. It should have arrived at Hugson's Siding at midnight, but it was already five o'clock and the gray dawn was breaking in the east when the little train slowly rumbled up to the open shed that served for the station-house. As it came to a stop the conductor called out in a loud voice:

"Hugson's Siding!"

At once a little girl rose from her seat and walked to the door of the car, carrying a wicker suit-case in one hand and a round birdcage covered up with newspapers in the other, while a parasol was tucked under her arm. The conductor helped her off the car and then the engineer started his train again, so that it puffed and groaned and moved slowly away up the track. The reason he was so late was because all through the night there were times when the solid earth shook and trembled under him, and the engineer was afraid that at any moment the rails might spread apart and an accident happen to his passengers. So he moved the cars slowly and with caution.

The little girl stood still to watch until the train had disappeared around a curve; then she turned to see where she was.

The shed at Hugson's Siding was bare save for an old wooden bench, and did not look very inviting. As she peered through the soft gray light not a house of any sort was visible near the station, nor was any person in sight; but after a while the child discovered a horse and buggy standing near a group of trees a short distance away. She walked toward it and found the horse tied to a tree and standing motionless, with its head hanging down almost to the ground. It was a big horse, tall and bony, with long legs and large knees and feet. She could count his ribs easily where they showed through the skin of his body, and his head was long and seemed altogether too big for him, as if it did not *fit*. His tail was short and scraggly, and his harness had been broken in many places and fastened together again with cords and bits of wire. The buggy seemed almost new, for it had a shiny top and side curtains. Getting around in front, so that she could look inside, the girl saw a boy curled up on the seat, fast asleep.

She set down the bird-cage and poked the boy with her parasol. Presently he woke up, rose to a sitting position and rubbed his eyes briskly.

"Hello!" he said, seeing her, "are you Dorothy Gale?"

"Yes," she answered, looking gravely at his tousled hair and blinking gray eyes. "Have you come to take me to Hugson's Ranch?"

"Of course," he answered. "Train in?"

"I couldn't be here if it wasn't," she said.

He laughed at that, and his laugh was merry and frank. Jumping out of the buggy he put Dorothy's suit-case under the seat and her bird-cage on the floor in front.

"Canary-birds ?" he asked.

"Oh, no; it's just Eureka, my kitten. I thought that was the best way to carry her."

The boy nodded.

"Eureka's a funny name for a cat," he remarked.

"I named my kitten that because I found it," she explained. "Uncle Henry says 'Eureka' means 'I have found it.' "

"All right; hop in."

She climbed into the buggy and he followed her. Then the boy picked up the reins, shook them, and said "Gid-dap!"

The horse did not stir. Dorothy thought he just wiggled one of his drooping ears, but that was all.

"Gid-dap !" called the boy, again.

The horse stood still.

"Perhaps," said Dorothy, "if you untied him, he would go."

The boy laughed cheerfully and jumped out.

"Guess I'm half asleep yet," he said, untying the horse.

"But Jim knows his business all right—don't you, Jim?" patting the long nose of the animal.

Then he got into the buggy again and took the reins, and the horse at once backed away from the tree, turned slowly around, and began to trot down the sandy road which was just visible in the dim light.

"Thought that train would never come," observed the boy. "I've waited at that station for five hours."

"We had a lot of earthquakes," said Dorothy. "Didn't you feel the ground shake?"

"Yes; but we're used to such things in California," he replied. "They don't scare us much."

"The conductor said it was the worst quake he ever knew."

"Did he? Then it must have happened while I was asleep," he said, thoughtfully.

"How is Uncle Henry?" she enquired, after a pause during which the horse continued to trot with long, regular strides.

"He's pretty well. He and Uncle Hugson have been having a fine visit."

"Is Mr. Hugson your uncle?" she asked.

"Yes. Uncle Bill Hugson married your Uncle Henry's wife's sister; so we must be second cousins," said the boy, in an amused tone. "I work for Uncle Bill on his ranch, and he pays me six dollars a month and my board."

"Isn't that a great deal?" she asked, doubtfully.

"Why, it's a great deal for Uncle Hugson, but not for me. I'm a splendid worker. I work as well as I sleep," he added, with a laugh.

"What is your name ?" asked Dorothy, thinking she liked the boy's manner and the cheery tone of his voice.

"Not a very pretty one," he answered, as if a little ashamed. "My whole name is Zebediah; but folks just call me 'Zeb.' You've been to Australia, haven't you?"

"Yes; with Uncle Henry," she answered. "We got to San Francisco a week ago, and Uncle Henry went right on to Hugson's Ranch for a visit while I stayed a few days in the city with some friends we had met."

"How long will you be with us?" he asked.

"Only a day. Tomorrow Uncle Henry and I must start back for Kansas. We've been away for a long time, you know, and so we're anxious to get home again."

The boy flicked the big, boney horse with his whip and looked thoughtful. Then he started to say something to his little companion, but before he could speak the buggy began to sway dangerously from side to side and the earth seemed to rise up before them. Next minute there was a roar and a sharp crash, and at her side Dorothy saw the ground open in a wide crack and then come together again.

"Goodness!" she cried, grasping the iron rail of the seat. "What was that?"

"That was an awful big quake," replied Zeb, with a white face. "It almost got us that time, Dorothy."

The horse had stopped short, and stood firm as a rock. Zeb shook the reins and urged him to go, but Jim was stubborn. Then the boy cracked his whip and touched the animal's flanks with it, and after a low moan of protest Jim stepped slowly along the road. Neither the boy nor the girl spoke again for some minutes. There was a breath of danger in the very air, and every few moments the earth would shake violently. Jim's ears were standing erect upon his head and every muscle of his big body was tense as he trotted toward home. He was not going very fast, but on his flanks specks of foam began to appear and at times he would tremble like a leaf.

The sky had grown darker again and the wind made queer sobbing sounds as it swept over the valley.

Suddenly there was a rending, tearing sound, and the earth split into another great crack just beneath the spot where the horse was standing. With a wild neigh of terror the animal fell bodily into the pit, drawing the buggy and its occupants after him.

Dorothy grabbed fast hold of the buggy top and the boy did the same. The sudden rush into space confused them so that they could not think.

Blackness engulfed them on every side, and in breathless silence they waited for the fall to end and crush them against jagged rocks or for the earth to close in on them again and bury them forever in its dreadful depths.

The horrible sensation of falling, the darkness and the terrifying noises, proved more than Dorothy could endure and for a few moments the little girl lost consciousness. Zeb, being a boy, did not faint, but he was badly frightened, and clung to the buggy seat with a tight grip, expecting every moment would be his last.

THE GLASS CITY

When Dorothy recovered her senses they were still falling, but not so fast. The top of the buggy caught the air like a parachute or an umbrella filled with wind, and held them back so that they floated downward with a gentle motion that was not so very disagreeable to bear. The worst thing was their terror of reaching the bottom of this great crack in the earth, and the natural fear that sudden death was about to overtake them at any moment. Crash after crash echoed far above their heads, as the earth came together where it had split, and stones and chunks of clay rattled around them on every side. These they could not see, but they could feel them pelting the buggy top, and Jim screamed almost like a human being when a stone overtook him and struck his boney body. They did not really hurt the poor horse, because everything was falling together; only the stones and rubbish fell faster than the horse and buggy, which were held back by the pressure of the air, so that the terrified animal was actually more frightened than he was injured.

How long this state of things continued Dorothy could not even guess, she was so greatly bewildered. But bye and bye, as she stared ahead into the black chasm with a beating heart, she began to dimly see the form of the horse Jim—his head up in the air, his ears erect and his long legs sprawling in every direction as he tumbled through space. Also, turning her head, she found that she could see the boy beside her, who had until now remained as still and silent as she herself.

Dorothy sighed and commenced to breathe easier. She began to realize that death was not in store for her, after all, but that she had merely started upon another adventure, which promised to be just as queer and unusual as were those she had before encountered.

With this thought in mind the girl took heart and leaned her head over the side of the buggy to see where the strange light was coming from. Far below her she found six great glowing balls suspended in the air. The central and largest one was white, and reminded her of the sun. Around it were arranged, like the five points of a star, the other five brilliant balls; one being rose colored, one violet, one yellow, one blue and one orange. This splendid group of colored suns sent rays darting in every direction, and as the horse and buggy—with Dorothy and Zeb—sank steadily downward and came nearer to the lights, the rays began to take on all the delicate tintings of a rainbow, growing more and more distinct every moment until all the space was brilliantly illuminated.

Dorothy was too dazed to say much, but she watched one of Jim's big ears turn to violet and the other to rose, and wondered that his tail should be yellow and his body striped with blue and orange like the stripes of a zebra. Then she looked at Zeb, whose face was blue and whose hair was pink, and gave a little laugh that sounded a bit nervous.

"Isn't it funny?" she said.

The boy was startled and his eyes were big. Dorothy had a green streak through the center of her face where the blue and yellow lights came together, and her appearance seemed to add to his fright.

"I—I don't s-s-see any-thing funny—'bout it!" he stammered.

Just then the buggy tipped slowly over upon its side, the body of the horse tipping also. But they continued to fall, all together, and the boy and girl had no difficulty in remaining upon the seat, just as they were before. Then they turned bottom side up, and continued to roll slowly over until they were right side up again. During this time Jim struggled frantically, all his legs kicking the air; but on finding himself in his former position the horse said, in a relieved tone of voice:

"Well, that's better."

Dorothy and Zeb looked at one another in wonder.

"Can your horse talk?" she asked.

"Never knew him to, before," replied the boy.

"Those were the first words I ever said," called out the horse, who had overheard them, "and I can't explain why I happened to speak then. This is a nice scrape you've got me into, isn't it?"

"As for that, we are in the same scrape ourselves," answered Dorothy, cheerfully. "But never mind; something will happen pretty soon."

"Of course," growled the horse; "and then we shall be sorry it happened."

Zeb gave a shiver. All this was so terrible and unreal that he could not understand it at all, and so had good reason to be afraid.

Swiftly they drew near to the flaming colored suns, and passed close beside them. The light was then so bright that it dazzled their eyes, and they covered their faces with their hands to escape being blinded. There was no heat in the colored suns, however, and after they had passed below them the top of the buggy shut out many of the piercing rays so that the boy and girl could open their eyes again.

"We've got to come to the bottom some time," remarked Zeb, with a deep sigh. "We can't keep falling forever, you know."

"Of course not," said Dorothy. "We are somewhere in the middle of the earth, and the chances are we'll reach the other side of it before long. But it's a big hollow, isn't it?"

"Awful big!" answered the boy.

"We're coming to something now," announced the horse.

At this they both put their heads over the side of the buggy and looked down. Yes; there was land below them; and not so very far away, either. But they were floating very, very slowly—so slowly that it could no longer be called a fall—and the children had ample time to take heart and look about them.

They saw a landscape with mountains and plains, lakes and rivers, very like those upon the earth's surface; but all the scene was splendidly colored by the variegated lights from the six suns. Here and there were groups of houses that seemed made of clear glass, because they sparkled so brightly.

"I'm sure we are in no danger," said Dorothy, in a sober voice. "We are falling so slowly that we can't be dashed to pieces when we land, and this country that we are coming to seems quite pretty."

"We'll never get home again, though!" declared Zeb, with a groan.

"Oh, I'm not so sure of that," replied the girl. "But don't let us worry over such things, Zeb; we can't help ourselves just now, you know, and I've always been told it's foolish to borrow trouble."

The boy became silent, having no reply to so sensible a speech, and soon both were fully occupied in staring at the strange scenes spread out below them. They seemed to be falling right into the middle of a big city which had many tall buildings with glass domes and sharp-pointed spires. These spires were like great spear-points, and if they tumbled upon one of them they were likely to suffer serious injury.

Jim the horse had seen these spires, also, and his ears stood straight up with fear, while Dorothy and Zeb held their breaths in suspense. But no; they floated gently down upon a broad, flat roof, and came to a stop at last.

Anonymous Chinese Immigrants

1910–1940

What follows is a selection of poetry by anonymous Chinese writers from two sources: Island *(1980), edited by Him Mark Lai, Genny Lim, and Judy Yung; and* Songs of Gold Mountain *(1987), edited by Marlon K. Hom. There have been many recent rediscoveries of the buried contributions of people of color in California, but few so moving as these two collections. In the San Francisco earthquake and fire of 1906, all immigration records were destroyed, and entrants seeking citizenship on the basis of their connections to families already in legal residence were no longer able to document their claims. From 1910 until 1940, U.S. immigration authorities used Angel Island in San Francisco Bay as the port of entry for all Chinese arrivals, detaining some for "review" for as long as four months. Many immigrants carved their pain in poems in the wooden doors and walls of "Building," as the quarters were bitterly named, and as many were turned back from "Gold Mountain" (the Chinese term for California) as gained entry. Through photographs of the panels, showing the original Chinese characters, along with translations and editorial explanations,* Island *humanizes this phenomenon. Similarly, from the two major Chinatown Cantonese newspapers of the time, Marlon K. Hom drew a collection of unsigned poems and songs by ordinary citizens. Hom's commentary offers an accessible and intelligent introduction to the anonymous Chinese literature of this dark era.*

1

Over a hundred poems are on the walls.
Looking at them, they are all pining at the delayed progress.
What can one sad person say to another?
Unfortunate travelers everywhere wish to commiserate.
Gain or lose, how is one to know what is predestined?
Rich or poor, who is to say it is not the will of heaven?
Why should one complain if he is detained and imprisoned here?
From ancient times, heroes often were the first ones to face adversity.

2

I count on my fingers: a year is about to end.
In the embroidery room, a young woman laments:

I am still somewhat young—
Yet time passes ever so quickly, in the blink of an eye,
Gone and never to return;
No one can detain it.
Enjoy life when the time is right, don't ever delay.
Alas, no thanks to Husband, who has yet to come home.

3

Face haggard, turning yellow and puffy,
Waist, bent like a drawn bow.
Lying on his side next to a small lit lamp,
He holds the pipe as his family fortune goes down its hole.
Look at him:
Soon he will be six feet underground.
Lazy, remiss, he won't move even if you drag him.
He's about to meet King Yimlo at Hell's tenth palace.

4

It's a summerlike first month of the new year.
Ten thousand houses are decorated with New Year scrolls.
In a foreign country, we celebrate the joyous festival in springtime clothes;
We greet each other by the door, with auspicious sayings:
May you claim a mine full of gold.
May wealth soothe your soul.
Hosts and guests, so gaily, raise the jade winecups,
Sipping the spring wine, toasting merrily the swift, rosy clouds.

Anonymous Chinese Immigrants

Jack London
1876–1916

One of America's most popular writers, still widely read around the world, London was born in San Francisco. He grew up in poverty, the illegitimate son of a traveling astrologer and a spiritualist mother. From the age of fourteen, he supported himself by means of a series of rugged jobs at a cannery, as an oyster pirate, and as a merchant seaman on a Pacific sealing expedition. During these years he read constantly, guided at times by the poet Ina Coolbrith. With fierce energy, he also began to try writing as a way of improving his lot in life, like the hero of his autobiographical novel Martin Eden *(1909). In 1897 he joined the Klondike gold rush, and the stories he brought back finally earned some recognition. The first was published in the* Overland Monthly *in 1899. His collection* The Son of the Wolf *(1900) was followed by* The Call of the Wild *(1903), a bestseller that made London wealthy at age twenty-seven. A man of enormous appetites and enormous contradictions, he soon became the most highly paid writer of his time. His fans admired the passion of his prose and the raw energy of his characters. His critics said that he wrote too much and too fast and that he never reconciled two competing beliefs: the socialist triumph of the working class and the more Darwinian doctrine of the survival of the superior individual. Obsessed and driven, London lectured, traveled widely, and pushed himself to deliver a thousand words a day, six days a week. In twenty years of writing, he produced dozens of stories, hundreds of articles, and some fifty books, among them* The Sea Wolf *(1904),* White Fang *(1906), and* The Iron Heel *(1908). He died on his Sonoma County ranch near Glen Ellen at age forty, apparently by his own hand.*

From *Martin Eden*

CHAPTER 15

"The first battle, fought and finished," Martin said to the looking-glass ten days later. "But there will be a second battle, and a third battle, and battles to the end of time, unless—"

He had not finished the sentence, but looked about the mean little room and let his eyes dwell sadly upon a heap of returned manuscripts, still in their long envelopes, which lay in a corner on the floor. He had no stamps with which to continue them on their travels, and for a week they had been piling up. More of them would come in on the morrow, and on the next day, and the next, till they were all in. And he would be unable to start them out again. He was a month's rent behind on the type-writer, which be could not pay, having barely enough for the week's board which was due and for the employment office fees.

He sat down and regarded the table thoughtfully. There were ink stains upon it, and he suddenly discovered that he was fond of it.

"Dear old table," he said, "I've spent some happy hours with you, and you've been a pretty good friend when all is said and done. You never turned me down, never passed me out a reward-of-unmerit rejection slip, never complained about working overtime."

He dropped his arms upon the table and buried his face in them. His throat was aching, and he wanted to cry. It reminded him of his first fight, when he was six years old, when he punched away with the tears running down his cheeks while the other boy, two years his elder, had beaten and pounded him into exhaustion. He saw the ring of boys, howling like barbarians as he went down at last, writhing in the throes of nausea, the blood streaming from his nose and the tears from his bruised eyes.

"Poor little shaver," he murmured. "And you're just as badly licked now. You're beaten to a pulp. You're down and out."

But the vision of that first fight still lingered under his eyelids, and as he watched he saw it dissolve and reshape into the series of fights which had followed. Six months later Cheese-Face (that was the boy) had whipped him again. But he had blacked Cheese-Face's eye that time. That was going some. He saw them all, fight after fight, himself always whipped and Cheese-Face exulting over him. But he had never run away. He felt strengthened by the memory of that. He had always stayed and taken his medicine. Cheese-Face had been a little fiend at fighting, and had never once shown mercy to him. But he had stayed! lie had stayed with it!

Next, he saw a narrow alley, between ramshackle frame buildings. The end of the alley was blocked by a one-story brick building, out of which issued the rhythmic thunder of the presses, running off the first edition of the *Enquirer*. He was eleven, and Cheese-Face was thirteen, and they both carried the *Enquirer*. That was why they were there, waiting for their papers. And, of course, Cheese-Face had picked on him again, and there was another fight that was indeterminate, because at quarter to four the door of the press-room was thrown open and the gang of boys crowded in to fold their papers.

"I'll lick you to-morrow," he heard Cheese-Face promise; and he heard his own voice, piping and trembling with unshed tears, agreeing to be there on the morrow.

And he had come there the next day, hurrying from school to be there first, and beating Cheese-Face by two minutes. The other boys said he was all right, and gave him advice, pointing out his faults as a scrapper and promising him victory if he carried out their instructions. The same boys gave Cheese-Face advice, too. How they had enjoyed the fight! He paused in his recollections long enough to envy them the spectacle he and Cheese-Face had put up. Then the fight was on, and it went on, without rounds, for thirty minutes, until the press-room door was opened.

He watched the youthful apparition of himself, day after day, hurrying from school to the *Enquirer* alley. He could not walk very fast. He was stiff and lame from the incessant fighting. His forearms were black and blue from wrist to elbow, what of the countless blows he had warded off, and here and there the tortured flesh was beginning to fester. His head and arms and shoulders ached, the small of his back ached,—he ached all over, and his brain was heavy and dazed. He did not play at school. Nor did he study. Even to sit still all day at his desk, as he did, was a torment. It seemed centuries since he had begun the round of daily fights, and time stretched away into a nightmare and infinite future of daily fights. Why couldn't Cheese-Face be licked? he often thought; that would put him, Martin, out of his misery. It never entered his head to cease fighting, to allow Cheese-Face to whip him.

And so he dragged himself to the *Enquirer* alley, sick in body and soul, but learning the long patience, to confront his eternal enemy, Cheese-Face, who was just as sick as he, and just a bit willing to quit if it were not for the gang of newsboys that looked on and made pride painful and necessary. One afternoon, after twenty minutes of desperate efforts to annihilate each other according to set rules that did not permit kicking, striking below the belt, nor hitting when one was down, Cheese-Face, panting for breath and reeling, offered to call it quits. And Martin, head on arms, thrilled at the picture he caught of himself, at that moment in the afternoon of long ago, when he reeled and panted and choked with the blood that ran into his mouth and down his throat from his cut lips; when he tottered toward Cheese-Face, spitting out a mouthful of blood so that he could speak, crying out that he would never quit, though Cheese-Face could give in if he wanted to. And Cheese-Face did not give in, and the fight went on.

The next day and the next, days without end, witnessed the afternoon fight. When he put up his arms, each day, to begin, they pained exquisitely, and the first few blows, struck and received, racked his soul; after that things grew numb, and he fought on blindly, seeing as in a dream, dancing and wavering, the large features and burning, animal-like eyes of Cheese-Face. He concentrated upon that face; all else about him was a whirling void. There was nothing else in the world but that face, and he would never know rest, blessed rest, until he had beaten that face into a pulp with his bleeding knuckles, or until the bleeding knuckles that somehow belonged to that face had beaten him into a pulp. And then, one way or the other, he would have rest. But to quit,—for him, Martin, to quit,—that was impossible!

Came the day when he dragged himself into the *Enquirer* alley; and there was no Cheese-Face. Nor did Cheese-Face come. The boys congratulated him, and told him that he had licked Cheese-Face. But Martin was not satisfied. He had not licked Cheese-Face, nor had Cheese-Face licked him. The problem had not been solved. It was not until afterward that they learned that Cheese-Face's father had died suddenly that very day.

Martin skipped on through the years to the night in the nigger heaven at the Auditorium. He was seventeen and just back from sea. A row started. Somebody was bullying somebody, and Martin interfered, to be confronted by Cheese-Face's blazing eyes.

"I'll fix you after de show," his ancient enemy hissed.

Martin nodded. The nigger-heaven bouncer was making his way toward the disturbance.

"I'll meet you outside, after the last act," Martin whispered, the while his face showed undivided interest in the buck-and-wing dancing on the stage.

The bouncer glared and went away.

"Got a gang?" he asked Cheese-Face, at the end of the act.

"Sure."

"Then I got to get one," Martin announced.

Between the acts he mustered his following—three fellows he knew from the nail works, a railroad fireman, and half a dozen of the Boo Gang, along with as many more from the dread Eighteen-and-Market Gang.

When the theatre let out, the two gangs strung along inconspicuously on opposite sides of the street. When they came to a quiet corner, they united and held a council of war.

"Eighth Street Bridge is the place," said a red-headed fellow belonging to Cheese-Face's gang. "You kin fight in the middle, under the electric light, an' whichever way the bulls come in we kin sneak the other way."

"That's agreeable to me," Martin said, after consulting with the leaders of his own gang.

The Eighth Street Bridge, crossing an arm of San Antonio Estuary, was the length of three city blocks. In the, middle of the bridge, and at each end, were electric lights. No policeman could pass those end-lights unseen. It was the safe place for the battle that revived itself under Martin's eyelids. He saw the two gangs, aggressive and sullen, rigidly keeping apart from each other and backing their respective champions; and he saw himself and Cheese-Face stripping. A short distance away lookouts were set, their task being to watch the lighted ends of the bridge. A member of the Boo Gang held Martin's coat, and shirt, and cap, ready to race with them into safety in case the police interfered. Martin watched himself go into the centre, facing Cheese-Face, and he heard himself say, as he held up his hand warningly:—"They ain't no hand-shakin' in this. Understand? They ain't nothin' but scrap. No throwin' up the sponge. This is a grudge-fight an' it's to a finish. Understand? Somebody's goin' to get licked."

Cheese-Face wanted to demur,—Martin could see that,—but Cheese-Face's old perilous pride was touched before the two gangs.

"Aw, come on," he replied. "Wot's the good of chewin' de rag about it? I'm wit' cheh to de finish."

Then they fell upon each other, like young bulls, in all the glory of youth, with naked fists, with hatred, with desire to hurt, to maim, to destroy. All the painful thousand years' gains of man in his upward climb through creation were lost. Only the electric light remained, a milestone on the path of the great human adventure. Martin and Cheese-Face were two savages, of the stone age, of the squatting place and the tree refuge. They sank lower and lower into the muddy abyss, back into the dregs of the raw beginnings of life, striving blindly and chemically, as atoms strive, as the star-dust of the heavens strives, colliding, recoiling, and colliding again and eternally again.

"God! We are animals! Brute-beasts!" Martin muttered aloud, as he watched the progress of the fight. It was to him, with his splendid power of vision, like gazing into a kinetoscope. He was both onlooker and participant. His long months of culture and refinement shuddered at the sight; then the present was blotted out of his consciousness and the ghosts of the past possessed him, and he was Martin Eden, just returned from sea and fighting Cheese-Face on the Eighth Street Bridge. He suffered and toiled and sweated and bled, and exulted when his naked knuckles smashed home.

They were twin whirlwinds of hatred, revolving about each other monstrously. The time passed, and the two hostile gangs became very quiet. They had never witnessed such intensity of ferocity, and they were awed by it. The two fighters were greater brutes than they. The first splendid velvet edge of youth and condition wore off, and they fought more cautiously and deliberately. There had been no advantage gained either way. "It's anybody's fight," Martin heard some one saying. Then he followed up a feint, right and left, was fiercely countered, and felt his cheek laid open to the bone. No bare knuckle had done that. He heard mutters of amazement at the ghastly damage wrought, and was drenched with his own blood. But he gave no sign. He became immensely wary, for he was wise with knowledge of the low cunning and foul vileness of his kind. He watched and waited, until he feigned a wild rush, which he stopped midway, for he had seen the glint of metal.

"Hold up yer hand!" he screamed. "Them's brass knuckles, an' you hit me with 'em !"

Both gangs surged forward, growling and snarling. In a second there would be a free-for-all fight, and he would be robbed of his vengeance. He was beside himself.

"You guys keep out!' he screamed hoarsely. "Understand? Say, d'ye understand?"

They shrank away from him. They were brutes, but he was the arch-brute, a thing of terror that towered over them and dominated them.

"This is my scrap, an' they ain't goin' to be no buttin' in. Gimme them knuckles."

Cheese-Face, sobered and a bit frightened, surrendered the foul weapon.

"You passed 'em to him, you red-head sneakin' in behind the push there," Martin went on, as he tossed the knuckles into the water. "I seen you, an' I was wonderin' what you was up to. If you try anything like that again, I'll beat cheh to death. Understand?"

They fought on, through exhaustion and beyond, to exhaustion immeasurable and inconceivable, until the crowd of brutes, its blood-lust sated, terrified by what it saw, begged them impartially to cease. And Cheese-Face, ready to drop and die, or to stay on his legs and die, a grisly monster out of whose features all likeness to Cheese-Face had been beaten, wavered and hesitated; but Martin sprang in and smashed him again and again.

Next, after a seeming century or so, with Cheese-Face weakening fast, in a mix-up of blows there was a loud snap, and Martin's right arm dropped to his side. It was a broken bone. Everybody heard it and knew; and Cheese-Face knew, rushing like a tiger in the other's extremity and raining blow on blow. Martin's gang surged forward to interfere. Dazed by the rapid succession of blows, Martin warned them back with vile and earnest curses sobbed out and groaned in ultimate desolation and despair.

He punched on, with his left hard only, and as he punched, doggedly, only half-conscious, as from a remote, distance he heard murmurs of fear in the gangs, and one who said with shaking voice: "This ain't a scrap, fellows. It's murder, an' we ought to stop it."

But no one stopped it, and he was glad, punching on wearily and endlessly with his one arm, battering away at a bloody something before him that was not a face but a horror, an oscillating, hideous, gibbering, nameless thing that persisted before his wavering vision and would not go away. And he punched on and on, slower and slower, as the last shreds of vitality oozed from him, through centuries and eons and enormous lapses of time, until, in a dim way, he became aware that the nameless thing was sinking, slowly sinking down to the rough board-planking of the bridge. And the next moment he was standing over it, staggering and swaying on shaky legs, clutching at the air for support, and saying in a voice he did not recognize:—

"D'ye want any more? Say, d'ye want any more?" He was still saying it, over and over,—demanding, entreating, threatening, to know if it wanted any more,—when he felt the fellows of his gang laying hands on him, patting him on the back and trying to put his coat on him. And then came a sudden rush of blackness and oblivion.

The tin alarm-clock on the table ticked on, but Martin Eden, his face buried on his arms, did not hear it. He heard nothing. He did not think. So absolutely had he relived life that he had fainted just as he fainted years before on the Eighth Street Bridge. For a full minute the blackness and the blankness endured. Then, like one from the dead, he sprang upright, eyes flaming, sweat pouring down his face, shouting :—"I licked you, Cheese-Face! It took me eleven years, but I licked you!"

His knees were trembling under him, he felt faint, and he staggered back to the bed, sinking down and sitting on the edge of it. He was still in the clutch of the past. He looked about the room, perplexed, alarmed, wondering where he was, until he caught sight of the pile of manuscripts in the corner. Then the wheels of memory slipped ahead through four years of time, and he was aware of the present, of the books he had opened and the universe he had won from their pages, of his dreams and ambitions, and of his love for a pale wraith of a girl, sensitive and sheltered and ethereal, who would die of horror did she witness but one moment of what he had just lived through— one moment of all the muck of life through which he had waded.

He arose to his feet and confronted himself in the looking-glass.

"And so you arise from the mud, Martin Eden," he said solemnly. "And you cleanse your eyes in a great brightness, and thrust your shoulders among the stars, doing what all life has done, letting the 'ape and tiger die' and wresting highest heritage from all powers that be."

He looked more closely at himself and laughed.

"A bit of hysteria and melodrama, eh?" he queried. "Well, never mind. You licked Cheese-Face, and you'll lick the editors if it takes twice eleven years to do it in. You can't stop here. You've got to go on. It's to a finish, you know."

"Say, Joe," was his greeting to his old-time working-mate next morning, "there's a Frenchman out on Twenty-eighth Street. He's made a pot of money, and he's going back to France. It's a dandy, well-appointed, small steam laundry. There's a start for you if you want to settle down. Here, take this; buy some clothes with it and be at this man's office at ten o'clock. He looked up the laundry for me, and he'll take you out and show you around. If you like it, and think it is worth the price—twelve thousand—let me know and it is yours. Now run along. I'm busy. I'll see you later."

"Now look here, Mart," the other said, slowly, with kindling anger, "I come here this mornin' to see you. Savve? I didn't come here to get no laundry. I come here for a talk for old friends' sake, and you shove a laundry at me. I tell you what you can do. You can take that laundry and go to hell."

He was starting to fling out of the room when Martin caught him by the shoulder and whirled him around.

"Now look here, Joe," he said; "if you act that way, I'll punch your head. And for old friends' sake I'll punch it hard. Savve?—you will, will you?"

Joe had clinched and attempted to throw him, and he was twisting and writhing out of the advantage of the other's hold. They reeled about the room, locked in each other's arms, and came down with a crash across the splintered wreckage of a wicker chair. Joe was underneath, with arms spread out and held and with Martin's knee on his chest. He was panting and gasping for breath when Martin released him.

"Now we'll talk a moment," Martin said. "You can't get fresh with me. I want that laundry business finished first of all. Then you can come back and we'll talk for old times' sake. I told you I was busy. Look at that."

A servant had just come in with the morning mail, a great mass of letters and magazines.

"How can I wade through that and talk to you? You go and fix up with the laundry, and then we'll get together."

"All right," Joe admitted reluctantly. "I thought you was turning me down, but I guess I was mistaken. But you can't lick me, Mart, in a stand-up fight. I've got the reach on you."

"We'll put on the gloves sometime and see," Martin said with a smile.

"Sure; as soon as I get that laundry going." Joe extended his arm. "You see that reach? "It'll make you go a few."

Martin heaved a sigh of relief when the door closed behind the laundry-man. He was becoming anti-social. Daily he found it a severer strain to be decent with people. Their presence perturbed him, and the effort of conversation irritated him. They made him restless, and no sooner was he in contact with them than he was casting about for excuses to get rid of them.

He did not proceed to attack his mail, and for a half hour he lolled in his chair, doing nothing, while no more than vague, half-formed thoughts occasionally filtered though his intelligence, or rather, at wide intervals, themselves constituted the flickering of his intelligence.

He roused himself and began glancing through his mail. There were a dozen requests for autographs—he knew them at sight; there were professional begging letters; and there were letters from cranks, ranging from the man with a working model of perpetual motion, and the man who demonstrated that the surface of the earth was the inside of a hollow sphere, to the man seeking financial aid to purchase the Peninsula of Lower California for the purpose of communist colonization. There were letters from women seeking to know him, and over one such he smiled, for enclosed was her receipt for pew-rent, sent as evidence of her good faith and as proof of her respectability.

Editors and publishers contributed to the daily heap of letters, the former on their knees for his manuscripts, the latter on their knees for his books—his poor disdained manuscripts that had kept all he possessed in pawn for so many dreary months in order to find them in postage. There were unexpected checks for English serial rights and for advance payments on foreign translations. His English agent announced the sale of German translation rights in three of his books, and informed him that Swedish editions, from which he could expect nothing because Sweden was not a party to the Berne Convention, were already on the market. Then there was a nominal request for his permission for a Russian translation, that country being likewise outside the Berne Convention.

He turned to the huge bundle of clippings which had come in from his press bureau, and read about himself and his vogue, which had become a furor. All his creative output had been flung to the public in one magnificent sweep. That seemed to account for it. He had taken the public off its feet, the way Kipling had, that time when he lay near to death and all the mob, animated by a mob-mind thought, began suddenly to read him. Martin remembered how that same world-mob, having read him and acclaimed him and not understood him in the least, had, abruptly, a few months later, flung itself upon him and torn him to pieces. Martin grinned at the thought. Who was he that he should not be similarly treated in a few more months? Well, he would fool the mob. He would be away, in the South Seas, building his grass house, trading for pearls and copra, jumping reefs in frail outriggers, catching sharks and bonitas, hunting wild goats among the cliffs of the valley that lay next to the valley of Taiohae.

In the moment of that thought the desperateness of his situation dawned upon him. He saw, cleared-eyed, that he was in the Valley of the Shadow. All the life that was in him was fading, fainting, making toward death. He realized how much he slept, and how much he desired to sleep. Of old, he had hated sleep. It had robbed him of precious moments of living. Four hours of sleep in the twenty-four had meant being robbed of four hours of life. How he had grudged sleep! Now it was life he grudged. Life was not good; its taste in his mouth was without tang, and bitter. This was his peril. Life that did not yearn toward life was in a fair way toward ceasing. Some remote instinct for preservation stirred in him, and he knew he must get away. He glanced about the room, and the thought of packing was burdensome. Perhaps it would be better to leave that to the last. In the meantime he might be getting an outfit.

He put on his hat and went out, stopping in at a gunstore, where he spent the remainder of the morning buying automatic rifles, ammunition, and fishing tackle. Fashions changed in trading, and he knew he would have to wait till he reached Tahiti before ordering his trade-goods. They could come up from Australia, anyway. This solution was a source of pleasure. He had avoided doing something, and the doing of anything just now was unpleasant. He went back to the hotel gladly, with a feeling of satisfaction in that the comfortable Morris chair was waiting for him; and he groaned inwardly, on entering his room, at sight of Joe in the Morris chair.

Joe was delighted with the laundry. Everything was settled, and he would enter into possession next day. Martin lay on the bed, with closed eyes, while the other talked on. Martin's thoughts were far away—so far that he was rarely aware that he was thinking. It was only by an effort that he occasionally responded. And yet this was Joe, whom he had always liked. But Joe was too keen with life. The boisterous impact of it on Martin's jaded mind was a hurt. It was an aching probe to his tired sensitiveness. When Joe reminded him that sometime in the future they were going to put on the gloves together, he could almost have screamed.

"Remember, Joe, you're to run the laundry according to those old rules you used to lay down at Shelly Hot Springs," he said. "No overworking. No working at night. And no children at the mangles. No children anywhere. And a fair wage."

Joe nodded and pulled out a note-book.

"Look at here. I was workin' out them rules before breakfast this A.M. What d'ye think of them?"

He read them aloud, and Martin approved, worrying at the same time as to when Joe would take himself off.

It was late afternoon when he awoke. Slowly the fact of life came back to him. He glanced about the room. Joe had evidently stolen away after he had dozed off. That was considerate of Joe, he thought. Then he closed his eyes and slept again.

In the days that followed Joe was too busy organizing and taking hold of the laundry to bother him much; and it was not until the day before sailing that the newspapers made the announcement that he had taken passage on the *Mariposa*. Once, when the instinct of preservation fluttered, he went to a doctor and underwent a searching physical examination. Nothing could be found the matter with him. His heart and lungs were pronounced magnificent. Every organ, so far as the doctor could know, was normal and was working normally.

"There is nothing the matter with you, Mr. Eden," he said, "positively nothing the matter with you. You are in the pink of condition. Candidly, I envy you your health. It is superb. Look at that chest. There, and in your stomach, lies the secret of your remarkable constitution. Physically, you are a man in a thousand—in ten thousand. Barring accidents, you should live to be a hundred."

And Martin knew that Lizzie's diagnosis had been correct. Physically he was all right. It was his "think-machine" that had gone wrong, and there was no cure for that except to get away to the South Seas. The trouble was that now, on the verge of departure, he had no desire to go. The South Seas charmed him no more than bourgeois civilization. There was no zest in the thought of departure, while the act of departure appalled him as a weariness of the flesh. He would have felt better if he were already on board and gone.

The last day was a sore trial. Having read of his sailing in the morning papers, Bernard Higginbotham, Gertrude, and all the family came to say good-by, as did Hermann von Schmidt and Marian. Then there was business to be transacted, bills to be paid, and everlasting reporters to be endured. He said good-by to Lizzie Connolly, abruptly, at the entrance to night school, and hurried away. At the hotel he found Joe, too busy all day with the laundry to have come to him earlier. It was the last straw, but Martin gripped the arms of his chair and talked and listened for half an hour.

"You know, Joe," he said, "that you are not tied down to that laundry. There are no strings on it. You can sell it any time and blow the money. Any time you get sick of it and want to hit the road, just pull out. Do what will make you the happiest."

Joe shook his head. . . .

From the deck of the *Mariposa,* at the sailing hour, he saw Lizzie Connolly hiding on the skirts of the crowd on the wharf. Take her with you, came the thought. It is easy to be kind. She will be supremely happy. It was almost a temptation one moment, and the succeeding moment it became a terror. He was in a panic at the thought of it. His tired soul cried out in protest. He turned away from the rail with a groan, muttering, "Man, you are too sick, you are too sick."

He fled to his stateroom, where he lurked until the steamer was clear of the dock. In the dining saloon, at luncheon, he found himself in the place of honor, at the captain's right; and he was not long in discovering that he was the great man on board. But no more unsatisfactory great man ever sailed on a ship. He spent the afternoon in a deck-chair, with closed eyes, dozing brokenly most of the time, and in the evening went early to bed.

After the second day, recovered from seasickness, the full passenger list was in evidence, and the more he saw of the passengers the more he disliked them. Yet he knew that he did them injustice. They were good and kindly people, he forced himself to acknowledge, and in the moment of acknowledgment he qualified—good and kindly like all the bourgeoisie, with all the psychological cramp and intellectual futility of their kind. They bored him when they talked with him, their little superficial minds were so filled with emptiness; while the boisterous high spirits and the excessive energy of the younger people shocked him. They were never quiet, ceaselessly playing deck-quoits, tossing rings, promenading, or rushing to the rail with loud cries to watch the leaping porpoises and the first schools of flying fish.

He slept much. After breakfast he sought his deck-chair with a magazine he never finished. The printed pages tired him. He puzzled that men found so much to write about, and, puzzling, dozed in his chair. When the gong awoke him for luncheon, he was irritated that he must awaken. There was no satisfaction in being awake.

Once, he tried to arouse himself from his lethargy, and went forward into the forecastle with the sailors. But the breed of sailors seemed to have changed since the days he had lived in the forecastle. He could find no kinship with these stolid-faced, ox-minded bestial creatures. He was in despair. Up above nobody had wanted Martin Eden for his own sake, and he could not go back to those of his own class who had wanted him in the past. He did not want them. He could not stand them any more than he could stand the stupid first-cabin passengers and the riotous young people.

Life was to him like strong, white light that hurts the tired eyes of a sick person. During every conscious moment life blazed in a raw glare around him and upon him. It hurt. It hurt intolerably. It was the first time in his life that Martin had travelled first-class. On ships at sea he had always been in the forecastle, the steerage, or in the black depths of the coal-hold, passing coal. In those days, climbing up the iron ladders from out of the pit of stifling heat, he had often caught glimpses of the passengers, in cool white, doing nothing but enjoy themselves, under awnings spread to keep the sun and wind away from them, with subservient stewards taking care of their every want and whim, and it had seemed to him that the realm in which they moved and had their being was nothing else than paradise. Well, here he was, the great man on board, in the midmost centre of it, sitting at the captain's right hand, and yet vainly harking back to forecastle and stoke-hole in quest of the Paradise he had lost. He had found no new one, and now he could not find the old one. . . .

Miserable as he was on the steamer, a new misery came upon him. What when the steamer reached Tahiti? He would have to go ashore. He would have to order his trade-goods, to find a passage on a schooner to the Marquesas, to do a thousand and one things that were awful to contemplate. Whenever he steeled himself deliberately to think, he could see the desperate peril in which he stood. In all truth, he was in the Valley of the Shadow, and his danger lay in that he was not afraid. If he were only afraid, he would make toward life. Being unafraid, he was drifting deeper into the shadow. He found no delight in the old familiar things of life. The *Mariposa* was now in the northeast trades, and this wine of wind, surging against him, irritated him. He had his chair moved to escape the embrace of this lusty comrade of old days and nights.

The day the *Mariposa* entered the doldrums, Martin was more miserable than ever. He could no longer sleep. He was soaked with sleep, and perforce he must now stay awake and endure the white glare of life. He moved about restlessly. The air was sticky and humid, and the rain-squalls were unrefreshing. He ached with life. He sat in around the deck until that hurt too much, then his chair until he was compelled to walk again. He forced himself at last to finish the magazine, and from the steamer library he culled several volumes of poetry. But they could not hold him, and once more he took to walking.

He stayed late on deck, after dinner, but that did not help him, for when he went below, he could not sleep. This surcease from life had failed him. It was too much. He turned on the electric light and tried to read. One of the volumes was a Swinburne. He lay in bed, glancing through its pages, until suddenly he became aware that he was reading with interest. He finished the stanza, attempted to read on, then came back to it. He rested the face downward on his breast and fell to thinking. That was it. The very thing. Strange that it had never come to him before. That was the meaning of it all; he had been drifting that way all the time, and now Swinburne showed him that it was the happy way out. He wanted rest, and here was rest awaiting him. He glanced at the open port-hole. Yes, it was large enough. For the first time in weeks he felt happy. At last he had discovered the cure of his ill. He picked up the book and read the stanza slowly aloud—

> From too much love of living,
> From hope and fear set free
> We thank with brief thanksgiving
> Whatever gods may be
> That no life live forever;
> That dead men rise up never;
> That even the weariest river
> Winds somewhere safe to sea.

He looked again at the open port. Swinburne had furnished the key. Life was ill, or, rather, it had become ill—an unbearable thing. "That dead men rise up never!" That line stirred him with a profound feeling of gratitude. It was the one beneficent thing in the universe. When life became an aching weariness, death was ready to soothe away to everlasting sleep. But what was he waiting for? It was time to go.

He arose and thrust his head out the port-hole, looking down into the milky wash. The *Mariposa* was deeply loaded, and, hanging by his hands, his feet would be in the water. He could slip in noiselessly. No one would hear. A smother of spray dashed up, wetting his face. It tasted salt on his lips, and the taste was good. He wondered if he ought to write a swan-song, but laughed the thought away. There was no time. He was too impatient to be gone.

Turning off the light in his room so that it might not betray him, he went out the port-hole feet first. His shoulders stuck, and he forced himself back so as to try it with one arm down by his side. A roll of the steamer aided him, and he was through, hanging by his hands. When his feet touched the sea, he let go. He was in a milky froth of water. The side of the *Mariposa* rushed past him like a dark wall, broken here and there by lighted ports. She was certainly making time. Almost before he knew it, he was astern, swimming gently on the foam-crackling surface.

A bonita struck at his white body, and he laughed aloud. It had taken a piece out, and the sting of it reminded him of why he was there. In the work to do he had forgotten the purpose of it. The lights of the *Mariposa* were growing dim in the distance, and there he was, swimming confidently, as though it were his intention to make for the nearest land a thousand miles or so away.

It was the automatic instinct to live. He ceased swimming, but the moment he felt the water rising above his mouth the hands struck out sharply with a lifting movement. The will to live, was his thought, and the thought was accompanied by a sneer. Well, he had will,—ay, will strong enough that with one last exertion it could destroy itself and cease to be.

He changed his position to a vertical one. He glanced up at the quiet stars, at the same time emptying his lungs of air. With swift, vigorous propulsion of hands and feet, he lifted his shoulders and half his chest out of water. This was to gain impetus for the descent. Then he let himself go and sank without movement, a white statue, into the sea. He breathed in the water deeply, deliberately, after the manner of a man taking an anaesthetic. When he strangled, quite involuntarily his arms and legs clawed the water and drove him up to the surface and into the clear sight of the stars.

The will to live, he thought disdainfully, vainly endeavoring not to breathe the air into his bursting lungs. Well, he would have to try a new way. He filled his lungs with air, filled them full. This supply would take him far down. He turned over and went down head first, swimming with all his strength and all his will. Deeper and deeper he went. His eyes were open, and he watched the ghostly, phosphorescent trails of the darting bonita. As he swam, he hoped that they would not strike at him, for it might snap the tension of his will. But they did not strike, and he found time to be grateful for this last kindness of life.

Down, down, he swam till his arms and legs grew tired and hardly moved. He knew that he was deep. The pressure on his ear-drums was a pain, and there was a buzzing in his head. His endurance was faltering, but he compelled his arms and legs to drive him deeper until his will snapped and the air drove from his lungs in a great explosive rush. The bubbles rubbed and bounded like tiny balloons against his cheeks and eyes as they took their upward flight. Then came pain and strangulation. This hurt was not death, was the thought that oscillated through his reeling consciousness. Death did not hurt. It was life, the pangs of life, this awful, suffocating feeling; it was the last blow life could deal him.

His wilful hands and feet began to beat and churn about, spasmodically and feebly. But he had fooled them and the will to live that made them beat and churn. He was too deep down. They could never bring him to the surface. He seemed floating languidly in a sea of dreamy vision. Colors and radiances surrounded him and bathed him and pervaded him. What was that? It seemed a lighthouse; but it was inside his brain—a flashing, bright white light. It flashed swifter and swifter. There was a long rumble of sound, and it seemed to him that he was falling down a vast and interminable stairway. And somewhere at the bottom he fell into darkness. That much he knew. He had fallen into darkness. And at the instant he knew, he ceased to know.

FRANK NORRIS

1870–1902

Born in Chicago, Norris moved to San Francisco with his family in 1884. While a student at UC Berkeley he began writing stories and sketches, some of which were published in the Argonaut *and the* Overland Monthly. *At Berkeley he discovered the works of Émile Zola and the literary naturalism that would shape his artistic vision. After a year at Harvard studying writing and a year as a correspondent in South Africa, Norris returned to the Bay Area to continue work on* McTeague, *the novel he had begun as an undergraduate. In San Francisco, he edited a prominent literary magazine, the* Wave, *in which he published much of his own work, including the novel* Moran of the Lady Letty (1898) *and some stories later gathered in* The Third Circle (1909). *In 1898 he moved to New York to work for McClure's magazine and soon began to publish the novels that made his reputation.* McTeague *appeared in 1899. Set in San Francisco, the Sierra, and the high desert near Death Valley, it became the basis for Erich von Stroheim's classic film* Greed (1923). *It was followed by* The Octopus (1901), *which Norris conceived as the first volume in a trilogy, "The Epic of the Wheat." "When complete," he wrote in the introduction to* The Octopus, *"they will form the story of a crop of wheat from the time of its sowing as seed in California to the time of its consumption as bread in a village of Western Europe." His meteoric career ended suddenly: after an appendectomy, he died of peritonitis at the age of thirty-two. The second volume of his trilogy,* The Pit, *was published posthumously in 1903.*

From *The Octopus*

FROM BOOK 2, CHAPTER 9

Presley came out upon the Country Road. At a little distance to his left he could see the group of buildings where once Broderson had lived. These were being remodelled, at length, to suit the larger demands of the New Agriculture. A strange man came out by the road gate; no doubt, the new proprietor. Presley turned away, hurrying northwards along the County Road by the mammoth watering-tank and the long wind-break of poplars.

He came to Caraher's place. There was no change here. The saloon had weathered the storm, indispensable to the new as well as to the old régime. The same dusty buggies and buckboards were tied under the shed, and as

Presley hurried by he could distinguish Caraher's voice, loud as ever, still proclaiming his creed of annihilation.

Bonneville Presley avoided. He had no associations with the town. He turned aside from the road, and crossing the northwest corner of Los Muertos and the line of the railroad, turned back along the Upper Road till he came to the Long Trestle and Annixter's,—Silence, desolation, abandonment.

A vast stillness, profound, unbroken, brooded low over all the place. No living thing stirred. The rusted windmill on the skeleton-like tower of the artesian well was motionless; the great barn empty; the windows of the ranch house, cook house, and dairy boarded up. Nailed upon a tree near the broken gateway was a board, white painted, with stencilled letters, bearing the inscription:

"Warning. ALL PERSONS FOUND TRESPASSING ON THESE PREMISES WILL BE PROSECUTED TO THE FULLEST EXTENT OF THE LAW. By order P. and S. W. R. R."

As he had planned, Presley reached the hills by the head waters of Broderson's Creek late in the afternoon. Toilfully he climbed them, reached the highest crest, and turning about, looked long and for the last time at all the reach of the valley unrolled beneath him. The land of the ranches opened out forever and forever under the stimulus of that measureless range of vision. The whole gigantic sweep of the San Joaquin expanded Titanic before the eye of the mind, flagellated with heat, quivering and shimmering under the sun's red eye. It was the season after the harvest, and the great earth, the mother, after its period of reproduction, its pains of labour, delivered of the fruit of its loins, slept the sleep of exhaustion in the infinite repose of the colossus, benignant, eternal, strong, the nourisher of nations, the feeder of an entire world.

And as Presley looked there came to him strong and true the sense and the significance of all the enigma of growth. He seemed for one instant to touch the explanation of existence. Men were nothings, mere animalculae, mere ephemerides that fluttered and fell and were forgotten between dawn and dusk. Vanamee had said there was no death. But for one second Presley could go one step further. Men were naught, death was naught, life was naught; FORCE only existed—FORCE that brought men into the world, FORCE that crowded them out of it to make way for the succeeding generation, FORCE that made the wheat grow, FORCE that garnered it from the soil to give place to the succeeding crop.

It was the mystery of creation, the stupendous miracle of re-creation; the vast rhythm of the seasons, measured, alternative, the sun and the stars keeping time as the eternal symphony of reproduction swung in its tremendous cadences like the colossal pendulum of an almighty machine—primordial energy flung out from the hand of the Lord God himself, immortal, calm, infinitely strong.

But as he stood thus looking down upon the great valley he was aware of the figure of a man, far in the distance, moving steadily towards the Mission of San Juan. The man was hardly more than a dot, but there was something unmistakably familiar in his gait; and besides this, Presley could fancy that he was hatless. He touched his pony with his spur. The man was Vanamee beyond all doubt, and a little later Presley, descending the maze of cow-paths and cattle-trails that led down towards the Broderson Creek, overtook his friend.

Instantly Presley was aware of an immense change. Vanamee's face was still that of an ascetic, still glowed with the rarefied intelligence of a young seer, a half-inspired shepherd-prophet of Hebraic legends; but the shadow of that great sadness which for so long had brooded over him was gone; the grief that once he had fancied deathless was, indeed, dead, or rather swallowed up in a victorious joy that radiated like sunlight at dawn from the deep-set eyes, and the hollow, swarthy cheeks. They talked together till nearly sundown, but to Presley's questions as to the reasons for Vanamee's happiness, the other would say nothing. Once only he allowed himself to touch upon the subject.

"Death and grief are little things," he said. "They are transient. Life must be before death, and joy before grief. Else there are no such things as death or grief. These are only negatives. Life is positive. Death is only the absence of life, just as night is only the absence of day, and if this is so, there is no such thing as death. There is only life, and the suppression of life, that we, foolishly, say is death. 'Suppression,' I say, not extinction. I do not say that life returns. Life never departs. Life simply *is*. For certain seasons, it is hidden in the dark, but is that death, extinction, annihilation? I take it, thank God, that it is not. Does the grain of wheat, hidden for certain seasons in the dark, die? The grain we think is dead *resumes again;* but how? Not as one grain, but as twenty. So all life. Death is only real for all the detritus of the world, for all the sorrow, for all the injustice, for all the grief. Presley, the good never dies; evil dies, cruelty, oppression, selfishness, greed—these die; but nobility, but love, but sacrifice, but generosity, but truth, thank God for it, small as they are, difficult as it is to discover them—these live forever, these are eternal. You are all broken, all cast down by what you have seen in this valley, this hopeless struggle, this apparently hopeless despair. Well, the end is not yet.

What is it that remains after all is over, after the dead are buried and the hearts are broken? Look at it all from the vast height of humanity—'the greatest good to the greatest numbers.' What remains? Men perish, men are corrupted, hearts are rent asunder, but what remains untouched, unassailable, undefiled? Try to find that, not only in this, but in every crisis of the world's life, and you will find, if your view be large enough, that it is *not* evil, but good, that in the end remains."

There was a long pause. Presley, his mind full of new thoughts, held his peace, and Vanamee added at length:

"I believed Angéle dead. I wept over her grave; mourned for her as dead in corruption. She has come back to me, more beautiful than ever. Do not ask me any further. To put this story, this idyll, into words, would, for me, be a profanation. This must suffice you. Angéle has returned to me, and I am happy. *Adios.*"

He rose suddenly. The friends clasped each other's hands.

"We shall probably never meet again," said Vanamee; "but if these are the last words I ever speak to you, listen to them, and remember them, because I know I speak the truth. Evil is short-lived. Never judge of the whole round of life by the mere segment you can see. The whole is, in the end, perfect."

Abruptly he took himself away. He was gone. Presley, alone, thoughtful, his hands clasped behind him, passed on through the ranches—here teeming with ripened wheat—his face set from them forever.

Not so Vanamee. For hours he roamed the country-side, now through the deserted cluster of buildings that had once been Annixter's home; now through the rustling and, as yet, uncut wheat of Quien Sabe! now treading the slopes of the hills far to the north, and again following the winding courses of the streams. Thus he spent the night.

At length, the day broke, resplendent, cloudless. The night was passed. There was all the sparkle and effervescence of joy in the crystal sunlight as the dawn expanded roseate, and at length flamed dazzling to the zenith when the sun moved over the edge of the world and looked down upon all the earth like the eye of God the Father.

At the moment, Vanamee stood breast-deep in the wheat in a solitary corner of the Quien Sabe rancho. He turned eastward, facing the celestial glory of the day and sent his voiceless call far from him across the golden grain out towards the little valley of flowers.

Swiftly the answer came. It advanced to meet him. The flowers of the Seed ranch were gone, dried and parched by the summer's sun, shedding their seed by handfuls to be sown again and blossom yet another time. The Seed ranch was no longer royal with colour. The roses, the lilies, the carnations, the hyacinths, the poppies, the violets, the mignonette, all these had vanished, the little valley was without colour; where once it had exhaled the most delicious perfume, it was now odourless. Under the blinding light of the day it stretched to its hillsides, bare, brown, unlovely. The romance of the place had vanished, but with it had vanished the Vision. It was no longer a figment of his imagination, a creature of dreams that advanced to meet Vanamee. It was Reality—it was Angéle in the flesh, vital, sane, material, who at last issued forth from the entrance of the little valley. Romance had vanished, but better than romance was here. Not a manifestation, not a dream, but her very self. The night was gone, but the sun had risen; the flowers had disappeared, but strong, vigorous, noble, the wheat had come.

In the wheat he waited for her. He saw her coming. She was simply dressed. No fanciful wreath of tube-roses was about her head now, no strange garment of red and gold enveloped her now. It was no longer an ephemeral illusion of the night, evanescent, mystic, but a simple country girl coming to meet her lover. The vision of the night had been beautiful, but what was it compared to this? Reality was better than Romance. The simple honesty of a loving, trusting heart was better than a legend of flowers, an hallucination of the moonlight. She came nearer. Bathed in sunlight, he saw her face to face, saw her hair hanging in two straight plaits on either side of her face, saw the enchanting fullness of her lips, the strange, balancing movement of her head upon her slender neck. But now she was no longer asleep. The wonderful eyes, violet blue, heavy-lidded with their perplexing, oriental slant towards the temples, were wide open and fixed upon his.

From out the world of romance, out of the moonlight and the star sheen, out of the faint radiance of the lilies and the still air heavy with perfume, she had at last come to him. The moonlight, the flowers, and the dream were all vanished away. Angéle was realised in the Wheat. She stood forth in the sunlight, a fact, and no longer a fancy.

He ran forward to meet her and she held out her arms to him. He caught her to him, and she, turning her face to his, kissed him on the mouth.

"I love you, I love you," she murmured. . . .

.   .   .

Upon descending from his train at Port Costa, S. Behrman asked to be directed at once to where the bark "Swanhilda" was raking on grain. Though he had bought and greatly enlarged his new elevator at this port, he had never seen it. The work had been carried on through agents, S. Behrman having far too many and more pressing occupations to demand his presence and attention. Now, however, he was to see the concrete evidence of his success for the first time.

He picked his way across the railroad tracks to the line of warehouses that bordered the docks, numbered with enormous Roman numerals and full of grain in bags.

The sight of these bags of grain put him in mind of the fact that among all the other shippers he was practically alone in his way of handling his wheat. They handled the grain in bags; he, however, preferred it in the bulk. Bags were sometimes four cents apiece, and he had decided to build his elevator and bulk his grain therein, rather than to incur this expense. Only a small part of his wheat—that on Number Three division—had been sacked. All the rest, practically two-thirds of the entire harvest of Los Muertos, now found itself warehoused in his enormous elevator at Port Costa.

To a certain degree it had been the desire of observing the working of his system of handling the wheat in bulk that had drawn S. Behrman to Port Costa. But the more powerful motive had been curiosity, not to say downright sentiment. So long had he planned for this day of triumph, so eagerly had he looked forward to it, that now, when it had come, he wished to enjoy it to its fullest extent, wished to miss no feature of the disposal of the crop. He had watched it harvested, he had watched it hauled to the railway, and now would watch it as it poured into the hold of the ship, would even watch the ship as she cleared and got under way.

He passed through the warehouses and came out upon the dock that ran parallel with the shore of the bay. A great quantity of shipping was in view, barks for the most part, Cape Horners, great, deep sea tramps, whose iron-shod forefeet had parted every ocean the world round from Rangoon to Rio de Janeiro, and from Melbourne to Christiania. Some were still in the stream, loaded with wheat to the Plimsoll mark, ready to depart with the next ride. But many others laid their great flanks alongside the docks and at that moment were being filled by derrick and crane with thousands upon thousands of bags of wheat. The scene was brisk; the cranes creaked and swung incessantly with a rattle of chains; stevedores and wharfingers toiled and perspired; boatswains and dock-masters shouted orders, drays rumbled, the water lapped at the piles; a group of sailors, painting the flanks of one of the great ships, raised an occasional chanty; the trade wind sang aeolian in the cordages, filling the air with the nimble taint of salt. All around were the noises of ships and the feel and flavor of the sea.

S. Behrman soon discovered his elevator. It was the largest structure discernible, and upon its red roof, in enormous white letters, was his own name. Thither, between piles of grain bags, halted drays, crates and boxes of merchandise, with an occasional pyramid of salmon cases, S. Behrman took his way. Cabled to the dock, close under his elevator, lay a great ship with lofty masts and great spars. Her stern was toward him as he approached, and upon it, in raised golden letters, he could read the words "Swanhilda—Liverpool."

He went aboard by a very steep gangway and found the mate on the quarter deck. S. Behrman introduced himself.

"Well," he added, "how are you getting on?"

"Very fairly, sir," returned the mate, who was an Englishman. "We'll have her all snugged down tight by this time, day after to-morrow. It's a great saving of time shunting the stuff in her like that, and three men can do the work of seven."

"I'll have a look 'round, I believe," returned S. Behrman.

"Right-oh," answered the mate with a nod.

S. Behrman went forward to the hatch that opened down into the vast hold of the ship. A great iron chute connected this hatch with the elevator, and through it was rushing a veritable cataract of wheat.

It came from some gigantic bin within the elevator itself, rushing down the confines of the chute to plunge into the roomy, gloomy interior of the hold with an incessant, metallic roar, persistent, steady, inevitable. No men were in sight. The place was deserted. No human agency seemed to be back of the movement of the wheat. Rather, the grain seemed impelled with a force of its own, a resistless, huge force, eager, vivid, impatient for the sea.

S. Behrman stood watching, his ears deafened with the roar of the hard grains against the metallic lining of the chute. He put his hand once into the rushing tide, and the contact rasped the flesh of his fingers and like an undertow drew his hand after it in its impetuous dash.

Cautiously he peered down into the hold. A musty odour rose to his nostrils, the vigorous, pungent aroma of the raw cereal. It was dark. He could see nothing; but all about and over the opening of the hatch the air was full of a fine, impalpable dust that blinded the eyes and choked the throat and nostrils.

As his eyes became used to the shadows of the cavern below him, he began to distinguish the grey mass of the wheat, a great expanse, almost liquid in its texture, which, as the cataract from above plunged into it, moved and shifted in long, slow eddies. As he stood there, this cataract of a sudden increased in volume. He turned about, casting his eyes upward toward the elevator to discover the cause. His foot caught in a coil of rope, and he fell headforemost into the hold.

The fall was a long one and he struck the surface of the wheat with the sodden impact of a bundle of damp clothes. For the moment he was stunned. All the breath was driven from his body. He could neither move nor cry out. But, by degrees, his wits steadied themselves and his breath returned to him. He looked about and above him. The daylight in the hold was dimmed and clouded by the thick chaff-dust thrown off by the pour of grain, and even this dimness dwindled to twilight at a short distance from the opening of the hatch, while the remotest quarters were lost in impenetrable blackness. He got upon his feet only to find that he sunk ankle deep in the loose packed mass underfoot.

"Hell," he muttered, "here's a fix."

Directly underneath the chute, the wheat, as it poured in, raised itself in a conical mound, but from the sides of this mound it shunted away incessantly in thick layers, flowing in all directions with the nimbleness of water. Even as S. Behrman spoke, a wave of grain poured around his legs and rose rapidly to the level of his knees. He stepped quickly back. To stay near the chute would soon bury him to the waist.

No doubt, there was some other exit from the hold, some companion ladder that led up to the deck. He scuffled and waded across the wheat, groping in the dark with outstretched hands. With every inhalation he choked, filling his mouth and nostrils more with dust than with air. At times he could not breathe at all, but gagged and gasped, his lips distended. But search as he would, he could find no outlet to the hold, no stairway, no companion ladder. Again and again, staggering along in the black darkness, he bruised his knuckles and forehead against the iron sides of the ship. He gave up the attempt to find any interior means of escape and returned laboriously to the space under the open hatchway. Already he could see that the level of the wheat was raised.

"God," he said, "this isn't going to do at all." He uttered a great shout. "Hello, on deck there, somebody. For God's sake."

The steady, metallic roar of the pouring wheat drowned out his voice. He could scarcely hear it himself above the rush of the cataract. Besides this, he found it impossible to stay under the hatch. The flying grains of wheat, spattering as they fell, stung his face like wind-driven particles of ice. It was a veritable torture; his hands smarted with it. Once he was all but blinded. Furthermore, the succeeding waves of wheat, rolling from the mound under the chute, beat him back, swirling and dashing against his legs and knees, mounting swiftly higher, carrying him off his feet.

Once more he retreated, drawing back from beneath the hatch. He stood still for a moment and shouted again. It was in vain. His voice returned upon him, unable to penetrate the thunder of the chute, and horrified, he discovered that so soon as he stood motionless upon the wheat, he sank into it. Before he knew it, he was knee-deep again, and a long swirl of grain sweeping outward from the ever-breaking, ever-reforming pyramid below the chute, poured around his thighs, immobilising him.

A frenzy of terror suddenly leaped to life within him. The horror of death, the Fear of The Trap, shook him like a dry reed. Shouting, he tore himself free of the wheat and once more scrambled and struggled towards the hatchway. He stumbled as he reached it and fell directly beneath the pour. Like a storm of small shot, mercilessly, pitilessly, the unnumbered multitude of hurtling grains flagellated and beat and tore his flesh. Blood streamed from his forehead and, thickening with the powder-like chaff-dust, blinded his eyes. He struggled to his feet once more. An avalanche from the cone of wheat buried him to his thighs. He was forced back and back and back, beating the air, falling, rising, howling for aid. He could no longer see; his eyes, crammed with dust, smarted as if transfixed with needles whenever he opened them. His mouth was full of the dust, his lips were dry with it; thirst tortured him, while his outcries choked and gagged in his rasped throat.

And all the while without stop, incessantly, inexorably, the wheat, as if moving with a force all its own, shot downward in a prolonged roar, persistent, steady, inevitable.

He retreated to a far corner of the hold and sat down with his back against the iron hull of the ship and tried to collect his thoughts, to calm himself. Surely there must be some way of escape; surely he was not to die like this, die in this dreadful substance that was neither solid nor fluid. What was he to do? How make himself heard?

But even as he thought about this, the cone under the chute broke again and sent a great layer of grain rippling and tumbling toward him. It reached him where he sat and buried his hand and one foot.

He sprang up trembling and made for another corner.

"By God," he cried, "by God, I must think of something pretty quick!"

Once more the level of the wheat rose and the grains began piling deeper about him. Once more he retreated. Once more he crawled staggering to the foot of the cataract, screaming till his ears sang and his eyeballs strained in their sockets, and once more the relentless tide drove him back.

Then began that terrible dance of death; the man dodging, doubling, squirming, hunted from one corner to another, the wheat slowly, inexorably flowing, rising, spreading to every angle, to every nook and cranny. It reached his middle. Furious and with bleeding hands and broken nails, he dug his way out to fall backward, all but exhausted, gasping for breath in the dust-thickened air. Roused again by the slow advance of the tide, he leaped up and stumbled away, blinded with the agony in his eyes, only to crash against the metal hull of the vessel. He turned about, the blood streaming from his face, and paused to collect his senses, and with a rush, another wave swirled about his ankles and knees. Exhaustion grew upon him. To stand still meant to sink; to lie or sit meant to be buried the quicker; and all this in the dark, all this in an air that could scarcely be breathed, all this while he fought an enemy that could not be gripped, toiling in a sea that could not be stayed.

Guided by the sound of the falling wheat, S. Behrman crawled on hands and knees toward the hatchway. Once more he raised his voice in a shout for help. His bleeding throat and raw, parched lips refused to utter but a wheezing moan. Once more he tried to look toward the one patch of faint light above him. His eye-lids, clogged with chaff, could no longer open. The Wheat poured about his waist as he raised himself upon his knees.

Reason fled. Deafened with the roar of the grain, blinded and made dumb with its chaff, he threw himself forward with clutching fingers, rolling upon his back, and lay there, moving feebly, the head rolling from side to side. The Wheat, leaping continuously from the chute, poured around him. It filled the pockets of the coat, it crept up the sleeves and trouser legs, it covered the great, protuberant stomach, it ran at last in rivulets into the distended, gasping mouth. It covered the face.

Upon the surface of the Wheat, under the chute, nothing moved but the Wheat itself. There was no sign of life. Then, for an instant, the surface stirred. A hand, fat, with short fingers and swollen veins, reached up, clutching, then fell limp and prone. In another instant it was covered. In the hold of the "Swanhilda" there was no movement but the widening ripples that spread flowing from the ever-breaking, ever-reforming cone; no sound, but the rushing of the Wheat that continued to plunge incessantly from the iron chute in a prolonged roar, persistent, steady, inevitable. . . .

FROM THE CONCLUSION

The "Swanhilda" lifted and rolled slowly, majestically on the ground swell of the Pacific, the water hissing and boiling under her forefoot, her cordage vibrating and droning in the steady rush of the trade winds. It was drawing towards evening and her lights had just been set. The master passed Presley, who was leaning over the rail smoking a cigarette, and paused long enough to remark:

"The land yonder, if you can make it out, is Point Gordo, and if you were to draw a line from our position now through that point and carry it on about a hundred miles further, it would just about cross Tulare County not very far from where you used to live."

"I see," answered Presley, "I see. Thanks. I am glad to know that."

The master passed on, and Presley, going up to the quarter deck, looked long and earnestly at the faint line of mountains that showed vague and bluish above the waste of tumbling water.

Those were the mountains of the Coast range and beyond them was what once had been his home. Bonneville was there, and Guadalajara and Los Muertos and Quien Sabe, the Mission of San Juan, the Seed ranch, Annixter's desolated home and Dyke's ruined hop-fields.

Well, it was all over now, that terrible drama through which he had lived. Already it was far distant from him; but once again it rose in his memory, portentous, sombre, ineffaceable. He passed it all in review from the day of his first meeting with Vanamee to the day of his parting with Hilma. He saw it all—the great sweep of country opening to view from the summit of the hills at the head waters of Broderson's Creek; the barn dance at Annixter's, the harness room with its jam of furious men; the quiet garden of the Mission; Dyke's house, his flight upon the engine, his brave fight in the chaparral; Lyman Derrick at bay in the dining-room of the ranch house; the rabbit drive; the fight at the irrigating ditch, the shouting mob in the Bonneville Opera House.

The drama was over. The fight of Ranch and Railroad had been wrought out to its dreadful close. It was true, as Shelgrim had said, that forces rather than men had locked horns in that struggle, but for all that the men of the Ranch and not the men of the Railroad had suffered. Into the prosperous valley, into the quiet community of farmers, that galloping monster, that terror of steel and steam had burst, shooting athwart the horizons, flinging the echo of its thunder over all the ranches of the valley, leaving blood and destruction in its path.

Yes, the Railroad had prevailed. The ranches had been seized in the tentacles of the octopus; the iniquitous burden of extortionate freight rates had been imposed like a yoke of iron. The monster had killed Harran, had killed Osterman, had killed Broderson, had killed Hooven. It had beggared Magnus and had driven him to a state of semi-insanity after he had wrecked his honour in the vain attempt to do evil that good might come. It had enticed Lyman into its toils to pluck from him his manhood and his honesty, corrupting him and poisoning him beyond redemption; it had hounded Dyke from his legitimate employment and had made of him a highwayman and criminal. It had cast forth Mrs. Hooven to starve to death upon the City streets. It had driven Minna to prostitution. It had slain Annixter at the very moment when painfully and manfully he had at last achieved his own salvation and stood forth resolved to do right, to act unselfishly and to live for others. It had widowed Hilma in the very dawn of her happiness. It had killed the very babe within the mother's womb, strangling life ere yet it had been born, stamping out the spark ordained by God to burn through all eternity.

What then was left? Was there no hope, no outlook for the future, no rift in the black curtain, no glimmer through the night? Was good to be thus overthrown? Was evil thus to be strong and to prevail? Was nothing left?

Then suddenly Vanamee's words came back to his mind. What was the larger view, what contributed the greatest good to the greatest numbers? What was the full round of the circle whose segment only he beheld? In the end, the ultimate, final end of all, what was left? Yes, good issued from this crisis, untouched, unassailable, undefiled.

Men—motes in the sunshine—perished, were shot down in the very noon of life, hearts were broken, little children started in life lamentably handicapped; young girls were brought to a life of shame; old women died in the heart of life for lack of food. In that little, isolated group of human insects, misery, death, and anguish spun like a wheel of fire.

But the WHEAT *remained.* Untouched, unassailable, undefiled, that mighty world-force, that nourisher of nations, wrapped in Nirvanic calm, indifferent to the human swarm, gigantic, resistless, moved onward in its appointed grooves. Through the welter of blood at the irrigation ditch, through the sham charity and shallow philanthropy of famine relief committees, the great harvest of Los Muertos rolled like a flood from the Sierras to the Himalayas to feed thousands of starving scarecrows on the barren plains of India.

Falseness dies; injustice and oppression in the end of everything fade and vanish away. Greed, cruelty, selfishness, and inhumanity are short-lived; the individual suffers, but the race goes on. Annixter dies, but in a far distant corner of the world a thousand lives are saved. The larger view always and through all shams, all wickednesses, discovers the Truth that will, in the end, prevail, and all things, surely, inevitably, resistlessly work together for good.

Mary Austin
1868–1934

Born in Illinois, Mary Hunter crossed the Sierra by train in 1888. Although she wrote more than thirty books, her first, The Land of Little Rain (1903), remains her most memorable. She married Stafford Austin in 1891 and moved to the Owens Valley, where he worked in the irrigation business. There she had her first sustained exposures to the Mojave Desert, the area's Indians, and the small towns along what is now Highway 395. Austin was among the first scientifically literate nature writers, by predilection and training, but she was also a poet, connecting desert topography, backcountry Latino and Anglo characters, and Indian folktales through a mystic sense of the female. Austin became a primary figure in the Carmel Colony, where she wrote many of her best works, including The Basket Woman (1905) and The Arrow-Maker (1912), both of which are dominated by strong female Indian figures. Lost Borders (1909), her second collection, makes an even more vivid link between Southwest drylands and resolute Indian women. After 1912, Austin spent as much time in New York as in the West. Her autobiography, Earth Horizon (1932), details her evolution as a feminist and environmentalist. She settled in New Mexico, and Willa Cather wrote her classic evocation of Southwest spirit, Death Comes for the Archbishop (1927), in Austin's Santa Fe home. On her death in 1934, Mary Austin was eulogized as one of the most significant American writers of the era. As personally thorny as her beloved desert, she was rediscovered in the environmental awakening of the 1990s, and her writing and philosophy have attracted new enthusiasts and scholars. Her novel The Ford (1917), one of five major works set in California, was recently republished by the University of California Press.

From *The Land of Little Rain*

East away from the Sierras, south from Panamint and Amargosa, east and south many an uncounted mile, is the Country of Lost Borders.

Ute, Paiute, Mojave, and Shoshone inhabit its frontiers, and as far into the heart of it as a man dare go. Not the law, but the land sets the limit. Desert is the name it wears upon the maps, but the Indian's is the better word. Desert is a loose term to indicate land that supports no man; whether the land can be bitted and broken to that purpose is not proven. Void of life it never is, however dry the air and villainous the soil.

This is the nature of that country. There are hills, rounded, blunt, burned, squeezed up out of chaos, chrome and vermilion painted, aspiring to the snow-line. Between the hills lie high level-looking plains full of intolerable sun glare, or narrow valleys drowned in a blue haze. The bill surface is streaked with ash drift and black, unweathered lava flows. After rains water accumulates in the hollows of small closed valleys, and, evaporating, leaves hard dry levels of pure desertness that get the local name of dry lakes. Where the mountains are steep and the rains heavy, the pool is never quite dry, but dark and bitter, rimmed about with the efflorescence of alkaline deposits. A thin crust of it lies along the marsh over the vegetating area, which has neither beauty nor freshness. In the broad wastes open to the wind the sand drifts in hummocks about the stubby shrubs, and between them the soil shows saline traces. The sculpture of the hills here is more wind than water work, though the quick storms do sometimes scar them past many a year's redeeming. In all the Western desert edges there are essays in miniature at the famed, terrible Grand Cañon, to which, if you keep on long enough in this country, you will come at last.

Since this is a hill country one expects to find springs, but not to depend upon them; for when found they are often brackish and unwholesome, or maddening, slow dribbles in a thirsty soil. Here you find the hot sink of Death Valley, or high rolling districts where the air has always a tang of frost. Here are the long heavy winds and breathless calms on the tilted mesas where dust devils dance, whirling up into a wide, pale sky. Here you have no rain when all the earth cries for it, or quick downpours called cloud-bursts for violence. A land of lost rivers, with little in it to love; yet a land that once visited must be come back to inevitably. If it were not so there would be little told of it.

This is the country of three seasons. From June on to November it lies hot, still, and unbearable, sick with violent unrelieving storms; then on until April, chill, quiescent, drinking its scant rain and scanter snows; from April to the hot season again, blossoming, radiant, and seductive. These months are only approximate; later or earlier the rain-laden wind may drift up the water gate of the Colorado from the Gulf, and the land sets its seasons by the rain.

The desert floras shame us with their cheerful adaptations to the seasonal limitations. Their whole duty is to flower and fruit, and they do it hardly, or with tropical luxuriance, as the rain admits. It is recorded in the report of the Death Valley expedition that after a year of abundant rains, on the Colorado desert was found a specimen of Amaranthus ten feet high. A year later the same species in the same place matured in the drought at four inches. One hopes the land may breed like qualities in her human offspring, not tritely to "try," but to do. Seldom does the desert herb attain the full stature of the type. Extreme aridity and extreme altitude have the same dwarfing effect, so that we find in the high Sierras and in Death Valley related species in miniature that reach a comely growth in mean temperatures. Very fertile are the desert plants in expedients to prevent evaporation, turning their foliage edgewise toward the sun, growing silky hairs, exuding viscid gum. The wind, which has a long sweep, harries and helps them. It rolls up dunes about the stocky stems, encompassing and protective, and above the dunes, which may be, as with the mesquite, three times as high as a man, the blossoming twigs flourish and bear fruit.

There are many areas in the desert where drinkable water lies within a few feet of the surface, indicated by the mesquite and the bunch grass (*Sporobolus airoides*). It is this nearness of unimagined help that makes the tragedy of desert deaths. It is related that the final breakdown of that hapless party that gave Death Valley its forbidding name occurred in a locality where shallow wells would have saved them. But how were they to know that? Properly equipped it is possible to go safely across that ghastly sink, yet every year it takes its toll of death, and yet men find there sun-dried mummies, of whom no trace or recollection is preserved. To underestimate one's thirst, to pass a given landmark to the right or left, to find a dry spring where one looked for running water—there is no help for any of these things.

Along springs and sunken watercourses one is surprised to find such water-loving plants as grow widely in moist ground, but the true desert breeds its own kind, each in its particular habitat. The angle of the slope, the frontage of a hill, the structure of the soil determines the plant. South-looking hills are nearly bare, and the lower tree-line higher here by a thousand feet. Cañons running east and west will have one wall naked and one clothed. Around dry lakes and marshes the herbage preserves a set and orderly arrangement. Most species have well-defined areas of growth, the best index the voiceless land can give the traveler of his whereabouts.

If you have any doubt about it, know that the desert begins with the creosote. This immortal shrub spreads down into Death Valley and up to the lower timberline, odorous and medicinal as you might guess from the name, wandlike, with shining fretted foliage. Its vivid green is grateful to the eye in a wilderness of gray and greenish white shrubs. In the spring it exudes a resinous gum which the Indians of those parts know how to use with pulverized rock for cementing arrow points to shafts. Trust Indians not to miss any virtues of the plant world!

Nothing the desert produces expresses it better than the unhappy growth of the tree yuccas. Tormented, thin forests of it stalk drearily in the high mesas, particularly in that triangular slip that fans out eastward from the meeting of the Sierras and coastwise hills where the first swings across the southern end of the San Joaquin Valley. The yucca bristles with bayonet-pointed leaves, dull green, growing shaggy with age, tipped with panicles of fetid, greenish bloom. After death, which is slow, the ghostly hollow network of its woody skeleton, with hardly power to rot, makes the moonlight fearful. Before the yucca has come to flower, while yet its bloom is a creamy cone-shaped bud of the size of a small cabbage, full of sugary sap, the Indians twist it deftly out of its fence of daggers and roast it for their own delectation. So it is that in those parts where man inhabits one sees young plants of *Yucca arborensis* infrequently. Other yuccas, cacti, low herbs, a thousand sorts, one finds journeying east from the coastwise hills. There is neither poverty of soil nor species to account for the sparseness of desert growth, but simply that each plant requires more room. So much earth must be preëmpted to extract so much moisture. The real struggle for existence, the real brain of the plant, is underground; above there is room for a rounded perfect growth. In Death Valley, reputed the very core of desolation, are nearly two hundred identified species.

Above the lower tree-line, which is also the snow-line, mapped out abruptly by the sun, one finds spreading growth of piñon, juniper, branched nearly to the ground, lilac and sage, and scattering white pines.

There is no special preponderance of self-fertilized or wind-fertilized plants, but everywhere the demand for and evidence of insect life. Now where there are seeds and insects there will be birds and small mammals and where these are, will come the slinking, sharp-toothed kind that prey on them. Go as far as you dare in the heart of a lonely land, you cannot go so far that life and death are not before you. Painted lizards slip in and out of rock crevices, and pant on the white hot sands. Birds, hummingbirds even, nest in the cactus scrub; woodpeckers befriend the demoniac yuccas; out of the stark, treeless waste rings the music of the nightsinging mockingbird. If it be summer and the sun well down, there will be a burrowing owl to call. Strange, furry, tricksy things dart across the open places, or sit motionless in the conning towers of the creosote. The poet may have "named all the birds without a gun," but not the fairy-footed, ground-inhabiting, furtive, small folk of the rainless regions. They are too many and too swift; how many you would not believe without seeing the footprint tracings in the sand. They are nearly all night workers, finding the days too hot and white. In mid-desert where there

Mary Austin

387

are no cattle, there are no birds of carrion, but if you go far in that direction the chances are that you will find yourself shadowed by their tilted wings. Nothing so large as a man can move unspied upon in that country, and they know well how the land deals with strangers. There are hints to be had here of the way in which a land forces new habits on its dwellers. The quick increase of suns at the end of spring sometimes overtakes birds in their nesting and effects a reversal of the ordinary manner of incubation. It becomes necessary to keep eggs cool rather than warm. One hot, stifling spring in the Little Antelope I had occasion to pass and repass frequently the nest of a pair of meadowlarks, located unhappily in the shelter of a very slender weed. I never caught them sitting except near night, but at midday they stood, or drooped above it, half fainting with pitifully parted bills, between their treasure and the sun. Sometimes both of them together with wings spread and half lifted continued a spot of shade in a temperature that constrained me at last in a fellow feeling to spare them a hit of canvas for permanent shelter. There was a fence in that country shutting in a cattle range, and along its fifteen miles of posts one could be sure of finding a bird or two in every strip of shadow; sometimes the sparrow and the hawk, with wings trailed and beaks parted, drooping in the white truce of noon.

If one is inclined to wonder at first how so many dwellers came to be in the loneliest land that ever came out of God's hands, what they do there and why stay, one does not wonder so much after having lived there. None other than this long brown land lays such a hold on the affections. The rainbow hills, the tender bluish mists, the luminous radiance of the spring, have the lotus charm. They trick the sense of time, so that once inhabiting there you always mean to go away without quite realizing that you have not done it. Men who have lived there, miners and cattlemen, will tell you this, not so fluently, but emphatically, cursing the land and going back to it. For one thing there is the divinest, cleanest air to be breathed anywhere in God's world. Some day the world will understand that, and the little oases on the windy tops of hills will harbor for healing its ailing, house-weary broods. There is promise there of great wealth in ores and earths, which is no wealth by reason of being so far removed from water and workable conditions, but men are bewitched by it and tempted to try the impossible.

You should hear Salty Williams tell how he used to drive eighteen and twenty-mule teams from the borax marsh to Mojave, ninety miles, with the trail wagon full of water-barrels. Hot days the mules would go so mad for drink that the clank of the water bucket set them into an uproar of hideous, maimed noises, and a tangle of harness chains, while Salty would sit on the high seat with the sun glare heavy in his eyes, dealing out curses of pacification in a level, uninterested voice until the clamor fell off from sheer exhaustion. There was a line of shallow graves along that road; they used to count on dropping a man or two of every new gang of coolies brought out in the hot season. But when he lost his swamper, smitten without warning at the noon halt, Salty quit his job; he said it was "too durn hot." The swamper he buried by the way with stones upon him to keep the coyotes from digging him up, and seven years later I read the penciled lines on the pine headboard, still bright and unweathered.

But before that, driving up on the Mojave stage, I met Salty again crossing Indian Wells, his face from the high seat, tanned and ruddy as a harvest moon, looming through the golden dust above his eighteen mules. The land had called him.

The palpable sense of mystery in the desert air breeds fables, chiefly of lost treasure. Somewhere within its stark borders, if one believes report, is a hill strewn with nuggets; one seamed with virgin silver; an old clayey waterbed where Indians scooped up earth to make cooking pots and shaped them reeking with grains of pure gold. Old miners drifting about the desert edges, weathered into the semblance of the tawny hills, will tell you tales like these convincingly. After a little sojourn in that land you will believe them on their own account. It is a question whether it is not better to be bitten by the little horned snake of the desert that goes sidewise and strikes without coiling, than by the tradition of a lost mine.

And yet—and yet—is it not perhaps to satisfy expectation that one falls into the tragic key in writing of desertness? The more you wish of it the more you get, and in the mean time lose much of pleasantness. In that country which begins at the foot of the east slope of the Sierras and spreads out by less and less lofty hill ranges toward the Great Basin, it is possible to live with great zest, to have red blood and delicate joys, to pass and repass about one's daily performance an area that would make an Atlantic seaboard State, and that with no peril, and, according to our way of thought, no particular difficulty. At any rate, it was not people who went into the desert merely to write it up who invented the fabled Hassaympa, of whose waters, if any drink, they can no more see fact as naked fact, but all radiant with the color of romance. I, who must have drunk of it in my twice seven years' wanderings, am assured that it is worth while.

For all the toll the desert takes of a man it gives compensations, deep breaths, deep sleep, and the communion of the stars. It comes upon one with new force in the pauses of the night that the Chaldeans were a desertbred people. It is hard to escape the sense of mastery as the stars move in the wide clear heavens to risings and settings unobscured. They look large and near and palpitant; as if they moved on some stately service not needful to declare. Wheeling to their stations in the sky, they make the poor world-fret of no account. Of no account you who lie out there watching, nor the lean coyote that stands off in the scrub from you and howls and howls.

John Rollin Ridge (c. 1860). Courtesy Bancroft Library, University of California at Berkeley.

California Geological Survey field party of 1864: Howard Gardiner, Richard Cotter, Joseph Henry Brewer, and Clarence King. Courtesy Bancroft Library, University of California at Berkeley.

Mark Twain (center), at the Third Territorial Legislature in Carson City, Nevada, in early 1864, before he left for San Francisco. The caption (in Twain's hand), "Three of the suspected men still in confinement at Aurora," is an ironic comment on the nature of political figures and the wild-and-woolly era. Courtesy Mark Twain Papers, Bancroft Library, University of California at Berkeley.

Ina Coolbrith (seated at center). An anonymous inscription reads: "Miss Coolbrith with Mrs. Verneille de Witter, aviatrix Lillian Gatlin (who flew to the Mother Lode for branches), Mrs. Genevieve Newmark, and unknown woman. Taken at birthday celebration for Ina, March 31, 1925."

Thocmetony (Sarah Winnemucca) in lecture attire of her own design (c. 1870s). Courtesy Nevada Historical Society.

Theodore Roosevelt and John Muir at Half Dome, Yosemite (1903).
Courtesy Bancroft Library, University of California at Berkeley.

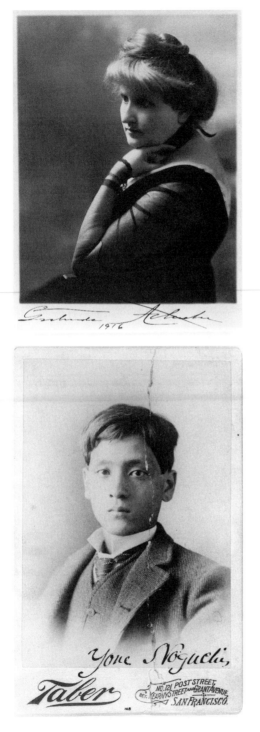

Gertrude Atherton (1916).
Courtesy Bancroft Library,
University of California at
Berkeley.

Yone Noguchi in postcard
pose shortly after arrival
in San Francisco (1894).
Courtesy Bancroft Library,
University of California at
Berkeley.

Charles Fletcher Lummis in New Mexico (1888).
Courtesy Southwest Museum, Los Angeles.

"on the Beach at Waikiki" 1915

Jack London and his wife
Charmian in Honolulu
(1915). Courtesy Bancroft
Library, University of
California at Berkeley.

Robinson Jeffers,
actress Dame Judith
Anderson, and Una
Jeffers at Hawk
Tower, Tor House
(1945). Anderson
visited to discuss
the poet's dramatic
translation of
Euripides' *Medea*, in
which she starred.
Courtesy Bancroft
Library, University of
California at Berkeley.

Jaime de Angulo (c. 1940s).
Photo by Harold Luck.
Courtesy University of
California at Santa Cruz,
Special Collections.

William Saroyan (1940).
Courtesy Bancroft Library,
University of California at
Berkeley.

John Steinbeck. An
inscription by his first wife,
Gwendolyn Conger
Steinbeck, reads: "This
picture taken approximately
at the time of the
publishing of In Dubious
Battle. Very poor—note
overcoat. I have original of
this, which he glued into a
little book of his love
poems to me dated 1938."
Courtesy Bancroft Library,
University of California at
Berkeley.

Josephine Miles (1984).
Courtesy Oakland Museum
of California, Oakland
Tribune Collection, gift of
the Alameda Newspaper
Group.

John Fante (1952). Courtesy Oakland Museum of California, Oakland Tribune Collection, gift of the Alameda Newspaper Group.

Raymond Chandler (1962). Courtesy Oakland Museum of California, Oakland Tribune Collection, gift of the Alameda Newspaper Group.

Idwal Jones (c. 1947). The architect of California wine writing, Jones sits among the founders of the wine industry: from second from left, Charles Beringer, Louis Martini, Jones, and Herman Wente. Courtesy Bancroft Library, University of California at Berkeley.

Toshio Mori (1979). Courtesy Oakland Museum of California, Oakland Tribune Collection, gift of the Alameda Newspaper Group.

Jade Snow Wong at her potting wheel (1950). Courtesy Oakland Museum of California, Oakland Tribune Collection, gift of the Alameda Newspaper Group.

Chester Himes (1954). Courtesy Oakland Museum of California, Oakland Tribune Collection, gift of the Alameda Newspaper Group.

PART FOUR

Dreams and Awakenings

1915–1945

INTRODUCTION

Modern California literature starts with Robinson Jeffers, and Jeffers started with the cold Pacific Ocean and the hard granite of the Carmel coast. Home to the original Ohlone peoples, Carmel was explored (and named) by the Spaniard Sebastián Vizcaino in 1603. Rugged, isolated, and eerily beautiful, it was known as *el puerto perdido* (the lost coast), an empty space on maps for almost two hundred years, until Serra and Crespí arrived to found the Carmel Mission in 1771. Although Bay Area writers and artists summered in an arts colony nearby and real estate interests thrived, Carmel itself was still a modest outpost when Jeffers arrived from Los Angeles in 1914.

The wildness and the elemental power of the place triggered an enormous creative energy in Jeffers. The landscape fed the poet; and the poet in turn took such fierce possession of the place itself that one might argue he still owns it, from Point Pinos, the Monterey Peninsula's northern tip, to Sycamore Canyon, south of the town of Big Sur—the long coastal corridor often called Jeffers Country.

In engaging the landscape, Jeffers created himself. He built his home on Carmel Point from great blocks of granite hauled up from the Pacific shoreline below, first as an apprentice on the family residence, Tor House, then as the stonemason on Hawk Tower, a forty-foot aerie inspired by Irish towers he visited. He walked his territory—the juncture of the Coast Range and the Pacific Ocean—absorbed the region, and released himself in a rigorous five-year practice of setting stone. A flood of poetry came in the next twenty years: *Tamar* (1924), *Roan Stallion* (1925), and four more volumes were published by 1930, and they made Jeffers perhaps the most popular serious poet of his time.

American poetry came of age in the decade surrounding World War I with the works of Robert Frost, Ezra Pound, William Carlos Williams, Marianne Moore, Wallace Stevens, and e. e. cummings, and Robinson Jeffers joined them as a major figure in the rise of American literary modernism. Almost single-handedly, he set California literature in the national eye. Solitary in his tower at Carmel as the Depression descended, Jeffers grew to be a legend, appearing on the cover of *Time* magazine in 1932.

His fame (and notoriety) grew in a succession of long dramatic narrative poems, among them "Cawdor," "Thurso's Landing," and "The Roan Stallion" (in which the protagonist is a female mixed-blood Indian named California). He believed that an immense state with a titanic history demanded big books and epic poems, a conviction also manifested in Steinbeck's *The Grapes of Wrath* and in contemporary long poems such as Gary Snyder's *Mountains and Rivers without End*. Frank Norris saw the wheat and the octopus as complex metaphors for the struggles transforming California into a Darwinian new world. For Jeffers, the forces and conflicts were even vaster and required a more expansive canvas. He created the literary region and drew it larger, as myth; and against a background of granite and hawk, winter gales and steelhead, he dramatized remnant families—father and son, brother and sister— in desperate struggle. They were doomed, Jeffers made clear, to destroy each other and themselves in the final paroxysms of Western civilization.

In poems such as "Continent's End," he imagined North America as the national body politic, and he saw physical California and the geographic West as the last site for American dreams of eternal renewal and progress. It was as if, in Kevin Starr's words, "the continent insisted that we enter into a dialog with it." Jeffers was a profoundly tragic poet, and if he felt that "the continent itself had its own mythopoeic dimension," he saw the Pacific coast as an ironic ending point for a misbegotten manifest destiny.

If Hawk Tower loomed over the psychic landscape in the North, the giant "Hollywoodland" sign (mounted in 1923, with stark white letters fifty feet tall and illuminated by four thousand lightbulbs, it was later shortened by storm to "Hollywood") was a beacon in the raffish southern sky. The South boomed between World War I and the financial crash of October 1929, fed by the pumping of oil, the capture of Owens Valley water, the burgeoning film industry (*The Jazz Singer*, the first "talkie," appeared in 1927), and commerce arising from the automobile age. Los Angeles doubled in population (to 1,230,000) between 1920 and 1930, and as it outstripped San Francisco in growth, it also developed in high contrast to the older northern city. As early as the Civil War, Northern and Southern California had been polar opposites. The San Francisco Bay Area was a Union hotbed, and the region south of the Grapevine harbored Rebel support. By the turn of the century, Northern California was Democratic, pro-labor, and Catholic in demography, while the South leaned toward Republican, pro-business, and Protestant beliefs. Modern California emerged as a confederacy of regions, often a conflicted one, and the friction between North and South was nowhere more evident than in the two rival World Expositions of 1915–1916— both celebrating the opening of the Panama Canal—in San Francisco and San Diego.

The surge of new citizens to Southern California—more than 80 percent of them Anglos from the Midwest—was a second gold rush. The tide of new money aside, Los Angeles seemed a crazy quilt of sudden towns, "screwy," downright schizoid in some Eastern eyes. For many, the City of Angels was an overgrown province, in Kevin Starr's words the "slobbering civic idiot in the family of American communities," united only in common yearning for a little bungalow ringed by palm trees. To others, it was a corrupted utopia in which nothing was true and everything permitted, a deceitful lie of quick money, tanned youth, and endless orange groves—perfect for cults like the "Mighty I Am" movement and religious "prophets" such as Amy Semple McPherson to gather legions of followers.

The Jazz Age in Los Angeles was a time of spectacle and excess, but the South lagged in developing a lasting literary culture. A handful of major works endures, speaking more to the failure of dreams than to any sort of triumph. Upton Sinclair's *Oil!* (1927) and Wallace Thurman's *The Blacker the Berry* (1929) are notable examples. Sinclair's novel is a serious and detailed account of the Signal Hill oil scandal of 1921 and of the slick of moral contamination and economic disaster that spread from it. Thurman's work, a classic of modern African American fiction, is set partially at the University of Southern California in Los Angeles in the mid-1920s, a bitter exploration of white racism, black class and caste prejudices, and their corrosive influence on the emerging urban black middle class.

The Great Depression stunned California, and from late 1929 until the mobilization for World War II, the economy and social fabric were devastated. The fields of El Centro, studios of Hollywood, boardrooms of San Francisco, and timber forests in Humboldt County were all disrupted. Bottomed out, margined away, wiped out, tractored off, or simply let go—such coinages speak of an entire population suffering and powerless. One-third of the work force was unemployed. A powerful documentary literature emerged as the scope of economic collapse became clear, and writers throughout the country engaged in a discourse, to the nation at large, about the nation at large. John Dos Passos, Richard Wright, James T. Farrell, Meridel Le Sueur, Clifford Odets, and Henry Roth, working side by side with photographers like Dorothea Lange, wrote graphic accounts of human misery and survival. John Steinbeck's *The Grapes of Wrath* (1939) was foremost in the group. A bestseller and source of enormous political controversy, it was the basis for a popular film that drove home the brutality of the Depression. *The Grapes of Wrath* became an enduring classic of American literature and its author an international figure.

Steinbeck lived early in Pacific Grove, where he wrote the first of his thirty novels, short story collections, plays, and nonfiction books. Like William Faulkner, he was deeply rooted in place and its literary reflection; and as with Faulkner and Mississippi, John Steinbeck and Central California have been linked ever since. Hard by Jeffers territory, Steinbeck country is bounded on the east and west by the Gabilan Mountain range and the Pacific Ocean, running north to San Jose and south to the end of the Salinas Valley. It emerged through many of his fifteen California books, mainly in the cadences of have-nots and social marginals, driven by powers that well from deep in the land.

The Grapes of Wrath, the work that won Steinbeck the Nobel Prize twenty-five years later, is set a few hundred miles away, in the Kern County growing fields and labor camps around Arvin, Shafter, and Weedpatch. It tells of the exodus of the Joad family from the Dust Bowl, and it was Steinbeck's vision of the tragedy and redemption of the largest single human migration in state history. The Okies hailed from a quadrangle carved from Oklahoma, Missouri, Arkansas, and Texas, driven west by drought, mechanization, and foreclosure. They came on Route 66, the "Mother Road" (now Interstate 40), a river of asphalt that brought half a million people in failing jalopies to California between 1934 and 1939. Route 66 had a fabled power—it was the subject of popular songs and kids' jump-rope rhymes—and it promised to deliver another tribe to the Promised Land.

"It's California," Ruthie Joad whispers as the family stops their car in the middle of a Tehachapi pass for their first look at the Golden State. Instead of a heaven on earth, the Okies reached a state with rampant unemployment, in an economic and political mess, and they found themselves handy targets for explosive anger and social hysteria. Steinbeck drew the Great Central Valley in epic strokes and grand fictional architecture, and he explored the ties between humans and landscape in agrarian terms. In raising the Joads— embracing them fully in downclass origins, illiteracy, and racist tendencies— to the stature of a biblical people, he was a voice for the rights of migrant cultures. In his drama of exile, suffering, and survival, he documented a national ordeal in uniquely Californian terms. As popular and praised as it was, *The Grapes of Wrath* was also highly controversial, banned and burned in communities in both Oklahoma and California.

The late 1930s also saw the arrival of several major works of modern nonfiction, including Carey McWilliams's *Factories in the Field* (1939) and George R. Stewart's *Ordeal by Hunger* (1936). While Steinbeck portrayed the Okies through the Joads, McWilliams traced the history and conditions of migrant farm laborers. He chronicled the treatment of Mexican, Filipino, and other workers in the fields of California, highlighting farm labor strikes and the efforts of public officials and agribusiness to crush them. McWilliams's work was also a best-seller, and it brought the same "official" responses as Steinbeck's: it was burned, banned from public libraries, denounced by elected figures, and attacked by chambers of commerce. Works by writers such as Steinbeck and McWilliams, with Dorothea Lange's haunting portraits of suffering men and women, documented the Depression in California. They keep its jagged grain vivid sixty years later.

In the midst of the chaos of 1930s, Steinbeck and McWilliams—for all their partisan anger—saw justice in the written word and the potential in awakened human decency. Simultaneously, a much darker, more seductive literary form emerged: the new detective novel. This genre, as it was shaped by Dashiell Hammett, James M. Cain, and Raymond Chandler, originated with Hammett's first efforts in San Francisco. Chandler transplanted it to Los Angeles, and it thrived in both cities on the urban conjunctions of dangerous streets and tony suburbs.

The hard-boiled private eye, epitomized by Hammett's Sam Spade and Chandler's Philip Marlowe, inhabited a world very different from that of Sherlock Holmes or Hercule Poirot. In the European tradition, crime was an aberration: the murderer was caught, justice prevailed, and order was restored. Society was stable; the detective came from a respectable class and sleuthed by wit and applied intelligence. In the world according to Hammett and Chandler, crime was the norm, justice was unexpected, and order was temporary, mainly because their heroes lived, as Chandler wrote, "in a world gone wrong," in which "the law was something to manipulate for profit and power." Police and criminals were in league, their complicity hidden behind façades shielding corruption. Spade and Marlowe were outsiders, garnering grudging respect by doing business with both sides on the integrity of their word, ultimately trusting no one. The new detectives solved their cases—with or without the aid of authorities—by cunning, leveraging knowledge of where which skeletons were buried and by whom, wielding solitary authority, and sometimes by brute violence. Tough-talking survivors, they were existential heroes of a peculiarly Western American sort.

San Francisco and Los Angeles proved perfect for hard-boiled sleuthing. A ghost of the frontier lingered in both cities, and they still harbored a struggle between nostalgia for a stable society and an urge to destroy and reinvent it every minute. They were picturesque—by the ocean and near Mexico—and already resonant in the popular mind. They had various ethnic groups to provide cultural conflict, and they contained neighborhoods whose zoning and architecture changed in the blink of an eye. And San Francisco and Los Angeles shared baroque histories of violence and corruption inseparable from the politics and plundering of the wide open West. "Most things in San Francisco," as Sam Spade viewed it laconically in 1929, "can be bought, or taken."

It remained for Raymond Chandler, the master of the new detective novel, to imagine the modern city as a dominant character in fiction. For him, Los Angeles itself is the alpha beast, a garish, foregrounded metaphor of California self-invention run wild. The cityscape is a jumble of movie sets in the mind of a bemused and evil creator, an architectural collision that masks a contemptible society. The opening of *The Big Sleep* draws a miniature Los Angeles in the Sternwood estate and hothouse, an inspired rendering of a whole city in which purchased family coats of arms and leased chauffeur's livery cannot hide the greed, twisted sexuality, and insanity that form its core. For Chandler, such antic disorder can be countered only by a man alone. He sees his hero as a modern knight-errant whose fierce self-possession is a moral stance in a world of poseurs. "Down these mean streets a man must go," he wrote of Marlowe, "who is not himself mean, who is neither tarnished nor afraid."

In Chandler's City of Fallen Angels, the California detective story merged with a third literary response to the troubled times: the Hollywood novel. Fiction set in or around Hollywood, targeting movies and their cultural influence, appeared as early as 1922 with Harry Leon Wilson's *Merton of the Movies*, and it soon proliferated. Money was short for nearly everyone in the 1930s, but the film industry, supplier of dreams in a desperate time, still had a lot of it. Nathanael West, Aldous Huxley, F. Scott Fitzgerald, William Faulkner, Christopher Isherwood, and Horace McCoy were the first of many serious artists lured to "the Coast" by the high prices paid for film scripts. They were then lured, by the very nature of the bizarre and contradictory world in which they found themselves, to write about their experiences. In such novels, the glamour of the movies merges with a titillating southern California concoction of fantasy, eccentricity, self-delusion, and excess.

Hollywood was a poisoned kingdom at the edge of the world, and each writer seized a corner of it to describe. West's *The Day of the Locust* makes Hollywood a site where the worst possibilities of California find grotesque expression, where movie sets mirror empty lives (and vice versa), where people confused by false promises and crazed with disappointment turn to mass violence, where the California Dream becomes a nightmare. "They realize that they've been tricked and burn with resentment," West seethes near the apocalyptic end of his novel. "The sun was a joke. Oranges can't titillate their jaded palates. Nothing can ever be violent enough to make taut their slack minds and bodies. They have slaved and worked for nothing." Enraged at how little their lives have amounted to, the crowd at the opening of Kahn's Pleasure Palace Theatre degenerates into a mob, wrecking everything in a frenzy of nihilistic self-destruction.

F. Scott Fitzgerald, sick and broke, found no magic in Tinseltown. His Pat Hobby stories were a semicomic look at a life wasted writing for schlock films. *The Love of the Last Tycoon* was more ambitious. While others developed characters to explore the contradictory facets of filmland, Fitzgerald used Hollywood's excesses to reveal the complex dimensions of film magnate Monroe Stahr, the ultimate insider. The author knew the studios, the sets, the offices, the dynamics of the industry, and he drew them with a cold eye. But it was Stahr who fascinated him—brilliant manipulator, charming tyrant, driven but solitary, still boyish in his thirties. In the words of Kathleen Moore, the British woman star Stahr thinks he loves, "You're three or four different men, but each of them is out in the open. Like all Americans." Fitzgerald died before completing the novel, but he clearly saw, in Stahr's rise, misspent power, and decline, a corrupt California version of the American Dream.

They Shoot Horses, Don't They? (1935) was the only major fictional work by the screenwriter Horace McCoy. Set during a marathon dance contest on the Santa Monica pier, at the heart of which occurs a senseless (or merciful) murder, the novel dwells on movie-fringe hangers-on. Like thousands of others, Robert Syverten and Gloria Beatty leave Dust Bowl Arkansas and West Texas in pursuit of the distinctively California fantasy of movie fame. They end up in a shabby arcade with a tired band of other aspirants, dancing out their hopes like wind-up toys. The ocean menaces in such novels, earthquakes shake from deep in the earth, and fire is always on the nervous near edge. Suspended over the Pacific Ocean, the dancers feel the surf pounding at the pilings below as nature threatens to chew away the spectacle and the hucksters who prey on it. Born of outrage at the betrayal of dreams, the Hollywood novel remains vibrant into our time with works like Joan Didion's *Play It As It Lays*.

In poetry, Robinson Jeffers ruled into the mid-1930s, when his work grew darker and isolationist in mood, and a field of modern verse slowly blossomed. William Everson (his Central Valley poems emerged) and Kenneth Rexroth (a leader of the San Francisco Renaissance) proved two important talents and influences on the later literary development of the state. Rexroth's first collection came out in 1940, and he struck a friendship with the publisher James Laughlin. Laughlin, who founded New Directions Books on the East Coast in

1936, turned to Rexroth for literary counsel and soon included California poets on his distinguished list. He charitably hired state writers—including Kenneth Patchen and Weldon Kees—as temporary help, and the Rexroth-Laughlin link forged a lasting Western connection. New Directions quickly became the principal literary platform for many international avante-garde figures, from Ezra Pound to Robert Duncan and Gary Snyder, and it gave California poetry and poetics a place in global literature.

Three major poets emerged, all continuing to write well into the late twentieth century. Hildegarde Flanner published her first book in 1920 and her last in 1987. She was influenced early by the Jesuit poet Gerard Manley Hopkins, but she turned her eyes from heaven to the spirit in the land—"the dry western earth . . . its arid and cryptic literalness"—first in the south, in Altadena, then later in Calistoga. *If There Is Time* (1942) established her reputation as she experimented with tight forms and a range of female voices atypical of the time. She was ultimately a poet of dry places, extending the line of rooted nature verse begun by Jeffers and continuing in the work of such figures as Robert Hass and Jane Hirshfield. Flanner saw the California poet's place in the landscape as "A grain of sensibility in native light, / Barely lodged upon a granite hill," but as poetry moved into the universities, she faded from view. Fresh audiences rediscovered her thirty years later with the growth of the environmental movement.

Josephine Miles was an urban poet and scholar, and her first book, *Lines from Intersection* (1939), came out just before she joined the faculty at UC Berkeley, where she taught for almost forty years. The collection, praised by one reviewer as "a world of small pictures brightly illuminated," established her interest in the quotidian matters of the city (shopping and street life, theaters and hotels, encroaching subdivisions) and the poetry of plain talk by ordinary people. Miles espoused an accessible public poetry, and her verse and scholarship were grounded in details of daily life. She was an inspiration to students, writers, and colleagues alike and a central figure in the rise of the Bay Area as a literary mecca in the decades after World War II.

The third major poet emerging from the 1930s, Yvor Winters, came to Stanford University as a student in 1928 and stayed for half a century as professor, poet, and critic. Insistently Californian, young Winters was shaped by arid landscape, Western and Indian history, and modernist aesthetics, a blend that yielded inspired and evocative poetry: "The Slow Pacific Swell" and "The California Oaks" are among the finest poems in the California canon and minor American classics. He grew to be a major intellectual presence, an old-fashioned man of letters with great influence in New York who was also one of the most incisive literary critics of his generation. As World War II neared, he reacted against the populist tide, growing markedly conservative in politics and neoclassic in aesthetics, a development mirrored in his literary tastes (he attacked Jeffers, Yeats, and Pound for their mysticism, poetic slackness, and corrupting influence) and his verse, which became far more controlled in form, rhythm, and rhyme.

With Everson and Rexroth, these three poets exemplified the growing multiplicity of California poetry. They were classicists and anarchists, rooted in country and cities; they peered into the future of a nation on the brink of war and revisited national and state history, reflecting on received historical and literary texts—especially the visions of California and the West. They traced their lineages from Walter Raleigh and Walt Whitman, Catullus and William Carlos Williams, Lao-Tse and the Marx Brothers. They took up old battles with the Eastern literary establishment and touted new voices that recovered Indian ways and saw a California linked not only to the continent but also to the Pacific Rim. In short, the poetry that gathered in the 1930s displayed cultural maturity, and the fact that all these poets worked well beyond the Vietnam era said much about the enduring power of their work. They also positioned California to be instrumental in the coming developments of American and world poetry.

Miles and Flanner, with M. F. K. Fisher and Jade Snow Wong, reflected the increasing prominence of California literature by women, and there were more significant women writers on the horizon. Tillie Olsen, for example, began publishing leftist journalism and short fiction in the mid-1930s. She also wrote *Yonnondio*—a remarkable account of women and families in the grip of the Depression—but locked it away, unfinished, as too crude. It was hidden for forty years, until after she became known as author of *Tell Me a Riddle* and respected as an icon of the women's movement, and it was published unrevised in 1974. Her work is represented in volume 2 of *The Literature of California*.

California was the sixth state to extend suffrage to women, in 1911, and the profound cultural shifts of the 1920s and 1930s seemed to promise a climate in which female professionals—including writers—could flourish at last. But Amy Semple McPherson and the actress Clara Bow did not a generation make, and there were no more female surgeons, lawyers, and concert violinists—and published writers—in San Francisco than there were in New York. Even in the arts in "open" California, visible female talents and feminist sensibilities such as Tillie Olsen's were the exceptions.

In prose only William Saroyan could see hope in a starving man's last hours in San Francisco circa 1934, and he became a national sensation for doing just that in "The Daring Young Man on the Flying Trapeze." Tom Joad, Philip Marlowe, and Nathanael West's Tod Hackett made a grim triangle, but Saroyan's young man chose another path: savoring the pure joy of being alive. "It was then he became thoroughly awake: at the thought of dying," he wrote, and the sentence was a splash of cold water. Saroyan's alter egos were trapeze artists, gamblers, bicycle messengers, and jazz musicians—all improvisers of life on the high wire of the Depression. The stories are virtuoso pieces, kaleidoscopes of shards of starvation and first love, shooting craps in an alley, and listening to jazz alone in a dingy room, finding that more work wouldn't get you more money yet still banging out a story in a fever at the typewriter. Saroyan was twenty-six and the darling of San Francisco when the collection *The Daring Young Man on the Flying Trapeze* (1934) appeared and became a national best-seller.

If William Saroyan was the prime optimist and San Francisco's darling, he was also Fresno's favorite son. *My Name Is Aram* (1940) celebrated the area's Armenian community, spirited survivors who fled centuries of persecution for the California heartland. His Armenians were romanticized and sentimental, a passionate people quick to love and anger, with a penchant for eccentrics. Like "my cousin Mourad, who enjoyed being alive more than anybody else" in "The Summer of the Beautiful White Horse," they tore off life like a chunk of warm bread. In a world gone cruel and mad, Saroyan implied, only the nutty ones could show us how to live happily in the ruins. He was among the earliest writers speaking from inside an immigrant culture to find wide acclaim and a national audience.

Saroyan, hungry and high on life, was not alone. John Fante, his friend and less famous counterpart, fell drunk in love with winner-take-all L.A. in *Ask the Dust* (1942). She is a strange woman with a dangerous past, but Arturo Bandini is smitten. "Los Angeles, give me some of you!," he begs from Bunker Hill. "Come to me the way I came to you . . . you pretty town I loved so much, you sad flower in the sand." Even the earthquake of 1933 is seen not as a terror or an apocalyptic omen but as just another crazy ride on the midway, as Bandini whoops his way through the Great Carnival of Life.

Jaime de Angulo was another yea-sayer. A cosmopolitan maverick, he came to the Golden State by way of Spain and France to emerge as one of the great characters in the annals of California literature. A linguistic anthropologist, he set out to do fieldwork in 1921 in a world unimaginably distant from the urban milieu of Saroyan and Fante: the Pit River country of the Atchumawi Indians in the remotest northeast corner of the state. De Angulo went to transcribe their language, but he fell astonished into a realm that seemed not simply ancient but outside time itself. He emerged with an innocent's tale of discovery—frequently hilarious—that dramatized a worldview all but lost to us, and the first transcriptions of the saga of Coyote. Joyous, outrageous, and suffused with wonder, *Indians in Overalls* (composed in the 1920s but unpublished until 1950) was a slim volume that went unremarked on publication. But it rescued and celebrated the way and the stories of a people in danger of extinction. De Angulo is now seen as central in the restoration of American Indian culture.

In many ways, the Great Depression cracked open the state and the canon of California literature. With Saroyan's bittersweet human comedies as a wedge, a new generation of immigrant and then ethnic writers came into print. Dire times sensitized a readership to "bottom dogs," and the support of Steinbeck, McWilliams, Saroyan, and Fante—who lobbied for young talents and introduced their works—helped launch the careers of Toshio Mori, Jade Snow Wong, Chester Himes, and Carlos Bulosan. Ironically, this work by writers from the social margins accumulated to form a literature of hope in a turbulent time.

The dialectic between welcome and exclusion was familiar to migrants and ethnic minorities. Since the near-extermination of the Indians and the plundering of the *Californios,* people of color had faced a disparity between the California Dreams that lured them and the facts of legislative and social rejection that locked them out or sought to drive them home. Some migrant groups assimilated, but to have a Japanese, Chinese, Mexican, Filipino, or African American face in the Golden State of 1940 was to live with contradiction: on one hand, to harbor the belief that it really was a land of fresh starts and handmade success, and on the other, to live with the fact that ethnic otherness meant injustice.

In this paradox a culturally diverse literature was born, a body of work blending multiple histories to produce new and vigorous hybrids. This development energized state letters as World War II approached, and it promised a cultural richness that would refigure life and art. It was a complex literature of hope, neither simplistic and pollyannaish nor preacherly. Most of its voices affirmed that the best potentials of life were not bankrupt promises or impossible dreams. And they shared the exhilaration of energy that welled up in groups and individuals going out each morning into the shops, fields, and factories of California, determined to win their share. For Mori, Wong, Himes, and Bulosan, hope was a large container that held joy, pain, rage, and strength.

The title of Toshio Mori's first book, *Yokohama, California*, speaks to the mixture of the two cultures at its core. A nisei, he made the last turns in a wrenching, one-hundred-year journey that had been taken by many of Japanese ancestry in California. By mid-1941 he was a rising star, and his collection was scheduled for release in spring 1942, with a preface by William Saroyan proclaiming Mori as "one of the most important new writers in the country." The stories had already attracted attention in magazines and contests. They were fresh and Zen-like in catching the surprise and soft quirkiness of the California moment, and they reached back to the Japanese *shibai* tradition of mingling folk drama and goofy skits. But the book was canceled after the Japanese bombed Pearl Harbor on December 7, 1941, and Mori was soon on his way from Oakland to Topaz, Utah—one of 111,000 citizens of Japanese descent held in Western internment camps between 1942 and late 1945. *Yokohama, California* was finally published in 1949, after anti-Japanese sentiments had abated, and the collection has since been rediscovered and republished. It remains a highlight not only of early modern California fiction but also of an Asian American literature that has reshaped the national literary terrain.

"Chinatown was agog," Jade Snow Wong comments near the end of *Fifth Chinese Daughter* (1950). "A woman in the window, her legs astride a potter's wheel, her hair in braids, her hands perpetually messy with sticky California clay, her finished products such things as coolies used in China, the daughter of a conservative family." She began her memoir after graduating from Mills College in 1943, had almost completed it by the end of World War II, and finally saw it published in 1950. Wong wrote of herself in the third person, and the understatement of her self-portrait, opening a pottery shop in San Francisco's Chinatown, is still arresting. She mixed an artful blend of East and West, old China and new California, at a time when Asian American women did not go to college, throw pots, open their own businesses, or write the story of their lives. *Fifth Chinese Daughter* endures as a groundbreaking narrative of cultural assimilation in America. The first major work by a modern Asian American author, it was an instance of an emerging multicultural paradigm, a literature struggling to incorporate two worlds, in a tradition that finds its full flowering in the works of Maxine Hong Kingston and Amy Tan.

Against the worlds of Mori and Wong, Chester Himes's wartime Los Angeles was a harsh contrast. Working in defense industry factories from 1941 to 1945, Himes grew so embittered that he later wrote, "I was thirty-one and whole when I went to Los Angeles, and thirty-five and shattered when I left for New York." *If He Hollers Let Him Go* (1945) was and is among the most forceful fictional accounts of black urban disillusionment in California. African Americans played prominent roles in the very making of the state: among the fourteen families of the 1793 pueblo that grew to be Los Angeles, several were black or of mixed black and Indian blood. But the population remained small in the state until well into the Depression, when African Americans began to stream in. Drawn west by the promise of factory jobs and greater freedom, their numbers quadrupled between 1935 and 1945. Many settled around the steel mills, shipyards, and aircraft plants of Oakland and Los Angeles, and the black communities of West Oakland and Watts were soon crowded. Jazz and blues clubs thrived, and a burgeoning black film industry grew with the population.

Himes's protagonist, leaderman Bob Jones, is a strong figure, relishing the rowdy energy of black culture in wartime Los Angles but most compelling in the accounts of his on-the-job struggles with white racism. Solid and hardworking, Jones is finally trapped in a duplicitous sexual snare by an Anglo woman coworker. Himes was dismayed that Western promises of freedom proved to be unfounded rumors, and *If He Hollers Let Him Go* and *Lonely Crusade* (1947), his second novel, dramatized the Dream denied to workers of color. Like Wallace Thurman, Chester Himes served his literary apprenticeship in California, and he demanded in these early novels—as he did throughout an illustrious career—that society reconcile the great divide between what it promised and what it delivered.

Like Mori and Wong, Carlos Bulosan was of Asian origin and evidenced California's growing ties to the Pacific Rim. He also knew the specific brutality his Filipino peers found in California. As new immigration laws restricted Japanese and Mexican entry (and the cheap labor vital to agribusiness), Filipinos were imported on the promises of work and the good life. By 1930, there were thirty-five thousand Pinoy in the state, but with no stable government at home to follow their progress in the new world and no established community to help newcomers on arrival, they were easy targets for segregation, riots, and the antilabor and exclusionary laws that followed. They lived in a vise, and by 1935, scarcely a decade after they had come to the Golden State, Filipinos were formally urged to repatriate and new arrivals were barred from entry into the United States.

Bulosan lived this terrible drama, which he etched in *America Is in the Heart* (1946), a quasi-autobiography spanning his arrival on the West Coast in 1931 and the Japanese invasion of Bataan during World War II. It endures as an ethnic memoir of conflict and accommodation with America, a tradition that began with *The Narrative of the Life of Frederick Douglass* (1845), by a former slave, and continued through prewar works by Saroyan and Wong. A people's fledgling literary efforts often appear as "embroidered" nonfiction, and *America Is in the Heart* brought a buried and shameful story to the surface. The author traced a decade of Filipino privation in California, but he was sharpest in drawing the daily life of a generation of mercurial working men and the pattern of isolation, rootlessness, and psychic erosion that defined them. It was the first significant literary account of Filipino culture in California, a streaky chronicle of suffering and loss, suffused with an angry refusal to stay mute or to quit.

As terrible as the decade had been for Bulosan and the Pinoy, they clung to remnants of hope. There was no going back to Binalonan village in the Philippines: Japanese tanks had crushed it. As awful and degrading as the Nipomo labor camps and Los Angeles barrios might be, they were all that remained. For Carlos Bulosan, life in the American West still held the possibility of transformation, of becoming a place worth the struggle. In *America Is in the Heart,* California becomes a metaphor for the entire country—the promises of the Golden State are American Dreams writ bolder in a time of war—and he quickly transforms the nation itself to an interior landscape of yearning and release. "The world is an island," his brother Macario reminds him. "We are cast upon the sea of life hoping to land somewhere in the world. *But there is only one island, and it is in the heart.*"

ROBINSON JEFFERS

1887–1962

*Born to an educated family in Pennsylvania, young Robinson Jeffers
moved with them to Europe, where he attended private schools. The family
returned in 1903 to settle in Long Beach, and he entered Occidental College.
Already publishing poetry, he graduated at seventeen. He enrolled in the University of
Southern California in 1905, where he met Una Call Kuster, a married woman. Jeffers
emphasized classics and science at USC, completing medical school, and he and Una
wed in 1913. They moved to Carmel shortly afterward. After great success in the 1920s
and 1930s, he lost public favor with a succession of book-length dramatic poems, and
many critics attacked them as lurid, reactionary throwbacks to the Romantic era. He
espoused "inhumanism," a "shifting of emphasis from man to not-man"* (The Double
Axe) *and condemned Western society as anthropocentric, introverted, and fated to perish
soon. During World War II, his bitter attacks on Roosevelt and Churchill as the moral
peers of Hitler and Mussolini outraged many, and in 1948, Random House agreed to
publish* The Double Axe *only in an expurgated edition, with a strong editorial dis-
claimer. On his death in 1962, the author of twenty books was seen by many poets and
critics as an archaic memory. An enduring favorite of lay readers, he was rediscovered
by the Beat Generation and the later environmental movement. As the poet Gary Snyder
observes in a recent letter: "I read Jeffers when I was a teenager, again in my twenties,
and have read him on and off ever since. My generation mostly admired him—Whalen,
Welch, Parkinson, Everson. Even Robert Duncan (speaking for many poets) rolled his
eyes and said, 'Oh, Jeffers. He's too much!' but then grudged him his due. I found him
inspiring for his unrelenting critique of western civilization, mainly right on. Also, for
his great poetic evocations of the Pacific Ocean and West Coast landscapes and people.
And for his exploration of the long narrative poem: who else has done it with as much
energy as Robinson Jeffers? The recent environmental movement has taken him much
to heart. He will continue with us for a long time—as a thinker as much as a poet."
Stanford University Press recently issued the three-volume* Collected Poetry of Robinson Jeffers, Tor House *and* Hawk Tower *are open to the public as national historic
sites, and Jeffers influences many recent poets.*

Continent's End

At the equinox when the earth was veiled in a late rain, wreathed with wet
    poppies, waiting spring,
The ocean swelled for a far storm and beat its boundary, the ground-swell
    shook the beds of granite.

I gazing at the boundaries of granite and spray, the established sea-marks,
    felt behind me
Mountain and plain, the immense breadth of the continent, before me the
    mass and doubled stretch of water.

I said: You yoke the Aleutian seal-rocks with the lava and coral sowings that
    flower the south,
Over your flood the life that sought the sunrise faces ours that has followed
    the evening star.

The long migrations meet across you and it is nothing to you, you have for-
    gotten us, mother.
You were much younger when we crawled out of the womb and lay in the
    sun's eye on the tideline.

It was long and long ago; we have grown proud since then and you have
    grown bitter; life retains
Your mobile soft unquiet strength; and envies hardness, the insolent quiet-
    ness of stone.

The tides are in our veins, we still mirror the stars, life is your child, but
    there is in me
Older and harder than life and more impartial, the eye that watched before
    there was an ocean.

That watched you fill your beds out of the condensation of thin vapor and
    watched you change them,
That saw you soft and violent wear your boundaries down, eat rock, shift
    places with the continents.

Mother, though my song's measure is like your surf-beat's ancient rhythm I
    never learned it of you.
Before there was any water there were tides of fire, both our tones flow
    from the older fountain.

To the Stone Cutters

Stone-cutters fighting time with marble, you foredefeated
Challengers of oblivion
Eat cynical earnings, knowing rock splits, records fall down,
The square-limbed Roman letters
Scale in the thaws, wear in the rain. The poet as well
Builds his monument mockingly;
For man will be blotted out, the blind earth die, the brave sun
Die blind and blacken to the heart:
Yet stones have stood for a thousand years, and pained thoughts found
The honey of peace in old poems.

Tor House

If you should look for this place after a handful of lifetimes:
Perhaps of my planted forest a few
May stand yet, dark-leaved Australians or the coast cypress, haggard
With storm-drift; but fire and the axe are devils.
Look for foundations of sea-worn granite, my fingers had the art
To make stone love stone, you will find some remnant.
But if you should look in your idleness after ten thousand years:
It is the granite knoll on the granite
And lava tongue in the midst of the bay, by the mouth of the Carmel
River-valley, these four will remain
In the change of names. You will know it by the wild sea-fragrance of wind
Though the ocean may have climbed or retired a little;
You will know it by the valley inland that our sun and our moon were born
    from
Before the poles changed; and Orion in December
Evenings was strung in the throat of the valley like a lamp-lighted bridge.
Come in the morning you will see white gulls
Weaving a dance over blue water, the wane of the moon
Their dance-companion, a ghost walking
By daylight, but wider and whiter than any bird in the world.
My ghost you needn't look for; it is probably
Here, but a dark one, deep in the granite, not dancing on wind
With the mad wings and the day moon.

Robinson Jeffers

Hurt Hawks

I

The broken pillar of the wing jags from the clotted shoulder,
The wing trails like a banner in defeat,
No more to use the sky forever but live with famine
And pain a few days: cat nor coyote
Will shorten the week of waiting for death, there is game without talons.
He stands under the oak-bush and waits
The lame feet of salvation; at night he remembers freedom
And flies in a dream, the dawns ruin it.
He is strong and pain is worse to the strong, incapacity is worse.
The curs of the day come and torment him
At distance, no one but death the redeemer will humble that head,
The intrepid readiness, the terrible eyes.
The wild God of the world is sometimes merciful to those
That ask mercy, not often to the arrogant.
You do not know him, you communal people, or you have forgotten him;
Intemperate and savage, the hawk remembers him;
Beautiful and wild, the hawks, and men that are dying, remember him.

II

I'd sooner, except the penalties, kill a man than a hawk; but the great
    redtail
Had nothing left but unable misery
From the bone too shattered for mending, the wing that trailed under his
    talons when he moved.
We had fed him six weeks, I gave him freedom,
He wandered over the foreland hill and returned in the evening, asking for
    death,
Not like a beggar, still eyed with the old
Implacable arrogance. I gave him the lead gift in the twilight. What fell was
    relaxed,
Owl-downy, soft feminine feathers; but what
Soared: the fierce rush: the night-herons by the flooded river cried fear at
    its rising
Before it was quite unsheathed from reality.

Rock and Hawk

Here is a symbol in which
Many high tragic thoughts
Watch their own eyes.

This gray rock, standing tall
On the headland, where the seawind
Lets no tree grow,

Earthquake-proved, and signatured
By ages of storms: on its peak
A falcon has perched.

I think, here is your emblem
To hang in the future sky;
Not the cross, not the hive,

But this; bright power, dark peace;
Fierce consciousness joined with final
Disinterestedness;

Life with calm death; the falcon's
Realist eyes and act
Married to the massive

Mysticism of stone,
Which failure cannot cast down
Nor success make proud.

The Purse-Seine

Our sardine fishermen work at night in the dark of the moon; daylight or
    moonlight
They could not tell where to spread the net, unable to see the phosphores-
    cence of the shoals of fish.
They work northward from Monterey, coasting Santa Cruz; off New Year's
    Point or off Pigeon Point
The look-out man will see some lakes of milk-color light on the sea's night-
    purple; he points, and the helmsman
Turns the dark prow, the motor-boat circles the gleaming shoal and drifts
    out her seine-net. They close the circle
And purse the bottom of the net, then with great labor haul it in.

Robinson Jeffers

I cannot tell you
How beautiful the scene is, and a little terrible, then, when the crowded
    fish
Know they are caught, and wildly beat from one wall to the other of their
    closing destiny the phosphorescent
Water to a pool of flame, each beautiful slender body sheeted with flame,
    like a live rocket
A comet's tail wake of clear yellow flame; while outside the narrowing
Floats and cordage of the net great sea-lions come up to watch, sighing in
    the dark; the vast walls of night
Stand erect to the stars.

Lately I was looking from a night mountain-top
On a wide city, the colored splendor, galaxies of light: how could I help but
    recall the seine-net
Gathering the luminous fish? I cannot tell you how beautiful the city ap-
    peared, and a little terrible.
I thought, We have geared the machines and locked all together into inter-
    dependence; we have built the great cities; now
There is no escape. We have gathered vast populations incapable of free
    survival, insulated
From the strong earth, each person in himself helpless, on all dependent.
    The circle is closed, and the net
Is being hauled in. They hardly feel the cords drawing, yet they shine al-
    ready. The inevitable mass-disasters
Will not come in our time nor in our children's, but we and our children
Must watch the net draw narrower, government take all powers—or revolu-
    tion, and the new government
Take more than all, add to kept bodies kept souls—or anarchy, the mass-
    disasters.

These things are Progress;
Do you marvel our verse is troubled or frowning, while it keeps its reason?
    Or it lets go, lets the mood flow
In the manner of the recent young men into mere hysteria, splintered
    gleams, crackled laughter. But they are quite wrong.
There is no reason for amazement: surely one always knew that cultures
    decay, and life's end is death.

Carmel Point

The extraordinary patience of things!
This beautiful place defaced with a crop of suburban houses—
How beautiful when we first beheld it,
Unbroken field of poppy and lupin walled with clean cliffs;
No intrusion but two or three horses pasturing,
Or a few milch cows rubbing their flanks on the outcrop rockheads—
Now the spoiler has come: does it care?
Not faintly. It has all time. It knows the people are a tide
That swells and in time will ebb, and all
Their works dissolve. Meanwhile the image of the pristine beauty
Lives in the very grain of the granite,
Safe as the endless ocean that climbs our cliff.—As for us:
We must uncenter our minds from ourselves;
We must unhumanize our views a little, and become confident
As the rock and ocean that we were made from.

Robinson Jeffers

413

JAIME DE ANGULO
1887–1950

Born in France to Spanish expatriate parents, Jaime de Angulo was a rebellious child, and age did not mellow him. He arrived in Colorado in 1905 and worked as a cowboy. He was a wanderer throughout his life, moving from Colorado to South America and then to Honduras, ostensibly to mine silver. He completed medical school at Johns Hopkins University, and he came to California to take a job as a genetic researcher at Stanford University. Bored with medicine and science, he quit and used the remainder of a family inheritance to buy a cattle ranch in Alturas. This venture soon failed, but de Angulo made the acquaintance of some local Atchumawi (Pit River) Indians, and they opened a world to him that never closed. After World War I, he made his way to UC Berkeley, where the distinguished linguistic anthropologists Alfred Kroeber and Paul Radin taught. Under their direction he rekindled his fascination with the Atchumawi and plunged into serious study. His bohemian ways made Kroeber distinctly uneasy, but by 1921 de Angulo had prepared himself for field study of the Atchumawi culture and language. He took off for Modoc County, and his adventures are recounted in Indians in Overalls *(1950), a lively immersion into a timeless and perplexing way of life. The book was delayed in publication for almost thirty years, but with works such as* Indian Tales *(1953)—many reprinted since his death—de Angulo has come to be regarded as a pivotal figure in the rediscovery of California Indian peoples and their oral culture. Maddeningly idiosyncratic and a true California original, he is portrayed in* The Old Coyote of Big Sur: The Life of Jaime de Angulo, *a 1995 memoir by his daughter, Gui.*

From *Indians in Overalls*

Wild Bill said he would stay here and wait for Jack Folsom and the rest of the party to come back from the *atsuge* country. That evening he told me a lot about Coyote and the Coyote saga. The Coyote stories form a regular cycle, a saga. This is true of all of California; and it extends eastward even as far as the Pueblos of Arizona and New Mexico. Coyote has a double personality. He is at once the Creator, and the Fool. This antinomy is very important. Unless you understand it you will miss the Indian psychology completely—at least you will miss the significance of their literature (because I call their tales, their "old time stories," literature).

The wise man and the buffoon: the two aspects of Coyote, Coyote Old Man. Note that I don't call them the good and the evil, because that conception of morality does not seem to play much part in the Pit River attitude to life. Their mores are not much concerned with good and evil. You have a definite attitude toward moral right and moral wrong. I don't think the Pit River has. At least, if he has, he does not try to coerce. I have heard Indians say: "That's not right what he is doing, that fellow . . ."

"What do you mean it's not right?" ". . . Well . . . you ain't supposed to do things that way . . . it never was done that way . . . there'll be trouble." "Then why don't you stop him?" "Stop him? How can I stop him? It's his way."

The Pit Rivers (except the younger ones who have gone to the Government School at Fort Bidwell) don't ever seem to get a very clear conception of what you mean by the term God. This is true even of those who speak American fluently, like Wild Bill. He said to me: "What is this thing that the white people call God? They are always talking about it. It's goddamn this and this and goddamn that, and in the name of god, and the god made the world. Who is that god, Doc? They say that Coyote is the Indian God, but if I say to them that God is Coyote, they get mad at me. Why?"

"Listen, Bill, tell me . . . Do the Indians think, really think that Coyote made the world? I mean, do they really think so? Do you really think so?"

"Why of course I do . . . Why not? . . . Anyway . . . that's what the old people always said . . . only they don't all tell the same story. Here is one way I heard it: it seems like there was nothing anywhere but a kind of fog. Fog and water mixed, they say, no land anywhere, and this here Silver Fox . . ."

"You mean Coyote?"

"No, no, I mean Silver Fox. Coyote comes later. You'll see, but right now, somewhere in the fog, they say, Silver Fox was wandering and feeling lonely. *Tsikuellaaduwi maandza tsikualaasa.* He was feeling lonely, the Silver Fox. I wish I would meet someone, he said to himself, the Silver Fox did. He was walking along in the fog. He met Coyote. 'I thought I was going to meet someone,' he said. The Coyote looked at him, but he didn't say anything. 'Where are you traveling?' says Fox. 'But where are YOU traveling? Why do you travel like that?' 'Because I am worried.' 'I also am wandering,' said the Coyote, 'I also am worrying and traveling.' 'I thought I would meet someone. Let's you and I travel together. It's better for two people to be traveling together, that's what they always say. . . .' "

"Wait a minute, Bill. . . . Who said that?"

"The Fox said that. I don't know who he meant when he said: *that's what they always say.* It's funny, isn't it? How could he talk about *other* people since there had never been anybody before? I don't know . . . I wonder about that sometimes, myself. I have asked some of the old people and they say: That's what I have been wondering myself, but that's the way we have always heard it told. And then you hear the Paiutes tell it different! And our own people down the river, they also tell it a little bit different from us. Doc, maybe the whole thing never happened . . . And maybe it did happen but everybody tells it different. People often do that, you know. . . .

"Well, go on with the story. You said the Fox had met the Coyote. . . ."

"Oh, yah, . . . Well, this Coyote he says: 'What are we going to do now?' 'What do you think?' says the Fox. 'I don't know,' says Coyote. 'Well, then,' says Fox, 'I'll tell you: LET'S MAKE THE WORLD.' 'And how are we going to do that?' 'WE WILL SING,' says the Fox."

"So, there they were singing up there in the sky. They were singing and stomping and dancing around each other in a circle. Then the Fox he thought in his mind: CLUMP OF SOD, come!! That's the way he made it come: *by thinking*. Pretty soon he had it in his hands. And he was singing, all the while he had it in his hands. They were both singing and stomping. All of a sudden the Fox threw that clump of sod, that *tsapettia*, he threw it down into the clouds. 'Don't look down!' he said to the Coyote. 'Keep on singing! Shut your eyes, and keep them shut until I tell you.' So they kept on singing and stomping around each other in a circle for quite a while. Then the Fox said to the Coyote: 'Now look down there. What do you see?' 'I see something . . . I see something . . . but I don't know what it is.' 'All right. Shut your eyes again!' Now they started singing and stomping again, and the Fox thought and wished: Stretch! Stretch! 'Now look down again. What do you see?' 'Oh! It's getting bigger!' 'Shut your eyes again and don't look down!' And they went on singing and stomping up there in the sky. 'Now look down again!' 'Oooh! now it's big enough!' said the Coyote."

"That's the way they made the world, Doc. Then they both jumped down on it and they stretched it some more. Then they made mountains and valleys; they made trees and rocks and everything. It took them a long time to do all that!"

"Didn't they make people, too?"

"No. Not people. Not Indians. The Indians came much later, after the world was spoiled by a crazy woman, Loon. But that's a long story . . . I'll tell you some day."

"All right, Bill, but tell me just one thing now: there was a world now; then there were a lot of animals living on it, but there were no people then. . . ."

"Yes, they are . . . but . . . they are not Indians, but they are people, they are alive . . . Whad'you mean animal?"

"Well . . . how do you say 'animal' in Pit River?"

". . . I dunno . . ."

"But suppose you wanted to say it?"

"Well . . . I guess I would say something like *teeqaade-wade toolol aakaadzi* (world-over, all living) . . . I guess that means animals, Doc."

"I don't see how, Bill. That means people, also. People are living aren't they?"

"Sure they are! that's what I am telling you. Everything is living, even the rocks, even that bench you are sitting on. Somebody *made that bench for a purpose*, didn't he? Well then it's *alive*, isn't it? Everything is alive. That's what we Indians believe. White people think everything is dead . . ."

"Listen, Bill. How do you say 'people'?"

"I don't know . . . just *is,* I guess."

"I thought that meant 'Indian.' "

"Say . . . Ain't we *people?!*"

"So are the whites!"

"Like hell they are!! We call them *inillaaduwi,* 'tramps,' nothing but tramps. They don't believe anything is alive. They are dead themselves. I don't call that 'people.' They are smart, but they don't know anything. . . . Say, it's getting late, Doc. I am getting sleepy. I guess I'll go out and sleep on top of the haystack. . . ."

"But you'll die of cold! It's already freezing, these nights."

"Naw, I won't. I am an Indian. I am used to it."

"But, why don't you sleep here, inside?"

"WHAT?! Are you crazy? That woman might come and kill me."

"You mean Lena?"

"Shh! . . . Doc. For God's sake don't call her, don't call her name! Just say: the woman who died. That's bad enough. She is probable somewhere around, somewhere around here. They haven't burnt her things yet, you know, her baskets, her blankets, her clothes . . . all these things are calling her, are calling her shadow, her *de'lamdzi.*"

"But why should she hurt you?"

"She don't want to hurt me."

"But you just said she might kill you . . ."

"Well, she's take my shadow away with her, and then I'll die."

"What for would she take your shadow away with her?"

"Oh, to keep from getting lonely on the road to the land of the dead people."

"Where is that?"

"I dunno. Nobody knows. Somewhere out west. They say there is a big lake there, no end to it, and the dead people live there on an island . . . I dunno . . . that's what I've heard.

"But, Bill, I still don't see what she should want to take you there . . ."

"I just told you, Doc: to keep from getting lonely on the trip to the land of the dead. You would do the same thing yourself if you were going to a strange place. You would take along someone you knew and liked."

"Well then, she might take me, Bill. I know she liked me."

"Sure! That's why I tell you that you are a damn fool to sleep here!"

"Listen, Bill, tell me something else before you go . . . about the shadow, what do you call it, the *dalilamdzi*?"

"Naw, that means 'to make a shadow,' for instance *salilamdzi*, that means I am making a shadow. . . . No, Doc, I know what you are thinking about, that's the *de'lamdzi*, the shadow, that's not the same thing *dalilamdzi*, that's the shadow . . . oh, hell, I dunno what's the difference, it kind of sounds the same, don't it? Lissen: I remember when I was a little boy I used to hear the old men when they woke in the morning, they used to sing:

dalilamdzi walilamdzi de'lamdzi seena seena

the dawn   is dawning   a shadow   I come home, I come home

"So the *dalilamdzi*, that means the dawn, also! The old people they would hum like that when they woke up in the morning and they said: My shadow is liable to go wandering during the night and mebbe get lost and not find me again in the morning, that's why I sing to show him where I am! . . . Well, I think you are foolish to sleep here in this shack where she is liable to come back and take another look at her baskets that she made herself, and her stove, and everything, her shadow is, and it may ask your shadow to go along, and there will be no more Buckaroo Doc, and we will bury you and burn all your things, your saddle, and your book, and everything, and everybody will cry . . . well, good night, Doc!"

Wild Bill stayed there several days, waiting for Jack Folsom and the other people to come back from the Hat Creek country where they had buried "the woman who had died." He was an excellent raconteur and told me many old-time stories. There are tribes where the old-time stories and "myths" (as the anthropologists call them) are stereotyped, may even be cast in a rigid form and must be recited verbatim. But not so with the Pit Rivers! A poor storyteller gives you the barest outline, in short sentences (nearly all beginning with "and then"), in a monotonous voice. But a good raconteur like Wild Bill or old Mary tells it gestures, mimicry, imitation noises—a regular performance. If there are several people in the audience they grunt in approval after each telling passage. Instead of the applauding by clapping as we do, they raise their chins and say: Hunh. . . .

Finally, one day about noon, Jack and all the relatives returned; five or six wagons full of them, and immediately everything was confusion and pandemonium in this quiet corner of the sagebrush behind the little hill. They started a big bonfire. There was a lot of argument going on. Some of the people were still wailing. A woman would come dragging things out of the house, maybe two or three baskets, maybe an armful of clothes, and throw them into the fire; then she would go out a little way into the sagebrush and wail. The men were mostly silent and preoccupied; some of them wailed in man fashion: a sort of deep grunt, Honh-ho-ho, honh-ho-ho. . . . They carried things swiftly out of the house, threw them into the fire, and went back for more. Some of them were arguing (they wouldn't have been Pit Rivers if there hadn't been some kind of argument going on!); there was a little man who kept coming to me and complaining that they ought to burn the house, also. That seemed to be a moot point because in the old days there were no individual houses. And besides, according to Wild Bill, it was Jack's house, as well as the woman's who had died . . . But the little old man was all for destruction. At least they should throw the stove into the fire. "But it won't burn!" said Wild Bill. "Well, throw it into the creek, then," said the fundamentalist.

I was sitting in my little tent, trying to keep out of the way. All this happened so fast, like a whirlwind out of the sagebrush, that I was dazed. But everybody kept coming into my tent either to prove to me or to themselves that they were right, or to ask me if this or that object were mine, before throwing it into the fire. My copy of *Moby Dick* nearly went, and a horse's hackamore that belonged to me. Wild Bill stuck in my tent most of the time, sardonic as usual: "That's Indians for you! Just watch them, Doc. . . . Crazy goddamn bunch. Always argue, always argue; argue all the time . . . I wish they would get through with that burning. I have three colts I am breaking, at *Tuluukupi*, I left them in the corrals, I guess them fellows will feed them . . . still, I ought to be getting back to them."

Jack Folsom himself didn't seem to be doing anything except going around, wailing, crying, grunting. He came into my tent and sat on my cot and sobbed like a little child. "She was very good, that woman, Doc. She never quarreled. I have had four, no, five before her. We have been together a long time now. You know my daughter Jessie, well she raised her. Jessie has got grandchildren now."

"But Jack, I thought Jessie was this woman's daughter. . . ."

"No, another woman's. I have had three women already, no, four. No, two only, according to the Indian way. This woman I paid for her and she paid for me. That's according to the Indian law. I gave Jack Wilson, you know . . . the old fellow who was singing that night, I gave him a white mare, she was awful fast, she had won several races for me, and her people gave me the right to fish on Hat Creek. . . . But you noticed that woman that's come in with them? She is ordering everything around, she is bossing everybody. . . ."

"Yes, I noticed her. Who is she?"

"She is younger sister of woman who died, what we call *enun*, same as what you call 'cousin.' So, she has come to claim me."

"What do you mean, claim you?"

"It's this way, Doc: according to Indian law, *the dead people have got the say; the relations of the dead person have got the right.* If I had died, then my people, my relations, they are the ones who have the right to bring another man in my place. It don't matter he is an old man good for nothing. They say: We bought that woman, she belongs to us now; here's a man for her; she take him, or give us back our present; we gave you a horse for her; where is that horse? Now, this woman who died I married according to Indian law. So, her people, her relations, they come here with this other woman, and they say to me: You lost one, here's another, you got no claim against us."

"Well, then, it's all right, isn't it?

"No, it ain't all right, Doc. I don't want that woman. She is all right. She is young, I know. She is clean; she is a good worker . . . but she is bossy as hell! She'll boss me . . . I am too old to be bossed!"

Afterwards I took Jack down to my little ranch in the mountains south of Monterey. We had to go fifty miles by horse-stage, then fifteen miles more by trail over the ridges. When we were on top of the highest ridge the sun was dipping into the ocean, and we stopped to eat some sandwiches and make a little coffee. But before he ate, Jack chewed a piece and spat some to the east, and to the north, and to the south, and to the west. "See, Doc, I am doing that because I am in a new country. Them people you don't see, them coyotes and foxes and all kinds of *dinihowis* and *damaagomes* that live around here, they don't know me, because I am a stranger. They might hurt me. So I am telling them: I am all right, I don't mean no harm to you people, see, I am feeding you; and you people don't hurt me neither, because I am a stranger but I want to be friends with you. That's the way to do, Doc, that's the good way."

Night overtook us, and we went down the steep trail in the dark. Jack was stumbling. "Say, Doc, you sure picked you a darn steep country for your homestead." We reached the cabin at last, and I lit a fire in the hearth. There was an old rock mortar, of the kind the Indians use to pound acorns with a stone pestle. They still use them in Central California, but, for some reason which I don't understand, they don't use them anymore in Pit River country. Indeed, the Pit River Indians are afraid to touch them. "Them things are dangerous, Doc, them things are full of power. You come across one lying on the ground, some place; and next day you'll find him mebbe a mile further away! He moved during the night!" Whether it was only the ones who were lying abandoned "some place," or whether it was *all* mortars, I never found out. Anyway, I never saw any in use among the Pit Rivers. And now, Jack was very much shocked because I had one of these mortars lying near the hearth! "You shouldn't do that, Doc! He is getting too hot there, near the fire ... make him mad ... he is liable to hurt you, bring you bad luck, maybe make your children sick ..."

But Jack did not stay very long at my little ranch. He was having bad dreams. "I have been dreaming of blood, Doc. It's those people working against me, my wife's people, the one who died. They have got powerful doctors on their side. I should have married that sister of hers when she came to claim me. That's Indian law. I can't get out of it!"

So I put him on the stage and he went back to Modoc and the joys of matrimony.

When I saw him the next summer he looked subdued. He greeted me with his usual warmth, but when I asked him how he was getting along with quondam sister-in-law, he said, "Oh, it's hell, Doc, just hell. I don't draw a free breath of my own."

I saw him again the next summer. He was radiant. "I got rid of her, Doc. I was camped at Davis Creek, and her brother come and see me, and he says: Jack, I wouldn't stay with that woman, it I were you. She is too damn bossy! ... Well, Doc, that's all I wanted to hear. He was her elder brother, so he had the say. So I called my own boy, Millard, you know him, and I said: I am going—when that woman comes back to camp, don't tell her where I am gone—you don't know nothing about it, *sabe?*"

A few years later I found her married to Sukmit, of all people! But she had found her mate. They were yelling at each other, while old Mary smiled on complacently. Old Mary had earned her rest.

Upton Sinclair
1878–1968

Invited to visit California in 1909 by the bohemian poet George Sterling and the eccentric real estate developer Gaylord Wilshire, Upton Sinclair settled in Pasadena, where he lived for the rest of his life. He was a prominent writer when he arrived: The Jungle *(1906), his classic muckraking account of the corruption and brutality of the Chicago stockyards, had assured him a lasting place in American literary history. Sinclair was a writing machine, the author of more than one hundred books, and at last count he was also the most widely translated author in the history of the United States, with works appearing in more than fifty languages. His* Oil! *(1927) remains the most comprehensive account of the discovery of oil and the development of Los Angeles circa 1920. It focuses on the Signal Hill strike of 1921 that produced 250,000 barrels a day and poured immense wealth into Southern California— and on the ensuing corruption that reached to the top of the Harding administration and into the centers of international power. A lifelong teetotaler and vegetarian, Upton Sinclair was a utopian and a political zealot, and he fought an incessant battle against corporate capitalism and the social inequity it fostered in the United States. His crusades attracted considerable support in California, and he ran as a Socialist for Congress in 1920, for the Senate in 1922, and for governor of California in 1926. He waged his strongest campaign as the Democratic nominee for governor in 1934, running on the EPIC (End Poverty in California) platform as a remedy for the statewide ravages of the Great Depression.*

From *Oil!*

CHAPTER 1, PART 7. THE RIDE

The road was asphalt now; it shimmered in the heat, and whenever it fell away before you, a mirage made it look like water. It was lined with orange-groves; dark green shiny trees, golden with a part of last year's crop, and snowy-white with the new year's blossoms. Now and then a puff of breeze blew out, and you got a ravishing sweet odor. There were groves of walnuts, broad trees with ample foliage, casting dark shadows on the carefully culti-vated, powdery brown soil. There were hedges of roses, extending for long distances, eight or ten feet high, and covered with blossoms. There were wind-breaks of towering thin eucalyptus trees, with long wavy leaves and bark that scales off and leaves them naked; all the world is familiar with them in the moving pictures, where they do duty for sturdy oaks and ancient elms and spreading chestnuts and Arabian date-palms and cedars of Lebanon and whatever else the scenario calls for.

You had to cut your speed down here, and had to watch incessantly; there were intersections, and lanes coming in, and warning signs of many sorts; there was traffic both ways, and delicate decisions to he made as to whether you could get past the car ahead of you, before one coming in the other direction would bear down on you and shut you in a pair of scissors. It was exciting to watch Dad's handling of these emergencies, to read his intentions and watch him carry them out.

There were towns every five or ten miles now, and you were continually being slowed up by traffic, and continually being warned to conform to a rate of movement which would have irritated an able-bodied snail. The highway passed through the main street of each town; the merchants arranged that, Dad said, hoping you would get out and buy something at their places; if the highway were shifted to the outskirts of the town, to avoid traffic congestion, all the merchants would forthwith move to the highway! Sometimes they would put up signs, indicating a turn in the highway, attempting to lure the motorist onto a business street; after you had got to the end of that street, they would steer you back to the highway! Dad noted such tricks with the amused tolerance of a man who had worked them on others, but did not let anyone work them on him.

Each town consisted of some tens, or hundreds, or thousands of perfectly rectangular blocks, divided into perfectly rectangular lots, each containing a strictly modern bungalow, with a lawn and a house-wife holding a hose. On the outskirts would be one or more "subdivisions," as they were called; "acreage" was being laid out onto lots, and decorated with a row of red and yellow flags fluttering merrily in the breeze; also a row of red and yellow signs which asked questions and answered them with swift efficiency: "Gas? Yes." "Water? Best ever." "Lights? Right." "Restrictions? You bet." "Schools? Under construction." "Scenery? Beats the Alps."—and so on. There would be an office or a tent by the roadside, and in front of it an alert young man with a writing pad and a fountain-pen, prepared to write you a contract of sale after two minutes conversation. These subdividers had bought the land for a thousand dollars an acre, and soon as they had set up the fluttering little flags and the tent it became worth $1675 per lot. This also Dad explained with amused tolerance. It was a great country!

They were coming to the outskirts of Angel City. Here were trolley tracks and railroads, and subdivisions with no "restrictions"—that is, you might build any kind of house you pleased, and rent it to people of any race or color; which meant an ugly slum, spreading like a great sore, with shanties of tin and tar-paper and unpainted boards. There were great numbers of children playing here—for some strange reason there seemed to be more of them where they were least apt to thrive.

By dint of constant pushing and passing every other car, Dad had got on his schedule again. They skirted the city, avoiding the traffic crowds in its centre, and presently came a sign: "Beach City Boulevard." It was a wide asphalt road, with thousands of speeding cars, and more subdivisions and suburban home-sites, with endless ingenious advertisements designed to catch the fancy of the motorist, and cause him to put on brakes. The real estate men had apparently been reading the Arabian Nights and Grimm's fairy-tales; they were housed in little freak offices that shot up to a point, or tilted like a drunken sailor; their colors orange and pink, or blue and green, or with separately painted shingles, spotted with various colors. There were "good eats" signs and "barbecue" signs—the latter being a word which apparently had not been in the spelling-books when the sign-painters went to school. There were stands where you got orange-juice and cider, with orange-colored wicker chairs out in front for you to sit in. There were fruit and vegetable stands kept by Japs, and other stands with signs inviting you to "patronize Americans." There was simply no end of things to look at, each separate thing bringing its separate thrill to the mind of a thirteen-year old boy. The infinite strangeness and fascinatingness of this variegated world! Why do people do this, Dad? And why do they do that?

They came to Beach City, with its wide avenue along the ocean-front. Six-thirty, said the clock on the carts running-board—exactly on the schedule. They stopped before the big hotel, and Bunny got out of the car, and opened the hack compartment, and the bell-hop came hopping—you bet, for he knew Dad, and the dollars and half dollars that were jingling in Dad's pockets. The bell-hop grabbed the suit-cases and the overcoats, and carried them in, and the boy followed, feeling responsible and important, because Dad couldn't come yet, Dad had to put the car in a parking place. So Bunny strode in and looked about the lobby for Ben Skutt, the oil-scout, who was Dad's "lease-hound." There he was, seated in a big leather chair, puffing at a cigar and watching the door; he got up when he saw Bunny, and stretched his long, lean body, and twisted his lean, ugly face into a grin of welcome. The boy, very erect, remembering that he was J. Arnold Ross, junior, and representing his father in an important transaction, shook hands with the man, remarking: "Good evening, Mr. Skutt. Are the papers ready ?"

CHAPTER 2, PART 1

The number of the house was 5746 Los Robles Boulevard, and you would have had to know this land of hope in order to realize that it stood in a cabbage field. Los Robles means "the oaks"; and two or three miles away, where this boulevard started in the heart of Beach City, there were four live oak trees. But out here a bare slope of hill, quite steep, yet not too steep to be plowed and trenched and covered with cabbages, with sugar beets down on the flat. The eye of hope, aided by surveyors' instruments, had determined that some day a broad boulevard would run on this line; and so there was a dirt road, and at every corner white posts set up, with a wing north and a wing east—Los Robles Blvd.—Palomitas Ave.; Los Robles Blvd—El Centro Ave.; and so on.

Two years ago the "subdividers" had been here, with their outfit of little red and yellow flags; there had been full-page advertisements in the newspapers, and free auto rides from Beach City, and a free lunch, consisting of "hot dog" sandwiches, a slice of apple pie, and a cup of coffee. At that time the fields had been cleared of cabbages, and graded, and the lots had blossomed with little signs: "Sold." This was supposed to refer to the lot, but in time it came to refer to the purchaser. The company had undertaken to put in curbs and sidewalks, water and gas and sewers; but somebody made off with the money, and the enterprise went into bankruptcy, and presently new signs began to appear, "For Sale, by Owner," or "Bargain: See Smith and Headmutton, Real Estate." And when these signs brought no reply, the owners sighed, and reflected that some day when little Willie grew up he would make a profit out of that investment. Meantime, they would accept the proposition of Japanese truck-gardeners, to farm the land for one-third of the crop.

But three or four months ago something unexpected had happened. A man who owned an acre or two of land on the top of the hill had caused a couple of motor-trucks to come toiling up the slope, loaded with large square timbers of Oregon pine; carpenters had begun to work on these, and the neighborhood had stared, wondering what strange kind of house it could be. Suddenly the news had spread, in an explosion of excitement: an oil derrick!

A deputation called upon the owner, to find out what it meant. It was pure "wild-catting," he assured them; he happened to have a hundred thousand dollars to play with, and this was his idea of play. Nevertheless, the bargain signs came down from the cabbage fields, and were replaced by "Oil Lot for

Sale." Speculators began to look up the names and addresses of owners, and offers were made—there were rumors that some had got as high as a thousand dollars, nearly twice the original price of the lots. Motor-cars took to bumping out over the dirt roads, up and down the lanes; and on Saturday and Sunday afternoons there would be a crowd staring at the derrick.

The drilling began, and went on, monotonously and uneventfully. The local newspapers reported the results: the D. H. Culver Prospect No. 1 was at 1478 feet, in hard sandstone formation and no signs of oil. It was the same at 2,000, and at 3,000; and then for weeks the rig was "fishing" for a broken drill, and everybody lost interest; it was nothing but a "dry hole," and people who had refused double prices for their lots began to curse themselves for fools. "Wild-catting" was nothing but gambling anyhow—quite different from conservative investments in town lots. Then the papers reported that D. H. Culver Prospect No. 1 was drilling again; it was at 3059 feet, but the owners had not yet given up hope of striking something.

Then a strange thing happened. There came trucks, heavily loaded with stuff, carefully covered with canvas. Everybody connected with the enterprise had been warned or bribed to silence; but small boys peered under the canvas while the trucks were toiling up the hill with roaring motors, and they reported big sheets of curved metal, with holes along the edges for bolts. That could be only one thing, tanks. And at the same time came rumors that D. H. Culver had purchased another tract of land on the hill. The meaning of all this was obvious: Prospect No. 1 had got into oil sands!

The whole hill began to blossom with advertisements, and real estate agents swarmed to the "field." A magic word now—no longer cabbage field or sugar-beet field, but "*the* field!" Speculators set themselves up in tents, or did business from automobiles drawn up by the roadside, with canvas signs on them. There was coming and going all day long, and crowds of people gathered to stare up at the derrick, and listen to the monotonous grinding of the heavy drill that went round all day—"Ump-um–ump-um–ump-um–ump-um"—varied by the "puff puff" of the machine. "Keep out—this means you!" declared a conspicuous sign; Mr. D. H. Culver and his employees had somehow lost all their good breeding.

But suddenly there was no possibility of secrecy; literally all the world knew—for telegraph and cable carried the news to the farthest corners of civilization. The greatest oil strike in the history of Southern California, the Prospect Hill field! The inside of the earth seemed to burst out through that hole; a roaring and rushing, as Niagara, and a black column shot up into the air, two hundred feet, two hundred and fifty—no one could say for sure—-

and came thundering down to earth as a mass of thick, black, slimy, slippery fluid. It hurled tools and other heavy objects this way and that, so the men had to run for their lives. It filled the sump-hole, and poured over, like a sauce-pan boiling too fast, and went streaming down the hillside. Carried by the wind, a curtain of black mist, it sprayed the Culver homestead, turning it black, and sending the women of the household flying across the cabbage-fields. Afterwards it was told with Homeric laughter how these women had been heard to lament the destruction of their clothing and their window-curtains by this million-dollar flood of "black gold"!

Word spread by telephone to Beach City; the newspapers bulletined it, the crowds shouted it on the street, and before long the roads leading to Prospect Hill were black with a solid line of motor-cars. The news reached Angel City, the papers there put out "extras," and before nightfall the Beach City boule-vard was crowded with cars, a double line, all coming one way. Fifty thousand people stood in a solid ring at what they considered a safe distance from the gusher, with emergency policemen trying to drive them further back, and shouting: "Lights out! Lights out!" All night those words were chanted in a chorus; everybody realized the danger some one fool might forget and light a cigarette, and the whole hill-side would leap into flame; a nail in your shoe might do it, striking on a stone; or a motor-truck, with its steel-rimmed tires. Quite frequently these gushers caught fire at the first moment.

But still the crowds gathered; men put down the tops of their automobiles, and stood up in the seats and conducted auction rooms by the light of the stars. Lots were offered for sale at fabulous prices, and some of them were bought; leases were offered, companies were started and shares sold—the traders would push their way out of the crowd to a safe distance on the wind-ward side, where they could strike a match, and see each other's faces, and scrawl a memorandum of what they agreed. Such trading went on most of the night, and in the morning came big tents that had been built for revival meetings, and the cabbage fields became gay with red and black signs:

"Beach Co-operative No. 1," "Skite Syndicate, No. 1, ten thousand units, $10."

Meantime the workmen were toiling like mad to stop the flow of the well; they staggered here and there, half blinded by the black spray—and with no place to brace themselves, nothing they could hold onto, because everything was greased, streaming with grease. You worked in darkness, groping about, with nothing but the roar of the monster, his blows upon your body, his spitting in your face, to tell you where he was. You worked at high tension, for there were bonuses offered—fifty dollars for each man if you stopped the flow before midnight, a hundred dollars if you stopped it before ten o'clock. No one could figure how much wealth that monster was wasting, but it must be thousands of dollars every minute. Mr. Culver himself pitched in to help, and in his reckless efforts lost both of his ear-drums. "Tried to stop the flow with his head," said a workman, unsympathetically. In addition the owner discovered, in the course of ensuing weeks, that he had accumulated a total of forty-two suits for damages to houses, clothing, chickens, goats, cows, cabbages, sugar-beets, and automobiles which had skidded into ditches on too well-greased roads.

Dashiell Hammett

1894–1961

With Raymond Chandler, Hammett fashioned a new kind of detective story and hero, spawned in the cities of the West Coast, shaped by the cynicism that followed the excesses of post–World War I America. In Chandler's view the tone and style were largely Hammett's doing, as he wrote in a 1948 letter: "I did not invent the hardboiled murder story and I have never made any secret that Hammett deserves most or all of the credit." Born in Maryland, Hammett never finished high school, working at odd jobs until a four-year stint with the Pinkerton National Detective Agency. During World War I, he served in the U.S. Army Ambulance Corps. There he contracted influenza, leading to a lifelong series of lung ailments. By 1919, he was once again a Pinkerton agent, a job that brought him west to San Francisco. When poor health forced him to give up detective work, he started writing stories based on his experience. Soon his fictional "Continental Op," world-weary and unflappable, was rubber-soling around the city's streets. Between 1923 and 1927, thirty-two of these stories appeared in Black Mask, *the famous mystery magazine founded by H. L. Mencken and George Jean Nathan. An installment of his first novel,* Red Harvest, *appeared there in 1927. With* The Dain Curse, *it was published by Knopf in 1929. His most famous novel,* The Maltese Falcon, *soon followed, starring the Satan-faced San Francisco private eye Sam Spade. Both the novel and the 1941 film, directed by John Huston, are considered American classics. After* The Glass Key *(1930) and* The Thin Man *(1934), Hammett stopped writing fiction. He moved south to Hollywood and worked in film until after World War II, when he returned permanently to New York.*

Chapter 6
from *The Maltese Falcon*

For half an hour after Joel Cairo had gone Spade sat alone, still and frowning, at his desk. Then he said aloud in the tone of one dismissing a problem, "Well, they're paying for it," and took a bottle of Manhattan cocktail and a paper drinking-cup from a desk-drawer. He filled the cup two-thirds full, drank, returned the bottle to the drawer, tossed the cup into the wastebasket, put on his hat and overcoat, turned off the lights, and went down to the night-lit street.

An undersized youth of twenty or twenty-one in neat grey cap and overcoat was standing idly on the corner below Spade's building.

Spade walked up Sutter Street to Kearny, where he entered a cigar-store to buy two sacks of Bull Durham. When he came out the youth was one of four people waiting for a street-car on the opposite corner.

Spade ate dinner at Herbert's Grill in Powell Street. When he left the Grill, at a quarter to eight, the youth was looking into a nearby haberdasher's window.

Spade went to the Hotel Belvedere, asking at the desk for Mr. Cairo. He was told that Cairo was not in. The youth sat in a chair in a far corner of the lobby.

Spade went to the Geary Theatre, failed to see Cairo in the lobby, and posted himself on the curb in front, facing the theatre. The youth loitered with other loiterers before Marquard's restaurant below.

At ten minutes past eight Joel Cairo appeared, walking up Geary Street with his little mincing bobbing steps. Apparently he did not see Spade until the private detective touched his shoulder. He seemed moderately surprised for a moment, and then said: "Oh. yes, of course you saw the ticket."

"Uh-huh. I've got something I want to show you." Spade drew Cairo back towards the curb a little away from the other waiting theatre-goers. "The kid in the cap down by Marquard's."

Cairo murmured, "I'll see," and looked at his watch. He looked up Geary Street. He looked at a theatre-sign in front of him on which George Arliss was shown costumed as Shylock, and then his dark eyes crawled sidewise in their sockets until they were looking at the kid in the cap, at his cool pale face with curling lashes hiding lowered eyes.

"Who is he?" Spade asked.

Cairo smiled up at Spade. "I do not know him."

"He's been tailing me around town."

Cairo wet his lower lip with his tongue and asked: "Do you think it was wise, then, to let him see us together?"

"How do I know?" Spade replied. "Anyway, it's done."

Cairo removed his hat and smoothed his hair with a gloved hand. He replaced his hat carefully on his head and said with every appearance of candor: "I give you my word I do not know him, Mr. Spade. I give you my word I have nothing to do with him. I have asked nobody's assistance except yours, on my word of honor."

"Then he's one of the others?"

"That may be."

"I just wanted to know, because if he gets to be a nuisance I may have to hurt him."

"Do as you think best. He is not a friend of mine."

"That's good. There goes the curtain. Good night." Spade said, and crossed the street to board a westbound street-car.

The youth in the cap boarded the same car.

Spade left the car at Hyde Street and went up to his apartment. His rooms were not greatly upset, but showed unmistakable signs of having been searched. When Spade had washed and had put on a fresh shirt and collar he went out again, walked up to Sutter Street, and boarded a westbound car. The youth boarded it also.

Within half a dozen blocks of the Coronet Spade left the car and went into the vestibule of a tall brown apartment-building. He pressed three bell-buttons together. The street-door-lock buzzed. He entered, passed the elevator and stairs, went down a long yellow-walled corridor to the rear of the building, found a back door fastened by a Yale lock, and let himself out into a narrow court. The court led to a dark back street, up which Spade walked for two blocks. Then he crossed over to California Street and went to the Coronet. It was not quite half-past nine o'clock.

The eagerness with which Brigid O'Shaughnessy welcomed Spade suggested that she had been not entirely certain of his coming. She had put on a satin gown of the blue shade called Artoise that season, with chalcedony shoulder-straps, and her stockings and slippers were Artoise.

The red and cream sitting-room had been brought to order and livened with flowers in squat pottery vases of black and silver. Three small rough-barked logs burned in the fireplace. Spade watched them burn while she put away his hat and coat.

"Do you bring me good news?" she asked when she came into the room again. Anxiety looked through her smile, and she held her breath.

"We won't have to make anything public that hasn't already been made public."

"The police won't have to know about me?"

"No."

She sighed happily and sat on the walnut settee. Her face relaxed and her body relaxed. She smiled up at him with admiring eyes. "However did you manage it?" she asked more in wonder than in curiosity.

"Most things in San Francisco can be bought, or taken."

"And you won't get into trouble? Do sit down." She made room for him on the settee.

"I don't mind a reasonable amount of trouble," he said with not too much complacence.

He stood beside the fireplace and looked at her with eyes that studied, weighed, judged her without pretense that they were not studying, weighing, judging her. She flushed slightly under the frankness of his scrutiny, but she seemed more sure of herself than before, though a becoming shyness had not left her eyes. He stood there until it seemed plain that he meant to ignore her invitation to sit beside her, and then crossed to the settee.

"You aren't," he asked as he sat down, "exactly the sort of person you pretend to be, are you?"

"I'm not sure I know what you mean," she said in her hushed voice, looking at him with puzzled eyes.

"Schoolgirl manner," he explained, "stammering and blushing and all that."

She blushed and replied hurriedly, not looking at him: "I told you this afternoon that I've been bad—worse than you could know."

"That's what I mean," he said. "You told me that this afternoon in the same words, same tone. It's a speech you've practiced."

After a moment in which she seemed confused almost to the point of tears she laughed and said: "Very well, then, Mr. Spade. I'm not at all the sort of person I pretend to be. I'm eighty years old, incredibly wicked, and an iron-molder by trade. But if it's a pose it's one I've grown into, so you won't expect me to drop it entirely, will you?"

"Oh, it's all right," he assured her. "Only it wouldn't be all right if you were actually that innocent. We'd never get anywhere."

"I won't be innocent," she promised with a hand on her heart.

"I saw Joel Cairo tonight," he said in the manner of one making polite conversation.

Gaiety went out of her face. Her eyes, focused on his profile, became frightened, then cautious. He had stretched his legs out and was looking at his crossed feet. His face did not indicate that he was thinking about anything.

There was a long pause before she asked uneasily:

"You—you know him?"

"I saw him tonight." Spade did not look up and he maintained his light conversational tone. "He was going to see George Arliss."

"You mean you talked to him?"

"Only for a minute or two, till the curtain-bell rang.

She got up from the settee and went to the fireplace to poke the fire. She changed slightly the position of an ornament on the mantelpiece, crossed the room to get a box of cigarettes from a table in a corner, straightened a curtain, and returned to her seat. Her face now was smooth and unworried.

Spade grinned sidewise at her and said: "You're good. You're very good."

Her face did not change. She asked quietly: "What did he say?"

"About what?"

She hesitated. "About me."

"Nothing." Spade turned to hold his lighter under the end of her cigarette. His eyes were shiny in a wooden satan's face.

"Well, what did he say?" she asked with half-playful petulance.

"He offered me five thousand dollars for the black bird."

She started, her teeth tore the end of her cigarette, and her eyes, after a swift alarmed glance at Spade, turned away from him.

"You're not going to go around poking at the fire and straightening up the room again, are you?" he asked lazily.

She laughed a clear merry laugh, dropped the mangled cigarette into a tray, and looked at him with clear merry eyes. "I won't," she promised. "And what did you say?"

"Five thousand dollars is a lot of money."

She smiled, but when, instead of smiling, he looked gravely at her, her smile became faint, confused, and presently vanished. In its place came a hurt, bewildered look "Surely you're not really considering it," she said.

"Why not? Five thousand dollars is a lot of money."

"But, Mr. Spade, you promised to help me." Her hands were on his arm. "I trusted you. You can't—" She broke off, took her hands from his sleeve and worked them together.

Spade smiled gently into her troubled eyes. "Don't let's try to figure out how much you've trusted me," he said. "I promised to help you—sure—but you didn't say anything about any black birds."

"But you must've known or—or you wouldn't have mentioned it to me. You do know now. You won't—you can't—treat me like that." Her eyes were cobalt-blue prayers.

"Five thousand dollars is," he said for the third time, "a lot of money."

She lifted her shoulders and hands and let them fall in a gesture that accepted defeat. "It is," she agreed in a small dull voice. "It is far more than I could ever offer you, if I must bid for your loyalty."

Spade laughed. His laughter was brief and somewhat bitter. "That is good," he said, "coming from you. What have you given me besides money? Have you given me any of your confidence? any of the truth? any help in helping you? Haven't you tried to buy my loyalty with money and nothing else? Well, if I'm peddling it, why shouldn't I let it go to the highest bidder?"

"I've given you all the money I have." Tears glistened in her white-ringed eyes. Her voice was hoarse, vibrant. "I've thrown myself on your mercy, told you that without your help I'm utterly lost. What else is there?" She suddenly moved close to him on the settee and cried angrily: "Can I buy you with my body?"

Their faces were a few inches apart. Spade took her face between his hands and he kissed her mouth roughly and contemptuously. Then he sat back and said: "I'll think it over." His face was hard and furious.

She sat still holding her numbed face where his hands had left it.

He stood up and said: "Christ! there's no sense to this." He took two steps towards the fireplace and stopped, glowering at the burning logs, grinding his teeth together.

She did not move.

He turned to face her. The two vertical lines above his nose were deep clefts between red wales. "I don't give a damn about your honesty," he told her, trying to make himself speak calmly. "I don't care what kind of tricks you're up to, what your secrets are, but I've got to have something to show that you know what you're doing."

"I do know. Please believe that I do, and that it's all for the best, and—"

"Show me," he ordered. "I'm willing to help you. I've done what I could so far. If necessary I'll go ahead blindfolded, but I can't do it without more confidence in you than I've got now. You've got to convince me that you know what it's all about, that you're not simply fiddling around by guess and by God, hoping it'll come out all right somehow in the end."

"Can't you trust me just a little longer?"

"How much is a little? And what are you waiting for?"

She bit her lip and looked down. "I must talk to Joel Cairo," she said almost inaudibly.

"You can see him tonight," Spade said, looking at his watch. "His show will be out soon. We can get him on the phone at his hotel."

She raised her eyes, alarmed. "But he can't come here. I can't let him know where I am. I'm afraid."

"My place," Spade suggested.

She hesitated, working her lips together, then asked: "Do you think he'd go there?"

Spade nodded.

"All right," she exclaimed, jumping up, her eyes large and bright. "Shall we go now?"

She went into the next room. Spade went to the table in the corner and silently pulled the drawer out. The drawer held two packs of playing-cards, a pad of score-cards for bridge, a brass screw, a piece of red string, and a gold pencil. He had shut the drawer and was lighting a cigarette when she returned wearing a small dark hat and a grey kidskin coat, carrying his hat and coat.

Their taxicab drew up behind a dark sedan that stood directly in front of Spade's street-door. Iva Archer was alone in the sedan, sitting at the wheel. Spade lifted his hat to her and went indoors with Brigid O'Shaughnessy. In the lobby he halted beside one of the benches and asked: "Do you mind waiting here a moment? I won't be long."

"That's perfectly all right," Brigid O'Shaughnessy said, sitting down. "You needn't hurry."

Spade went out to the sedan. When he had opened the sedan's door Iva spoke quickly. "I've got to talk to you, Sam. Can't I come in?" Her face was pale and nervous.

"Not now."

Iva clicked her teeth together and asked sharply, "Who is she?'

"I've only a minute, Iva," Spade said patiently. "What is it?"

"Who is she?" she repeated, nodding at the street-door.

He looked away from her, down the street. In front of a garage on the next corner an undersized youth of twenty or twenty-one in neat grey cap and overcoat loafed with his back against a wall. Spade frowned and returned his gaze to Iva's insistent face. "What is the matter?" he asked. "Has anything happened? You oughtn't to be here at this time of night."

"I'm beginning to believe that," she complained. "You told me I oughtn't to come to the office, and now I oughtn't to come here. Do you mean I oughtn't to chase after you? If that's what you mean why don't you say it right out?"

"Now, Iva, you've got no right to take that attitude."

"I know I haven't. I haven't any rights at all, it seems, where you're concerned. I thought I did. I thought your pretending to love me gave me—"

Spade said wearily: "This is no time to be arguing about that, precious. What was it you wanted to see me about?"

"I can't talk to you here, Sam. Can't I come in?"

"Not now."

"Why can't I?"

Spade said nothing.

She made a thin line of her mouth, squirmed around straight behind the wheel, and started the sedan's engine, staring angrily ahead.

When the sedan began to move Spade said, "Good night, Iva," shut the door, and stood at the curb with his hat in his hand until it had been driven away. Then he went indoors again.

Brigid O'Shaughnessy rose smiling cheerfully from the bench and they went up to his apartment.

Wallace Thurman

1902–1934

Wallace Thurman was a native of Salt Lake City, and he came to the University of Southern California in 1922. He used USC as a principal setting for his first novel, The Blacker the Berry (1929), a widely praised indictment of intraracial color prejudice. He modeled his protagonist, Emma Lou Morgan, after his own experiences as a dark-skinned African American, and the novel is a rare and accurate picture of black middle-class life in Los Angeles during Prohibition. Working as a postal worker (as did Arna Bontemps), he was excited by the news from New York of the Harlem Renaissance and spent his free hours trying to spark a parallel West Coast literary movement. He founded Outlet, a magazine that survived for only a year and a half. Discouraged, he moved to New York in 1925. With Bontemps, he became a major figure in the black art, drama, music, and literary movement that influenced American culture in the 1920s and established African American arts in many forms. Gay, gifted, and versatile, iconoclastic and hard-drinking, Thurman became managing editor of the Messenger, the literary journal of the NAACP, publishing first works by Zora Neale Hurston, Langston Hughes, and many others. Shortly before the end of his short and turbulent life, he moved back to California to earn a huge salary as a screenwriter. He wrote two scripts, both of which were made into feature films: Tomorrow's Children (1934) and High School Girl (1935). Prolific during his short life and now a key figure in modern black literature, Thurman also wrote two other novels, of which Infants of Spring (1932) is the more significant.

From The Blacker the Berry

She had arrived in Los Angeles a week before registration day at the university, and had spent her time in being shown and seeing the city. But whenever these sightseeing excursions took her away from the sections where Negroes lived, she immediately lost all interest in what she was being shown. The Pacific Ocean in itself did not cause her heart beat to quicken, nor did the roaring of its waves find an emotional echo within her. But on coming upon Bruce's Beach for colored people near Redondo, or the little strip of sandied shore they had appropriated for themselves at Santa Monica, the Pacific Ocean became an intriguing something to contemplate as a background for their activities. Everything was interesting as it was patronized, reflected through, or acquired by Negroes.

Her Uncle Joe had been right. Here, in the colored social circles of Los Angeles, Emma Lou was certain that she would find many suitable companions, intelligent, broad-minded people of all complexions, intermixing and being too occupied otherwise to worry about either their own skin color or the skin color of those around them. Her Uncle Joe had said that Negroes were Negroes whether they happened to be yellow, brown, or black, and a conscious effort to eliminate the darker elements would neither prove or solve anything. There was nothing quite so silly as the creed of the blue veins: "Whiter and whiter, every generation. The nearer white you are the more white people will respect you. Therefore all light Negroes marry light Negroes. Continue to do so generation after generation, and eventually white people will accept this racially, bastard aristocracy, thus enabling those Negroes who really matter to escape the social and economic inferiority of the American Negro."

Such had been the credo of her grandmother and of her mother and of their small circle of friends in Boise. But Boise was a provincial town, given to the molding of provincial people with provincial minds. Boise was a backwoods town out of the main stream of modern thought and progress. Its people were cramped and narrow, their intellectual concepts stereotyped and static. Los Angeles was a happy contrast in all respects.

.   .   .

On registration day, Emma Lou rushed out to the campus of the University of Southern California one hour before the registrar's office was scheduled to open. She spent the time roaming around, familiarizing herself with the layout of the campus and learning the names of the various buildings, some old and vineclad, others new and shiny in the sun, and watching the crowds of laughing students, rushing to and fro, greeting one another and talking over their plans for the coming school year. But her main reason for such an early arrival on the campus had been to find some of her fellow Negro students. She had heard that there were to be quite a number enrolled, but in all her hour's stroll she saw not one, and finally somewhat disheartened she got into the line stretched out in front of the registrar's office, and, for the moment, became engrossed in becoming a college freshman.

All the while, though, she kept searching for a colored face, but it was not until she had been duly signed up as a student and sent in search of her advisor that she saw one. Then three colored girls had sauntered into the room where she was having a conference with her advisor, sauntered in, arms interlocked, greeted her advisor, then sauntered out again. Emma Lou had wanted to rush after them – to introduce herself, but of course it had been impossible under the circumstances. She had immediately taken a liking to all three, each of whom was what is known in the parlance of the black belt as high brown, with modishly-shingled bobbed hair and well formed bodies, fashionably attired in flashy sport garments. From then on Emma Lou paid little attention to the business of choosing subjects and class hours, so little attention in fact that the advisor thought her exceptionally tractable and some-what dumb. But she liked students to come that way. It made the task of being advisor easy. . . .

Hazel Mason was the girl's name. Emma Lou had fully expected it to be either Hyacinth or Geranium. Hazel was from Texas, Prairie Valley, Texas, and she told Emma Lou that her father, having become quite wealthy when oil had been found on his farm lands, had been enabled to realize two life ambitions—obtain a Packard touring car and send his only daughter to a "fust-class" white school.

Emma Lou had planned to loiter around the campus. She was still eager to become acquainted with the colored members of the student body, and this encounter with the crass and vulgar Hazel Mason had only made her the more eager. She resented being approached by any one so flagrantly inferior, any one so noticeably a typical southern darky, who had no business obtruding into the more refined scheme of things. Emma Lou planned to lose her un-welcome companion somewhere on the campus so that she could continue unhindered her quest for agreeable acquaintances.

But Hazel was as anxious to meet some one as was Emma Lou, and having found her was not going to let her get away without a struggle. She, too, was new to this environment and in a way was more lonely and eager for the companionship of her own kind than Emma Lou, for never before had she come into such close contact with so many whites. Her life had been spent only among Negroes. Her fellow pupils and teachers in school had always been colored, and as she confessed to Emma Lou, she couldn't get used "to all these white folks."

"Honey, I was just achin' to see a black face," she had said, and, though Emma Lou was experiencing the same ache, she found herself unable to sympathize with the other girl, for Emma Lou classified Hazel as a barbarian who had most certainly not come from a family of best people. No doubt her mother had been a washerwoman. No doubt she had innumerable relatives and friends all as ignorant and as ugly as she. There was no sense in any one having a face as ugly as Hazel's, and Emma Lou thanked her stars that though she was black, her skin was not rough and pimply, nor was her hair kinky, nor were her nostrils completely flattened out until they seemed to spread all over her face. No wonder people were prejudiced against dark skinned people when they were so ugly, so haphazard in their dress, and so boisterously mannered as was this present specimen. She herself was black, but nevertheless she had come from a good family, and she could easily take her place in a society of the right sort of people.

The two strolled along the lawn-bordered gravel path which led to a vine-covered building at the end of the campus. Hazel never ceased talking. She kept shouting at Emma Lou, shouting all sorts of personal intimacies as if she were desirous of the whole world hearing them. There was no necessity for her to talk so loudly, no necessity for her to afford every one on the crowded campus the chance to stare and laugh at them as they passed. Emma Lou had never before been so humiliated and so embarrassed. She felt that she must get away from her offensive companion. What did she care if she had to hurt her feelings to do so. The more insulting she could be now, the less friendly she would have to be in the future.

"Good-by," she said abruptly, "I must go home." With which she turned away and walked rapidly in the opposite direction. She had only gone a few steps when she was aware of the fact that the girl was following her. She quickened her pace, but the girl caught up with her and grabbing hold of Emma Lou's arm, shouted,

"Whoa there, Sally."

It seemed to Emma Lou as if every one on the campus was viewing and enjoying this minstrel-like performance. Angrily she tried to jerk away, but the girl held fast.

"Gal, you sure walk fast. I'm going your way. Come on, let me drive you home in my buggy."

And still holding on to Emma Lou's arm, she led the way to the side street where the students parked their cars. Emma Lou was powerless to resist. The girl didn't give her a chance, for she held tight, then immediately resumed the monologue which Emma Lou's attempted leave-taking had interrupted. They reached the street, Hazel still talking loudly, and making elaborate gestures with her free hand.

"Here we are," she shouted and releasing Emma Lou's arm, salaamed before a sport model Stutz roadster. "Oscar," she continued, "meet the new girl friend. Pleased to meetcha, says he. Climb aboard."

And Emma Lou had climbed aboard, perplexed, chagrined, thoroughly angry, and disgusted. What was this little black fool doing with a Stutz road-ster? And of course, it would be painted red—Negroes always bedecked them-selves and their belongings in ridiculously unbecoming colors and orna-ments. It seemed to be a part of their primitive heritage which they did not seem to have sense enough to forget and deny. Black girl—white hat—red and white striped sport suit—white shoes and stockings—red roadster. The picture was complete. All Hazel needed to complete her circus-like appear-ance, thought Emma Lou, was to have some purple feathers stuck in her hat.

Still talking, the girl unlocked and proceeded to start the car. As she was backing it out of the narrow parking space, Emma Lou heard a chorus of semi-suppressed giggles from a neighboring automobile. In her anger she had failed to notice that there were people in the car parked next to the Stutz. But as Hazel expertly swung her machine around, Emma Lou caught a glimpse of them. They were all colored and they were all staring at her and at Hazel. She thought she recognized one of the girls as being one of the group she had seen earlier that morning, and she did recognize the two broth-ers she had passed on the stairs. And as the roadster sped away, their laughter echoed in her ears, although she hadn't actually heard it. But she had seen the strain in their faces, and she knew that as soon as she and Hazel were out of sight, they would give free rein to their suppressed mirth.

Although Emma Lou had finished registering, she returned to the univer-sity campus on the following morning in order to continue her quest for collegiate companions without the alarming and unwelcome presence of Ha-zel Mason. She didn't know whether to be sorry for the girl and try to help her or to be disgusted and avoid her. She didn't want to be intimately asso-ciated with any such vulgar person. It would damage her own position, cause her to be classified with some one who was in a class by herself, for Emma Lou was certain that there was not, and could not be, any one else in the university just like Hazel. But despite her vulgarity, the girl was not all bad. Her good nature was infectious, and Emma Lou had surmised from her monologue on the day before how utterly unselfish a person she could be and was. All of her store of the world's goods were at hand to be used and enjoyed by her friends. There was not, as she had said, "a selfish bone in her body." But even that did not alter the disgusting fact that she was not one who would be welcome by the "right sort of people." Her flamboyant style of dress, her loud voice, her raucous laughter, and her flagrant disregard or ignorance of English grammar seemed inexcusable to Emma Lou, who was unable to un-derstand how such a person could stray so far from the environment in which she rightfully belonged to enter a first class university. Now Hazel, according to Emma Lou, was the type of Negro who should go to a Negro college. There were plenty of them in the South whose standard of scholarship was not beyond her ability. And then, in one of those schools, her darky-like clownishness would not have to be paraded in front of white people, thereby causing discomfort and embarrassment to others of her race, more civilized and circumspect than she.

The problem irritated Emma Lou. She didn't see why it had to be. She had looked forward so anxiously, and so happily to her introductory days on the campus, and now her first experience with one of her fellow colored students had been an unpleasant one. But she didn't intend to let that make her unhappy. She was determined to return to the campus alone, seek out other companions, see whether they accepted or ignored the offending Hazel, and govern herself accordingly.

. . .

Two weeks of school had left Emma Lou's mind in a chaotic state. She was unable to draw any coherent conclusions from the jumble of new things she had experienced. In addition to her own social strivings, there had been the academic routine to which she had had to adapt herself. She had found it all bewildering and overpowering. The university was a huge business proposition and every one in it had jobs to perform. Its bigness awed her. Its blatant reality shocked her. There was nothing romantic about going to college. It was, indeed, a serious business. One went there with a purpose and had several other purposes inculcated into one after school began. This getting an education was stern and serious, regulated and systematized, dull and unemotional.

Besides being disappointed at the drabness and lack of romance in college routine, Emma Lou was also depressed by her inability to make much headway in the matter of becoming intimately associated with her colored campus mates. They were all polite enough. They all acknowledged their introductions to her and would speak whenever they passed her, but seldom did any of them stop for a chat, and when she joined the various groups which gathered on the campus lawn between classes, she always felt excluded and out of things because she found herself unable to participate in the general conversation. They talked of things about which she knew nothing, of parties and dances, and of people she did not know. They seemed to live a life off the campus to which she was not privy, and into which they did not seem particularly anxious to introduce her.

She wondered why she never knew of the parties they talked about, and why she never received invitations to any of their affairs. Perhaps it was because she was still new and comparatively unknown to them. She felt that she must not forget that most of them had known one another for a long period of time and that it was necessary for people who "belonged" to be wary of strangers. That was it. She was still a stranger, had only been among them for about two weeks. What did she expect? Why was she so impatient?

The thought of the color question presented itself to her time and time again, but she would always dismiss it from her mind. Verne Davis was dark and she was not excluded from the sacred inner circle. In fact, she was one of the most popular colored girls on the campus. The only thing that perplexed Emma Lou was that although Verne too was new to the group, had just recently moved into the city, and was also just beginning her first year at the University, she had not been kept at a distance or excluded from any of the major extra-collegiate activities. Emma Lou could not understand why there should be this difference in their social acceptance. She was certainly as good as Verne.

In time Emma Lou became certain that it was because of her intimacy with Hazel that the people on the campus she really wished to be friendly with paid her so little attention. Hazel was a veritable clown. She went scooting about the campus, cutting capers, playing the darky for the amused white students. Any time Hazel asked or answered a question in any of the lecture halls, there was certain to be laughter. She had a way of phrasing what she wished to say in a manner which was invariably laugh provoking. The very tone and quality of her voice designated her as a minstrel type. In the gymnasium she would do buck and wing dances and play low-down blues on the piano. She was a pariah among her own people because she did not seem to know, as they knew, that Negroes could not afford to be funny in front of white people even if that was their natural inclination. Negroes must always be sober and serious in order to impress white people with their adaptability and non-difference in all salient characteristics save skin color. All of the Negro students on the campus, except Emma Lou, laughed at her openly and called her Topsy. Emma Lou felt sorry for her although she, too, regretted her comic propensities and wished that she would be less the vaudevillian and more the college student.

Besides Hazel, there was only one other person on the campus who was friendly with Emma Lou. This was Grace Giles, also a black girl, who was registered in the School of Music. The building in which she had her classes was located some distance away, and Grace did not get over to the main campus grounds very often, but when she did, she always looked for Emma

Lou and made welcome overtures of friendship. It was her second year in the university, and yet, she too seemed to be on the outside of things. She didn't seem to be invited to the parties and dances, nor was she a member of the Greek letter sorority which the colored girls had organized. Emma Lou asked her why.

"Have they pledged you?" was Grace Giles' answer.

"Why no."

"And they won't either."

"Why?" Emma Lou asked surprised.

"Because you are not a high brown or half-white." Emma Lou had thought this too, but she had been loath to believe it.

"You're silly, Grace. Why—Verne belongs."

"Yeah," Grace had sneered, "Verne, a bishop's daughter with plenty of coin and a big Buick. Why shouldn't they ask her?"

Emma Lou did not know what to make of this. She did not want to believe that the same color prejudice which existed among the blue veins in Boise also existed among the colored college students. Grace Giles was just hyper-sensitive. She wasn't taking into consideration the fact that she was not on the campus regularly and thus could not expect to be treated as if she were. Emma Lou fully believed that had Grace been a regularly enrolled student like herself, she would have found things different, and she was also certain that both she and Grace would be asked to join the sorority in due time.

But they weren't. Nor did an entire term in the school change things one whit. The Christmas holidays had come and gone and Emma Lou had not been invited to one of the many parties. She and Grace and Hazel bound themselves together and sought their extra-collegiate pleasures among people not on the campus. Hazel began to associate with a group of housemaids and mature youths who worked only when they had to and played the pool rooms and the housemaids as long as they proved profitable. Hazel was a welcome addition to this particular group what with her car and her full pocketbook. She had never been proficient in her studies, had always found it impossible to keep pace with the other students, and, finally realizing that she did not belong and perhaps never would, had decided to "go to the devil," and be done with it.

It was not long before Hazel was absent from the campus more often than she was present. Going to cabarets and parties, and taking long drunken midnight drives made her more and more unwilling and unable to undertake the scholastic grind on the next morning. Just before the mid-term examinations, she was advised by the faculty to drop out of school until the next year, and to put herself in the hands of a tutor, during the intervening period. It was evident that her background was not all that it should be; her preparatory work had not been sufficiently complete to enable her to continue in college. As it was, they told her, she was wasting her time. So Hazel disappeared from the campus and was said to have gone back to Texas. "Serves her right, glad she's gone," was the verdict of her colored campus fellows. . . .

The holidays over, Emma Lou returned to school a little reluctantly. She wasn't particularly interested in her studies, but having nothing else to do kept up in them and made high grades. Meanwhile she had been introduced to a number of young men and gone out with them occasionally. They too were friends of Grace's and of the same caliber as Grace's other friends. There were no college boys among them except Joe Lane who was flunking out in the School of Dentistry. He did not interest Emma Lou. As it was with Joe, so it was with all the other boys. She invariably picked them to pieces when they took her out, and remained so impassive to their emotional advances that they were soon glad to be on their way and let her be. Emma Lou was determined not to go out of her class, determined either to associate with the "right sort of people" or else to remain to herself.

Had any one asked Emma Lou what she meant by the "right sort of people" she would have found herself at a loss for a comprehensive answer. She really didn't know. She had a vague idea that those people on the campus who practically ignored her were the only people with whom she should associate. These people, for the most part, were children of fairly well-to-do families from Louisiana, Texas and Georgia, who, having made nest eggs, had journeyed to the West for the same reasons that her grandparents at an earlier date had also journeyed West. They wanted to live where they would have greater freedom and greater opportunity for both their children and themselves. Then, too, the World War had given impetus to this westward movement. There was more industry in the West and thus more chances for money to be made, and more opportunities to invest this money profitably in property and progeny.

The greater number of them were either mulattoes or light brown in color. In their southern homes they had segregated themselves from their darker skinned brethren and they continued this practice in the North. They went to the Episcopal, Presbyterian, or Catholic churches, and though they were not as frankly organized into a blue vein society as were the Negroes of Boise, they nevertheless kept more or less to themselves. They were not insistent that their children get "whiter and whiter every generation," but they did want to keep their children and grandchildren from having dark complexions. A light brown was the favored color; it was therefore found expedient to exercise caution when it came to mating.

The people who, in Emma Lou's phrase, really mattered, the business men, the doctors, the lawyers, the dentists, the more moneyed pullman porters, hotel waiters, bank janitors, and majordomos, in fact all of the Negro leaders and members of the Negro upper class, were either light skinned themselves or else had light skinned wives. A wife of dark complexion was considered a handicap unless she was particularly charming, wealthy, or beautiful. An ordinary looking dark woman was no suitable mate for a Negro man of prominence. The college youths on whom the future of the race depended practiced this precept of their elders religiously. It was not the girls in the school who were prejudiced—they had no reason to be, but they knew full well that the boys with whom they wished to associate, their future husbands, would not tolerate a dark girl unless she had, like Verne, many things to compensate for her dark skin. Thus they did not encourage a friendship with some one whom they knew didn't belong. Thus they did not even pledge girls like Grace, Emma Lou, and Hazel into their sorority, for they knew that it would make them the more miserable to attain the threshold only to have the door shut in their faces. . . .

Summer vacation time came and Emma Lou went back to Boise. She was thoroughly discouraged and depressed. She had been led to expect so much pleasure from her first year in college and in Los Angeles; but she had found that the people in large cities were after all no different from people in small cities. Her Uncle Joe had been wrong—her mother and grandmother had been right. There was no place in the world for a dark girl.

YVOR WINTERS

1900–1968

*Born in Chicago, Yvor Winters spent his childhood in Southern Cali-
fornia. He returned to Illinois to study at the University of Chicago until
a bout of tuberculosis sent him to convalesce in Santa Fe. Self-consciously
Western, he often emphasized that he was a product of the California of his youth and
the New Mexican desert landscape of his young adulthood. His early influences included
the American Indian poetry he discovered during his recovery and, later, more formal
poets such as Emily Dickinson and Wallace Stevens. "See Los Angeles First" shows the
influence of the spare, free-verse lines of William Carlos Williams and his eye for the
shards of modern city life. As Winters matured as a poet and critic, though, he grew
anti-Romantic and antimodernist. After he came to Stanford University to complete his
Ph.D. in 1927, he joined the faculty and founded the "Gyroscope Group," a movement
that promoted a return to the neoclassic ideals of intellectual reason, control, and formal
literary tropes. He turned to Elizabethan poetry, especially Walter Raleigh and Fulke
Greville, for his models, insisting on a rigorous formal discipline and an unyielding
moral and intellectual responsibility. His many books chart this development, from
collections such as* The Immobile Wind *(1921) to* The Giant Weapon *(1943) and* In
Defense of Reason *(1947), a controversial volume of criticism. In 1961 his* Collected
Poems *was awarded Yale's prestigious Bollingen Prize. Married to the fiction writer
Janet Lewis (1899–1998), Winters was a challenging intellect at Stanford for almost
forty years. A number of his students went on to literary prominence, including the poets
J. V. Cunningham, Alan Stephens, Donald Hall, Thom Gunn, and Robert Hass.*

See Los Angeles First

Rosyfingered cocklehouses
burst from burning
rock red plaster hollyhocks
spit crackling mamas
tickled pink

      on tiptoe
yawn into the dewy dawn
dark wettish plushy lawn

MIZPAH
                    The Temple glittergates
Ask God He Knows
                         O pyramid of Sunoil Dates

The mockingbird is singing
eighty languages a minute
swinging by his toes from
highpower
                    jagged geometric currents
roar along aluminum gashed
out of gulleys rending
night to one blind
                         halo for your cold

concrete Egyptian nakedness
O watertower of cleanliness

The Slow Pacific Swell

Far out of sight forever stands the sea,
Bounding the land with pale tranquillity.
When a small child, I watched it from a hill
At thirty miles or more. The vision still
Lies in the eye, soft blue and far away:
The rain has washed the dust from April day;
Paint-brush and lupine lie against the ground;
The wind above the hill-top has the sound
Of distance water in unbroken sky;
Dark and precise the little steamers ply—
Firm in direction they seem not to stir.
That is illusion. The artificer
Of quiet, distance holds me in a vise
And holds the ocean steadily to my eyes.

Once when I rounded Flattery, the sea
Hove its loose weight like sand to tangle me
Upon the washing deck, to crush the hull;
Subsiding, dragged flesh at the bone. The skull

Felt the retreating wash of dreaming hair.
Half drenched in dissolution, I lay bare.
I scarcely pulled myself erect; I came
Back slowly, slowly knew myself the same.
That was the ocean. From the ship we saw
Gray whales for miles: the long sweep of the jaw,
The blunt head plunging clean above the wave.
And one rose in a tent of sea and gave
A darkening shudder; water fell away;
The whale stood shining, and then sank in spray.

A landsman, I. The sea is but a sound.
I would be near it on a sandy mound,
And hear the steady rushing of the deep
While I lay stinging in the sand with sleep.
I have lived inland long. The land is numb.
It stands beneath the feet, and one may come
Walking securely, till the sea extends
Its limber margin, and precision ends.
By night a chaos of commingling power,
The whole Pacific hovers hour by hour.
The slow Pacific swell stirs on the sand,
Sleeping to sink away, withdrawing land,
Heaving and wrinkled in the moon, and blind;
Or gathers seaward, ebbing out of mind.

John Sutter

I was the patriarch of the shining land,
Of the blond summer and metallic grain;
Men vanished at the motion of my hand,
And when I beckoned they would come again.

The earth grew dense with grain at my desire;
The shade was deepened at the springs and streams;
Moving in dust that clung like pillared fire,
The gathering herds grew heavy in my dreams.

Across the mountains, naked from the heights,
Down to the valley broken settlers came,

And in my houses feasted through the nights,
Rebuilt their sinews and assumed a name.

In my clear rivers my own men discerned
The motive for the ruin and the crime—
Gold heavier than earth, a wealth unearned,
Loot, for two decades, from the heart of Time.

Metal, intrinsic value, deep and dense,
Preanimate, inimitable, still,
Real, but an evil with no human sense,
Dispersed the mind to concentrate the will.

Grained by alchemic change, the human kind
Turned from themselves to rivers and to rocks;
With dynamite broke metal unrefined;
Measured their moods by geologic shocks.

With knives they dug the metal out of stone;
Turned rivers back, for gold through ages piled,
Drove knives to hearts, and faced the gold alone;
Valley and river ruined and reviled;

Reviled and ruined me, my servant slew,
Strangled him from the figtree by my door.
When they had done what fury bade them do,
I was a cursing beggar, stripped and sore.

What end impersonal, what breathless age,
Incontinent of quiet and of years,
What calm catastrophe will yet assuage
This final drouth of penitential tears?

Moonlight Alert

Los Altos, California, June 1943

The sirens, rising, woke me; and the night
Lay cold and windless; and the moon was bright,
Moonlight from sky to earth, untaught, unclaimed,
An icy nightmare of the brute unnamed.

This was hallucination. Scarlet flower
And yellow fruit hung colorless. That hour
No scent lay on the air. The siren scream
Took on the fixity of shallow dream.
In the dread sweetness I could see the fall,
Like petals sifting from a quiet wall,
Of yellow soldiers through indifferent air,
Falling to die in solitude. With care
I held this vision, thinking of young men
Whom I had known and should not see again,
Fixed in reality, as I in thought.
And I stood waiting, and encountered naught.

The California Oaks

Spreading and low, unwatered, concentrate
Of years of growth that thickens, not expands,
With leaves like mica and with roots that grate
Upon the deep foundations of these lands,
In your brown shadow, on your heavy loam
—Leaves shrinking to the whisper of decay—
What feet have come to roam,
                     what eyes to stay?
Your motion has o'ertaken what calm hands?

Quick as a sunbeam, when a bird divides
The lesser branches, on impassive ground,
Hwui-Shan, the ancient, for a moment glides,
Demure with wisdom, and without a sound;
Brown feet that come to meet him, quick and shy,
Move in the flesh, then, browner, dry to bone;
The brook-like shadows lie
                    where sun had shone;
Ceaseless, the dead leaves gather, mound on mound.

And where they gather, darkening the glade,
In hose and doublet, and with knotty beard,
Armed with the musket and the pirate's blade,
Stern as the silence by the savage feared,

Drake and his seamen pause to view the hills,
Measure the future with a steady gaze.
But when they go naught fills
                              the patient days;
The bay lies empty where the vessels cleared.

The Spaniard, learning caution from the trees,
Building his dwelling from the native clay,
Took native concubines: the blood of these
Calming his blood, he made a longer stay.
Longer, but yet recessive, for the change
Came on his sons and their sons to the end;
For peace may yet derange
                              and earth may bend
The ambitious mind to an archaic way.

Then the invasion! and the soil was turned,
The hidden waters drained, the valleys dried;
And whether fire or purer sunlight burned,
No matter! one by one the old oaks died.
Died or are dying! The archaic race—
Black oak, live oak, and valley oak—ere long
Must crumble on the place
                              which they made strong
And in the calm they guarded now abide.

JAMES M. CAIN

1892–1977

With Dashiel Hammett and Raymond Chandler, James M. Cain was a founding father of the hard-boiled school of American fiction. Born in Maryland, he attended Washington College, where his father had been president. After army service in World War I, he worked for newspapers in Baltimore and spent a year as professor of journalism at St. John's College in Annapolis. He moved on to an eight-year stint with the New York World, *followed by a year as a managing editor at the* New Yorker. *In the 1920s, Cain began writing short fiction, making his first sale to H. L. Mencken's* American Mercury. *In 1931, when his stories came to the attention of Hollywood producers, he headed west. Six months later he was fired by Paramount. In desperation he began to craft a story from the beguiling Southern California world he had recently entered. Sun-drenched and volatile,* The Postman Always Rings Twice *(1934) made him famous. Tried for obscenity and banned in Boston, the novel has been the basis for four films—the first made in France in 1939—and is now regarded as a classic* roman noir. *The French novelist Georges Simenon acknowledged Cain's influence, and Albert Camus said that* Postman *inspired his novel* The Stranger. *In southern California, Cain wrote three more novels that secured his reputation, all of them later adapted for film:* Serenade *(1937),* Mildred Pierce *(1941), and* Double Indemnity *(1943). He wrote for film until 1947, when he abruptly returned to Maryland. He wrote nine more novels there, of which only three were published, none recapturing the audience found by the work he had done in California.*

From *The Postman Always Rings Twice*

I caught a ride to San Bernardino. It's a railroad town, and I was going to hop a freight east. But I didn't do it. I ran into a guy in a poolroom, and begun playing him one ball in the side. He was the greatest job in the way of a sucker that God ever turned out, because he had a friend that could really play. The only trouble with him was, he couldn't play good enough. I hung around with the pair of them a couple of weeks, and took $250 off them, all they had, and then I had to beat it out of town quick.

I caught a truck for Mexicali, and then I got to thinking about my $250, and how with that much money we could go to the beach and sell hot dogs or something until we got a stake to take a crack at something bigger. So I dropped off, and caught a ride back to Glendale. I began hanging around the market where they bought their stuff, hoping I would bump into her. I even called her up a couple of times, but the Greek answered and I had to make out it was a wrong number.

In between walking around the market, I hung around a poolroom, about a block down the street. One day a guy was practicing shots alone on one of the tables. You could tell he was new at it from the way he held his cue. I began practicing shots on the next table. I figured if $250 was enough for a hot dog stand, $350 would leave us sitting pretty.

"How you say to a little one ball in the side?"

"I never played that game much."

"Nothing to it. Just the one ball in the side pocket."

"Anyhow, you look too good for me."

"Me? I'm just a punk."

"Oh well. If it's just a friendly game."

We started to play, and I let him take three or four, just to feel good. I kept shaking my head, like I couldn't understand it.

"Too good for you hey. Well, that's a joke. But I swear, I'm really better than this. I can't seem to get going. How you say we put $1 on it, just to make it lively?"

"Oh well. I can't lose much at a dollar."

We made it $1 a game, and I let him take four or five, maybe more. I shot like I was pretty nervous, and in between shots I would wipe off the palm of my hand with a handkerchief, like I must be sweating.

"Well, it looks like I'm not doing so good. How about making it $5, so I can get my money back, and then we'll go have a drink?"

"Oh well. It's just a friendly game, and I don't want your money. Sure. We'll make it $5, and then we'll quit."

I let him take four or five more, and from the way I was acting, you would have thought I had heart failure and a couple more things besides. I was plenty blue around the gills.

"Look. I got sense enough to know when I'm out of my class all right, but let's make it $25, so I can break even, and then we'll go have that drink."

"That's pretty high for me."

"What the hell? You're playing on my money, aren't you ?"

"Oh well. All right. Make it $25."

Then was when I really started to shoot. I made shots that Hoppe couldn't make. I banked them in from three cushions, I made billiard shots, I had my english working so the ball just floated around the table, I even called a jump shot and made it. He never made a shot that Blind Tom the Sightless Piano Player couldn't have made. He miscued, he got himself all tangled up on position, he scratched, he put the one ball in the wrong pocket, he never even called a bank shot. And when I walked out of there, he had my $250 and a $3 watch that I had bought to keep track of when Cora might be driving in to the market. Oh, I was good all right. The only trouble was I wasn't quite good enough.

. . .

"Hey, Frank!"

It was the Greek, running across the street at me before I had really got out the door.

"Well Frank, you old son a gun, where you been, put her there, why you run away from me just a time I hurt my head I need you most?"

We shook hands. He still had a bandage around his head and a funny look in his eyes, but he was dressed up in a new suit, and had a black hat cocked over on the side of his head, and a purple necktie, and brown shoes, and his gold watch chain looped across his vest, and a big cigar in his hand.

"Well Nick! How you feeling, boy?"

"Me, I feel fine, couldn't feel better if was right out a the can, but why you run out on me? I sore as hell at you, you old son a gun."

"Well, you know me, Nick. I stay put a while, and then I got to ramble."

"You pick one hell of a time to ramble. What you do, hey? Come on, you don't do nothing, you son a gun, I know you, come on over while I buy'm steaks I tell you all about it."

"You alone?"

"Don't talk so dumb, who the hell you think keep a place open now you run out on me, hey? Sure I'm alone. Me a Cora never get to go out together now, one go, other have to stay."

"Well then, let's walk over."

It took him an hour to buy the steaks, he was so busy telling me how his skull was fractured, how the docs never saw a fracture like it, what a hell of a time he's had with his help, how he's had two guys since I left and he fired one the day after he hired him, and the other one skipped after three days and took the inside of the cash register with him, and how he'd give anything to have me back.

"Frank, I tell you what. We go to Santa Barbara tomorrow, me a Cora. Hell boy, we got to step out a little, hey? We go see a fiesta there, and you come with us. You like that, Frank? You come with us, talk about you come back a work for me. You like a fiesta a Santa Barbara?"

"Well, I hear it's good."

"Is a girls, is a music, is a dance in streets, is swell. Come on, Frank, what you say?"

"Well, I don't know."

"Cora be sore as hell at me if I see you and no bring you out. Maybe she treat you snotty, but she think you fine fellow, Frank. Come on, we all three go. We have a hell of a time."

"O.K. If she's willing, it's a go."

There were eight or ten people in the lunchroom when we got there, and she was back in the kitchen, washing dishes as fast as she could, to get enough plates to serve them.

"Hey. Hey Cora, look. Look who I bring."

"Well for heaven's sake. Where did he come from?"

"I see'm today a Glendale. He go to Santa Barbara with us."

"Hello, Cora. How you been?"

"You're quite a stranger around here."

She wiped her hands quick, and shook hands, but her hand was soapy. She went out front with an order, and me and the Greek sat down. He generally helped her with the orders, but he was all hot to show me something, and he let her do it all alone. It was a big scrapbook, and in the front of it he had pasted his naturalization certificate, and then his wedding certificate, and then his license to do business in Los Angeles County, and then a picture of himself in the Greek Army, and then a picture of him and Cora the day they got married, and then all the clippings about his accident. Those clippings in the regular papers, if you ask me, were more about the cat than they were about him, but anyway they had his name in them, and how he had been brought to the Glendale Hospital, and was expected to recover. The one in the Los Angeles Greek paper, though, was more about him than about the cat, and had a picture of him in it, in the dress suit he had when he was a waiter, and the story of his life. Then came the X-Rays. There were about a half dozen of them, because they took a new picture every day to see how he was getting along. How he had them fixed up was to paste two pages together, along the edges, and then cut out a square place in the middle, where the X-Ray was slipped in so you could hold it up to light and look through it. After the X-Rays came receipted hospital bills, the receipted doctors' bills and the receipted nurses' bills. That rap on the conk cost him $322, believe it or not.

"Is a nice, hey?"

"Swell. It's all there, right on the line."

"Of course, is a not done yet. I fix'm up red, a white, a blue, fix'm up fine. Look."

He showed me where he had put the fancy stuff on a couple of the pages. He had inked in the curley cues, and then colored it with red, white, and blue. Over the naturalization certificate, he had a couple of American flags, and an eagle, and over the Greek Army picture he had crossed Greek flags, and another eagle, and over his wedding certificate he had a couple of turtle doves on a twig. He hadn't figured out yet what to put over the other stuff, but I said over the clippings he could put a cat with red, white, and blue fire coming out of its tail, and he thought that was pretty good. He didn't get it, though, when I said he could have a buzzard over the Los Angeles County license, holding a couple of auctioneer's flags that said Sale Today, and it didn't took like it would really be worth while to try to explain it to him. But I got it, at last, why he was all dressed up, and not carrying out the chow like he used to, and acted so important. This Greek had had a fracture of the skull, and a thing like that don't happen to a dumb cluck like him every day. He was like a wop that opens a drug store. Soon as he gets that thing that says Pharmacist, with a red seal on it, a wop puts on a gray suit, with black edges on the vest, and is so important he can't even take time to mix the pills, and wouldn't even touch a chocolate icecream soda. This Greek was all dressed up for the same reason. A big thing had happened in his life.

It was pretty near supper time when I got her alone. He went up to wash, and the two of us were left in the kitchen.

"You been thinking about me, Cora?"

"Sure. I wouldn't forget you all that quick."

"I thought about you a lot. How are you?"

"Me? I'm all right."

"I called you up a couple of times, but he answered and I was afraid to talk to him. I made some money."

"Well, gee, I'm glad you're getting along good."

"I made it, but then I lost it. I thought we could raise it to get started with, but then I lost it.

"I declare, I don't know where the money goes."

"You sure you think about me, Cora?"

"Sure I do."

"You don't act like it."

"Seems to me I'm acting all right."

"Have you got a kiss for me?"

"We'll be having supper pretty soon. You better get ready, if you've got any washing to do."

That's the way it went. That's the way it went all evening. The Greek got out some of his sweet wine, and sang a bunch of songs, and we sat around, and so far as she was concerned, I might just as well have been just a guy that used to work there, only she couldn't quite remember his name. It was the worst flop of a home-coming you ever saw your life.

.   .   .

When it came time to go to bed, I let them go up, and then I went outside to try and figure out whether to stay there and see if I couldn't get going with her again, or blow and try to forget her. I walked quite a way off, and I don't know how long it was, or far away I was, but after a while I could hear a row going on in the place. I went back, and when I got close I could hear some of what they were saying. She was yelling like hell and saying I had to leave. He was mumbling something, probably that he wanted me to stay and go back to work. He was trying to shut her up, but I could tell she was yelling so I would hear it. If I had been in my room, where she thought I was, I could have heard it plain enough, and even where I was I could hear plenty.

Then all of a sudden it stopped. I slipped in the kitchen, and stood there listening. But I couldn't hear anything, because I was all shook up, and all I could get was the sound of my own heart, going bump-bump, bump-bump, bump-bump, like that. I thought that was a funny way for my heart to sound, and then all of a sudden I knew there was two hearts in that kitchen, and that was why it sounded so funny.

I snapped on the light.

She was standing there, in a red kimono, as pale milk, staring at me, with a long thin knife in her hand. I reached out and took it away from her. When she spoke, it was in a whisper that sounded like a snake licking its tongue in and out.

"Why did you have to come back?"

"I had to, that's all."

"No you didn't. I could have gone through with it. I was getting so I could forget you. And now you have to come back. God damn you, you have to come back!"

"Go through with what?"

"What he's making that scrapbook for. *It's to show to his children!* And now he wants one. He wants one right away."

"Well, why didn't you come with me?"

"Come with you for what? To sleep in box cars? Why would I come with you? Tell me that."

I couldn't say anything. I thought about my $250, but what good was it telling her that I had some money yesterday, but today I lost it playing one ball in the side?

"You're no good. I know that. You're just no good. Then why don't you go away and let me alone instead of coming back here again? Why don't you leave me be?"

"Listen. Stall him on this kid stuff just a little while. Stall him, and we'll see if we can't figure something out. I'm not much good, but I love you, Cora. I swear it."

"You swear it, and what do you do? He's taking me to Santa Barbara, so I'll say I'll have the child, and you—you're going right along with us. You're going to stay at the same hotel with us! You're going right along in the car. You're—"

She stopped, and we stood there looking at each other. The three of us in the car, we knew what that meant. Little by little we were nearer, until we were touching.

"Oh, my God, Frank, isn't there any other way out for us than that?"

"Well. You were going to stick a knife in him just now."

"No. That was for me, Frank. Not him."

"Cora, it's in the cards. We've tried every other way out."

"I can't have no greasy Greek child, Frank. I can't, that's all. The only one I can have a child by is you. I wish you were some good. You're smart, but you're no good."

"I'm no good, but I love you."

"Yes, and I love you."

"Stall him. Just this one night."

"All right, Frank. Just this one night."

WILLIAM SAROYAN

1908–1981

Born in Fresno, California, Saroyan grew up in a large transplanted Armenian community. At age twelve he quit school and went to work as a telegraph messenger boy. Self-educated and a self-taught writer, he was living from hand to mouth in San Francisco when he wrote the stories in his first book, The Daring Young Man on the Flying Trapeze *(1934), a collection of monologues and freewheeling tales that was an instant critical and popular success. More stories followed, in collections such as* Inhale and Exhale *(1936),* Love, Here Is My Hat *(1937), and* My Name Is Aram *(1940). His play* The Time of Your Life, *set in a San Francisco waterfront saloon, won the 1940 Pulitzer Prize as well as the New York Drama Critics' Circle Award.*

During a career that spanned half a century, Saroyan wrote with an expansiveness and generosity of spirit that drew on his rich cultural and personal background. His works include over a dozen plays and forty works of fiction and nonfiction, among them The Human Comedy *(1952),* Bicycle Rider in Beverly Hills *(1952),* Boys and Girls Together *(1963), and* Places Where I've Done Time *(1972). In the opening pages of his first book, he voiced an attitude that fittingly introduces himself and his life's work: "I am out here in the far west, in San Francisco, in a small room on Carl Street, writing a letter to common people, telling them in simple language things they already know. I am merely making a record, so if I wander around a little, it is because I am in no hurry and because I do not know the rules. If I have any desire at all, it is to show the brotherhood of man."*

The Daring Young Man on the Flying Trapeze

1. SLEEP

Horizontally wakeful amid universal widths, practicing laughter and mirth, satire, the end of all, of Rome and yes of Babylon, clenched teeth, remembrance, much warmth volcanic, the streets of Paris, the plains of Jericho, much gliding as of reptile in abstraction, a gallery of watercolors, the sea and the fish with eyes, symphony, a table in the corner of the Eiffel Tower, jazz, at the opera house, alarm clock and the tap-dancing of doom, conversation with a tree, the river Nile, Cadillac coupe to Kansas, the roar of Dostoyevsky, and the dark sun.

This earth, the face of one who lived, the form without the weight, weeping upon snow, white music, the magnified flower twice the size of the universe, black clouds, the caged panther staring, deathless space, Mr. Eliot with rolled sleeves baking bread, Flaubert and Guy de Maupassant, a wordless rhyme of early meaning. Finlandia, mathematics highly polished and slick as a green onion to the teeth, Jerusalem, the path to paradox.

The deep son of man, the sly whisper of someone unseen but vaguely known, the hurricane in the cornfield, a game of chess, hush the queen, the king, Karl Franz, black Titanic, Mr. Chaplin weeping, Stalin, Hitler, a multitude of Jews, tomorrow is Monday, no dancing in the streets.

O swift moment of life: it is ended, the earth is again now.

2. WAKEFULNESS

He (the living) dressed and shaved, grinning at himself in the mirror. Very unhandsome, he said: where is my tie? (He had but one.) Coffee and a gray sky, Pacific Ocean fog, the drone of a passing streetcar, people going to the city, time again, the day, prose and poetry. He moved swiftly down the stairs to the street and began to walk, thinking suddenly, *It is only in sleep that we may know that we live. There only, in that living death, do we meet ourselves and the far earth, God and the saints, the names of our fathers, the substance of remote moments; it is there that the centuries merge in the moment, that the vast becomes the tiny, tangible atom of eternity.*

He walked into the day as alertly as might be, making a definite noise with his heels, perceiving with his eyes the superficial truth of streets and structures, the trivial truth of reality. Helplessly his mind sang, *He flies through the air with the greatest of ease; the daring young man on the flying trapeze;* then laughed with all the might of his being. It was really a splendid morning: gray, cold, and cheerless, a morning for inward vigor; ah, Edgar Guest, he said, how I long for your music.

In the gutter he saw a coin which proved to be a penny dated 1923, and placing it in the palm of his hand he examined it closely, remembering that year and thinking of Lincoln whose profile was stamped on the coin. There was almost nothing a man could do with a penny. I will purchase a motorcar, he thought. I will dress myself in the fashion of a fop, visit the hotel strumpets, drink and dine, and then return to the quiet. Or I will drop the coin into a slot and weigh myself.

It was good to be poor, and the Communists—but it was no good to be hungry. What appetites they had, how fond they were of food! Empty stomachs. He remembered how greatly he needed food. Every meal was bread and coffee and cigarettes, and now he had no more bread. Coffee without bread could never honestly serve as supper, and there were no weeds in the park that could be cooked as spinach is cooked.

If the truth were known, he was half starved, and yet there was still no end of books he ought to read before he died. He remembered the young Italian Brooklyn Hospital, a small sick clerk named Mollica, who had said desperately, I would like to see California once before I die. And he thought earnestly, I ought at least to read *Hamlet* once again; or perhaps *Huckleberry Finn*.

It was then that he became thoroughly awake: at the thought of dying. Now wakefulness was a state in the nature of the sustained shock. A young man could perish rather unostentatiously, he thought; and already he was very nearly starved. Water and prose were fine, they filled much inorganic space, but they were inadequate. If there were only some work he might do for money, some trivial labor in the name of commerce. If they would only allow him to sit at a desk all day and add trade figures, subtract and multiply and divide, then perhaps he would not die. He would buy food, all sorts of it: untasted delicacies from Norway, Italy, and France; all manner of beef, lamb, fish, cheese, grapes, figs, pears, apples, melons, which he would worship when he had satisfied his hunger. He would place a bunch of red grapes on a dish beside two black figs, a large yellow pear, and a green apple. He would hold a cut melon to his nostrils for hours. He would buy green loaves of French bread, vegetables of all sorts, meat; he would buy life.

From a hill he saw the city standing majestically in the east, great towers, dense with his kind, and there he was suddenly outside of it all, almost definitely certain that he should never gain admittance, almost positive that somehow he had ventured upon the wrong earth, or perhaps into the wrong age, and now a young man of twenty-two was to be permanently ejected from it. This thought was not saddening. He said to himself, Sometime soon I must write *An Application for Permission to Live*. He accepted the thought of dying without pity for himself or for man, believing that he would at least sleep another night. His rent for another day was paid; there was yet another tomorrow. And after that he might go where other homeless men went. He might even visit the Salvation Army—sing to God and Jesus (unlover of my soul), be saved, eat and sleep. But he knew that he would not. His life was a private life. He did not wish to destroy this fact. Any other alternative would be better.

Through the air on the flying trapeze, his mind hummed. Amusing it was, astoundingly funny. A trapeze to God, or to nothing, a flying trapeze to some sort of eternity; he prayed objectively for strength to make the flight with grace.

I have one cent, he said. It is an American coin. In the evening I shall polish it until it glows like a sun and I shall study the words.

He was now walking in the city itself, among living men. There were one or two places to go. He saw his reflection in the plate-glass windows of stores and was disappointed with his appearance. He seemed not at all as strong as he felt; he seemed, in fact, a trifle infirm in every part of his body, in his neck, in his shoulders, arms, trunk, and knees. This will never do, he said, and with an effort he assembled all his disjointed parts and became tensely, artificially erect and solid.

He passed numerous restaurants with magnificent discipline, refusing even to glance into them, and at last reached a building which he entered. He rose in an elevator to the seventh floor, moved down a hall, and, opening a door, walked into the office of an employment agency. Already there were two dozen young men in the place; he found a corner where he stood waiting his turn to be interviewed. At length he was granted this great privilege and was questioned by a thin, scatterbrained miss of fifty.

Now tell me, she said, what can you do?

He was embarrassed. I can write, he said pathetically.

You mean your penmanship is good? Is that it? said the elderly maiden.

Well, yes, he replied. But I mean I can write.

Write what? said the miss, almost with anger.

Prose, he said simply.

There was a pause. At last the lady said:

Can you use a typewriter?

Of course, said the young man.

All right, went on the miss, we have your address; we will get in touch with you. There is nothing this morning, nothing at all.

It was much the same at the other agency, except that he was questioned by a conceited young man who closely resembled a pig. From the agencies he went to the large department stores: there was a good deal of pomposity, some humiliation on his part, and finally the report that work was not available. He did not feel displeased, and strangely did not even feel that he was personally involved in the foolishness. He was a living young man who was in need of money with which to go on being one, and there was no way of getting it except by working for it; and there was no work. It was purely an abstract problem which he wished for the last time to attempt to solve. Now he was pleased that the matter was closed.

William Saroyan

463

He began to perceive the definiteness of the course of his life. Except for moments, it had been largely artless, but now at the last minute he was determined that there should be as little imprecision as possible.

He passed countless stores and restaurants on his way to the Y.M.C.A., where he helped himself to paper and ink and began to compose his *Application*. For an hour he worked on his document, then suddenly, owing to the bad air in the place and to hunger, he became faint. He seemed to be swimming away from himself with great strokes, and hurriedly left the building. In the Civic Center Park, across from the Public Library Building, he drank almost a quart of water and felt himself refreshed. An old man was standing in the center of the brick boulevard surrounded by sea gulls, pigeons, and robins. He was taking handfuls of bread crumbs from a large paper sack and tossing them to the birds with a gallant gesture.

Dimly he felt impelled to ask the man for a portion of the crumbs, but he did not allow the thought even nearly to reach consciousness; he entered the Public Library and for an hour read Proust, then, feeling himself to be swimming away again, he rushed outdoors. He drank more water at the fountain in the park and began the long walk to his room.

I'll go and sleep some more, he said; there is nothing else to do. He knew now that he was much too tired and weak to deceive himself about being all right, and yet his mind seemed somehow lithe and alert. It, as if it were a separate entity, persisted in articulating impertinent pleasantries about his very real physical suffering. He reached his room early in the afternoon and immediately prepared coffee on the small gas range. There was no milk in the can, and the half pound of sugar he had purchased a week before was all gone; he drank a cup of the hot, black fluid, sitting on his bed and smiling.

From the Y.M.C.A. he had stolen a dozen sheets of letter paper upon which he hoped to complete his document, but now the very notion of writing was unpleasant to him. There was nothing to say. He began to polish the penny he had found in the morning, and this absurd act somehow afforded him great enjoyment. No American coin can be made to shine so brilliantly as a penny. How many pennies would he need to go on living? Wasn't there something more for him to sell? He looked about the bare room. No. His watch was gone; also his books. All those fine books; nine of them for eighty-five cents. He felt ill and ashamed for having parted with his books. His best suit he had sold for two dollars, but that was all right. He didn't mind at all about clothes. But the books. That was different. It made him angry to think that there was no respect for men who wrote.

He placed the shining penny on the table, looking upon it with the delight of a miser. How prettily it smiles, he said. Without reading them he looked at the words *E Pluribus Unum One Cent United States of America,* and turning the penny over, he saw Lincoln and the words, *In God We Trust 1923.* How beautiful it is, he said.

He became drowsy and felt a ghastly illness coming over his blood, a feeling of nausea and disintegration. Bewildered, he stood beside his bed, thinking, *There is nothing to do but sleep.* Already he felt himself making great strides through the fluid of the earth, swimming away to the beginning. He fell face down on the bed, saying, I ought first at least to give the coin to some child. A child could buy any number of things with a penny.

Then swiftly, neatly, with the grace of the young man on the trapeze, he was gone from his body. For an eternal moment he was all things at once: the bird, the fish, the rodent, the reptile, and man. An ocean of print undulated endlessly and darkly before him. The city burned. The herded crowd rioted. The earth circled away, and knowing that he did so, he turned his lost face to the empty sky and became dreamless, unalive, perfect.

From *Quarter, Half, Three-Quarter and Whole Notes*

The minutes and the hours and the years, the mornings and the noons and the nights, the Saturdays and the Sundays and the Mondays, the Januarys and the Junes and the Augusts and the Decembers: the change in the landscape the new grass, the new buildings, the new faces: and the new voices, birds and men: and all the smiling of sky and pavement, all the anguish of house and door, all the despair of place in time.

Wisdom Crieth in the Streets: a story.

I have found one mob as bad as another, and I have put it down plainly, and a lot of the professional proletarians don't like it. This fool, they feel, is a mob himself, and how can you have a resolution when one man's mob is greater than the collective mob?

What revolution? Any revolution, *the revolution,* the one they are always talking about, writing bad poems about. You know: poor man walking into rich man's house without wiping shoes. Knocking over vases, and smoking expensive cigars: heaven on earth. Well. I think mine is the better mob. And I think it will win the better revolution.

He made a world of the streetcar and explored it, pulling open the slide door, going around in the thing while it moved, and running back to his mother, with a rapt expression on his face, he told her how remarkable it was: a small boy: a story.

Hello, Rat.

Miseries of 1935.

Comparison of Pains.

The Man with the Glass Eye, Hare Lip, and Wooden Leg: a story. What a man.

A Brief Life: a short novel of a boy, born to poor parents, whose wisdom is instinctive and profound: he sees, understands, knows, wordlessly: with sensibility: he prefers death to life, and dies at the age of eight, swimming alone in Kings River, the chapter on his death closing the story: an historic death, the death of all things, through this boy who is all things: a great character: articulations of unworded wisdom.

Lady, You Were a Riot: a story.

A man is silly to walk in a parade unless he has a drum to beat, because it is no fun to walk quietly and gradually become sullen-faced, and have people look at you and maybe think you are a little loose upstairs, or maybe pity you, or maybe laugh, so when they told me I could have a drum in the parade I said all right, I would join the party and be a Communist, although at heart I am an Anarchist and believe the worst is yet to come. The drum: a story. (They'll kill me.)

Errors of Man: a story of people who steal or kill or perform cruel acts: as paining small animals or hurting the feelings of children. Theft and murder.

Pity. Awake.

Vultures in this world, evil-eyed, filthy, glutted, yet starving: rats, racing in the underparts of the body of man: snakes, frogs, spiders. Clammy things, half-plant and half-animal. Worms. A story of the filthiness in the heart of man. (A heart which is pure, too.)

Character: What I got is personality, I guess.

O Jesus, if you could see the things I am seeing in this crazy town you would get drunker than I am drunk and you would do crazier things than the things I am doing, running around everywhere trying to straighten everything out.

Streetcar to the sun.

Unwritten.

A number of sheets of paper bound or stitched together. A moment of a man. Something said. A word. A word. And silence. An implication. The smile of mortality. Holy, holy, holy, which was, and is, and is to come.

Night. Day. (Repeat endlessly.) If any have ears let them hear. Rivers. Seas. Continents. Cities. Plains. Hills. The face of one or two living. Arrangement.

Never there, the heart, sadly, and the sorrowing peasants springing from the hot earth, crying for one thing, to live, begging for it, Mexican life, turning, inwardly to themselves, outwardly, to the earth and to the Aztec sun, to the heart itself. Dark and mad with it, Mexican blood crying for Mexican life, weeping for it. The bleeding heart of the world-peasant.

Legs chorus-girls dancers whores movie-stars: parenthetical music: a novel.

So I visited my friend, and he was a great Wop, solid, all there, Italy itself, the broad geniality, the fine laughter, loud and easy, the clear thinking, the violent generosity, and he said he was of the streets, not of the polished floors, and I said I am of the streets, and we drank wine, being of the same universe, the everlastingly street level: Italy.

Brawn and birth: and gasp: and mighty wail. This is the moment of another face: mortality implied. And movement: pain and madness: the face distorted. Mortal suffering. Great expectations, although it is only another birth.

William Saroyan

He died. She died. The earth swarms with him and with her, and each rots alone in the earth: unhappy ending.

If you laugh loudly, you are bound to weep bitterly. Walk in the valley, and through the dark city walk. See.

Suddenly the whole town was in motion, not only people running, but houses and streets. A big light in heaven. The church on fire. God and flame. How beautiful. How appropriate. Church Burning.

Sea burial. The cow and the train. The meadow and the track. Earth and steel. A sudden fury of train smash, meadow flash of flower, and myself walking up the aisle saying, You sons of bitches. Tree shadows across the meadow: my mortality. Sheep and anger. Waiting for arrival: the train going.

Pages lost. I said nothing. I thought nothing. My own unwritten works coming across the broad black valley of time, a mountain of silence in my ear, thick with snow and fog, and lost somewhere, in such and such a city: the great book unwritten, novel.

My country, it is of thee I sing: existence in space. Essence. Sweet land, thy rocks I love. To stand and to be and to have time in the flesh: let rocks their silence break. Let pebbles speak. They are thyself, and every morning the sun occurs and every evening the moon and every moment the face of man. This continent. These cities. And the big machines. They weep. They sleep. Thy rocks in silence weep. Thy pebbles sleep. America.

In 1926 they were singing Valencia, in my dreams. Do you remember the cigarettes? The traffic turning the corner? Mirage of earthfaces? Eyes of living stone? Whistle? Gasoline? The roar of sudden machinery? Boy, we have been alive: sweet land. Shadows calm upon the rocks. Summer carols.

Irish songs: Oh, didn't you hear the glorious news that happened in Bally-hooly? Dan Tutty the gauger was caught and thrashed by Paddy and Timothy Dooly. Farewell for evermore. O give me your hand. With my Ballinamona Oro, the girl of Cullen for me. Gaily we went and gaily we came. In the new-mown meadows. The dear black white-backed cow. Get up, my darling, and come with me. Go home, go home, dear heart. A kiss in the kitchen. Shall we ever be in one lodging? O Mary my darling. Last night I was thinking of the ways of the world. In deepest sorrow I think of home. When my old hat was new.

If I haven't got the best job in America, I'd like to know who has. The hours are lousy. There is no pay. Even so.

You do not have to be a composer in order to hear music everywhere, and it is impossible not to hear American music everywhere, wherever you may be. And you remember music that you once heard and you remember music that was never composed and never played by an orchestra or sung by a singer. It is the music of this continent and the music of these times and the music of these people who have their lives on this continent in the cities and in the small towns in the country, on the farms, in the places of the mobs and in the places of the quiet, Manhattan and the great southwestern desert, the subway and the sleeping lizard, Carnegie Hall, and the wagonwheel road that leads to the abandoned house. Notes for an American symphony.

A work of prose may be said to be good (though not necessarily great) when it has wholeness, for it is wholeness that man instinctively desires in works of art, and this wholeness been not be purely technical, as many writers imagine. As a matter of fact, the logical growth of the story form would seem to be toward a dismissal, or at least a relegation to a position of minor importance, of technical virtuosity, and a more powerful emphasis of the spiritual or emotional intensity and wholeness of a piece of writing involving man. A narrative in order to be a narrative need no longer concern itself solely with physical events in the lives of men (this is history); on the contrary, it should concern itself with the subtlest and most evanescent of universal meanings evolving from all the facts which make for consciousness in man; that is to say, from his being conscious in the first place, which is certainly an immense thing alone, from his awareness of the world (and every man is aware of the world in a way of his own, which furnishes the sincere writer with an endless source of material), from his awareness of his fellow man, from his very chemistry (that is to say, his organic make-up, his physical structure, the thickness of his blood, the quality of his nervous system, the sharpness or dullness of his perception), from (and this is very important) the manner in which he dreams, the substances and rhythms of his sleep, and from the thoughts that run through his mind when he is not exactly the civilized being he would pretend to be when he is abroad in the world, and so on almost endlessly.

William Saroyan

469

So long as a work of prose is about man, and so long as it is brief and tends to emphasize one phase of the reality of man, it may be called a short story, provided it possesses this wholeness. Plot, atmosphere, style, and all the rest of it may be regarded as so much nonsense: it is impossible to write one paragraph about man without having plot, and atmosphere, and what is known as style.

Horace McCoy

1897–1955

Born in Tennessee, McCoy served in France as a member of the American Air Service during World War I, seeing action in which he was wounded and awarded the Croix de Guerre. Later, as a Texas newspaperman, he moonlighted many stories in Black Mask *magazine, and by the time he came to California in 1931 he had adopted the hard-boiled mannerisms espoused by the magazine's editor, Joseph T. Shaw. An established actor in Texas, he came to Los Angeles to seek a career in movies, but he found that the Depression had occasioned a glut of others like him, with twenty thousand extras vying for bit parts in Hollywood. He began writing screenplays in 1932, and Columbia Studios filmed his original scenario for* Dangerous Crossroads *in 1933. Soon made financially independent by marriage, McCoy returned to fiction, and* They Shoot Horses, Don't They? *appeared in 1935. He had intermittent success thereafter until* I Should Have Stayed Home, *a bitter Hollywood novel also about the world of jobless extras, was published in 1938. Although he did not publish another novel for ten years, in the late 1940s* They Shoot Horses, Don't They? *began to draw the attention of European intellectuals, helping to establish its reputation as the first American existential novel and a major example of the Hollywood novel.*

From *They Shoot Horses, Don't They?*

THE
PRISONER
WILL
STAND.

1

I stood up. For a moment I saw Gloria again, sitting on that bench on the pier. The bullet had just struck her in the side of the head; the blood had not even started to flow. The flash from the pistol still lighted her face. Everything was plain as day. She was completely relaxed, was completely comfortable. The impact of the bullet had turned her head a little away from me; I did not have a perfect profile view but I could see enough of her face and her lips to know she was smiling. The Prosecuting Attorney was wrong when he told the jury she died in agony, friendless, alone except for her brutal murderer, out there in that black night on the edge of the Pacific. He was wrong as a man can be. She did not die in agony. She was relaxed and comfortable and she was smiling. It was the first time I had ever seen her smile. How could she have been in agony then? And she wasn't friendless. I was her best friend. I was her only friend. So how could she have been friendless?

IS THERE

ANY LEGAL CAUSE

WHY

SENTENCE

SHOULD NOT NOW

BE PRONOUNCED?

2

What could I say? . . . All those people knew I had killed her; the only other person who could have helped me at all was dead too. So I just stood there, looking at the judge and shaking my head. I didn't have a leg to stand on.

"Ask the mercy of the court," said Epstein, the lawyer they had assigned to defend me.

"What was that?" the judge said.

"Your Honor," Epstein said, "—we throw ourselves an the mercy of the court. This boy admits killing the girl, but he was only doing her a personal favor—"

The judge banged on the desk, looking at me.

THERE BEING

NO LEGAL CAUSE

WHY SENTENCE

SHOULD NOT NOW

BE PRONOUNCED . . .

3

It was funny the way I met Gloria. She was trying to get into pictures too, but I didn't know that until later. I was walking down Melrose one day from the Paramount studios when I heard somebody hollering, "Hey! Hey!" and I turned around and there she was running towards me and waving. I stopped, waving back. When she got up to me she was all out of breath and excited and I saw I didn't know her.

"Damn that bus," she said.

I looked around and there was the bus half a block down the street going towards Western.

"Oh," I said, "I thought you were waving at me . . ."

"What would I be waving at you for?" she asked.

I laughed. "I don't know," I said. "You going my way?"

"I may as well walk on down to Western," she said; and we began to walk on down towards Western.

That was how it all started and it seems very strange to me now. I don't understand it at all. I've thought and thought and still I don't understand it. This wasn't murder. I try to do somebody a favor and I wind up getting killed myself. *They are going to kill me. I know exactly what the judge is going to say. I can tell by the look of him that he is going to be glad to say it and I can tell by the feel of the people behind me that they are going to be glad to hear him say it.*

Take that morning I met Gloria. I wasn't feeling very good; I was still a little sick, but I went over to Paramount because von Steinberg was making a Russian picture and I thought maybe I could get a job. I used to ask myself what could be nicer than working for von Steinberg, or Mamoulian or Boles-lawsky either, getting paid to watch him direct, learning about composition and tempo and angles . . . so I went over to Paramount.

I couldn't get inside, so I hung around the front until noon when one of his assistants came out for lunch. I caught up with him and asked what was the chance to get some atmosphere.

"None," he said, telling me that von Steinberg was very careful about his atmospheric people.

I thought that was a lousy thing to say but I knew what he was thinking, that my clothes didn't look any too good. "Isn't this a costume picture?" I asked.

"All our extras come through Central," he said, leaving me.

I wasn't going anywhere in particular; I was just riding along in my Rolls-Royce, having people point me out as the greatest director in the world, when I heard Gloria hollering. You see how those things happen? . . .

So we walked on down Melrose to Western, getting acquainted all the time; and when we got to Western I knew she was Gloria Beatty, an extra who wasn't doing well either, and she knew a little about me. I liked her very much.

She had a small room with some people over near Beverly and I lived only a few blocks from there, so I saw her again that night. That first night was really what did it but even now I can't honestly say I regret going to see her. I had about seven dollars I had made squirting soda in a drug store (subbing for a friend of mine. He had got a girl in a jam and had to take her to Santa Barbara for the operation) and I asked her if she'd rather go to a movie or sit in the park.

"What park?" she asked.

"It's right over here a little way," I said.

"All right," she said. "I got a bellyful of moving pictures anyway. If I'm not a better actress than most of those dames I'll eat your hat—Let's go sit and hate a bunch of people . . .

I was glad she wanted to go to the park. It was always nice there. It was a fine place to sit. It was very small, only one block square, but it was very dark and very quiet and tilled with dense shrubbery. All around it palm trees grew up, fifty, sixty feet tall, suddenly tufted at the top. Once you entered the park you had the illusion of security. I often imagined they were sentries wearing grotesque helmets: my own private sentries, standing guard over my own private island . . .

The park was a fine place to sit. Through the palms you could see many buildings, the thick, square silhouettes of apartment houses, with their red signs on the roofs, reddening the sky above and everything and everybody below. But if you wanted to get rid of these things you had only to sit and stare at them with a fixed gaze . . . and they would begin receding. That way you could drive them as far into the distance as you wanted to . . .

"I never paid much attention to this place before," Gloria said.

". . . I like it," I said, taking off my coat and spreading it on the grass for her. "I come here three or four times a week."

"You do like it," she said, sitting down.

"How long you been in Hollywood?" I asked.

"About a year. I been in four pictures already. I'd have been in more," she said, "but I can't get registered by Central."

"Neither can I," I said.

Unless you were registered by Central Casting Bureau you didn't have much chance. The big studios call up Central and say they want four Swedes or six Greeks or two Bohemian peasant types or six Grand Duchesses and Central takes care of it. I could see why Gloria didn't get registered by Central. She was too blonde and too small and looked too old. With a nice wardrobe she might have looked attractive, but even then I wouldn't have called her pretty.

"Have you met anybody who can help you?" I asked.

"In this business how can you tell who'll help you?" she said. "One day you're an electrician and the next day you're a producer. The only way I could ever get to a big shot would be to jump on the running board of his car as it passed by. Anyway, I don't know whether the men stars can help me as much as the women stars. From what I've seen lately I've about made up my mind that I've been letting the wrong sex try to make me . . ."

"How'd you happen to come to Hollywood," I asked.

"Oh, I don't know," she said in a moment—"but anything is an improvement over the life I led back home." I asked her where that was. "Texas," she said. "West Texas. Ever been there?"

"No," I said, "I come from Arkansas."

"Well, West Texas is a hell of a place," she said. "I lived with my aunt and uncle. He was a brakeman on a railroad. I only saw him once or twice a week, thank God . . ."

She stopped, not saving anything, looking at the red, vaporish glow above the apartment buildings.

"At least," I said, "you had a home—"

"That's what you call it," she said. "Me, I got another name for it. When my uncle was home he was always making passes at me and when he was on the road my aunt and I were always fighting. She was afraid I'd tattle on her—"

"Nice people," I said to myself.

"So I finally ran away," she said, "to Dallas. Ever been there?"

"I've never been to Texas at all," I said.

"You haven't missed anything," she said. "I couldn't get a job, so I decided to steal something in a store and make the cops take care of me."

"That was a good idea," I said.

"It was a swell idea," she said, "only it didn't work. I got arrested all right but the detectives felt sorry for me and turned me loose. To keep from starving to death I moved in with a Syrian who had a hot-dog place around the corner from the City Hall. He chewed tobacco. He chewed tobacco all the time . . . Have you ever been in bed with a man who chewed tobacco?"

"I don't believe I have," I said.

"I guess I might even have stood that," she said, "but when he wanted to make me between customers, on the kitchen table, I gave up. A couple of nights later I took poison."

"Jesus," I said to myself.

"I didn't take enough," she said. "I only got sick. Ugh, I can still taste the stuff. I stayed in the hospital a week. That was where I got the idea of coming to Hollywood."

"It was?" I said.

"From the movie magazines," she said. "After I got discharged I started hitchhiking. Is that a laugh or not?"

"That's a good laugh," I said, trying to laugh.

"Haven't you got any parents?"

"Not any more," she said. "My old man got killed in the war in France. I wish I could get killed in a war."

"Why don't you quit the movies?" I asked.

"Why should I?" she said. "I may get to be a star overnight. Look at Hepburn and Margaret Sullavan and Josephine Hutchinson . . . but I'll tell you what I would do if I had the guts: I'd walk out of a window or throw myself in front of a street car or something."

"I know how you feel," I said; "I know exactly how you feel."

"It's peculiar to me," she said, "that everybody pays so much attention to living and so little to dying. Why are these high-powered scientists always screwing around trying to prolong life instead of finding pleasant ways to end it? There must be a hell of a lot of people in the world like me—who want to die but haven't got the guts—"

"I know what you mean," I said; "I know exactly what you mean."

Neither of us said anything for a couple of seconds.

"A girl friend of mine has been trying to get me to enter a marathon dance down at the beach," she said. "Free food and free bed as long as you last and a thousand dollars if you win."

"The free food part of it sounds good," I said.

"That's not the big thing," she said. "A lot of producers and directors go to those marathon dances. There's always the chance they might pick you out and give you a part in a picture . . . what do you say?"

"Me?" I said . . . "Oh, I don't dance very well . . ."

"You don't have to. All you have to do is keep moving."

"I don't think I better try it," I said. "I been pretty sick. I just got over the intestinal flu. I almost died. I was so weak I used to have to crawl to the john on my hands and knees. I don't think I better try it," I said, shaking my head.

"When was all this?"

"A week ago," I said.

"You're all right now," she said.

"I don't think so—I better not try it. I'm liable to have a relapse."

"I'll take care of that," she said.

". . . Maybe in a week—" I said.

"It'll be too late then. You're strong enough now," she said. . . .

4

The marathon dance was held on the amusement pier at the beach in an enormous old building that once had been a public dance hall. It was built out over the ocean on pilings, and beneath our feet, beneath the floor, the ocean pounded night and day. I could feel it surging through the balls of my feet, as if they had been stethoscopes.

Inside there was a dance space for the contestants, thirty feet wide and two hundred feet long, and around this on three sides were loge seats, behind these were the circus seats, the general admission. At the end of the dance space was a raised platform for the orchestra. It played only at night and was not a very good orchestra. During the day we had what music we could pick up with the radio, made loud by the amplifiers. Most of the time it was too loud, filling the hall with noise. We had a master of ceremonies, whose duty it was to make the customers feel at home; two floor judges who moved around on the floor all the time with the contestants to see that everything went all right, two male and female nurses, and a house doctor for emergencies. The doctor didn't look like a doctor at all. He was much too young.

One hundred and forty-four couples entered the marathon dance but sixty-one dropped out the first week. The rules were you danced for an hour and fifty minutes, then you had a ten-minute rest period in which you could sleep if you wanted to. But in those ten minutes you also had to shave or bathe or get your feet fixed or whatever was necessary.

The first week was the hardest. Everybody's feet and legs swelled—and down beneath the ocean kept pounding, pounding against the pilings all the time. Before I went into this marathon dance I used to love the Pacific Ocean: its name, its size, its color, its smell—I used to sit for hours looking at it, wondering about the ships that had sailed it and never returned, about China and the South Seas, wondering all sorts of things . . . But not any more. I've had enough of the Pacific. I don't care whether I ever see it again or not. *I probably won't. The judge is going to take care of that.*

Gloria and I had been tipped off by some old-timers that the way to beat a marathon dance was to perfect a system for those ten minute rest periods: learning to eat your sandwich while you shaved, learning to eat when you went to the john, when you had your feet fixed, learning to read newspapers while you danced, learning to sleep on your partner's shoulder while you were dancing; but these were all tricks of the trade you had to practice. They were very difficult for Gloria and me at first.

I found out that about half of the people in this contest were professionals. They made a business of going in marathon dances all over the country, some of them even hitchhiking from town to town. The others were just girls and boys who came in like Gloria and me.

Couple No. 13 were our best friends in the dance. This was James and Ruby Bares, from some little town in northern Pennsylvania. It was their eighth marathon dance; they had won a $1500 prize in Oklahoma, going 1253 hours in continuous motion. There were several other teams in this dance who claimed championships of some kind, but I knew James and Ruby would be right in there for the finish. That is, if Ruby's baby didn't come first. She expected a baby in four months.

"What's the matter with Gloria?" James asked me one day as we came back from the floor of the sleeping quarters.

"Nothing. What do you mean?" I asked. But I knew what he mean. Gloria had been singing the blues again.

"She keeps telling Ruby what a chump she would be to have the baby," he said. "Gloria wants her to have an abortion."

"I can't understand Gloria talking like that," I said, trying to smooth things over.

"You tell her to lay off Ruby," he said.

When the whistle started us off on the 216th hour I told Gloria what James had said.

"Nuts to him," she said. "'What does he know about it?"

"I don't see why they can't have a baby if they want to. It's their business," I said. "I don't want to make James sore. He's been through a lot of these dances and he's already given us some good tips. Where would we be if he got sore?"

"It's a shame for that girl to have a baby," Gloria said. "What's the sense of having a baby unless you got dough enough to take care of it?"

"How do you know they haven't?" I asked.

"If they have what're they doing here? . . . That's the trouble now," she said. "Everybody is having babies—"

"Oh, not everybody," I said.

"A hell of a lot you know about. You'd been better off if you'd never been born—"

"Maybe not," I said. "How do you feel?" I asked, trying to get her mind off her troubles.

"I always feel lousy," she said. "God, the hand on that clock moves slow." There was a big strip of canvas on the master of ceremonies' platform, painted in the shape of a clock, up to 2500 hours. The hand now pointed to 216. Above it was a sign: ELAPSED TIME—216. COUPLES REMAINING—83.

"How are your legs?"

"Still pretty weak," I said. "That flu is awful stuff . . ."

"Some of the girls think it'll take 2000 hours to win," Gloria said.

"I hope not," I said. "I don't believe I can hold out that long."

"My shoes are wearing out," Gloria said. "If we don't hurry up and get a sponsor I'll be barefooted." A sponsor was a company or a firm that gave you sweaters and advertised their names of products on the backs. Then they took care of your necessities.

James and Ruby danced over beside us. "Did you tell her?" he asked, looking at me. I nodded.

"Wait a minute," Gloria said, as they started to dance away. "What's the big idea of talking behind my back?"

"Tell that twist to lay off me," James said, still speaking directly to me.

Gloria started to say something else but before she could get it out I danced her away from there. I didn't want any scenes.

"The son of a bitch," she said.

"He's sore," I said. "Now where are we?"

"Come on," she said, "I'll tell him where he gets off—"

"Gloria," I said, "will you please mind your own business?"

"Soft pedal that loud cussing," a voice said. I looked around. It was Rollo Peters, the floor judge.

"Nuts to you," Gloria said. Through my fingers I could feel the muscles twitching in her back, just like I could feel the ocean surging through the balls of my feet. . . .

. . . THAT

FOR THE CRIME

OF MURDER

IN

THE FIRST DEGREE . . .

George R. Stewart

1895–1980

Born in Pennsylvania, Stewart served with the U.S. Army in World War I, then in 1922 completed graduate study at Columbia. He spent nearly forty years as professor of English at the University of California at Berkeley (1923–1962). With a lifelong passion for western American history, he published twenty-six works of fiction and nonfiction, including the novels East of the Giants *(1938), which explored California before the Gold Rush,* Fire *(1948), and* The Earth Abides *(1949). Both in* Fire *and in his most successful novel,* Storm *(1941), enormous forces of nature come alive as he charts their impact on the region and on human life. In an introduction to the Modern Library edition he wrote, "A storm itself had most of the qualities of a living thing. A storm could be a character, even the protagonist."*

Stewart's nonfiction interests ranged from Bret Harte *(1931) and* Committee of Vigilance *(1964), dealing with San Francisco lawlessness in the 1850s, to* Ordeal by Hunger *(1936), still his best-known work. The Donner Party saga was a formative event in the history of Western settlement. Books about it had been appearing since J. Quinn Thornton's account in* California and Oregon *(1848) and continue to this day. But Stewart, by absorbing all prior materials available as of the mid-1930s, and by calling on skills he honed as a novelist, transformed this epic tale of survival into a classic historical narrative that is still the account most often turned to for a dramatization of one of California's most celebrated cautionary sagas: the Donner Party's ordeal in the Sierra Nevada in the winter of 1846–1847.*

From *Ordeal by Hunger*

The last desert was crossed! Whatever else might still happen, they would never again be beyond reach of water. Here the cool stream from the Sierra rushed past, fifty feet broad, swift-running, sweet water with no taint of alkali. In the bottom-land grass and wild peas gave luxurious pasture, and trees were growing, actual trees, tall cottonwoods in whose shade a man might rest, the first trees which the emigrants had enjoyed in five hundred miles of scrubby sage brush. Such loveliness following upon such desolation inspired one emigrant-poet, casting about for a metaphor, to hail the Truckee as the River of Heaven itself.

As they rested for a day in the bottom and let the cattle feed up, they were not altogether without reason, hard as their situation was, to think well of themselves. Since they had first struck the Humboldt, they had been no longer forced to camp each night where Hastings had camped, and in full knowledge of the lateness of the season they had begun to stretch out their daily marches. And they had done well in spite of oxen whose hip-bones loomed through the tight-stretched skin, in spite of troubles with the Diggers and of troubles among themselves. Down the Humboldt they had made it to the sink in twelve days, and they could count that an average of twenty miles a day even without allowing for the half-day they had halted on account of Snyder's death. They could tell pretty well from Hastings's camps that he had spent sixteen days in making the same distance. Four days' gain in twelve was good going!

They and the cattle, too, deserved a rest, but they were not going to get it for a while. Lingering in this little paradise by the river was not for them. To cross the desert was only to solve one problem, and two others at once pressed forward—to pass the mountains before the snow flew, and to avoid the present danger of actual starvation. The latter was more imminent. Had Stanton and McCutchen failed—or deserted? The emigrants must have begun to eye Mrs. McCutchen and the baby a little queerly. Wasn't Mac going to come back even for *them?*

Eddy had not eaten for forty-eight hours. Eleanor was almost as badly off, and even the babies had had nothing but the sugar and some coffee since leaving the sink. He applied to Mrs. Graves and Mrs. Breen for a little meat, but they refused him. Hearing some wild geese, he borrowed a gun, and after two hours along the river returned with nine fine birds. This sudden surfeit he shared with the other emigrants. During the day also the Indians again killed some cattle, so that the need of food was supplied at the expense of transport.

After only a day's rest for the oxen, the train pressed on up the Truckee. The bottom land lasted for only two or three miles, and then narrowed into a canyon winding straightly between high rocky mountains, red, brown, and black in color. To follow the plentifully flowing, green-banked river and look up at these parched desert heights was like sitting comfortably in a warm room at home and looking out into a raging snow-storm.

Unfortunately the going was hard, doubly so for the worn-down oxen, many of them still suffering from arrow-wounds. The road ducked and dodged almost as badly as the one which they themselves had cut through the Wahsatch. They had to ford the river more than once to the mile.

On this day Reinhardt and Spitzer came up. Wolfinger was not with them, and they told a briefly tragic story. The Indians had come down from the hills; they had killed Wolfinger and driven the others away; then they had rifled and burned the wagons. Mrs. Wolfinger almost collapsed at the news. The story had an ugly look. To return without your companion was a bad business by western standards. Wolfinger was believed to be rich, and to have much money with him; every one remembered the rich clothes and the jewelry which Mrs. Wolfinger had worn at the beginning of the journey. But it was just as well perhaps for Mrs. Wolfinger to believe the story. The ever-charitable Donners took her in, and the train moved on. They might all be with Wolfinger soon enough.

For three days, scraping at the bottom of the flour-barrels, they labored up the canyon, and then suddenly he came! Three riders and seven pack-mules clumping down the trail. It was little Stanton.

Food in camp again, boys! Flour and jerked beef! And bread baking in the Dutch ovens! You never could tell. Here they had sent out a married man and a single man, and it was the single man who came back. Good little Stanton!

Where was McCutchen? He was taken sick, had to stay at Sutter's. Yes, they had both got through all right; nothing much had happened on the way; they had passed Hastings's company. McCutchen had found friends with Hastings, and they had tried to get him to go back, had even offered him food, to go back and get Amanda and the baby. They thought the Donners were not far enough along, and couldn't ever get across before the snow. McCutchen had gone on. He decided to stick to his promise to the whole company instead of trying to pull out his own family.

Yes, Sutter had given all the food and the mules, gladly. And these two others—they were Indians, good fellows though. They were two of the ones that Sutter had to herd his cattle, *vaqueros* they called them in Spanish. They could catch steers in the most curious ways you ever saw, by throwing a noose. No use trying to talk English to them; Luis understood a few words, that was all. The other one was called Salvador. Spanish was their lingo, and they were Christians, Catholics, that is. You could trust them, even if they were Indians, for they were afraid of Captain Sutter, and he had said he would hang them if they lost his mules.

Yes, he had seen Reed, too; Reed and Herron had just managed to get through. Four days ago as he came into Bear Valley on the way back, he had found part of Hastings's company camped. And that day, down the steep mountainside where the wagons were let down with ropes, two men had come falling rather than walking. A gray mare, tottery and gaunt, too weak even to carry a saddle, came with them. The two were so worn with fatigue and starvation that no one recognized them, but they turned out to be Reed and Herron.

The pair had gone on from the Donners' camp, it seemed, riding turn and turn, until the mare failed. After their few days' rations were ended, they had been able to kill geese by the rivers, and so get along from day to day. But after leaving the Truckee they had had nothing. They decided not to stop and hunt, for fear that they might have no success and would starve by delaying. For several days they pressed ahead, eating nothing but a few wild onions, and at last Herron demanded that they kill the now useless animal. Reed pled for his favorite mare, but promised to sacrifice her if they did not find help soon. They went on. Herron became delirious. That afternoon Reed found in the road a treasure which had spilled from some wagon—*one bean!* He gave it to Herron. After that they walked with their eyes keen for anything more which might have filtered through that wagon-bed, and held themselves well rewarded by finding four more beans. This was their ration for the day, but Herron ate more heavily than Reed, for he had three beans to Reed's two. Next morning they struggled on, and soon came to some abandoned wagons. They searched eagerly for food, but emigrant wagons at the end of the trail were always as bare as Mother Hubbard's cupboard. Reed found the usual tar-bucket beneath one of the axles, but scraping away with the tar-paddle on a despairing hope he discovered that the bucket had previously held tallow and that a little rancid fat still stuck to the bottom! Close by, Herron was sitting on a wagon-rack, but at Reed's words he got up hallooing joyfully. Reed handed him the tar-paddle on which he had scraped together some tallow to the size of a walnut. Herron swallowed it without even a smell. Then Reed ate a little, but even in his starving condition could hardly swallow the ill-smelling filth. The stouter-stomached Herron ate a second helping, and demanded still more. Reed refused, out of fear that to a starving man more of such food ought be fatal. Strangely enough, Herron digested the meal, but Reed had scarcely left the wagons before he became so sick that his companion for a few moments thought him dying. When he recovered somewhat, they proceeded. Not far from the scene of the tar-bucket, they came to the steep descent into Bear Valley, and when part way down caught sight of more wagons. Stumbling down the mountainside, shouting weakly, they at last got to the camp and found food. There, too, they had met Stanton.

That had been four days ago, and since then Stanton had crossed the pass, finding it still open in spite of some early snows. He himself now went on with part of the pack-train to meet and relieve the rear-guard of the train, a day's journey down the canyon. Afterwards he traveled with the Reeds, and the Reeds themselves marched on a little more hopefully for knowing that the family protector did not lie scalped in some gully. Moreover Stanton took them under his care, and they no longer had to walk. They had one of Sutter's mules for their clothing and blankets, and one for Mrs. Reed and Tommy. Patty and Jim each rode behind an Indian, and Virginia behind Stanton.

To the plucky little rescuer the condition of the company which he had come to save must have been a shock. He himself in the noblest spirit of self-sacrifice and social duty had ridden back across the fateful pass, to save— what? It was no longer even the fairly unified party which he had left. Now under the stress of circumstance almost too great to be borne, the cruel individualism of the westerner had gained the upper hand, at least with many of the emigrants. These, more and more, fought wolfishly for their families alone. An old man had been allowed to die on the trail; babies with tongues thick from thirst had been refused water. To rescue these people Stanton had come riding like a knight upon a quest. Having once delivered his provisions, he would have been justified, any one would think, in taking Indians and mules, spurring for the pass. Three days would have taken him to safety in Bear Valley. Instead, he took up Virginia Reed behind him on the mule, and thus they came into the broad-stretching Truckee Meadows.

Here the company reassembled, and the emigrants encamped in the fine grassland which reached along the river for several miles. They were really leaving the arid country behind now; on the mountains round about the meadows pine trees were growing. This was the best place to recruit cattle before attempting the passage of the mountains, and so the emigrants faced another dilemma. It had come to October 20. The weather was cloudy and threatening, and some snow had fallen on the higher mountains around them. Prudence bade them press on with all haste. But prudence also bade them stay, and let the oxen rest and build up their strength. To attempt the passage of the mountains with worn-out teams was only to invite catastrophe. Above Truckee Lake, as Stanton could tell them, the trail went right up over broken domes of granite. It was steep, worse even than the Wahsatch, much worse. Even with the strongest oxen it was a struggle. Every one had to double or triple teams, and many used windlasses and all sorts of devices with ropes.

And more strongly than even the threat of snow, what had happened in the last few days must be considered. On the Humboldt they had gained four days on Hastings, but coming up the canyon of the Truckee he had made it in three days and they had taken four, some of them even five. The teams had been pressed too hard and were at the breaking point. Then, too, Stanton, who of all the company had the best right to make the decision, spoke out for their taking the chance of waiting a few days. At Sutter's the people said that the pass would really not be closed till the middle of November. Hastings, every one knew, had got through on horseback the year before, toward the end of December. This season his company crossing the summit about October 7 had met a heavy snow-storm, but had got through all right. At this time of year the snow would melt between storms. So they took Stanton's advice, although some of them had misgivings, and they let their cattle pasture upon the rich grass of Truckee Meadows.

Then death struck again. The two brothers-in-law, Pike and Foster, sat by their camp-fire as Pike cleaned a pepper-box pistol. Some one called for wood to replenish the fire, and Pike rose to get it. He handed the pistol to Foster, but as he did so, it exploded, and he himself got the bullet in the back. In an hour he was dead.

They buried Pike, and his burial showed the progressing rout of the company. Halloran had been laid to rest in a made coffin; Snyder had been wrapped in a shroud with a board above and a board beneath; but Pike was merely laid into the ground. Sorrow fell on the company with his death. Halloran, Snyder, and Hardkoop had been unmarried; Wolfinger had been childless; but Pike left a widow and two babies. Foster, the accidental slayer, was now the only grown man left among the twelve members of the Murphy family.

Snow fell as they buried Pike. Still they stayed in Truckee Meadows, restless, their eyes shifting from the clouded wintry sky to the gaunt, rib-lined flanks of the oxen. To go or to stay? Stanton's reasoning still held them, but after about five days they began to get under way. They did not leave in a body, but the more nervous and those with the better cattle got off first. No one thought much any more of having the company act as a whole.

First of all were the Breens. The luck of the Irish had been with them; they had lost fewest cattle from the Indians and being in the best condition to move had fretted most at having to halt. With them went their friend Dolan, the Kesebergs, and the wagonless Eddys. Stanton, the Reeds, the Graveses, and the Murphys made a second section. The Donners, solid people and not to be stampeded, took their time, and brought up the rear.

For the first time, from Stanton's story, they had some detail of the road ahead. A day's journey above the meadows it crossed the river for the forty-ninth time in eighty miles, then swung sharply to the right, left the river to avoid another canyon, and crossed a fairly easy range of mountains. Next it descended into a beautiful little valley, crossed a divide, and went on southwards over rolling, heavily forested country with the main range of the Sierra looming up on the right. Then it came to a cabin built two years before by winter-bound emigrants. A quarter of a mile above the cabin was Truckee Lake, and from the lake you could look up at the great wall of the pass. The whole distance from the meadows to the pass was close to fifty miles.

At the first camp which the leading section made after finally leaving the river, an Indian crept up to the cattle and began shooting arrows. He struck nineteen oxen, but failed to kill any of them. Eddy caught him in the act, and drew a bead. At the crack of the rifle the Indian leaped high into the air and with a horrible shriek fell down a bank into some willows. The score was evened a little for so many cattle.

But in the game which the emigrants were playing against Time, the score could not be evened by a rifle bullet, and it stood heavily against them. During those last days of October snow fell as they moved along. The cattle had to nose through it for grass. On the distant mountains it lay white upon the bare branches. Winter was in the air; it was bitter cold, and the sky was bleak.

On a steep downward pitch a front axle broke on George Donner's family wagon. They hauled little Georgia out through the back of the wagon-sheets, and then dug madly into the heaped-up mass of household goods, calling to baby Eliza, who did not answer. At last they pulled her out, limp, smothered, and unconscious for the moment, but not really hurt.

Abandon the broken wagon! Abandon all the wagons! Let the cattle fend for themselves. Take the children and the horses amid push on for life. Get across the pass at any cost—the only chance! Perhaps such thoughts of panic ran through their minds. But the German farmer is not the man lightly to surrender his household goods. Hastily the two brothers cut timber for an axle. Just as they were finishing its shaping, a chisel slipped, and the blood spurted from along gash across the back of George Donner's hand. It was bound up, and he made light of it; there were other things, he said, more to be worried about than a cut hand. There were!

By the time of this accident the Breens far ahead must have been approaching the lake which lay beneath the pass. As they marched, clouds rested upon the high mountains to their right, but occasionally the clouds lifted displaying solid masses of snow. On the night of October 31 they made camp shortly before reaching the cabin. Snow lay on the ground, an inch or more deep. The cattle could not find grass, and made a poor meal of boughs which the men and boys cut for them.

The morning was very cold, and the clouds still hung over the mountains ahead. The Breens and Dolan, the Eddys and the Kesebergs, pushed on. Then the clouds, as if in mockery, rolled away and revealed towering peaks and the pass itself solidly covered with snow. This sight almost sank the emigrants into despair, but still they went on. They passed the deserted cabin, and followed along the north shore of the lake, where the road ran so close that at times the wagons almost seemed to be toppling into the water. They worked on beyond the head of the lake, but the snow was soft and deep, and deepened still as the road rose toward the pass. They reached a point which they thought to be only three miles from the summit, but the snow was five feet deep, and they had no way of telling where the trail was. They could go no further. They turned about and go back to the cabin, which was only a mile in advance of where they had camped the night before. It seemed the end.

The Breens took possession of the cabin. The others camped as best they could. The day had been clear, and in the evening the sky was bright with nearly a full moon. But around it was a ring, and by that sign everyone knew that they should expect a storm. Their folklore was right, and the Breens soon found that the cabin roof of pine boughs merely impeded the rain slightly. They took refuge in their wagons. The rain fell in torrents. All the next day they remained in camp, saying hopefully, like the plains-dwellers that they were, that the rain would wash away the snow and melt it down so they could cross. At dark those of the second section came up, Stanton with them. The Donners did not arrive.

On the next morning the weather was better. Some of the emigrants were in despair and made no further effort, but with Stanton and the Indians as guides those who had previously made the trial and some of the others turned their faces toward the pass. They yoked up the teams, and started with the wagons. But even near the lake the snow was three feet deep by this time, and the oxen after three days of browsing upon branches were weaker than ever. As the men laboriously broke out a way for the wagons, the snow seemed to grow deeper with every yard of advance toward the pass. Soon even the mules were floundering, up to their sides in snow. The emigrants saw now how foolish their hope had been that the rain would beat down the snow, and they realized, what mountaineers would have known before, that at this time of year rain in the valleys meant snow on the heights. As soon as this knowledge had been forced upon them, every one saw that they must abandon the wagons, pack what goods they could upon the oxen, and press on afoot.

Already it was getting late in the day, and indecision over what should be taken along and what left behind caused still further delay. One spoke for a box of tobacco, and another argued for a bale of calico. The packing of the oxen took more time, for the animals were unused to such procedure and objected by bucking off the unskillfully slung packs, or by lying down in the snow and wallowing. Children were so numerous that almost every adult was burdened by carrying one of them. Keseberg had to have a horse, for he had hurt his foot and could not walk. They hoisted him up, and tied his leg up to the saddle in a sort of sling.

At last they got under way again. Clear ahead was the gap of the summit, and it seemed no great distance as one looked at it. Carrying children, driving unruly oxen, and floundering through snow waist-deep, they got ahead but slowly. The road, if here on the pass it could be called a road at all, was buried deep under snow, so that Stanton and the Indians could follow only its general route. A certain mule proved to be the best trail-breaker; so with the little Patty Reed clinging on behind him one of the Indians went ahead, the mule plunging through drifts but making progress. The emigrants advanced on foot for a distance which they though to be two or three miles; they must by this time have been well beyond and above the lake; the summit as they guessed from looking ahead was anywhere from one to three miles farther. But the labor of the advance was killing, and it came near evening. The leading mule began to plunge headlong into snow-filled gullies, and the Indian could no longer keep to any sort of road. So everyone halted while this Indian and Stanton went ahead to find a route. The two pushed on, located the road, and actually reached the summit. For the second time Stanton came back in the face of death to rescue the company.

In the meantime the halted emigrants had become somewhat demoralized. They were all so worn out with carrying children, that resting seemed best of all. Then someone found a dead pine full of pitch, and set fire to it. The flame leaped up into the higher branches, and the poor, half-frozen women and children gathered about its comfort. The oxen, untended, were rubbing off their packs against the tree-trunks. By the time Stanton returned, the emigrants were half encamped, and only the strongest pressure could make them move. Twilight was already at hand. And Stanton's report was not the most encouraging; they could get through, he thought, if it did not snow any more. Sensing the crisis, some of the emigrants urged a bold push forward, but most of them were too exhausted to make a further effort.

So they prepared to the spend the night as best they could upon the snow. They gathered about the fire, and had something to eat. Then they laid blankets and buffalo-robes on the snow, put the children to bed bundled up as well as possible. The men and women huddled about, some making themselves beds, and some sitting crouched by the fire. They were too weary now; they would cross in the morning.

Then it began to snow.

The children slept as the snow covered their blankets warmly. The men and women also slept, or else drew close about the fire. One of the Indians stoically wrapped himself in his blanket, and all night stood leaning against a tree. Now and then a mother shook off the snow from the children's beds as it grew too deep. The night was freezing cold. The wind hissed through the pine trees. The snow fell steadily and fast, mixed with cutting sleet. No one needed to say anything; all knew what had happened. By morning a foot of new snow had fallen. The drifts around them were ten feet deep.

They turned back, and even working down-hill they had consumed the morning and the afternoon until four when they finally reached the cabin. The Donners had not yet come up. Back across the lake, as they looked through the darkening atmosphere of the short winter afternoon, they could see the solid rampart of the pass, a mass of snow unbroken except where bare precipices stood darkly out. It was November 4. The trap which had clicked behind them at Fort Bridger had closed in front.

George R. Stewart

John Steinbeck

1902–1968

One of the foremost writers of the twentieth century, Steinbeck was born in Salinas. His formal education was sketchy: in the 1920s he intermittently attended Stanford University but never finished. His first novel, Cup of Gold, *a historical romance written partly while he worked at a Lake Tahoe fish hatchery, appeared in 1929. His next two books,* Pastures of Heaven *(1932) and* To a God Unknown *(1934), announced the intense involvement with the terrain of central California that would permeate his later and more important works. Like William Saroyan, he grew up in an agricultural community, with an abiding affection for the soil and a respect for those who lived by their hands. His first popular success,* Tortilla Flat *(1935), was followed by three powerful novels that probed the plight of the working man and forever linked Steinbeck with the proletarian struggles of the 1930s:* In Dubious Battle *(1936),* Of Mice and Men *(1937), and* The Grapes of Wrath *(1939), which won a Pulitzer Prize for fiction and has been in print for over half a century. In a very different vein,* The Log From the Sea of Cortez *(1941), written after a trip into the Gulf of California with his best friend, the marine biologist Ed Ricketts, was a signal nonfiction work on marine ecology. Many scholars see that journey and the influence of Ricketts as significant factors in Steinbeck's philosophical development. A playwright and film writer, Steinbeck adapted some of his own works for the screen, including "The Red Pony" and* The Pearl. *He also wrote the script for* Viva Zapata!, *set during the Mexican Revolution, which once again voiced his concern for social justice.* East of Eden, *one of the most important American novels to emerge from the West Coast, and the novel he considered his masterwork, was published in 1952. In 1962 Steinbeck was awarded the Nobel Prize for literature.*

From *The Grapes of Wrath*

The sun sank low in the afternoon, but the heat did not seem to decrease. Tom awakened under his willow, and his mouth was parched and his body was wet with sweat, and his head was dissatisfied with his rest. He staggered to his feet and walked toward the water. He peeled off his clothes and waded into the stream. And the moment the water was about him, his thirst was gone. He lay back in the shallows and his body floated. He held himself in place with his elbows in the sand, and looked at his toes, which bobbed above the surface.

A pale skinny little boy crept like an animal through the reeds and slipped off his clothes. And he squirmed into the water like a muskrat, and pulled himself along like a muskrat, only his eyes and nose above the surface. Then suddenly he saw Tom's head and saw that Tom was watching him. He stopped his game and sat up.

Tom said, "Hello."

"'Lo!"

"Looks like you was playin' mushrat."

"Well, I was." He edged gradually away toward the bank; he moved casually, and then he leaped out, gathered his clothes with a sweep of his arms, and was gone among the willows.

Tom laughed quietly. And then he heard his name called shrilly. "Tom, oh, Tom!" He sat up in the water and whistled through his teeth, a piercing whistle with a loop on the end. The willows shook, and Ruthie stood looking at him.

"Ma wants you," she said. "Ma wants you right away."

"Awright." He stood up and strode through the water to the shore; and Ruthie looked with interest and amazement at his naked body.

Tom, seeing the direction of her eyes, said, "Run on now, Git!" And Ruthie ran. Torn heard her calling excitedly for Winfield as she went. He put the hot clothes on his cool, wet body and he walked slowly up through the willows toward the tent.

Ma had started a fire of dry willow twigs, and she had a pan of water heating. She looked relieved when she saw him.

"What's a matter, Ma?" he asked.

"I was scairt," she said. "They was a policeman here. He says we can't stay here. I was scairt he talked to you. I was scairt you'd hit him if he talked to you."

Tom said, "What'd I go an' hit a policeman for?" Ma smiled. "Well—he talked so bad—I nearly hit him myself."

Tom grabbed her arm and shook her roughly and loosely, and he laughed. He sat down on the ground, still laughing. "My God, Ma. I knowed you when you was gentle. What's come over you?"

She looked serious. "I don' know, Tom."

"Fust you stan' us off with a jack handle, and now you try to hit a cop." He laughed softly, and he reached out and patted her bare foot tenderly. "A ol' hell-cat," he said.

"Tom."

"Yeah?"

She hesitated a long time. "Tom, this here policeman—he called us—Okies. He says, 'We don' want you goddamn Okies settlin' down.' "

Tom studied her, and his hand still rested gently on her bare foot. "Fella tol' about that," he said. "Fella tol' how they say it." He considered, "Ma, would you say I was a bad fella? Oughta be locked up—like that?"

"No," she said. "You been tried—No. What you ast me for?"

"Well, I dunno. I'd a took a sock at that cop."

"Ma smiled with amusement. "Maybe I oughta ast you that, 'cause I nearly hit 'im with a skillet."

"Ma, why'd he say we couldn' stop here?"

"Jus' says they don' want no damn Okies settlin' down. Say's he's gonna run us in if we're here tomorra."

"But we ain't use' ta gettin' shoved aroun' by no cops."

"I tol' him that," said Ma. "He says we ain't home now. We're in California, and they do what they want."

Tom said uneasily, "Ma, I got somepin to tell ya. Noah—he went on down the river. He ain't a-goin' on."

It took a moment for Ma to understand. "Why?" she asked softly.

"I don' know. Says he got to. Says he got to stay. Says for me to tell you."

"How'll he eat?" she demanded.

"I don' know. Says he'll catch fish."

Ma was silent a long time. "Family's fallin' apart," she said. "I don' know. Seems like I can't think no more. I jus' can't think. They's too much."

Tom said lamely, "He'll be awright, Ma. He's a funny kind a fella." Ma turned stunned eyes toward the river. "I jus' can't seem to think no more."

Tom looked down the line of tents and he saw Ruthie and Winfield standing in front of a tent in decorous conversation with someone inside. Ruthie was twisting her skirt in her hands, while Winfield dug a hole in the ground with his toe. Tom called, "You, Ruthie!" She looked up and saw him and trotted toward him, with Winfield behind her. When she came up, Tom said, "You go get our folks. They're sleepin' down the willows. Get 'em. An' you, Winfiel'. You tell the Wilsons we're gonna get rollin' soon as we can." The children spun around and charged off.

Tom said, "Ma, how's Granma now?"

"Well, she got a sleep today. Maybe she's better. She's still a-sleepin'."

"Tha's good. How much pork we got?"

"Not very much. Quarter hog."

"Well, we got to fill that other kag with water. Got to take water along."
They could hear Ruthie's shrill cries for the men down in the willows.

Ma shoved willow sticks into the fire and made it crackle up about the
black pot. She said, "I pray God we gonna get some res'. I pray Jesus we
gonna lay down in a nice place."

The sun sank toward the baked and broken hills to the west. The pot over
the fire bubbled furiously. Ma went under the tarpaulin and came out with
an apronful of potatoes, and she dropped them into the boiling water. "I pray
God we gonna be let to wash some clothes. We ain't never been dirty like
this. Don't even wash potatoes 'fore we boil 'em. I wonder why? Seems like
the heart's took out of us."

The men came trooping up from the willows, and their eyes were full of
sleep, and their faces were red and puffed with daytime sleep.

Pa said, "What's a matter?"

"We're goin'," said Tom. "Cop says we got to go. Might's well get her over.
Get a good start an' maybe we'll be through her. Near three hunderd miles
where we're goin'."

Pa said, "I thought we was gonna get a rest."

"Well, we ain't. We got to go. Pa," Tom said. "Noah ain't a-goin'. He walked
on down the river."

"Ain't goin'? What the hell's the matter with him?" And then Pa caught
himself. "My fault," he said miserably. "That boy's all my fault."

"No."

"I don't wanta talk about it no more," said Pa. "I can't—my fault."

"Well, we got to go," said Tom.

Wilson walked near for the last words. "We can't go, folks," he said. "Sairy's
done up. She got to res'. She ain't gonna git acrost that desert alive."

They were silent at his words; then Tom said, "Cop says he'll run us in if
we're here tomorra."

Wilson shook his head. His eyes were glazed with worry, and a paleness
showed through his dark skin. "Jus' hafta do 'er, then. Sairy can't go. If they
jail us, why, they'll hafta jail us. She got to res' an' get strong."

Pa said, "Maybe we better wait an all go together."

"No," Wilson said. "You been nice to us; you been kin', but you can't stay
here. You got to get on an' get jobs and work. We ain't gonna let you stay."

Pa said excitedly, "But you ain't got nothing"

Wilson smiled. "Never had nothin' when you took us up. This ain't none
of your business. Don't you make me git mean. You got to go, or I'll get mean
an' mad."

Ma beckoned Pa into the cover of the tarpaulin and spoke softly to him.

Wilson turned to Casy. "Sairy wants you should go see."

"Sure," said the preacher. He walked to the Wilson tent, tiny and gray, and he slipped the flaps aside and entered. It was dusky and hot inside. The mattress lay on the ground, and the equipment was scattered about, as it had been unloaded in the morning. Sairy lay on the mattress, her eyes wide and bright. He stood and looked down at her, his large head bent and the stringy muscles of his neck tight along the sides. And he took off his hat and held it in his hand.

She said, "Did my man tell ya we couldn' go on?"

"Tha's what he said."

Her low, beautiful voice went on, "I wanted us to go. I knowed I wouldn' live to the other side, but he'd be acrost anyways. But he won't go. He don' know. He thinks it's gonna be all right. He don' know."

"He says he won't go."

"I know," she said. "An' he's stubborn. I ast you to come to say a prayer."

"I ain't a preacher," he said softly. "My prayers ain't no good."

She moistened her lips. "I was there when the ol' man died. You said one then."

"It wasn't no prayer."

"It was a prayer," she said.

"It wasn't no preacher's prayer."

"It was a good prayer. I want you should say one for me."

"I don' know what to say."

She closed her eyes for a minute and then opened them again. "Then say one to yourself. Don't use no words to it. That'd be awright."

"I got no God," he said.

"You got a God. Don't make no difference if you don' know what he looks like." The preacher bowed his head. She watched him apprehensively. And when he raised his head again she looked relieved. "That's good," she said. "That's what I needed. Somebody close enough—to pray."

He shook his head as though to awaken himself. "I don' understan' this here," he said.

And she replied, "Yes—you know, don't you?"

"I know," he said, "I know, but I don't understan'. Maybe you'll res' a few days an' then come on."

She shook her head slowly from side to side. "I'm jus' pain covered with skin. I know what it is, but I won't tell him. He'd be too sad. He wouldn' know what to do anyways. Maybe in the night, when he's a-sleepin'—when he waked up, it won't be so bad."

"You want I should stay with you an' not go on?"

"No," she said. "No. When I was a little girl I use' ta sing. Folks roun' about use' ta say I sung as nice as Jenny Lind. Folks use' ta come an' listen when I sung. An'—when they stood—an' me a-singin', why, me an' them was together more'n you could ever know. I was thankful. There ain't so many folks can feel so full up, so close, an' them folks standin' there an me a-singin'. Thought maybe I'd sing in theaters, but I never done it. An' I'm glad. They wasn't nothin' got in between me an' them. An'—that's why I wanted you to pray. I wanted to feel that clostness, oncet more. It's the same thing, singin' an' prayin', jus' the same thing. I wisht you could a-heerd me sing."

He looked down at her, into her eyes. "Good-by," he said.

She shook her head slowly back and forth and closed her lips tight. And the preacher went out of the dusky tent into the blinding light.

The men were loading up the truck, Uncle John on top, while the others passed equipment up to him. He stowed it carefully, keeping the surface level. Ma emptied the quarter of a keg of salt pork into a pan, and Tom and Al took both little barrels to the river and washed them. They tied them to the running boards and carried water in buckets to fill them. Then over the tops they tied canvas to keep them from slopping the water out. Only the tarpaulin and Granma's mattress were left to be put on.

Tom said, "With the load we'll take, this ol' wagon'll boil her head off. We got to have plenty water."

Ma passed the boiled potatoes out and brought the half sack from the tent and put it with the pan of pork. The family ate standing, shuffling their feet and tossing the hot potatoes from hand to hand until they cooled.

Ma went to the Wilson tent and stayed for ten minutes, and then she came out quietly. "It's time to go," she said.

The men went under the tarpaulin. Granma still slept, her mouth wide open. They lifted the whole mattress gently and passed it up on top of the truck. Granma drew up her skinny legs and frowned in her sleep, but she did not awaken.

Uncle John and Pa tied the tarpaulin over the cross-piece, making a little tight tent on top of the load. They lashed it down to the side-bars. And then they were ready. Pa took out his purse and dug two crushed bills from it. He went to Wilson and held them out.

"We want you should take this, an' "—he pointed to the pork and potatoes—"an' that."

Wilson hung his head and shook it sharply. "I ain't a-gonna do it," he said. "You ain't got much."

"Got enough to get there," said Pa. " 'We ain't left it all. We'll have work right off."

"I ain't a-gonna do it," Wilson said. "I'll git mean if you try."

Ma took the two bills from Pa's hand. She folded them neatly and put them on the ground and placed the pork pan over them. "That's where they'll be," she said. "If you don' get 'em, somebody else will." Wilson, his head still down, turned and went to his tent; he stepped inside and the flaps fell behind him.

For a few moments the family waited, and then, "We got to go," said Tom. "It's near four, I bet."

The family climbed on the truck, Ma on top, beside Granma. Tom and Al and Pa in the seat, and Winfield on Pa's lap. Connie and Rose of Sharon made a nest against the cab. The preacher and Uncle John and Ruthie were in a tangle on the load.

Pa called, "Good-by, Mister and Mis' Wilson." There was no answer from the tent. Tom started the engine and the truck lumbered away. And as they crawled up the rough road toward Needles and the highway, Ma looked back. Wilson stood in front of his tent, staring after them, and his hat was in his hand. The sun fell full on his face. Ma waved her hand at him, but he did not respond.

Tom kept the truck in second gear over the rough road, to protect the springs. At Needles he drove into a service station, checked the worn tires for air, checked the spares tied to the back. He had the gas tank filled, and he bought two five-gallon cans of gasoline and a two-gallon can of oil. He filled the radiator, begged a map, and studied it.

The service-station boy, in his white uniform, seemed uneasy until the bill was paid. He said, "You people sure have got nerve."

Tom looked up from the map. "What you mean?"

"Well, crossin' in a jalopy like this."

"You been acrost?"

"Sure, plenty, but not in no wreck like this."

Tom said, "If we broke down maybe somebody'd give us a han'."

"Well, maybe. But folks are kind of scared to stop at night. I'd hate to be doing it. Takes more nerve than I've got."

Tom grinned. "It don't take no nerve to do somepin when there ain't nothin' else you can do. Well, thanks. We'll drag on." And he got in the truck and moved away.

The boy in white went into the iron building where his helper labored over a book of bills. "Jesus, what a hard-looking outfit!"

"Them Okies? They're all hard-lookin'."

"Jesus, I'd hate to start out in a jalopy like that."

"Well, you and me got sense. Them goddamn Okies got no sense and no feeling. They ain't human. A human being wouldn't live like they do. A human being couldn't stand it to be so dirty and miserable. They ain't a hell of a lot better than gorillas."

"Just the same I'm glad I ain't crossing the desert in no Hudson Super-Six. She sounds like a threshing machine."

The other boy looked down at his book of bills. And a big drop of sweat rolled down his finger and fell on the pink bills. "You know', they don't have much trouble. They're so goddamn dumb they don't know it's dangerous. And, Christ Almighty, they don't know any better than what they got. Why worry?"

"I'm not worrying. Just thought if it was me, I wouldn't like it."

"That's 'cause you know better. They don't know any better." And he wiped the sweat from the pink bill with his sleeve.

. . .

The truck took the road and moved up the long hill, through the broken, rotten rock. The engine boiled very soon and Tom slowed down and took it easy. Up the long slope, winding and twisting through dead country, burned white and gray, and no hint of life in it. Once Tom stopped for a few moments to let the engine cool, and then he traveled on. They topped the pass while the sun was still up, and looked down on the desert—black cinder mountains in the distance, and the yellow sun reflected on the gray desert. The little starved bushes, sage and greasewood, threw bold shadows on the sand and bits of rock. The glaring sun was straight ahead. Tom held his hand before his eyes to see at all. They passed the crest and coasted down to cool the engine. They coasted down the long sweep to the floor of the desert, and the fan turned over to cool the water in the radiator. In the driver's seat, Tom and Al and Pa, and Winfield on Pa's knee, looked into the bright descending sun, and their eyes were stony, and their brown faces were damp with perspiration. The burnt land and the black, cindery hills broke the even distance and made it terrible in the reddening light of the setting sun.

Al said, "Jesus, what a place. How'd you like to walk acrost her?"

"People done it," said Tom. "Lots a people done it; an' if they could, we could."

"Lots must a died," said Al.

"Well, we ain't come out exac'ly clean."

Al was silent for a while, and the reddening desert swept past. "Think we'll ever see them Wilsons again?" Al asked. Tom flicked his eyes down to the oil gauge. "I got a hunch nobody ain't gonna see Mis' Wilson for long. Jus' a hunch I got."

Winfleld said, "Pa, I wanta get out."

Tom looked over at him. "Might's well let ever'body out 'fore we settle down to drivin' tonight." He slowed the car and brought it to a stop. Winfield scrambled out and urinated at the side of the road. Tom leaned out. "Anybody else?"

"We're holdin' our water up here," Uncle John called.

Pa said, "Winfiel', you crawl up on top. You put my legs to sleep a-settin' on 'em." The little boy buttoned his overalls and obediently crawled up the back board and on his hands and knees crawled over Granma's mattress and forward to Ruthie.

The truck moved on into the evening, and the edge of the sun struck the rough horizon and turned the desert red.

Ruthie said, "Wouldn' leave you set up there, huh?"

"I didn' want to. It wasn't so nice as here. Couldn' lie down."

"Well, don' you bother me, a-squawkin' an' a-talkin'," Ruthie said, " 'cause I'm goin' to sleep, an' when I wake up, we gonna be there! 'Cause Tom said so! Gonna seem funny to see pretty country."

The sun went down and left a great halo in the sky. And it grew very dark under the tarpaulin, a long cave with light at each end—a flat triangle of light.

Connie and Rose of Sharon leaned back against the cab, and the hot wind tumbling through the tent struck the backs of their heads, and the tarpaulin whipped and drummed above them. They spoke together in low tones, pitched to the drumming canvas, so that no one could hear them. When Connie spoke he turned his head and spoke into her ear, and she did the same to him. She said, "Seems like we wasn't never gonna do nothin' but move. I'm so tar'd."

He turned his head to her ear. "Maybe in the mornin'. How'd you like to be alone now?" In the dusk his hand moved out and stroked her hip.

She said, "Don't. You'll make me crazy as a loon. Don't do that." And she turned her head to hear his response.

"Maybe—when ever'body's asleep."

"Maybe," she said. "But wait till they get to sleep. You'll make me crazy, an' maybe they won't get to sleep."

"I can't hardly stop," he said.

"I know. Me neither. Le's talk about when we get there; an' you move away 'fore I get crazy."

He shifted away a little. "Well, I'll get to studyin' nights right off," he said. She sighed deeply. "Gonna get one a them books that tells about it an' cut the coupon, right off."

"How long, you think?" she asked.

"How long what?"

"How long 'fore you'll be makin' big money an' we got ice?"

"Can't tell," he said importantly. "Can't really rightly tell. Fella oughta be studied up pretty good 'fore Christmas."

"Soon's you get studied up we could get ice an' stuff, I guess."

He chuckled. "It's this here heat," he said. "What you gonna need ice roun' Christmas for?"

She giggled. "Tha's right. But I'd like ice any time. Now don't. You'll get me crazy!"

The dusk passed into dark and the desert stars came out in the soft sky, stars stabbing and sharp, with few points and rays to them, and the sky was velvet. And the heat changed. While the sun was up, it was a beating, flailing heat, but now the heat came from below, from the earth itself, and the heat was thick and muffling. The lights of the truck came on, and they illuminated a little blur of highway ahead, and a strip of desert on either side of the road. And sometimes eyes gleamed in the lights far ahead, but no animal showed in the lights. It was pitch dark under the canvas now. Uncle John and the preacher were curled in the middle of the truck, resting on their elbows, staring out the back triangle. They could see the two bumps that were Ma and Granma against the outside. They could see Ma move occasionally, and her dark arm moving against the outside.

Uncle John talked to the preacher. "Casy," he said, "you're a fella oughta know what to do."

"What to do about what?"

"I dunno," said Uncle John.

Casy said, "Well, that's gonna make it easy for me!"

"Well, you been a preacher."

"Look, John, ever'body takes a crack at me 'cause I been a preacher. A preacher ain't nothin' but a man."

"Yeah, but—he's—a *kind* of a man, else he wouldn' be a preacher. I wanna ast you—well, you think a fella could bring bad luck to folks?"

"I dunno," said Casy. "I dunno."

"Well—see—I was married—fine, good girl. An' one night she got a pain in her stomach. An' she says, 'You better get a doctor.' An' I says, 'Hell, you jus' et too much.'" Uncle John put his hand on Casy's knee and he peered through the darkness at him. "She give me a *look*. An' she groaned all night, an' she died the next afternoon." The preacher mumbled something. "You see," John went on, "I kil't her. An' sence then I tried to make it up—mos'ly to kids. An' I tried to be good, an' I can't. I get drunk, an' I go wild."

"Ever'body goes wild," said Casy. "I do too."

"Yeah, but you ain't got a sin on your soul like me."

Casy said gently, "Sure I got sins. Ever'body got sins. A sin is somepin you ain't sure about. Them people that's sure about ever'thing an' ain't got no sin—well, with that kind a son-of-a-bitch, if I was God I'd kick their ass right outa heaven! I couldn' stand 'em!"

Uncle John said, "I got a feelin' I'm bringin' bad luck to my own folks. I got a feelin' I oughta go away an' let 'em be. I ain't comf'table bein' like this."

Casy said quickly, "I know this—a man got to do what he got to do. I can't tell you. I can't tell you. I don't think they's luck or bad luck. On'y one thing in this worl' I'm sure of, an' that's I'm sure nobody got a right to mess with a fella's life. He got to do it all hisself. Help him, maybe, but not tell him what to do."

Uncle John said disappointedly, "Then you don' know?"

"I don' know."

"You think it was a sin to let my wife die like that?"

"Well," said Casy, "for anybody else it was a mistake, but if you think it was a sin—then it's a sin. A fella builds his own sins right up from the groun'."

"I got to give that a goin'-over," said Uncle John, and he rolled on his back and lay with his knees pulled up.

The truck moved on over the hot earth, and the hours passed. Ruthie and Winfield went to sleep. Connie loosened a blanket from the load and covered himself and Rose of Sharon with it, and in the heat they struggled together, and held their breaths. And after a time Connie threw off the blanket and the hot tunneling wind felt cool on their wet bodies.

On the back of the truck Ma lay on the mattress beside Granma, and she could not see with her eyes, but she could feel the struggling body and the struggling heart; and the sobbing breath was in her ear. And Ma said over and over, "All right. It's gonna be all right." And she said hoarsely, "You know the family got to get acrost. You know that."

Uncle John called, "You all right?"

It was a moment before she answered. "All right. Guess I dropped off to sleep." And after a time Granma was still, and Ma lay rigid beside her.

The night hours passed, and the dark was in against the truck. Sometimes cars passed them, going west and away; and sometimes great trucks came up out of the west and rumbled eastward. And the stars flowed down in a slow cascade over the western horizon. It was near midnight when they neared Daggett, where the inspection station is. The road was floodlighted there, and a sign illuminated, "KEEP RIGHT AND STOP." The officers loafed in the office, but they came out and stood under the long covered shed when Tom pulled in. One officer put down the license number and raised the hood.

Tom asked, "What's this here?"

"Agricultural inspection. We got to look over your stuff. Got any vegetables or seeds?"

"No," said Tom.

"Well, we got to look over your stuff. You got to unload." Now Ma climbed heavily down from the truck. Her face was swollen and her eyes were hard. "Look, mister. We got a sick ol' lady. We got to get her to a doctor. We can't wait." She seemed to fight with hysteria. "You can't make us wait."

"Yeah? Well, we got to look you over."

"I swear we ain't got any thing!" Ma cried. "I swear it. An' Granma's awful sick."

"You don't look so good yourself," the officer said.

Ma pulled herself up the back of the truck, hoisted herself with huge strength. "Look," she said.

The officer shot a flashlight beam up on the old shrunken face. "By God, she is," he said. "You swear you got no seeds or fruits or vegetables, no corn, no oranges?"

"No, no. I swear it!"

"Then go ahead. You can get a doctor in Barstow. That's only eight miles. Go on ahead."

Tom climbed in and drove on.

The officer turned to his companion. "I couldn' hold 'em."

"Maybe it was a bluff," said the other.

"Oh, Jesus, no! You should of seen that ol' woman's face. That wasn't no bluff."

Tom increased his speed to Barstow, and in the little town he stopped, got out, and walked around the truck. Ma leaned out. "It's awright," she said. "I didn' wanta stop there, fear we wouldn' get acrost."

"Yeah! But how's Granma?"

"She's awright—awright. Drive on. We got to get acrost."

Tom shook his head and walked back.

"Al," he said, "I'm gonna fill her up, an' then you drive some." He pulled to an all-night gas station and filled the tank and the radiator, and filled the crankcase. Then Al slipped under the wheel and Tom took the outside, with Pa in the middle. They drove away into the darkness and the little hills near Barstow were behind them.

Tom said, "I don' know what's got into Ma. She's flighty as a dog with a flea in his ear. Wouldn' a took long to look over the stuff. An' she says Granma's sick; an' now she says Granma's awright. I can't figger her out. She ain't right. S'pose she wore her brains out on the trip."

Pa said, "Ma's almost like she was when she was a girl. She was a wild one then. She wasn' scairt of nothin'. I thought havin' all the kids an' workin' took it out a her, but I guess it ain't. Christ! When she got that jack handle back there, I tell you I wouldn' wanna be the fella took it away from her."

"I dunno what's got into her," Tom said. "Maybe she's jus' tar'd out."

Al said, "I won't be doin' no weepin' an a-moanin' to get through. I got this goddamn car on my soul."

Tom said, "Well, you done a damn good job a pickin'. We ain't had hardly no trouble with her at all."

All night they bored through the hot darkness, and jack-rabbits scuttled into the lights and dashed away in long jolting leaps. And the dawn came up behind them when the lights of Mojave were ahead. And the dawn showed high mountains to the west. They filled with water and oil at Mojave and crawled into the mountains, and the dawn was about them.

Tom said, "Jesus, the desert's past! Pa, Al, for Christ sakes! The desert's past!"

"I'm too goddamn tired to care," said Al.

"Want me to drive?"

"No, wait awhile."

They drove through Tehachapi in the morning glow, and the sun came up behind them, and then—suddenly they saw the great valley below them. Al jammed on the brake and stopped in the middle of the road, and, "Jesus Christ! Look!" he said. The vineyards, the orchards, the great flat valley, green and beautiful, the trees set in rows, and the farm houses.

And Pa said, "God Almighty!" The distant cities, the little towns in the orchard land, and the morning sun, golden on the valley. A car honked behind them. Al pulled to the side of the road and parked.

"I want ta look at her." The grain fields golden in the morning, and the willow lines, the eucalyptus trees in rows.

Pa sighed, "I never knowed they was anything like her." The peach trees and the walnut groves, and the dark green patches of oranges. And red roofs among the trees, and barns—rich barns. Al got out and stretched his legs.

He called, "Ma—come look. We're there!"

Ruthie and Winfield scrambled down from the car, and then they stood, silent and awestruck, embarrassed before the great valley. The distance was thinned with haze, and the land grew softer and softer in the distance. A windmill flashed in the sun, and its turning blades were like a little helio-graph, far away. Ruthie and Winfield looked at it, and Ruthie whispered, "It's California."

Winfield moved his lips silently over the syllables. "There's fruit," he said aloud.

Casy and Uncle John, Connie and Rose of Sharon climbed down. And they stood silently. Rose of Sharon had started to brush her hair back, when she caught sight of the valley and her hand dropped slowly to her side.

Tom said, "Where's Ma? I want Ma to see it. Look, Ma! Come here, Ma." Ma was climbing slowly, stiffly, down the back board Tom looked at her. "My God, Ma, you sick?" Her face was stiff and putty-like, and her eyes seemed to have sunk deep into her head, and the rims were red with weariness. Her feet touched the ground and she braced herself by holding the truck-side.

Her voice was a croak. "Ya say we're acrost?"

Tom pointed to the great valley. "Look!"

She turned her head, and her mouth opened a little. Her fingers went to her throat and gathered a little pinch of skin and twisted gently. "Thank God!" she said. "The fambly's here." Her knees buckled and she sat down on the running board.

"You sick, Ma?"

"No, jus' tar'd."

"Didn' you get no sleep?"

"No."

"Was Granma bad?"

Ma looked down at her hands, lying together like tired lovers in her lap. "I wisht I could wait an' not tell you. I wisht it could be all—nice."

Pa said, "Then Granma's bad."

Ma raised her eyes and looked over the valley. "Granma's dead."

They looked at her, all of them, and Pa asked, "When?"

"Before they stopped us las' night."

"So that's why you didn' want 'em to look."

"I was afraid we wouldn' get acrost," she said. "I tol' Granma we couldn' he'p her. The fambly had ta get acrost. I tol' her, tol' her when she was a-dyin'. We couldn' stop in the desert. There was the young ones—an' Rosasharn's baby. I tol' her." She put up her hands and covered her face for a moment. "She can get buried in a nice green place," Ma said softly. "Trees aroun' an a nice place. She got to lay her head down in California."

The family looked at Ma with a little terror at her strength.

Tom said, "Jesus Christ! You layin' there with her all night long!"

"The fambly hadda get acrost," Ma said miserably.

Tom moved close to put his hand on her shoulder.

"Don' touch me," she said. "I'll hol' up if you don' touch me. That'd get me."

Pa said, "We got to go on now. We got to go on down."

Ma looked up at him. "Can—can I set up front? I don' wanna go back there no more—I'm tar'd. I'm awful tar'd."

They climbed back on the load, and they avoided the long stiff figure covered and tucked in a comforter, even the head covered and tucked. They moved to their places and tried to keep their eyes from it—from the hump on the comforter that would be the nose, and the steep cliff that would be the jut of the chin. They tried to keep their eyes away, and they could not. Ruthie and Winfield, crowded in a forward corner as far away from the body as they could get, stared at the tucked figure.

And Ruthie whispered, "Tha's Granma, an' she's dead."

Winfield nodded solemnly. "She ain't breathin' at all. She's awful dead."

And Rose of Sharon said softly to Connie, "She was a-dyin' right when we—"

"How'd we know?" he reassured her.

Al climbed on the load to make room for Ma in the seat. And Al swaggered a little because he was sorry. He plumped down beside Casy and Uncle John. "Well, she was ol'. Guess her time was up," Al said. "Ever'body got to die." Casy and Uncle John turned eyes expressionlessly on him and looked at him as though he were a curious talking bush. "Well, ain't they?" he demanded. And the eyes looked away, leaving Al sullen and shaken.

Casy said in wonder, "All night long, an' she was alone." And he said, "John, there's a woman so great with love—she scares me. Makes me afraid an' mean."

John asked, "Was it a sin? Is they any part of it you might call a sin?"

Casy turned on him in astonishment, "A sin? No, there ain't no part of it that's a sin."

"I ain't never done nothin' that wasn't part sin," said John, and he looked at the long wrapped body.

Tom and Ma and Pa got into the front seat. Tom let the truck roll and started on compression. And the heavy truck moved, snorting and jerking and popping down the hill. The sun was behind them, and the valley golden and green before them. Ma shook her head slowly from side to side. "It's purty," she said. "I wisht they could of saw it."

"I wisht so too," said Pa.

Tom patted the steering wheel under his hand. "They was too old," he said. "They wouldn't of saw nothin' that's here. Grampa would a been a-seein' the Injuns an' the prairie country when he was a young fella. An' Granma would a remembered an' seen the first home she lived in. They was too ol'. Who's really seein' it is Ruthie an Winfiel'."

Pa said, "Here's Tommy talkin' like a growed-up man, talkin' like a preacher almos'."

And Ma smiled sadly. "He is. Tommy's growed way up—way up so I can't get aholt of 'im sometimes."

They popped down the mountain, twisting and looping, losing the valley sometimes, and then finding it again. And the hot breath of the valley came up to them, with hot green smells on it, and with resinous sage and tar-weed smells. The crickets crackled along the road. A rattlesnake crawled across the road and Tom hit it and broke it and left it squirming.

Tom said, "I guess we got to go to the coroner, wherever he is. We got to get her buried decent. How much money might be lef', Pa?"

"'Bout forty dollars," said Pa.

Tom laughed. "Jesus, are we gonna start clean! We sure ain't bringin' nothin' with us." He chuckled a moment, and then his face straightened quickly. He pulled the visor of his cap down low over his eyes. And the truck rolled down the mountain into the great valley.

CAREY MCWILLIAMS

1905–1980

One of California's most distinguished modern men of letters, Carey McWilliams was born in Colorado. After graduating from the University of Southern California, he began a lucrative career as an oil rights lawyer in Pasadena. Early literary interests yielded his first book, the biography Ambrose Bierce (1929). One of the first true experts on California history and literature, McWilliams wrote a monthly column for Westways in the late 1930s, and they remain a treasure chest for any serious Californiophile.

As with many intellectuals of the period, the disastrous events of the Great Depression radicalized him and diverted his personal course. As the 1930s progressed, McWilliams shifted his legal interests to farm labor law, and his research led to a series of exposés of the treatment of California migrant fieldworkers in the Nation and the New Republic. He was appointed state commissioner of housing and immigration by Governor Culbert Olson, and his outspoken advocacy for the rights of the agrarian underclass and ethnic minorities enmeshed him in controversy. As a lawyer and an indefatigable scholar, McWilliams had the facts on his side, but by the time Factories in the Field appeared in 1939, he was public enemy number one for the California Associated Farmers, the association for corporate agribusiness. McWilliams continued publishing serious studies of the treatment of workers and immigrant minorities in California after World War II and also produced two broader nonfiction books: Southern California Country: An Island on the Land (1946) and California: The Great Exception (1949) remain valuable studies. He served as editor of the Nation from 1955 to 1975.

From *Factories In the Field*

The erratic and violent development of agriculture in California has been paralleled by the sporadic turbulence which has characterized the history of farm labor in the State. The story of migratory labor is one of violence: harsh repression interrupted by occasional outbursts of indignation and protest. Nor is there much probability that the future will be one of peaceful adjustment to new social conditions; no one familiar with the dominant interests in California agriculture can have any illusions on this score. Violence, and more violence, is clearly indicated. It is indicated not only by the established patterns of industrialized agriculture, but, more explicitly, by the past record of violence in the industry. This record, it should be observed, stems from the early social behavior of the Californians. The history of the Vigilance Committees of 1850 and 1856 is well known and requires no repetition. While it is true that these early committees were organized to cope with crime, it is indisputable that they were largely representative of the "merchants and propertied" classes and that, at least in 1856, their activities were directed in part against organized labor. During the period when the vigilantes were in action, they completely usurped the functions of governmental officials, defied the Governor of the State, conducted their own trials, equipped and drilled an armed force, and operated in effect as an insurrectionary junta. The story of the vigilantes entered deeply into the consciousness of the merchants, businessmen, and industrialists of California. They never forgot the experience and their successors have never hesitated to constitute themselves "vigilantes" whenever the occasion has demanded "action." In 1934 "vigilante committees" appeared in practically every city, town, and rural district in California during the "Red" hysteria of that year. The significance of this deeply rooted tradition of violence must constantly be kept in mind. Insurrection was once sanctioned—violence was once glorified in the historical annals of the State—these facts have been remembered. Hence present-day industrialists are quick to drape themselves in the cloak of the vigilante tradition. Mining camps throughout the West, in Montana, Idaho, and Nevada, quickly improvised Vigilance Committees, on the San Francisco pattern, when they were first faced with a strong labor movement. Vigilantism, as such, had its origin in California.

The eruptions of farm labor have been at infrequent intervals and, in every instance, they have been violently suppressed, each incident provoking a long chain of prosecutions in the courts. No tearful glorification of the occasional protests of farm labor, however, is to he found in the official histories. Whatever theoretical considerations may be entertained concerning the use of violence in labor disputes, it is evident that, from a historical point of view, migratory labor has made gains in California when it has been militant. It has been potentially militant for a great many years, but, when strong protest movements have occurred, they have, in each instance, been directed by a clearly class-conscious leadership. One of the earliest instances of the stirring of deep-seated unrest in migratory labor was the Wheatland Riot, which occurred on the ranch of a large hop grower named Durst, near Wheatland, California, on August 3, 1913. Wheatland, clearly marked as one of the most significant episodes in the history of migratory labor in the West, also forms an important chapter in the social history of California. In the lurid illumination which the fires of the riot cast forth, the ugly facts about the condition of farm labor in California were, for the first time, thoroughly exposed. The riot and the subsequent trial attracted national attention. It resulted in two important public documents bearing on the subject of farm labor (Report on the Wheatland Riot, issued June 1, 1914, and the Section titled "The Seasonal Labor Problem in Agriculture," Vol. V, Reports of the United States Commission on Industrial Relations), and one of the first serious studies of migratory labor *(The Casual Laborer,* 1920, by Carleton H. Parker).

The Wheatland affair marked the culmination of several years of agitational and organizational work on the part of the Industrial Workers of the World. To see the affair in proper perspective, therefore, it is necessary to indicate something of the background of these activities.

In the years between the Chicago convention at which the I.W.W. was formed in 1905 and 1913, the wobblies had been active in the fields, along the highways, on the trains, and in the jungle camps, with their spectacular propaganda and vivid agitation. The roots of the I.W.W.—if the organization may be said to have had any roots—were to be found among the migratory workers of West. Not only were these workers unmercifully exploited—the conditions under which they worked making them highly susceptible to the inflammatory agitation of wobblies—but they followed, in general, the routes pursued by the I.W.W. organizers. Organizers, coming from the timber camps of the Northwest, drifted south into agricultural fields. Always on the move, the wobblies, themselves essentially migratory, moved naturally into the currents of farm labor. Their organizational techniques—action, organizing on the job, low dues or no dues at all—were well adapted to the circumstances under which farm labor was employed. They moved with the workers and organized them, so to speak, in transit.

During the years 1905–1913, the wobblies had demonstrated considerable strength in California. They had, example, conducted two sensational "free-speech" fights: in San Diego and in Fresno. The fight in Fresno was of particular importance, as Fresno has long been the center of agricultural labor in California, located as it is in the heart of the San Joaquin Valley. In Fresno the wobblies fought for the right to maintain a headquarters, distribute literature, and to hold public meetings. For months, through one fall and winter in 1910, they battled the Fresno authorities. As often as they were crushed, they launched new campaigns, finally succeeding in winning a kind of tolerance for their activities. The courage and tenacity of the wobblies in Fresno attracted the attention of many migratory workers and made a deep impression throughout the State.

The San Diego fight was, if anything, even more sensational. Beginning in January, 1912, the San Diego authorities began to suppress wobbly meetings, the campaign culminating in a remarkable ordinance which outlawed free speech throughout the city (San Diego then had a population of about 40,000). The wobblies promptly sent out word for a "concentration" on San Diego, the idea being to crowd the jails and to raise such a fracas that the city fathers would despair of making arrests. Newspapers, at the time, carried scare headlines about "thousands" of workers converging on San Diego; in fact, only about 150 wobblies were involved. To cope with the situation, the authorities sponsored a local vigilance committee which established camps and posted armed guards along the highways leading to San Diego (one of the first California "border patrols"), turning back all transients. In San Diego itself the vigilantes rounded up all persons even remotely suspected of being wobblies and marched them, one night, to Sorrento. There the wobblies were made to mount an improvised platform, kiss the American flag, and sing the national anthem, while hundreds of vigilantes stood about armed with revolvers, knives, clubs, blackjacks, and black snake whips. Then they were marched to San Onofre and driven into a cattle pen and systematically slugged and beaten. After a time, they were taken out of the pen and beaten with clubs and whips as, one at a time, they were made "to run the gantlet." One wobbly subsequently died in jail; scores received serious injuries. Not only was this performance sanctioned by the authorities, but the Merchants Association and the Chamber of Commerce passed resolutions praising the vigilantes. Speaking on behalf of San Diego, the *San Diego Tribune,* in its issue of March 4, 1912, spoke of the wobblies as follows: "Hanging is none too good for them and they would be much better dead; for they are absolutely useless in the human economy; they are the waste material of creation and should be drained off into the sewer of oblivion there to rot in cold obstruction like any other excrement." When one local editor protested, the vigilantes attempted to lynch him. The facts, as I have given them, merely summarize the findings of Mr. Harris Weinstock who was appointed by Governor Hiram Johnson to investigate the incident.

After the San Diego free-speech fight, wobbly locals established throughout California: in Fresno, Bakersfield, Los Angeles, San Diego, San Francisco and Sacramento. From these locals, camp delegates were sent into the fields to organize workers "on the job." Many "job strikes" called and, frequently, they were successful. Largely because of the sensational character of their propa-

ganda the militancy of their free-speech fights, the wobblies built up a reputation in California out of all relation to their actual numerical strength. The
I.W.W. had less than 5000 members in the State in 1913 and less than 8 per
cent of the migratory farm workers were members. Nevertheless, the wobblies
were a great influence. Whenever "labor trouble" occurred in the fields or in
the construction camps, it was usually discovered that a "camp delegate" had
been on the ground. The songs of the I.W.W. were frequently heard in the
fields and in the jungle camps under the railroad bridges. To such an extent
had this agitation permeated the mass of farm laborers that when the Wheatland incident occurred the I.W.W. was able to assume complete leadership
of the workers. Conditions similar to those which existed on the Durst ranch
in 1913 had existed in California for twenty years or longer, but militant action
awaited the arrival of the wobblies.

1. THE RIOT

Immediately prior to August 3, 1913, some 2800 men, women and children
were camped on a low, unshaded hill near the Durst hop ranch at Wheatland.
Of this number, approximately 1500 were women and children. Over half the
total number of workers in this miserable camp were aliens; at one of the
subsequent mass meetings seven interpreters had to be used; and a field boss
made note of twenty-seven nationalities represented in one working gang of
235 men on the ranch. Following the established practice of his fellow growers, Durst had advertised in newspapers throughout California and Nevada
for workers. He had asked for 2700 workers when, as he subsequently admitted, he could only supply employment for about 1500. Within four days
after his fanciful advertisements had appeared, this strange aggregation of
workers had assembled. They came by every conceivable means of transportation; many of them had walked from near-by towns and cities. A great
number had no blankets and slept on piles of straw thrown on tent floors.
The tents, incidentally, were rented from Durst at seventy-five cents a week.
Many slept in the fields. One group of 45 men, women and children slept
packed closely together on a single pile of straw. There were nine outdoor
toilets for 2800 people. The stench around the camp was nauseating, with
children and women vomiting; dysentery was prevalent to an alarming degree. Between 200 and 300 children worked in the fields; and hundreds of
children were seen around the camp "in an unspeakably filthy condition."
The workers entered the fields at four o'clock in the morning, and by noon
the heat was terrific, remaining, as it did, around 105 degrees. The water wells
were "absolutely insufficient for the camp," with no means provided of bring-

ing water to the fields. "Numerous instances of sickness and partial prostration among children from 5 to 10 years of age were mentioned in the testimony." One reason for Durst's chariness about providing water was that his cousin, Jim Durst, had a lemonade concession, selling lemonade to the workers at a nickel a glass. There was no organization for sanitation, no garbage disposal. Local Wheatland stores were forbidden to send delivery wagons to the camp, so that the workers were forced to buy what supplies they could afford from a "concession" store on the ranch.

The commission of inquiry which investigated the incident found that Durst had intentionally advertised for more workers than he needed in order to force wages down and that he purposely permitted the camp to remain in a filthy condition so that some of the workers would leave before the season was over, thereby forfeiting 10 per cent of their wages which he insisted on holding back. Carleton Parker stated that the amount paid, per hundred pounds of hops picked, fluctuated daily in relation to the number of workers on hand. Earnings varied between $1.00 and $.78 a day. Over half the workers were destitute and were forced to cash their checks each night. Throughout the season, at least a thousand workers, unable to secure employment, remained idle in the camp.

The foregoing is a very meager and abbreviated statement of the conditions which were found to have existed at the camp, on and prior to August third. Of the workers assembled, about a third came from California towns and cities; another third were "quasi-gypsies" from the Sierra foothills, with ramshackle wagons and carts; the remaining third were "hoboes," or their "California exemplars, the fruit tramps," with many foreigners among this group, including Japanese, Hindus, and Puerto Ricans. Of this strange assortment, about 100 men were I.W.W "card men," i.e. they had, at one time or another, carried a wobbly card. Some of the wobblies had organized a loosely formed local in the camp in which some thirty workers had been enrolled. "It is a deeply suggestive fact," reads the official report, "that these thirty men, through their energy, technique and skill in organization, unified and dominated an unskilled mass of 2,800 unskilled laborers" within two days. It was subsequently estimated that about 400 workers of those assembled knew, in a rough way, something of the philosophy of the I.W.W. and could sing some of its songs. Of the hundred card men, some had been in the San Diego fight, some had been soap-boxers in Fresno. Among these men were Blackie Ford—an experienced I.W.W. organizer—and Herman Suhr.

Resentment had been steadily mounting in the camp for several days prior to August third. For the most part, the workers were indignant over living conditions; they were not primarily interested in wages. On August third, the wobblies called a mass meeting, Blackie Ford (he was unarmed) addressed the workers, and, among other remarks, told them to "knock the blocks off the scissor bills." He took a sick baby from its mother's arms and, holding it before the eyes of about 2000 workers, shouted: "It's for the kids we are doing this." The meeting had come to a close with the singing of "Mr. Block"—a wobbly song—when the sheriff and his posse arrived with the district attorney (who was, also, Durst's private attorney). The sheriff and a few of his men started through the crowd to arrest Ford. One deputy, on the fringe of the crowd, fired a shot in air "to sober the mob," and, as he fired, the fighting started. The district attorney, a deputy sheriff, and two workers, a Puerto Rican and an English boy, were killed, and many more persons were injured, in the riot which followed. The posse, apparently astonished at the resistance they had encountered, fled the scene. Shocked beyond measure by reports of the riot, the State was immediately up in arms. The Governor dispatched four companies of the National Guard to Wheatland. The guardsmen marched to the workers' camp, surrounded it, and assisted the local officers in arresting about a hundred workers. Most of the workers had left the camp the night of August third, the "roads out of Wheatland being filled all that night with pickers leaving camp." The townspeople of Wheatland were so badly frightened by the incident that the National Guard remained on the scene for over a week.

Feeling that they had a revolutionary situation to cope with, the authorities were panicstricken and promptly launched a campaign of wild and irresponsible persecution. The Burns Detective Agency was called in and a hundred or more of its operatives were deputized. There followed one of the most amazing reigns of terror that California has ever witnessed. Wobblies were arrested literally in every part of the State. No one was ever able to make an accurate estimate of the number of arrests; many cases were subsequently reported of men being arrested and held by local authorities incommunicado for seventy and eighty days. The total number of arrests ran well into the hundreds. Private detectives seized Suhr in Arizona (he was not even present when the riot occurred) and, without legal formalities, loaded him into a box car and brought him back to California. En route to Marysville, California, where the trial was held, Suhr was kept from consulting his attorney, being taken from hotel to hotel by night. Stool pigeons were placed with him to elicit confessions and he was beaten on an average of once a night with rubber bludgeons. It was several weeks after his "arrest" before his attorneys could even discover his whereabouts. Many other defendants were arrested and hurried from county to county in order to elude defense attorneys who were scurrying about trying to find their clients. So terrible was the treatment of these prisoners that one committed suicide and another went insane. An operative of the Burns Agency was, in fact, later convicted in Contra Costa County for a violent assault upon one of the men who was arrested but never tried. Eight months after the Wheatland riot occurred, Ford and Suhr were convicted of murder and sentenced to life imprisonment and this conviction was sustained on appeal, the first California labor *cause célèbre*. During the trial sixty or more wobblies rented a house in Marysville, which they used as headquarters. Every day of the trial, they marched from this house to the courtroom. When Austin Lewis, the defense attorney, needed a witness, he merely scribbled the name and address of the witness on a card and handed it to one of these men. Sympathetic brakemen and conductors on the trains invariably honored the cards as passenger tickets and allowed wobblies to travel about the State hunting witnesses.

Wheatland was not a strike, but a spontaneous revolt. It stands out as one of the significant episodes in the long and turgid history of migratory labor in California. For the first time, the people of California were made to realize, even if vaguely, the plight of its thousands of migratory workers. It had been customary to assume the existence of these laborers, but never to recognize the fact of their existence. The deplorable conditions under which they lived and worked were, also, brought to light for the first time. Although the immediate public reaction was one of horror over the I.W.W. menace, so-called, the incident made an impression. It created an opportunity for effective investigation by the Commission on Immigration and Housing in California which, under the distinguished chairmanship of Simon J. Lubin, did much to improve living and housing conditions among migratory workers in the State. As the annual reports of this commission began to appear after 1914, the Californians were given some interesting facts about labor conditions in the State's most important industry. It was discovered, for example, that, in 1914, there were about 75,000 migratory farm laborers in the State; and that, when employed, these people worked on ranches "devoid of the accommodations given horses." Sample studies indicated that about a fourth of them were suffering from one type of sickness or another and that about an equal percentage were feebleminded.

2. KELLEY'S ARMY

Following the Wheatland affair, and during the winter of 1914, an incident occurred, which for the first time, threw considerable light on the question of what happened to 75,000 migratory farm laborers during the winter months. The number of unemployed in San Francisco that winter was unusually large and the city authorities soon discovered that "General Kelley," a gentleman of mysterious antecedents, had organized an army of the unemployed. About two thousand men had enrolled in the army and were living in abandoned warehouses and store buildings; quite a number were camped in tents in the Mission district. Kelley had his men organized into companies and squads and put them through regular military maneuvers. As the size of the army increased, Kelley became more outspoken in his demands upon the authorities for relief, or "charitable assistance," as it was then called. The officials, and the business interests of the city, soon became alarmed over the situation, and, seizing upon Kelley's desire to stage a "march on the capitol," they escorted his army to the ferries and sent them across the bay to Oakland. The Mayor of Oakland, not at all delighted by this visitation of "rainsoaked, sick, and coughing" men, hurriedly arranged for their transportation to Sacramento. In Sacramento, they organized a "camp" and were to march on the capitol building, 1500 strong, when a rival "army," of eight hundred special deputy sheriffs, arrived with pick handles and drove them across the river, burned their blankets and equipment, and mounted an armed guard along the bridge to keep them out. In the process of ousting the army, the deputies were none too gentle. E. Guy Talbott, a local clergyman, states that many of Kelley's men "were beaten into insensibility and the most atrocious and barbarous methods were used." Within three weeks, the Army, "rained on and starved out," melted away. For years afterwards, however, the story of Kelley's Army lingered in the social consciousness of the Californian as a grim portent of the days to come.

When the Industrial Relations Commission arrived in California in August, 1914, they took testimony both on the Wheatland affair and on the strange rise and fall of General Kelley's Army, and the connection between the two incidents was clearly indicated. "You can't analyze the Wheatland affair and the riot that took place," testified Carleton Parker, "or the problem of the unemployed in San Francisco last winter without bringing into the analysis the seasonal character of employment in California." Testifying further, he said: "The fact that San Francisco is said to have in winter thirty-five to forty thousand men lying up until the earlier season when the first agricultural demand for labor occurs, is explained by the fact that along in November and December, especially in November, agricultural work practically ceases. The State being fundamentally an agricultural State, the industrial life of the State not being of tremendous importance, and the fact that the State is geographically isolated, means that we have to nurse our own casual labor class through the winter. Witness after witness testified as to the instability of employment, the lack of co-ordination, and the refusal of the agricultural interests of the State to assume any measure of responsibility for the situation which they had created. It is interesting to note that one witness did suggest that if the growers continued to shirk their responsibility, it might be well for the State to condemn some of their holdings and settle the unemployed on the land so that they could earn a living. At about the same time, San Diego, faced with a serious unemployment problem, took over four thousand acres of "waste" land, and gave food and lodging to hundreds of unemployed, and paid them fifty cents a day, while they worked in improving and cultivating the tract. The experiment was quite successful and was continued until 1916, when the demand for labor increasing, it was abandoned. August Vollmer, describing the operation of the plan in the *Christian Science Monitor,* advocated its extension throughout the State and claimed that there were approximately 11,000,000 acres of "waste" lands in the State that might be put to constructive social use in this manner.

The recognition of an acute social problem in migratory farm labor, a problem so serious as to shake the foundations of the State, which the Wheatland Riot and the appearance of General Kelley's Army had forced upon the people of California, was, unfortunately, destroyed by the World War. Both incidents passed into history. Even the beginning toward a solution of the problem, as indicated by the creation of the State Commission on Immigration and Housing, was soon nullified. Reactionary postwar administrations proceeded to undermine the work of the commission (Simon J. Lubin resigned in protest), and the chaos of former years once more prevailed.

Carey McWilliams

HILDEGARDE FLANNER

1899–1987

Born into a progressive Indianapolis family, June Hildegarde Flanner was, like her sister Janet (the author of the Paris letters published in the New Yorker), something of a prodigy. She enrolled at the University of California at Berkeley at the age of twenty, and her first book of poems came out shortly thereafter. A student of the poet Witter Bynner, Flanner developed an abiding love of the natural world of California, undiminished even by the infamous Berkeley hills fire that destroyed her family home in 1923. She married the designer Frederick Monhoff, whose engravings graced many of her books, and took up residence in Altadena, where she lived for thirty-six years.

Flanner's early poetry, which expressed a variety of female voices unusual at the time, displayed a passionate connection to the Southern California landscape and recorded her alarm as her pristine adopted region was transformed by urban development. The publication of her chapbook If There is Time by New Directions in 1942 signaled her stature as a serious poet, but other interests and a gradually dwindling readership interrupted her career, and no major collection followed for almost forty years. Even after she and Monhoff fled urbanization to renovate an old Napa estate in 1962, she despaired that "even the earth itself is altered . . . threatens to become a memory" (A Vanishing Land, 1980). In the last eight years of her life, her prose and poetry found new audiences through four books published by John Daniel.

Noon on Alameda Street

Sun, when it shines on traffic, has a look
Of loaded radiance that might explode,
Yet keeps its kindle like a meaning known
Only to motors in the city road,

Only to fury lifted of all horns
Mourning to themselves a thing to come,
For we have heard delirium in a claxon,
Seen revelation lit on chromium.

On Alameda Street the earth is turning
Secret among old sluices and their kind:

The voice of men among machines at noon
Comes like a sigh from history to the mind,

For in this noon there is no light like light,
(Oh, tell us, dark on asphalt, of the sun)
But brightness spawning upon dirty glass,
But fever smoking at meridian,

But men and women riding in their graves
With hands upon a wheel they cannot keep
Clear in the rapt confusion of the crowd,
Crowd and the fate of motion and of sleep.

12 O'Clock Freight

Away, four miles, I heard the Santa Fe
Go down the track, and I could see the sight,
A freighter pulling out with cryptic cars,
So sealed and sullen in the flowered night.

At home and in my mind I saw her draw
Her secrets where black fences line the rail,
And choking orange groves abandoned to
No rain and flaky pestilence of scale.

And then by palmy drives and boulevards
Where stucco gleams beside the carob-tree,
And Spanish patios in vain enclose
Lone hearts from Iowa and Kankakee.

And past Anita's wealthy meadows where
Her smouldering pea-cocks doze among her hounds
With sapphire laces folded in the dark
That daily trail and twitch about the grounds.

On by the oaks whose forest stoops upon
The listing hills where once the drift of deer
Drew down with winter's waters green,
A herd of dreams in glassy atmosphere.

Hildegarde Flanner

Lava Has Meaning

Here lies an ancient, that black rock
Fierce thing so black, black lava sere.
It burns my brain to think the awful shock
Of fire on fundament. Thus it got here.
Thus mountains boiled and liquid altitude
Roared running red, earth's fused earth at the skies
Loud lunged, and valleys in their hot laps brewed
The huge fume like a burning brute. Here lies,
From some old fainted fiery night long gone,
Fraught likeness to this hour, these agonies.
For after havoc, staggering through his chilled
Terrors extinct and black things left in view,
Man has like sable ground to tread upon,
Yet cries (what matter, wild master, could not do)
Cries to his morbid stones, *Stand up, and build!*

The Buck

Heard him from the cliff where the fern dripped,
Faint, deep, he's calling to the doe.
Heard, where the brook ran cold and subtle
Straight from icy vitals of the snow.
Heard him from the trail where summer smells
So soft, and the large air is brightened balm,
Voice like blunt horns in caverns blown, the buck,
In granite silence and cliff glittering calm.
Bell bell that rings in middle of a rock,
His cry of green wood lifted hot and dense,
Till forest feels it in the least, the leaf,
A murmurous knowledge out of sun and sense.
Rumor rolled on mountain wind, heard
From far in wood's black glamour and the place
Witness to such wild beatitude
And the clear startle of Sierran grace.
Somewhere, sheer hope assured, by snow's white side
And the bright dangle of dewed glacier lilies,
Desire does overtake its own at last,

Blithe among cedar slopes the running bride:
Not desperate disunion gaunt on stone,
Not the chilled heart left louder and alone.

Hawk Is a Woman

I saw a hawk devour a screaming bird,
Devour the little ounce sugared with song.
First bent and ate the pretty eyes both out,
One eye and twice, stooping to taste the pang.
Then her dripping tongue she cleaned, then
Into the winsome breast she plied her beak,
Took at a gulp the rosy heart, a pinch
Of too great innocence, drank the whole lark
Down, the inmost blood down, licked the lark down
With vicious dainty pick, oh the damned thief!
To break! into the beating bird! and tear
The veins out, out the joy, flesh out of life.
May hawk be hawked upon, I say,
May she be spied and nailed upon the ground
And feel herself divided and devoured
To ease the gullet of some casual fiend.
She, she! before her agony lapse quite,
Before her breast is eaten to her back,
May she, the very she, may that hawk hear
The ugly female laughter of a hawk.

Hildegarde Flanner

Josephine Miles

1911–1985

Born in Chicago, Josephine Miles suffered from chronic arthritis and was physically challenged from age four. She spent her childhood near the California desert. Her mind set early on being a poet, she was educated in Los Angeles and at UCLA. In 1936, at the age of twenty-five, she won the coveted James D. Phelan Award for poetry, and when her first collection, Lines at Intersection, *was published in 1939, she reached the first plateau of her childhood dream. After completing a Ph.D. in English at UC Berkeley Miles became one of the first female faculty members at that institution, and she remained there for almost forty years as a poet, teacher, and scholar. She published nearly a dozen books of poetry and was also a scholar of English poetic syntax, notably for her three-part study* The Primary Language of Poetry *(1948–1951). She took an active role in local Berkeley poetry groups and encouraged young poets, much as Ina Coolbrith had done seventy-five years before her. For the last twenty years of her life, Josephine Miles was an enthusiastic and much-admired activist in the literary, environmentalist, and antiwar political ferment that came to define Berkeley and the Bay Area.*

Tehachapi South

Tehachapi south down with dust in the mouth
And hills that spin under wheels,
Wild lilac gray, and sunflowers sick of the sun,
And the grade run.

Faint in the ears like a shout the shifting of gears
High on the grade behind, and ahead
Easing out on the road that takes again
The smooth speed of the plain.

The earth bent up into folds yellow and spent
Now passes in pale grass
To a new horizon, farther and more neat,
Cut clean with heat.

The round high pipes following low ground,
Lying apart, bear at heart
Water, water, for men's throats. And the breath
Of the town is in the teeth.

The Directors

See the roofs bend down at behest of moving picture,
We are in montage up to plain omniscience,
The plot pieced, set to be sung and acted in,
And we act in it.

See the trees bend to the reel of moving picture,
The road unwind like plot not neat but nimbly,
The roofs come in, in crowd of complication:
We know the ending.

Not guess what goes behind the hundred windows
Or in the hundred trees that crack the curbstone,
But take it all up into plot and call it
Coming attraction.

We are in simple silence of excitement
Seeing the night unwind as we direct it,
Moving, under impress of moving picture,
Plot into morrow.

Now That April's Here

Coming up to the boulevard stop on the slant,
The poplars standing off along,
The white proceeding and as white crossed,
One would have to look a west sun in the eye.

Picking up after La Cienega the long quiet,
The porch lights flying, still as they are.
The cars staying along the curb north and south quiet,
One would have to go straight chin deep in light on the level tracts.

Stopping for ice, bouncing in short against the red paint,
The store building facing up like a bastille,
One would have to get breath to look off down the street,
Down the low roofs, races of pavement, meadows of evening.

And so I would if there I were, there I would take
One into another the long flat avenues of the angels,
Lower than the west light, the luminous levels,
There through the shiny shallows remember that one dimension.

City

What is my home, what is my city and home,
My avenue of palms, where the traffic ever
Rides and rides,
My Telegraph Avenue where the message filters,
My Shattuck Square of stores?

You are my home, you are my city lights
In which the morning sun entangles when it comes
Over our shoulder like an Easter.
You are my western loss
That brings the city back into its shine.

And I am my home, I am my country town
Through which the highway roars that 101
Leads on its way.
I am the town that to your highway turns
And goes along with it a little while.

Subdivision

Three dogs bark at the street end, hear, this
Is a wild region, animals talk in audible sound,
What if one called it baying, then for 1104
Or 1107A or 1126½
Death were inevitably taking up the ground.

But ground here? ground with its growl and limitation
Not here at avenue. The poorest is paved and scaped.

And lift eyes, one will see the fuel of perpetual dawn
Over 1100 block as over
The civil civic center where it is shaped.

Dog again, it is disturbed. In this briefest meantime
Municipal hum has taken itself close in
And does not as on milder nights accompany
To the 1100 bed and board
The soft-soled progress of the citizen.

Dog answers and agrees; o pioneer,
Five blocks to windward hear the click of rails
Bearing their car away, hear faulting up
Near to 1100 block and nearer
The hoary quarries and the scrub of hills.

Josephine Miles

JOHN FANTE
1909–1983

Born in Colorado into an Italian American family whose experiences figured centrally in his early work, John Fante hitchhiked to Los Angeles in 1930. His mother and younger siblings followed, and he soon found himself living with them near the Los Angeles harbor and supporting them by working on the docks and in the fish canneries. Early in the 1930s he began an extensive correspondence with H. L. Mencken, who became his idol, mentor, and finally his editor when he accepted "Altar Boy" for American Mercury *in 1932. Seven other stories appeared in Mencken's magazine between 1932 and 1937, and they later constituted the core of Fante's collection* Dago Red *(1940). The persona of Arturo Bandini emerged in his letters to Mencken. That artist-as-a-young-man, who rollicked through the L.A. demi-monde of the late 1930s, became the recurrent, self-disparaging hero of four novels, of which* Ask the Dust *(1939) is the most accomplished. The spirit of Fante's work was often compared to that of William Saroyan, and he was popular and respected in the Los Angeles literary set. In 1940 he began a career as a successful screenwriter and saw ten of his scenarios receive major film credits. Late in his life he was rediscovered as a fiction writer—by Charles Bukowski, among others—and Black Sparrow republished five of his books.*

Chapter 12
from *Ask the Dust*

The name on the mailbox was Vera Rivken, and that was her full name. It was down on the Long Beach Pike, across the street from the Ferris Wheel and the Roller Coaster. Downstairs a pool hall, upstairs a few single apartments. No mistaking that flight of stairs; it possessed her odor. The banister was warped and bent, and the grey wallpaint was swollen, with pulled places that cracked open when I pushed them with my thumb.

When I knocked, she opened the door.

"So soon?" she said.

Take her in your arms, Bandini. Don't grimace at her kiss, break away gently, with a smile, say something. "You look wonderful," I said. No chance to speak, she was over me again, clinging like a wet vine, her tongue like a frightened snake's head, searching my mouth. Oh great Italian Lover Bandini, reciprocate! Oh Jewish girl, if you would be so kind, if you would approach these matters more slowly! So I was free again, wandering to the window, saying something about the sea and the view beyond. "Nice view," I said. But she was taking off my coat, leading me to a chair in the corner, taking off my shoes. "Be comfortable," she said. Then she was gone, and I sat with my teeth gritted, looking at a room like ten million California rooms, a bit of wood here and a bit of rag there, the furniture, with cobwebs in the ceiling and dust in the corners, her room, and everybody's room, Los Angeles, Long Beach, San Diego, a few boards of plaster and stucco to keep the sun out.

She was in a little white hole called the kitchen, scattering pans and rattling glasses, and I sat and wondered why she could be one thing when I was alone in my room and something else the moment I was with her. I looked for incense, that saccharine smell, it had to come from somewhere, but there was no incense burner in the room, nothing in the room but dirty blue over-stuffed furniture, a table with a few books scattered over it, and a mirror over the paneling of a Murphy bed. Then she came out of the kitchen with a glass of milk in her hand. "Here, " she offered. "A cool drink."

But it wasn't cool at all, it was almost hot, and there was a yellowish scum on the top, and sipping it I tasted her lips on the strong food she ate, a taste of rye bread and Camembert cheese. "It's good," I said, "delicious."

She was sitting at my feet, her hands on my knees, staring at me with the eyes of hunger, tremendous eyes so large I might have lost myself in them. She was dressed as I saw her the first time, the same clothes, and the place was so desolate I knew she had no others, but I had come before she had had a chance to powder or rouge and now I saw the sculpture of age under her eyes and through her cheeks. I wondered that I had missed these things that night, and then I remembered that I had not missed them at all, I had seen them even through rouge and powder, but in the two days of reverie and dream about her they had concealed themselves, and now I was here, and I knew I should not have come.

We talked, she and I. She asked about my work and it was a pretense, she was not interested in my work. And when I answered it was a pretense. I was not interested in my work either. There was only one thing that interested us, and she knew it, for I had made it plain by my coming.

But where were all the words, and where were all the little lusts I had brought with me? And where were those reveries, and where was my desire, and what had happened to my courage, and why did I sit and laugh so loudly at things not amusing? So come, Bandini—find your heart's desire, take your passion the way it says in the books. Two people in a room; one of them a woman; the other, Arturo Bandini, who is neither fish, fowl, nor good red herring.

Another long silence, the woman's head on my lap, my fingers playing in the dark nest, sorting out strands of grey hair. Awake, Arturo! Camilla Lopez should see you now, she with the big black eyes, your true love, your Mayan princess. Oh Jesus, Arturo, you're marvelous! Maybe you did write *The Little Dog Laughed*, but you'll never write Casanova's Memoirs. What are you doing, sitting here? Dreaming of some great masterpiece? Oh you fool, Bandini!

She looked up at me, saw me there with eyes closed, and she didn't know my thoughts. But maybe she did. Maybe that was why she said, "You're tired. You must take a nap. Maybe that was why she pulled down the Murphy bed and insisted that I lie upon it, she beside me, her head in my arms. Maybe, studying my face, that was why she asked, "You love somebody else?"

I said, "Yes. I'm in love with a girl in Los Angeles."

She touched my face.

"I know," she said. "I understand."

"No you don't."

Then I wanted to tell her why I had come, it was right there at the tip of my tongue, springing to be told, but I knew I would never speak of that now. She lay beside me and we watched the emptiness of the ceiling, and I played with the idea of telling her. I said, "There's something I want to tell you. Maybe you can help me out." But I got no farther than that. No, I could not say it to her; but I lay there hoping she would somehow find out for herself, and when she kept asking me what it was that bothered me I knew she was handling it wrong, and I shook my head and made impatient faces. "Don't talk about it," I said. "It's something I can't tell you."

"Tell me about her," she said.

I couldn't do that, be with one woman and speak of the wonders of another. Maybe that was why she asked, "Is she beautiful?" I answered that she was. Maybe that was why she asked, "Does she love you?" I said she didn't love me. Then my heart pounded in my throat, because she was coming nearer and nearer to what I wanted her to ask, and I waited while she stroked my forehead.

"And why doesn't she love you?"

There it was. I could have answered and it would have been in the clear, but I said, "She doesn't love me, that's all."

"Is it because she loves somebody else?"

"I don't know. Maybe."

Maybe this and maybe that, questions, questions, wise, wounded woman, groping in the dark, searching for the passion of Arturo Bandini, a game of hot and cold, with Bandini eager to give it away. "What is her name?"

"Camilla," I said.

She sat up, touched my mouth.

"I'm so lonely," she said. "Pretend that I am she."

"Yes," I said. "That's it. That's your name. It's Camilla." I opened my arms and she sank against my chest.

"My name is Camilla," she said.

"You're beautiful," I said. "You're a Mayan princess."

"I am Princess Camilla."

"All of this land and this sea belongs to you. All of California. There is no California, no Los Angeles, no dusty streets, no cheap hotels, no stinking newspapers, no broken, uprooted people from the East, no fancy boulevards. This is your beautiful land with the desert and the mountains and the sea. You're a princess, and you reign over it all."

"I am Princess Camilla," she sobbed. "There are no Americans, and no California. Only deserts and the mountains and the sea, and I reign over it all."

"Then I come."

"Then you come."

"I'm myself. I'm Arturo Bandini. I'm the greatest writer the world ever had."

"Ah yes," she choked. "Of course! Arturo Bandini, the genius of the earth." She buried her face in my shoulder and her warm tears fell on my throat. I held her closer.

"Kiss me, Arturo."

But I didn't kiss her. I wasn't through. It had to be my way or nothing. "I'm a conqueror," I said. "I'm like Cortez, only I'm an Italian."

I felt it now. It was real and satisfying, and joy broke through me, the blue sky through the window was a ceiling, and the whole living world was a small thing in the palm of my hand. I shivered with delight.

"Camilla, I love you so much!"

There were no scars, and no desiccated place. She was Camilla, complete and lovely. She belonged to me, and so did the world. And I was glad for her tears, they thrilled me and lifted me, and I possessed her. Then I slept, serenely weary, remembering vaguely through the mist of drowsiness that she was sobbing, but I didn't care. She wasn't Camilla anymore. She was Vera Rivken, and I was in her apartment and I would get up and leave just as soon as I had some sleep.

She was gone when I woke up. The room was eloquent with her departure. A window open, curtains blowing gently. A closet door ajar, a coat-hanger on the knob. The half-empty glass of milk where I had left it on the arm of the chair. Little things accusing Arturo Bandini, but my eyes felt cool after sleep and I was anxious to go and never come back. Down in the street there was music from a merry-go-round. I stood at the window. Below two women passed, and I looked down upon their heads.

Before leaving I stood at the door and took one last look around the room. Mark it well, for this was the place. Here too history was made. I laughed. Arturo Bandini, suave fellow, sophisticated; you should hear him on the subject of women. But the room seemed so poor, pleading for warmth and joy. Vera Rivken's room. She had been nice to Arturo Bandini, and she was poor. I took the small roll from my pocket, peeled off two one dollar bills, and laid them on the table. Then I walked down the stairs, my lungs full of air, elated, my muscles so much stronger than ever before.

But there was a tinge of darkness in the back of my mind. I walked down the street, past the Ferris Wheel and canvassed concessions, and it seemed to come stronger; some disturbance of peace, something vague and nameless seeping into my mind. At a hamburger stand I stopped and ordered coffee. It crept upon me—the restlessness, the loneliness. What was the matter? I felt my pulse. It was good. I blew on the coffee and drank it: good coffee. I searched, felt the fingers of my mind reaching out but not quite touching whatever it was back there that bothered me. Then it came to me like crashing and thunder, like death and destruction. I got up from the counter and walked away in fear, walking fast down the boardwalk, passing people who seemed strange and ghostly: the world seemed a myth, a transparent plane, and all things upon it were here for only a little while; all of us, Bandini, and Hackmuth and Camilla and Vera, all of us were here for a little while, and then we were somewhere else; we were not alive at all; we approached living, but we never achieved it. We are going to die. Everybody was going to die. Even you, Arturo, even you must die.

I knew what it was that swept over me. It was a great white cross pointing into my brain and telling me I was a stupid man, because I was going to die, and there was nothing I could do about it. *Mea Culpa, mea culpa, mea maxima culpa.* A mortal sin, Arturo. Thou shalt not commit adultery. There it was, persistence to the end, assuring me that there was no escape from what I had done. I was a Catholic. This was a mortal sin against Vera Rivken.

At the end of the row of concessions the sand beach began. Beyond were dunes. I waded through the sand to a place where the dunes hid the boardwalk. This needed thinking about. I didn't kneel; I sat down and watched the breakers eating the shore. This is bad, Arturo. You have read Nietzsche, you have read Voltaire, you should know better. But reasoning wouldn't help. I could reason myself out of it, but that was not my blood. It was my blood that kept me alive, it was my blood pouring through me, telling me it was wrong. I sat there and gave myself over to my blood, let it carry me swimming back to the deep sea of my beginnings. Vera Rivken, Arturo Bandini. It was not meant that way: it was never meant that way. I was wrong. I had committed a mortal sin. I could figure it mathematically, philosophically, psychologically: I could prove it a dozen ways, but I was wrong, for there was no denying the warm even rhythm of my guilt.

Sick in my soul I tried to face the ordeal of seeking forgiveness. From whom? What God, what Christ? They were myths I once believed, and now they were beliefs I felt were myths. This is the sea, and this is Arturo, and the sea is real, and Arturo believes it real. Then I turn from the sea, and everywhere I look there is land; I walk on and on, and still the land goes stretching away to the horizons. A year, five years, ten years, and I have not seen the sea. I say unto myself, but what has happened to the sea? And I answer, the sea is back there, back in the reservoir of memory. The sea is a myth. There never was a sea. But there *was* a sea! It gave me food and it gave me peace, and its fascinating distances fed my dreams! No, Arturo, there never was a sea. You dream and you wish, but you go on through the wasteland. You will never see the sea again. It was a myth you once believed. But, I have to smile, for the salt of the sea is in my blood, and there may be ten thousand roads over the land, but they shall never confuse me, for my heart's blood will ever return to its beautiful source.

Then what shall I do? Shall I lift my mouth to the sky, stumbling and burbling with a tongue that is afraid? Shall I open my chest and beat it like a loud drum, seeking the attention of my Christ? Or is it not better and more reasonable that I cover myself and go on? There will be confusions, and there will be hunger; there will be loneliness with only my tears like wet consoling little birds, tumbling to sweeten my dry lips. But there shall be consolation, and there shall be beauty like the love of some dead girl. There shall be some laughter, a restrained laughter, and quiet waiting in the night, a soft fear of the night like the lavish, taunting kiss of death. Then it will be night, and the sweet oils from the shores of my sea, poured upon my senses by the captains I deserted in the dreamy impetuousness of my youth. But I shall be forgiven for that, and for other things, for Vera Rivken, and for the ceaseless flapping of the wings of Voltaire, for pausing to listen and watch that fascinating bird, for all things there shall be forgiveness when I return to my homeland by the sea.

. . .

I got up and plodded through the deep sand toward the boardwalk. It was the full ripeness of evening, with the sun a defiant red ball as it sank beyond the sea. There was something breathless about the sky, a strange tension. Far to the south sea gulls in a black mass roved the coast. I stopped to pour sand from my shoes, balanced on one leg as I leaned against a stone bench. Suddenly I felt a rumble, then a roar.

The stone bench fell away from me and thumped into the sand, I looked at the row of concessions: they were shaking and cracking. I looked beyond to the Long Beach skyline; the tall buildings were swaying. Under me the sand gave way; I staggered, found safer footing. It happened again.

It was an earthquake.

Now there were screams. Then dust. Then crumbling and roaring. I turned round and round in a circle. I had done this. I had done this. I stood with my mouth open, paralyzed, looking about me. I ran a few steps toward the sea. Then I ran back.

You did it, Arturo. This is the wrath of God. You did it.

The rumbling continued. Like a carpet over oil, the sea and land heaved. Dust rose. Somewhere I heard a booming of debris. I heard screams, and then a siren. People running out of doors. Great clouds of dust.

You did it, Arturo. Up in that room on that bed you did it.

Now the lamp posts were falling. Buildings cracked like crushed crackers. Screams, men shouting, women screaming. Hundreds of people rushing from buildings, hurrying out of danger. A woman lying on the sidewalk, beating it. A little boy crying. Glass splintering and shattering. Fire bells. Sirens. Horns. Madness.

Now the big shake was over. Now there were tremors. Deep in the earth the rumbling continued. Chimneys toppled, bricks fell and a grey dust settled over all. Still the temblors. Men and women running toward an empty lot away from buildings.

I hurried to the lot. An old woman wept among the white faces. Two men carrying a body. An old dog crawling on his belly, dragging his hind legs.

Several bodies in the corner of the lot, beside a shed, blood-soaked sheets covering them. An ambulance. Two high school girls, arms locked, laughing. I looked down the street. The building fronts were down. Beds hung from walls. Bathrooms were exposed. The street was piled with three feet of debris. Men were shouting orders. Each temblor brought more tumbling debris. They stepped aside, waited, then plunged in again.

I had to go. I walked to the shed, the earth quivering under me.

I opened the shed door, felt like fainting. Inside were bodies in a row, sheets over them, blood oozing through. Blood and death. I walked off and sat down. Still the temblors, one after another.

Where was Vera Rivken? I got up and walked to the street. It had been roped off. Marines with bayonets paroled the roped area. Far down the street I saw the building where Vera lived. Hanging from the wall, like a man crucified, was the bed. The floor was gone and only one wall stood erect. I walked back to the lot. Somebody had built a bonfire in the middle of the lot. Faces reddened in the blaze. I studied them, found nobody I knew. I didn't find Vera Rivken. A group of old men were talking. The tall one with the beard said it was the end of the world; he had predicted it a week before. A woman with dirt smeared over her hair broke into the group. "Charlie's dead," she said. Then she wailed. "Poor Charlie's dead. We shouldn't have come! I told him we shouldn't come!" An old man seized her by the shoulders, swung her around. "What the hell you sayin'?" he said. She fainted in his arms.

I went off and sat on the curbing. Repent, repent before it's too late. I said a prayer but it was dust in my mouth. No prayers. But there would be some changes made in my life. There would be decency and gentleness from now on. This was the turning point. This was for me, a warning to Arturo Bandini.

Around the bonfire people were singing hymns. They were in circle, a huge woman leading them. Lift up thine eyes to Jesus, for Jesus is coming soon. Everybody was singing. A kid with a monogram on his sweater handed me a hymn book. I walked over. The woman in the circle swung her arms with wild fervor, and the song tumbled with the smoke toward the sky. The temblors kept coming. I turned away. Jesus, these Protestants! In my church we didn't sing cheap hymns. With us it was Handel and Palestrina.

It was dark now. A few stars appeared. The temblors were ceaseless, coming every few seconds. A wind rose from the sea and it grew cold. People huddled in groups. From everywhere sirens sounded. Above, airplanes droned, and detachments of sailors and marines poured through the streets. Stretcher-bearers dashed into ruined buildings. Two ambulances backed toward the shed. I got up and walked away. The Red Cross had moved in. There was an emergency headquarters at one corner of the lot. They were handing out big tins of coffee. I stood in line. The man ahead of me was talking.

"It's worse in Los Angeles," he said. "Thousands dead."

Thousands. That meant Camilla. The Columbia Buffet would be the first to tumble. Sure, she was dead. She worked from four until eleven. She had been caught in the midst of it. She was dead and I was alive. Good. I pictured her dead: she would lie still in this manner; her eyes closed like this, her hands clasped like that. She was dead and I was alive. We didn't understand one another, but she had been good to me, in her fashion. I would remember her a long time. I was probably the only man on earth who would remember her. I could think of so many charming things about her; her huaraches, her shame for her people, her absurd little Ford.

All sorts of rumors circulated through the lot. A tidal wave was coming. A tidal wave wasn't coming. All of California had been struck. Only Long Beach had been struck. Los Angeles was a mass of ruins. They hadn't felt it in Los Angeles. Some said the dead numbered fifty thousand. This was the worst quake since San Francisco. This was much worse than the San Francisco quake. But in spite of it all, everybody was orderly. Everybody was frightened, but it was not a panic. Here and there people smiled: they were brave people. They were a long way from home, but they brought their bravery with them. They were tough people. They weren't afraid of anything.

The marines set up a radio in the middle of the lot, with big loudspeakers yawning into the crowd. The reports came through constantly, outlining the catastrophe. The deep voice bellowed instructions. It was the law and everybody accepted it gladly. Nobody was to enter or leave Long Beach until further notice. The city was under martial law. There wasn't going to be a tidal wave. The danger was definitely over. The people were not to be alarmed by the temblors, which were to be expected, now that the earth was settling once more.

The Red Cross passed out blankets, food, and lots of coffee. All night we sat around the loudspeaker, listening to developments. Then the report came that the damage in Los Angeles was negligible. A long list of dead was broadcast. But there was no Camilla Lopez on the list. All night I swallowed coffee and smoked cigarets, listening to the names of the dead. There was no Camilla; not even a Lopez.

RAYMOND CHANDLER

1888–1959

Born in Chicago, Raymond Chandler was reared and educated in England. He settled in Southern California after World War I, working as an oil company executive. He began writing mysteries during the Depression, publishing his first Black Mask *stories when he was almost fifty. Hard drinking and the economic crash ended his management career prematurely, but, with the publication of* The Big Sleep *(1939) and the introduction of its detective hero Philip Marlowe, he began a distinguished run as California's foremost detective novelist. Chandler and his wife, Cissy, lived in fifteen different places in Los Angeles. He came to know the city intimately, and the changes of scenery informed his feel for the urban scape as a vivid character. His other Marlowe novels include* Farewell, My Lovely *(1940),* The Lady in the Lake *(1943), and* The Long Goodbye *(1953), all of which were made as films.* The Simple Art of Murder *(1950) is a classic nonfiction commentary on literary sleuth narratives and his own work. During the 1940s Chandler was also a successful screenwriter, and his credits include* The Blue Dahlia *and* Double Indemnity. *He died in La Jolla on March 26, 1959.*

From *The Big Sleep*

1

It was about eleven o'clock in the morning, mid October, with the sun not shining and a look of hard wet rain in the clearness of the foothills. I was wearing my powder-blue suit, with dark blue shirt, tie and display handkerchief, black brogues, black wool socks with dark blue clocks on them. I was neat, clean, shaved and sober, and I didn't care who knew it. I was everything the well-dressed private detective ought to be. I was calling on four million dollars.

The main hallway of the Sternwood place was two stories high. Over the entrance doors, which would have let in a troop of Indian elephants, there was a broad stained-glass panel showing a knight in dark armor rescuing a lady who was tied to a tree and didn't have any clothes on but some very long and convenient hair. The knight had pushed the vizor of his helmet back to be sociable, and he was fiddling with the knots on the ropes that tied the lady to the tree and not getting anywhere. I stood there and thought that if I lived in the house, I would sooner or later have to climb up there and help him. He didn't seem to be really trying.

There were French doors at the back of the hall, beyond them a wide sweep of emerald grass to a white garage, in front of which a slim dark young chauffeur in shiny black leggings was dusting a maroon Packard convertible. Beyond the garage were some decorative trees trimmed as carefully as poodle dogs. Beyond them a large greenhouse with a domed roof. Then more trees and beyond everything the solid, uneven, comfortable line of the foothills.

On the east side of the hall a free staircase, tile-paved, rose to a gallery with a wrought-iron railing and another piece of stained-glass romance. Large hard chairs with rounded red plush seats were backed into the vacant spaces of the wall round about. They didn't look as if anybody had ever sat in them. In the middle of the west wall there was a big empty fireplace with a brass screen in four hinged panels, and over the fireplace a marble mantel with cupids at the corners. Above the mantel there was a large oil portrait, and above the portrait two bullet-torn or moth-eaten cavalry pennants crossed in a glass frame. The portrait was a stiffly posed job of an officer in full regimentals of about the time of the Mexican war. The officer had neat black imperial mustachios, hot hard coal-black eyes, and the general look of a man it would pay to get along with. I thought this might be General Sternwood's grandfather. It could hardly be the General himself, even though I had heard he was pretty far gone in years to have a couple of daughters still in the dangerous twenties.

I was still staring at the hot black eyes when a door opened far back under the stairs. It wasn't the butler coming back. It was a girl.

She was twenty or so, small and delicately put together, but she looked durable. She wore pale blue slacks and they looked well on her. She walked as if she were floating. Her hair was a fine tawny wave cut much shorter than the current fashion of pageboy tresses curled in at the bottom. Her eyes were slate-gray, and had almost no expression when they looked at me. She came over near me and smiled with her mouth and she had little sharp predatory teeth, as white as fresh orange pith and as shiny as porcelain. They glistened between her thin too taut lips. Her face lacked color and didn't look too healthy.

"Tall, aren't you?" she said.

"I didn't mean to be."

Her eyes rounded. She was puzzled. She was thinking. I could see, even on that short acquaintance, that thinking was always going to be a bother to her.

"Handsome too," she said. "And I bet you know it."

I grunted.

"What's your name?"

"Reilly," I said. "Doghouse Reilly."

"That's a funny name." She bit her lip and turned her head a little and looked at me along her eyes. Then she lowered her lashes until they almost cuddled her cheeks and slowly raised them again, like a theater curtain. I was to get to know that trick. That was supposed to make me roll over on my back with all four paws in the air.

"Are you a prizefighter?" she asked, when I didn't.

"Not exactly. I'm a sleuth."

"A—a—" She tossed her head angrily, and the rich color of it glistened in the rather dim light of the big hall. "You're making fun of me."

"Uh-uh."

"What?"

"Get on with you," I said. "You heard me."

"You didn't say anything. You're just a big tease." She put a thumb up and bit it. It was a curiously shaped thumb, thin and narrow like an extra finger, with no curve in the first joint. She bit it and sucked it slowly, turning it around in her mouth like a baby with a comforter.

"You're awfully tall," she said. Then she giggled with secret merriment. Then she turned her body slowly and lithely, without lifting her feet. Her hands dropped limp at her sides. She tilted herself towards me on her toes. She fell straight back into my arms. I had to catch her or let her crack her head on the tessellated floor. I caught her under her arms and she went rubber-legged on me instantly. I had to hold her close to hold her up. When her head was against my chest she screwed it around and giggled at me.

"You're cute," she giggled. "I'm cute too."

I didn't say anything. So the butler chose that convenient moment to come back through the French doors and see me holding her.

It didn't seem to bother him. He was a tall, thin, silver man, sixty or close to it or a little past it. He had blue eyes as remote as eyes could be. His skin was smooth and bright and he moved like a man with very sound muscles. He walked slowly across the floor towards us and the girl jerked away from me. She flashed across the room to the foot of the stairs and went up them like a deer. She was gone before I could draw a long breath and let it out.

The butler said tonelessly: "The General will see you now, Mr. Marlowe."

I pushed my lower jaw up off my chest and nodded at him. "Who was that?"

"Miss Carmen Sternwood, sir."

"You ought to wean her. She looks old enough."

He looked at me with grave politeness and repeated what he had said.

2

We went out at the French doors and along a smooth red-flagged path that skirted the far side of the lawn from the garage. The boyish-looking chauffeur had a big black and chromium sedan out now and was dusting that. The path took us along to the side of the greenhouse and the butler opened a door for me and stood aside. It opened into a sort of vestibule that was about as warm as a slow oven. He came in after me, shut the outer door, opened an inner door and we went through that. Then it was really hot. The air was thick, wet, steamy and larded with the cloying smell of tropical orchids in bloom. The glass walls and roof were heavily misted and big drops of moisture splashed down on the plants. The light had an unreal greenish color, like light filtered through an aquarium tank. The plants filled the place, a forest of them, with nasty meaty leaves and stalks like the newly washed fingers of dead men. They smelled as overpowering as boiling alcohol under a blanket.

The butler did his best to get me through without being smacked in the face by the sodden leaves, and after a while we came to a clearing in the middle of the jungle, under the domed roof. Here, in a space of hexagonal flags, an old red Turkish rug was laid down and on the rug was a wheel chair, and in the wheel chair an old and obviously dying man watched us come with black eyes from which all fire had died long ago, but which still had the coal-black directness of the eyes in the portrait that hung above the mantel in the hall. The rest of his face was a leaden mask, with the bloodless lips and the sharp nose and the sunken temples and the outward-turning earlobes of approaching dissolution. His long narrow body was wrapped—in that heat—in a traveling rug and a faded red bathrobe. His thin clawlike hands were folded loosely on the rug, purple-nailed. A few locks of dry white hair clung to his scalp, like wild flowers fighting for life on a bare rock.

The butler stood in front of him and said: "This is Mr. Marlowe, General."

The old man didn't move or speak, or even nod. He just looked at me lifelessly. The butler pushed a damp wicker chair against the backs of my legs and I sat down. He took my hat with a deft scoop.

Then the old man dragged his voice up from the bottom of a well and said: "Brandy, Norris. How do you like your brandy, sir?"

"Any way at all," I said.

The butler went away among the abominable plants. The General spoke again, slowly, using his strength as carefully as an out-of-work show-girl uses her last good pair of stockings.

"I used to like mine with champagne. The champagne as cold as Valley Forge and about a third of a glass of brandy beneath it. You may take your coat off, sir. It's too hot in here for a man with blood in his veins."

I stood up and peeled off my coat and got a handkerchief out and mopped my face and neck and the backs of my wrists. St. Louis in August had nothing on that place. I sat down again and I felt automatically for a cigarette and then stopped. The old man caught the gesture and smiled faintly.

"You may smoke, sir. I like the smell of tobacco."

I lit the cigarette and blew a lungful at him and he sniffed at it like a terrier at a rathole. The faint smile pulled at the shadowed corners of his mouth.

"A nice state of affairs when a man has to indulge his vices by proxy," he said dryly. "You are looking at a very dull survival of a rather gaudy life, a cripple paralyzed in both legs and with only half of his lower belly. There's very little that I can eat and my sleep is so close to waking that it is hardly worth the name. I seem to exist largely on heat, like a newborn spider, and the orchids are an excuse for the heat. Do you like orchids?"

"Not particularly," I said.

The General half-closed his eyes. "They are nasty things. Their flesh is too much like the flesh of men. And their perfume has the rotten sweetness of a prostitute."

I stared at him with my mouth open. The soft wet heat was like a pall around us. The old man nodded, as if his neck was afraid of the weight of his head. Then the butler came pushing back through the jungle with a tea-wagon, mixed me a brandy and soda, swathed the copper ice bucket with a damp napkin, and went away softly among the orchids. A door opened and shut behind the jungle.

I sipped the drink. The old man licked his lips watching me, over and over again, drawing one lip slowly across the other with a funereal absorption, like an undertaker dry-washing his hands.

"Tell me about yourself, Mr. Marlowe. I suppose I have a right to ask?"

"Sure, but there's very little to tell. I'm thirty-three years old, went to college once and can still speak English if there's any demand for it. There isn't much in my trade. I worked for Mr. Wilde, the District Attorney, as an investigator once. His chief investigator, a man named Bernie Ohls, called me and told me you wanted to see me. I'm unmarried because I don't like policemen's wives."

"And a little bit of a cynic," the old man smiled. "You didn't like working for Wilde?"

"I was fired. For insubordination. I test very high on insubordination, General."

"I always did myself, sir. I'm glad to hear it. What do you know about my family?"

"I'm told you are a widower and have two young daughters, both pretty and both wild. One of them has been married three times, the last time to an ex-bootlegger who went in the trade by the name of Rusty Regan. That's all I heard, General."

"Did any of it strike you as peculiar?"

"The Rusty Regan part, maybe. But I always got along with bootleggers myself."

He smiled his faint economical smile. "It seems I do too. I'm very fond of Rusty. A big curly-headed Irishman from Clonmel, with sad eyes and a smile as wide as Wilshire Boulevard. The first time I saw him I thought he might be what you are probably thinking he was, an adventurer who happened to get himself wrapped up in some velvet."

"You must have liked him," I said. "You learned to talk the language."

He put his thin bloodless hands under the edge of the rug. I put my cigarette stub out and finished my drink.

"He was the breath of life to me—while he lasted. He spent hours with me, sweating like a pig, drinking brandy by the quart and telling me stories of the Irish revolution. He had been an officer in the I.R.A. He wasn't even legally in the United States. It was a ridiculous marriage of course, and it probably didn't last a month, as a marriage. I'm telling you the family secrets, Mr. Marlowe."

"They're still secrets," I said. "What happened to him?"

The old man looked at me woodenly. "He went away, a month ago. Abruptly, without a word to anyone. Without saying good-bye to me. That hurt a little, but he had been raised in a rough school. I'll hear from him one of these days. Meantime I am being blackmailed again."

I said: "Again?"

He brought his hands from under the rug with a brown envelope in them. "I should have been very sorry for anybody who tried to blackmail me while Rusty was around. A few months before he came—that is to say about nine or ten months ago—I paid a man named Joe Brody five thousand dollars to let my younger daughter Carmen alone."

"Ah," I said.

He moved his thin white eyebrows. "That means what?"

"Nothing," I said.

He went on staring at me, half frowning. Then he said: "Take this envelope and examine it. And help yourself to the brandy."

I took the envelope off his knees and sat down with it again. I wiped off the palms of my hands and turned it around. It was addressed to General Guy Sternwood, 3765 Alta Brea Crescent, West Hollywood, California. The address was in ink, in the slanted printing engineers use. The envelope was slit. I opened it up and took out a brown card and three slips of stiff paper. The card was of thin brown linen, printed in gold: "Mr. Arthur Gwynn Geiger." No address. Very small in the lower left-hand corner: "Rare Books and De Luxe Editions." I turned the card over. More of the slanted printing on the back. "Dear Sir: In spite of the legal uncollectibility of the enclosed, which frankly represent gambling debts, I assume you might wish them honored. Respectfully, A. C. Geiger."

I looked at the slips of stiffish white paper. They were promissory notes filled out in ink, dated on several dates early in the month before, September. "On Demand I promise to pay to Arthur Gwynn Geiger on Order the sum of One Thousand Dollars ($1000.00) without interest. Value Received. Carmen Sternwood."

The written part was in a sprawling moronic handwriting with a lot of fat curlicues and circles for dots. I mixed myself another drink and sipped it and put the exhibit aside.

"Your conclusions?" the General asked.

"I haven't any yet. Who is this Arthur Gwynn Geiger?"

"I haven't the faintest idea."

"What does Carmen say?"

"I haven't asked her. I don't intend to. If I did, she would suck her thumb and look coy."

I said: "I met her in the hall. She did that to me. Then she tried to sit in my lap."

Nothing changed in his expression. His clasped hands rested peacefully on the edge of the rug, and the heat, which made me feel like a New England boiled dinner, didn't seem to make him even warm.

"Do I have to be polite?" I asked. "Or can I just be natural?"

"I haven't noticed that you suffer from many inhibitions, Mr. Marlowe."

"Do the two girls run around together?"

"I think not. I think they go their separate and slightly divergent roads to perdition. Vivian is spoiled, exacting, smart and quite ruthless. Carmen is a child who likes to pull wings off flies. Neither of them has any more moral sense than a cat. Neither have I. No Sternwood ever had. Proceed."

"They're well educated, I suppose. They know what they're doing."

"Vivian went to good schools of the snob type and to college. Carmen went to half a dozen schools of greater and greater liberality, and ended up where she started. I presume they both had, and still have, all the usual vices. If I sound a little sinister as a parent, Mr. Marlowe, it is because my hold on life is too slight to include any Victorian hypocrisy." He leaned his head back and closed his eyes, then opened them again suddenly. "I need not add that a man who indulges in parenthood for the first time at the age of fifty-four deserves all he gets."

I sipped my drink and nodded. The pulse in his lean gray throat throbbed visibly and yet so slowly that it was hardly a pulse at all. An old man two-thirds dead and still determined to believe he could take it.

"Your conclusions?" he snapped suddenly.

"I'd pay him."

"Why?"

"It's a question of a little money against a lot of annoyance. There has to be something behind it. But nobody's going to break your heart, if it hasn't been done already. And it would take an awful lot of chiselers an awful lot of time to rob you of enough so that you'd even notice it."

"I have pride, sir," he said coldly.

"Somebody's counting on that. It's the easiest way to fool them. That or the police. Geiger can collect on these notes, unless you can show fraud. Instead of that he makes you a present of them and admits they are gambling debts, which gives you a defense, even if he had kept the notes. If he's a crook, he knows his onions, and if he's an honest man doing a little loan business on the side, he ought to have his money. Who was this Joe Brody you paid the five thousand dollars to?"

"Some kind of gambler. I hardly recall. Norris would know. My butler."

"Your daughters have money in their own right, General?"

"Vivian has, but not a great deal. Carmen is still a minor under her mother's will. I give them both generous allowances."

I said: "I can take this Geiger off your back, General, if that's what you want. Whoever he is and whatever he has. It may cost you a little money, besides what you pay me. And of course it won't get you anything. Sugaring them never does. You're already listed on their book of nice names."

"I see." He shrugged his wide sharp shoulders in the faded red bathrobe. "A moment ago you said pay him. Now you say it won't get me anything."

"I mean it might be cheaper and easier to stand for a certain amount of squeeze. That's all."

"I'm afraid I'm rather an impatient man, Mr. Marlowe. "What are your charges?"

"I get twenty-five a day and expenses—when I'm lucky."

"I see. It seems reasonable enough for removing morbid growths from people's backs. Quite a delicate operation. You realize that. I hope. You'll make your operation as little of a shock to the patient as possible? There might be several of them, Mr. Marlowe."

I finished my second drink and wiped my lips and my face. The heat didn't get any less hot with the brandy in me. The General blinked at me and plucked at the edge of his rug.

"Can I make a deal with this guy, if I think he's within hooting distance of being on the level?"

"Yes. The matter is now in your hands. I never do things by halves."

"I'll take him out," I said. "He'll think a bridge fell on him."

"I'm sure you will. And now I must excuse myself. I am tired." He reached out and touched the bell on the arm of his chair. The cord was plugged into a black cable that wound along the side of the deep dark green boxes in which the orchids grew and festered. He closed his eyes, opened them again in a brief bright stare, and settled back among his cushions. The lids dropped again and he didn't pay any more attention to me.

I stood up and lifted my coat off the back of the damp wicker chair and went off with it among the orchids, opened the two doors and stood outside in the brisk October air getting myself some oxygen. The chauffeur over by the garage had gone away. The butler came along the red path with smooth light steps and his back as straight as an ironing board. I shrugged into my coat and watched him come.

He stopped about two feet from me and said gravely:

"Mrs. Regan would like to see you before you leave, sir. And in the matter of money the General has instructed me to give you a check for whatever seems desirable."

"Instructed you how?"

He looked puzzled, then he smiled. "Ah, I see, sir. You are, of course, a detective. By the way he rang his bell."

"You write his checks?"

"I have that privilege."

"That ought to save you from a pauper's grave. No money now, thanks. What does Mrs. Regan want to see me about?"

His blue eyes gave me a smooth level look. "She has a misconception of the purpose of your visit, sir."

"Who told her anything about my visit?"

"Her windows command the greenhouse. She saw us go in. I was obliged to tell her who you were."

"I don't like that," I said.

His blue eyes frosted. "Are you attempting to tell me my duties, sir?"

"No. But I'm having a lot of fun trying to guess what they are."

We stared at each other for a moment. He gave me a blue glare and turned away.

Nathanael West

1903–1940

Born Nathan Wallenstein Weinstein in New York, West came to Cali-fornia late in the 1930s to write film scripts. Primed by earlier satirical works such as Miss Lonelyhearts *(1933), he was a connoisseur of disenchant-ment with American dreams, and what he found in Hollywood did not disappoint him. The Day of the Locust (1939) was initially titled* The Cheated, *and it dealt with the hordes of people—especially those from the Midwest—who came to Southern California for breathy excitement but found that life was a numbing succession of perfect, empty, cloudless days. Whereas F. Scott Fitzgerald was fascinated by the studios and movie impresarios, Horace McCoy and Nathanael West worked the fringes of Hollywood. McCoy saw a faded dream in the world of aspiring film extras, and West focused on "losers" like Homer Simpson and "freaks" such as the boy-star Divine. A wickedly gifted cartoonist and caricaturist, West saw misfits everywhere, people who never quite felt they were getting what was promised them when they left Des Moines, people who felt, in short, cosmically cheated. Set designer Tod Hackett's absentminded fantasy of paint-ing the apocalyptic masterpiece "The Burning of Los Angeles" becomes all too real when the cheated erupt in outrage at the showy vacuousness of another luxury theater grand opening and turn on Hackett himself. West and his wife were killed in an automobile accident in 1940, as they hurried from Mexico to attend Fitzgerald's funeral in Los Angeles.*

Chapter 27
from *The Day of the Locust*

When Tod reached the street, he saw a dozen great violet shafts of light mov-ing across the evening sky in wide crazy sweeps. Whenever one of the fiery columns reached the lowest point of its arc, it lit for a moment the rose-colored domes and delicate minarets of Kahn's Persian Palace Theatre. The purpose of this display was to signal the world premiere of a new picture.

Turning his back on the searchlights, he started in the opposite direction, toward Homer's place. Before he had gone very far, he saw a clock that read a quarter past six and changed his mind about going back just yet. He might as well let the poor fellow sleep for another hour and kill some time by looking at the crowds.

When still a block from the theatre, he saw an enormous electric sign that hung over the middle of the street. In letters ten feet high he read that—

MR. KAHN A PLEASURE DOME DECREED

Although it was still several hours before the celebrities would arrive, thousands of people had already gathered. They stood facing the theatre with their backs toward the gutter in a thick line hundreds of feet long. A big squad of policemen was trying to keep a lane open between the front rank of the crowd and the facade of the theatre.

Tod entered the lane while the policeman guarding it was busy with a woman whose parcel had torn open, dropping oranges all over the place. Another policeman shouted for him to get the hell across the street but he took a chance and kept going. They had enough to do without chasing him. He noticed how worried they looked and how careful they tried to be. If they had to arrest someone, they joked good-naturedly with the culprit, making light of it until they got him around the corner, then they whaled him with their clubs. Only so long as the man was actually part of the crowd did they have to be gentle.

Tod had walked only a short distance along the narrow lane when he began to get frightened. People shouted, commenting on his hat, his carriage, and his clothing. There was a continuous roar of catcalls, laughter and yells, pierced occasionally by a scream. The scream was usually followed by a sudden movement in the dense mass and part of it would surge forward wherever the police line was weakest. As soon as that part was rammed back, the bulge would pop out somewhere else.

The police force would have to be doubled when the stars started to arrive. At the sight of their heroes and heroines, the crowd would turn demoniac. Some little gesture, either too pleasing or too offensive, would start it moving and then nothing but machine guns would stop it. Individually the purpose of its members might simply to be to get a souvenir, but collectively it would grab and rend.

A young man with a portable microphone was describing the scene. His rapid, hysterical voice was like that of a revivalist preacher whipping his congregation toward the ecstasy of fits.

"What a crowd, folks! What a crowd! There must be ten thousand excited, screaming fans outside Kahn's Persian tonight. The police can't hold them. Here, listen to them roar."

He held the microphone out and those near it obligingly roared for him.

"Did you hear it? It's a bedlam, folks. A veritable bedlam! What excitement! Of all the premieres I've attended, this is the most . . . the most . . . stupendous, folks. Can the police hold them? Can they? It doesn't look so, folks . . ."

Another squad of police came charging up. The sergeant pleaded with the announcer to stand further back so the people couldn't hear him. His men threw themselves at the crowd. It allowed itself to be bustled and shoved out of habit and because it lacked an objective. It tolerated the police, just as a bull elephant does when he allows a small boy to drive him with a light stick.

Tod could see very few people who looked tough, nor could he see any working men. The crowd was made up of the lower middle classes, every other person one of his torchbearers.

Just as he came near the end of the lane, it closed in front of him with a heave, and he had to fight his way through. Someone knocked his hat off and when he stooped to pick it up, someone kicked him. He whirled around angrily and found himself surrounded by people who were laughing at him. He knew enough to laugh with them. The crowd became sympathetic. A stout woman slapped him on the back, while a man handed him his hat, first brushing it carefully with his sleeve. Still another man shouted for a way to be cleared.

By a great deal of pushing and squirming, always trying to look as though he were enjoying himself, Tod finally managed to break into the open. After rearranging his clothes, he went over to a parking lot and sat down on the low retaining wall that ran along the front of it.

New groups, whole families, kept arriving. He could see a change come over them as soon as they had become part of the crowd. Until they reached the line, they looked diffident, almost furtive, but the moment they had become part of it, they turned arrogant and pugnacious. It was a mistake to think them harmless curiosity seekers. They were savage and bitter, especially the middle-aged and the old, and had been made so by boredom and disappointment.

All their lives they had slaved at some kind of dull, heavy labor, behind desks and counters, in the fields and at tedious machines of all sorts, saving their pennies and dreaming of the leisure that would be theirs when they had enough. Finally that day came. They could draw a weekly income of ten or fifteen dollars: Where else should they go but California, the land of sunshine and oranges?

Once there, they discover that sunshine isn't enough. They get tired of oranges, even of avocado pears and passion fruit. Nothing happens. They don't know what to do with their time. They haven't the mental equipment for leisure, the money nor the physical equipment for pleasure. Did they slave so long just to go to an occasional Iowa picnic? What else is there? They watch the waves come in at Venice. There wasn't any ocean where most of them came from, but after you've seen one wave, you've seen them all. The same is true of the airplanes at Glendale. If only a plane would crash once in a while so that they could watch the passengers being consumed in a "holocaust of flame," as the newspapers put it. But the planes never crash.

Their boredom becomes more and more terrible. They realize that they've been tricked and burn with resentment. Every day of their lives they read the newspapers and went to the movies. Both fed them on lynchings, murder, sex crimes, explosions, wrecks, love nests, fires, miracles, revolutions, wars. This daily diet made sophisticates of them all. The sun is a joke. Oranges can't titillate their jaded palates. Nothing can ever be violent enough to make taut their slack minds and bodies. They have been cheated and betrayed. They have slaved and saved for nothing.

Tod stood up. During the ten minutes he had been sitting on the wall, the crowd had grown thirty feet and he was afraid that his escape might be cut off if he loitered much longer. He crossed to the other side of the street and started back.

He was trying to figure what to do if he were unable to wake Homer, when suddenly he saw his head bobbing above the crowd. He hurried toward him. From his appearance, it was evident that there was something definitely wrong.

Homer walked more than ever like a badly made automaton and his features were set in a rigid, mechanical grin. He had his trousers on over his nightgown and part of it hung out of his open fly. In both of his hands were suitcases. With each step, he lurched to one side then the other, using the suitcases for balance weights.

Tod stopped directly in front of him, blocking his way.

"Where're you going?"

"Wayneville," he replied, using an extraordinary jaw movement to get out this single word.

"That's fine. But you can't walk to the station from here. It's in Los Angeles."

Homer tried to get around him, but he caught his arm.

"We'll get a taxi. I'll go with you."

The cabs were all being routed around the block because of the preview. He explained this to Homer and tried to get him to walk to the corner.

"Come on, we're sure to get one on the next street."

Once Tod got him into a cab, he intended to tell the driver to go to the nearest hospital. But Homer wouldn't budge, no matter how hard he yanked and pleaded. People stopped to watch them, others turned their heads curiously. He decided to leave him and get a cab.

"I'll come right back," he said.

He couldn't tell from either Homer's eyes or expression whether he heard, for they both were empty of everything, even annoyance. At the corner he looked around and saw that Homer had started to cross the street, moving blindly. Brakes screeched and twice he was almost run over, but he didn't swerve or hurry. He moved in a straight diagonal. When he reached the other curb, he tried to get on the sidewalk at a point where the crowd was very thick and was shoved violently back. He made another attempt and this time a policeman grabbed him by the back of the neck and hustled him to the end of the line. When the policeman let go of him, he kept on walking as though nothing had happened.

Tod tried to get over to him, but was unable to cross until the traffic lights changed. When he reached the other side, he found Homer sitting on a bench, fifty or sixty feet from the outskirts of the crowd.

He put his arm around Homer's shoulder and suggested that they walk a few blocks further. When Homer didn't answer, he reached over to pick up one of the valises. Homer held on to it.

"I'll carry it for you," he said, tugging gently.

"Thief!"

Before Homer could repeat the shout, he jumped away. It would be extremely embarrassing if Homer shouted thief in front of a cop. He thought of phoning for an ambulance. But then, after all, how could he be sure that Homer was crazy? He was sitting quietly on the bench, minding his own business.

Tod decided to wait, then try again to get him into a cab. The crowd was growing in size all the time, but it would be at least half an hour before it over-ran the bench. Before that happened, he would think of some plan. He moved a short distance away and stood with his back to a store window so that he could watch Homer without attracting attention.

About ten feet from where Homer was sitting grew a large eucalyptus tree and behind the trunk of the tree was a little boy. Tod saw him peer around it with great caution, then suddenly jerk his head back. A minute later he repeated the maneuver. At first Tod thought he was playing hide and seek, then noticed that he had a string in his hand which was attached to an old purse that lay in front of Homer's bench. Every once in a while the child would jerk the string, making the purse hop like a sluggish toad. Its torn lining hung from its iron mouth like a furry tongue and a few uncertain flies hovered over it.

Tod knew the game the child was playing. He used to play it himself when he was small. If Homer reached to pick up the purse, thinking there was money in it, he would yank it away and scream with laughter.

When Tod went over to the tree, he was surprised to discover that it was Adore Loomis, the kid who lived across the street from Homer. Tod tried to chase him, but he dodged around the tree, thumbing his nose. He gave up and went back to his original position. The moment he left, Adore got busy with his purse again. Homer wasn't paying any attention to the child, so Tod decided to let him alone.

Mrs. Loomis must he somewhere in the crowd, he thought. Tonight when she found Adore, she would give him a hiding. He had torn the pocket of his jacket and his Buster Brown collar was smeared with grease.

Adore had a nasty temper. The completeness with which Homer ignored both him and his pocketbook made him frantic. He gave up dancing it at the end of the string and approached the bench on tiptoes, making ferocious faces, yet ready to run at Homer's first move. He stopped in when about four feet away and stuck his tongue out. Homer ignored him. He took another step forward and ran through a series of insulting gestures.

If Tod had known that the boy held a stone in his hand, he would have interfered. But he felt sure that Homer wouldn't hurt the child and was waiting to see if he wouldn't move because of his pestering. When Adore raised his arm, it was too late. The stone hit Homer in the face. The boy turned to flee, but tripped and fell. Before he could scramble away, Homer landed on his back with both feet, then jumped again.

Tod yelled for him to stop and tried to yank him away. He shoved Tod and went on using his heels. Tod hit him as hard as he could, first in the belly, then in the face. He ignored the blows and continued to stamp on the boy. Tod hit him again and again, then threw both arms around him and tried to pull him off. He couldn't budge him. He was like a stone column.

The next thing Tod knew, he was torn loose from Homer and sent to his knees by a blow in the back of the head that spun him sideways. The crowd in front of the theatre had charged. He was surrounded by churning legs and feet. He pulled himself erect by grabbing a man's coat, then let himself be carried along backwards in a long backwards in a long, curving swoop. He saw Homer rise above the mass for a moment, shoved against the sky, his jaw hanging as though he wanted to scream but couldn't. A hand reached up and caught him by his open mouth and pulled him forward and down.

There was another dizzy rush. Tod closed his eyes and fought to keep upright. He was jostled about in a hacking cross surf of shoulders and backs, carried rapidly in one direction and then in the opposite. He kept pushing and hitting out at the people around him, trying to face in the direction he was going. Being carried backwards terrified him.

Using the eucalyptus tree as a landmark, he tried to work toward it by slipping sideways against the tide, pushing hard when carried away from it and riding the current when it moved toward his objective. He was within only a few feet of the tree when a sudden, driving rush carried him far past it. He struggled desperately for a moment, then gave up and let himself be swept along. He was the spearhead of a flying wedge when it collided with a mass going in the opposite direction. The impact turned him around. As the two forces ground against each other, he was turned again and again, like a grain between millstones. This didn't stop until he became part of the opposing force. The pressure continued to increase until he thought he must collapse. He was slowly pushed into the air. Although relief for his cracking ribs could be gotten by continuing to rise, he fought to keep his feet on the ground. Not being able to touch was an even more dreadful sensation than being carried backwards.

There was another rush, shorter this time, and he found himself in a dead spot where the pressure was less and equal. He became conscious of a terrible pain in his left leg, just above the ankle, and tried to work it into a more comfortable position. He couldn't turn his body, but managed to get his head around. A very skinny boy, wearing a Western Union cap, had his back wedged against his shoulder. The pain continued to grow and his whole leg as high as the groin throbbed. He finally got his left arm free and took the back of the boy's neck in his fingers. He twisted as hard as he could. The boy began to jump up and down in his clothes. He managed to straighten his elbow, by pushing at the back of the boy's head, and so turn half way around and free his leg. The pain didn't grow less.

There was another wild surge forward that ended in another dead spot. He now faced a young girl who was sobbing steadily. Her silk print dress had been torn down the front and her tiny brassiere hung from one strap. He tried by pressing back to give her room, but she moved with him every time he moved. Now and then, she would jerk violently and he wondered if she was going to have a fit. One of her thighs was between his legs. He struggled to get free of her, but she clung to him, moving with him and pressing against him.

She turned her head and said, "Stop, stop," to someone behind her.

He saw what the trouble was. An old man, wearing a Panama hat and horn-rimmed glasses, was hugging her. He had one of his hands inside her dress and was biting her neck.

Tod freed his right arm with a heave, reached over the girl and brought his fist down on the man's head. He couldn't hit very hard but managed to knock the man's hat off, also his glasses. The man tried to bury his face in the girl's shoulder, but Tod grabbed one of his ears and yanked. They started to move again. Tod held on to the ear as long as he could, hoping that it would come away in his hand. The girl managed to twist under his arm. A piece of her dress tore, but she was free of her attacker.

Another spasm passed through the mob and he was carried toward the curb. He fought toward a lamp-post, but he was swept by before he could grasp it. He saw another man catch the girl with the torn dress. She screamed for help. He tried to get to her, but was carried in the opposite direction. This rush also ended in a dead spot. Here his neighbors were all shorter than he was. He turned his head upward toward the sky and tried to pull some fresh air into his aching lungs, but it was all heavily tainted with sweat.

In this part of the mob no one was hysterical. In fact, most of the people seemed to be enjoying themselves. Near him was a stout woman with a man pressing hard against her from in front. His chin was on her shoulder, and his arms were around her. She paid no attention to him and went on talking to the woman at her side.

"The first thing I knew," Tod heard her say, "there was a rush and I was in the middle."

"Yeah. Somebody hollered, 'Here comes Gary Cooper,' and then wham!"

"That ain't it," said a little man wearing a cloth cap and pull-over sweater. "This is a riot you're in."

"Yeah," said a third woman, whose snaky gray hair was hanging over her face and shoulders. "A pervert attacked a child."

"He ought to be lynched."

Everybody agreed vehemently.

"I come from St. Louis," announced the stout woman, "and we had one of them pervert fellers in our neighborhood once. He ripped up a girl with a pair of scissors."

"He must have been crazy," said the man in the cap. "What kind of fun is that?"

Everybody laughed. The stout woman spoke to the man who was hugging her.

"Hey, you," she said. "I ain't no pillow."

The man smiled beatifically but didn't move. She laughed, making no effort to get out of his embrace.

"A fresh guy," she said.

The other woman laughed.

"Yeah," she said, "this is a regular free-for-all."

The man in the cap and sweater thought there was another laugh in his comment about the pervert.

"Ripping up a girl with scissors. That's the wrong tool."

He was right. They laughed even louder than the first time.

"You'd a done it different, eh, kid?" said a young man with a kidney-shaped head and waxed mustaches.

The two women laughed. This encouraged the man in the cap and he reached over and pinched the stout woman's friend. She squealed.

"Lay off that," she said good-naturedly.

"I was shoved," he said.

An ambulance siren screamed in the street. Its wailing moan started the crowd moving again and Tod was carried along in a slow, steady push. He closed his eyes and tried to protect his leg. This time, when the movement ended, he found himself with his back to the theatre wall. He kept his eyes closed and stood on his good leg. After what seemed like hours, the pack began to loosen and move again with a churning motion. It gathered momentum and rushed. He rode it until he was slammed against the base of an iron rail which fenced the driveway of the theatre from the street. He had the wind knocked out of him by the impact, but managed to cling to the rail. He held on desperately, fighting to keep from being sucked back. A woman caught him around the waist and tried to hang on. She was sobbing rhythmically. Tod felt his fingers slipping from the rail and kicked backwards as hard as he could. The woman let go.

Despite the agony in his leg, he was able to think clearly about this picture, "The Burning of Los Angeles." After his quarrel with Faye, he had worked on it continually to escape tormenting himself, and the way to it in his mind had become almost automatic.

As he stood on his good leg, clinging desperately to the iron rail, he could see all the rough charcoal strokes with which he had blocked it out on the big canvas. Across the top, parallel with the frame, he had drawn the burning city, a great bonfire of architectural styles, ranging from Egyptian to Cape Cod colonial. Through the center, winding from left to right, was a long hill street and down it, spilling into the middle foreground, came the mob carrying baseball bats and torches. For the faces of its members, he was using the innumerable sketches he had made of the people who come to California to die; the cultists of all sorts, economic as well as religious, the wave, airplane, funeral and preview watchers—all those poor devils who can only be stirred by the promise of miracles and then only to violence. A super "Dr. Know-All Pierce-All" had made the necessary promise and they were marching behind his banner in a great united front of screw-balls and screwboxes to purify the land. No longer bored, they sang and danced joyously in the red light of the flames.

In the lower foreground, men and women fled wildly before the vanguard of the crusading mob. Among them were Faye, Harry, Homer, Claude and himself. Faye ran proudly, throwing her knees high. Harry stumbled along behind her, holding on to his beloved derby hat with both hands. Homer seemed to be falling out of the canvas, his face half-asleep, his big hands clawing the air in anguished pantomime. Claude turned his head as he ran to thumb his nose at his pursuers. Tod himself picked up a small stone to throw before continuing his flight.

He had almost forgotten both his leg and his predicament, and to make his escape still more complete he stood on a chair and worked at the flames in an upper corner of the canvas, modeling the tongues of fire so that they licked even more avidly at a corinthian column that held up the palmleaf roof of a nutburger stand.

He had finished one flame and was starting on another when he was brought back by someone shouting in his ear. He opened his eyes and saw a policeman trying to reach him from behind the rail to which he was clinging. He let go with his left hand and raised his arm. The policeman caught him by the wrist, but couldn't lift him. Tod was afraid to let go until another man came to aid the policeman and caught him by the back of his jacket. He let go of the rail and they hauled him up and over it.

When they saw that he couldn't stand, they let him down easily to the ground. He was in the theatre driveway. On the curb next to him sat a woman crying into her skirt. Along the wall were groups of other disheveled people. At the end of the driveway was an ambulance. A policeman asked him if he wanted to go to the hospital. He shook his head no. He then offered him a lift home. Tod had the presence of mind to give Claude's address.

He was carried through the exit to the back street and lifted into a police car. The siren began to scream and at first he thought he was making the noise himself. He felt his lips with his hands. They were clamped tight. He knew then it was the siren. For some reason this made him laugh and he began to imitate the siren as loud as he could.

F. Scott Fitzgerald
1896–1940

One of America's most elegant writers of literary prose, F. Scott Fitzgerald reached greatness with The Great Gatsby *(1925), but when he came to work for MGM Studios in Hollywood in 1937 he arrived in emotional, economic, and professional turmoil. He had two previous stints as a screenwriter, neither of them productive, and the studio hired him—with much trepidation—on a short contract but at a premium salary of $1,000 a week. Fitzgerald spent eighteen months at MGM. For* The Love of the Last Tycoon *(1941 [1994]) he drew on an inside view of the studios, and he developed a sense of the flawed grandeur of studio impresarios that was embodied in the most admirable of his fictional protagonists: the last tycoon, Monroe Stahr. The novel was unfinished when Fitzgerald died at age forty-four of a heart attack, just before Christmas 1940. It was pieced together by his Princeton friend and former classmate, the critic Edmund Wilson, who termed it Fitzgerald's "most mature piece of work." Wilson, who wrote brilliantly on California literature in* Classics and Commercials *(1950), also edited* The Crack-Up *(1945), which sheds further light on his friend's later career. Sheilah Graham, Fitzgerald's companion during his Hollywood days, gives a frank account of his life in those years in her controversial* Beloved Infidel *(1958).* The Love of the Last Tycoon, *a restored version of* The Last Tycoon *(with stylistic idiosyncrasies), edited by Matthew J. Bruccoli, appeared in 1994, and these excerpts come from that text.*

From *The Love of the Last Tycoon*

EPISODES 4 AND 5

It was nine o'clock of a July night and there were still some extras in the drugstore across from the studio—I could see them bent over the pin-games inside—as I parked my car. "Old" Johnny Swanson stood on the corner in his semi-cowboy clothes, staring gloomily past the moon. Once he had been as big in pictures as Tom Mix or Bill Hart—now it was too sad to speak to him, and I hurried across the street and through the front gate.

There is never a time when a studio is absolutely quiet. There is always a night shift of technicians in the laboratories and dubbing rooms and people on the maintenance staff dropping in at the commissary. But the sounds are all different—the padded hush of tires, the quiet tick of a motor running idle, the naked cry of a soprano singing into a nightbound microphone. Around a corner I came upon a man in rubber boots washing down a car in a wonderful white light—a fountain among the dead industrial shadows. I slowed up as I saw Mr. Marcus being hoisted into his car in front of the administration building, because he took so long to say anything, even good night—and while I waited I realized that the soprano was singing, *Come, come, I love you only* over and over; I remember this because she kept singing the same line during the earthquake. That didn't come for five minutes yet.

Father's offices were in the old building with the long balconies and iron rails with their suggestion of a perpetual tightrope. Father was on the second floor, with Stahr on one side and Mr. Marcus on the other—this evening there were lights all along the row. My stomach dipped a little at the proximity to Stahr, but that was in pretty good control now—I'd seen him only once in the month I'd been home.

There were a lot of strange things about Father's office, but I'll make it brief. In the outer part were three poker-faced secretaries who had sat there like witches ever since I could remember—Birdy Peters, Maude something, and Rosemary Schmiel; I don't know whether this was her name, but she was the dean of the trio, so to speak, and under her desk was the kick-lock that admitted you to Father's throne room. All three of the secretaries were passionate capitalists, and Birdy had invented the rule that if typists were seen eating together more than once in a single week, they were hauled up on the carpet. At that time the studios feared mob rule.

I went on in. Nowadays all chief executives have huge drawing rooms, but my father's was the first. It was also the first to have one-way glass in the big French windows, and I've heard a story about a trap in the floor that would drop unpleasant visitors to an oubliette below, but believe it to be an invention. There was a big painting of Will Rogers, hung conspicuously and intended, I think, to suggest Father's essential kinship with Hollywood's St. Francis; there was a signed photograph of Minna Davis, Stahr's dead wife, and photos of other studio celebrities and big chalk drawings of mother and me. Tonight the one-way French windows were open and a big moon, rosy-gold with a haze around, was wedged helpless in one of them. Father and Jacques La Borwitz and Rosemary Schmiel were down at the end around a big circular desk.

What did Father look like? I couldn't describe him except for once in New York when I met him where I didn't expect to; I was aware of a bulky, middle-aged man who looked a little ashamed of himself, and I wished he'd move on—and then I saw he was Father. Afterward I was shocked at my impression. Father can be very magnetic—he has a tough jaw and an Irish smile.

But as for Jacques La Borwitz, I shall spare you. Let me just say he was an assistant producer, which is something like a commissar, and let it go at that. Where Stahr picked up such mental cadavers or had them forced upon him— or especially how he got any use out of them—has always amazed me, as it amazed everyone fresh from the East who slapped up against them. Jacques La Borwitz had his points, no doubt, but so have the submicroscopic protozoa, so has a dog prowling for a bitch and a bone. Jacques La—oh my!

From their expressions I was sure they had been talking about Stahr. Stahr had ordered something or forbidden something, or defied Father or junked one of La Borwitz' pictures or something catastrophic, and they were sitting there in protest at night in a community of rebellion and helplessness. Rosemary Schmiel sat pad in hand, as if ready to write down their dejection.

"I'm to drive you home dead or alive," I told Father. "All those birthday presents rotting away in their packages!"

"A birthday!" cried Jacques in a flurry of apology. "How old? I didn't know."

"Forty-three," said Father distinctly.

He was older than that—four years—and Jacques knew it; I saw him note it down in his account book to use some time. Out here these account books are carried open in the hand. One can see the entries being made without recourse to lip-reading, and Rosemary Schmiel was compelled in emulation to make a mark on her pad. As she rubbed it out, the earth quaked under us.

We didn't get the full shock like at Long Beach, where the upper stories of shops were spewed into the streets and small hotels drifted out to sea— but for a full minute our bowels were one with the bowels of the earth—like some nightmare attempt to attach our navel cords again and jerk us back to the womb of creation.

Mother's picture fell off the wall, revealing a small safe—Rosemary and I grabbed frantically for each other and did a strange screaming waltz across the room. Jacques fainted or at least disappeared, and Father clung to his desk and shouted, "Are you all right?" Outside the window the singer came to the climax of *I love you only,* held it a moment and then, I swear, started it all over. Or maybe they were playing it back to her from the recording machine.

The room stood still, shimmying a little. We made our way to the door, suddenly including Jacques, who had reappeared, and tottered out dizzily through the anteroom on to the iron balcony. Almost all the lights were out, and from here and there we could hear cries and calls. Momentarily we stood waiting for a second shock—then, as with a common impulse, we went into Stahr's entry and through to his office.

The office was big, but not as big as Father's. Stahr sat on the side of his couch rubbing his eyes. When the quake came he had been asleep, and he wasn't sure yet whether he had dreamed it. When we convinced him he thought it was all rather funny—until the telephones began to ring. I watched him as unobtrusively as possible.

He was grey with fatigue while he listened to the phone and dictograph; but as the reports came in, his eyes began to pick up shine.

"A couple of water mains have burst," he said to Father, "—they're heading into the back lot."

"Gray's shooting in the French Village," said Father.

"It's flooded around the Station, too, and in the Jungle and the City Corner. What the hell—nobody seems to be hurt." In passing, he shook my hands gravely: "Where've you been, Cecilia?"

"You going out there, Monroe?" Father asked.

"When all the news is in. One of the power lines is off, too—I've sent for Robinson."

He made me sit down with him on the couch and tell about the quake again.

"You look tired," I said, cute and motherly.

"Yes," he agreed, "I've got no place to go in the evenings, so I just work."

"I'll arrange some evenings for you."

"I used to play poker with a gang," he said thoughtfully, "before I was married. But they all drank themselves to death."

Miss Doolan, his secretary, came in with fresh bad news.

"Robby'll take care of everything when he comes," Stahr assured Father. He turned to me. "Now there's a man—that Robinson. He was a trouble-shooter—fixed the telephone wires in Minnesota blizzards—nothing stumps him. He'll be here in a minute—you'll like Robby."

He said it as if it had been his life-long intention to bring us together, and he had arranged the whole earthquake with just that in mind.

"Yes, you'll like Robby," he repeated. "When do you back to college?"

"I've just come home."

"You get the whole summer?"

"I'm sorry," I said. "I'll go back as soon as I can."

I was in a mist. It hadn't failed to cross my mind that he might have some intention about me, but if it was so, it was in an exasperatingly early stage—I was merely "a good property." And the idea didn't seem so attractive at that moment—like marrying a doctor. He seldom left the studio before eleven.

"How long—" he asked my father, "—before she graduates from college. That's what I was trying to say."

And I think I was about to sing out eagerly that I needn't go back at all, that I was quite educated already—when the totally admirable Robinson came in. He was a bowlegged young redhead, all ready to go.

"This is Robby, Cecilia," said Stahr. "Come on, Robby."

So I met Robby. I can't say it seemed like fate—but it was. For it was Robby who later told me how Stahr found his love that night.

EPISODE 6

Under the moon the back lot was thirty acres of fairyland—not because the locations really looked like African jungles and French chateaux and schooners at anchor and Broadway by night, but because they looked like the torn picture books of childhood, like fragments of stories dancing in an open fire. I never lived in a house with an attic, but a back lot must be something like that, and at night of course in an enchanted distorted way, it all comes true.

When Stahr and Robby arrived, clusters of lights had a picked out the danger spots in the flood.

"We'll pump it out into the swamp on Thirty-Sixth Street, said Robby after a moment. "It's city property—but isn't this an act of God? Say—look there!"

On top of a huge head of the Goddess Siva, two women were floating down the current of an impromptu river. The idol had come unloosed from a set of Burma, and it meandered earnestly on its way, stopping sometimes to waddle and bump in the shallows with the other debris of the tide. The two refugees had found sanctuary along a scroll of curls on its bald forehead and seemed at first glance to be sightseers on an interesting bus-ride through the scene of the flood.

"Will you look at that, Monroe!" said Robby. "Look at those dames!"

Dragging their legs through sudden bogs, they made their to the bank of the stream. Now they could see the women, looking a little scared but brightening at the prospect of rescue.

"We ought to let 'em drift out to the waste pipe," said Robby gallantly, "but DeMille needs that head next week."

He wouldn't have hurt a fly, though, and presently he was hip deep in the water, fishing for them with a pole and succeeding only in spinning it in a dizzy circle. Help arrived, and the impression quickly got around that one of them was very pretty, and then that they were people of importance. But they were just strays, and Robby waited disgustedly to give them hell while the thing was brought finally into control and beached.

"Put that head back!" he called up to them. "You think it's a souvenir?"

One of the women came sliding smoothly down the cheek of the idol, and Robby caught and set her on solid ground; the other one hesitated and then followed. Robby turned to Stahr for judgment.

"What'll we do with them, chief?"

Stahr did not answer. Smiling faintly at him from not four feet away was the face of his dead wife, identical even to the expression. Across the four feet of moonlight, the eyes he knew looked back at him, a curl blew a little on a familiar forehead; the smile lingered, changed a little according to pattern; the lips parted—the same. An awful fear went over him, and he wanted to cry aloud. Back from the still sour room, the muffled glide of the limousine hearse, the falling concealing flowers, from out there in the dark—here now warm and glowing. The river passed him in a rush, the great spotlights swooped and blinked—and then he heard another voice speak that was not Minna's voice.

"We're sorry," said the voice. "We followed a truck in through a gate."

A little crowd had gathered—electricians, grips, truckers, and Robby began to nip at them like a sheep dog.

". . . get the big pumps on the tanks on Stage 4 . . . put a cable around this head . . . raft it up on a couple of two by fours . . . get the water out of the jungle first, for Christ's sake . . . that big 'A' pipe, lay it down . . . all that stuff is plastic. . . ."

Stahr stood watching the two women as they threaded their way after a policeman toward an exit gate. Then he took a tentative step to see if the weakness had gone out of his knees. A loud tractor came bumping through the slush, and men began streaming by him—every second one glancing at him, smiling, speaking: "Hello, Monroe. . . . Hello, Mr. Stahr . . . wet night, Mr. Stahr . . . Monroe . . . Monroe . . . Stahr . . . Stahr . . . Stahr."

He spoke and waved back as the people streamed by in the darkness, looking, I suppose, a little like the Emperor and the Old Guard. There is no world so but it has its heroes, and Stahr was the hero. Most of these men had been here a long time—through the beginnings and the great upset, when sound came, and the three years depression, he had seen that no harm came to them. The old loyalties were trembling now, there were clay feet everywhere; but he was their man, the last of the princes. And their greeting was a sort of low cheer as they went by.

Between the night I got back and the quake, I'd made many observations.

About Father, for example. I loved Father—in a sort of irregular graph with many low swoops—but I began to see that his strong will didn't fill him out as a passable man. Most of what he accomplished boiled down to shrewd. He had acquired with luck and shrewdness a quarter interest in a booming circus—together with young Stahr. That was his life's effort—all the rest was an instinct to hang on. Of course, he talked that double talk to Wall Street about how mysterious it was to make a picture, but Father didn't know the ABC's of dubbing or even cutting. Nor had he learned much about the feel of America as a bar boy in Ballyhegan, nor did he have any more than a drummer's sense of a story. On the other hand, he didn't have concealed paresis like——; he came to the studio before noon, and, with a suspicious-ness developed like a muscle, it was hard to put anything over on him.

Stahr had been his luck—and Stahr was something else again. He was a marker in industry like Edison and Lumiere and Chaplin. He led pictures way up past the range and power of the theatre, reaching a sort of golden age, before the censorship.

Proof of his leadership was the spying that went on around him—not just for inside information or patented process secrets—but spying on his scent for a trend in taste, his guess as to how things were going to be. Too much of his vitality was taken by the mere parrying of these attempts. It made his work secret in part, often devious, slow—and hard to describe as the plans of a general, where the psychological factors become too tenuous and we end by merely adding up the successes and failures. But I have determined to give you a glimpse of him functioning, which is my excuse for what follows. It is drawn partly from a paper I wrote in college on *A Producer's Day* and partly from my imagination. More often I have blocked in the ordinary events my-self, while the stranger ones are true.

In the early morning after the flood, a man walked up to the outside bal-cony of the Administration Building. He lingered the some time, according to an eyewitness, then mounted to the iron railing and dove head first to the pavement below. Breakage—one arm.

Miss Doolan, Stahr's secretary, told him about it when he buzzed for her at nine. He had slept in his office without hearing the small commotion.

"Pete Zavras!" Stahr exclaimed, "—the camera man?"

"They took him to a doctor's office. It won't be in the paper."

"Hell of a thing," he said. "I knew he'd gone to pot—but I don't know why. He was all right when we used him two years ago—why should he come here? How did he get in?"

"He bluffed it with his old studio pass," said Catherine Doolan. She was a dry hawk, the wife of an assistant director. "Perhaps the quake had something to do with it."

"He was the best camera man in town," Stahr said. When he had heard of the hundreds dead at Long Beach, he was still haunted by the abortive suicide at dawn. He told Catherine Doolan to trace the matter down.

The first dictograph messages blew in through the warm morning. While he shaved and had coffee, he talked and listened. Robby had left a message: "If Mr. Stahr wants me tell him to hell with it I'm in bed." An actor was sick or thought so; the Governor of California was bringing a party out; a supervisor had beaten up his wife for the prints and must be "reduced to a writer"— these three affairs were Father's job—unless the actor was under personal contract to Stahr. There was early snow on a location in Canada with the company already there—Stahr raced over the possibilities of salvage, reviewing the story of the picture. Nothing. Stahr called Catherine Doolan.

"I want to speak to the cop who put two women off the back lot last night. I think his name's Malone."

"Yes, Mr. Stahr. I've got Joe Wyman—about the trousers."

"Hello, Joe," said Stahr. "Listen—two people at the sneak preview complained that Morgan's fly was open for half the picture . . . of course they're exaggerating, but even if it's only ten feet . . . no, we can't find the people, but I want that picture run over and over until you find that footage. Get a lot of people in the projection room—somebody'll spot it."

Tout passe.—L'art robuste
Seul a l'éternité.

"And there's the Prince from Denmark," said Catherine Doolan. "He's very handsome." She was impelled to add pointlessly, "—for a tall man."

"Thanks," Stahr said. "Thank you, Catherine, I appreciate it that I am now the handsomest small man on the lot. Send the Prince out on the sets and tell him we'll lunch at one."

"And Mr. George Boxley—looking very angry in a British way."

"I'll see him for ten minutes."

As she went out, he asked: "Did Robby phone in?"

"No."

"Call sound, and if he's been heard from, call him and ask him this. Ask him this—did he hear that woman's name last night? Either of those women. Or anything so they could be traced."

"Anything else?"

"No, but tell him it's important while he still remembers. What were they? I mean what kind of people—ask him that, too. I mean were they—"

She waited, scratching his words on her pad without looking.

"—oh, were they—questionable? Were they theatrical? Never mind—skip that, just ask if he knows how they can be traced."

The policeman, Malone, had known nothing. Two dames, and he had hustled 'em, you betcha. One of them was sore. Which one? One of them. They had a car, a Chevy—he thought of taking the license. Was it—the good looker who was sore? It was one of them.

Not which one—he had noticed nothing. Even on the lot here Minna was forgotten. In three years. So much for that, then.

EPISODE 8

Stahr smiled at Mr. George Boxley. It was a kindly fatherly smile Stahr had developed inversely when he was a young man pushed into high places. Originally it had been a smile of respect toward his elders, then as his own decisions grew rapidly to displace theirs, a smile so that they should not feel it—finally emerging as what it was: a smile of kindness—sometimes a little hurried and tired but always there—toward anyone who had not angered him within the hour. Or anyone he did not intend to insult, aggressive and outright.

Mr. Boxley did not smile back. He came in with the air of being violently dragged, though no one apparently had a hand on him. He stood in front of a chair, and again it was as if two invisible attendants seized his arms and set him down forcibly into it. He sat there morosely. Even when he lit a cigarette on Stahr's invitation, one felt that the match was held to it by exterior forces he disdained to control.

Stahr looked at him courteously.

"Something not going well, Mr. Boxley?"

The novelist looked back at him in thunderous silence.

"I read your letter," said Stahr. The tone of the pleasant young headmaster was gone. He spoke as to an equal, but with a faint two-edged deference.

"I can't get what I write on paper," broke out Boxley. "You've all been very decent, but it's a sort of conspiracy. Those two hacks you've teamed me with listen to what I say, but they spoil it—seem to have a vocabulary of about a hundred words."

"Why don't you write it yourself?" asked Stahr.

"I have. I sent you some."

"But it was just talk, back and forth," said Stahr mildly. "Interesting talk but nothing more."

Now it was all the two ghostly attendants could do to hold Boxley in the deep chair. He struggled to get up; he uttered a single quiet bark which had some relation to laughter but none to amusement, and said:

"I don't think you people read things. The men are duelling when the conversation takes place. At the end one of them falls into a well and has to be hauled up in a bucket."

He barked again and subsided.

"Would you write that in a book of your own, Mr. Boxley?"

"What? Naturally not."

"You'd consider it too cheap."

"Movie standards are different," said Boxley, hedging.

"Do you ever go to them?"

"No—almost never."

"Isn't it because people are always duelling and falling down wells?"

"Yes—and wearing strained facial expressions and talking incredible and unnatural dialogue."

"Skip the dialogue for a minute," said Stahr. "Granted your dialogue is more graceful than what these hacks can write—that's why we brought you out here. But let's imagine something that isn't either bad dialogue or jumping down a well. Has your office got a stove in it that lights with a match?"

"I think it has," said Boxley stiffly, "—but I never use it."

"Suppose you're in your office. You've been fighting duels or writing all day and you're too tired to fight or write any more. You're sitting there staring—dull, like we all get sometimes. A pretty stenographer that you've seen before comes into the room and you watch her—idly. She doesn't see you, though you're very close to her. She takes off her gloves, opens her purse and dumps it out on a table—"

Stahr stood up, tossing his key-ring on his desk,

"She has two dimes and a nickle—and a cardboard match box. She leaves the nickle on the desk, puts the two dimes back into her purse and takes her black gloves to the stove, opens it and puts them inside. There is one match in the match box and she starts to light it kneeling by the stove. You notice that there's a stiff wind blowing in the window—but just then your telephone rings. The girl picks it up, says hello—listens—and says deliberately into the phone, 'I've never owned a pair of black gloves in my life.' She hangs up, kneels by the stove again, and just as she lights the match, you glance around very suddenly and see that there's another man in the office, watching every move the girl makes—"

Stahr paused. He picked up his keys and put them in his pocket.

"Go on," said Boxley smiling. "What happens?"

"I don't know," said Stahr. "I was just making pictures."

Boxley felt he was being put in the wrong.

"It's just melodrama," he said.

"Not necessarily," said Stahr. "In any case, nobody has moved violently or talked cheap dialogue or had any facial expression at all. There was only one bad line, and a writer like you could improve it. But you were interested."

"What was the nickle for?" asked Boxley evasively.

"I don't know," said Stahr. Suddenly he laughed. "Oh, yes—the nickle was for the movies."

The two invisible attendants seemed to release Boxley. He relaxed, leaned back in his chair and laughed.

"What in hell do you pay me for?" he demanded. "I don't understand the damn stuff."

"You will," said Stahr grinning, "or you wouldn't have asked about the nickle."

M. F. K. Fisher

1908–1992

Born in Albion, Michigan, Mary Frances Kennedy was four years old when she came to Whittier, where her father, Rex Kennedy, owned, edited, and published the Whittier News. *Taken with the cookbooks she read in the Los Angeles Public Library, she began writing articles on food and region, and her first publication was "Pacific Village" (on Laguna Beach) in* Westways *in 1934, signed cryptically "M. F. K. Fisher." Fisher earned her baccalaureate at the University of Dijon in 1931 and lived for more than twenty years in Europe. After her immersion in French culture she returned to find her métier as an American essayist on food, region, and human foibles in four startlingly original books—*Serve It Forth *(1937),* Consider the Oyster *(1941),* How to Cook a Wolf *(1942), and* The Gastronomical Me *(1943)— raising food writing to a literary art. "The First Oyster," based on her experience at Bishop's Preparatory School in 1925, appeared in the last volume. Distinctive for its wedding of gastronomic initiation with an adolescent's first erotic experiences, it presented her—and California life—as at once fresh and sophisticated, a marriage of old world and new. She moved to Saint Helena in the wine country in 1953 and to "Last House" in Glen Ellen in 1970, where she continued to write until her death from Parkinson's disease in 1992. Considered the dean of American food writers, Fisher worked with Jack Shoemaker—an eminent editor of many California writers—to have her later works published by North Point and Counterpoint Press.*

The First Oyster

The intramural complexities of the faculty at Miss Huntingdon's School for Girls have become much clearer to me since I left there, but even at sixteen I knew that Mrs. Cheever's social position was both uncomfortable and lonely.

She had her own office, which was certainly more than any snobbish Latin teacher could boast. She was listed as part of the school's administration in the discreet buff and sepia catalog; I cannot remember now just what her title was, except that it implied with high-sounding ambiguity that she was the housekeeper without, of course, using that vulgar word itself.

She was a college graduate, even though it was from some domestic science school instead of Smith or Mount Holyoke.

She was, above all, a lady.

She was almost a super-lady, mainly because it was so obvious that the rest of the faculty, administration as well as teachers, considered her a cook. When she stepped occasionally after dinner into the library, where I as an honor Sophomore was privileged to carry demitasses to the Seniors and the teachers on alternate Wednesday nights, I could see that she was snubbed almost as thoroughly as her well-fed colleagues snubbed the school nurse, one notch below the housekeeper on the social scale but also a colleague as far as the catalog went.

No malicious, inverted, discontented boarding-school teacher on God's earth, however, could snub the poor nurse as much as Mrs. Cheever could. Her coarsely genteel face under its Queen Mary coiffure expressed with shocking clarity the loathing she felt for that gentle ninny who dealt out pills and sticking plasters, and all the loneliness and bitter social insecurity of her own position showed in the way Mrs. Cheever stood proudly alone in the crowded library, smiling with delicacy and frightful pleasure at the nurse, whose hand trembled clumsily as she sipped at her little coffee cup and tried to look like a college graduate.

The two women studiously spoke to no one, mainly because no one spoke to them. Perhaps once or twice, long since, the nurse may have said a timid nothing to the housekeeper, but Mrs. Cheever would have bitten out her own tongue before loosening it in charity toward a sister outcast.

Once it almost looked as if she would have a friend on the faculty, when a new gym teacher came. So often athletic people were not exactly . . . that is, they seldom had MA's, even if they seemed really quite lady-like at times. And Mrs. Cheever felt sure that the new colleague would be as scornful as she was herself of all the pretentious schoolma'ams, with their airs and graces.

But after the first week, during which the little gym teacher stood shyly by the housekeeper for coffee, or nibbled in her room on the pink grapes and small frosted cakes that Mrs. Cheever sent her, the other women discovered that not only was she from Barnard . . . *summa cum laude, parbleu!* . . . but that she had the most adorable little cracked voice, almost like a boy's. It was perfect with her hair, so short and boyish too, and by the end of the second week three of the teachers were writing passionate notes to her, and Mrs. Cheever once more stood magnificently alone on her occasional visits to the library after dinner.

Perhaps loneliness made her own food bitter to her, because Mrs. Cheever was an obvious dyspeptic. The rest of us, however: Miss Huntingdon herself, remote and saint-like; Miss Blake, her shadow, devoted, be-wigged, a skin-and-bone edition of Krafft-Ebing; all the white women of the school, fat, thin, frantic or calm, and all the Filipino servants, . . . ; all the girls, who felt like victims but were really the *raison d'être* of this strange collection within the high walls . . . Mrs. Cheever fed us four times a day with probably the best institutional food in America.

She ran her kitchens with such skill that in spite of ordinary domestic troubles like flooded basements and soured cream, and even an occasional extraordinary thing like the double murder and harakiri committed by the head-boy one Good Friday, our meals were never late and never bad.

There were about seventy boarders and twenty-five women, and for morning-recess lunch a pack of day-girls, and most of us ate with the delicacy and appreciation of half-starved animals. It must have been sickening to Mrs. Cheever to see us literally wolfing her well-planned, well-cooked, well-served dishes. For in spite of doing things wholesale, which some gastronomers say is impossible with any finesse, the things we ate at Miss Huntingdons were savory and interesting.

Mrs. Cheever, for instance, would get a consignment of strange honey from the Torrey pine trees, honey which only a few people in the world were supposed to have eaten. I remember it now with some excitement, as a grainy greenish stuff like some I once ate near Adelboden in the Bernese Alps, but then it was to most of us just something sweet and rather queer to put on hot biscuits. Tinned orange marmalade would have done as well.

At Thanksgiving she would let the Filipinos cover the breakfast tables with dozens of odd, beautiful little beasts they had made from vegetables and fruits and nuts, so that the dining room became for a while amazingly funny to us, and we were allowed to make almost as much noise as we wanted while we ate forbidden things like broiled sausage and played with the crazy toys. The boys would try not to laugh too, and even Mrs. Cheever would incline her queenly topknot less scornfully than usual when spoken to.

Saturday noons we could eat sandwiches and cocoa or pink punch on the hockey field, and have ice cream from the soda fountain in the village if we told Mrs. Cheever between eight and nine that morning. I sometimes went without it, or got another girl to order for me, simply because I could not bear to go into the little office and have the housekeeper look at me. She made me feel completely unattractive, which is even worse at sixteen than later.

She would sit stiffly at her desk, waiting for orders with an expression of such cold impersonal nausea on her face that I could hardly believe the gossip that she had made a fat sum weekly by charging us almost double what the drug store got for its cartons of ice cream and its incredibly sweet sauces.

She would make precise notations on a sheet of paper while we mumbled our orders, and sometimes even suggested in her flat clear voice that salted pecans might be better than strawberry syrup on chocolate ice-cream-with-butter-scotch-sauce. Her expression of remote anguish never changed, even when she reminded us, with her eyes resting coldly on a bulging behind or a spotty chin, that we were limited to one pint apiece.

It was for festivals like Easter and Old Girls' Day, though, that she really exercised her talents. Now I can see that she must have filled many hours of snubbed isolation in plans for our pleasure, but then I only knew that parties at Miss Huntingdon's School for Girls were really fun, mostly because the food was so good. Mrs. Cheever, callously ignored by the girls except for a few minutes each Saturday morning, and smiled at condescendingly by her unwilling colleagues with university degrees, turned out rare bats into what could truly be called small gastronomic triumphs . . . and the more so because they were what they were within high walls.

Old Girls' Day, for instance, meant to all but the Seniors, who had to be nice to the returning alumnae, that we spent a long gray warm June day on the sand and the rocks, and that we could wear our full pleated gym-bloomers and *no stockings,* and take pictures of each other with our Brownies, and, best of all, that at half past noon a procession of house-boys would come down the cliffs from the school with our lunch for us in big baskets.

There would be various things, of course, like pickles and napkins and knives and probably sandwiches and fruit, although how Mrs. Cheever managed it with the school full of hungry shrieking postgraduates is more than I can guess. Perhaps she even sent down devilled eggs to make it a real picnic.

I don't remember, because all that we thought about then, or could recall now if we ever dared to think at all of those day's, were the hot crisp fried halves of young chickens, stiff and tempting. We could have all we wanted, even three or four, and we could eat with our fingers, and yell, and gobble. It was wonderful.

There must have been chaperones, but they seemed not to exist down there in the warmth and the silly freedom, and when a stately figure stood for an instant on the cliff top, wrapped fussily in an afternoon gown for the Old Girls, and looked down at us with her face set in a sour chill smile, we waved our greasy drumsticks hilariously up at her, and cried,

> Miss-is Chee-ver
> Miss-is Chee-ver
> Miss-is Chee-ver
> Rah-ah-ah-ah,

almost as if she were a whole basketball game between the Golds and the Purples. For one moment, at least, in the year, we were grateful to her for our deliciously full mouths.

She did her conscientious best to be sensible in her menus, and fed us better garden things and fresher cream and milk than most of us have eaten since, but there must have been a dreadful impatience in her for such pap, so that occasionally she would give us the Torrey pine-honey for breakfast, or have the Chinese cook put chives over the Friday fish instead of a cream sauce.

Once, for the Christmas Party, she served Eastern oysters, fresh oysters, oysters still in their shells.

Nothing could have been more exotic in the early twenties in Southern California. The climate was still considered tropical, so that shellfish imported alive from the East were part of an oil-magnate's dream, or perhaps something to be served once or twice a year at Victor Hugo's, in a private room with pink candleshades and a canary. And of course any local mollusks were automatically deemed inedible, at least by *nice* people.

The people, that Christmas Party night, were indeed nice. We wore our formals: skirts not less than eight nor more than fifteen inches from the floor, dresses of light but not bright colors and of materials semi-transparent or opaque, neck-lines not more than three inches below the collar bone and sleeves long or elbow-length. We all passed the requirements of the catalog, but with such delectable additions as long chiffon scarves twined about our necks in the best Nita-Naldi-bronchitic manner, or great artificial flowers pinned with holiday abandon on our left shoulders. Two or three of the Seniors had fox furs slung nonchalantly about them, with the puffy tails dangling down over their firmly flattened young breasts in a most fashionable way.

There may even have been a certain amount of timid make-up in honor of Kris Kringle and the approaching libertinage of Christmas vacation, real or devoutly to be hoped for, but fortunately the dining room was lighted that night by candles only.

Mrs. Cheever had outdone herself, although all we thought then was that the old barn had never looked so pretty. The oblong tables, usually in ranks like dominoes in their box, were pushed into a great horseshoe, with a little table for Miss Huntingdon and Miss Blake and the minister and the president of the trustees in the middle, and a sparkling Christmas tree, and . . . yes! . . . a space for dancing! And there were candles, and the smells of pine branches and hot wax, and place cards all along the outer edge of the horseshoe so that the Freshmen would not sit in one clot and the other groups in theirs.

We marched once around the beautiful room in the flickering odorous candlelight, singing, "God Rest You Merry, Gentlemen" or some such thing to the scrapings of the assistant violin instructor and two other musicians, who in spite of their trousers had been accurately judged unable to arouse unseemly longings in our cloistered hearts.

Then we stood by the chairs marked with our names, and waited for the music to stop and Miss Huntingdon and the minister to ask the blessings in their flinty voices. It was all very exciting.

When I saw that I was to sit between a Senior and a Junior, with not a Freshman in sight, I felt almost uplifted with Christmas joy. It must mean that I was Somebody, to be thus honored, that perhaps I would even be elected to the Altar Guild next semester.

I knew enough not to speak first, but could not help looking sideways at the enormous proud nose of Olmsted, who sat at my left. She was president of the Seniors, and moved about the school in a loose-limbed dreamy way that seemed to me seraphic. Inez, the Junior, was less impressive, but still had her own string of horses in Santa Barbara and could curse with great concentration, so many words that I only recognized *damn* and one or two others. Usually she had no use for me, but tonight she smiled, and the candlelight made her beady eyes look almost friendly.

The grace done with, we pulled our chairs in under the unaccustomed silkiness of our party-dress bottoms with less noise than usual, and the orchestra flung itself into a march. The pantry doors opened, and the dapper little house-boys pranced in, their smooth faces pulled straight and their eyes snapping with excitement.

They put a plate in front of each of us. We all looked mazily at what we saw, and waited with mixed feelings until Miss Huntingdon had picked up her fork (where, I wonder now, did Mrs. Cheever ever find one hundred oyster forks in a California boarding school?), before we even thought of eating. I heard Inez mutter under her breath, several more words I did not recognize except as such, and then Olmsted said casually, "How charming! Blue Points!"

There was a quiet buzz . . . we were being extremely well-bred, all of us, for the party . . . and I know now that I was not the only Westerner who was scared shaky at the immediate prospect of eating her first raw oyster, and was putting it off for as long as possible.

I remembered hearing Mother say that it was vulgar as well as extremely unpleasant to do anything with an oyster but swallow it as quickly as possible, without *thinking*, but that the after-taste was rather nice. Of course it was different with tinned oysters in turkey dressing: they could be chewed with impunity, both social and hygienic, for some reason or other. But raw, they must be swallowed whole, and rapidly.

And alive.

With the unreasoning and terrible persnicketiness of a sixteen-year-old I knew that I would be sick if I had to swallow any thing in the world alive, but especially a live oyster.

Olmsted picked up one deftly on the prongs of her little fork, tucked it under her enormous nose, and gulped, "Delicious," she murmured.

"Jesus," Inez said softly. "Well, here goes. The honor of the old school. Oi!" And she swallowed noisily. A look of smug surprise crept into her face, and she said in my ear, "Try one, Baby-face. It ain't the heat, it's the humidity. Try one. Slip and go easy." She cackled suddenly, watching me with sly bright eyes.

"Yes, do," Olmsted said.

I laughed lightly, tinklingly, like Helen in *Helen and Warren,* said, "Oh, I *love* Blue Points!", and got one with surprising neatness into my mouth.

At that moment the orchestra began to play, with sexless abandon, a popular number called, I think, "Horses." It sounded funny in Miss Huntingdon's dining room. Olmsted laughed, and said to me, "Come on, Kennedy. Let's start the ball rolling, shall we?"

The fact that she, the most wonderful girl in the whole school, and the most intelligent, and the most revered, should ask me to dance when she knew very well that I was only a Sophomore, was so overwhelming that it made even the dream-like reality that she had called me Kennedy, instead of Mary Frances, seem unimportant.

The oyster was still in my mouth. I smiled with care, and stood up, reeling at the thought of dancing the first dance of the evening with the senior-class president.

The oyster seemed larger. I knew that I must down it, and was equally sure that I could not. Then, as Olmsted put her thin hand on my shoulder blades, I swallowed once, and felt light and attractive and daring, to know what I had done. We danced stiffly around the room, and as soon as a few other pairs of timid girls came into the cleared space by the tree, headed toward Miss Huntingdon's table.

Miss Huntingdon herself spoke to me by name, and Miss Blake laughed silently so that her black wig bobbled, and cracked her knuckles as she always did when she was having a good time, and the minister and Olmsted made a little joke about Silent Sophomores and Solemn Seniors, and I did not make a sound, and nobody seemed to think it strange. I was dumb with pleasure at my own importance . . . practically the Belle of the Ball I was . . . and with a dawning gastronomic hunger. Oysters, my delicate taste buds were telling me, oysters are *simply marvelous!* More, more!

I floated on, figuratively at least, in Olmsted's arms. The dance ended with a squeaky but cheerful flourish, and the girls went back to their seats almost as flushed as if they were returning from the arms of the most passionate West Point cadets in white gloves and coats.

The plates had been changed. I felt flattened, dismayed, as only children can about such things.

Olmsted said, "You're a funny kid, Kennedy. Oh, green olives!" when I mumbled how wonderful it had been to dance with her, and Inez murmured in my ear, "Dance with me next, will you, Baby-face? There are a couple of things boys can do I can't, but I can dance with you a damn sight better than that bitch Olmsted."

I nodded gently, and smiled a tight smile at her, and thought that she was the most horrible creature I had ever known. Perhaps I might kill her some day. I was going to be sick.

I pushed back my chair.

"Hey, Baby-face!" The music started with a crash, and Inez put her arms surely about me, and led me with expert grace around and around the Christmas Tree, while all the candles fluttered in time with my stomach.

"Why don't you talk?" she asked once. "You have the cutest little ears I ever saw, Baby-face . . . like a pony I had, when I was in Colorado. How do you like the way I dance with you?"

Her arm tightened against my back. She was getting a crush on me, I thought, and here it was only Christmas and I was only a Sophomore! What would it be by April, the big month for them? I felt somewhat flattered, because Inez was a Junior and had those horses in Santa Barbara, but I hated her. My stomach felt better.

Miss Huntingdon was watching me again, while she held her water glass in her white thin fingers as if it had wine in it, or the Holy Communion. She leaned over and said something to Miss Blake, who laughed silently like a gargoyle and cracked her knuckles with delight, not at what Miss I Huntingdon was saying but that she was saying anything at all. Perhaps they were talking about me, saying that I was nice and dependable and would be a good Senior president in two more years, or that I had the cutest ears. . . .

"Relax, kid," Inez murmured. "Just pretend . . ."

The pantry door swung shut on a quick flash of gray chiffon and pearls, almost at my elbow, and before I knew it myself I was out of Inez' skillful arms and after it. I had to escape from her; and the delightful taste of oyster in my mouth, my new-born gourmandise, sent me toward an unknown rather than a known sensuality.

The thick door shut out almost all the sound from the flickering, noisy dining room. The coolness of the pantry was shocking, and Mrs. Cheever was even more so. She stood, queenly indeed in her beautiful gray evening dress and her pearls and her snowy hair done in the same lumpy rhythm as Mary of England's, and her face was all soft and formless with weeping.

Tears trickled like colorless blood from her eyes, which had always been so stony and now looked at me without seeing me at all. Her mouth, puckered from years of dyspepsia and disapproval, was loose and tender suddenly, and she sniffed with vulgar abandon.

She stood with one arm laid gently over the scarlet shoulders of the fat old nurse, who was dressed fantastically in the ancient costume of Saint Nicholas. It became her well, for her formless body was as generous as his, and her ninny-simple face, pink-cheeked and sweet, was kind like his and neither male nor female. The ratty white wig sat almost tidily on her head, which looked as if it hardly missed its neat black-ribboned nurse's cap, and beside her on the pantry serving table lay the beard, silky and monstrous, ready to be pulled snug against her chins when it was time to give us all our presents under the Christmas tree.

She looked through me without knowing that I stood staring at her like a paralyzed rabbit. I was terrified, of her the costumed nurse and of Mrs. Cheever so hideously weeping and of all old women.

Mrs. Cheever did not see me either. For the first time I did not feel unattractive in her presence, but rather completely unnecessary. She put out one hand, and for a fearful moment I thought perhaps she was going to kiss me: her face was so tender. Then I saw that she was putting oysters carefully on a big platter that sat before the nurse, and that as she watched the old biddy eat them, tears kept running bloodlessly down her soft ravaged cheeks, while she spoke not a word.

I backed toward the door, hot as fire with shock and the dread confusion of adolescence, and said breathlessly, "Oh, excuse me, Mrs. Cheever! But I . . . that is, *all* the Sophomores . . . on behalf of the Sophomore Class I want to thank you for this beautiful, this *simply marvelous* party! Oysters . . . and . . . and everything . . . It's all *so* nice!"

But Mrs. Cheever did not hear me. She stood with one hand still on the wide red shoulders of the nurse, and with the other she put the oysters left from the Christmas Party on a platter. Her eyes were smeared so that they no longer looked hard and hateful, and as she watched the old woman eat steadily, voluptuously, of the fat cold mollusks, she looked so tender that I turned anxiously toward the sureness and stability of such small passions as lay in the dining room.

The pantry door closed behind me. The orchestra was whipping through "Tales from the Vienna Woods," with the assistant violin instructor doubling on the artificial mocking bird. Filipino boys skimmed . . . into the candlelight, with great trays of cranberry sauce and salted nuts and white curled celery held above their heads, and I could tell by their faces that whatever they had seen in the pantry was already tucked far back behind their eyes, perhaps forever.

If I could I still taste my first oyster, if my tongue still felt fresh and excited, it was perhaps too bad. Although things are different now, I hoped then, suddenly and violently, that I would never see one again.

IDWAL JONES
1887–1964

The son of a Welsh slate quarryman, Idwal Jones was reared in Pennsylvania and New York. He came to California in 1911. Jones was a professional writer: a newspaper journalist, magazine columnist, novelist and
writer of nonfiction books, and at one time a publicity writer for Paramount Pictures.
He found his largest audience in the monthly column he wrote for Westways magazine
from 1935 until his death, contributing more than two hundred stylish articles on the
state's life, history, and folklore. His books included China Boy (1936), a novel about
the Chinese in California; Vermilion (1947), the saga of a quicksilver mining family
that he based on the New Almaden mine in the Santa Cruz mountains; and Ark of
Empire (1951), Jones's account of bohemian San Francisco—at the center of which
was the poet George Sterling—and the Montgomery Block, a fabled building that lasted
through multiple fires and the great earthquake of 1906. His greatest love was the wine
country. In The Vineyard (1942) Jones offers an absorbing account of the viticulture
of the Napa and Sonoma areas and the families that developed it until the coming of
Prohibition in 1919. In his California Classics, Lawrence Clark Powell pronounced
the book "that most lyrically beautiful, enchanting of all novels in California's literature." Lost for years, The Vineyard was recently republished by the University of California Press.

Chapter 5
from *The Vineyard*

In a week of rain and drizzle, white fogs from the sea and conquering black
fogs from the tule marshes pushed into the valley. They sought egress, rose
to the crown of the slope and the shoulder of Mount St. Helena, found a
ceiling of high winds, then surrendered to lie densely on the soggy, black
fields. A furlong of the highway was under water, and the road from the forks
to the Montino gate was a swamp, hubdeep, but the villa was not marooned.
Visitors came and went, or they stayed. They came to pay their respects to
Giorgio, and their wives to Carola. Hector hid out in his refuge off the vat
room.[. . .]

Hector thought back to the days when another boy lived on Montino, and
the same Wing gave him fish hooks to catch trout in the gully. Wing did until

Giorgio, despotic even in his middle years, forbade him under pain of expulsion. Hector was forbidden to go anywhere near the pool, for fear he might tumble in and drown. He could not swim. He had never been allowed to play near deep water.

One August day his mother had sent him to the post office, and he returned by a shortcut through the Mission field. The basin of water in the gully, shaded by tall firs, was cool and enticing. Wing had planted lily roots far beneath in tubs, and on the surface, nibbled at by carp and trout, floated the pads and white blossoms. Hector lay flat and hung his face over the brim; with a switch he tickled the sides of the fat carp. All things moved in that deep water; the stick might have been a weed swaying in the current. The red-waisted goldfish came up his fingers, shaking out their tails that were like swatches of silk. In the spear of sunlight that came through the foliage, their beauty was almost unbearable. But it was the carp that fascinated him: the fat, indolent carp, their gills working, like so many pompous aldermen blowing out their cheeks, their eyes glazed, as if sated after a banquet. A group of them hovered behind a mossy rock, just out of his reach. He hooked his foot on a root, stretched himself out and poked down the stick. The root was firm, the water below him, ten feet deep, looked as solid as glass. He kept perfectly still, oblivious to the world about him, looking into that abyss.

Even more still, like one paralyzed, lay his father, watching him. Giorgio, awakening from a doze in his fever, saw him from a bed in the villa. He called out, but his shout was too feeble to penetrate the wall. No one was upstairs, and he was supposed to be fast asleep. He stared helplessly at the child hanging above the pool, face to the water, his foot precariously held by a root. Horror froze him. Then his hand moved, he managed to reach his cane, lifted it to the fowling piece above the book case, and pulled it towards him. Somehow, he contrived to point the gun over the footboard of the bed.

The blast rocked the villa. The women came running, found the room smoke-filled, the window blown out, and Giorgio waiting.

"The boy is at the pool. Bring him here."

Hector, stiff with fear, was brought in. "Women leave the room," said Giorgio. "Out! *Fuori!*" Rage enabled him to crack his fingers. "Lock that door now, boy."

Giorgio drew himself up on the pillows. "Come here!" The child drew nearer, hands lifted, whimpering.

The first Mrs. Regola, a rebel for once, beat at the door with her small hands, and screamed. But nothing could interrupt what Giorgio had to say in the room, no pleading could unlock that door and release her child before the end of that hour in which something in his breast was forever broken.

For weeks after that, the child rose crying in the night; by day he had the eyes of a frightened spaniel, and hid whenever Giorgio came into the house or the vineyard.

The storm had quieted, and Hector, turning Chess about, drove back through the Gamays. At the end of this tract was a rail fence, which separated Montino from a field that once had been part of it, but which Giorgio had sold to the Lanes. Here the Regolberg had grown. It was now leased to a cattleman; a pasture with here and there jungly thickets of cane, twenty to thirty feet long, that never bore fruit. Elsewhere the livestock had eaten the green shoots as soon as they appeared, and the vines had died out. There was small likelihood of it being planted again. Hector sometimes dreamed of buying it, but the land he tilled hardly more than kept Montino going. And the Lanes set an inordinate value on their holdings.

Hector turned Chess into the corral. The ground had been heavy, and they were tired. Little remained to be done in the vineyard. Drip from trees was still flurrying in the wind, but holes had been torn in the fog. Tomorrow might be fine, and he thought of the bucks. Up he went past the winery, then into the black entrance of the cave in the hillside.

The laboratory was one of his private haunts, the cave was another. It had been started when he was small—the Chinese help, between seasons, hacking out the limestone—and he himself had carried further the excavating. The Montino wines had always been hauled to the city for storing in one of the great warehouses, a reservoir that the trade tapped at need. The cave had room for fifty barrels; it now held twenty, and when the next vintage came in, space would be lacking. So Hector worked away in his tunnel. It had always troubled him that his reserve should be sent away for storage. To Giorgio, wine was something that could be regarded in the abstract, like drafts or bills of sale, and could be disposed of with no involving of sentiment. Those twenty barrels of Malbec he would have sold at a price made acceptable by its sprightliness, its bright youth. But Hector had been aware in it of a fine note, a determination, a finish to come with age. Malbec vines were temperamental; they had quirks, they were tricksy, they sulked if they were not pruned one way this spring, and quite another way next spring. They were often ungrateful enough to die before their fruits could be gathered.

But last summer had been cloudless, with heat reflecting from the ground, and Hector had coddled the vines slavishly. He packed the wines into the tunnel, not even Giorgio knowing of them, and here they were mellowing, within reach of him. He had the small vigneron's dislike of relinquishing grasp on his wealth in hand.

Lighting a pair of tallow candles, he spiked them on the rough wall, turned up his sleeves, and began to cut into the rock. It was limestone, easy to work, hardening on exposure to air. The tunnel was already a hundred feet long; on this slope only the Schram place had a larger cave, and like the Regola's, its temperature varied no more than five degrees in the cycle of the year. Hector worked massively, with hammer and chisel, but through the cave doors not a sound of the mining carried on to the villa.

The guests had come back from tea at Calistoga, and a fire burned in the parlor, where Carola and Miss Lane sat over their embroidery, and Vic played lotto with Jule. Giorgio was in his den, smoking a cheroot, his quill moving rapidly. The tasks of posting books, writing letters and dispatching them he compressed all in one particular day, as was the custom of the older merchants in San Francisco; and this was steamer day, a survival of the time when the packet sailed out of Meiggs' Wharf for the East. The smoke was asphyxiating, the room stuffy and just right, like his office in the old Montgomery Building; he wrote off a dozen letters, and was in excellent, crisp form. On the whole, this had been a good day. In Calistoga he had been recognized, he had liked the tea, rewarded the Ladies' Aid by purchasing a cake and a jar of spiced peaches. Also, he had heard a pleasing comment as he walked by the veranda of the Calistoga Hotel, where some villagers sat lounging in chairs.

"That's him! That's Mr. Regola of Montino. He made the Comet, and the Regolberg."

Giorgio had marched on finely with his stick, between Carola and Miss Marthe Lane, old Wildcat Lane's daughter. Oblivion had swallowed up most of his contemporaries, but he was still remembered. He had made a big smash in his day, set off a lot of fireworks, and necks still craned as he passed by.

He stamped the letters, then went into the kitchen. Alda was pressing out a shirt for Cleve.

"Where's Hector? I want these taken to the post office."

"He must be in the field somewhere."

"In the wet! Well, then, I'll have the Chinaman take them in. Oh, by the way—" He frowned. "That boy of yours, he's been down in the gully. Fishing! I saw him come up with a rod and a fish as we were coming through the gate. We don't stand for that in Montino. Never did!"

Alda, trying the iron at her cheek, looked at him thoughtfully. "You just can't keep your hands off other folks' business, can you?" she wanted to say.

"You must forbid it at once!" he said peremptorily, with the aspect of an indignant schoolmaster, the ribbon of his pince-nez tangled in his beard that was vibrant like antennae. "He will drown there!"

"He's swum in deeper water than that since he was five," she smiled, clumping with the iron. "Cleve just took to water like an eel."

"Hrrumph!" Giorgio paraded up and down the floor, then gave another snort. "Well, this isn't getting my letters posted. Hector not around, nor Port. Nobody around!"

"There won't be any mail going out tonight, but Wing'll take the letters down in the morning."

"Steamer day, and they ought to be off now."

The sky had cleared a little, and the damp air was sharp, full of oxygen. A stroll would do him good. Anything was better than hanging about the house, with all these women getting on his nerves. He had a notion of calling Vic, but Vic would have to change his clothes first, and there he was, sitting before the fire playing games, pampered like a girl. Boys of that age, when not at their books, should be kept outside.

"I'm going up to the shack."

Giorgio turned up his coat collar as he walked through the yard, picking up Lobo, who went up before him in a shambling trot. The air was velvety, but indeed cool, and he was glad he had on his heavy suit of broadcloth, his Sunday best. He climbed the hill, ducked under some wet alders, and rapped at the door. At a shout from within, he entered. The shack was as hot as blazes from a stove on which pots were steaming. There was a Chinesey smell, laundryish, something like camphor, but without the smell of camphor; and overlaid with a reek of feathers and sour wine. Mike was snuggled in the wood-box; before him was a pan of bread soaked in wine dregs. He looked drunk; in fact, he was drunk. The shack, otherwise, was orderly and clean.

"You have chair," said Wing, and Giorgio seated himself.

Wing and Cleve were at the table, playing a game that must have been going a long while; it was also very intricate and solemn. The Chinaman, with eyelids drawn down, as if he had relinquished the external world, sat like an antique statue in ivory, holding a long pipe to his lips. The greyhounds fixed their gaze on the turkey. Cleve played with gravity and a detachment from surroundings rather like that of the dogs. Giorgio edged his chair closer. Cleve dealt. His hands were small and grubby, but dexterous.

They played for markers, which were *ch'iens,* coins of unrivalled fine casting, aquamarine blue, very thin and old. When cast into the pot they rang with a wan, dulcet music.

Idwal Jones

"You want to get in, Giorgio?"

"What are you at? Spit-in-the-ocean?"

Cleve dealt him a hand, and kept the pack face down. "Shasta Sam."

Wing, tapping his pipe, spoke also with brevity. "Ten points. High, low, and the jack."

They played round after round; Giorgio, a cheroot in his teeth, elbows flat on the table, playing with the animateness of a terrier. Both he and Wing puffed cheroots. The pot rang with dollars and silver.

"Gobble-gobble-gobble!"

Mike, rising majestically from the wood-box, addressed the dogs that were under Cleve's chair. They were aggrieved, they rolled their eyes and backed off with yelps of fear. The din was hideous, befitting a barnyard more than a house.

"Here, you!" chided Cleve, fetching Mike a smack on the feathers with his bare foot. "Quiet!"

Mike made an onslaught, and the dogs tripled their protests. Giorgio peered over his glasses. "That turkey looks crazy to me."

"He's just tanked," said Cleve.

"I don't like to be near any turkey, drunk or sober."

"I'll put him in the woodshed," said Cleve, opening the door. The greyhounds scuttled out. With the broom he pushed Mike towards the lean-to, but this time the bird, gobbling in an apoplectic rage, his barred tail feathers spread out, was not to be imprisoned. The dogs, dismayed, but resolved to fight back, were inside it; and Mike was not accustomed to roost this early. He turned and sped downhill. Cleve yelled frantically.

"He's gone to the old stable! He's gone home!"

Wing, his slippers flying, hurled his corpulence out of the shack. Then he pelted down after Cleve. There was no help for it. Mike faced death, or worse. He would be unstitched—his scornful kin would pull all the stitches out of him, and drive him out, an outcast from the society of all right-minded turkeys. Cleve got to the old stable first, and headed off Mike, who vaulted to the fence.

The corral was mud under a film of green slime. It had islands of rocks. He bumped from one island to another, as wary as a condor, but wobbly on his pins. Wing led the chase, holding up his trouser legs; he had again lost his slippers, this time in the mud. He howled execrations. A steady drizzle was closing the afternoon, and pelting on his face.

"There he goes!" yelled Giorgio. "Corner him now!"

Strategy was futile. Mike sailed over their heads to the next rock or stump.

It was like a game of battledore, the shuttlecock a drunken, twenty-pound turkey in erratic flight. The dogs came in, and the pursuers splashed about, breathless and mud-soaked. Mike perched on a log in the furthest corner, a redoubt in deep slime. He was an adversary terrible in splendor, tail fanning, chest bursting with rage and defiance, his red wattles swinging like a metronome. The dogs wilted, their eyes going limpid with fear. Even Wing hesitated. Giorgio clung to the fence, helpless from excess of mirth.

There was a truce. Cleve took deep breaths. Wing recoiled his pigtail, clapped it atop his head in a bun, and skewered it with a pencil. Giorgio, his shoes plopping out of the mud like corks, crawled along the fence into ambush.

"If that wino sobers up, we're lost. Rush him in that corner."

At the right moment Cleve made a leap and a snatch at Mike's tail, and plopped face down in muck. A cry of triumph broke out as he struggled upright. Giorgio had collared the bird with the cane handle.

"Got him! I've got the hellion!"

"Hold him now!" yelled Cleve, pulling off his suspender. "He's slipping!"

He tied the suspender about Mike's neck, and urged him, with Wing's help, through the bars of the corral. All trooped up the hill, Cleve, hair plastered over his face, miserably holding up his pants. Giorgio, weak from mirth, tottered helplessly on his cane, gasping for breath. Mike's rage was unquenched; he clamored, pinions going like an electric fan, and was pushed into the woodshed. Wing, cursing hard, fastened the door with wire. Whether it was strong enough to hold in such desperate villainy was doubtful. He reinforced the door by propping logs against it. Giorgio exploded again, groped into the shack, and moaned feebly as he shook out a handkerchief and dropped into a chair.

Behind the woodshed were a barrel and dipper. Cleve washed himself blue and clean, drew the poncho over his head, and went in. The poncho stuck to him, he was worm-naked under it, and his teeth chattered. Wing, who had made a pot of tea, gave him a hot cup. They all had cups, all talked at once, and the elders lighted cheroots.

"Never saw such a hunt in my life," said Giorgio. "It was like catching an eagle." He guffawed again. "An eagle with tail feathers riveted on." He emptied his cup. "Now for that game. We've got to finish that game. It was your play, Wing."

It was finished on the edge of dusk, just as a voice floated up from the villa. It was Concha's voice. Giorgio, eyebrows wagging, the Toscano cheroot rolling in his teeth, totted up the winnings.

"You're four-bits to the good, Wing." He slid over the money, then a dime to Cleve. "Yours. Me, I got skunked."

They left, Wing staying to change his slippers. On the step was a dripping handful of pants and shirt, which Giorgio speared with his cane.

"I'll pack 'em along."

Cleve had the dime locked in his fist. Thoughts of a fish hook set at the Busy Bee—twelve hooks for a dime—tantalized him. It was either fish hooks or one of those marvellous camel's-hair brushes, good for watercolors, that Lum Yat sold in his shop. Wing caught up with them. Giorgio handed him a packet of letters.

"Don't bother with them now," he said. "Tomorrow will do."

"Tomollow," said Wing impersonally, "not steamuh day. I go post office tonight."

Alda, in white bibbed apron, met them on the veranda. Her forehead rose in amused query. Giorgio's suit was rumpled and moss-stained, his shoes pulpy, the blacking washed out of them.

"Been chasing that damned turkey," he said. "I'll have to scrub."

If Carola and Marthe, to say nothing of the guests, saw him in the hallway, he would be in for a twitting. He looked like something fished up out of the creek. Alda held open the screen door.

"There's nobody this end of the house. You can slip up the back stairs. Wing will take you up a hot claret, and bring your suit down to press. And after dinner he can post your letters."

So she remembered the letters, too. He nodded and obeyed; went through the kitchen gratefully, and upstairs. She had saved him, and done it quietly, without fussing like a hen and making a to-do. If only he had someone to look after him like that at home. . . . He couldn't for the life of him see her transplanted to the city, any more than if she were a deer. She was no ordinary, strapping country wench, the kind needed to scrub in the kitchen and put up with the imbecilities and pettish exactions of Signora Bettina. Even Carola could see that, unless Carola were stupider than her brother—which she wasn't. Let her fight it out for herself if she wanted to get the girl away from Montino—she'd soon learn how far that would get her. Giorgio, hauling off his boots, was grinning diabolically at the thought as the door opened and Wing entered with the hot claret.

Toshio Mori

1910–1980

Mori was the first American writer of Japanese ancestry to be recognized for his literary talent and the first to publish a book of fiction. Born in Oakland of immigrant parents, he grew up dreaming of a baseball career. He earned a tryout with the Chicago Cubs but had to give up the idea to run his family's florist business. Mori started writing and publishing stories about the Japanese American community in the Bay Area, stories tinged with a mix of zaniness and 1930s melancholy that called to mind his contemporaries William Saroyan and John Fante. His work had begun to appear in important collections, such as New Directions Annual and Best American Short Stories of 1943, when World War II sent Mori and his family to an internment camp for Japanese Americans in Utah. He spent three years there, serving as camp historian and cofounding the literary magazine Trek, issues of which are now collectors' items. After the war he returned to the Bay Area and continued to write.

Before the bombing of Pearl Harbor, a collection of his stories had been accepted, but publication of his landmark book Yokohama, California was delayed until 1949. A new generation of readers discovered these stories when they appeared again in the 1970s in early anthologies charting the emergence of Asian American writing. In 1978 UCLA's Asian American Studies Center published a second collection, The Chauvinist and Other Stories. Mori's 1980 novel, Woman from Hiroshima, won the Honor Award from the Women's International League for Peace and Freedom.

The Woman Who Makes Swell Doughnuts

There is nothing I like better to do than to go to her house and knock on the door and when she opens the door, to go in. It is one of the experiences I will long remember—perhaps the only immortality that I will ever be lucky to meet in my short life—and when I say experience I do not mean the actual movement, the motor of our lives. I mean by experience the dancing of emotions before our eyes and inside of us, the dance that is still but is the roar and the force capable of stirring the earth and the people.

Of course, she, the woman I visit, is old and of her youthful beauty there is little left. Her face of today is coarse with hard water and there is no question that she has lived her life: given birth to six children, worked side by side with her man for forty years, working in the fields, working in the house, caring for the grandchildren, facing the summers and winters and also the springs and autumns, running the household that is completely her little world. And when I came on the scene, when I discovered her in her little house on Seventh Street, all of her life was behind, all of her task in this world was tabbed, looked into, thoroughly attended, and all that is before her in life and the world, all that could be before her now was to sit and be served; duty done, work done, time clock punched; old-age pension or old-age security; easy chair; soft serene hours till death take her. But this was not of her, not the least bit of her.

When I visit her she takes me to the coziest chair in the living room, where are her magazines and books in Japanese and English. "Sit down," she says. "Make yourself comfortable. I will come back with some hot doughnuts just out of oil."

And before I can turn a page of a magazine she is back with a plateful of hot doughnuts. There is nothing I can do to describe her doughnuts; it is in a class by itself, without words, without demonstration. It is a doughnut, just a plain doughnut just out of oil but it is different, unique. Perhaps when I am eating her doughnuts I am really eating her; I have this foolish notion in my head many times and whenever I catch myself doing so I say, that is not so, that is not true. Her doughnuts really taste swell, she is the best cook I have ever known, Oriental dishes or American dishes.

I bow humbly that such a room, such a house exists in my neighborhood so I may dash in and out when my spirit wanes, when hell is loose. I sing gratefully that such a simple and common experience becomes an event, an event of necessity and growth. It is an event that is a part of me, an addition to the elements of the earth, water, fire, and air, and I seek the day when it will become a part of everyone.

All her friends, old and young, call her Mama. Everybody calls her Mama. That is not new, it is logical. I suppose there is in every block of every city in America a woman who can be called Mama by her friends and the strangers meeting her. This is commonplace, it is not new and the old sentimentality may be the undoing of the moniker. But what of a woman who isn't a mama but is, and instead of priding in the expansion of her little world, takes her little circle, living out her days in the little circle, perhaps never to be exploited in a biography or on everybody's tongue, but enclosed, shut, excluded from world news and newsreels; just sitting, just moving, just alive, planting the plants in the fields, caring for the children and the grandchildren and baking the tastiest doughnuts this side of the next world.

When I sit with her I do not need to ask deep questions, I do not need to know Plato or The Sacred Books of the East or dancing. I do not need to be on guard. But I am on guard and foot-loose because the room is alive.

"Where are the grandchildren?" I say. "Where are Mickey, Tadao, and Yaeko?"

"They are out in the yard," she says. "I say to them, play, play hard, go out there and play hard. You will be glad later for everything you have done with all your might."

Sometimes we sit many minutes in silence. Silence does not bother her. She says silence is the most beautiful symphony, she says the air breathed in silence is sweeter and sadder. That is about all we talk of. Sometimes I sit and gaze out the window and watch the Southern Pacific trains rumble by and the vehicles whizz with speed. And sometimes she catches me doing this and she nods her head and I know she understands that I think the silence in the room is great, and also the roar and the dust of the outside is great, and when she is nodding I understand that she is saying that this, her little room, her little circle, is a depot, a pause, for the weary traveler, but outside, outside her little world there is dissonance, hugeness of another kind, and the travel to do. So she has her little house, she bakes the grandest doughnuts, and inside of her she houses a little depot.

She is still alive, not dead in our hours, still at the old address on Seventh Street, and stopping the narrative here about her, about her most unique doughnuts, and about her personality, is the best piece of thinking I have ever done. By having her alive, by the prospect of seeing her many more times, I have many things to think and look for in the future. Most stories would end with her death, would wait till she is peacefully dead and peacefully at rest but I cannot wait that long. I think she will grow, and her hot doughnuts just out of the oil will grow with softness and touch. And I think it would be a shame to talk of her doughnuts after she is dead, after she is formless.

Instead I take today to talk of her and her wonderful doughnuts when the earth is something to her, when the people from all parts of the earth may drop in and taste the flavor, her flavor, which is everyone's and all flavor; talk to her, sit with her, and also taste the silence of her room and the silence that is herself; and finally go away to hope and keep alive what is alive in her, on earth and in men, expressly myself.

Toshio Mori

The Eggs of the World

Almost everyone in the community knew Sessue Matoi as the heavy drinker. There was seldom a time when one did not see him staggering full of drink. The trouble was that the people did not know when he was sober or drunk. He was very clever when he was drunk and also very clever when sober. The people were afraid to touch him. They were afraid of this man, sober or drunk, for his tongue and brains. They dared not coax him too solicitously or make him look ridiculous as they would treat the usual tipsy gentleman. The people may have had only contempt for him but they were afraid and silent. And Sessue Matoi did little work. We always said he practically lived on sake and wit. And that was not far from truth.

I was at Mr. Hasegawa's when Sessue Matoi staggered in the house with several drinks under his belt. About the only logical reason I could think of for his visit that night was that Sessue Matoi must have known that Mr. Hasegawa carried many bottles of Japan-imported sake. There was no other business why he should pay a visit to Hasegawa's. I knew Mr. Hasegawa did not tolerate drinking bouts. He disliked riotous scenes and people.

At first I thought Mr. Hasegawa might have been afraid of this drinker, and Sessue Matoi had taken advantage of it. But this was not the case. Mr. Hasegawa was not afraid of Sessue Matoi. As I sat between the two that night I knew I was in the fun, and as likely as any minute something would explode.

"I came to see you on a very important matter, Hasegawa," Sessue Matoi said without batting an eye. "You are in a very dangerous position. You will lose your life."

"What are you talking about?" Mr. Hasegawa said.

"You are in an egg," Sessue Matoi said. "You have seen nothing but the inside of an egg and I feel sorry for you. I pity you."

"What are you talking about? Are you crazy?" Mr. Hasegawa said.

"I am not crazy. I see you very clearly in an egg," Sessue Matoi said. "That is very bad. Pretty soon you will be rotten."

Mr. Hasegawa was a serious fellow, not taking to laughter and gaiety. But he laughed out loud. This was ridiculous. Then he remembered Sessue Matoi was drunk.

"What about this young fellow?" Mr. Hasegawa said, pointing at me.

Sessue Matoi looked me over quizzically. He appeared to study me from all angles. Then he said, "His egg is forming. Pretty soon he must break the shell of his egg or little later will find himself too weak to do anything about it."

I said nothing. Mr. Hasegawa sat with a twinkle in his eyes.

"What about yourself, Sessue Matoi?" he said. "Do you live in an egg?"

"No," Sessue Matoi said. "An egg is when you are walled in, a prisoner within yourself. I am free, I have broken the egg long ago. You see as I am. I am not hidden beneath a shell and I am not enclosed in one either. I am walking on this earth with my good feet, and also I am drinking and enjoying, but am sad on seeing so many eggs in the world, unbroken, untasted, and rotten."

"Are you insulting the whole world or are you just insulting me?" Mr. Hasegawa said.

"I am insulting no one. Look, look me in the eye, Hasegawa. See how sober I am," he said. "I am not insulting you. I love you. I love the whole world and sober or drunk it doesn't make a bit of difference. But when I say an egg's an egg I mean it. You can't very well break the eggs I see."

"Couldn't you break the eggs for us?" Mr. Hasegawa said. "You seem to see the eggs very well. Couldn't you go around and break the shells and make this world the hatching ground?"

"No, no!" Sessue Matoi said. "You have me wrong! I cannot break the eggs. You cannot break the eggs. You can break an egg though."

"I don't get you," said Mr. Hasegawa.

"An egg is broken from within," said Sessue Matoi. "The shell of an egg melts by itself through heat or warmth and it's natural, and independent."

"This is ridiculous," said Mr. Hasegawa. "An egg can be broken from outside. You know very well an egg may be broken by a rap from outside."

"You can rape and assault too," said Sessue Matoi.

"This is getting to be fantastic," Mr. Hasegawa said. "This is silly! Here we are getting all burned up over a little egg, arguing over nonsense."

"This is very important to me," Sessue Matoi said. "Probably the only thing I know about. I study egg culture twenty-four hours. I live for it."

"And for sake," Mr. Hasegawa said.

"And for sake," Sessue Matoi said.

"Shall we study about sake tonight? Shall we taste the sake and you tell me about the flavor?" Mr. Hasegawa said.

"Fine, fine, fine!" said Mr. Matoi.

Mr. Hasegawa went back in the kitchen and we heard him moving about. Pretty soon he came back with a steaming bottle of sake. "This is Hakushika," he said.

"Fine, fine," Sessue Matoi said. "All brands are the same to me, all flavors match my flavor. When I drink I am drinking my flavor."

Mr. Hasegawa poured him several cups which Sessue Matoi promptly gulped down. Sessue Matoi gulped down several more. "Ah, when I drink sake I think of the eggs in the world," he said. "All the unopened eggs in the world."

"Just what are you going to do with all these eggs lying about? Aren't you going to do something about it? Can't you put some of the eggs aside and heat them up or warm them and help break the shells from within?" Mr. Hasegawa said.

"No," Sessue Matoi said. "I am doing nothing of the sort. If I do all you think I should do, then I will have no time to sit and drink. And I must drink. I cannot go a day without drinking because when I drink I am really going outward, not exactly drinking but expressing myself outwardly, talking very much and saying little, sadly and pathetically."

"Tell me, Sessue Matoi," said Mr. Hasegawa. "Are you sad at this moment? Aren't you happy in your paganistic fashion, drinking and laughing through twenty-four hours?"

"Now, you are feeling sorry for me, Hasegawa," Sessue Matoi said. "You are getting sentimental. Don't think of me in that manner. Think of me as the mess I am. I am a mess. Then laugh very hard, keep laughing very hard. Say, oh what an egg he has opened up! Look at the shells, look at the drunk without a bottle."

"Why do you say these things?" Mr. Hasegawa said. "You are very bitter."

"I am not bitter, I am not mad at anyone," Sessue Matoi said. "But you are still talking through the eggshell."

"You are insulting me again," Mr. Hasegawa said. "Do not allow an egg to come between us."

"That is very absurd," Sessue Matoi said, rising from his chair. "You are very absurd, sir. An egg is the most important and the most disturbing thing in the world. Since you are an egg you do not know an egg. That is sad. I say, good night, gentlemen."

Sessue Matoi in all seriousness bowed formally and then tottered to the door.

"Wait, Sessue Matoi," said Mr. Hasegawa. "You didn't tell me what you thought of the flavor of my sake."

"I did tell you," Sessue Matoi said. "I told you the flavor right along."

"That's the first time I ever heard you talking about the flavor of sake tonight," said Mr. Hasegawa.

"You misunderstand me again," said Sessue Matoi. "When you wish to taste the flavor of sake which I drank then you must drink the flavor which I have been spouting all evening. Again, good night, gentlemen."

Again he bowed formally at the door and staggered out of the house.

I was expecting to see Mr. Hasegawa burst out laughing the minute Sessue Matoi stepped out of the house. He didn't. "I suppose he will be around in several days to taste your sake. This must happen every time he comes to see you," I said.

"No," Mr. Hasegawa said. "Strangely, this is the first time he ever walked out like that. I cannot understand him. I don't believe he will be back for a long time."

"Was he drunk or sober tonight?" I said.

"I really don't know," said Mr. Hasegawa. "He must be sober and drunk at the same time."

"Do you really think we will not see him for awhile?" I said.

"Yes, I am very sure of it. To think that an egg would come between us!"

He Who Has the Laughing Face

The simplest thing to say of him is that he is sad and alone but is laughing all the time. It would definitely put him in a hole and everybody would understand and say what a sad story, what an unhappy man he is, what bravery there is in the world. But that is not the story. He is a very common man. His kind is almost everywhere, his lot is the ordinary, the most common, and that is why he is so lost and hidden away from the spotlight.

He, the Japanese, was sitting on the park bench on Seventh and Harrison, looking and gazing at the people without much thought but looking just the same and this being Sunday he was taking his time about it, taking all the time in the world, to belong to this great world or to discover why he is so unhappy, sad and alone. But he did not think for long, he did not sit down and probe like great philosophers do. Instead he simply sat and pretty soon from his sadness, and aloneness, he began to smile, not from happiness, not from sadness, and this is where I saw his face, not a handsome one but common and of everyday life.

His name does not matter, it makes no difference, although it is Tsumura. I found him sitting on the park bench on Seventh and Harrison when I looked up from a book I was reading under a tree. And before one begins to guess and attempt to judge a person right who is a stranger, there is an adventure. I sat, pretending to read the book, and all the time watching this individual who was like all or any of the park bench sitters on Sundays. By the time I began to guess who he was and what he did, he was someone of immense proportions, someone living close to me or someone I know and talk to. And then suddenly, unexpectedly, he would laugh. Not a crazy laugh. He would laugh the kind no one pays attention to. Or if someone pays attention and hear him that someone will believe the man had seen something funny in the park or in the street or had listened to something amusing, and let it go. But that is not all. He did not look queer, he looked the part of others—out for rest.

When I began to guess who he was and what he did there was no stopping of human curiosity and there was no end of mental adventure that is inward and centralized on intuition. What was he laughing at? I wanted to know. Who was he, what does he do for a living? I sat and guessed many times.

He looked like a writer or an artist or a composer with his sad face detached from laughter. But he was laughing almost all the time and smiling as if the world was a part of him. He looked like an idiot, laughing when there was no outward evidence of laughing matter and sense. But idiot he could not be—he was too polished, too well groomed to lead a causeless life. Could he be a priest, a clergy? Could he be the one to lead others and could he by chance come among the people to mix without identity, without the strings attached to him? But on Sunday! Sunday is the clergyman's busy day and also, Sunday is the day any one may possibly be in the park. At one time I believe he was a grocer or a manager of a dry goods store or the proprietor of a flower shop. So it went but it did not end.

One Monday morning I saw him out early in the park, sitting and looking the same as he did the day before and on other Sundays, watching the race of people and of machinery and of time passing through the earth with the same lazy, easy eyes of Sunday and looking unhurried and unflustered and still living, in spite of the fact that this was the restless weekday, the day of sweat and toil and misery and no church bells ringing. He sat without words, like other days, simply sitting and laughing at intervals unconsciously, unaware of human ears and human eyes listening and noticing and probing him. He sat without austerity, without a wit of sadness, sitting, basking, drinking, not singing dramatically in the opera or in the arena, not writing to bring tears or happiness, not using, not playing, not living heroically in one word perhaps, but alive, basking today, a living presence, a phenomenon of life that is here awhile and gone without an answer.

And then on Tuesday I saw him again, and again on Wednesday, Thursday, Friday till I began to believe I have been following a man of leisure or a man out of work or on pension. This assumption, however, was short lived. He did not make an appearance for a week, leaving myself sitting under a tree, waiting with anticipation and with nervousness that the man will not appear again. When I sat and watched for a week and he did not come, I was certain I had lost him, the individual who had become someone big, the man who instantly had charged the park on Seventh and Harrison with life and interest. I sat and read my book regretting the opportunity I had lost to identify him, to put him down as he was, to seek him out through words and gestures the man he really was in the material atmosphere.

But the Japanese returned to the park bench one Sunday, returning with laughter intact and with the sadness creased in his face, looking unchanged as the time I had first noticed him, looking and laughing at intervals, unexpectedly and inconspicuously, occupying a place on the park bench, occupying simply and quietly and lost in the mass of Sunday faces.

This time I did not hesitate to go up to the park bench and address him. I said hello and he looked at me not surprised and smiled. I told him I had been sitting under the tree reading books for weeks and that I had seen him come and sit down on the park bench for weeks and that for a week I had missed him and feared that something must have happened or more dreadful, that he was not to appear at the park bench again.

"Sit down," he said.

He made room for me. We sat and talked a good hour or more. He said his name was Tsumura, and he was from Shinano prefecture in Japan. I said my parents were from Hiroshima prefecture and he said he knew a number of people from Hiroshima.

"I was afraid I had lost you, that I would not see you again," I said.

The man laughed. "You need not be afraid," he said. "I am always here. I am not rich and I do not travel.

"What do you do?" I said.

He said he worked for Hinode Laundry Co. He said he was a truck driver calling at the houses and offices all over the East Bay. He said he had been working for fourteen years at the same place and sometimes he worked only part time which was why I saw him on weekdays for a long stretch.

A moment later he said he had to go. He said the supper at the laundry house was at six and he must go now to be on time. We said good-bye and promised that we would meet again. Not a word did he say about the sadness of his face and his life. And I did not ask why he is sad and why he is laughing all the time. We did not speak a word of it, we did not like to be foolish and ask and answer the problem of the earth, and we did not have to. Every little

Toshio Mori

observation, every little banal talk or laughing matter springs from the sadness of the earth that is reality; every meeting between individuals, every meeting of society, every meeting of a gathering, of gaiety or sorrow, springs from sadness that is the bed of earth and truth.

And so when he said he was a laundry truck driver and had come to the park for a breath of air which is no different from the wind that hits him while driving, all that matters is that he is a laundry truck driver, a man living in the city, coming to the park for a pause, not for great thoughts or to escape the living of life, but to pause and laugh, unbitterly and unsentimentally, not wishing for dreams, not expecting a miracle, not even accepting the turn of the next hour or the next second.

And this is the greatest thing happening today: that of a laundry truck driver or an equivalent to such who is living and coming in and out of parks, the homes, the alleys, the dives, the offices, the rendezvous, the vices, the churches, the operas, the movies; all seeking unconsciously, unawaredly, the hold of this sadness, the loneliness, the barrenness, which is not elusive but hovering and pervading and seeping into the flesh and vegetation alike, churning out potentially the greatness, the weakness, and the heroism, the cowardice; and therefore, leaving unfinished all the causes of sadness, unhappiness, and sorrows of the earth behind in the laughter and the mute silence of time.

JADE SNOW WONG

1922–

Born in San Francisco of Chinese immigrant parents, Jade Snow Wong attended schools in Chinatown, where her father ran a small garment factory. In 1943, she graduated from Mills College in Oakland. Soon after, at the age of twenty-two, she began work on her autobiographical narrative, Fifth Chinese Daughter. It became the first book by an Asian American woman to receive national recognition. Portions appeared as early as 1945, and the book was published by Harper and Row in 1950. Widely recognized as a pioneering work, it has remained in print for half a century and been translated into several foreign languages. At a time when women of color had almost no presence in the world of books and publishing, Wong set out to tell the story of her early years, before and during World War II, as a woman of Chinese ancestry coming of age in a land that prizes self-assertion. In an author's note to the first edition, her comment on voice is also a comment on the transplanted culture from which she was emerging: "Although a 'first person singular' book, this story is written in the third person from Chinese habit. The submergence of the individual is literally practiced. In written Chinese, prose or poetry, the word 'I' almost never appears." While she has published two more works of nonfiction, The Immigrant Experience (1971) and No Chinese Stranger (1975), Wong has never considered writing her main calling. Soon after World War II she began a long and successful career making and selling ceramics in San Francisco, where she still lives.

From *Fifth Chinese Daughter*

A PERSON AS WELL AS A FEMALE

After graduation from the Chinese school, Jade Snow seriously sought a solution to her money problem. For two reasons, she decided that she would try working outside their factory-home. She thought that she could make a little more money, and even if she didn't, she would at least escape from some of the continuous family friction. She sought help from the state employment service, which found openings for her in housework. Within the following six months, Jade Snow worked in seven different homes and was exposed to a series of candid views of the private lives of these American families. Jade Snow made her own decisions. At no time did she consult her family about the various jobs; she simply told them when her mind was made up. . . . By word-of-mouth referrals, she made four contacts which kept her busy. She really liked these odd jobs better, since all that was involved was serving party dinners and washing dishes, which was not so tiring as the entire management of a household.

Mentally she tabulated these four families by type rather than by name—"the horsy family," "the apartment-house family," "the political couple," and the "bridge-playing group."

The "horsy family" was composed of an elderly, mild father who said scarcely a word, an ambitious, tense mother, and two equally ambitious and mutually antagonistic daughters in their thirties, whose chief purpose in life was to be "smart." They were unrelenting in their efforts to get their names on the social page of the local newspapers, and their method was horses. They had their pictures taken in horsy poses, and they gave parties, but only for guests who "mattered." They owned a large house patterned after English cottage architecture, which the mother tried to keep in perfect order as a setting for her daughters' activities. The father, who worked all day, said nothing when he came home, but the daughters argued continuously about the best means to achieve their common goal.

The "political" middle-aged couple gave dinners in honor of up-and-coming young California political figures; there were always many men but few women at these parties. Here, Jade Snow was initiated into a new wrinkle in the American pattern—the off-color story.

Needless to say, the Wong household, if not always gentle, had high standards. Between Confucian decorum and Christian ideals, even unessential or boisterous laughing was dissonant. There an off-color story had never reared its ugly head. However, at this home, toward ten o'clock when everyone had had many cocktails, and the waiting dinner was turning to ruin in the oven, a group of men, including the political star of honor, howling with laughter, would burst into the kitchen to get away from the women in the living room. Here they would start on their gleeful "Have you heard the latest one?" slap each other, and roar with gales of laughter over each tale.

The small, lone female, Jade Snow, must have been to them merely another kitchen fixture for they never recognized her. Stoically she continued her work, trying not to blush at their remarks and double talk and to drive them out of her memory.

What would Daddy and Mama think about this? They never knew that in these months their fifth daughter saw and heard things that broadened and humanized the American world beyond the realm of typewriters and stenographers, which had provided her first and only childhood associations with

Caucasians. Needless to say, she never talked about these new experiences at home. Mama and Daddy were comfortable in their knowledge that Jade Snow had found honest work and was performing it satisfactorily. She was making about twenty dollars a month, and now paid for her own lunches, carfare, clothes, and all the other necessities of a fifteen-year-old schoolgirl. She had completed Chinese school, was about to complete the American high school, and was apparently establishing firm habits for earning a living and being a good homemaker, in accordance with the traditional Chinese pattern for women.

The "apartment-house" dwellers had one little girl about three, who was the light of their life. Everything Arleen did or said was the most astounding thing in the world, and had never been done or said so well before. If Arleen threw her dinner at the window of the kitchen door, she was not reproved or punished; she was excused for being "full of spirit." The only reason Jade Snow continued to oblige Arleen's fond parents was that once their angel child was asleep, she could use the evening to study, while being paid.

Finally, there were the Gilberts, or rather, Mrs. Gilbert, who loved bridge parties. The Gilberts' home was large, beautiful, adequately landscaped, and they were very proud of it. Gilbert liked golf. "Nothing like it in the world for relaxation and public relations," he always said. Every Saturday afternoon which did not see a downpour of rain found him at his favorite activity.

Mrs. Gilbert's passion for bridge demanded every Saturday, rain or shine. On the afternoons when she entertained "the girls" in her own home, Jade Snow helped her. On other Saturdays, she was at "the other girls' " homes.

When Mrs. Gilbert was hostess for a "simple" buffet luncheon, she set her table with her best lace cloth and polished silver. It was Jade Snow's first acquaintance with buffet meals. "The girls," from thirty-five to fifty in years, arrived, gushed, giggled, gossiped, ate, and played bridge all afternoon—and what was most amazing to Jade Snow—all the while with their hats on! It was always the same crowd of faces under different hats. Jade Snow wondered what it would be like to be one of them, to have so much time that you would try to spend it playing bridge, and so much money that you could pay someone to come in and wash the dishes while you played.

Jade Snow now concentrated intensely on her American school work, since there were no more Chinese lessons to divide her energy. As her graduation was approaching, she began inquiries about qualifications for college entrance. She found that she had met the academic requirements for the state university; but the registration and other fees, together with commutation and books, would be beyond her part-time earning capacity, and more than she could possibly save, since she was using all her earnings for current expenses.

But if not college, what was her future?

"Education is your path to freedom," Daddy had said. "In China, you would have had little private tutoring and no free advanced schooling. Make the most of your American opportunity."

"Be a good girl—and study hard," Grandmother had said.

"Daddy thinks that Jade Snow is so intelligent," she had overheard her older sisters say skeptically, "but let's see if she can bring any honors home to our family."

"I resolve to be a credit to Mama and prove that the unkind predictions about her children were wrong," she had vowed once when Daddy was ill.

"Give me the strength and the ability to prove to my family that they have been unjust and make them prouder of me than anyone else," Jade Snow had pleaded later in unnumbered prayers.

Constantly, she remembered these challenges.

Moreover, she was most curious about college, and eager to earn more about the new worlds which her high school subjects were just opening up to her.

Yes, Jade Snow agreed with Daddy that education was the path to freedom. Forgotten was her early ambition to be a stenographer. She resolved to ask Daddy to help her with the college fees. After all, he had financed Older Brother's education.

Her next free night, when she was alone with Daddy in the dining room after dinner, Jade Snow broached the subject.

"Daddy, I have been studying the state university catalogue, and I should like to continue my education there, but it will cost more than I can manage, even though I still worked all I could. Would you help me to meet the college expenses?"

Daddy reluctantly pulled himself away from his evening paper and settled back in the large, square, straight, black armchair that was his alone. He took off his dark-rimmed reading glasses, and looked thoughtfully but distractedly at the figure standing respectfully before him. Then he chose his words seriously and deliberately.

"You are quite familiar by now with the fact that it is the sons who perpetuate our ancestral heritage by permanently bearing the Wong family name and transmitting it through their blood line, and therefore the sons must have priority over the daughters when parental provision for advantages must be limited by economic necessity. Generations of sons, bearing our Wong name, are those who make pilgrimages to ancestral burial grounds and preserve them forever. Our daughters leave home at marriage to give sons to their husbands' families to carry on the heritage for other names.

"Jade Snow, you have been given an above-average Chinese education for an American-born Chinese girl. You now have an average education for an American girl. I must still provide with all my powers for your older brother's advanced medical training."

"But Daddy, I want to be more than an average Chinese or American girl. If I stay here, I want to be more than average. If I go to China, I shall advance further with an American college degree," Jade Snow pleaded earnestly.

"I have no other means even though you desire to be above average," Daddy replied evenly, and Jade Snow could not detect either regret or sympathy in his statement of fact. She did not know whether his next words were uttered in challenge or in scorn as he added, "If you have the talent, you can provide for your own college education."

Daddy had spoken. He returned to his Chinese paper with finality and clamped on his glasses again. By habit, Jade Snow questioned aloud no more. She had been trained to make inquiry of Daddy with one question, and to accept his answer; she never asked twice. But her mind was full of questions as it echoed his words, "If you have the talent, you can provide for your own college education."

Tonight his statement did not leave Jade Snow with the customary reaction, "Daddy knows better. Daddy is fair. Even though I do not like what he says, he has eaten more salt than I have eaten rice, and in time I shall understand why this is my own problem and must be endured."

No, his answer tonight left Jade Snow with a new and sudden bitterness against the one person whom she had always trusted as fair to her.

"How can Daddy know what an American advanced education can mean to me? Why should Older Brother be alone in enjoying the major benefits of Daddy's toil? There are no ancestral pilgrimages to be made in the United States! I can't help being born a girl. Perhaps, even being a girl, I don't want to marry, *just* to raise sons! Perhaps I have a right to want more than sons! I am a person, besides being a female! Don't the Chinese admit that women also have feelings and minds?"

Jade Snow retreated to her little bedroom, but now she felt imprisoned. She was trapped in a mesh of tradition woven thousands of miles away by ancestors who had had no knowledge that someday one generation of their progeny might be raised in another culture. Acknowledging that she owed her very being and much of her thinking to those ancestors and their tradition, she could not believe that this background was meant to hinder her further development either in America or in China.

Beyond this point, she could not think clearly. Impulsively, she threw on her coat and left the house—the first time that she had done so without notifying Mama.

In a lonely walk, she wandered in the darkness over the San Francisco hills. She went first to the waterfront, saw a few tramps sleeping in empty railroad cars, hid from some drunken brawlers in front of the saloons, climbed up Telegraph Hill, came down and went up again over Russian Hill, to Van Ness Avenue, then back to Chinatown and home.

As she walked, she pushed away her bitterness in order to organize a practical course of action. To begin with, she was not going to give up her education. She felt that it was right to go on with it, and she must try to provide for it alone. She would try to get a scholarship to college.

But Daddy had also said, "If you have the talent." Jade Snow reasoned: talent is what you were born with—in combination with what you have learned. Did she have talent? Older Brother had said that she had no imagination nor personality, but did she have talent? She reasoned further: she had always tried to make the most of her ability. Often her classmates seemed to get the right answer much more quickly than she did, but she always hung on, and eventually she caught up with them. If she continued to do her very best, and if what she had set her eyes on was the right thing for her to do, she had to believe that the talent part would somehow be taken care of . . .

"LEARNING CAN NEVER BE POOR OR EXHAUSTED"—CHINESE PROVERB

Jade Snow's years at Mills College were inseparably colored by living at "Kapiolani," the dean's little brown-shingled home.

This simple structure located on a hillside road wore a charming crown: a garden of gaily colored fuchsias, bamboo, camellias, azaleas, and species of geraniums and pelargoniums—all thriving in pots bordering the flat roof. At night, the mellow glow from a string of electrically lighted Japanese lanterns extended the tropical setting into evening enjoyment.

On one corner of this roof garden was a miniature penthouse room, surrounded by a ribbon of windows. These pleasant quarters gave Jade Snow her first complete privacy in studying and in personal living, and at last gave her inner peace.

The various rooms of the house downstairs were like the exterior, simple and without clutter. Jade Snow helped operate the house and manage the meals to enable the dean and herself to carry on their respective campus responsibilities and activities with maximum dispatch. Sometimes, she also helped attend to the house or dinner guests. But though these duties filled her days with busyness, she never felt too rushed and she never felt herself to be merely a servant. All who lived in that home, including a pair of cocker spaniels named Pupuli and Papaia, a black cat named Bessie, and Jade Snow, were recipients of the dean's kindness and consideration.

Unexpectedly, life shone with a new glow. Jade Snow returned home each day to a friend who was never too tired to think through a problem with her, who could explain the many new experiences peculiar to a residential women's college, and who shed a mature light on the art of living. With humor, honesty, and affection, Jade Snow was given guidance and comfort without judgment pronounced, and by daily example she was impressed with the marvel of inner spiritual strength and the meaning of gentleness.

Now, living became fun! The fun was partly in being able to participate in the home activities of one of the campus' central figures. At their house, there were teas for parents of students, apple and doughnut parties for seniors, breakfasts for residence-hall mothers, and a host of other unorganized, impromptu, but memorable little gatherings. Here Jade Snow met celebrated musicians, scholars, and speakers who visited the college. . . .

What was disturbing in the first weeks at Mills was that her lifelong perfected system of learning failed her. At the end of several weeks, she had only a handful of lecture notes. The instructor of the labor course, a brilliant and direct man as interested in the practical workings of theory as in the theory itself, taught by encouraging questions. But at the end of every never-dull class period, Jade Snow did not have one lecture note.

How was she going to study without notes? Accustomed to specific assignments in orderly fashion, and habitually thorough, she became concerned by the vagueness of these subjects which defeated her ability to memorize—an ability carefully perfected by her Chinese studies and which had heretofore always worked.

Impressed by the informality and approachability of her professors she gathered her courage to speak to her labor instructor. "I have a problem in not being able to take any lecture notes from you. At junior college, we were given definite outlines to follow and study for examinations."

Her instructor seemed amused. "Why do you think that you learn only from lecture notes?"

Jade Snow had no answer to this unexpected question.

He continued, "Here we want to know each one individually. Instead of reading a set of prepared notes, I study my students minds and ideas. By the conversational method, I try to develop your minds, not give you sets of facts. Don't you know that you can always go to the library to look up facts?"

Jade Snow could not immediately grasp this new concept of individual training. She had never thought of the purpose of academic training as being anything else than that of disseminating superior information.

All she could say in defense was, "But I learned a lot from junior college."

The instructor came back neatly, "Sure, you learned a lot. But now I am trying to teach you to think!"

Jade Snow, at a complete loss, mumbled a "Thank you" and trailed off in a state of mental indigestion.

The first midterm gave ample exercise in how to think. Jade Snow arrived at class in a fog of memorized dates, names, and places, and found that one essay question comprised the entire midterm. It was: "You are (choose any one) a Palestinian potter; an Anatolian farmer; an Athenian shoemaker; a Carthaginian clerk; a Roman cook; a West-Saxon weaver; an Italian goldsmith. You are transferred, buckrogerswise, to Oakland in 1940, and try to get a job in your trade. What problems do you face?"

A buzz of excitement went around the astounded class. Incredulous and confused, Jade Snow reread the question and floundered miserably to find a passably imaginative answer. After spending half an hour figuring what trade to select, she chose the Palestinian potter simply because it was the first one listed, but she didn't know a thing about pottery, let alone Palestinian pottery. In the ensuing hour, her heretofore unshaken faith in the effectiveness of the Chinese study method collapsed completely.

Gradually, through successive examinations and successive classroom discussions, she learned the true meaning of her instructor's remarks, and at the end of a year's study she found that from slow beginnings she was learning to analyze and to evaluate what she heard and read, and to express more readily in English what she thought. She found that her curious mind was being disciplined to work quickly and to find relationships between problems.

She was being led gradually to reverse her lifelong practice, enforced by her parents, of keeping to herself what she thought. Her mind sprang from its tightly bound concern with facts and the Chinese absolute order of things, to concern with the reasons behind the facts, their interpretations, and the imminence of continuous change.

This release did not mean that her imagination soared to new heights on unfurled wings, but it did cause her to search for new answers, to fail painfully before classmates, to grope inwardly for the right expression and find herself and try again—because sometimes in her eagerness with this newfound freedom she said only the wrong thing.

The labor-problems course included a number of field trips. First, the class attended some real union meetings. Next, the instructor—learning that Jade Snow's father owned a small garment factory—interrupted a conversation about piecework factories and workers to ask her one day:

"Do you think that our class might visit your father's factory?"

Jade Snow was startled. "I don't know."

"If you will arrange for a visit to your father's factory," he continued, "I'll arrange for a visit to a large factory manufacturing a famous national brand of overalls and we can compare notes on the two."

"I'll ask my father," Jade Snow promised.

That evening she telephoned Daddy. Not wasting words in pleasantries, she began, "Daddy, one of my instructors would like our class to visit our factory as a field-trip project."

Daddy was disconcerting. "What is there remarkable to see in my factory?"

Jade Snow explained, "The teacher says that he wishes to contrast your factory with a large one. Most of the class members have never seen garment manufacturing in progress."

Daddy asked, "What kind of a person is your teacher?"

"Why, it's hard to say exactly . . . He is honest and has humility . . ." And then she was inspired by remembering some biographical facts. "His father was a missionary in China, where he was born. He is, moreover, a Ph.D. in Religion and a Methodist."

In response came a favorable and thoughtful "Is that so?" Then, "Be sure to give me adequate notice before you come, so that the floor will be newly swept."

"Good, Daddy." Chinese parents and children seldom thanked each other in so many words.

At the arranged time, the class toured Daddy's factory, while Jade Snow explained the different processes, familiar to her since childhood. All the while, the Chinese women workers stared at the young, healthy Caucasian girls just as curiously as the students stared at the native costumes and the Chinese babies who played and napped comfortably as their mothers worked.

Jade Snow also showed the class through their living quarters, where Mama and Daddy were waiting for them. In warm greeting Daddy extended his hand and a big smile to the instructor, while Mama hovered shyly but keenly observant in the background. In the Chinese spirit of hospitality, she had made extra tea besides the quart in the thermos bottle which was always on hand to greet unexpected callers, quench thirst, or pacify fright. Now she invited everyone to have tea and tea cakes in the dining room. The girls had their tea standing, and gazed curiously at the numerous photographs of cousins and ancestral graves in China, which Daddy was proud to hang on all the walls. Daddy sat in his customary chair. Although everyone seemed more or less at home, the parents as well as guests, Jade Snow suddenly felt estranged, for while she was translating conversation between instructor and parents, she was observing the scene with two pairs of eyes—Fifth Daughter's, and those of a college junior.

The subsequent trip to the American factory at least twenty times larger than Daddy's brought the contrast sharply home to her. This firm, unlike Daddy's, marketed as well as manufactured its own brand of jeans. The most striking difference to Jade Snow, however, was not merely the size of operations, which impressed her fellow class members. It was the intensity of the Caucasian men and women piece-workers, who did not chat or stop one moment. No one looked around, ready to laugh and relieve his boredom. A baby would have been unhappy and entirely out of place there. What a difference between the relaxed attitude of the Chinese pieceworkers and the frantic preoccupation of the Caucasians! Instead of thinking of the economic significance of a big business as against Daddy's small one, Jade Snow was thinking that the boss of this vast establishment could not give his personal attention to train each apprentice to correct habits, nor could he repair a bassinette for a tired worker's baby; nor could his wife sew alongside his employees and invite a hungry worker to have some soup in her factory kitchen.

Field trips like these were infrequent, but one requirement common to all courses was the term paper, the quality of which tipped the final grade of a course tremendously. It was an opportunity for the individual student to do a unified piece of original thinking at her own pace, but no student seemed to appreciate such an opportunity. Groans, not cries of delight, greeted the instructor's reminder that term papers were expected or due.

Fortunately Jade Snow found that her previous practice in creative writing helped now in preparing a term paper for a year's course in the English novel. Her subject, "The Chinese Novel," offered opportunity for comparing the English and Chinese treatment of novels. At last, she had an opportunity to link her past and present learning.

Coincidentally with her work on this paper came the publication of an English translation of the historically famous Chinese classic novel, *Chin Ping Mei*, written anonymously in the sixteenth century. Jade Snow was therefore able to review a typical Chinese novel, to prove her thesis that the Chinese novel differed completely from the English or Continental novel in its development, form, and purpose.

Jade Snow thought hard, wove her best Chinese and English knowledge into the paper, and felt satisfied with her work. Her English professor was also satisfied. He told her that he had chosen the paper for reading at an English conference to be held at the college, where representatives from three other bay area colleges and universities would gather.

Jade Snow heard this announcement, smiled, but could find no words to answer when her classmates congratulated her. How could she tell them that for a year she had been watching and listening with wonder to catch every movement and sound of these Caucasian girls who participated so easily in the college scene, who absorbed and contributed while she remained a mere spectator? Now at last she too could claim to be a participant.

CARLOS BULOSAN

1913–1956

Born in Binalonan, Luzon, the Philippines, Carlos Bulosan arrived in
Seattle in 1931, chasing a dream of freedom and prosperity in the New
World. Working in West Coast restaurants and fields at the height of the Depression—from California to Alaska—he was overwhelmed by the recognition that Filipinos in America were the ultimate victims of exploitation and discrimination, systematically denied the right to become citizens, vote, own property, or marry whom they
chose. He became a labor organizer and a radical intellectual. As editor of the New Tide
in 1934, he met Richard Wright, Carey McWilliams, and many other kindred spirits.
He schooled himself at the Los Angeles Public Library, and, encouraged by Harriet Monroe, the editor of Poetry, he began to write satirical, comic folk fables that were collected
in the best-selling Laughter of My Father (1934). Well aware of the brutal treatment of
the Pinoy in California, he nonetheless embraced the allied cause in World War II, publishing impassioned poems in books such as Letter from America (1942), insisting that
his adopted home hold true to its promises and potential. By the time America Is in the
Heart was published in 1946, Bulosan was an outspoken advocate for multiculturalism
in the United States. He stayed politically committed and productive for the rest of his
life, returning to the Philippines to write favorably in support of the Huk insurrection.
Virtually blacklisted by the media during the cold war, he was threatened with deporta-
tion, but because of his international stature the action was quietly dropped.

Chapter 16
from *America Is in the Heart*

I began to be afraid, riding alone in the freight train. I wanted suddenly to
go back to Stockton and look for a job in the tomato fields, but the train was
already traveling fast. I was in flight again, away from an unknown terror that
seemed to follow me everywhere. Dark flight into another place, toward other
enemies. But there was a clear sky and the night was alive with stars. I could
still see the faint blaze of Stockton's lights in the distance, a halo arching
above it and fading into a backdrop of darkness.

In the early morning the train stopped a few miles from Niles, in the midst
of a wide grape field. The grapes had been harvested and the bare vines were
falling to the ground. The apricot trees were leafless. Three railroad detectives

jumped out of a car and ran toward the boxcars. I ran to the vineyard and hid behind a smudge pot, waiting for the next train from Stockton. A few bunches of grapes still hung on the vines, so I filled my pockets and ran for the tracks when the train came. It was a freight and it stopped to pick up carloads of grapes; when it started moving again the empties were full of men.

I crawled to a corner of a car and fell asleep. When I awakened the train was already in San Jose. I jumped outside and found another freight going south. I swung aboard and found several hoboes drinking cans of beer. I sat and watched them sitting solemnly, as though there were no more life left in the world. They talked as though there were no more happiness left, as though life had died and would not live again. I could not converse with them, and this barrier made me a stranger. I wanted to know them and to be a part of their life. I wondered what I had in common with them beside the fact that we were all on the road rolling to unknown destinations.

When I reached Salinas, I walked to town and went to a Mexican restaurant on Soledad Street. I was drinking coffee when I saw the same young girl who had disappeared in the night. She was passing by with an old man. I ran to the door and called to her, but she did not hear me. I went back to my coffee wondering what would become of her.

I avoided the Chinese gambling houses, remembering the tragedy in Stockton. Walking on the dark side of the street as though I were hunted, I returned eagerly to the freight yards. I found the hoboes sitting gloomily in the dark. I tried a few times to jump into the boxcars, but the detectives chased me away. When the freights had gone the detectives left.

Then an express from San Francisco came and stopped to pick up a few passengers. The hoboes darted out from the dark and ran to the rods. When I realized that I was the only one left, I grabbed the rod between the coal car and the car behind it. Then the express started, gathering speed as it nosed its way through the night.

I almost fell several times. The strong, cold wind lashed sharply at my face. I put the crook of my arm securely about the rod, pinching myself when I feared that I was going to sleep. It was not yet autumn and the sky was clear, but the wind was bitter and sharp and cut across my face like a knife. When my arm went to sleep, I beat it to life with my fist. It was the only way I could save myself from falling to my death.

I was so exhausted and stiff with the cold when I reached San Luis Obispo that I could scarcely climb down. I stumbled when I reached the ground, rolling over on my stomach as though I were headless. Then I walked to town, where I found a Filipino who took me in his car to Pismo Beach. The Filipino community was a small block near the sea—a block of poolrooms, gambling houses, and little green cottages where prostitutes were doing business. At first I did not know what the cottages were, but I saw many Filipinos going into them from the gambling houses near by. Then I guessed what they were, because cottages such as these were found in every Filipino community.

I went into one of the cottages and sat in the warm little parlor where the Filipinos were waiting their turn to go upstairs. Some of the prostitutes were sitting awkwardly in the men's laps, wheedling them. Others were dancing cheek to cheek, swaying their hips suggestively. The Filipinos stood around whispering lustily in their dialects. The girls were scantily dressed, and one of them was nude. The nude girl put her arms around me and started cooing lasciviously.

I was extricated from her by the same Filipino who had taken me into his car in San Luis Obispo. He came into the house and immediately took the girl upstairs. In ten minutes he was down again and asked me if I would like to ride with him to Lompoc. I had heard of the place when I was in Seattle, so naturally I was interested. We started immediately and in about two hours had passed through Santa Maria.

Beyond the town, at a railroad crossing, highway patrolmen stopped our car. Speaking to me in our dialect, Doro, my companion, said:

"These bastards probably want to see if we have a white woman in the car."

"Why?" I asked him, becoming frightened.

"They think every Filipino is a pimp," he said. "But there are more pimps among them than among all the Filipinos in the world put together. I will kill one of these bastards someday!"

They questioned Doro curtly, peered into the car, and told us to go on.

I came to know afterward that in many ways it was a crime to be a Filipino in California. I came to know that the public streets were not free to my people: we were stopped each time these vigilant patrolmen saw us driving a car. We were suspect each time we were seen with a white woman. And perhaps it was this narrowing of our life into an island, into a filthy segment of American society, that had driven Filipinos like Doro inward, hating everyone and despising all positive urgencies toward freedom.

When we reached the mountains to the right of the highway, we turned toward them and started climbing slowly, following the road that winds around them like a taut ribbon. We had been driving for an hour when we reached the summit, and suddenly the town of Lompoc shone like a constellation of stars in the deep valley below. We started downward, hearing the strong wind from the sea beating against the car. Then we came to the edge of the town, and church bells began ringing somewhere near a forest.

It was the end of the flower season, so the Filipino workers were all in town. They stood on the sidewalks and in front of Japanese stores showing their fat rolls of money to the girls. Gambling was going on in one of the old buildings, in the Mexican district, and in a cafe across the street Mexican girls and Filipinos were dancing. I went inside the cafe and sat near the counter, watching the plump girls dancing drunkenly.

I noticed a small Filipino sitting forlornly at one of the tables. He was smoking a cigar and spitting like a big man into an empty cigar box on the floor. When the juke box stopped playing he jumped to the counterman for some change. He put the nickels in the slot, waving graciously to the dancers although he never danced himself. Now and then a Filipino would go into the back room where the gamblers were playing cards and cursing loudly.

The forlorn Filipino went to the counter again and asked for change. He put all the nickels in the slot and bought several packages of cigarettes. He threw the cigarettes on the table near the juke box and then called to the old Mexican men who were sitting around the place. The Mexicans rushed for the table, grabbing the cigarettes. The Filipino went out lighting another big cigar.

I followed him immediately. He walked slowly and stopped now and then to see if I was following him. There was some mysterious force in him that attracted me. When he came to a large neon sign which said Landstrom Café, he stopped and peered through the wide front window. Then he entered a side door and climbed the long stairs.

I opened the door quietly and entered. I heard him talking to a man in one of the rooms upstairs. When I reached the landing a hard blow fell on my head. I rolled on the floor. Then I saw him with a gun in his hand, poised to strike at my head again. Standing behind him was my brother Amado, holding a long-bladed knife.

I scrambled to my feet screaming: "Brother, it is me! It is Allos! Remember?"

My brother told his friend to stop. He came near me, walking around me suspiciously. He stepped back and folded the blade of the knife. There was some doubt in his face.

"I am your brother," I said again, holding back the tears in my eyes. "I am Allos! Remember the village of Mangusmana? Remember when you beat our *carabao* in the rain? When you touched my head and then ran to Binalonan? Remember, Amado?" I was not only fighting for my life, but also for a childhood bond that was breaking. Frantically I searched in my mind for other remembrances of the past which might remind him of me, and re-establish a bridge between him and my childhood.

"Remember when I fell from the coconut tree and you were a janitor in the *presidencia?*" I said. "And you brought some magazines for me to read? Then you went away to work in the sugar plantations of Bulacan?"

"If you are really my brother tell me the name of our mother," he said casually.

"Our mother's name is Meteria," I said. "That is what the people call her. But her real name is Autilia Sampayan. We used to sell salted fish and salt in the villages. Remember?"

My brother grabbed me affectionately and for a long time he could not say a word. I knew, then, that he had loved my mother although he had had no chance to show it to her. Yes, to him, and to me afterward, to know my mother's name was to know the password into the secrets of the past, into childhood and pleasant memories; but it was also a guiding star, a talisman, a charm that lights us to manhood and decency.

"It has been so long, Allos," Amado said at last. "I had almost forgotten you. Please forgive me, brother . . ."

"My name is Alfredo," said his friend. "I nearly killed you!"

He laughed guiltily, putting the gun in his pocket. "Yes, I almost killed you, Allos!"

My brother opened the door of their room. it was a small room, with one broken chair and a small window facing the street. Their clothes were hanging on a short rope that was strung between the door and the cracked mirror. I sat on the edge of the bed, waiting for my brother to speak. Alfredo started playing solitaire on the table, laughing whenever he cheated himself.

"Go out in the hall and wash your hands," said my brother. "Then we will go downstairs for something to eat. Where is your suitcase?"

"I don't have any—now," I said. "I lost it when I was in Seattle."

"Have you been in Seattle?" he asked.

"I have been in Alaska, too," I said. "And other places."

"You should have written to me," he said. "You shouldn't have come to America. But you can't go back now. You can never go back, Allos."

I could hear men shouting in a bar two blocks down the street. Then church bells started ringing again, and the wind from the sea carried their message to the farmhouses in the canyon near the river. I knew that as long as there was a hope for the future somewhere I would not stop trying to reach it. I looked at my brother and Alfredo and knew that I would never stay with

CHESTER HIMES

1909–1984

Born in Jefferson City, Missouri, of schoolteacher parents (his father was a wheelwright who taught at black Southern A & M colleges), Himes studied briefly at Ohio State, dropping out to hustle in the criminal underbelly of Cleveland. Convicted of armed robbery in 1928, he served seven years in prison but began to write while he was incarcerated. Himes came to California in 1942 to work in the Los Angeles shipyards, and his encounters are sharply engraved in two early novels: If He Hollers Let Him Go *(1945) and* The Lonely Crusade *(1947). He brought life to the literal dark side of the California Dreamland just as its wealth and population began to soar. He details these years in the first volume of his autobiography,* The Quality of Hurt *(1972): "Los Angeles hurt me racially as much as any city I have ever known—much more than any city I remember from the South. Black people were treated much the same as they were in an industrial city of the South. . . . The only thing that surprised me about the race riots in Watts in 1965 was that they waited so long to happen. We are a very patient people."*

*Like Richard Wright and James Baldwin, Chester Himes was so embittered by American racism that he expatriated to France in 1953, returning infrequently over the next thirty years. He became noted as a writer of popular black detective novels set in Harlem (*Cotton Comes to Harlem *among them), several of which were made into films. Himes was reintroduced to American audiences by the perseverance of Charles Harris at Random House and the author and editor Ishmael Reed. With Al Young, Reed founded the influential 1980s Berkeley journal* Yardbird *(later* Y'Bird*), in which Himes was frequently praised.*

From *If He Hollers Let Him Go*

FROM CHAPTER 2

Homer and Conway were waiting in front of the drugstore at the corner of Fifty-fourth and Central.

"You're kinda tardy, playboy," Homer said, climbing in beside Conway.

I turned the corner into Central and started digging. "She wouldn't let me go," I said.

"You mean you had that last dollar left," Conway said.

I squeezed between a truck and an oncoming streetcar, almost brushing, and Homer said, "See that. Now he's tryna kill us. He don't mind dying hisself, but why he got to kill you and me too?"

"Just like that safety man said, gambling thirty seconds against thirty years," Conway said.

I pulled up in front of the hotel at Fifty-seventh and my other three riders climbed in the back.

"Is you ready to face the enemy, that's what I wanna know," Smitty said in his loud, grating voice, trying to be jolly. "Is you ready to meet the man, that's what I mean."

"Conway gonna show the man some teeth first thing," Pigmeat said. "That man done looked in Conway's mouth so much he know every time he have neck bones."

Before I started I turned to Pigmeat and said, "I own some parts of you, don't I, buddy?"

"Get over, goddammit!" Johnson snarled at Smitty in the back seat and pushed him. "You want all the seat?"

"Don't call me no 'buddy,' man," Pigmeat said to me. "When I escaped from Mississippi I swore I'd lynch the first sonabitch that called me a 'buddy.' "

"There these niggers is fighting already," Homer said, shaking his head. "Whenever niggers gets together that's the first thing they gonna do."

Smitty squirmed over to give Johnson more room. "By God, here's a man wakes up evil every morning. Ain't just *some* mornings; this man wakes up evil *every* morning." He looked around at Johnson. "What's the matter with you, man, do your old lady beat you?"

Homer thought they were going to fight. He decided to be peacemaker. "Now you know how Johnson is," he said to Smitty. "That's just his way. You know he don't mean no harm."

As soon as Smitty found out somebody was holding him he began getting bad sure enough. "How do I know how he is?" he shouted. "Does he know how I is? Hell, everybody evil on Monday morning. I'm evil too. He ain't no eviler'n me."

"Shut up!" Conway yelled. "Bob's tryna say something." Then he turned to me. "Don't you know what a 'buddy' is, Bob? A 'buddy' drinks bilge water, eats crap, and runs rabbits. That's what a peckerwood means when he calls you 'buddy.' "

"I ain't kidding, fellow," I told Pigmeat.

He started scratching for his wallet. "Now that's a Senegalese for you," he complained. "Gonna put me out his car 'bout three lousy bucks. Whatcha gonna do with a fellow like that?" He passed me three ones.

"This is for last week," I said, taking them. "What about this week?"

"Aw, man, I'll give it to you Friday," he grumbled. "You raise more hell 'bout three lousy bucks—" . . .

The red light caught me at Manchester; and that made me warm. It never failed; every time I got in a hurry I got caught by every light. I pulled up in the outside lane, abreast a V-8 and an Olds, shifted back to first, and got set to take the lead. When the light turned green it caught a white couple in the middle of the street. The V-8 full of white guys dug off and they started to run for it; and the two white guys in the Olds blasted at them with the horn, making them jump like grasshoppers. But when they looked up and saw we were colored they just took their time, giving us a look of cold hatred.

I let out the clutch and stepped on the gas. Goddamn 'em, I'll grind 'em into the street, I thought. But just before I hit them something held me. I tamped the brake.

"What the hell!" Johnson snarled, picking himself up off the floor.

I sat there looking at the white couple until they had crossed the sidewalk, giving them stare for stare, hate for hate. Horns blasted me from behind, guys in the middle lanes looked at me as they passed; but all I could see was two rebbish pecks who didn't hate me no more than I hated them. Finally I went ahead, just missed sideswiping a new Packard Clipper. My arms were rubbery and my fingers numb; I was weak as if I'd been heaving sacks of cement all day in the sun.

After that everything got under my skin. I was coming up fast in the middle lane and some white guy in a Nash coupe cut out in front of me without signaling. I had to burn rubber to keep from taking off his fender; and the car behind me tapped my bumper. I didn't know whether he had looked in the rear-view mirror before he pulled out or not, but I knew if he had he could have seen we were a carful of colored—and that's the way I took it. I kept on his tail until I could pull up beside him, then I leaned out the window and shouted, "This ain't Alabama, you peckerwood son of a bitch. When you want to pull out of line, stick out your hand."

He gave me a quick glance, then looked straight ahead. After that he ignored me. That made me madder than if he'd talked back. I stuck with him clear out to Compton. A dozen times I had a chance to bump him into an oncoming truck. Then I began feeling virtuous and let him go.

But at the entrance to the Shell Refinery the white cop directing traffic caught sight of us and stopped me on a dime. The white workers crossing the street looked at the big new car full of black faces and gave off cold hostility. I gave them look for look.

"What's the matter with these pecks this morning?" Homer said. "Is everybody evil?"

By now it was a quarter of eight. It was twelve miles to the yard. I gritted my teeth and started digging again; I swore the next person who tried to stop me I'd run him down. But traffic on all harbor roads was heavy the whole day through, and during the change of shifts at the numerous refineries and shipyards it was mad, fast, and furious. Cars were strung out in both directions as far as you could see; drivers jockeyed for position. Shipyard workers are reckless drivers. Handling tons of steel all day long makes cars seem as small as scooters and flexible as cables. I had to fight and bluff for every foot. Although I knew they did everyone like that, I got to feeling that the white guys were trying to push me around. I got mad and started bulling.

It was a bright June morning. The sun was already high. If I'd been a white boy I might have enjoyed the scramble in the early morning sun, the tight competition for a twenty-foot lead on a thirty-mile highway. But to me it was racial. The huge industrial plants flanking the ribbon of road—shipyards, refineries, oil wells, steel mills, construction companies—the thousands of rushing workers, the low-hanging barrage balloons, the close hard roar of Diesel trucks and the distant drone of patrolling planes, the sharp, pungent smell of exhaust that used to send me driving clear across Ohio on a sunny summer morning, and the snowcapped mountains in the background, like picture post cards, didn't mean a thing to me. I didn't even see them; all I wanted in the world was to push my Buick Roadmaster over some peckerwood's face.

Time and again I cut in front of some fast-moving car, making rubber burn and brakes scream and drivers curse, hoping a paddy would bump my fender so I'd have an excuse to get out and clip him with my tire iron. My eyes felt red and sticky and my mouth tasted brown. I turned into the tightly patrolled harbor road, doing a defiant fifty.

Conway said at large, "Oh, Bob's got plenny money, got just too much money. He don't mind paying a fine."

Nobody answered him. By now we were all too evil to do much talking. We came into the stretch of shipyards—Consolidated, Bethlehem, Western Pipe and Steel—caught an open mile, and I went up to sixty. White guys looked at us queerly as we went by. We didn't get stopped but we didn't make it. It was five after eight when we pulled into the parking lot at Atlas Ship. I found a spot and parked and we scrambled out, nervous because we were late, and belligerent because we didn't want anybody to say anything about it.

The parking-lot attendant waited until I had finished locking the car, then came over and told me I had to move, I'd parked in the place reserved for company officials. I looked at him with a cold, dead fury, too spent even to hit him. I let my breath out slowly, got back in the car, and moved it. The other fellows had gone into the yard. I had to stop at Gate No. 2 to get a late card.

The gatekeeper said, "Jesus Christ, all you colored boys are late this morning."

A guard standing near by leered at me. "What'd y'all do last night, boy? I bet y'all had a ball down on Central Avenue."

I started to tell him I was up all night with his mother, but I didn't feel up to the trouble. I punched my card without giving a sign that I had heard. Then I cut across the yard to the outfitting dock. We were working on a repair ship—it was called a floating dry dock—for the Navy. My gang was installing the ventilation in the shower compartment and the heads, as the toilets were called.

At the entrance to the dock the guard said, "Put out that cigarette, boy. What's the matter you colored boys can't never obey no rules?"

I tossed it over on the wooden craneway, still burning. He muttered something as he went over to step on it.

The white folks had sure brought their white to work with them that morning.

FROM CHAPTER 3

The decks were low, and with the tools and equipment of the workers, the thousand and one lines of the welders, the chippers, the blowers, the burners, the light lines, the wooden staging, combined with the equipment of the ship, the shapes and plates, the ventilation trunks and ducts, reducers, dividers, transformers, the machines, lathes, mills, and such, half yet to be installed, the place looked like a littered madhouse. I had to pick every step to find a foot-size clearance of deck space, and at the same time to keep looking up so I wouldn't tear off an ear or knock out an eye against some overhanging shape. Every two or three steps I'd bump into another worker. The only time anybody ever apologized was when they knocked you down.

Bessie, one of the helpers in my gang, met me at the midship bulkhead with the time cards.

"Are you evil too?" she greeted.

"Not at you, beautiful," I grimaced.

All I knew about her was that she was brown-skinned, straightened-haired, and medium-sized; she wore a hard hat, clean cotton waists, blue denim slacks, and a brown sweater. I'd never looked at her any closer.

"You folks got me almost scared to come to work," she was saying.

I ducked through the access opening without answering, came to a manhole, went down a jack ladder to the second deck, threaded through a maze of shapes to the sheet-metal toolroom. The Kelly that Conway had been whipping in the car was our supervisor. He was a thin, wiry, nervous Irishman with a blood-red, beaked face and close-set bright blue eyes. He had fought like hell to keep me from being made a leaderman, and we never had much to say to each other.

I tossed the cards on the desk before the clerk with the late cards on top. She picked them up without saying anything. Kelly looked up from a blueprint he was studying with Chuck, a white leaderman, and his face got redder. He turned back to the print without saying anything, and I turned to go out. He had given me enough jobs to last my gang another week and I didn't see any need to say anything to him either. But before I got out he stopped me.

"How's that colored gang of yours coming along, Bob?"

It was a moment before I turned around. I had to decide first whether to tell him to go to hell or not. Finally I said, "Fine. Kelly, fine! My colored gang is coming along fine." I started to ask him how were the white gangs coming along, but I caught myself in time.

"You colored boys make good workers when you learn how." he said. "I ain't got no fault to find with you at all."

Chuck gave me a sympathetic grin.

"Now that's fine," I said. I opened my mouth to say, "What do you think about the way we're blasting at Ireland?" but I didn't say it.

I turned to the crib girl and said, "Let me have S-14."

She was a fat, ducky, blue-eyed farm girl with round red cheeks and brownish hair. She widened her eyes with an inquiring look. "What's that?"

"A print."

"What's a print?" she asked.

She hadn't been on the job very long so I said patiently, "A print is a blueprint. They're in that cabinet there. You have the key. Will you unlock the cabinet and give me the print—the blueprint—marked S-14."

She unlocked the cabinet reluctantly, giving quick side glances at Kelly to see if he'd say anything, and when she saw that S-14 was marked "Not to be taken from office," she turned to Kelly and asked. "Can he see this?"

My head began heating up again. Kelly looked up and nodded. She took down the print and handed it to me. "You'll have to look at it here," she said.

All the leadermen took out prints. I wanted to explain it to her, knowing that she was new on the job. But she had tried my patience, so I said, "Listen, little girl, don't annoy me this morning."

She looked inquiringly at Kelly again, but he didn't look up. I walked out with the print. She called, "Hey!" indecisively, but I didn't look around.

A white helper was soldering a seam in a trunk while a white mechanic looked on. The mechanic and I had been in the department together for the past two years, but we had never spoken. He looked at me as I passed. I looked at him; we kept the record straight. I went up the jack ladder and came out on the third deck again.

There were a lot of women workers on board, mostly white. Whenever I passed the white women looked at me, some curiously, some coyly, some with open hostility. Some just stared with blank hard eyes. Few ever moved aside to let me pass; I just walked around them. On the whole the older women were friendlier than the younger. Now and then some of the young white women gave me an opening to make a pass, but I'd never made one: at first because the colored workers seemed as intent on protecting the white women from the colored men as the white men were, probably because they wanted to prove to the white folks they could work with white women without trying to make them; and then, after I'd become a leaderman, because I, like a damn fool, felt a certain responsibility about setting an example. Now I had Alice and the white chicks didn't interest me; I thought Alice was better than any white woman who ever lived.

When I ducked to pass through the access opening in the transverse bulkhead I noticed some words scrawled above and straightened up to read them: "Don't duck, Okie, you're tough." I was grinning when I ducked through the hole and straightened up, face to face with a tall white girl in a leather welder's suit.

She was a peroxide blonde with a large-featured, overly made-up face, and she had a large, bright-painted, fleshy mouth, kidney-shaped, thinner in the middle than at the ends. Her big blue babyish eyes were mascaraed like a burlesque queen's and there were tiny wrinkles in their corners and about the flare of her nostrils, calipering down about the edges of her mouth. She looked thirty and well sexed, rife but not quite rotten. She looked as if she might have worked half those years in a cat house, and if she hadn't she must have given a lot of it away.

We stood there for an instant, our eyes locked, before either of us moved; then she deliberately put on a frightened, wide-eyed look and backed away from me as if she was scared stiff, as if she was a naked virgin and I was King Kong. It wasn't the first time she had done that. I'd run into her on board a half-dozen times during the past couple of weeks and each time she'd put on that scared-to-death act. I was used to white women doing all sorts of things to tease or annoy the colored men so I hadn't given it a second thought before.

But now it sent a blinding fury through my brain. Blood rushed to my head like gales of rain and I felt my face burn white-hot. It came up in my eyes and burned at her; she caught it and kept staring at me with that wide-eyed phony look. Something about her mouth touched it off, a quirk made the curves change as if she got a sexual thrill and her mascaraed eyelashes fluttered.

Lust shook me like an electric shock; it came up in mouth, filling it with tongue, and drained my whole stomach down into my groin. And it poured out of me in a sticky rush and spurred over her from head to foot.

The frightened look went out of her eyes and she blushed right down her face and out of sight beneath the collar of her leather jacket, and I could imagine it going down over her overripe breasts and spreading out over her milk-white stomach. When she turned out of my stare I went sick to the stomach and felt like vomiting. I had started toward the ladder going to the upper deck, but instead I turned past her, slowing down and brushing her. She didn't move. I kept on going, circling.

Someone said, "Hiya, Bob," but I didn't hear him until after I'd half climbed, half crawled a third of the way up the jack ladder. Then I said, "Yeah." I came out on the fourth deck, passed two white women who looked away disdainfully, climbed to the weather deck. A little fat brown-skinned girl with hips that shook like jelly leaned against the bulwark in the sun. "Hello," she cooed, dishing up everything she had to offer in that first look.

"Hello, baby," I said. The sickness went. I leaned close to her and whispered, "Still keeping it for me?"

She giggled and said half seriously, "You don't want none."

I'd already broken two dates with her and I didn't want to make another one. "I'll see you at lunch," I said, moving quickly off.

I found a clean spot in the sun and spread out the print. I wanted an overall picture of the whole ventilation system; I was tired of having my gang kicked down in first one stinking hole and then another. But before I'd gotten a chance to look George came up and said Johnson and Conway were about to get into a fight.

"Hell, let 'em fight," I growled. "What the hell do I care, I ain't their papa."

But I got up and went down to the third deck again to see what it was all about. It was cramped quarters aft, a labyrinth of narrow, hard-angled companionways, jammed with staging, lines, shapes, and workers who had to be contortionists first of all. I ducked through the access opening, squeezed by the electricians' staging, pushed a helper out of my way, and started through the opening into the shower room. Just as I stuck my head inside a pipe fitter's tacker struck an arc and I jerked out of the flash. Behind me someone moved the nozzle of the blower that was used to ventilate the hole, and the hard stream of air punched my hard hat off like a fist. In grabbing for it I bumped my head against the angle of the bulkhead. My hat sailed into the middle of the shower room where my gang was working, and I began cursing in a steady streak.

Bessie gave me a dirty look, and Pigmeat said, "We got Bob throwing his hat in before him. We're some tough cats."

The air was so thick with welding fumes, acid smell, body odor, and cigarette smoke even the stream from the blower couldn't get it out. I had fifteen in my gang, twelve men and three women, and they were all working in the tiny, cramped quarters. Two fire pots were going, heating soldering irons. Somebody was drilling. Two or three guys were hand-riveting. A chipper was working on the deck above. It was stifling hot, and the din was terrific.

I picked up my hat and stuck it back on my head. Peaches was sitting on the staging at the far end, legs dangling, eating an apple and at peace with the world. She was a short-haired, dark brown, thick-lipped girl with a placid air—that's as much as I'd seen.

"Where's Smitty?" I asked her. She was his helper.

"I don't know," she said without moving.

Willie said, "While you're here, Bob, you can show me where to hang these stays and save me having to go get the print." He was crouched on the staging beneath the upper deck, trying to hang his duct.

I knew he couldn't read blueprints, but he was drawing a mechanic's pay. I flashed my light on the job and said, "Hang the first two by the split and the other two just back of the joint. What's your X?"

"That's what I don't know," he said. "I ain't seen the print yet."

"It's three-nine off the bulkhead," I said.

Behind me Arkansas said, "Conway, you're an evil man. You don't get along with nobody. How you get along with him, Zula Mae?"

"He's all right," she said. She was Conway's helper. "You just got to understand him."

"See," Conway said. "She's my baby."

Arkansas gave her a disdainful look. "That's 'cause she still think you her boss. Don't you let this guy go boss you 'round, you hear."

"He don't boss me 'round," she defended.

"You just tryna make trouble between me and my helper," Conway said. "I'm the easiest man here to get along with. Everybody gets along with me."

"You from Arkansas?" Arkansas asked.

"How you know I ain't from California?" Conway said.

"Ain't nobody in here from California," Arkansas said. "What city in Arkansas you from?"

"He's from Pine Bluff," Johnson said. "Can't you tell a Pine Bluff nig— Pine Bluffian when you see him?"

"Hear the Moroccan," Conway sneered. "Johnson a Moroccan, he ain't no colored man."

"You got any folks in Fort Worth, Conway?" Arkansas asked.

"I ain't got many folks," Conway said. "We a small family."

"You got a grandpa, ain't you?" Arkansas persisted.

"Had one," Conway said.

"Then how you know?" Arkansas pointed out.

Peaches was grinning.

"You going back?" Homer asked.

Arkansas looked at him. "Who you talking to? Me?"

"You'll do. You going back?"

"Back where?"

"Back to Arkansas?"

"Yeah, I'm going back—when the horses, they pick the cotton, and the mules, they cut the corn; when the white chickens lay black eggs and the white folks is Jim Crowed while the black folks is—"

He broke off as Smitty came in with a white leaderman named Donald. They didn't see me. He showed Donald where he had cut an opening in his duct for an intake vent, and Donald said he'd cut four inches off the X.

"That's where Bob told me to cut," he said.

Donald shook his head noncommittally; he was a nice guy and he didn't want to say I was wrong. I'd often wondered if he was a Communist. He had a round moonface, pleasant but unsmiling, and that sharp speculative look behind rimless spectacles that some Communists have.

I stepped into the picture then. "When did I tell you to cut out there?" I asked Smitty.

Donald turned red. "Hello Bob," he said. "Smitty said you was off today."

"Jesus Christ, can't you colored boys do anything right?" Kelly said from behind me. He had slipped in unnoticed.

Air began lumping in my chest and my eyes started burning. I looked at Kelly. I ought to bust him right on the side of his scrawny red neck, I thought. I'd kill him as sure as hell. Instead I ground out, "Any mechanic might have made the same mistake. Any mechanic but a white mechanic," I added.

He didn't get it. "Yeah, but you boys make too many mistakes. You got to cut it out."

Donald started moving off. "I ain't made a single mistake this month, Mr. Kelly." Conway grinned up at him from where he knelt on the floor, soldering a seam.

Pigmeat nudged me. "See what I mean? Got 'em skunt back to his ears. He thinks the man a dentist."

Kelly heard him but acted as if he didn't. He said to Conway, "I wasn't talking about you. You're a good boy, a good worker. I was talking 'bout some of these other boys."

In the silence that followed Peaches said, "Oh, Conway gonna get a raise," before she could catch herself, having thought we'd keep on talking and she wouldn't be heard. Somebody laughed.

I kept looking at Kelly without saying anything. He turned suddenly and started out. When he had gone Smitty said, "How come he always got to pick on you? He don't never jump on none of these white leadermen. You know as much as they do."

I unfolded my rule and tapped the duct he was working on. "Cut your bottom line ten inches from the butt joint," I directed, trying to keep my voice steady. He was just a simple-minded, Uncle Tom-ish nigger, I told myself; he couldn't help it. "You'll have a four-inch gap. Take this duct over to the shop and get a production welder to weld in an insert plate and grind the burrs down as smooth as possible." I turned and started out, then stopped. "And remember I'm your leaderman," I added.

Further Reading

This select bibliography is limited to general critical materials (chronological, generic, thematic, or regional in approach) on the literature of California to 1945. Original editions are cited, but more recent editions are often available.

Egli, Ida. *No Rooms of Their Own: Women Writers of Early California.* Berkeley: Heyday Books, 1992.

Everson, William. *Archetype West.* Berkeley: Oyez Press, 1976.

Ferlinghetti, Lawrence, and Nancy J. Peters. *Literary San Francisco.* San Francisco: Harper and Row, 1980.

Fine, David, ed. *Los Angeles in Fiction.* Albuquerque: University of New Mexico Press, 1984.

Fine, David, and Paul Skenazy, eds. *San Francisco in Fiction.* Albuquerque: University of New Mexico Press, 1995.

Haslam, Gerald, ed. *Many Californias: Literature from the Golden State,* rev. ed. Reno: University of Nevada Press, 1999.

Jackson, Joseph Henry, ed. *Continent's End: A Collection of California Writing.* New York: McGraw-Hill, 1944.

Kowalewski, Michael, ed. *Reading the West: New Essays on the Literature of the American West.* New York: Cambridge University Press, 1996.

———, ed. *Gold Rush: A Literary Exploration.* Berkeley: Heyday Books, 1997.

Lyon, Tom, ed. *Updating the Literary West.* Fort Worth: Texas Christian University Press, 1997.

McWilliams, Carey. *Southern California: An Island on the Land.* New York: Duell, Sloan, and Pearce, 1946.

———. *California: The Great Exception.* New York: Current Books, 1949.

Margolin, Malcolm. *The Way We Lived: California Indian Stories, Songs, and Reminiscences,* rev. ed. Berkeley: Heyday Books, 1993.

Powell, Lawrence Clark. *California Classics.* Los Angeles: Ward Ritchie Press, 1971.

Reed, Ishmael, and Al Young, eds. *Calafia: The California Poetry.* Berkeley: Y'Bird Books, 1979.

Starr, Kevin. *Americans and the California Dream, 1850–1915.* New York: Oxford University Press, 1973.

———. *Inventing the Dream: California through the Progressive Era.* New York: Oxford University Press, 1986.

———. *Material Dreams: Southern California through the 1920s.* New York: Oxford University Press, 1991.

————. *The Dream Endures: California Enters the 1940s.* New York: Oxford University Press, 1997.

————. *Endangered Dreams: The Great Depression in California.* New York: Oxford University Press, 1997.

Walker, Franklin. *San Francisco's Literary Frontier.* New York: Alfred A. Knopf, 1939.

————. *A Literary History of Southern California.* Berkeley: University of California Press, 1950.

————. *The Seacoast of Bohemia: An Account of Early Carmel.* San Francisco: Book Club of California, 1966.

Wilson, Edmund. "The Boys in the Back Room." In *Classics and Commercials.* New York: Farrar, Straus, 1950.

Wyatt, David. *The Fall into Eden: Landscape and Imagination in California.* New York: Cambridge University Press, 1986.

About the Editors

JACK HICKS teaches at the University of California at Davis, where he directs the Graduate Creative Writing Program and teaches courses on the literature of California. The author of two previous books and many articles on contemporary American fiction, nonfiction, and popular culture, he is also director of "The Art of the Wild," an annual national conference on writing with nature, wilderness, and environment, which meets each July at Lake Tahoe.

JAMES D. HOUSTON is the author of seven novels and several nonfiction books, all of which explore the history and culture of the American West and the Asia Pacific Rim. *The Last Paradise* (1998), his most recent novel, won the 1999 American Book Award in fiction. *Snow Mountain Passage*, a novel, is forthcoming in 2001. Houston is a frequent contributor to books on California, and he has edited other anthologies, including *West Coast Fiction* (Bantam).

MAXINE HONG KINGSTON is the author of *The Woman Warrior*, *China Men*, and *Tripmaster Monkey*, and she has won many awards, including honorary doctorates (from Brandeis, the University of Massachusetts, and other institutions) and a United States Presidential Medal in 1998. On the faculty at the University of California at Berkeley, she will teach at Harvard in late 2001. Kingston recently completed her fourth novel, *The Fifth Book of Peace*.

AL YOUNG is a novelist, poet, essayist, and musicologist with almost twenty books to his credit. They include *Who is Angelina?* (a novel), *Heaven* (collected poems), *Mingus/Mingus* (musical memoirs), and *African American Literature* (an anthology). His works have been translated into more than a dozen languages. Young has been a visiting writer at many institutions, most recently at the University of California at Davis, the University of Michigan, and the University of Pennsylvania.

Permissions and Credits

"The Creation" (Maidu) from *The Maidu Indian Myths and Stories of Hanc'ibyjim* by William Shipley. Reprinted by permission of Heyday Books.

Three Love Songs (Wintu) from *The Way We Lived* by Malcolm Margolin. Reprinted by permission of Heyday Books.

"About-the-House Girl" (Karok) from *The Inland Whale* by Theodora Kroeber, reprinted by permission of Indiana University Press.

Four Dream Cult Songs (Wintu): "Down West" (Sadie Marsh, Wintu), "There Above" (Wintu), and "It Is Above" (Harry Marsh, Wintu) from Dorothy Demetracopoulou, "Wintu Songs"; "Above Where the Minnow Maiden Sleeps" (Wintu) from Cora Du Bois, "The 1870 Ghost Dance." All from *The Way We Lived* by Malcolm Margolin. Reprinted by permission of Heyday Books.

"Dancing on the Brink of the World" (Costanoan), "Rattlesnake Ceremony Song" (Yokuts), and "Dream Time" (Ohlone) from Alfred Kroeber, *Handbook of the Indians of California.*

Excerpts by Yone Noguchi from *The Story of Yone Noguchi* (1915) and *Seen and Unseen; or, Monologues of a Homeless Snail* (1920). Reprinted by permission of Associated University Press.

Poems by anonymous Chinese immigrants: No. 1 from *Island: Poetry and History of Chinese Immigrants on Angel Island, 1910–1940*, ed. Him Mark Lai, Genny Lim, and Judy Yung. © 1991. Reprinted by permission of University of Washington Press. Nos. 2–4 from *Songs of Gold Mountain: Cantonese Rhymes from San Francisco Chinatown*, ed. Marlon K. Hom. © 1987. Reprinted by permission of University of California Press.

"Continent's End," © 1924 and renewed 1952 by Robinson Jeffers; "To the Stone Cutters," © 1938 and renewed 1966 by Robinson Jeffers; "Tor House," © 1928 and renewed 1956 by Robinson Jeffers; "Hurt Hawks," © 1928 and renewed 1956 by Robinson Jeffers; "Rock and Hawk," © 1934 and renewed 1962 by Donnan Jeffers and Garth Jeffers; "The Purse-Seine," © 1937 and renewed 1965 by Donnan Jeffers and Garth Jeffers; "Carmel Point," © 1954 by Robinson Jeffers. All from *The Selected Poems of Robinson Jeffers.* Reprinted by permission of Random House, Inc.

Chapter 3 from *Indians in Overalls* by Jaime de Angulo, © 1990 by Gui de Angulo. Reprinted by permission of City Lights Books.

Excerpts from *Oil!* by Upton Sinclair, © 1927. Reprinted by permission of John Weidman and Jeff Weidman, c/o Elizabeth Berney, Esq., The Literary Resources Agency, Great Neck, N.Y.

Chapter 6 from *The Maltese Falcon* by Dashiell Hammett, © 1929, 1930 by Alfred A. Knopf, Inc., and renewed 1957, 1958 by Dashiell Hammett. Reprinted by permission of Alfred A. Knopf, Inc.

"See Los Angeles First," "The Slow Pacific Swell," "John Sutter," "Moonlight Alert," and "The California Oaks" from *Collected Poems* by Yvor Winters, © 1978. Reprinted by permission of Carcanet Press Limited.

Chapter 6 from *The Postman Always Rings Twice* by James M. Cain, © 1934 and renewed 1962 by James M. Cain. Reprinted by permission of Alfred A. Knopf, Inc.

"The Daring Young Man on the Flying Trapeze" from *The Daring Young Man on the Flying Trapeze*, © 1934, and "Quarter, Half, Three-Quarter and Whole Notes" from *Three Times Three* by William Saroyan, © 1936. Reprinted by permission of the Trustees of Leland Stanford Junior University.

Chapter 1 from *They Shoot Horses, Don't They?* by Horace McCoy, © 1935. Reprinted by permission of Harold Matson Company, Inc.

Excerpt from *Ordeal by Hunger* by George R. Stewart, © 1936, 1960, renewed 1963 by George R. Stewart, renewed 1988 by Theodosia B. Stewart. Reprinted by permission of Houghton Mifflin Company. All rights reserved.

Excerpt from *The Grapes of Wrath* by John Steinbeck, © 1939, renewed 1967 by John Steinbeck. Used by permission of Viking Penguin, a division of Penguin Putnam, Inc.

Chapter 9 from *Factories in the Field* by Carey McWilliams, © 1939 by Carey McWilliams, renewed 1966 by Carey McWilliams. Reprinted by permission of Harold Ober Associates.

Poems by Hildegarde Flanner from *Poems: Collected and Selected,* by Hildegarde Flanner, © 1988. Reprinted by permission of John Daniel, Publisher.

Poems by Josephine Miles from *Josephine Miles: Collected Poems, 1930–83,* © 1983. Reprinted by permission of University of Illinois Press.

Chapter 12 from *Ask the Dust,* © 1980 by John Fante. Reprinted by permission of Black Sparrow Press.

Chapters 1 and 2 from *The Big Sleep* by Raymond Chandler. © 1939 by Raymond Chandler, renewed 1967 by Helga Greene, executrix of the estate of Raymond Chandler. Reprinted by permission of Alfred A. Knopf, Inc.

Chapter 27 from *Miss Lonelyhearts and The Day of the Locust* by Nathanael West. © 1939 by Estate of Nathanael West. Reprinted by permission of New Directions Publishing Corp.

Excerpts from *The Love of the Last Tycoon* by F. Scott Fitzgerald, © 1994. Reprinted by permission of Simon & Schuster, Inc.

"The First Oyster" from *The Gastronomical Me* by M. F. K. Fisher, © 1937, 1941, 1942, 1943, 1948, 1949, 1954, 1990 by M. F. K Fisher. Reprinted by permission of MacMillan General Reference USA.

INDEX OF AUTHORS AND TITLES

TEXT: SCALA

DISPLAY: SCALA SANS

DESIGN: NICOLE HAYWARD

COMPOSITION: BINGHAMTON VALLEY COMPOSITION

PRINTING + BINDING: FRIESENS CORPORATION